W9-BKS-140

LETITIA BALDRIGE'S
⤚ NEW ⤙
Complete Guide To
EXECUTIVE
MANNERS

Other Books by Letitia Baldrige

Roman Candle
Tiffany Table Settings
Of Diamonds and Diplomats
Home
Juggling
Amy Vanderbilt's Everyday Etiquette
The Entertainers
The 1978 revision of *The Amy Vanderbilt Complete Book of Etiquette*
Letitia Baldrige's Complete Guide to Executive Manners
Letitia Baldrige's Complete Guide to a Great Social Life
Letitia Baldrige's Complete Guide to the New Manners for the Nineties
Public Affairs, Private Relations

LETITIA BALDRIGE'S

~ NEW ~

Complete Guide To

EXECUTIVE

MANNERS

RAWSON ASSOCIATES
NEW YORK

MAXWELL MACMILLAN CANADA
TORONTO

MAXWELL MACMILLAN INTERNATIONAL
NEW YORK   OXFORD   SINGAPORE   SYDNEY

Rawson Associates   Maxwell Macmillan Canada, Inc.
Macmillan Publishing Company   1200 Eglinton Avenue East
866 Third Avenue   Suite 200
New York, NY 10022   Don Mills, Ontario M3C 3N1

Macmillan Publishing Company is part of the Maxwell Communication Group of Companies.

Library of Congress Cataloging-in-Publication Data

Baldrige, Letitia.
    Letitia Baldrige's new Complete guide to executive manners / by
Letitia Baldrige.
        p.   cm.
    Rev. ed. of: Letitia Baldrige's Complete guide to executive
manners. © 1985.
    Includes index.
    ISBN 0-89256-362-1
    1. Business etiquette.   I. Baldrige, Letitia. Complete guide to
executive manners.   II. Title.   III. Title: New complete guide to
executive manners.   IV. Title: Complete guide to executive manners.
    HF5389.B34   1993
    395'.52—dc20   93-14166
                                                            CIP

Portions of this book appeared in *Letitia Baldrige's Complete Guide to Executive Manners*

Macmillan books are available at special discounts for bulk purchases for sales promotions, premiums, fundraising, or educational use. For details, contact:

                        Special Sales Director
                        Macmillan Publishing Company
                        866 Third Avenue
                        New York, NY 10022

10 9 8 7 6 5 4 3 2 1

Printed in the United States of America

This book is dedicated to the youngest member of our family, grandson Luke Smyth, who may someday be a great doctor, like his father, or perhaps he will become a well-mannered but dynamic executive. Since he's two years old, he still has a way to go, and time to decide.

Contents

PART I
THE EXECUTIVE AT EASE

Knowing When to Say "Please" • How Many Times a Day Should One Say
"Please?" • Knowing How to Apologize • Knowing How to Say "Thank
You" • Ways in Which to Say "Thank You" for Substantive Favors or
Gifts • Compliments—The Best Way to Accept and Give Them • A Smart
Manager Compliments His Staff • Compliment Your Peers • Compliments Are
to Be Accepted, Not Rejected • If You're a Mean Person, Eventually You'll Get
Caught Being Mean • When You're the New Kid on the Block • When You
Have Moved from a Large to a Small Company

What's in a Name? • The Art of Introducing People • When People
Mis-Introduce You, Do You Correct Them? • Remembering Names
Takes Practice • Using Nicknames in the Workplace • What's in a
Handshake? • When Do You Shake Hands? • When Do You Not Shake
Hands? • Points of Protocol in Handshaking • When You Have Clammy
Hands • Hugging and Kissing in Greeting

5 The Executive Faces Problems in Today's Working World Which Never Existed Before

PART II

THE PERSON-TO-PERSON SIDE OF
BUSINESS LIFE

Techniques Managers Should Know • The Right Way for a Secretary to Announce Her Boss' Calls • When You Participate in a Conference Call • Putting People on Hold • Call-Waiting • For People Who Work at Home • Answering Machines • Voice Mail • Handling Calls of Complaint • When You Have Bad News to Impart • Dealing with an Answering Service

PART III

THE PROTOCOL OF BUSINESS LIFE

12 Business Protocol

13 Running and Attending Meetings and Conferences, From Inter-Office to International

Serving Alcohol • Helping Control Costs When You Serve Alcohol • The Cash
Bar • The Service of Wine • The Decanter: When You Give a Business Dinner
at Home • When a Waiter or Waitress Serves the Wine • The Wines at a Formal
Dinner • The Wines at an Informal Dinner • After-Dinner Drinks • If You're
Ordering Wine for Your Guests in a Restaurant • Tasting the Wine in a Fine
Restaurant • The Proper Wineglass • Serving Beer • Beer
Etiquette • Entertaining a Recovering Alcoholic

16 The Important Business of the Nonprofit World and the Duties of the Nonprofit Board

17 Celebrations and Rites of Passage 538

Acknowledgments

My deepest thanks, of course, go to my old friend and co-conspirator on all of my books on manners since 1985, Eleanor Rawson, head of Rawson Associates. She is not only my publisher, but a paragon of patience and a terrific editor, too. She should be in diplomatic service, because she's a master of the art of diplomacy. Every time I would come up with an absolutely wild scheme when writing this book, she would not react to it as such. She would simply say, "Well, Tish, let's think that one over just a bit. Let's talk about it tomorrow."

She has labored long and hard with me on this project for the past year and a half. It's been a stimulating trip, concentrating on the world of the new behavior and interaction of people at work. But there has been a sadness, too. This is my first book on manners that has not received the warm final touch of another publishing eye, that of Eleanor's husband, Ken Rawson, who left us last year.

I am grateful to Sandra Choron and Cyndi Marsico, who helped to speed into shape what has seemed at times to be the entire contents of the Library of Congress. I am thankful, too, to Grace Shaw, who has assisted on previous books, and who pitched in on this one with her usual "grace," and to Carol Cook, of Rawson Associates, whose tact and efficiency helped so much to move this project along. I also wish to thank Page Kjellstron, who was one of my vice-presidents before going on to much loftier positions, who brought me valuable new information on corporate entertaining and meetings. And, of course, I am indebted to my Executive Assistant, Helen Brown, who was always at my side, and to artists Remo Bramante and Denise Fike for their helpful illustrations.

It does not stop there. The following are but a handful of the people I have questioned ad infinitum to find out what is going on in the workplace *today*, particularly what is going on *that never happened before*. I made notes of their comments on the backs of letters, paper napkins, and in the narrow white spaces of the margins of newspapers:

A. Robert Abboud, Yuko Arai, James G. Babb, Margaret Baldrige, Robert C. Baldrige, Mohammed Bin Hussein Al-Shaali, John Boyd, Mabel Brandon, Evangeline Bruce, Gahl Burt, Lyn Butler, Deborah W. Callard, Irene P. Cohn, Jeffrey Cole, Barbara L. Collins, Brian Crawford, Patrick Daly, Shiv Dasani, Mary Davis, Daniel P. Davison, Eleanor Elliott, Louis Emmery, Lorre Erlick, Barbara Ettore, Carmine Fabrizio, Raymond F. Farley, Linda Faulkner, Paul Fay, Jr., Yoshiharu Fukuhara, Martin Garbisu, Fernanda K. Gilligan, Neal R. Goodman, Elizabeth T. Greenberg, Werner

Gundersheimer, Elbert O. Hand, Paul D. Hill, Talal Hoffman, Malcolm Hollensteiner, Neil Horstman, Syeda Abida Hussain, Donald P. Jacobs, Philip H. Jordan, Jr., Yue-Sai Kan, Henry Kaufman, Young-Joo Kim, Julius Koppelman, Richard Krasno, Brian Lange, Eppie Lederer, Paul E. Lego, Becky Little, Josephine Lyons, Sirio Maccioni, Emily Malino, Miles L. Marsh, Charles Marshall, John L. McCoy, Johann Meesman, Agnes Mouton, Rick Musi, Margaret Norvell, Thomas O'Connor, Charles K. Olson, Steven D. Pagano, Diane Paton, Vivanne Pommier, Lewis T. Preston, Sue Railey, George Raymond, Haskell Rhett, Frank E. Richardson, Judith K. Rogers, Barry Salvi, Vincent A. Sarni, Gerald Schneiderman, Richard Schubert, M.D., Sam F. Segnar, Meera Shankar, Mary Claire Shipp, Carey Shoemaker, Robert Showfety, James and Clare Smyth, Mary Snow, Guang Ming Song, Ann Stock, Ellen Sweet, Richard L. Thomas, Jay Treadwell, Nancy Tuckerman, Abigail Van Buren, Linda Verschelden, Thomas Watkins, Tracy Wellington, Lawson Willard, Nanette Wiser, Dana Witt, Roger Zissu.

There are many more who have helped me, and they know who they are.

Author's Note

For twenty years I have tried to find one or two new pronouns that could slip with ease into our language and which would signify "he or she," "his or hers," "him or her." A few years ago, I suggested "hes" (pronounced "hess") as a solution and was immediately advised by the wordsmiths to whom I wrote to stick to my knitting. They felt my bright idea was a disaster. My answer to them was that my solution may be a disaster in their eyes, but at least I was trying to find one!

I categorically refuse to keep repeating "him or her," "he or she," "his or hers," except occasionally. Therefore, I'm asking the reader to assume that each time I say "he" in a general sense, I mean both genders.

Why We Need a New Book on Business Manners

The research for the book you hold in your hands is something I have been doing all my working life in the United States Embassies in Paris and Rome; in the boardrooms of corporations where I have served as their first woman director; in the corridors of the White House, where I was a member of the Kennedy administration, as Jacqueline Kennedy's Chief of Staff and later as a consultant to four other First Ladies; in corporations where I have been retained as a marketing and public relations consultant; in companies where I have assisted in management training courses; and in the nonprofit world, where I have served on numerous boards.

Through these many decades of a jam-packed, energized life in several countries, I have witnessed the very best and the very worst of behavior. The role of writers on behavior today seems to be to help people recognize the difference. A concern for helping people move easily through life, the relationship between kindness and success, whether in business or social life, has always held a high priority for me.

So, as a consequence of my deep involvement in the cutting edge of human social and business relations, I began a new career: writing several works on manners and launching a life as a lecturer and TV and media commentator and advisor on manners and protocol at every level.

In the late 1970s I totally revised another author's famous book of manners, in which were met head-on the social issues of the day, such as what to do with abusive drunks at your dinner party, how to send an invitation to an unmarried couple living together, and more.

After that, with the explosion of women and most of the adult population into the world of work-for-pay, the next focus of attention obviously was the *workplace*. Eleanor Rawson of Rawson Associates, my publisher, saw this need, too, and the result in 1985 was *Letitia Baldrige's Complete Guide to Executive Manners*.

That book has now sold over half a million copies and has won a constituency all over the world. But since it first appeared, life at work has changed dramatically for all of us, from CEO to entry level. New problems that never existed before face managers and workers alike today.

There is a new informality at work in how we meet and greet, entertain, dress, and socialize with one another, and yet a new formality as we deal with a diversity of people from and in other countries, where we increasingly do business.

The needs of families, of women and men who are parents as well as respected workers, are increasingly sensitive issues in the workplace. The relations of men and women working together not only as equals, but also as new configurations of peer and superior in terms of gender and age, changes a lot of preconceived behavior codes. Also transforming life at work are the new concerns for the rights of the disabled, for more attention to ethnic equality, diversity, and pluralism.

And the techno-electronic explosion is affecting everything about how we communicate with one another, which profoundly affects how we interact with one another in our work world.

These are only some of the revolutionary changes taking place in our business and business-social lives. Every day I get letters, faxes, and telephone calls asking me to delineate the new guidelines and parameters that everyone from the Chief Executive Officer on down can refer to, to guide them through this maze of change.

This book is my answer.

Many traditional customs and rituals remain in place in the codes of behavior that can make or break the future of a rising star on the business horizon. They, too, are covered here.

Happiness is never mentioned in business school, but it is a term that appears often in this newly revised book. We need to be happy, we even deserve to be happy. In these pages I have tried to spell out the challenges those of us involved in business face in the new society in which we live and, more importantly, to supply some solutions. There are many ways in which our knowledge of how to move through life with grace is the key to our happiness on the job, and also in our social lives. Our business and social lives are frequently inextricably wrapped together today.

The world around us is dynamic. It's important to be a whiz kid on a computer, but ultimately it is more important to be a whiz kid in managing people. *It's people who matter.* It's people who tie us together. It's people who inject humanity into our world.

Success at work does not happen without good human relations. A team does not function without people skills. And the real purpose of this book is to provide you with those people skills and to help you take yourself and your endeavors to the peak.

PART I

THE EXECUTIVE AT EASE

1

The Executive at Ease
on the Job

Everyone has qualms when they're starting out in the business world. Even senior managers who have excelled in the workplace for decades confess to concern when plunged into strange, new territory, entering unknown situations, dealing with strangers about whom they know nothing other than their brief bios and some second-hand opinions.

The purpose of a book like this on human interactions and behavior is to give you information that can become a useful set of tools to help make life at work easier and more successful.

Everyone who goes to work wants to feel at ease (or "socially comfortable") in his or her surroundings. An executive known as someone at ease is a person who makes others around him comfortable too.

No one wants to be conspicuous by acting unsophisticated or unknowing. A person at ease walks with grace through the workplace. He thinks about other people, and that unconsciously takes his mind off himself and gives him poise. The fact that others get along well with him is not defined by his designer-made clothes or car of the moment. Rather, it's defined by something as simple as using three common phrases that are automatic, instinctive parts of his everyday vocabulary: "Please," "I'm sorry," and "Thank you." It's that simple. He doesn't have to own Cartier panthère cufflinks, know how to gossip in a foreign language, or choose the perfect wine every time in a restaurant.

A cold, ill-at-ease person would say to an employee, "Sorry, but you're going to have to stay tonight until you've analyzed this report and made the required number of copies. We need it for tomorrow's seven o'clock meeting." An at-ease executive would say, "Jim, I hate to have to ask you to stay late to finish the report and the *copies tonight, but you're the only one who knows how to make sense out of this. We'll make it up to you for messing up your evening, I promise."*

BEING AT EASE ANYWHERE IN THE BUSINESS WORLD

There is no rest when you are helping to manage a business. You have an excess of responsibility. You must motivate and guide people; watch over their safety, benefits, and health; realize profits; keep morale high; and avoid any criticism of the firm for exploitation of its employees or racism, sexism, or discrimination.

Luckily, a good manager usually has a good mindset, a positive attitude that is inherent in his actions toward the company, its employees, and the common goals they all share. This attitude is natural and automatic. A good manager does not have to force himself to summon up superhuman strength or a feeling of compassion, or dose of courage, to handle the inevitable people problems that arise in day-to-day work situations. He handles them quickly, fairly, and with insight and understanding.

A good manager is constantly concerned about the morale of the people on his watch. His employees, in turn, care about his morale, too, and enjoy doing a good job for him. That's teamwork!

Here are some of the components of an executive's behavior that make others want to be on his team:

Knowing When to Say "Please"

Whether you're asking the waitress at the diner to bring you another cup of breakfast coffee or asking your secretary to go to the copy machine, "please" should come forth without self-prompting or even consciously thinking about it. Hollywood, unfortunately, has set a bad example: Network TV shows feature sitcom stars yelling orders to people in their offices as well as waiters or shopkeepers. (There's never a "please" at the beginning or end.) You should view with dismay America's favorite child TV stars ordering around their teachers and parents in their shows each week. These kids would last about four days on a job in the business world.

Fortunately, the real world bears little resemblance to the screen world, because no matter how bad the manners around us seem to be, most children come to learn that when they grow up, their jobs will depend on how well they behave, not how much they can get away with.

How Many Times a Day Should One Say "Please?"

If you are in the business world, it's impossible to count the number of times. When you make even the slightest request of someone, you should begin or end it with "please." For every favor you ask, "please" should be the entrance or exit word.

To your spouse: "*Please* help me entertain the boss at Sunday lunch. I need your help."

To the taxi driver: "Take me to La Guardia Airport, *please*."

To the hotel cashier: "*Please* give me my bill for room 803."

To your secretary: "*Please* fax this to John Garrett, with a copy also to Joan Scribner in New Orleans."

To the waiter: "I'd like to see the wine list, *please*."

To the CEO: "*Please* note his criticism of our strategy plan in the second paragraph. It's pretty strong."

Knowing How to Apologize
(*See also* "Letter of Apology," Chapter 7)

The short phrase "I'm sorry" means so much to the person to whom it is addressed, even when you have to push yourself to utter it. Whatever your motivation, when an apology is called for, make it! For example:

- If you misdial someone on the phone, say "I'm terribly sorry, wrong number," rather than just slam down the receiver in the other person's ear.
- If you do something really hurtful, such as forgetting an appointment:
  - Telephone your sincere apology.
  - Follow it up with a personal note of apology.
  - Send flowers or a gift of some kind, such as fruit, wine, or candy, to reinforce your apology.
- If a stranger does something nice, like picking up something you just dropped on the street but didn't notice, tell him with a warm smile of appreciation that he has really "made your day."
- If you arrive late at a meeting, apologize to the chairman or the host and to the others you have kept waiting.
- When you give someone in your office too much work to do on an emergency basis, use all three of these phrases:

  "Please do it."

  "I'm sorry to have to ask you to do this."

  "Thank you very much for doing it."

- If you do something like bump a person as you move rapidly through a hallway, react quickly with a sincere "I'm really sorry. I certainly didn't mean to do that." (Your words will diffuse the hostility your act may have engendered.)
- If you cause damage to a colleague's possession, apologize profusely, then offer to have it fixed or replaced. For example, when you're a guest in a co-worker's, client's, or your boss's home:

- If you stain your host's good tablecloth at dinner, arrange to take it to the best dry cleaner available.
- If you spill something on his pale-colored carpet, arrange to have it professionally cleaned.
- If you break something, arrange to have it repaired at the best repair shop in town.

No matter what damage you do in someone else's home or office, always do the best you can to make amends—and write a good letter of apology.

Knowing How to Say "Thank You"
(See also "Informal Business Letters" and "Letters
of Acknowledgment and Thanks," Chapter 7)

We should thank people a lot more than we do—automatically—but if we think about what we are thanking them for, we'll be more sincere. Some examples of the kinds of situations in our everyday lives where a little expression of gratitude can be very effective:

- When someone goes back to your office to get your glasses for a meeting
- When someone from the mailroom brings you the mail
- When a gas station attendant finishes filling your tank with gas
- When someone opens a door for you or holds the elevator door for you
- When someone serves you in any capacity, whether it's your secretary who brings papers to your desk or the person in the employee cafeteria who hands a plate of food across the counter
- When anyone gives you a gift of any kind
- When someone does a favor for you
- When someone praises you

Ways in Which to Say "Thank You"
for Substantive Favors or Gifts

- *Spoken*. Convenient if you happen to run into the person. Careless and not very effective.
- *Telephone*. Effective, but only if done within twenty-four hours; if the call is made after that, it seems like an afterthought, not a sincere gesture.
- *Written*. The most effective, because it's on the record and can be shown around and reread.

Compliments—The Best Way to Accept and Give Them
(*See also* "Acknowledging a Compliment," Chapter 7)

Nothing is more affirmative than a compliment. Naturally, that compliment should not be exaggerated, snide, or phony, because then it turns into a negative gesture.

Say it from the heart.

A Smart Manager Compliments The Staff

Employees may feel they're doing a good job, but they don't know it until they hear it. Praise your staff when they do good work—when they get things done on time, when they make an extra effort, when they deserve special recognition. Sure, you may see to it that they get a raise the next pay period, but say it with words, not just a personnel action for increased compensation. People need encouragement as they progress in their job. Of course, you should correct any errors or laxities in their work, but how about telling them what a good job they've done on this and that?

Complimenting Your Peers

Many of our parents brought us up according to the rule, "If you can't say anything nice about someone, just don't open your mouth." Not bad advice.

There's always something you can find to compliment about anyone. It may be the color of a fellow executive's tie, or the print of a woman executive's scarf; it might be an employee's new haircut or snappy looking briefcase; it could be the good looks of his children, as seen in the snapshot on his desk; or the amazing progress an executive in the international division has made with her weekend Japanese lessons. Open your eyes; you'll see it. Then it's up to you to comment on it. It makes people feel good; it lifts their spirits.

The people with whom you spend all day—your co-workers—deserve your praise and cheering up. You have no idea how much influence you can have when you make your peers happy in their jobs. It's another example of an individual's power for good.

Compliments Are to Be Accepted, Not Rejected

Nothing can take the wind out of a person's sails faster than to have one's compliment rejected. If someone says to you, "I think the proposal you presented this morning was first-rate," the last thing he wants to hear you say is, "I thought I did a lousy job of presenting it. I left out half the strong points." The fact that *you personally* felt you did not do a good job does not matter. *Take the compliment in the spirit in which it was given.*

If people compliment you on your appearance, don't correct them and point out all the negatives. For example, if someone says, "You look particularly bright and chipper this morning,'' don't make a retort, ''I feel terrible, my eyes are all puffy from allergies, and I think I look awful.''

What is the right way to accept a compliment? ''*Thank you*. That's really nice of you!''

When a manager walks with ease through a business day, he makes everyone around him feel more at ease in turn. When he sets an example of excellence, courtesy, and caring, others rise to meet his standards. This is true leadership, out of which teamwork develops.

If You're a Mean Person, Eventually You'll Get Caught Being Mean

It's amazing how often a person is caught in his private life, away from the office, when he thinks he's free to act as he darn well pleases. A prime example of this is the young, freshly recuited manager, top of his class at Harvard Business School, who was observed one Saturday (by the wife of the CEO of his new corporation) in the supermarket's overcrowded parking lot. The manager did not see her, however. He had recently been to his boss's home for a lunch where he had impressed everyone with his graceful manners and charm.

The young business school graduate, driving a fancy sports car and bursting with impatience, looked around the congested parking lot and quickly solved his parking problem by pulling into a spot clearly marked for the handicapped, next to the front door of the store, and shutting out a driver who really *was* handicapped. By the time the CEO heard the report of this incident from his furious wife, who had spent fifteen minutes trying to find a nonhandicapped parking space, he decided to fire the young newcomer while it was still legally possible. At work that week, the boss told him he had been seen by his wife pulling a fast one after lunch on Saturday. ''True meanness just isn't part of our corporate culture,'' he explained. ''You won't go very far in this company, so you'd be better off working elsewhere.''

The story has a happy ending, fortunately. The fired manager found another job and proceeded to work hard on weekends and at nighttime donating his services to the local hospital. At the end of a year he was given an award as the outstanding volunteer in the suburban community, which his old boss read about in the newspaper. He got his old job back.

When You're the New Kid on the Block

When you join a company, either in your first executive position or as a transfer from another company, you might as well accept the fact that you will be an object of curiosity and probably of some suspicion as well. You might also be a hate object for someone who thought he was going to obtain the position you have been retained to fill.

Remember, time is the great healer and dealer. It doesn't matter how cool the atmosphere may be when you arrive in your job. What matters is that you take your time to establish good personal relations and proceed slowly and carefully—the opposite of a shotgun approach. Here are some tips on how to handle yourself:

- *Listen and learn, rather than do all the talking.* Don't think you have to justify yourself to everyone. Spend your energies observing and asking smart questions rather than trying to let everyone know how much you know and how important you are.
- *Be equally nice to everyone.* The messenger may someday turn out to be your best friend in court. The receptionist may one day be able to give you the most important information of your life. The junior executive in the office next to yours whom you don't think is very important may one day be your boss.
- *Don't make snap judgments* about who's important, who's going to be your friend. You may change your mind about most of the people in the office, so it's smart not to form an opinion of anyone until you know them well and have seen them interact. Don't listen to negative stories about who's out to get whom, who's about to get fired, who's cheating. Resolve to keep an open mind and to make your own judgments later—much later.
- *Ask your peers to lunch, one by one* (one a week, for example). Get to know them on an easy, informal basis. It will be money well invested. Assume an "I honestly need your help to learn how this company works" attitude. If you make your peers understand that you need their assistance, that you know less than they do but need to know more in order to become a good *team member*, you will find they will help you. They won't mind your asking for information. What does *not* work is arrogance; what *does* work is modesty.
- *Don't ask prying personal questions about others in the office.* If you try to collect gossip, you'll instantly acquire the kind of reputation you don't want. You'll become known as a gossip yourself, someone not to be trusted.

When You Have Moved from a Large to a Small Company

An employee who changes from a large corporation to a small company may have difficulty adjusting and in making friends with a new set of peers. In a large corporation, an executive has set, defined responsibilities; in a small company, he or she may have to pinch-hit for anyone and everyone as necessity dictates. The newcomer who complains, acts uppity, or keeps talking about "how it was back at the other company" is in for trouble. If you keep making comparisons to your former company, others probably will find them pretty odious and superior sounding. As a newcomer, you should make a determined effort to "hang loose"—and to step in to help as needed. The opportunity to grow with a small company—to nurture it and enjoy the camaraderie as it prospers—is worth an exercise in humility on your part any time.

Being at Ease in Meeting and Greeting
in the Business World

The art of meeting and greeting people with charm and efficiency is one of the most effective tools with which anyone in business or the professions can be armed. Meeting someone requires making an effort, putting oneself out, stepping forward, saying and doing *something*. A manager (or potential manager) can show himself to be a smooth, secure, knowing executive by that first gesture—the way he acts when introduced, introduces himself, or introduces someone else. For example, Tony Cordier sees an old colleague approaching from the other end of the airport terminal. He jumps up from his seat near his flight gate, reaches out warmly to shake the hand of the newly arrived passenger, and says, "Gregg! Tony Cordier, great to see you again!" (He gives his own name, in case Gregg has forgotten it.)

What's in a Name?

Everything. It means everything to the person you are properly introducing to someone else in your business life. It means everything to the person to whom you are introducing the newcomer, who will want to learn the other person's name correctly so that she won't be embarrassed later by having to ask for it again.

We're a nation of name-mumblers when we introduce ourselves or other people. All we need do is slow down and pronounce our names slowly, clearly, and distinctly; we may feel as though we are exaggerating our names, but it eases the problem of communication. We also don't pay much attention to people's last names anymore. Perhaps the reason why we've become so first-name oriented, and casual and sloppy about names in general, is that we just don't want to make the effort. In business it is well worth the effort to conscientiously learn the names of everyone with whom you interact, in and out of the office. When a manager remembers his contacts' full names (not just their given ones), they are flattered, their egos are enhanced, and relationships become more cordial as a result.

The Art of Introducing People
(*See also* Chapter 12, "Business Protocol")

The protocol of making proper introductions is very logical: You properly introduce a lesser *to* a more important or senior person. For example, you would introduce:

- A younger person *to* an older person
- A peer in your company *to* a peer in another company
- A junior executive *to* a senior executive
- A fellow executive *to* a customer or client
- An unofficial person *to* an official person
- A fellow U.S. citizen *to* a peer from another country

Introductions can be hazardous. Here are some ways to sail through them:

· *Explain who people are when you introduce them:*

> "Mr. Cogswell, I want my daughter, Cynthia Warren, to meet you. Cynthia, this is Mr. Gregory Cogswell, the president of this company."

> "Jane, I'd like to introduce Harry Newman, my nephew. Harry, this is Dr. Jane Arrowsmith, head of our hospital's Pain Clinic."

> "Georgio, I wanted June Treacher and Anthony Reynolds to meet you. They're college interns from Stanford spending the summer with our company. June and Anthony, this is *Dottor* Georgio Rizzoli of the Montecatini Corporation in Milano."

> "Ambassador Ketchum, I'd like to present Liza Rawson, the Comptroller of our corporation. Liza, Ambassador Ketchum was formerly head of our embassy in Paris and is now a partner in Hockland and Crighton."

When you're introducing a younger person to an older one, for example, touch the arm of the older person and say his name first, then symbolically, in your mind, bring up to the person whose arm you are touching the junior person. This is the way you'll remember how to introduce people to people of rank and status.

Of course, if you are just introducing peers and friends to one another, a simple, "Bill, this is Andy Miller—Andy, meet Bill Laidlaw" will do it. And if you forget who is senior to whom and get all clutched up as to who to introduce to whom, take a deep breath and do the best you can. Even if you have forgotten names, just come up with the parts of the names you know, and no one will know the difference. Many is the time I've bluffed my way through introductions, because I remember either the first or the last name, but not both. "Mr. Parker, I'd like to introduce my old friend Steve from American Express. Steve, this illustrious gentleman is the head of the Jenkins Beer ad account." The fact that I could not remember Mr. Parker's first name nor Steve's last name simply didn't matter, because no one noticed it. They were too busy shaking hands and saying hello to one another.

· *Give information when you introduce someone.* Don't just call a person "Ambassador" without naming the country to which he or she is—or was—accredited. Don't just introduce people by name at a business party without giving their firm or profession or some piece of information that can serve as a jumping off point for conversation in that group.

· *Remember to use titles when introducing people.* You may know that woman well as "Jennifer Garrett." But when you are introducing her, it's important to give her title. Introduce her as "Dr. Jennifer Garrett." Your brother may be your brother, but when introducing him, if he is a judge, he should be referred to as "my brother, Judge William Doakes." A man you're introducing may have been your college roommate, but if he is of high political or appointive office, the people to whom you're presenting him should know it. Therefore, introduce him as "Steve Creighton, Congressman from California," instead of just "Steve Creighton." People want to know to whom they're speaking, so they can make appropriate comments.

· *Some titles accompany their owners to their graves.* Once an Ambassador, always an Ambassador. When a general retires, his family name is still preceded with his rank; when a high-ranking official no longer holds his post, he's introduced as "Governor," "Senator," or "Judge," all his life (*see also* "Proper Forms of Address," Chapter 12).

· *If you forget someone's entire name when you know that person well*, don't worry if you have a total lapse of memory. It happens to us all. Just laugh and make a joke of it. "Sometimes I can't even remember my own mother's name . . ." Confess on the spot. You will be forgiven, because every single person in this world forgets names. It's a very human failing. You will always be forgiven—unless you do it to your future mother-in-law, who is against the marriage.

· *Be a sport: Always give your own name.* Since there is a possibility—maybe even a probability—that the person you know, who is standing with some people you do not know, has forgotten your name and therefore cannot introduce you, help him out. Stick out your hand and give him your name ("Hello, Jim Schubert, good to see you"), to which he will reply, "Jim, did you think I had forgotten your name?" Of course, he has, but everyone is smiling, being introduced all around, everyone is happy, and you have saved the day by simply coming out with your name right away.

· *If your last name is different from your spouse's* (which, of course, occurs when a woman keeps her own name after marriage), *it is important to communicate this fact when you are at social events together.* I am a case in point, since I'm Letitia Baldrige during the day, but in the evening I'm Letitia Hollensteiner. If there is one thing my husband does not appreciate, it is to be introduced as Robert Baldrige, instead of Robert Hollensteiner. This lays the onus on me to introduce him properly whenever we're around people who know me but not him, and who always call me by my professional, maiden name of Baldrige. In these situations, I say very clearly, slowly, and distinctly, "This is my husband, Bob *Hollensteiner*," and if anyone starts to call him Mr. Baldrige, I jump right in and correct them (politely, of course). It's a question of communication. Men and women should be sensitive to their spouses' egos when they are in a business setting that is familiar to one but not the other.

When People Mis-Introduce You, Do You Correct Them?

If someone repeatedly mis-introduces you—giving you either the wrong name, title, or company name—don't make a dramatic episode out of it. Put a big smile on your face and whisper in the person's ear, "Just thought you'd like to know that my name is Jane Merson, not Mason" . . . "It's nothing at all serious, but I'm a lawyer with Simpson Thacher, not Covington & Burling'' . . . "Just a small correction—I'm Colonel Morris, not Major Morris."

I am famous for introduction mistakes, because of always being in a hurry and not concentrating enough. I have been known to introduce husbands to wives, brothers to sisters, and divorced couples as though they were still married (the latter is particularly grim if one or both have remarried).

Remembering Names Takes Practice

The ability to remember names is an outstanding asset. Concentration is the key to remembering a large number of them—at least for a short space of time, such as during a party or a weekend meeting.

When you meet a person, concentrate on his name as it is given to you. Repeat it mentally while you say it aloud. "Glad to meet you, Mr. McChesney," you might say as your mind repeats the name silently two or three times and you also search for an identifying word association. He may have one wisp of hair standing up straight on his head" ("McChesney, wisp on top of head"). He may have unusual colored eyes ("McChesney, green cat's eyes"), very broad shoulders ("McChesney, wrestler's shoulders"), or an unusual pattern in his suit ("McChesney, tic-tac-toe suit"). If the name can be used in a word association with the person himself, concentrate on that. For example: "Mr. Burns, red hair," "Mr. Long, very tall," "Mrs. McIntosh, wearing a raincoat," etc. Remember one salient detail and it will fasten to that person's name like Velcro, at least for a while.

If you don't understand a name when it's given to you (and many introducers are hopelessly inept at articulating names when making introductions), don't be shy about asking for the name again: "I'm sorry, I didn't understand your name, and I want to know it." The other person should be flattered that you care enough to want to know.

If the other person repeats it but you still do not understand, ask for a repetition, even more apologetically this time: "I'm sorry, I just can't seem to catch the name."

This time the person should pronounce his name slowly so that you are able to understand it. If you repeat it aloud, his name will now stick in your mind. If his name is very complicated (like Dobyczescowitz, for example), ask him for his business card; if he doesn't have one, ask him to write his name on your notepad. (When I am out on business, I always carry a thin notepad with me, as do many business people.) By now he will either be very irritated or immensely pleased by your interest.

If you see someone you've met before but can't remember the name, say something like, "I remember meeting you at that American Express lunch at the Hilton last spring. I'm Agnes Catwell." The other person will be flattered to have been remembered, even if you didn't recall his or her name.

If you are entrusted with the responsibility of introducing people to each other at a corporate function, you will have to go through a lot of hard work in order to remember people's names and in order to pronounce them properly. When you do a good job of it, you cast a fine reflection on your company and on your own talents. People like to have their names and titles remembered and stated correctly. It's one of the emoluments in life to which one feels entitled.

Using Nicknames in the Workplace

An unflattering, ugly-sounding, or just plain comical nickname has no place in a conservative business situation. This kind of informality is fine in an art director's office, but not in the office of the vice-president for corporate finance. Besides, a nickname is often a put-down of the person.

Some people have the misfortune to grow up with their childhood nicknames firmly attached—"Chuckles," "Bubba," "Pepper," "Pooch," "Pits," "Spritz," etc. Friends who insist upon calling an executive by this kind of nickname should be kindly reminded by the executive: "Look, I'm not called that anymore. I'd appreciate your calling me Bill."

Everyone has the right to be addressed by a dignified name in the office, one that is neither silly nor deprecating. If your nickname is a pleasing shortened version of your name (such as "Charlie," "Bob," "Dick," etc.), there is no problem. But if Charlie wants to be called "Charles" in the workplace, all he has to do is keep reminding people to call him that. Once his proper name is fixed in other people's minds, he will become "Charles" to them forever.

The head of an insurance company recently circulated a memo to his company executives decreeing that "names, not nicknames will be used in this office." He added, "I happen to love dogs, but dogs, not their owners, are known by nicknames."

What's in a Handshake?

Everything. It's your first physical contact with someone, flesh to flesh. Your handshake is important from the point of view of:

- How you do it
- When you do it
- How it feels to someone else

A DESIRABLE HANDSHAKE FEELS:	AN UNDESIRABLE HANDSHAKE FEELS:
Firm, strong, representative of a person who makes decisions, takes risks, and above all, *takes charge*	Hesitant, apologetic, almost as if you were saying, "I don't really want to shake your hand, nor am I a decision maker."
Warm and enthusiastic, as if you are really glad to meet that person	Weak, slippery, lifeless, like a handful of dead fish. Just as negative is the bone crusher handshake, which makes the other person feel in need of having his hand X-rayed.
Dry, pleasant to the touch	Wet and clammy, or cold, as though you have been holding an iced drink all day

When Do You Shake Hands?

All the time. For instance:

- When you run into someone you know
- When you say goodbye to the same person
- When someone comes in from the outside to see you in your office, and when he leaves, too
- When someone enters your home, or when you enter someone else's home (or when you take leave of one another)
- When you meet someone you know in a restaurant
- When you're introduced to people in any business or social situation, and when you take leave of them
- When you are congratulating someone—after a speech, after an award presentation
- When you are consoling someone (in this case you might hold the handshake for several seconds, then put your other hand on top of the two shaking hands—a gesture of transmitting sympathy through the two pairs of clasped hands
- When you greet someone with very arthritic hands or a prosthesis, rather than taking his hand, put your right hand on his forearm or upper arm as a sign of a salute while saying hello.

When Do You Not Shake Hands?

- When the other person has his or her hands full
- When the person you want to greet is someone much higher ranked than you and to whom you really have nothing to say. In this case, it would look pushy for you to rush up to shake his hand and introduce yourself.
- When the other person is eating a messy hors d'oeuvre in one hand and holding a drink in the other and doesn't have a hand free to indulge in this pleasantry. You should give him a half-salute in greeting that symbolizes "I know you can't shake hands now, but hello."

Points of Protocol in Handshaking

If you enter a group, shake hands first with your host, and then with the other most senior people in the room. If everyone is clustered together—people of all ranks—don't worry about whose hand you shake next, as long as you have shaken the hand of the host of this particular gathering.

Protocol decrees that you shake hands with your host when you leave. Sometimes this is not possible, as when the host of your gathering is surrounded by people and it would be rude for you to interrupt. Use your common sense. If you can easily get to the host to thank him for the meeting, social event, or whatever, fine, shake his hand in goodbye. If you can't easily get to him, leave and telephone your thanks or write him a note the next day.

If someone doesn't see your hand extended and doesn't offer his or her hand to you, just draw back your hand and smile. That person is not rejecting you on purpose; he or she simply doesn't see your extended hand. It's an embarrassing two or three seconds for you, but it happens to every person who shakes hands often.

When You Have Clammy Hands

- If you have a tendency to have cold hands, stick your right hand in your jacket pocket to warm it up as you approach a situation in which you'll be shaking hands. (You can also sit on your hand for a minute to warm it up!)
- Don't hold iced drinks in your right hand. Hold them in your left, so that your shaking hand is nice and dry.
- If you have perennially clammy hands, before you shake someone else's hand, give a quick swipe of your right hand on your skirt or trousers, so that when you present it, it's dry. You can do it so quickly and gracefully, no one will be aware that you made the gesture.

Hugging and Kissing in Greeting

Usually, we greet one another in our business environment with smiles, handshakes, and spoken greetings. Occasionally a bear-hug is in order between two close friends of either gender, when there is good news to celebrate ("I got my promotion," or, "We're going to be married"), or when there is a reunion after a long trip.

A warm hug is not grounds for a sexual harassment suit; it is a nice expression of friendship and affection by a warm, nice person. There is nothing sexual about it. It merely implies a closeness of interest and friendship between the two people.

A person in the office who kisses another on the mouth has stepped out of bounds (unless they are married to one another, and even then, that kiss is better given in private).

A person who air-kisses when greeting another person engages, in my opinion, in the worst kind of artificial behavior there is. An "air kiss" means a person puts a cheek alongside the other person's, while making a kissing sound into the air. It is phony. Two people air-kissing with cries of delight when they had seen one another only a week ago is silly, vacuous behavior, and it looks particularly poor as a form of greeting when someone comes into the office from the outside.

An American man who kisses a woman's hand is also setting himself up as the joke of the month. First of all, by cultural definition, an American man is not supposed to kiss a woman's hand; second, men from other countries know that only a married woman's hand is meant to be kissed. Third, American men don't know the art of hand-kissing anyway. Once I saw a young manager (just back from a three-day trip to Paris and feeling very continental) kiss the hand of the prettiest single woman in the company. Her reaction was marvelous. "First of all, I'm not a married woman, and second, you'll have to spend thirty years in Paris, not three days, if you're going to try that again.'' To this day he still doesn't know what she meant, only that she was displeased.

BEING AT EASE IN MOVING AROUND

Your good or bad manners are always with you, and when you move from one place to another, they become even more conspicuous. Whether you are moving through a living room, a darkened movie theater, a church pew, the corporate auditorium, or the narrow aisle of a Concorde jet on its way to Paris, the way you move tells a great deal about you.

Some people always move suddenly, jerkily, noisily. The right way to move is quietly and effortlessly, so no one is even aware of your movements.

People who speak loudly and laugh raucously as they move through an area upset the train of thought of others around them who may be trying to concentrate. (The noisy movers generally are people of low self-esteem, who are seeking to be noticed.)

Many parents today, I have observed, never have taught their children to ''take the least comfortable chair in the room when visitors come.'' Instead they grow up plopping into the most comfortable one or on the best part of the sofa, sprawling all over with arms and legs in every direction. This is the child who later grows up to be the man or woman who takes up two seats, instead of one, on the bus; grows up to be the one who grabs the comfortable chair in the room and leaves the spindly legged, creaky one for someone else. My father always used to whisper sternly at his children when we went to visit people, ''Heads up!'' meaning look about you, *think*, and then you'll do the right thing. When children today move through the aisle of a theater, wielding soda cans and popcorn containers like weapons, it's plain to see that no one ever told them, ''Heads up.'' Young managers need to be told what children used to be told in the days when parents taught their offspring manners:

- Keep your eyes open when you move among people in public. Look around you; be aware of others.
- When you enter a room or have people entering your office, give the best seat to your client or customer—or senior manager.
- When you must move quickly among people, perhaps carrying something that may hit them (like suitcases, backpacks, tote bags, briefcases, umbrellas, etc.), look where you're going, apologize left and right with sincerity, and smile at the people you are whacking. In most cases, their anger levels will be lowered by your apologetic behavior.

Going Through Doors

In the old days, ladies always preceded gentlemen in going through doors, and in addition, a door was always rather ceremoniously held open for her to sail through in a queenly fashion. It was an understood, accepted *politesse*. Little boys held doors for old ladies. Even frail old men on crutches always tended to the door of the ladies behind them. Today, chivalry counts for little. What you have to think about is not getting hit in the face by a door swung shut by the person ahead of you. In spite of the fact that no one will ever thank you or even notice your kindnesses, take a vow: *Be a door holder* for others. It doesn't matter if you are male or female, holding a door for the person coming behind is a common courtesy. It doesn't matter if it's the CEO or the bicycle messenger in his Spandex shorts, just do it. It brings so much pleasure—after the shock registers—to people, and it makes people remember and like you.

Always hold the elevator door for the people coming toward you in the hallway. It's enough to make people want to resign from the human race when they tear down an office building corridor carrying bags, red-faced and huffing, to catch the one elevator with its doors open—only to reach the spot just in time to see the door close on a car full of people who are standing there, eyes upward, pretending not to notice them. All one person on that car had to do was press the "Open" button.

Going Through Swinging Doors

- Regardless of your gender, let your guests—and anyone on staff who ranks considerably higher than you—precede you through the swinging door. Don't make a big thing of it.
- When a group of five or more comes to your offices, precede them, so you can show your guests where to go.
- If you know that a door is very heavy and difficult, precede any guest you may have with you by saying, "This is a heavy door; I'll go first and give it a shove."
- If someone, even a stranger, on crutches or in a wheel chair or with a cast on his arm, or just plain frail-looking and slow-moving, is approaching a swinging door, go first, tell him what you're doing, and hold the door so that it opens slowly. (Every year disabled people are knocked down and suffer head, leg, and arm injuries because of some thoughtless person racing through the door while the disabled person attempts to go through slowly.)
- In the evening, if a man and woman are away from the business world and he wishes to be gallant, he should let her go through first, and give the door a firm shove from behind. I have a little advice for an over-reactive woman's advocate who wishes to challenge my viewpoint on a man's desire to hold doors for his wife or girlfriend: Live a little longer, get more experience in working relationships, and lighten up!
- During the normal daytime movement of people, in office buildings or other kinds of buildings, whoever arrives first at the door should enter and go through it. It's as simple as that.

KEEPING YOUR SENSE OF HUMOR
ABOUT YOUR GAFFES

Unless you have practiced recovering your composure after making some serious gaffes, you will probably continue to suffer far too much. (By the time I was thirty, I had made enough serious ones to last a normal person's lifetime.) Young executives, when they discover something they've done wrong, are generally over-mortified. And the more mortified they are, the more uncomfortable everyone else is around them.

Step back from a gaffe, ask yourself some questions and seek some answers:

How serious was it? Your embarrassment may be more than that of the other people around you. Don't blow the episode out of proportion, because as soon as you recover your own dignity, the others will recover theirs.

Did anyone get hurt (other than you) and did your company lose face or suffer harm because of your actions? If so, take instant remedial action, which could be anything from making a simple apology to mounting a compensatory campaign.

Was there any humor to highlight in your faux pas situation? If there wasn't any, can you inject some, even at a later date, perhaps inserted into your letter of explanation or apology?

Many of my celebrated gaffes committed in high, important places (which I often have included in my writing and lectures) have given comfort to the people who have heard them, because they know they could never do anything that stupid and still remain employed. For example:

- At a White House State dinner the French ambassador concluded I had improperly seated him, according to protocol (which was not the case), so he walked out of the dining room in the middle of the first course, leaving everyone (including President and Mrs. Kennedy) in an astonished silence. All eyes were on me as I fluttered like a nervous chicken between the Kennedys and the ambassador, trying to keep the ambassador from leaving in a huff. I had carried out the Secretary of State's wishes in this diplomatic matter, but I couldn't exactly yell that out in the middle of the service of the *Filets de sole Marguery*, could I? I could feel the disapproval of my professionalism floating in the air of the State Dining Room that night.
- At a reception at the American Embassy in Rome, at a moment when India and Pakistan were at war over their borders, I introduced the new ambassador from Pakistan as the new ambassador from India to the entire diplomatic corps. The guest of honor, the Pakistani ambassador, fled the residence and returned to his own embassy to recover from the humiliation.
- I introduced a top Democratic contributor to President Kennedy at a White House reception, then I introduced his wife, using his mistress' first name instead of his wife's.
- I inadvertently produced an all-white menu for a very important diplomatic dinner in Rome given by Ambassador Clare Boothe Luce and her husband, Henry Luce.

It was white from the cream of celery soup through to the creme brulee dessert. Even the toast points around the white fish with its sauce were made of white bread. It caused Henry Luce to ask if I was perhaps color blind.

- I mixed up two of my typed letters in their envelopes and sent a letter chiding a friend (who had not done a job for a charity which he had promised to do) to the CEO of a company whose PR account I was trying to land. The friend, of course, received the PR proposal that was meant for the CEO. The real problem was that my friend's PR firm was also trying to land the same account that I was.
- I made three mistakes in introducing an illustrious guest speaker at an evening's banquet: I got his name, title, and state wrong!
- A letter with my facsimile signature on it went out to several hundred people in a Burlington Industries interior design award program that I ran. The recipients of this form letter were told they were winners in the prestigious Burlington annual competition, when in fact, they were the losers. The two lists had been switched. The real winners received form letters signed by me that consoled them for having lost. It was my fault as manager of the project for not having been at the mailing house to see that this disaster didn't happen.

I survived every single one of these faux pas, errors, gaucheries, gaffes, mistakes—whatever you wish to call them. For example:

- I crawled back into the French ambassador's good graces in the Kennedy Administration by begging his forgiveness in an impassioned letter, even though I was right and he was wrong.
- I followed the Pakistani ambassador back to his embassy, pleading for his mercy. When that didn't work, I sent roses and a letter of apology, which did work (very few people can resist the latter combination).
- I apologized profusely to the Democratic contributor whose wife I had misintroduced with his mistress' name, but President Kennedy took over, mentioned the stunned wife's real name, and saved the day for us all by making a big fuss over the married couple in the receiving line.
- I assured Henry Luce I was not color blind, and for a while after this incident, the food platters in the ambassador's residence in Rome were as colorful as a Mondrian painting. In fact, it was color over-kill, *tutti frutti*, Mr. Luce assured me.
- My friend never divulged the contents of my public relations plan to his own firm. Instead of being upset, the CEO was vastly amused by my chiding letter to my friend about his lack of charity, and both men, after my frantic telephone calls of passionate apology, laughed and thought the whole thing was funny. (I also won the CEO's PR account.)
- Although I had made such a complete shambles of introducing the senator, everyone in the ballroom had consumed enough wine and joviality to think I had done it on purpose. There was uproarious laughter, and by the time I realized the mis-

takes I had made, I was already receiving congratulations for "being so funny and clever." The audience was completely fooled, and even the senator congratulated me "for the only real laughs of the evening."

- After the design award winners had been notified in my letter that they were losers, and vice versa, I realized the people who had been falsely notified they were winners deserved our attention first. I hired several friends who can act with dramatic flair, in a Sarah Bernhardtian fashion, if required to. I brought "the apology squad" into my office, and together with my staff, we used a battery of telephones and called every number long distance until we reached each of the people who had received my letter. Day and night, we explained how the "ghastly" mistake (or should I say "*my* ghastly mistake?") had occurred. Our telephone voices transmitted our dismay, even our horror at having misled them with the wrong letters. (Computers and faxes do not convey emotions like voices do.) We sounded so upset and contrite, all of the people we called—with the exception of one (a troublemaker who threatened to sue)—were kind and understanding about the mailing house's—excuse me—*my* mistake.

A serious gaffe requires apologies—verbal and written (*see also* "Letter of Apology," Chapter 7). But for the occasional misstep, laugh about your own mistake, because everyone around you is miserable for you.

For example, when you are seriously late for an appointment with a client or customer: "You know, Dave, we have a competition going on back at the office where we list the most irritating and infuriating kinds of behavior in the business world. I think my keeping you waiting has probably won."

If you make a joke about yourself, the others present will quickly feel at ease themselves, and everyone can get on with their lives. *Humor, of course, should always follow, not lead, the obligatory apology.* Your timing must be right, or your joke could fall terribly flat. Humor can never replace an apology; it merely augments the effectiveness of it and lightens it at the same time. And the humor is always more effective *when turned toward yourself*, rather than someone else.

It's human to err. Remind the person you have inopportuned that to forgive is divine. I can tell you from years of experience that if it's your boss whom your gaffe has put on the spot, and if he or she doesn't fire you but instead tells you to "forget it," you are blessed and perhaps home free, not to mention fortunate to be working for such a secure person.

2

The Executive at Ease with Staff, Peers, and Superiors

A manager has a much larger responsibility than just the quality of his or her work. The manager of people is responsible for the morale of the office. It's a skill that, unfortunately, is not part of a business school curriculum.

A good manager shows the way: in giving credit where it is due, in defending those who need it; in encouraging staff when they are feeling down; and in showing by his or her own example how to treat people, including the support staff, from the ground up. There is no team without cooperation all along the line.

THE EXCELLENT MALE OR FEMALE MANAGER, WORKING SMART

A successful manager never loses sight of the importance of his team. He:

- Gives full credit to whomever deserves it—and does it in front of the staff
- Always uses "we" instead of "I" when representing a section or division
- Vigorously defends any staff member who has been unjustly accused; lobbies for another chance for any staff member who has been justly accused
- Never thoughtlessly encroaches on another manager's territory
- Sets an example for the staff in environmental behavior
- Runs meetings efficiently, and never calls one unless it is absolutely necessary

- Is an excellent meeting participant: pays attention to the agenda, refrains from wasting time, but adheres to the chairman's requests
- Knows how to motivate employees in work and in good causes
- Makes certain employees are in the best possible environment, with the proper ventilation, lighting, seating, sound, and desk efficiency
- Is a consummate personal note writer—to thank, encourage, console, inspire, or apologize to someone
- Goes out of the way, creatively, to help a colleague or friend who is in trouble
- Always returns borrowed property promptly and in good condition
- Discourages any hurtful rumor and plays a defense role when it comes to gossip
- Dresses appropriately for any occasion to reflect well on the company
- Is socially astute: answers all invitations promptly and attends any function on time and properly dressed
- Does not boast about invitations that others in the office have not received, nor discuss the event after it has occurred
- Is a considerate host, always mindful of his guests' comfort
- Is a considerate guest who keeps his eyes open and who helps when it is needed
- Is generous, and known for picking up the check at a difficult moment, when it is not his turn, to avoid a scene in the restaurant
- Knows protocol, adheres by its rules and understands deference to people of senior rank
- Knows how to give a compliment to others and to receive one graciously
- Understands that the quickest road to social failure is to be socially over-aggressive (i.e., pushy)
- Has excellent telephone, cellular phone, E-mail, beeper, and fax manners
- Encourages employees to better their lives, to further educate themselves and strive to be qualified for a higher level job
- Motivates employees, by example and financial support, to support and enjoy their area's cultural offerings
- Shows compassion for employees, and tries to help solve problems with an imaginative use of the programs or counseling services offered by the company. (Sometimes these services don't even exist—until a manager makes them happen!)
- Understands that when communicating, some people he manages have better skills in written explanations, while others do better with oral ones. It is only fair to ask them to do what they do best.
- Gives the support staff a good forum in which to exchange ideas and to ventilate complaints. He knows that if an employee is asked what he or she thinks should be done to cut costs, raise profitability, or improve product quality, the answers can be helpful, even brilliant, and morale-building in the process.
- Makes the support staff feel really important to the company, and constantly challenges them to do more.

- Coaches them on how to ask questions of customers, and how to answer customers' questions. Does some role-playing and devil's-advocating with staff members, so that they will not be surprised and stunned by interchanges with a sometimes rude and hostile public.
- When an employee has made a mistake, criticizes that person in private, but makes certain the employee understands exactly what was wrong. This requires great communication skills on the part of the manager, and also human skills—to reassure the employee that he is still of great value to the company, that everyone believes in that employee and that he should continue to work creatively and take risks, not just work gingerly for fear of making an error.
- Has a sense of humor, because, next to kindness, it is the greatest asset of all.

AN INTELLIGENT MANAGER HELPS
A NEW EMPLOYEE ADJUST

A good manager judges new colleagues fairly, according to the value of the new employee to the company. He:

- Shows the employee the ropes on joining the company or firm, assisting without patronizing
- Praises her good performances and criticizes the poor ones, giving fair and accurate feedback on job performance
- Honestly appraises what he contributes to the team effort, including his successes that make him look good, too
- Shows regard for her as a team member, includes her in all the division's or firm's activities, and metes out her major responsibilities
- If there is an "Old Boys' Network" operating within the office, he insists that the new female managerial employee be made a part of it. (This is when male managers gather informally at lunch to discuss business and share information and gossip garnered from many grapevines to which women managers usually do not have access.) If, however, once she has been welcomed by the men to their lunches, golf games, and more, and her peers consider her behavior nontraditional and unacceptable, her boss tells her the frank truth. She can either conform and remain in their group or do what she pleases and remain, uncomplainingly, outside it.
- If she will eventually be competing with him for the same higher position within the company, he treats her as he would any male competitor.

THE MANAGER'S STAFF AND PEERS

The competent executive who treats everyone in the office with equal respect and consideration *will* succeed, because everyone in that office will want that person to enjoy success, and will assist in that effort.

This means that when you walk into your office building you greet everyone who crosses your path, even if you don't feel like it. You may have indigestion, a bad cold, or have had a fight with your spouse that morning, or your teen-age son managed to wreck your car, so you had to come on a crowded bus. Others aren't interested in your troubles. They may have had a bad night and early morning, too. They may also be in need of cheering up, but instead of relaying your troubles to them, help them with theirs by putting on a positive face.

It may sound syrupy, but it's true: Smiles are immensely contagious. A sudden, warm, enthusiastic smile tossed at someone can change the whole temperature in the room at that moment. No matter how high-ranking you become within the organization, remember to say "Hello" to everyone and to start an epidemic of smiles as people start their workdays. This is a message yet to be understood by groups of well-educated, newly employed, young executives.

Years ago I became aware of how universally beloved a certain executive of Burlington Industries was, and so I questioned people at all levels in the New York headquarters as to why he was regarded as such a great guy.

They all said pretty much the same thing:

- He's so cheerful, always making everyone else feel good. He never gives you time to ask how *he* is.
- He knows everyone's name and never passes anyone in the building without saluting them and calling them by their names.
- He cares about the people he works with, always knows when they have had good or bad news, and always comments and inquires: "Mary, how's your mother doing this week? Good!" "Tony, I hear you guys are going to grab the softball league championship for us this year. Nice going!" "Mark, you saved all our hides at the meeting this morning. We appreciate what you did."
- He never tries to shunt off the dirty work on others; he's always deep in the middle of any emergency, helping out anyone who needs it.
- One division manager described him as "the perfect team member . . . A leader who always accepts criticism when it is merited, but who doles out praise effortlessly."
- He's just "always there" for everyone, which means he's there for the company, too.

A GOOD MANAGER MAKES FRIENDS AT WORK

For many people, the office is the primary arena of social life. Employees often do not have the resources, or perhaps the time, to make friends in their communities. The place of work, where so many hours in a week are spent, should be looked upon as a rich resource for establishing friendships. (If you are single, it is smart *not* to look upon it as a rich resource for romance, because it probably won't be.)

Good personal relationships at work are key to happy, productive executives, and to high morale in the entire workplace. In cultivating friendships, remember the following:

- *Be open and friendly to everyone*, not just to those who are especially popular or who have an almost celebrity status. Don't play favorites, in other words, or be overly aggressive in courting someone's friendship. It's fine to invite someone to lunch; it's not fine to invite someone to lunch five days in a row, which looks like an act of desperation. Let the friendship develop slowly.
- *Scout around for someone in the office who shares your passion in life*, whether it's playing tennis or golf, browsing around art galleries, watching foreign films, taking gourmet cooking lessons, bungee-jumping, attending concerts, or consulting astrologists. The person who shares your major extra-curricular interest is the most logical potential friend.
- *Be sensitive to the other person's schedule, such as work deadlines*. It's as annoying to your executive friend as it is to his boss if you interrupt him when he's hard at work, on a deadline. Just because you may not be busy for the moment, you should never hover over someone else's desk to make chit-chat.
- *Don't expect to share in your new friend's social life*, at least at first. A friendship must grow logically and easily in the office, before the other person will want you to share his or her out-of-the-office life. In fact, don't be upset if you never become part of someone's out-of-the-office life.
- *Don't be resentful of your friend's friendships in the office*. Jealousy is the quickest deterrent to a good social relationship.
- *Be supportive of your friend*. When he or she has had a success, bask in the reflected glory of it; when he has had a major disappointment, stand ready to cheer him up, encourage him and make him feel good about the future.
- *Lend a helping hand when it is really needed*. For a good friend, that might consist of any of the following:

  - Lend money if he has had a personal emergency.
  - Lend your car in the case of a breakdown of his car.
  - Stick up for him when he is unfairly criticized, whether by his peers or his boss.
  - Report a piece of information you have that will benefit him—even if it's a criticism he needs to hear.

- Assist him when he is in the midst of an office crisis. For example: copying documents he needs for an emergency meeting when the support staff has gone home for the day.

- *Be sensitive to your friend's family obligations, if they exist.* Don't feel neglected or spurned if you are not invited to join your new friend during family weekend activities.
- *You're much better off if you have several best friends.* Having only one puts you at a disadvantage, particularly if he or she disappoints you, has his or her own personal problems, or moves away.
- *Be discreet in the office about your friendships.* It is distracting, gossip-producing, and not very professional if you and your friends broadcast to your office environment your every joint activity.
- *Don't abuse your friendships.* This means that you're careful not to ask too many favors of friends, and you never put them on the spot.
- *Use your really good friends to improve yourself.* Ask them to give you frank answers to tough questions. ("Do I really have an overly loud voice?" "What about my handshake—is it really wishy-washy?" "Did I ramble too much in my presentation of the new plan this morning—should I have been more concise?" "Will you come with me when I order a new suit tomorrow, so I don't make a big mistake?")

THE FIRST PERSON TO PROJECT THE COMPANY'S IMAGE: THE RECEPTIONIST
(See also "Management Should Take an Interest in What the Public Hears When Calling the Company," Chapter 7)

The treatment afforded visitors by your company's receptionist (who may be primarily someone's secretary stationed near the office entrance) is as important as the first voice a caller hears upon phoning your office. The welcome should be warm and efficient. Make this person understand the importance of the job as keeper of the gate, the voice of the company greeting the public.

It is the duty of the company's personnel officers to make tough demands when screening applicants for this important assignment, to set strict rules, and to be very clear about the *do*'s and *don't*s of this job. If the applicant feels Personnel is being too restrictive of his or her rights, then the applicant should look for another job.

A receptionist's job is too important to be accorded a very low salary. The salary should be adequate, and only conscientious and capable people should be hired for the job, with a promise of promotion within a year or two if they do a good job and learn the company's business.

Since many more women than men fill the job of receptionist, I have used the female pronoun for simplification in the following set of behavior guides for the position:

- She dresses conservatively. She wears pants only if her figure is perfect and her pants are very well cut.
- Her makeup and hairstyle are neat, well done, and conservative; she does not fuss with her face or her hair once she is on the job.
- She wears little jewelry, and what she does wear is noiseless and unobtrusive.
- She does not eat, chew gum, smoke, or drink at her desk.
- She does not read newspapers at her desk, since they are so messy. She reads either magazines or a book hidden on her lap—and only when there is no activity in the area over which she is presiding.
- She keeps her hands and fingernails presentable.
- Her desk is neat, with everything in its proper place.
- She smiles when she greets each visitor and her demeanor shows she is glad to see each one. Her voice is cheerful when she uses the telephone to announce the visitor.
- She transmits orders and directions to the visitor in a very clear manner, so that she can be easily understood.
- She does not take personal calls of any length while on the job; she never continues a conversation she is having when a visitor approaches her desk, unless it is an important one. When she is on the telephone, she does not turn her back to the visitor, as though trying to shut him out.
- She makes sure that the reception area is clean at all times and equipped with good company reading materials, including company product catalogs, annual reports, and so on.
- If a visitor is kept waiting longer than usual, she herself calls to see what is happening and then reports to the visitor.
- She treats executives, visitors, and employees with equal courtesy as they enter and leave her area.
- She calls everyone by his or her last name, so that her reception area has an air of dignity.
- She fastidiously keeps the company directory up to date, with accurate names, numbers, and locations of all personnel.
- She knows senior management—their titles, what they do, and how they fit into the hierarchy—so she can intelligently answer any question asked by a visitor.
- She makes sure her area has everything it needs, including a guest telephone, sufficient closet space, an umbrella stand, etc., as well as the proper sign-in book, if signing in is company policy for security's sake.
- If the receptionist is responsible for fire and bomb evacuation drills, she takes this duty very seriously and informs herself of every single detail.

The receptionist should have a signal to press in an emergency as well as a number she can call to give a code signal meaning ''Come help. There's a suspicious looking individual here.''

The sophisticated executive understands what an important role a good receptionist plays in the organization and treats her with respect. He remembers the promise made to her to move her up within the company if she gives a stellar performance.

THE SYMBOL OF GOOD MANNERS AT WORK: THE ADMINISTRATIVE ASSISTANT OR EXECUTIVE SECRETARY

A secretary or administrative assistant with beautiful manners greatly enhances her organization, and she sets the tone for everyone in it. She elevates the entire corporate image by the tactful, considerate way in which she (or he) handles the relationships between the boss and the world inside and outside the company.

A good secretary handles people so gracefully that when they've been told ''no,'' they go away satisfied all the same.

I began my own career as a secretary. Women did not go to graduate schools of business in those days. I was bilingual, with most of my MA in psychology, and with experience living in Europe, but I was female, and therefore ineligible to join the Foreign Service. So I became a secretary in the Foreign Service. I don't regret it for a second. I sat in the offices of the great and powerful in many countries because I had those office skills. It opened the door to the worlds of diplomacy, politics, the White House—and real power. I had a view from the catbird seat overlooking American politics and history in the last half of the twentieth century, which few people have had, and all because at the age of twenty-one I was forced to learn how to pound a typewriter and use a little stenotype machine to take dictation.

The secretarial profession is one of the least appreciated and understood in the entire spectrum of jobs. The truth is that most of the true professionals in this field who have been with their companies for years know more than their bosses do about the business. That fact is accepted by their appreciative, high-ranking managers, who admit that they do their jobs more brilliantly because the person behind the desk in the outer offices is doing that job brilliantly.

Change the Title and Upgrade the Job

Technological advancements and changes in the business world have not obliterated the secretary's position; they have, instead, freed her from many tiresome, routine tasks and enabled her to assume responsibilities of a more diversified nature. *Efficient executive secretaries should be considered part of the management team.* As they advance in stature, they may want to have their titles changed to raise their status within the organization. Here are some options:

- Executive Assistant
- Personal Assistant to . . .

- Administrative Assistant
- Staff Assistant
- Staff Coordinator
- Executive Office Manager
- Executive Staff Assistant
- Executive Coordinator

Secretaries who are upgraded in position should have their salaries adjusted accordingly and receive increased benefits.

How to Introduce Your Secretary

It doesn't matter if today's office environment is basically informal. The secretary to a manager should be introduced by the boss as "Ms. Johnson," not as "Debbie Sue." To introduce her by her family name is to give her—and her job—a sense of dignity, a special status. When people from the outside are in and around this senior manager's office, even though they use given names in private, the boss and secretary should refer to one another by their family names.

"Ms. Johnson, will you please get Mr. Asquith on the telephone?"
"Certainly, Mr. Brainard."

Doesn't that create a much better image of the office to outside visitors present than this exchange?:

"Debbie Sue, get Bernie on the phone."
"Yeah, sure, Jerry."

Having Your Secretary Run Personal Errands for You

The company does not pay your secretary a salary to spend time outside the office on personal errands for you. Handling personal matters on the office telephone is certainly acceptable, since it makes your work load lighter and increases your efficiency. However, to have your assistant running around town during office hours to pick up this and that for you, to take the dog to the vet and to accompany a child to the dentist, are not tasks that she was hired by the company to perform.

If you ask your secretary to do personal business for you that requires her to leave the office, have her do it after work or on weekends, and pay a mutually agreed upon sum for performing these services.

Promote Your Secretary

Some senior managers become so attached to and dependent on their secretaries, they forget that they may have ambition and a desire to move up in the corporate world.

A sensitive boss is aware of his or her secretary's feelings about advancing to a managerial position, and helps achieve her goal. This means eventually letting her go, helping her to move up and out, and then having to adjust to her replacement. It's a tough call, but hopefully, the manager will help his secretary, motivate her, push her out of the comfortable nest she occupies, and then take great pride in her advancement.

One of the nicest CEOs I ever knew encouraged his executive secretary of fourteen years to go to graduate business school. He saw how incredibly bright she was, how knowledgable she was, and how interested in the company's business, and he respected her judgment. He personally paid out of his pocket for her tuition, as well as for books and other materials needed, because the company was downsizing and was no longer paying tuition for anyone. When she graduated, he was in the front row with her family. The nice ending was that she spent an entire month after graduation sitting by her old desk, carefully training her replacement, so that her boss would be well taken care of.

The secretary to a world-famous publisher and founder of a magazine empire whom I knew, told me once that "a secretary is only as good as the amount of respect she and the boss have for one another." Since, through the years, her boss gave her several thousand shares of the empire's stock at Christmas time, she had to know what she was talking about.

THE YOUNG MANAGER AND HIS OLDER EMPLOYEES

I once heard two young managers discussing who had the worse lot in life: One was a twenty-eight-year-old man, who had an entire office full of older women reporting to him, and the other was a thirty-year-old woman manager, who had two men in their fifties and one in his sixties reporting to her.

I have seen young managers handle this kind of situation beautifully. The first meeting of the new young manager with much older employees is always the most important. Sometimes the hostility and resentment is even overt, which is inexcusable. I was present, for example, when a fifty-some woman sniffed at her new young boss in answer to his question of what her job was, "I've been here for thirty years because I draw very good architectural plans. I suppose you're here because you graduated from Harvard."

"No," he quickly retorted, "I'm here because I helped found a company very much like this one in size, except that our company was healthy and strong, and your company—my new company—is weak and having terrible problems. I'm hoping you and everyone else will work hard with me to make it strong and profitable again." The women around him cheered at his answer, and I had the feeling that they themselves would take care of disciplining their sharp-tongued peer.

A new young manager should set his style of management immediately upon entering the room where the staff waits for their first meeting. (One young manager told me she could only think of a cage of pacing, angry lions when she entered that room the first time.)

The older employees may be hostile, but they may also just be fearful of losing their jobs to the younger generation. *The new young manager should therefore:*

- Greet and shake hands with every employee present, asking each person his name and job
- Read carefully beforehand the employee bios, so that he can profess admiration for the impressive backgrounds and job skills of the people he or she will now manage. He should memorize interesting tidbits about them, to prove when he meets them how well he did his homework, such as, "You're the one with nine children, aren't you? Wonderful! I'd like to see a picture of them some day." "You must be the one who transferred from Indianapolis. How do you like Denver in comparison?" "You won the company sales championship last year, didn't you? Great!"
- Explain to his workers they really need one another in order to work as a team, to bring increased profits
- Demonstrate why he is qualified to be in the new lead position he holds. He should talk about his background and his expertise, and how he expects to utilize it.
- End with a vigorous affirmation of how pleased he is to be in the new job, how much he admires his team already in place, and how successful he *knows* they will all be

YES, A WOMAN EXECUTIVE HAS SPECIAL NEEDS AND PROBLEMS—ALL OF THEM SOLVABLE

Whenever a woman today complains about "how bad she has it," I want to tell her what it was like to be a consultant in 1964 to a Fortune 100 company and to be expected, as the only woman member of the team, to make sandwiches and prepare thermoses of coffee and tea at home to bring to a meeting of the corporation's clients. I was being paid, I had thought, for my brain and my international experience, but obviously from their point of view, also for my egg-salad-on-whole-wheat sandwiches! (Actually, my sandwiches *were* quite good.)

An Intelligent Woman Manager Relates to Her Male Colleagues

- She has excellent manners. It is expected of her, and chauvinist though it may seem, bad manners are much more conspicuous on a woman than they are on a man. Part of good manners means that she is grateful to whomever trains her and gives her the time to settle in to the new office routine.

- She is pleasant to everyone in the office environment, not just to the big chiefs. She shows interest in them as people, not just in their jobs.
- She is punctual, well organized, thorough in her preparation.
- She refrains from whining and blaming others when she fails at what she tries to do.
- When she is invited to join the Old Boys' Network, she comes prepared with some interesting information or something very amusing, as her contribution to the conversation. She pays for her own meal (perhaps she even buys the table a bottle of wine) and thanks her fellow managers for having ushered her into their lunch group.

The Woman Executive Copes with Unwelcome Advances

A businesswoman or a professional woman may very well, in the course of her life, find herself in difficult situations with customers and clients. Some words of advice from someone who has been in the business world for many decades and feels as though she has seen it all:

- Don't be paranoid and think, on your business trip, that every man who looks at you is a potential rapist. Only very, very rarely are you going to be in danger, so enjoy meeting members of the opposite sex on your business trips. If a friend or acquaintance has had one too many drinks, joke him out of it. He will probably feel embarrassed tomorrow, if he even *remembers* it. Don't make a big issue out of one little pass. Forget it.
- Be wise and use your head. When you're in a potentially dangerous situation, you'll recognize the signs: liquor on a man's breath and his constant physical approaches, such as pulling you over to him with his arm around your shoulders, grabbing you constantly around the waist, trying to kiss you.
- If you feel someone is coming on to you at a business-social function, such as a restaurant meal or cocktail party, don't drink. You want to stay alert and articulate, so you can handle him with words and the actions of your brain, not with the physical defenses of your body.
- Don't go into his hotel room if you two are the only ones present, even if it's for a purported meeting with him. Just say "I'd feel much more comfortable if we held this meeting in the lobby. There are good places to sit down there. Come on." If you say these words as you head toward the elevator, he will get the message and accompany you, however sheepishly, to the meeting downstairs—in a public place.
- If he uses physical force to pull you into his room or if he forces himself into your room, call the hotel operator for help immediately. If he wrestles you to the floor or to the bed before you can reach the telephone, scream like crazy. Full-force howling is called for. (This is very off-putting to a man bent on having sex with you, and if he's a rapist, your calls will probably be heard and help will come.)

· If he begins to make sexual advances, don't stay alone with him in the back seat of a car or taxi. You are very vulnerable in these circumstances, so get out of the car at a stoplight. *Better yet,* don't get into the car with him in the first place, if he has been giving you the wrong signals. If you have a funny feeling about a man who has offered to transport you to a meeting or a place of business, simply don't go with him. Make excuses, tell a lie—do anything to get to the meeting by other means. Your funny feeling is probably good intuition. *Follow it.*

The main point here is that, as a woman, you should not find yourself in compromising situations with a man who has been coming on to you sexually, particularly if he's been drinking. Stay around other people until he has left or until you can get away safely. If you're traveling and are bothered by someone staying in your hotel, tell a couple of people nearby (strangers included) that you're afraid, and ask them to escort you to your room, so that he won't accompany you.

When a Woman Manager Doesn't Need or Want a Certain Friend

It could happen that another person in the office wants you for a friend, and the feeling is not reciprocated. We are talking about someone who is lonely and who begins to cling to you for security, because you were kind-hearted and nice. It may be that you are simply not attracted to that person as a friend, or she may get on your nerves or you may already have too many friends. Whatever the reason, having to worry about her feelings can become a big drag on your own morale and productivity at work.

I personally feel that a frank talk with her is best. To be up-front, but in a kind way, is the most successful tactic in letting someone down easily. You might use any of these ploys:

> "I would enjoy having lunch, but between my work schedule and my personal commitments, I just don't make many lunch dates. I need the time for personal business instead."

> "It's very nice of you to ask me to go out after work, but my personal schedule is a tight one and doesn't permit that, I'm sorry to say. From the moment I leave here I am committed to another agenda . . ."

Whatever conversational tactic you use, remember to leave the other person feeling good about herself or himself. Praise her, tell her she's a delightful person, but for her own sake, she should move on to someone who has a more flexible schedule.

When a Single Person Does Not Wish to Date Another Single Person Who Keeps Asking

When a single person in the office keeps asking you out, and a date with him or her is the farthest thing from your own wishes, don't just keep stringing that person along. Don't make lame excuses about being busy when he or she asks you out.

If the other person is abusive, or if sexual harassment enters into your relationship, of course, you must report it to a superior at once. But if it is simply someone who thinks you'd be fun to go out with for dinner and a movie, or to go dancing, or whatever, turning that person down diplomatically can sap your energy. You're telling little white lies that make you feel uncomfortable.

You must confront the situation. Use some of the conversational gambits listed for unwanted friends, if they fit. But the most graceful way to handle this situation, the way that is the least embarrassing to the other person, is to say that you would enjoy getting to know him under other circumstances, but that there is someone else very important in your life and thus you are committed elsewhere. (That someone else could be your dog, your would-be suitor—your boss doesn't have to know.)

Get up your courage, say it, tell him he's a wonderful person, look in his eyes and say, "Someone is going to be very fortunate to have you take her out. I really wish you well." Then get up and leave. It's tough to do, but it's better than falsely leading someone on.

A GOOD MANAGER DEALS WITH RATHER THAN AVOIDS EMPLOYEES' PERSONAL PROBLEMS

A good manager is like a good general in the field—he takes care of the troops. When it comes to the manager's attention that an employee is having a serious problem, he takes action.

For example, if an employee comes to you with a legitimate complaint about another employee's personal mannerisms, do what you can to help so that everyone has an easier time of it. Tact and diplomacy may be required here. Discuss the problem privately with the employee and encourage his input in the solution to the problem. Be sure to check on the employee's progress and congratulate him, as well as anyone who helped, when the problem is under control. For instance:

- John W. in the mail room may come into work every morning reeking of garlic, and without clean clothes. He is considered unpleasant to be around. Tell him that people have been complaining about his odor. Come right out and say, "You must use a deodorant every day and you must take a shower or bath every day. I'm sorry to have to tell you this—it's embarrassing to us both—but it had to be said." Then change the subject quickly. Tell him something he's been doing that's praiseworthy before you say goodbye to him. "John, I heard the mail room expenses are down this month. That's the way to go. Good work!" In other words, end your difficult discussion on a upbeat note.
- You hear people complaining about Suzie J. in the legal department—about her infuriating habit of interrupting everyone with whom she talks. She does this consistently and militantly; her peers don't want to hold conversations with her. You also know that Suzie deals a great deal with outside clients, and you do not want her interrupting them to the point of great annoyance. Again, in private, where no

one can hear, tell her that she must cease doing this. Later, if she continues to interrupt when you are talking privately with her, try giving her some of her own medicine. Begin interrupting her constantly yourself, always with a smile on your face, so she knows exactly what you are doing. Tell her she needs to know how it feels to others when she constantly interrupts them.

- George A. in the advertising department is rude to the clerical staff; he never speaks to them except to bark a command at someone. He opens his mouth only to criticize a staff member, never to praise for a job well done. As his manager, take him to lunch and while the atmosphere is pleasant and relaxed, tell him how those under him are intimidated and frustrated by his negative management style. Explain how easy it is for an employee to lose his motivation to do well if he can never please his boss. If you have a manager with a Superman complex, who mistakenly thinks he is perfect in his job and who makes unrealistic demands of others, he needs to learn that when a person is trying as hard as he is able, he can function only when criticism is merited. The intensity of a supervisor's praise when an employee does a job well should certainly match the intensity of the criticism leveled at him when he messes up.

3

The Executive Receives, Visits, and Dines with Others

S*ome people seem to move with fluid grace whether they are entering an elevator, getting out of a cab, coming into someone's office, or using their eating utensils during lunch. They are at ease, and if you watch them closely, you'll find they move efficiently, quietly, inconspicuously. It takes practice, the skill of careful observation of others, but it also requires a certain amount of unselfishness. They know what to do, but their movements also show they are considerate of others.*

THE PROPER WELCOME MAT FOR YOUR BUSINESS CALLERS

A polished manager gives priority attention to *how people are received* in his or her office.

If the visitor has no appointment and is just calling on you for an informal discussion, or to sell his products or services, he will be accustomed to having to wait. He should be treated with respect, however—a comfortable place to sit, something interesting to read (recent magazines, today's newspapers), and, of course, the company's annual report and special publications. Many offices offer refreshment—coffee or a cold soda.

A person with an appointment needs special treatment if kept waiting at your office. Sometimes, a series of emergencies will play havoc with your schedule. If you are keeping someone waiting for more than ten minutes, take another minute to leave your office and go to greet your appointment, shake his hand and apologize for the delay. (This will help soothe the *angst* that may be festering in the heart of an impatient person who hates to be kept waiting. It is particularly grievous when he has had a long-standing appointment with you and has come from far away or when he thinks he is more important than you.

Give your visitor the option of another appointment, which in most cases he will reject, hoping you are going to meet your obligation to him soon. Instruct your secretary or assistant to check with you every ten minutes and to report back to him: "It won't be long now. They're almost finished." A comforting smile will help, too.

What a waiting person hates most is to be forgotten and to have the receptionist or secretary ignore him and act as though they couldn't care less about his dilemma.

When you finally are able to receive your visitor, apologize again with sincerity, explain the nature of the emergency, and then give him your undivided attention.

"Undivided attention" means that you do not take telephone calls during the visit, that staff members may not interrupt you with papers to sign or questions to answer.

How to Gracefully Get Someone to Leave Your Office

It happens all the time. When you're the busiest you could be, a friend drops in and takes too much time, or an important customer comes in and wants a large dose of premium treatment.

At a certain moment, look at the clock or watch, and gasp with controlled horror. "Good Lord, it's eleven o'clock! I have a meeting coming up right now." Rise quickly from your chair, flushed with the recognition of a real emergency at hand. Your visitor will rise, too. Put out your hand, shake his warmly, and then apologize for having to finish the appointment so abruptly. "Please write me a letter concerning anything we haven't discussed" could be your next statement. "Thank you for coming in today; forgive me for this rush."

You have every right to look at your watch and say, "I'm so sorry—I have another meeting that started a few minutes ago," or, "I'm sorry, I have to go across town this very minute." Give the person the opportunity to get in a last word or two, then rise from your chair, stick out your hand and say, "It's been a rewarding discussion," or, "It's so nice to see you again," or, "Thank you for coming. I'll let you know as soon as I know" or whatever is appropriate. While you're offering your hand, you're also leading that person toward the coat closet or the exit door. Never be embarrassed about ending a meeting that has had its allotted time.

CUSTOMER TOURS

If you are often delayed by emergencies in greeting people with whom you have appointments, give them something to do, *if they have the time*. For example, aspects of your headquarters or plant may be interesting to others: a demonstration of a production technique, a display of company products, the splendid architecture and design of the new building, or an art collection on the walls. A well-managed, short tour (nothing longer will do) for customers and clients is an excellent public relations gesture. The guiding factors for success are:

- The area toured is clean and ship-shape.
- The workers are not disturbed by the visitors.
- The guide is knowledgeable, speaks well, knows what to say (which means that he or she gives a terrific sales pitch without the people on the tour even realizing it).
- A visitor's specific interests—usually known in advance—should be addressed in the guide's remarks.
- The visitors have a smart-looking piece of literature to take away with them, reinforcing what they saw on the tour.

A corporation comes across as modern and efficient when the right kind of customer tour is provided; for only a modern, efficient manager could have arranged it.

WHEN MANAGERS RECEIVE AND VISIT ONE ANOTHER

Good manners are conspicuously present (or absent) when a business person receives the visit of another in his or her office. Whether you are host to someone on your premises or you visit someone else, it's important to be gracious, alert, and organized.

When You Are the One Receiving a Business Visitor

- *Be on time with your appointments*—if you care about how people perceive you. If you keep someone waiting, he or she will resent it, particularly if that person feels as important as you (or perhaps more important). If you know you are going to keep someone waiting more than five minutes, go out to the reception area to apologize, explain why you're delayed, and most important, promise you are going to shorten the delay as much as possible. Make sure that the person you have kept waiting has coffee or a soft drink, something to read (other than a year-old magazine or a trade journal having nothing to do with your caller's business). Ask if he needs to use the telephone or send a fax.

    There needs to be a warning here. Some visiting executives take advantage of their hosts' amenities. They sit on the secretary's desk while using the telephone to make personal calls. They give her complicated and personal jobs to do for them in the duplicating and fax rooms. I broke off a working relationship with one executive, a fellow public relations counselor who shared a client with me, when my secretary informed me that while waiting ten minutes for a meeting to begin, he had helped himself to my postage meter machine. Without even asking, he used some thirty dollars worth of airmail postage for his own business letters.

- If you do not have a secretary or receptionist to escort your visitor to your office from the elevator lobby or reception area, when you are notified that your visitor has arrived, *go to the reception area yourself*, greet that person, and escort him to your office. It's elegant to defer to visitors and have them walk ahead of you, but it is much faster and more efficient if you precede them and lead the way. (I speak from experience. Once, when I arrived for an important appointment in Madrid, the Minister of Trade insisted I precede him—"Ladies first, in Spain"— and I walked at my usual high speed right into the men's room.)

- If a staff member brings the visitor to your office, *stand up, step out from behind your desk* and put out your hand to greet that person. There is something very cheerful and kind about making an effort to greet your visitor as though it were important to you.

- *If you are on the telephone when your appointment arrives, terminate the conversation immediately* and say you'll call back later to finish the business at hand. (Nothing is more off-putting than to have an appointment with someone, only to have him on the telephone constantly during the time he should be spending with you.)

- *If your visitor arrives wearing or carrying a coat, take it* and either hang it up in your office closet or give it to a staff member to hang up outside. You should, of course, have an umbrella stand of some kind in your outer office, so that anyone arriving with a wet umbrella will be able to stash it there without worrying about its dripping on the carpet.

- If you are expecting a group of people, *be prepared with sufficient chairs already in place*. Nothing eats up more time (and is more unwelcoming) than to have insufficient seats, and then be forced to search all over the place for others—and not very comfortable ones at that.

- If you have a sofa and some chairs in a corner of your office that you use for mini meetings, motion your visitors in that direction.

- Allow your office visitors to be seated before you are.

- *Walk your visitor to the elevator* if there is no secretary to do so, or if she is already busy doing something for you.

- If your visitor has no car, and *if it is intemperate weather or if your visitor is elderly or disabled, call a taxi for him*, or send someone down to locate one for him. If you are a junior staff member, you should go down and help find the taxi yourself.

When You Are the One Making the Business Visit

- *Be on time.* Even if you are only five minutes late, it is enough to start off the appointment on the wrong foot. (The person you have come to see may be exceedingly busy and may not want to see you at all.)
- *Do not make demands of the secretary or receptionist while you are waiting.* For example, "May I use your telephone?" "Can I borrow some stamps?" "Would you be able to get a check cashed for me?" It is perfectly all right if the person you have come to see offers you assistance of this nature, but do not ask for it yourself. You are there to see the boss, and that person's employees are not paid to do your bidding. Think ahead. Bring everything you need yourself. And never tie up your host's facilities. If you have your own cellular phone with you, do not hang on it incessantly, talking away, because you will ruin the secretary's work concentration.
- *Don't take it out on the secretary or receptionist if you're kept waiting.* After a delay of fifteen minutes, you certainly have the right to ask how much longer it will be, but don't keep interrupting, complaining about the delay. (The employee would probably like to have you out of the office even more than you would like it.) Always be polite, and when you leave the office, always say "Thank you." (It's most effective if you call her by her name, and don't forget to say something nice about the assistant to her boss if you have been treated well while waiting.)
- If your host must take a telephone call while you're sitting there, *ask if he would like privacy for the call.* "Should I go outside?" If he says no, stay where you are, don't stare at him while he's talking (very disconcerting), and instead of absentmindedly reading the documents on his desk (which looks too much like snooping), look everywhere else in the room—the pictures on the wall, the view out the window, the pattern in the rug, etc.
- Whether you accomplished your mission or not during the appointment, thank your host for having received you, shake hands, and *leave promptly when it is time.*

ELEVATOR ETIQUETTE

Everyone at the very front of a crowded elevator car should automatically get off, when the doors open, even if they are not at their destination floor. The people behind cannot possibly emerge with ease if the people in front do not exit to give them enough room to move. If everyone on the car is going to get off at the same floor, then the people in front should step off smartly and to the side, again to make it easier for those following behind.

Traditionally, it was customary for "gentlemen" to perform every kind of contortion necessary to allow the ladies behind them to leave the elevator car first. After the ladies, the man most senior in rank and importance was supposed to leave the car. In a few places today (e.g., in the homes of heads of state), these protocol customs are still rigorously followed.

The late playwright and friend of many famous people, Marc Connelly, used to tell the story of his visit to Stockholm for the performance of his play *The Green Pastures*. He was the guest of honor at a U.S. embassy reception following the performance and found himself with Sweden's Prince William in an elevator going to the reception floor of the American minister's home. (In those days we were represented by a minister instead of an ambassador in Stockholm.) When the elevator stopped, the prince deferred to Mr. Connelly, insisting the latter exit first. Connelly refused, "After you, Your Royal Highness." "No, no," replied Prince William. "Since you are my country's guest, you must let me be hospitable."

Connelly could not bring himself to do it; it was a denial of the code of manners with which he was reared. "Sir," he finally said, "do you realize that at this moment, we are on American territory and that, according to international law, you are now a guest of the United States?"

The prince was ready. "You have made an error, my dear friend. One foot ahead of us may technically be United States territory, but right now we are in a Swedish lift and right above Swedish ground."

So they emerged from the elevator shoulder to shoulder. No one was first, and no one was last, a compromise in the same sense that a round table, with no head or bottom place, is used for international conferences, so that no representative of a state will feel he and his country have been downgraded.

Fortunately, in today's workplace, he or she who is at the front of the elevator exits first, and no one should have to stand back or crunch against the side to allow another person to pass.

If you accidentally push against someone in an elevator, your saying "I'm sorry" or "Please excuse me"—quickly and with conviction—will calm the other person's hostility. As far as elevator etiquette goes, my own pet peeve, second to someone's smoking on an elevator (a federal offense), is a person on the car staring relentlessly at me. I begin to wonder if I have mascara dripping on my cheek or a bit of today's chicken salad on my chin. An elevator is much too close quarters for staring activities.

One more point of elevator etiquette: Keep talking to a minimum. Everyone on the car is listening and the only really safe topic of conversation is the weather. The mother of a friend of mine found out that her unmarried daughter was pregnant when she overheard an executive colleague of her daughter's discussing it between the 107th and 48th floors of New York's World Trade Center. It was not a fortunate elevator conversation!

THE EXECUTIVE AT EASE AT THE TABLE

No aspect of an executive's *persona* is as highly visible and capable of directing a sometimes cruel spotlight on him as the quality of his table manners. In the previous edition of this book, table manners were not discussed in any detailed way. Young executives were supposed to bring their good table manners right from school into the workplace. It was something that was always learned and practiced at home. It was knowledge a person was supposed to have.

Today, in the world of broken or extraordinarily busy families, teaching table manners at home has pretty well disappeared, along with the family dinner table. I was asked to include the subject in this revision of the book by popular demand—not only from CEOs and departments of human resources and training, but also from junior and mid-management executives themselves.

Famed humorist Erma Bombeck one day reminisced about her reasons for breaking up with a boyfriend in her youth. He "laughed with his jaw open and with cottage cheese in his mouth," she wrote in a column. It's a graphic description of a person with less than perfect table manners.

You can learn good table manners by being very observant of people who have good ones. Open your eyes, watch what they do, question them, ask them to give you an assist when you're eating together. (Another avenue of assistance is my general book on manners, *Letitia Baldrige's Complete Guide to the New Manners for the '90s.*) In addition, here are some solutions to the most common dilemmas that come up at the table.

When to Sit Down at the Table

If you are someone's guest, wait to sit down until you receive your host's signal. If your host sits down himself without signaling you where to sit, just take the chair nearest you. If you are the host, however, be smooth. Point out a chair for each guest and say, "Please sit here."

Beginning the Meal

Before you begin to eat, wait for your host to begin (or wait until the guest of honor, the person seated on the host's or hostess's right, starts to eat). This point of etiquette holds true for each main course served. In other words, if the waiter is passing a bowl of *mousse au chocolat* for dessert, watch out of the corner of your eye, and begin to eat your mousse when the host or the honored guest picks up his spoon.

When you have served yourself at a large buffet party, and you have found a place to sit at an unhosted table (or you have found a place card with your name on it), wait until two or three more people join you at that table. Then you can start in on the food in front of you. It looks pretty greedy if you are the first at your table and the other guests approach and find you gobbling everything in sight.

If you are one of the first people served by a waiter at a large table, and if the first course is hot, your host should urge you to begin eating at once "while it's still hot." In this case you are free to do just that. (I usually don't, however, even if it's proper etiquette, because I feel a little awkward when only one or two other people at the table are eating along with me.)

Napkins

Unfold your napkin all the way when you sit down; keep it on your lap throughout the meal. If it is extra large, fold it in half. If you must leave the table in the middle of the meal for any reason, put it on the seat of your chair, never upon the table. (The time to put your napkin on the table is when the meal is over and everyone stands up to leave.) The reason for this is logical: The other people eating their meal do not want to look at your soiled napkin on the table while you are temporarily away from it.

Your Posture at Table

Sit up straight. A lolling, slumped figure reminds the others of a Raggedy Ann doll—huggable, perhaps, but mostly collapsed, lacking energy, powerless. Your hands (at the wrists) may rest on the table top, if that's comfortable for you. Do not support yourself with your elbows resting on the table, except between courses or after the meal; in other words, when no one is eating. It is simply a remark of respect to the others.

Don't push back your chair and cross your legs in a position of comfort, away from the table, until after dessert is finished. It is perfectly all right to sit like that while people are talking at the end of the meal, but it is disconcerting to others *during* the meal.

Control Your Nervous Habits

If you have a nervous habit like drumming your fingers on the table or hitting your glass with a knife, cease and desist. Just because you are nervous is no reason to make the entire guest list feel like jumping out of their skins. If you know you have this kind of problem, tell all your close associates, friends, and family that you want to break the habit. Ask their help. Prearrange for your friend to lean across the table and stay your hand when it is fidgeting with something, or they might remind you of your habit with a whispered word, such as "fingers."

If you're left-handed, and are about to eat an informal meal with friends, it's all right if you ask your host if you might occupy a left-hand corner seat. But if you're at a seated dinner with people who are senior to you or who have official positions (the latter must be seated according to rank), don't mention it. If you're in tight quarters, joke about it to the dinner partner on your left. ("You're obviously aware of the fact

I'm left-handed. I hope you don't bruise easily, because my left elbow will hit you in the ribs every time I cut something on my plate!")

Like anything in life, the problems of eating left-handed are solvable. You can learn to eat with your elbows close to your body and manipulate your knife and fork with greater dexterity than you had before.

The Meal Is Served

Study your flatware, and eat from the outside in, if you have an array of flatware facing you at the table. Look at what's down there.

First Course

If you see a soup spoon on the far right side of your place setting, it signifies that soup will be the first course. Or, if you see a small salad fork on the far left side, you might be having salad for the first course, or something like shrimp cocktail, requiring a fork instead of a spoon.

FORMAL DINNER PLACE SETTING

LUNCH PLACE SETTING

Fish Course (optional)

At a fancy dinner party, you might next be served something like a *light fish course*, which would require a small fork on the left side of your plate and a small knife on the right.

Sorbet Course (optional)

Again, at a fancy dinner, you might be served next a tart-tasting *fruit sorbet*, a French affectation intended to clear the palate. You would eat this with a small spoon.

The Entree (or main course)

The *entree* is the main dish (meat, fowl, and sometimes fish), so you would find at your place setting a large dinner fork on the left and a large dinner knife on the right of your plate. (If the main course is fish, you would be given a smaller fork and knife.)

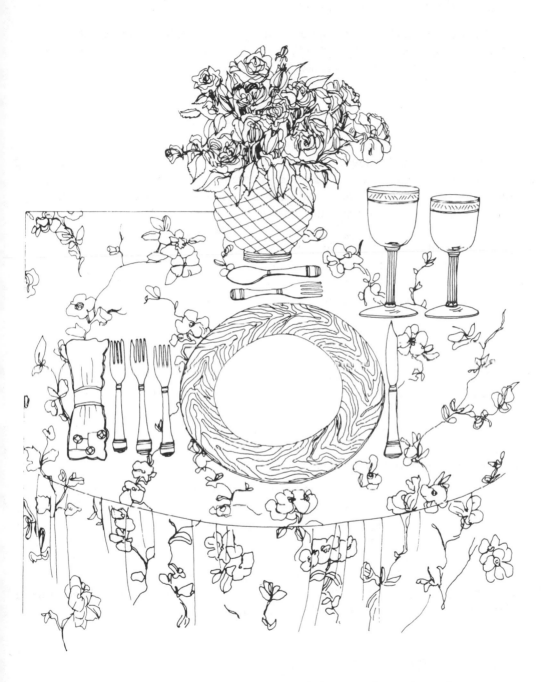

When fish is the main course for dinner, the table is set as shown above: On your left, the appetizer fork first, fish fork next, salad fork last. On your right, the fish knife. To the right of your water goblet is your white wine glass.

Salad and Cheese Course (optional)

If there is a separate salad (and often cheese) course after the entree, you will find a small fork and knife on the left and right of your plate, respectively. You have now used each utensil from the outside toward the plate.

Dessert

There is no mistaking your dessert utensils when you find them placed on the table above your plate, lying horizontally, the dessert spoon (bowl facing left) on top of the fork (tines facing right). The dessert implements for something like pie or cake would call for a fork lying horizontally above a knife. If the dessert is something like ice cream, pudding, or mousse, only a dessert spoon is needed at the top center of the plate. At a fancy dinner party, the waiter will lay down from the left your empty dessert plate with its fork and spoon on top, and then he will personally remove them from the plate and place them to the left and right of it. In this kind of service, the guest doesn't have to do anything but wait for the food to arrive. (You may very well get through a long life without seeing such formal service occur. Don't grieve over it.)

When You Are Served

The waiter will pass the platter of food from your left, or he will lay down your plate with the food already served on it from your left. When you have finished eating, he will remove your plate from the right.

When Salad Is a Separate Course Before Dessert

The salad plate will be placed in front of you by the waiter, and the bowl will be passed. At a more informal meal, the empty salad plate is already on the table—to the left of your forks—when you approach the table at the beginning of the meal, and you help yourself when the salad bowl is passed, while you are eating your entree. In a very informal situation, your salad plate on the left, with your portion of salad already adorning it, is at your place setting when you approach the table. In some parts of America, particularly southern California, salad is a first course and is already served on each person's plate when guests approach the table.

The Coffee Cup and Saucer

At a properly served dinner party, these do not appear until dessert has been eaten, although in many American homes coffee is served either before or during dessert.

For a formal dessert service, a waiter brings each guest a finger bowl filled with water. The bowl is set on a small lace or organdy doily (optional), which in turn sits on the dessert plate. The dessert fork and spoon are balanced on the plate in this case (instead of sitting at the top of the place setting throughout the meal, as is shown in most cases in this book). It's a nice touch to float a small, fresh flower in each finger bowl.

A guest should dip finger tips in the finger bowl, wipe them on his or her napkin, then remove the finger bowl and doily to the upper left of the place setting. He or she now moves the fork and spoon from the plate to the left and right side of the plate respectively. The empty plate is now ready to receive a helping of dessert.

The Finger Bowl

This is an object with which you might never have to cope, unless you go to a posh dinner party or a good fish restaurant. In this situation you will be presented with a small bowl of warm water after you have eaten a messy dish like boiled lobster, steamed clams, or raw oysters). Dip all your fingers in your bowl, wipe them on your napkin, and the waiter will remove all the fingerbowls from the table. (You can even pat your lips with your moistened fingers if you feel your mouth is messy, and then bring up your napkin to dry your mouth.) By the way, you're not supposed to take a bath at the table with the finger bowl water, although I've seen many people dip their napkins into their bowls and then use them as wet towels to sponge off their faces and necks!

At a dinner party in someone's home, a small crystal bowl of cool water (with something like a fresh flower or a small porcelain object, like a tiny fish, floating in it) might be presented to you at the beginning of the dessert course. The finger bowl in this case is placed on a small lace or organdy doily that rests on a dessert plate. Your first step is to dip the fingertips of each hand in the water, then dry your fingers on your napkin; next, transfer the finger bowl and its doily to the upper left of the place setting, near where the butter plate was (or just above where the forks originally were). Your empty dessert plate is now ready to receive the dessert.

I have seen many comical finger-bowl moments. One evening an executive, in a quandary over what to do with his white lace-trimmed doily, decided it was a souvenir gift from his host, so he jauntily tucked it into the upper left pocket of his suit coat as a pocket handkerchief. I have seen people forget to remove the doily when dessert is passed, with the result that the food is dumped onto a delicate piece of fabric that is not supposed to be stained. (It is also very hard to eat a dessert that is skittering about on a delicate doily!) One night a woman who had served herself a hot, gooey Apple Brown Betty onto her doily, brought a forkful to her lips, only to find that the doily came with it.

Our own daughter Clare, at the age of seven, in the very formal Williamsburg Inn dining room, daintily picked up her fingerbowl and drank all of the water in it. I watched her in disbelief, but she said solemnly, "This is a very pretty glass, Mom."

Serving Yourself

It's smart to take small portions the first time around. Platters are usually passed again, or if it's a buffet, the hosts will be flattered if you return to help yourself again.

Where Do You Leave Your Eating Utensils on the Plate?

In answer to one of the most often-asked questions on table etiquette, when a waiter serves you from a plate or bowl, always leave the pair of serving untensils neatly in a vertical position on the right hand rim of the platter (fork on the inside and knife or spoon on the outside), so that the next person can grasp them and serve himself with ease, without even changing the position of the serving pieces.

When You Have Paused in Eating

Whether you've stopped to catch your breath, listen to someone speaking, or leave the table to make a telephone call, put your fork and knife angled inward from the lower right and left outer rims of the plate respectively. The utensils should point toward one another, even touch at the top center of the plate. (Fork tines should be down). This signals the waiter not to take your plate and that you have only stopped eating for a short time.

When You Have Finished Eating a Course

As a signal to the waiter that your plate may be removed, put your fork and knife side by side on the right-hand rim of your plate, fork inside the knife, and with the fork tines up or down. The blade of the knife should be turned inward.

When you have paused in eating but have not finished, leave your knife and fork in this open position. A trained waiter will recognize that you are signaling him not to remove your plate.

Placing your fork and knife together on the side of your plate signals the waiter that you have finished eating and that the plate may be removed.

Holding Your Flatware Properly

It's wise to learn how to eat in the *continental* rather than the American style, because it is much more widely used around the world, more elegant, quieter, and vastly more practical. *In the continental style*, you hold your fork in the left hand, and the knife remains in the right throughout the meal, not just when you are cutting your meat.

No one knows why America is the only country in the world where the fork is changed from the left hand to the right after cutting each piece of food. In this style, it is difficult to keep from clanging one's flatware on the plates as the diner cuts a piece of meat, for example, puts down his knife, and then transfers his fork from the left to the right hand in order to eat his food.

If you prefer the American style and are going to cut something like meat, *grasp the fork with your left hand*, holding it *tines down* with your thumb beneath the handle, and the tip of your forefinger pushing from above at the center point of the base of the fork tines. Your other fingers act as a support to the two fingers actually holding the fork, and are comfortably curled in an ascending order around the bottom part of the handle.

Take the knife with your right hand, turn it blade down above the plate, and hold its handle between your thumb and middle finger (about two inches down from the point where the handle meets the blade). Your thumb and middle finger should be pushing toward one another on the handle, while your forefinger is on top of the blade, applying pressure from above, at the point where the blade meets the handle. This forefinger, bearing down on the top of the blade, provides the force with which the meat or whatever it is can be cut.

Like this . . .

Not like this . . .

The correct way to cut your meat, whether eating American or continental style, is shown at left. Note the hand positions. You should never grasp either knife or fork in a clenched fist, as shown at right.

In the American style of eating, after cutting your meat, you switch the fork to your right hand, place your knife on the plate, spear a piece of meat, and then eat it. It's a lot of work doing it that way!

In the continental eating style, you keep your fork in your left hand and convey the food to your mouth after cutting each piece. The knife remains in your right hand and may be subtly used to get meat or any other food onto your fork. This is a more graceful and more efficient way of eating.

To hold your fork properly (for eating, not cutting) grasp the handle where it's comfortable for you (for most people, that's halfway up the base of the fork). Hold the handle between your thumb and forefinger, with your three other fingers acting as support below.

How to Eat with Chopsticks

The Chinese may have invented the fork, but they have preferred over the centuries to use chopsticks instead. People in business spend so much time in the Far East, they may very well find themselves in restaurants where Western eating implements are unavailable. If you deal with the Far East, you would do well to become proficient with chopsticks. Attaining agility in wielding them is, like everything else in life, a question of practice.

It's also gracious to supply your guests with chopsticks in your home when you are entertaining guests from the Far East and are serving their dishes.

The bottom chopstick slides under the base of the thumb of your right hand, in the crook, and is supported by a gripping action between the third and fourth fingers. The top chopstick acts as a lever, firmly supported by the under side of the thumb and the under side of the index finger.

Use the pair as imaginary tweezers in picking up bits of food from your plate. The top chopstick does most of the work and moves the most; the bottom one plays more of a support role. At the beginning, you will be able to pick up only a small piece of meat or vegetable; later on, you will be able to pick up one tiny grain of rice and get it into your mouth with ease.

Hold the plate or bowl under your chin while eating until you become so adept, you don't spill all over the table and yourself. Even when you are adept, there will be times when it is perfectly appropriate to hold the bowl under your chin for the sake of fastidiousness.

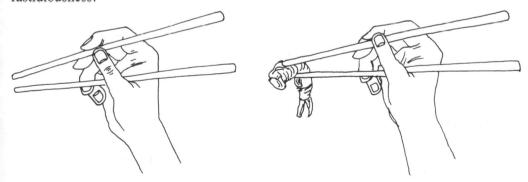

HOW TO USE CHOPSTICKS CORRECTLY

When you are eating oriental food, you may want to use chopsticks. A little practice makes perfect. The thumb and forefinger manipulating the upper chopstick act in a pincer movement, so that the food is grasped securely.

Maneuvering Around Difficult-to-Eat Foods

- The greatest dilemma many have is what to do when one does not wish to swallow something already in the mouth, like an olive pit or piece of gristle. Move it with your tongue onto the fork (which you have brought up to your mouth) and then bring the fork down to your plate and deposit it on the rim. No one should notice you doing this, because the fork-to-mouth motion is a common one made by anyone who is eating.

- Yes, you may pick up your *asparagus branches* and eat them down as far as you can, provided they are firm, not overcooked, or awash in a sauce that would drip all over you. (In the latter case, of course, you would eat them with a knife and fork.) Put the uneaten part of the asparagus branches back on the plate.

- *As for chicken, small birds, or lamb chops:* If you're out-of-doors, eat the piece with your fingers without hesitation. If you're indoors, eat it with your fork and knife until you reach the last succulent morsels next to the bones. Say to your hosts, "It's so delicious, do you mind if I pick this up?" They will say "Please do," and everyone at the table will probably follow suit. (Of course, it's easier on everyone if the host says, "Pick it up in your fingers" before any guest has to ask.)

- Never eat *greasy food with your fingers* when you're in evening clothes. It's not chic, but more important, it inevitably results in astronomical dry cleaning bills. *French fries and potato chips* are eaten with the fingers, however, no matter how you're dressed or where you are, unless the french fries are soggy with grease.

- *Spare ribs and corn on the cob* are meant to be eaten out of doors or at a very informal meal indoors. (Give each guest from two to three paper napkins along with their food.) If you're eating corn on the cob at a picnic, for example, butter and season a few rows at a time, and eat from one end of the cob to the other. At a party held indoors, a thoughtful host cuts the corn off the cob in the kitchen, seasons it, and serves it in a bowl.

- An *artichoke* is consumed leaf by leaf. First, dip the soft meaty end in the sauce provided, eat as much of the leaf as is edible, and then deposit the leaves in neat piles on your plate around the choke. When you have eaten down to the grey, feathery bottom of the choke, cut off the spiny feathers and then cut the smooth grey heart (the real delicacy) into bite-sized pieces. Dip each piece into the sauce and enjoy.

- *Peas* are difficult to eat because they keep escaping from the fork. (If you're eating continental style, you can use your knife to imprison the peas on your fork.) The easiest way to get them compactly onto the fork if you're eating American style is to push them on with a bit of roll held in the other hand. It sometimes requires great willpower not to use the fingers to assist you in eating them.

- *Small, very special pizzas* are sometimes served as a separate first course at dinner. Eat yours with a knife and fork in this case. Otherwise, the slice is meant to be eaten held in one hand, with care taken not to drip the topping all over the place.

- *Soup* should be spooned away from yourself, in order to keep from spilling. Tip the bowl or plate away from yourself, in order to get that last precious drop on your spoon. You may pick up the soup cup and drink the broth, once the vegetables, rice, pasta bits or whatever is floating in it has been consumed. (Otherwise, you might get a rush of croutons to your nose!)
- If *a stray bit of food* flies off your plate onto the table, use your fork to pick it up and put it back onto your plate. If it's too difficult to entrap with a fork or a spoon, like strands of greasy pasta, when no one at the table is looking, use your fingers. (Please remember to wipe your fingers afterward on your napkin.)
- If you don't wish to miss a morsel of a *special sauce,* spear a small piece of bread or roll with your fork, and then squish the bread around in the last remnants of the sauce and eat it. (Don't just hold the roll in your fingers and wipe up the sauce.) Hold up your napkin close to the front of your suit or dress when you do this, because it's easy to spill, slopping up the sauce in this manner.
- In the presence of senior management or a customer, you should not dunk your *donut* in your coffee or your *bagel* in your soup or your *croissant* in your wineglass. It's really tacky. Of course, what you do at home is your own business. Dunk away!
- Go easy on using *sauces, spices,* and such in front of others. If you ask for catsup in a good restaurant and then proceed to drown your filet mignon in it, your companions may consider you something of a dolt. Don't heavily season your food without first tasting it, even if you are accustomed to pouring on the condiments at home. (It is anything but complimentary to the cook.)
- *Picking your teeth at the table* is bad enough to lose you a promotion. If you have a food-sticking-in-the-teeth problem, try drinking a lot of water in the hopes of dislodging it, and if that doesn't work, excuse yourself and go to the restroom to take care of it.
- While we're on the subject of toothpicks, when you take an *hors d'oeuvre on a toothpick* from a waiter's tray, don't put your used one back on his tray, next to the food. Hopefully, he will have a container or small plate in his other hand for you to deposit the used toothpick. If there is none, stash it in an ashtray, wastebasket, or, if necessary, in your pocket or handbag until it can be properly disposed of.

No matter where you go or what group you are dining with, amusing or embarrassing things that will happen. When you make a mistake, don't get hung up on it. Laugh off your gaffe, and remember what famous British comedienne Bea Lillie once said: "You can criticize the way I eat, you can criticize the food I serve you, but never ever criticize the pleasure my company gives you!"

When You're on a Diet, Make It a State Secret

It's bad manners to discuss diets while you are at a table with people who are eating. You can offend your host by making remarks about the cholesterol content of her food; you can upset everyone by remarking that no one should be taking sugar with their coffee; you can infuriate a host by saying you never eat fried food; you can make your host resolve never to let you join his lunch group again if you rant and rave about fiber content, cancer-fighting vegetables, the fact that you've just lost another ten pounds, and why doesn't everyone else do the same? Mealtime is relaxation time. No one should be lectured to, made to feel less than perfect, or have their imperfections discussed and prescribed for. (If anyone at a dinner party remarks to me that he or she takes it for granted that I'm going to be strong and pass up the brownie-and-ice-cream hot fudge sauce dessert, I will retaliate by eating two of them.)

Eating-at-Your-Desk Etiquette

Many companies today permit employees to eat lunch at their desks today. (During the downsizing of many companies in the 1990s, this has become common, since some people are doing two people's jobs or living without the assistance that used to be available.)

In spite of the free and easy eat-at-your-desk rules, managers should be sensitive to their fellow human beings and keep the following in mind:

- Cans of soda sitting haphazardly and for endless hours on desks really visually pollute the office landscape. They should be drunk with the meal and then disposed of—or, if kept to drink later during the day, the cans should be tucked away inconspicuously.
- Noisy food ruins the concentration of those around you, including potato chips and popcorn. These food items also have the habit of escaping and traveling, so watch it when you eat the stuff. The sound of other people's footsteps crunching over your errant debris is not very aesthetic.
- Food that emanates a strong odor can annoy those sitting near you—for example, an overly strong pastrami sandwich and kosher pickles from the nearby deli, or garlic-flavored roast chicken, brought from home, or tacos filled with who knows what, or a salad topped by a quantity of freshly sliced red onions. It is preferable not to consume that kind of food indoors near your neighbors; if you want to anyway, take the garbage to a container out of doors, on the street, or spray the air around you with a deodorizing air spray.

    One executive I know forbids employees in the executive suite to eat or drink anything in the office that has a strong odor. To compensate for being such an "ogre," once a month he takes all twenty-eight of them to a nearby modest cafe for a short lunch during which they consume all the spicy food they want, and give him a splendid earful of office gossip at the same time.

4

The Executive at Ease
When Traveling

Safety and good manners go hand in hand—constant companions. It doesn't matter whether you are boarding a crowded plane in coach or swimming in a lane in a pool, consideration for others is key to getting through the experience safely, effectively, and kindly. When we're late and when we're bucking crowds and frustrations, it's hard to keep our cool. But let's face it: We must. This chapter will help you travel more easily and work with others while doing so.

THE POLITE TRAVELER

You carry your manners with you when you travel, whether it's in a rented car, on an overcrowded commercial plane or in a corporate jet. (Few of us have to worry about brushing up on our helicopter manners!)

Manners Concerning Automobiles

- *When you borrow someone's car, do not return it even five minutes later than you said you would*. Return it washed, with the interior cleaned, litter-free and with a full tank of gas plus a hand-written thank-you note (*see also* ''Thanking for a Favor, However Small,'' Chapter 7).
- *When you hit and fender-scrape an empty, parked car,* leave a note on that per-

son's windshield containing your name and telephone number, so that you or your insurance company can cover the cost of the expenses. (Ethics, anyone?)

- *Don't smoke in anyone else's car*, and if there are other people in your own car, don't smoke in their presence. There is no escape from the residue of smoking materials in the closed confines of an automobile.
- *Think of your fellow man and woman when you park your vehicle*. That means you don't take up two spaces instead of one; you don't block driveways and entrances (even for five minutes); and that if you're not disabled, you wouldn't even consider parking in a handicapped person's space.
- *Safety and manners go hand-in-hand when driving*. If you live by the rules of safe driving, including respecting speed limits, proper signalling, lane-changing etiquette, and so on, you will also be driving in a well-mannered, not just safe, way.

The Obnoxious Airplane Traveler

If you exhibit any of the awful behavior listed below, you do harm to your own reputation and to your company's, too, for having hired you. No one wants you on board if you:

- *Board early and stuff the overhead compartment with several suitcases or packages*, so other passengers cannot place anything else in the bin
- *Board with heavy suit bags and duffles slung over your shoulder*, so that as you move toward your seat, you whack every person sitting on the aisle with a swinging bag
- *Talk animatedly and boisterously to your seatmates during the flight attendant's safety lecture, since you know it so well*, thus endangering other passengers who are not as familiar with the safety procedures of the plane and who cannot hear the words coming over the loudspeaker
- *Take up the empty center seat with your own bulky articles*, so that the other person cannot put anything of his own in that seat
- *Read spread-out newspapers when you're sitting in a crowded three-seat row*, so that your arms and elbows completely imprison the people on either side of you, and they can neither move nor see in front of them
- *Talk incessantly to your seatmate, who obviously is trying to get work done*. (If *you* are the victim of an unwelcome chatterer, simply state up front, "I'm so sorry, I'm on a deadline and have to finish this whole thing before we land.") Then you can engross yourself in your work. If a meal is served, it is only polite, and humane, to have a five- or ten-minute conversation with your neighbor while you are eating.
- *Rush to the plane's magazine rack and take all the good magazines*, leaving little for the others to read
- *Ask the flight attendants for an exotic cocktail they couldn't possibly provide,*

which may make you think you look sophisticated and worldly but in reality makes you look terribly naive

- *Treat the flight attendants with disrespect.* They are not on board to cater to your every whim but to make everyone comfortable, and also to save lives in case of an emergency.
- *Put your seat back in a reclining position in coach.* If the person behind you is long-legged, all blood circulation will stop in his legs because of you, and he may be forced to exit the plane on his knees. Putting your seat all the way back also means that the person sitting behind you cannot easily exit from his row to go to the lavatory, or read properly, because the back of your seat is in his face and there's no room for him to hold his reading material properly.
- *Talk incessantly on the telephone that is set into the back of the seat in front,* thus depriving everyone around you of the opportunity to concentrate on their own work. If you have to use the phone make it fast and speak very softly. It's an intrusive noise to others.
- *Thoughtlessly leave the restroom on the plane in a messy condition*
- Do a lengthy *shaving or total makeup job in the restroom,* leaving an anxious planeload of people waiting outside to use the facilities before landing
- *Dress improperly.* You may think it's perfectly proper to appear sloppy when traveling. However, the other passengers probably do not share your feelings. Even if you don't give a hang what other people think, remember that the impression you make as an individual reflects on your company. Therefore, your company will care what other people think. Dirty sneakers, jeans with holes in them, men's sleeveless undershirts worn as shirts on the street, sweatsuits (often living up to their name) are not appropriate travel clothes. And when you're sitting on the plane, remember, please, to keep your shoes on if you're not wearing socks!

CORPORATE JET ETIQUETTE

Often a corporate jet brings directors and VIPs to headquarters for meetings. If you are someone's guest on a corporate jet, the most important thing to remember is not just to be on time, but to *be early.* If you hold up the departure of a jet by as much as ten minutes, you can cause the plane to wait in line for another hour or two before obtaining a new clearance.

As a guest you should wait to board until after your host has boarded; you should take the seat to which you are shown, and not try to choose your own.

There is usually only a limited amount of refreshment on board. The pilot, copilot, or steward (if there is one) will offer you what there is. Don't embarrass your corporate host by asking for something special; just take what is offered.

Treat the crew with great respect and carry your own baggage whenever you can—they are not your porters.

Don't use the jet to transport your Christmas packages and large personal items. Space is at a premium. If you are not the boss of the corporation, as a passenger you should travel light.

Be careful when eating and drinking on the plane. Organize your litter neatly. I heard a pilot complain one day that every time a certain person traveled with the flight group, it was necessary to vacuum the entire interior of the plane. Said the pilot, "Even the cages in the zoo look better than our plane when he's been aboard."

When you land, always thank the crew and compliment them on a "beautiful flight." If the flight was a rough one because of weather, mention what "skillful pilots" the crew are.

If you have received a ride on a corporate jet, write a thank-you note to the executive who was responsible for your getting a seat on the flight. Don't forget to praise the crew in that letter (*see also* "Helpful Hints on Thank-You Notes," Chapter 7).

Outside directors who are regularly flown in to board meetings at company headquarters on the corporate jet, always with the same crew, should remember each crew member with a small gift at holiday time.

WHEN JUNIOR AND SENIOR EXECUTIVES TRAVEL TOGETHER

When a young executive travels with a member of senior management, he should be helpful in handling details, but without being obsequious. He should offer to see to all transportation, including the limo, checking in and out of the hotel, tipping, managing all logistical aspects of the trip. The older executive may have a lot of important work to do and not wish to be disturbed. If she has time to talk, it is, of course, the perfect opportunity for the younger person to get to know her, to learn some important management lessons, perhaps even to make a few brownie points of his own with the boss. The younger person should be very careful before engaging in long conversations to make sure the senior executive wants them as much as he does. In other words, the junior executive should follow the senior executive's lead.

In the Limo

A younger executive should take it for granted that when a group travels in the limo, the junior occupies one of the uncomfortable jump seats. (The next most uncomfortable spot in the limo is in the middle of the back seat.)

The seat next to the limo driver is very comfortable; the only difficulty is that one is usually cut off from the conversation taking place in back. This negative is often a plus, because most limo drivers are fountains of information, and often a young executive can learn more about the company, the town, and future trends from the driver than he can from the manager of the local plant they are going to visit.

Someone exceedingly long-legged should be put in the front seat if the jump seats are in use, for the latter cut into the legs even of short people sitting behind them.

In an Executive's Own Car

A junior executive driving with his boss and others on a long trip should ask, "Where do you want me to sit?" instead of taking a choice seat himself. I once watched an aggressive young manager take the comfortable front seat next to the company president, who was driving his own car, while the chairman and two other executives were wedged into the small back seat. When I saw the CEO the next day at a North Carolina furniture plant and asked him how the three-hour drive had been, he said, "Fine, but I learned something about young _____ that I had never known before." Before I could ask what, he continued, "Anyone who is insensitive enough to hog the best seat in the car during a very hot, long ride either has to be the chairman of the company or someone on his way out of the company. I'll let you guess which one *he* is!"

CONVERSATION WHEN THE YOUNG EXECUTIVE IS ALONE WITH A SENIOR EXECUTIVE

Most young executives dread being alone with the big boss in his office, while both are waiting for a plane at the airport, or when riding a considerable distance in the company limo. Instead of dreading it, they should realize that this is an opportunity to seize, not only as a chance for recognition, but also to bring to light the things that never seem to be brought to senior management's attention.

A young person should "play it cool" and not force the conversation. The senior person may be tired, want to think, or prefer to read or work. A bubbling, enthusiastic young executive may be just the kind of company the senior executive is *not* seeking at that point.

There are obvious cues the younger person should notice. If the senior person seems distracted, lost in his thoughts, it is best not to disturb him. If he answers questions perfunctorily, that means he is not in the mood to talk. At a certain moment the senior executive will probably put down on his lap what he is reading and address a question to his younger companion. That is the time for the latter to answer with clarity and sincerity. If the senior person wants him to continue, he will give another cue, directing further questions to his companion, a signal that he is now ready to listen.

If the senior executive is ready for light talk—something not too serious—the younger person should be ready with some amusing stories of what is happening in the office or interesting news of competitors or of anyone associated with the business.

The young executive should follow his boss's lead as to whether he should talk about what is happening within the company or in his job in particular or whether he should talk about anything *but* business. He can tell by the kind of questions asked of him. If his boss asks about his squash game, it is not the time to talk about new information systems that are not working as well as they should.

YOUR MANNERS AT A HOTEL

If you have been to the hotel before, say "Hello" to the concierge, and send word to the general manager that you are back and wish to salute him, even if only by hand-written note. You will be treated as a first-class citizen if you remember these little niceties. If you receive a special treat from management, like fresh fruit or an iced bottle of white wine, remember to write a thank-you note, which you can leave at the front desk when you check out, or at least pen a word of thanks on the back of your business card.

Tipping at a First-Class, Big-City Hotel

- Tip the doorman from $1 to $5, according to how much baggage he takes from your car or taxi at the front door.
- Tip the doorman from $1 to $2 for each cab he gets you, depending upon the weather and the time and trouble he has hailing the cab for you.
- Tip the doorman from $1 to $2 when you leave, *after* he has supervised the installation of your bags in the car or taxi.
- Tip the bellman who brings your luggage to your room or from your room $5. If your family is with you, and a great deal of baggage is involved, give him $10.
- Tip the bellman from $1 to $2 for each message or package he delivers to your room.
- The room service charges are often on your bill, but give the waiter $2 extra, because he or she often does not share equitably in the service charge.
- Tip the valet from $2 to $5, according to how much work he does in fetching and returning your clothes.
- Tip the engineer (who comes to fix your TV, readjust your heat or air-conditioning, etc.) from $2 to $5.
- If the concierge got you theater tickets, had things delivered for you, arranged your plane reservations, made restaurant reservations, and so on, give him or her $10 or more, according to how much time the services took or how much skill was required.
- Tip whoever fetches your car for you in the garage from $1 to $2. Leave $2 per night per person for the maid when you check out. (Leave it in the bathroom or on your pillow).

Keeping Your Cool

Your cool may possibly be challenged from the minute you check in. Your bags may not arrive in your room until after you have had to leave it. Your suits may not come back from the valet in time for an important appointment. An all-important message may never get to you.

- Don't blame an innocent person for someone else's error. For example, don't read the riot act to the concierge for something the desk clerk did.
- Realize that not all hotels have speedy, on-time room service, so don't berate one hotel because the room service isn't as good as yesterday's hotel. (Hotel service typically changes, sometimes from year to year, or from manager to manager.)
- Realize that the hotels are all trying to do a good job, to serve you and make you happy. If you have one bad experience, don't let it sour you for months on end.
- The way to be effective is to write good letters. Express yourself on paper, with positive statements whenever they are relevant, and with the same passion you use when you are making complaints. Write to the general manager:
  - To complain, with a detailed description of what went wrong
  - To praise and extoll the efforts of certain members of the staff

A SMART WOMAN MANAGER KNOWS HOW TO TRAVEL SAFELY AND WELL

A woman alone doesn't mean an available woman. A woman on her own may be afraid of being perceived as an easy "pickup." To some unintelligent men, "alone" signifies "available," which is sexual discrimination in its most basic form.

Don't feel you have to be a prisoner in your hotel or motel room, which may be an unpleasant experience in itself. A decorating scheme of flowered gold wallpaper with a poison-green-colored bedspread is enough to send me to a movie all by myself when I am traveling on business. If you stay in your room because you don't feel safe, room service may be another enormous downer. (If you're not in a first-class hotel in a large city, room service may take forever to arrive and the food may be inedible.) If there's a restaurant or a coffee shop in your hotel, go downstairs and use it. You may certainly go into the bar of your hotel for a drink before dinner and not be considered a potential "pickup."

There are some things to remember, of course. First of all, *you should look like a professional* at all times when traveling for your company. Your conservative, business image is conveyed by the way you dress as well as by the way you behave.

Enter the bar with your briefcase or some files (a symbol of your status). Hold your head high, with a pleasant expression on your face, and without any embarrassment tell the person seating you, "Yes, a table for one, please." After you have ordered your drink, shuffle through a paper or two, to further establish yourself as someone who is stopping in his hotel on business.

If an attractive man comes over to your table and politely asks if he can join you, you may say yes, if you feel like it. Explain to him at the beginning, however, that you have only a few more minutes before you have to leave. This gives you a chance to desert him if you find his company less than satisfactory.

If he then offers to pay for your drink, it is proper for you to accept. If you both order a second round, make it clear that you are going to pay for *this* round. As for the third round of drinks, finesse it. This is the round that one (or both) of you will be sorry to have ordered.

If your companion invites you to join him for dinner and you wish to accept, make it clear that you will charge your dinner to your own bill and that you do not wish to leave the premises. By not becoming indebted to him, he and everyone else will know you are a no-nonsense woman who does not pick up men. Mention something like "Dinner will have to be a pretty speedy one, because I have a lot of work to prepare before the meetings tomorrow." With this statement you are emitting a clear signal that you will not continue through the night as his companion.

There have been some very unpleasant stories about businesswomen who have left their hotels or motels with strangers who invited them out to dinner. That's why it's smart to stay where you are.

When a Woman Dines Alone in Public

A woman often feels self-conscious dining in a good restaurant without an escort or a friend. Yet when she is on the road on business it is enjoyable to try out the restaurants for which that city is famous. If you wish to dine in a particular restaurant in another city, be sure to book a reservation beforehand. (Make certain your choice is not the night club–cabaret kind of place, because if you are typical, sitting alone while a floor show is in progress is uncomfortable.) When you reserve your table, give your name, your title, and company. It helps impress management of the restaurant. If you are fussed over and shown special attention, remember to be generous with your tips when you leave.

On rare occasions a maître d'hôtel will discriminate against solitary woman guests. If this happens to you, ask for a better table. If you have booked a reservation well in advance and you arrive early in the dining hour, you should be shown to a good table, not one directly in front of the kitchen, where you are in danger of being hit each time the door opens.

If you are shy about having others see you dining alone, you might pass some time by making notes in your office diary or by jotting down some notes on a pad. It doesn't look very nice—or appetizing—if you read your newspaper, because dirty newsprint means dirty fingers on a clean white tablecloth. An exception to this rule is of course the breakfast meal, when most people are too tired or sleepy to care about inky fingers, and the cuisine is not subtle enough to worry about what newsprint might do to the food.

You might take a small book to the table to peruse occasionally. Don't stick your nose in it the entire time, or others might think you have an inferiority complex and are afraid to be looked at. Glance up from your reading every so often; put a pleasant expression on your face. If you find someone staring at you, ignore it. You have a right to be there, to enjoy your meal and your surroundings. (Keep reminding yourself of this, and it will help you combat any possible shyness about being alone.)

One night a very attractive young woman traveling for Procter & Gamble was absorbedly reading a book through part of her dinner in a hotel dining room. An executive at a nearby table asked the waiter to find out discreetly what book was holding her interest so completely. When the headwaiter returned to give him the name of a book on Elizabethan England, the executive smiled broadly. He had written his college thesis on the subject. He had a very legitimate entree with which to begin a conversation. There was an immediate exchange of notes between the two tables; there were glasses of champagne shared after dinner; and there was a wedding six months later, which goes to prove that not all business trips are boring!

When a Woman Does Business in Her Hotel Suite

Many of the women on the road for business feel insecure about the *dos* and *don'ts* of business travel. The majority spend their days in meetings and their evenings unenthusiastically but safely, consuming a less-than-inspiring dinner on a tray in front of the television set in the room.

A woman doesn't have to hold all meetings in restaurants or hotel lobby bars when out of town. If a woman wants to use her room or suite for a business meeting, she can. She should make sure it is free of personal items—such as her clothing—before people arrive and should have anything left over from room service, like a breakfast tray, picked up before anyone arrives. If she has been smoking, she should air out the room.

A suite is by far the best arrangement for a meeting, but if one is unavailable or if her company cannot afford a suite, she should ask for a room with a bed that converts to a sofa. If that is not possible, she should pull up chairs and use the bed as a giant conference table, arranging papers, files, etc., on it. That will make the bed a very nonsexual object.

When people assemble for a meeting, she should offer them something nonalcoholic to drink. If the meeting is an afternoon one that drags on interminably, everyone might need a pickup, in which case a surprise tray of fresh fruit cut up into "finger food" and some glasses of iced soda water make a special treat. If the meeting is held in her room, she is the hostess, so to speak, and caring for the comfort of those sitting there should be considered part of her executive ability, not just a "womanly" gesture.

I talked at length to one extremely attractive woman who travels constantly and who inevitably has customer meetings in her hotel suite, to view the new lines her company manufacturers. Did she ever have anyone coming on to her, and was she ever frightened? She laughed and said, "Never! I'm always in a hurry and am very businesslike. I always leave the door open—just a crack—into the hall, but every visitor knows it's open. And then I always put this" (she points to a large framed photograph of her husband and three children) "in a very conspicuous place."

Speaking of suites, I know many women who share a suite with fellow male salesmen and managers on the road. They think nothing of it. The company saves money by getting a corporate discount on a small suite, each person has his or her own bedroom, the living room can be used for business meetings, and everyone concerned understands that this suite is for business only!

SOME ADVICE TO INTERNATIONAL TRAVELERS

- Always make copies of all documents, credit cards, and other items you generally carry in your wallet or cardcase so that if the horror of horrors should occur (i.e., the loss or theft of these items), you will know which credit cards to cancel.
- Never carry everything, including all your cash, in one place, such as your wallet, woman's handbag, or briefcase. Tuck each credit card in a different place, so that if one of them is stolen, it will not be the end of the world. (To be abroad without a credit card is, to put it in trite terms, like being in a rowboat without oars, but credit card issuers say they can get a replacement card to you within two days.)
- Always carry a couple of copies (kept in different locations) of the toll-free numbers to use in calling your credit card consumer relations departments to report the loss.
- Keep a copy of the first page of your passport in a place other than where your passport is kept. If you should lose your passport, the copy of the first page will make replacement at the nearest American Embassy or Consulate much easier.
- Carry some spare passport photos, too, just in case this disastrous loss should occur.
- If you need cash, have someone from home arrange to wire a transfer of it through your bank or the local American Express office in your foreign city. Or have someone send you at your hotel a cashier's check or money order by overseas courier, which usually takes two days. Or have someone give the money to Western Union (or use a credit card for the money) and have it wired to you. (It's more expensive than a bank wire, by the way)
- Cashing a check is difficult in a foreign country. (If you have an American Express card, you can cash a check for $200 at one of their offices if you have proper identification with you.)
- If you get sick, ask your local American Embassy or Consulate for a list of recommended doctors. Although they will not vouch for them, the fact that a doctor is on the Embassy list makes using him or her a wiser idea than just calling anyone

from the telephone book. If you have to check into a hospital ask the Embassy operator for advice; she will know to whom in the Embassy to transfer your call.

BEING AT EASE IN SPORTS AND AT PLAY WHEN AT MEETINGS, CONVENTIONS, OR COMPANY OUTINGS

A manager's manners are certainly visible in sports—whether he or she is a player or a spectator.

- *Remember that safety and good manners go hand-in-hand in sports*, just as they do in an automobile , when you're driving defensively. Watch what you're doing at all times. Be aware not only of your own actions, but of everyone else's at the same time. When you're on that surfboard, watch for someone in the water you might hit; check when you're swimming that you're not about to run into another swimmer; remember that children often don't know the most basic safety rules, so when they're around, be super-cautious and wary; go slowly in the boat you're steering, so that you will see swimmers in the water and other boats coming up from other directions; don't dive until the water beneath you is absolutely clear of people. If *consideration for others* is your watch phrase at all times, you'll be successful in sports as well as respected for putting *courtesy and safety* at a premium.
- *If you wish to be asked to join other enthusiasts of your particular sport, play it cool.* Don't be obvious or overly aggressive. If you would like to join a group that often plays golf on weekends, for example, there's a great difference between saying brashly, "I'm a very good golfer, so I'd like to join you next weekend" and saying offhandedly, "If you have room in your foursome for another person someday, I'd really appreciate the chance to join you."
- *Be modest about the way you play—never exaggerate your abilities*. Nothing upsets players more than to have someone who wants to join them brag that's he's great at the game, only to find out during a foursome or doubles match with three other excellent players that the newcomer is hopelessly inept.
- *When a match of some kind is arranged, be diligent about your own responsibilities*. Make sure:
  - You're properly dressed. Ask someone what the dress code is at that particular place; make sure you have the right shoes.
  - You arrive in advance, not just on time, so that you don't hold up the game.
  - If you should have some kind of emergency that will keep you from playing on a certain day, you find someone to take your place, so that the others' game will not be ruined.
  - You have a complete familiarity with the rules of the game, not just a casual knowledge of them.
  - Your language is devoid of curse words and expletives of any kind, whether they're whispered or loudly spoken.

- *Keep good sportsmanship first and foremost in your mind* which means that:
  - You never complain about your own playing—or anyone else's, but *particularly your partner's*.
  - You never hold up the game with interruptions (such as taking a telephone call or stopping for a drink when the others wish to continue playing).
  - You never challenge anyone's call or score, even if you're certain it was wrong. (You only lose by playing the injured victim of someone else's supposedly bad eyesight.)

- *Carry a good set of manners with you*, which means that:
  - You observe the rules of golf, tennis, squash, and other game etiquette. (If you don't know what the rules are, ask the pro on the courts or the course.)
  - You greet the others playing with you cordially (shake hands when you arrive), you congratulate them after the game for playing well, and you thank them for letting you be part of the action.
  - You keep your voice down, even silent, when necessary, such as when out hunting and fishing with others.
  - You always bring your own balls and equipment, so as not to slow up the game while people try to outfit you with the proper clothing, shoes, lend you balls, racquets.
  - You follow the rules of common sense and sensitivity to others. (For example, if you're riding, you do not cross through people's fields or through private property without first requesting permission, nor do you snowmobile or cross-country ski through others' property without their permission.)

- *Treat the environment with respect and care.* It's the only one we have, and its increasing fragility should be of great concern to every one of us.
  - It's very important, for example, that you leave the area where you play in as good condition as when you found it, or better. In other words, the net is stretched tight (ready for the next players), any divot has been replaced and smoothed on the green, croquet balls and mallets or badminton racquets and birdies are put back in their storage units in the shelter, any litter is picked up and removed from the grounds, and so on.
  - When you go camping, bring along bags to dispose of your garbage, so that every single remnant of the intrusion of civilization in the beautiful outdoors, from a paper tissue to a soda can, from a candy wrapper to the Sunday newspaper, from an empty catsup bottle to the empty cellophane bag for the hamburger rolls, is transported back home, and into one's own waste-disposal facilities. Mother Nature is not supposed to take care of our trash; *we* are.
  - If you've made a fire on the beach, remember to throw water on the coals and thoroughly douse them, then cover them with sand.

Your Swimming Pool Manners

If you're fortunate enough to be invited to a senior manager's home for a party by his pool, or if you join a group at a pool, there are many points of pool etiquette to remember. You and your company are on trial when you're a guest at a private pool.

- Don't ask to use someone's pool. Wait to be asked, and having been asked once, remember it does not mean that you can come by and use the pool any time you feel like it.
- Always take a shower before using the swimming pool, removing dirt, sweat, and suntan preparations that your host obviously does not want added to his water components.
- Don't ask to bring your children. If your kind host asks you to bring them, don't leave them there the entire day. Two hours is a long enough visit for one's children.
- Bring your own towels, along with your own suit. (A woman lawyer friend told me that in the summer of 1992, eighteen business friends arrived to use her pool without bringing suits; she lent them suits from her own collection and from those of the friends she called on the telephone. What an imposition!)
- Don't go into the house wearing your wet bathing suit and sit down in one of your host's prized chairs while you make some business telephone calls.
- Don't hang on your own telephone either, by the pool, droning on in a conversation that could interest only you and certainly not the other guests lounging about. (Someone complained to me recently: "You tell me not to use my cellular phone in a host's house, or by the pool. For heaven's sake, where *can* I use my telephone?" Answer: behind the bushes, far from the pool.
- If you're invited with other business guests, you are supposed to help entertain one another. That means you are not supposed to lie in the sun far away from the others in an "I'm better than anyone else here" pose, refusing to talk to or make an effort toward the other guests.
- Don't bring totally business-oriented materials with you to study by the pool when everyone else is supposedly socializing. It is very off-putting to the others around you to be enjoying the sun and water while you are conspicuously studying spreadsheets and flowcharts!
- Don't expect your host to feed you mid-morning snacks, lunch, tea, and perhaps even dinner. Stay from two to three hours and then leave. Your host might have another group of guests coming.
- Obviously you don't need a reminder not to splash people or try to throw them into the pool. We assume that you passed through that stage as a child and are now a sophisticated adult.

Sports Spectating

A young manager may be asked by a colleague or a member of senior management to attend a very special game with him. This is a great compliment to the young person, and if it should occur, it's important for the guest to note these points:

- He or she should be aware of which team the host is rooting for and therefore should not obstreperously root for the other side or make critical comments of the host's team. He should not act in an unnecessarily adversial manner. (It will not help his career). If he is a novice at the sport, he should do some research on the players for the upcoming game, so that he can make intelligent comments, but also follow the game more efficiently.
- He should be familiar with the rules of the game (having asked questions and read up on it if he was not already familiar with it).
- He should refrain from too much alcohol, so that he will be in control of his behavior.
- He should offer to buy lunch or supper at the stadium for his host (and any other guests present), an invitation that will probably not be accepted, but which should nevertheless be extended.
- He should be creative in offering sympathy to his boss if the boss's team went down in miserable, uncalled-for defeat.
- In his thank-you note sent the day after the game, he should make no reference to the poor performance of the team yesterday, but write an affirmative, upbeat comment about the success of the team previously or in next year's season—or some one spectacular play or player. (It will help his career.)

5

The Executive Faces Problems in Today's Working World Which Never Existed Before

When men had the executive suite pretty much to themselves, everyone knew their place; the rules were rigid and well understood. Today all that has changed. There has been a revolution at work that mirrors the revolution in our society at large.

New concepts about how we behave and think about our roles at work are on everyone's mind: pluralism, diversity, political correctness, collegiality, sexual harassment, equal opportunity, the rights of many special interest groups, the new relationships that must form as men and women work together at new levels of command—and much more—are with us to stay.

The chapter that follows is the first in a book of this kind to offer some guidelines for adjusting to these changes so that all concerned can live with them comfortably and beneficially.

A GOOD MANAGER DOES NOT USE SEXIST LANGUAGE

"Men," "Women," "Guys," and "Gals"

The Women's Movement in the latter part of the twentieth century brought to the fore many semantic problems. Sensitivities popped up all over the workplace. Women executives began to snap at their male colleagues when they used expressions male executives had innocently used for decades, such as, "I'll have *my girl* call *your girl* to make the appointment."

If a man was accustomed to referring to his employees as "my men," he now had to learn to refer to the women in the company, too, without using the term "the ladies." Many men today still have trouble with the terms used to denote the sexes. I tell executives to balance the terms on a teeter-totter, and if they balance, they're correct. For example, "ladies" goes with "gentlemen." You don't say, "I'm going to send the men through the training session today, and the ladies tomorrow." "Boys" balances with "girls," "men" with "women," "ladies" with "gentlemen."

The term "guys" has become unisexual, while the term "gals" has fallen out of use. "Guys" is admittedly slangy but is in constant use today by both men and women in referring to both genders. For example: "You guys had better leave quickly, we're late." (You would not say, "You guys and gals had better leave quickly," because that sounds more like the lyrics from a Broadway show than a manager's directive.)

"Chairman," "Chairwoman," "Chairperson," "Chair-Whatever"

In today's world the controversy over gender-oriented titles is still evolving. Some terms are logically adaptable to both genders and should be utilized: "congressman and congresswoman," for example, or "businessman and businesswoman."

When a woman reaches that revered pinnacle of "chairman," to be forced to call her "chair," "chairwoman," or "chairperson" is to me counter-productive, even harmful, because it separates women in top management instead of unifying them with men. We don't call a woman president a "presidentess," and a woman secretary or treasurer of a corporation is not a "secretaria" or a "treasuress" respectively. A woman general is not a "generaless." Men and women who serve on board commercial flights are "flight attendants," not "flight attendants and attendantesses." Women poets no longer wish to be called "poetesses"; women prefer "sculptor" to "sculptress." In my more than forty years in business, and during my experience in serving on corporate boards since 1977, I can say that "chairman of the board" suits most women just fine. We're all still trying to get there.

Terms of Endearment in the Office: A Definite Negative

If a male manager wishes to irritate a woman colleague very effectively, all he has to do is address her in a patronizing fashion, like calling her "honey," "sweetie," or "darling."

I remember when a visitor in my embassy office in Rome gave me a paper to give the ambassador. "Thanks, baby, for doing it right away." I looked at him angrily, and his reply was, "Be a nice baby, now." I got out from behind my desk and looked down at him with utter disdain. He was about 5'6" and I am 6'1".

"Guess I shouldn't have called you 'baby?' "

"You guessed right. But I have a fantastic suggestion for you."

"Yeah?" his eyes gleamed brightly. He probably thought I was going to give him a tip on where to find women, or something equally tempting.

"My fantastic suggestion is that you don't call any working woman 'baby,' regardless of her size, because some baby just might slug you hard for using disrespectful, put-down language like that."

"Slug me hard, huh?"

"Hard."

I have often wondered what kind of language he is using on women today.

Disrespectful language is a problem a woman must handle herself. She should not run to complain to Personnel, like a child running to her mother. She should have a frank, private conversation with any male colleague who continually puts her down with his pet names and terms for women. (Sometimes he is blissfully unaware of his chauvinist behavior; his father probably talked that way at home, and his mother probably never corrected him.) When the woman who has to work with him every day decides to correct him, she should keep smiling and advise him kindly, in a friendly way. "Al, would you like to do me a *big* favor?"

Al would probably return the smile. "Sounds ominous. Maybe I'd better hear what the favor is, first."

"It's a very simple one. Would you mind dropping a few words from that otherwise excellent vocabulary of yours, words I feel are a put-down to me and all women, like 'sweetie,' 'honey,' and 'kid?' "

He might laugh and say, "I'm relieved. I thought you were going to complain about my saying things like 'she has big hooters' and a 'butt like no other.' "

That would be her cue to say, "Oh, Al, I'm doing just a few words at a time. 'Sweetie,' 'honey,' and 'kid' are it for today. The other words and phrases will be mentioned in days to come. We're going to do this a little bit at a time.' "

He might be amazed that she could think these words were anything other than terms of affection. After she explains that they make her feel totally unprofessional and they make him sound patronizing, usually a man like Al will accept the lesson in good humor and cease referring to women in those terms. Most men really do not want to be perceived of as chauvinists. It's the last thing they want. Time, patience, and a sense of humor on the part of the women in the office are usually all that it takes to rid them of their sexist language, and their wives and daughters to come will thank the women in the office for shaping them up.

Chivalry Isn't Dead, It's Just No Longer Gender-Based

The tradition of exemplary behavior toward women did a double somersault in the last half of the twentieth century. By 1970 men were being told that their ancient code no longer held. A female colleague did not wish to be put up on a pedestal, to be considered a helpless creature in need of protection. I remember hearing a senior partner in an old-line, male-bastion law firm protesting to his youngest, most ambitious woman lawyer, "But why do you think I should not treat you in a chivalrous manner? What's wrong with *that*?"

Her answer was simple and to the point: "Because I'm after your job." Fortunately, she smiled when she said it.

What Was This Old-School Gallantry That Prevailed Until the 1970s?

A "polite" man was supposed to (and generally did) the following for every woman he respected:

· Hold open doors for her
· Hold her coat for her
· Light her cigarettes
· Never allow her to carry a package
· Walk curbside with her, to protect her from being splashed by passing cars
· Run around to open her car door
· Push in her chair at the table
· Never shake her hand unless she offered it first
· Jump up and remain standing for her until she sat down
· Refrain from discussing such subjects as business, because she probably wouldn't understand

Most women executives feel that men who treat them as "gentle ladies in need of protection" will not let those same gentle ladies make tough decisions in the board room. "In fact," one woman remarked, "gallant men won't let those 'gentle ladies' into the board room at all, except to provide the coffee, sodas, and waterglasses." This rather simplistic explanation of the death of chivalry in the workplace does not mean that good manners and consideration of others is not commendable, proper, or desirable. What it does mean is that now that the two sexes are to be treated equally, whoever is in need of help—*whoever* could use assistance—should receive it:

- An older woman who sees a young male executive trying unsuccessfully to hail a cab (because he's laden with luggage, briefcases, and an umbrella) should find and hail the cab for him.
- Whoever is first going down the corridor should hold open the door for other people walking behind.
- Whoever is on the front of the elevator gets off first, regardless of gender.
- If a man is having trouble getting his coat on in the minuscule airplane aisle, the woman standing behind him should help slip it over his shoulders.
- If a woman has trouble carrying many heavy files and notebooks down the hallway, a man coming behind her should step up and lift half of them from her, and carry them to her destination; if a man is having the same trouble carrying too many documents, and a woman happens to come up behind him, she should step up and help him in the same way.
- A woman should pick up the bar and food tab for herself and her male client or customer when she has done the inviting. A man should pick up the bill when he has done the inviting. If the woman host happens to be a twenty-two-year-old woman, just out of college, and her guest is a seventy-year-old chairman of the board, it does not change the rule: Whoever does the inviting, does the paying.
- A woman stands up for a male visitor to her office, and remains standing until he is seated; a man stands up for a female visitor to his office and remains standing until she is seated.

I ran into a Spanish businessman in New York fifteen years after I had given a speech at which he had also been present, in the grand palace that houses the Madrid Chamber of Commerce. At that presentation, the sixty manufacturers present refused to allow me to stand to give my speech, unless they stood also. (A true Spanish gentleman until recent days would never sit down before a lady present had seated herself.) I protested, I remonstrated, I begged them to let me stand while they sat. Their old world manners prevented them from allowing it. I had to give my speech seated, at an enormous table, where I could only see a small portion of the audience. The Spanish businessman I ran into told me that much had changed for business people's relationships in fifteen years. "But," he said softly, "there are some things that will never change in my country. For example, you would never this to do to me, I hope," and he raised my hand to kiss it.

Some things just never will change, and that's not all bad, either.

SEXUAL HARASSMENT
(*See also* "A Smart Woman Manager Knows
How to Travel Safely and Well," Chapter 4)

This is an emotional topic, one with infinite variations and degrees of seriousness, and therefore difficult to discuss. A man in the office may think nothing of engaging in a moment of locker-room humor, but that moment may gravely upset his female co-worker. One person sexually harassing another can be merely aggravating to the victim, or it can be seriously harmful in a psychological sense, or even in a physical sense, if she has to resist him.

Men should not joke about this subject (as many have in the past). They should take it seriously. The law mandates it. From the woman's point of view, sexual harassment can be disgusting, cruel, and frightening. It must be dealt with immediately, so that a woman on the job is not forced to enter into a relationship that makes her feel victimized.

Some Personal Observations

- *A woman should not label a colleague's easy-going, affectionate bantering in the office as harassment.* Men and women who have grown up with brothers and sisters and who have spent a great deal of time with their siblings' friends during their young years often tend to kid around in conversation with the opposite sex.
- *If you are the victim of legitimate harassment, take action.* Don't accept it; don't continue to be frightened and intimidated because you need your job. Tell yourself you have value and that you make real contributions to your family or society or your company or all three. Women who are self-confident, with a good self-image, simply do not allow themselves to become victims of this kind of behavior.
- *When you see someone in your office being sexually harassed by a bully, take action on that person's behalf.* Become that person's confidante, comforter, and give suggestions on what action to take. Go with the victim (ask others in your section to add to the group if allies are needed) to report the harassment to senior management.
- *If a woman in a two- or three-person office is being sexually harassed by her boss, there may be only one viable course of action for her to take: Get out of that office.* No matter how tough things are financially, she would be better off leaving that job and finding a new life.
- *Don't joke about sexual harassment.* Both men and women have been falsely accused of this kind of behavior because they were the butt of good-natured jokes. I remember when the women in one middle-sized company turned against a very popular member of senior management, because, during a ''roast'' of this executive (held in a restaurant on his birthday), several joking references to sexual harassment—none of which were true—were made about him by his male colleagues. By the time the stories were repeated and circulated among the corporate employees, they were all considered true. The victim of the ''roast'' never again regained the popularity and respect with which he had previously been held.

What Is Sexual Harassment?

It is important to understand—and to recognize—the many shadings of this onerous behavior.

IT IS NOT:	IT IS:
When he says offhandedly that you are wearing a lovely dress	When he compliments your dress, then leers down the front of it
When he puts an arm around your shoulders and gives you the same hug he gives everyone else	If he holds you and won't release you
When he tells a group a naughty story that is more amusing than it is seriously raunchy	When he tells you a story that goes into clinical sexual detail or when he brags about his sexual prowess
If he is single and asks you for a date, but you decline	If he is married and asks you for a date, or if he is single and asks you out, and when you decline, he threatens to have you fired if you don't "cooperate"
If he kisses you on the cheek as a mark of affection after returning from a trip, or in celebration of an office victory	If he kisses you hard on the mouth for any reason
If he pats your shoulder or arm as a mark of affection, upon hearing good news	If he suddenly touches your body suggestively, in public or in private
If he leaves a written compliment on your desk about your work	If he leaves repeated notes on your desk containing sexual innuendoes
If he says,"I feel so good, I could kiss you!" but he doesn't	If he says, "Show me more affection, or no more raises"

Defensive Responses to Sexual Harassment

- *Attack his ego.* She could smile and tell him his advances are comical, not sexually attractive.
- *Make him feel ashamed.* She could say that this kind of behavior is really pathetic and unworthy of him, and that she knows he is a far better person than his behavior would reveal.
- *Give him fair warning.* She could say, "I'm going to forget this occurred, provided you heed this warning. I will tell no one. Let's forget it ever happened."
- *Give him a second chance.* "You have received one warning, and you ignored it. This is my last warning. Try this again, and I'll report you to the top."
- *Take action* if he ignores the second warning. She should appeal to the most senior person in management she can find, and quickly.

When You Decide to Report Him to Senior Management

- First get control of your emotions. Don't go into the senior manager's office red-eyed and flushed. You won't be able to make your points that way.
- If you work for a large company, there may well be a sexual harassment counselor on staff in the Personnel or Human Resources department. If so, make your report to him or her.
- Have in your hand a detailed, clearly written list of the time, date, place, and type of harassing actions made against you by the perpetrator. Include an accurate report of the warnings you gave him, and of what he said and did in response.
- If the person who is continually sexually harassing you happens to be the CEO, the only higher authority is the board of directors, and for you to go to them takes great courage. If your company is publicly owned, you definitely should inform them of what is going on. Ask for a private meeting with at least three outside directors, because the shareholders would not want a person of your tormentor's calibre running their corporation.

    If you work for a small company, my advice is to resign. If you sue, you'll spend a great deal on legal fees, and the resulting negative publicity will probably nix your chances for getting a good job in the future. A woman with a litigious reputation is not on a fast track, to put it mildly. This is what I've learned through decades spent in the executive suite.

Men Who Are Sexually Harassed

More and more cases are surfacing each year of women executives accused of harassing male employees whom they supervise, and also of homosexual male executives harassing their male employees. This is as evil and disturbing as a woman being harassed by a man in the workplace. A man often feels even greater shame than a woman would in reporting this kind of offense.

A man's colleagues who notice him being harassed by a female boss or male executive should lend him their support in reporting the situation and acting as witnesses. Men and women should always stick up for one another when a grave injustice is being committed, and sexual harassment is one of the gravest there is.

A man being harassed in a large corporation should make an official complaint (with documentation of events, time, place, dialogue, etc.) to the head of Human Resources, or to the Sexual Harassment Counselor. In a small office, in such an instance, the atmosphere is usually so charged with stress and emotion that the victim should look for another job quickly and leave as soon as he has found one. Even moving to a much inferior job (on a temporary basis, until he can find something much more suitable) is better than staying where he was and having to submit to such indignities.

One friend of mine who left his job after suffering three weeks of harassment by a woman boss, knew that he should be careful what he wrote in his letter of resignation.

He certainly did not want to put his accusations on the record, for many reasons. He simply slipped one significant sentence into an otherwise standard letter and handed it to the head of Personnel who said "Oh, my God," and rose from behind his desk to shake my friend's hand warmly in a knowing gesture of sympathy. The sentence was, "Like my four male predecessors during these past two years, I am resigning to seek a position with better possibilities for advancement in the management of a communications company." Without making a direct accusation aimed at his boss, he implied for the record very neatly what the trouble was. (Two weeks after his departure, the head of Personnel in that company laid the files of the five men who had resigned that position on the desk of the second in command of the company, and a month after that, the woman boss was gone.)

A GOOD MANAGER FACES UP TO SEX
IN THE OFFICE TODAY

Dating Someone in the Office

If you find yourself attracted to a colleague whom you have met through your office life, go ahead. Ask that person for a date. A man or a woman executive might need someone to accompany him or her to a company business function, or for something that's fun, like using tickets to a football game or going to Sunday brunch at a friend's house. Before you ask someone for a date, make sure that:

· He or she is not married.
· This person is not a customer or client who might consider your invitation overly aggressive.
· You are not seeking anything other than companionship.

Remember that if you are a woman asking a man for a date, you are supposed to pay for everything on the first date: the dinner, any tickets used, parking or transportation, etc. On future dates, how you split the cost (or how you allow the man to pay) is up to the two of you.

Talking About Your Sex Life

In business your sex life should be left at home—before, during, and after marriage. If you have a real need to discuss it with people, find an appropriate professional counselor. If you tell all at work, people will perceive you as immature and unable to handle increased responsibilities. A person discussing his or her sexual prowess in the office embarrasses his or her peers, regardless of how they pretend to be fascinated. An office is not a locker room or a fraternity or sorority house.

Sex and Affairs in the Office

It will not help your career to become seriously, sexually involved with a client, because if the relationship sours, it will affect the company's relationship with that person too, and you'll be blamed for any breakdown in business relations or future loss of revenue from that source.

If you have an affair with one of your office colleagues, you can be certain that it will not remain a secret very long. The red warning lights will began to flash all over the place. A secret affair usually changes, rather quickly, into a known one. A whirlwind of gossip begins to circulate. People will think of you in terms of the affair, rather than in terms of how good you are at your job. People will smirk, and your colleagues will always be conjecturing on how often and where you meet, how much passion is exuded. They will become awkward in their relationships with you, and senior management will not be pleased with the gossip nor a serious loss in productivity of the two people sexually involved.

If you have an affair with someone who is married, usually there is an inevitable, simple result: You can kiss your career goodbye.

Showing Too Much Affection

- If you are dating someone in the office, it is very smart to be cool and not be seen hugging, kissing, or casting suggestive glances at one another.
- If you are engaged to someone in the office, the same advice applies.
- If you are married to someone in the office, the same advice applies.
- If you have a homosexual relationship with someone in the office, the same advice applies.

The sight of two people demonstrating physical attraction in the office stops people in their tracks, no matter how sweet or romantic they may find it. It distracts and stops work from progressing properly. There's an asset that every working person should possess, in fact, management should be able to demand it of its employees, and it's called "self control."

When You Know There's a Female Boss—Male Employee Problem, Take It to Lunch

From what I have observed, the executives who are the happiest and the most successful are the ones who relate with the greatest ease to the opposite sex. Men and women can make absolutely first-rate teams, and team spirit is what it's all about.

I am often called upon to advise women who are having trouble in their relationships with male cohorts, both with the men who supervise them and the men whom they supervise. "Devote a lunch hour to it," I am forever exhorting a troubled woman manager. "Make your problem accept your lunch invitation. You've got to get him out of the office, alone, away from interruptions and distractions, in order to delve into your problems with one another. Tell him (jokingly, of course) you'll kidnap him if he says no, and then take him to the best place in town. This lunch is on you.''

"That's fine," the woman being advised will reply, "that sounds like a good idea, but you haven't told me, once I get him to this incredibly good restaurant, what I say next."

Wait until you have both ordered your meals and then jump in, head first. Give him the benefit of the doubt. Initially take the blame, the blame of innocence, since you don't know what you've done wrong. First acknowledge that things haven't gone well and that he must feel uncomfortable, too, and you are sorry about that. Explain that you know he must not want this less than satisfactory relationship to continue either. "Look, we're not pulling together toward the same end, like we should be," you might explain to him regretfully. "I feel bad about it for three reasons: You are uncomfortable; the situation hurts our office productivity; and it makes me feel very bad, too. There they are, the three reasons why we should change what it is that is doing this to us. For my part I will do whatever is necessary. I want us to work well together, so tell me what my part will be. Whatever it takes, I'll do it.''

By being so openly frank, by taking the initiative to ventilate the problem, by taking the blame (sort of), and by initiating the solution, you have put him in the corner. He will have to come out with what is eating him. You need to hear it, too. You may have gone along all this time thinking you were the wronged party and that he was unfairly on your case, but when you make him blurt it out over the *paillard di vitello* you may learn something you have done or failed to do of which you were blissfully unaware. Listen carefully to him, to what he says outright, and to any hint of what else may lie beneath the surface. Don't meet him halfway in the solution to the problem. Give much more than he does, because that will make you win in the end.

Since the above scenario involves a woman having a problem with her male colleague, you might ask, What does a man say to a woman with whom *he* is having a problem? The answer: The same dialogue should take place. *Good communication* is the solution to most aspects of office life that break down. When it comes to people bearing grudges, refusing to bury hostilities, and setting off sparks of resentment when they work together, one person has to take the initiative to start the healing process. Women's problems get more play and attention because women are the newer minority in the workplace. But there is no gender difference when it comes to mending relationships. The glue that mends it and holds it together is not gender-based, but rather part of the workings of the same human spirit.

Homosexual Relationships

Two people of the same sex who live in a monogamous sexual relationship are a *couple* and should be treated as one, and with respect. A homosexual couple in the office is under the same restrictions as a heterosexual couple in regard to displays of affection or sexual flirtations in public.

A homosexual couple should be invited as a single unit to all social events. If your company has invited spouses and dates of employees to certain social or social-business meetings, conferences, tours, parties, and so on, a homosexual on staff should be invited with his or her partner as well. In other words, if you are hosting a corporate dinner where spouses will be present, do not treat a gay man as a single man. Invite him with his partner.

The details of anyone's sex life should be neatly filed *at home* and not brought into the office. A sexual move made by a heterosexual on another person in the office is inexcusable; so is a pass made in the office by a homosexual.

If you are not certain of the sexual orientation of a person, do not ask him or her unless you know that person extremely well. It is the kind of question that is no one else's business; however, if you work closely with someone who seems very lonely, and you're trying to introduce that person to some new friends, you have the right to ask that person privately if he or she would like to meet someone of the opposite sex before, with the best of intentions, you go charging off in the wrong direction.

If you find out confidentially from a colleague about his or her same-gender preference, preserve that confidence. Do not be the spreader of gossip that could be harmful to that person's career. You would only be adding to the abuse that person already may suffer at the hands of others.

At the same time, it is the responsibility of homosexual members of the staff to be rigorously private about their private lives, to bring no hint of scandal to the company that employs them, and to show by example the proper way to manage one's life outside the office—privately and discreetly.

If you, as a manager, fight to eradicate discrimination against your homosexual employees and to banish any vestiges of gay-bashing in your workplace, you have the right to expect—in fact, to insist upon—dignified, discreet behavior from your gay employees in return.

A GOOD MANAGER RECOGNIZES THE RIGHTS OF THE COMPANY'S DISABLED EMPLOYEES

Disabled employees are usually hard workers, totally loyal, completely dependable. You should be doing everything possible to make life easier for them. The corporation may be planning on taking new space, or remodeling part of the building. Ask what special aids are being built into the plans for the disabled. Start management thinking. In bad economic times, remodeling or ordering new furniture may be impossible, but put it in senior management's mind that it should have a priority when times aren't so tough and they begin to expand or renovate.

There are hundreds of details that should be taken care of. A designer who specializes in this field should be retained as a project consultant. Listen to the disabled employees' gripes—but a small part of a very big picture.

- Microwave ovens are often placed so high up in the kitchen that a wheelchair-bound person can't reach them.
- The same can be said for bathroom or kitchen faucets.
- Counters in the employee bathroom sinks should have drainage around them—a person in a wheelchair gets completely splashed every time he turns on a faucet.
- A new building should have a low water fountain for people in wheelchairs along with one of the regular height. Supply a wheelchair-disabled employee with some paper cups to keep in his drawer to use at a water fountain that's much too high for him to reach.
- Floors with steps and several threshholds and levels are a menace to people in wheelchairs. They should be designed out of any new office plans.
- What if a hearing-disabled employee is working alone in the office at night and a smoke alarm goes off? Why not have these alarms flash lights or create another visual alarm to attract the person's attention?
- Automatic doors often aren't properly timed to allow people on canes or crutches or in wheelchairs to get through the doorway in time.
- Marble floors are slippery at best, particularly when it rains. There should be some sort of floor covering somewhere in the marble expanse to allow the disabled to cross it safely.
- Curved walls would be very helpful to people in wheelchairs, instead of having to face sharp angles when turning a corner. Even shaving off the sharp existing edges would make the wall less dangerous.
- Designers should specify furniture that is flexible, so that shelving can be added to or deleted from mobile desk pedestals, and counters can be raised or lowered. Chair seats and backs should be adjustable.
- Instructions and signs on the walls and elevator buttons should be tactile, so that a visually impaired person can *feel* them.
- Telephones should be equipped with loudspeakers for the hearing impaired.

Thanks to the passage by Congress of the ADA (Americans with Disabilities Act), all new buildings for public use must now by law take into account the needs of the disabled. There is still a lot of room for improvement in the planning for new spaces and the architectural rehabilitation of old ones to make them barrier-free. Senior managers who are sensitive to this and do all they can in the planning stages are aware that disabled employees make *great* and loyal employees.

MANAGING THE HIV-POSITIVE EMPLOYEE OR STAFFER

When someone develops cancer or heart disease, people tend to become creative in thinking of ways to help and support the sick person and his family. When someone in the workplace develops AIDS, there is another element that suddenly darkens people's desire to help, and that is fear. Many people who are uninformed mistakenly fear they will contract AIDS from their colleague and die.

Here is one way of handling this situation: The supervisor of the person who tested HIV-positive and let his or her boss know it, would, with that person's permission, tell co-workers in a private meeting. Rather than allow distorted rumors to circulate, the manager would calm down everyone and offer straight answers to their questions. If he doesn't know enough himself to answer their questions with authority, he should have someone from the company's medical staff, or an AIDS counselor from a local hospital, be the spokesperson. It is the lack of information and the dominance of heresay that causes all the trouble in the workplace in relation to how people treat someone who is HIV-positive or who has AIDS. Several major points need to be made:

- People do not "catch" AIDS. It is spread through sexual contact or sharing the infected needles of drug abusers (or sometimes because of blood transfusions).
- People who have tested HIV-positive can live for many years, working at full speed, without showing any signs of the infection. They should be treated as normal people, capable of bearing the same responsibilities they did before the HIV-positive test finding.
- When someone eventually does come down with full-blown AIDS, he should be allowed to continue in his job until he is no longer able to work. Co-workers who are friends of the victim should volunteer assistance. This support might entail anything from cleaning house to bringing food, from writing letters to transportation to medical appointments. It above all entails keeping in touch through personal visits, telephone calls, and notes. The feeling of abandonment, AIDS patients say, is hardest of all to bear. A good manager does not let that happen to one of his or her staffers.

Places to call for information:

- National AIDS Hotline (1-800-342-AIDS), or you can write to GMHC [Gay Men's Health Crisis], 129 West 20th Street, New York, NY 10011. Ask to have their information packet sent to you.
- San Francisco AIDS Foundation (1-800-367-2437)
- Project Inform (1-800-822-7422)
- AIDS Clinical Trials (1-800-874-2572). You would call this number to inquire about joining a cure-testing program where you would become part of an experiment
- AMFAR [American Foundation for AIDS] (1-800-392-6327)
- AIDS Information Line, Whitman-Walker Clinic, 1407 S Street, Washington, DC 20009

A GOOD MANAGER KNOWS HOW IMPORTANT FAMILY BENEFITS ARE TO EMPLOYEES TODAY

Business today can no longer ignore the problems posed by family pressures on employees, and is working harder to find the solutions to those problems. There is even a new kind of job out there: a company manager responsible full-time for programs that balance and buttress work and family life. The mix of benefits, policies, labor laws — and the spirit of compassion, too — is too complex to be managed piecemeal.

Sometimes it takes the working children (who are also parents) of a seasoned, hard-nosed CEO to open his eyes to the stresses working parents are living under today. When he sees his own son and daughter and their working spouses trying to balance family and jobs, compassion finally comes into play.

One woman entrepreneur I know employs six people and pays for half of all day-care costs for her employees' seven children. She has been saluted by her city but, more importantly, she receives a hundred applications a month from people longing to work for her.

By the end of the twentieth century, granted a healthy economy, the menu of benefits companies offer employees will include many of the following:

- Near-site or on-site child care center support
- Subsidization of emergency and sick-child home care
- Unpaid leave for childbirth (anywhere from four weeks to six months)
- Unpaid paternal leave up to two months
- Flextime
- Job sharing
- Subsidization of elder care
- Adoption aid (up to two thousand dollars)
- Adoption leave
- Nursing mothers' room in the offices
- Supervised activities for children on holidays
- Low-cost family dinners to take home from the cafeteria
- Lunchtime workshops on child and elder care

Corporations are paying attention to "family-friendly benefits" for workers for more than just altruism. Happy employees show increased productivity, and the profit sheet is affected. Then, too, unions also are making demands in their new proposed contracts for these perks. A small company obviously cannot embrace all of these expensive provisions, but it can try to offer what is feasible.

A good, family-friendly manager:

- Knows what his people want
- Is familiar with every regulation of company policy regarding these family benefits
- Tries to bring his employees' needs and the company's policies closer together

THE PREGNANT WOMAN MANAGER
(*See also* "When an Employee Has a Baby," Chapter 17)

The entrance of so many women into the workplace has demanded from management a recognition of the importance of family relationships in an employee's performance. This was something that management previously had chosen to ignore, before legislation and public opinion began to change a woman's rights in the workplace. In the late 1940s, when I first started to work, women had no rights or perks. We were lucky to have our own bathrooms in offices. Twenty-five years later I was present when a marketing client of mine dismissed a high-performance woman executive from her job, just like that, because she had become pregnant. He looked at her and said straightforwardly, "You were an asset to our company. You have chosen not to be any more. It was your choice, not mine. I'm sorry it turned out this way, but no top sales executive of mine is going to go waddling around her sales territory, knitting booties as she goes!" (Today, two decades later, that same woman's daughter may be going to work with her baby in a basket by her desk.)

During the 1970s there was tremendous pressure on women not to have children, for the sake of their careers. Any woman who stayed home and away from the office for more than two weeks' maternity leave was considered a wimp and unambitious, and was therefore considered automatically ineligible for important promotions.

Then came the 1980s, with young women pouring out of graduate schools of business and suddenly beginning to worry about an even greater concern, their biological timeclocks.

Then came the 1990s, with fewer women graduates of graduate business school and with many fewer even considering it, not only because of a faltering economy, but also because of:

- A frustration at the total impenetrability of the glass ceiling regarding corporate women, which leads to a "why bother?" attitude
- An increase in babies being born to executive women
- Intensified worries over their biological timeclocks when they do not as yet have children
- Hysteria over the ineptness, even dangers, of the poor child-care system in our country

The pressures of the 1990s made it seem just too much. If a wife and mother could afford not to work, we saw her leaving her job to opt for motherhood; she also dropped out of the study of law, medicine, and other professions. As women managers retreated from the workplace, briefcases were replaced by activism on behalf of children. If this same women in the 1980s had stayed home to be with her children, she might have felt as though she were wearing a badge of shame—not exactly a scarlet letter, but a badge reading "corporate cop-out."

Hooray for the Baby!

It's wonderful to have a baby. If you think the problems of working full-time and having a baby are insurmountable, remember, historically thousands of women have found them not to be. Be smart, put on your thinking cap, stay healthy, and plan your life carefully. It will work, whatever your decision. Here are some tips:

- *If your decision is to continue working*, remember:
  - ○ Your boss should know before anyone else in the office does.
  - ○ Tell your boss your plans the same time you tell him or her about your pregnancy, i.e., the date you expect to return to work; how many months of unpaid pregnancy leave you are requesting; whether, once the baby is born, you will be requesting flextime or part-time hours; etc.
  - ○ If you are a man whose company has a policy regarding unpaid paternity leave to help his wife for the first few weeks, speak to the boss about it the minute your wife tells her boss about her pregnancy. Your company will have to make substitute provisions for you, just as your wife's company will have to for her.
  - ○ Inform your boss that you still expect to be considered for that promotion for which you are truly qualified, and that you will prove it by your increased productivity during these months before the baby is born, and most definitely after it.

- *Inform your office colleagues of your pregnancy only when you begin to really show.* This is to save you a few months of relentless questioning from colleagues and business associates: "Isn't that baby ever coming?" "What are you doing, taking twelve months instead of nine to have it?" (The latter question, when you're only four months pregnant, can be really debilitating to a hard-working executive.)

- Regardless of any favors you may ask of your boss in regard to vacation or leave, *be sure to reconfirm your devotion to your company,* and make the boss feel that if he holds your job for you, you will not cheat the company on your commitment of time or enthusiasm. it's important to profess your loyalty to the company—but it's also important to live up to your promise, if they hold your job.

- *Don't keep reminding customers and clients of your condition*: "I hope you won't be embarrassed to be seen with me" . . . "I hope the restaurant has chairs I can get in and out of" . . . "Excuse me, I'm off to the ladies' room again. You know how it is when you're pregnant." Just leave your condition and how you feel out of the office conversation. *Stick to business.* You may be the most gregarious, relaxed person in the world, but others may be very up-tight, perhaps slightly embarrassed, about your condition.

- *Don't go around the office lamenting your physical aches and pains*—everything from swollen ankles to gas pains, from a bad back to varicose veins. The quieter and the more discreet you are in your pregnancy mode, the less distracted the office will be and the more professional your image will remain.

· *Keep your Lamaze class details to yourself*, and other details such as weight gain, ultrasound information, etc.

· *Be more diligent than ever with your work*. Prove that you can keep up with anyone in the office in producing work as well as a baby. Never slough off anything on anyone else because you're tired; never leave anything undone until tomorrow. You can be a wonderwoman if you really try. (Naturally, this kind of pep talk is directed solely at women who are having healthy, normal pregnancies.)

· *If you plan to return after the birth of your child, prove that you care about your job*. When it comes time to leave the office, make certain that loose ends are tightened up, that all your projects are in good shape, that the people who will be taking them over on a temporary basis are well-briefed and ready to continue on your own good work. When you are home, taking care of the baby, keep up with your work. Ask that your important correspondence—memos, journals, etc.—be forwarded to you at home. Keep up on the news in trade papers in your field. Keep your interest sharpened, even in the general office news. Have people brief you and report to you what's going on, so that when you return to your job after maternity leave, you will be *au courant* and ready for action.

Tips to the Pregnant Executive's Co-Workers

· Once your colleague has announced her pregnancy, congratulate her with joy, but *don't even think about asking her any personal questions*.

· *Don't keep pressing her for information*: "How much do you weigh?" "Are you going to breast-feed?" "Does the baby kick yet?" "How are your stretch marks doing?" "Will you have to have a Caesarian?"

· *Nix on patting her stomach* or putting your head to her stomach to listen for the baby. This is personal, private behavior suitable for the mother-to-be's husband and children and no one else. One young mother told me, "Everyone in the whole corporation, from the CEO to the guys in the mailroom, all patted my stomach at least once and sometimes several times during the pregnancy. I really resented it, until I took to wearing a T-shirt that said, 'Don't Touch.' "

· *One baby shower is enough*. It should be hosted outside the office, because if held on the premises, it can disrupt productivity. A baby shower might be held (Dutch treat, except for the pregnant one, whose lunch is paid for) in a nearby restaurant or an employee's home on the weekend. Then things will not upset management.

A point of etiquette: The mother-to-be should write a thank-you note to every single person who gave her a present within two weeks of the shower—and she should send flowers to the person who organized it.

The Unmarried Pregnant Woman

When a colleague on your staff who is not married becomes pregnant, there is only one thing to do: Treat her as you do her wedded colleagues. Don't make an issue of it. Respect her dignity and rejoice in her happiness over the impending birth.

Announcing It to the Office When You Adopt

The adoption of a child merits the same joy, celebration, and interest that the birth of a biological child creates in the office. The announcement of the arrival of an adopted baby deserves a letter of congratulations, too, from the executive's boss and all good friends who receive it.

It is thoughtful for the parents (or single parent) of a adopted child to send out announcement cards to family, close personal friends, and business associates, imparting the happy news. The announcement might read:

> Mr. and Mrs. James Fenman Starkweather
> announce with great joy
> that their daughter Mary Louise
> born on March 12, 1998
> has joined the family

The card of a single parent might read:

> Suzanne Gregory Marchison
> takes pleasure in announcing that her son
> Marcantonio, born July 23, 1994
> was adopted on January 2, 1997

Infant Feeding and Breast-Feeding in the Office

Certain companies allow women employees to feed their babies at work. In fact, some even encourage it to the point of providing a special room with baby-changing tables, comfortable chairs for nursing mothers, plus a formula-heating device and refrigerator for storing bottles of formula.

Some offices do not have the space or financial resources to permit this service. A nursing mother, in my opinion, should not breast-feed her baby in public in the office. Most men are the ones who become upset, even though they are embarrassed to admit it. Men still look upon the female breast as a sex organ, and there is a certain amount of voyeurism that comes into play if they catch a glimpse, even a quick one, of a colleague's bare breast. I think company policy has the right to insist that a woman breast-feed her baby out of sight—in the ladies' room, in an empty office, wherever.

A company also has the right *not* to allow a woman to bring her baby to work. Some do allow it, most don't. A woman can sometimes change jobs and find a company that will give her more leeway for her motherhood needs if she can't accept the policy of the company where she works. I have seen companies with two or more babies in baskets by their mothers' desks, all of whom were howling in unison while their mothers unsuccessfully tried to shush them. Such a scene is not businesslike, it is very unprofessional, and unless the company is all-female and the boss brings her babies to work, or unless there is a child-care facility on the premises or nearby, a working mother should, in my opinion, find someone to care for her baby while she is at work. In a poor economy, companies have to cut costs rather than increase them, and mothers should become creative in solving their child-care problems themselves, until that wonderful day when companies have all found—or will have been forced by law to find—happy solutions for the problem of child care.

DIVERSITY, PLURALISM, AND RACISM IN THE WORKPLACE

There are four facts of life the American business community should face in the 1990s:

- Good manners mean good personal relationships.
- Good manners and prejudice are a contradiction in terms.
- We are living in a global economy, which makes prejudice against other nationalities more unacceptable than ever.
- We must not only admit the importance of the diversity of our society, *but we should be proud of it.*

An individual's attitude toward any group based on gender, pigmentation, nationality, age, religion, occupation, or disability is inextricably interwoven into his or her everyday actions.

A manager should realize that the result of a well-constructed program of pluralism in a company is not pure altruism nor a phony manufactured scene of happy employees getting along with one another. One of the pluses diversity brings (of major interest to senior management) is an *increase in profits*. A diversity of employees brings a better understanding and opening up of new markets.

People Have Different Preferences in How They're Referred To

It's important to be responsive to people's own preferences in reference terms. Although "whites" is still a generally accepted term, people who wish to be politically correct use "caucasian." Indians often prefer "Indian-Americans" to "Native Americans"; many prefer "Latin-Americans" to "Hispanics," and "Asian-Americans" to "Orientals." Many want the word "international" used to describe them, rather than "foreigner."

If you feel confused as to which term to use, ask your employees for a consensus of their preferences. You can even circulate a memo to the employees, listing the various options, entitled, "My Preference as to How I Wish to Be Identified". The company can then follow the majority opinion for the names to be used on their personnel forms, the company newsletter, press releases, etc.

Derisive Terms for People of a Specific Race, Gender, or Creed

Critical or snide references to people in the workplace (as, for example, calling someone a wop, kike, spic, pollack, nigger, fag, dyke, etc.) should be discouraged at all costs. Every manager should make certain first that he himself never refers to other cultures in a pejorative manner, and that the people he supervises do not, either. What employees say on their own time in their own homes is one thing; the language they use in referring to their peers at work is quite another.

I once taped a much-loved senior vice-president who, after a racial incident, called his factory workers into a meeting in the plant. "I'm not asking," he said, "I'm telling you that here, in this place, you're not going to show any prejudices to *anyone*. Offensive language against a minority or an international is unacceptable, because it can destroy the teams we've all worked so hard to build. And teams are what have put us ahead of the competition. This company needs all of you, every single one of you, regardless of your gender, color, shape, size, and preferences for blue cars or red cars. If you want to use (*!) terms in talking about me behind my back, okay, as long as I don't hear about it. But if you feel like hitting on one of the men or women you work with, I'm telling you to sit on it! If you put somebody down because that person is different from you, it's unfair, you're wrong, you make an enemy, and you could get it right back again in your face. So don't mess up the spirit of this company with your mouth. We are a *team*, remember?"

His employees cheered him when he finished the talk and yelled their agreement from different parts of the floor.

The Managerial Responsibility

As a manager, you can't be expected to really change a biased person who makes constant abusive statements about other groups. However, a manager can definitely influence the majority of his or her employees in their fair treatment of colleagues, *first by his or her own example*. Managers should be able to correct, motivate, and train those under their supervision in dealing with any insensitivities they have brought to work. *Managers must realize that often they don't recognize tension and simmering resentment in the workplace because they're not listening*, but also because the workers often are not expressing their true feelings for fear of losing their jobs. Relationships change for the worse if accusations of discrimination aren't dealt with at once. When managers respond too late, employees conclude that management is afraid to address the issue or doesn't know what to do, or worse, doesn't care.

As a manager, you can respond to an act of discrimination committed under your watch by firing the one who initiated the altercation, on the spot, without even making an investigation, so that your employees will see that you are a quick-action manager. This, too, is a poor reaction, since your employees will be looking to you for a judicious, calm way of handling crises, not a burst of machine-gun fire. There must *always* be an investigation.

Or, you can react in a constructive manner. For example:

- You can ask that *the offender make a complete apology* to the person who has been wronged, publicly or in private, whichever is more appropriate. If the offender doesn't know how to make an apology, show both spoken and written examples (*see also* "Letter of Apology," Chapter 7).
- You can *counsel the victim*, letting him ventilate his anger and hurt to you.
- You might *call together your employees in a group session* to discuss what happened, with the hope that the group will conclude on their own that this kind of behavior will not be tolerated among them.
- You might schedule *professional training sessions in diversity* for the employees in order to teach them tolerance, as well as push their boundaries of information far beyond what they were taught in school, and to make them understand why everyone is better off when people are sensitive to one another.
- You should be *careful in the way a minority newcomer is introduced to the staff*, in order to give the newcomer the dignity he or she deserves. People from other countries, particularly the developing ones, have a legitimate complaint when they are treated like entry-level employees, regardless of their job, education, and credentials. A manager should always introduce a newcomer to the group by voicing admiration for that person's accomplishments. Instant respect usually follows. It can mean the difference between a successful integration of a female or minority employee and an unheralded, unnoticed arrival of a new person whom everyone concludes is unimportant.
- *Talk in a natural, unselfconscious way with people from other cultures.* Some people, perhaps for fear of being unable to hit upon a common ground of conversational topics with African-Americans, may hover on a "safe" subject like basketball or black entertainers. That's all wrong, because it's sounds forced and unnatural.
- When you overhear someone making a bigoted remark against a colleague, cut him short and say at once, *"Jerry, we don't have that kind of talk around here. It's not what this company stands for."*
- *When serious racial trouble erupts*, even though it may occur in a part of America far removed from your company's location, your CEO should go direct to the employees to address it. It's not a time for someone else to serve as spokesperson. It's time to "go direct"—which might mean that the CEO should:

- Address an assembly of employees.
- Write a good strong letter to the employees in the house organ, expressing the company's philosophy, so that it's on the record.
- Make certain that good material is given to employees by Personnel to remind them of the importance of working together (such as making available the latest books on the subject, putting up posters in the cafeteria and restrooms, showing cassette tapes on racism as a required part of training, etc.).
- Encourage a greater diversity in the corporate-sponsored athletic teams or problem-addressing workshops, employee family outings, company volunteer work in the community, etc.

Apologizing for a Racial Slur
(*See also* "Knowing How to Apologize," Chapter 1)

Someone in the group, perhaps even you, has made an unfortunate remark directed against a certain group, and you haven't realized that a member of that group, or a relative of a member of that group, would take offense! You can't ignore what you've done, because no one else present is ignoring it. They are all as embarrassed as you are, although less so than the person who has been wronged. This is not a time for a symbolic wringing of hands; it is a time for action. *The apology should be swift and sure.*

- If you make the slur while giving a speech, you may suddenly realize what you have done. *Apologize first to your audience:* "I realize that I made a very unfair, unnecessary, and ugly remark a few minutes ago. I apologize to everyone here for having said it. It was unforgivable."
- *Next, apologize privately in person* to the one whose group you have slurred. If he or she is not present, write a letter, which you might conclude in this manner:
    "It's nice when something good can come out of a bad situation. The good in this case is that I promise I will never ever say or even think something like that again. It is a firm resolve, I hope you understand that."

A Good Manager Cares About Ethics

The public seems to have grown almost blasé about new reports of ethics scandals. In fact, unethical behavior is becoming quite acceptable in some quarters. What is unacceptable—"really nerdy," as one young Wall Street accountant explained it—"is to get caught."

It's no secret that manners, morals, and ethics are closely interrelated. If, when sitting in an airport, you eavesdrop on the business conversation of a competitor who does not know who you are, you are being unethical, immoral, and ill-mannered all at the same time. If, on the other hand, you are an ethical person and you hear a competitor talking over confidential matters, you would either move away, out of hearing distance, or you would interrupt the speaker by saying, "I am with Such-and-such company, and although I'm obviously very interested in what you are divulging, perhaps you would prefer that I not hear it."

I remember so well my own first remembered breach of ethics. I was five years old and had never won a game prize at a birthday party. I was therefore determined that somehow I would win a prize. I did, by cheating. When a blindfold was tied around my head during a game of "Pin the Tail on the Donkey," I managed to keep it loose enough to see under it. I therefore attached my grey paper tail to the donkey poster in just the right spot on the animal's posterior. Of course I won the prize, and later, puffed with pride, I showed it to my older brothers and parents, receiving the expected congratulations and praise for my efforts. That night, the rosy glow surrounding the day wore off, and after a sleepless night, immersed in guilt, I woke up my parents at six o'clock in the morning, and told them the terrible truth.

Mother got me down to breakfast a half-hour early. Together we rewrapped the wonderful game prize I had "won." Before school, she drove me over to the birthday girl's house, where I rang the bell, confessed, and apologized to the birthday girl's mother, and stood in the doorway, wallowing in misery over my sin. The girl's mother told me I was valiant to have confessed, and I went on to school, feeling wiser and suddenly much older. I had learned the value of public retribution for a "crime."

Expiating for unethical conduct in the business world should require more than just feeling guilty. It may require going to jail, but for the small transgression, admitting guilt is the first step. Then comes the sincere apology, and finally, a promise to make amends.

Management sometimes becomes consumed by a desire to pry. Some supervisors manage ethics by monitoring their employees' electronic mail, including messages that are confidential or highly personal. It's understandable that the company wishes to know what's going on, but these actions may go up against the individual's right to privacy. At times a company is itself unethical in its attempts to unmask the identical kind of behavior in employees.

"The Unethical" at Work, at Play, at Home

Many people don't understand what the term "ethics" implies. It's easily explained by pointing out the examples of unethical business behavior we see around us in the everyday world, such as:

- Management juggling the financial figures to make them seem more advantageous than they are
- A job-seeker lying on his resumé
- An employee helping himself to office supplies for his family's home use
- Anyone who files fraudulent health or accident claims
- The use of the postage meter for personal mail

- Charging endless long-distance personal calls to the company
- Substituting an old part for a new one in a product, without the consumer's being aware of it
- Using a company car for personal business
- Bad-mouthing someone who justifiably stands to be promoted ahead of you
- Hiring someone to work for you without being up-front with the truth
- Flying coach on a trip, but putting in for first-class airfare reimbursement on your travel expense report, after conveniently having lost your ticket receipt
- Persuading a colleague to withhold information about an error you made
- Claiming sole credit for a successful idea when it was not yours
- Stating your product or service has affirmative qualities it does not possess
- Giving or accepting an expensive gift (this smacks of bribery)
- Revealing someone's confidences
- Not adhering to your promises
- Hiring unqualified people because of patronage or because you can control them
- Covering up for a worker who continually abuses drugs, who is unable to perform his or her duties, and who causes the company considerable financial harm
- Damaging someone's property and failing to report it

A person who got away with cheating on his tests in school, as well as snitching things from the supermarket without paying for them, will not usually, as an adult, change his habits in the workplace. This makes the manager's task even tougher, for she has to become a police officer as well as a manager. When you supervise people, you are responsible for their physical welfare, their business manners with the customers and vendors, and also for their ethical conduct. (One tool of understanding and training in the field of ethics that many managers find helpful is the series of newsletters and publications produced by The Josephson Institute of Ethics, 310 Washington Boulevard, Suite 104, Marina del Rey, CA 90202.)

Teaching Ethics Begins in Childhood

In spite of the fact that concerned business leaders like John Shad (Harvard Graduate School of Business) have poured millions of dollars into graduate schools for teaching ethics, I firmly believe that an understanding of this set of values is rightfully learned at an early age *at home* from your parents, the same time you are learning how to eat properly at table and say "thank you" and "no, thank you." By the time someone is in graduate school, her behavior is molded and his conscience is already developed (or nonexistent, as the case may be). Something as simple as a parent pointing out good and evil to a child while reading a bedtime story is where the study of ethics begins.

Even the evening news can be interpreted to a child in terms of ethics. "Do you know why that man is going to prison, Nancy? He played around with money that wasn't his. He caused others to lose their money, when he thought he could make a lot of money for himself. He must pay for that. He is going to prison because of that.''

Ethics is hardly a subject to be learned in the home when children hear one or both of their parents talking about cheating on their income taxes; lying to a prospective buyer about the condition of their house when it is about to be sold; limping badly in court during an injury case hearing, when the parent does not limp at all at home; or trying to bribe a police officer to avoid getting a ticket. A good manager realizes that since ethics are not being taught at home in many situations today, it is time for management to do what it can to influence and educate company employees on the subject.

Just as parents should discuss with their children unethical behavior that is in the news, so managers should discuss it with employees. When talking about a news story concerning a breach of ethics in another company, it's an opportunity for a manager to say to his staff, ''No matter how bad business may be, we're *not* going to pull *that* around here.''

A smart manager is never afraid of being considered a wimp because he believes in ethics. Along with manners, caring, and self-control, it is part of the same synergistic goal.

The Ethics of Reporting Someone for a Crime

This section of this book is not about tattling on someone who stole two rolls of paper towels from the office supply cabinet to take home for a party; this section is about someone who committed a crime against another person or the company that perhaps no one else knows about. A serious misdemeanor or a crime of which you have knowledge must be brought to management's attention, in spite of your possible close relationship with the perpetrator. From an ethical point of view, it is the duty of an employee to share with management information when:

- One employee has sexually assaulted another employee, and the victim is afraid to mention it—out of shame, but mainly out of fear of acts of revenge by the perpetrator. Her best friend in the office who knows about it (and who knows it actually did happen) should summon enough courage to go quietly to a senior person to report it.
- Someone has been stealing equipment regulary from the office, and selling it to support his or her drug habit.
- Someone is selling drugs within the corporation.
- Someone has been selling company classified information on new products or services to outside interested parties.

We are taught as children not to rat on a friend or classmate, and there are times when it is immoral to do so. When one employee tells on another, particularly a friend, he should expect his supervisor to guard closely the source of the information and to handle the arrest of the accused, his punishment, or whatever the outcome, with compassion.

A good manager has the trust of his employees, and guards it with tremendous respect. A promise of secrecy extends even to refusing to share this kind of information with a spouse or secretary. Great skills are required for a manager to be able to solicit the necessary information with full protection of the sources. This art is not taught in most business schools.

ADDICTION AND SUBSTANCE ABUSE

When one of the people responsible to you stops showing up on time, or when he is constantly late in returning from lunch, or if there are frequent unexplained absences from the office, the word will eventually reach your ears. Someone on your staff is in trouble. You should not just sit by, passively absorbing the gossip and complaints from people who are tired of having their own work suffer because of a colleague's shirking his or her own duties. Your responsibility is to act:

- *Check to make certain the rumors of addiction are accurate,* an act of humanity but also a legal necessity. Talking privately to three or four of the employee's close colleagues should provide sufficient confirmation of the problem to cause you to talk to the person himself—at once.
- *Keep your discussions private,* unless your Human Resources should also be present. Confront the individual person with your suspicions and a critique of the quality of his work of late. Unless he is in complete denial, you might startle him into an admission that he is an alcohol or drug abuser or gambler. (If he is in complete denial, follow the advice of professional abuse counselors, which may possibly involve family and colleague intervention.)
- In a large corporation the Human Resources division either has on staff a counselor for the problem of addiction and substance abuse, or it brings in outside experts. If yours is a small company, or if you are just an entrepreneur with two or three employees, *be prepared before you talk to the employee.* Do some research on existing programs in the community, contact professional counselors, and be knowledgable about what for-profit and nonprofit facilities and programs there are. Know what the next step in seeking help should be for the employee in question, and make certain that he or she takes it.
- *Consult the employee's spouse or a close relative to assist or to be assisted by the company in this matter.*
- *Promise—and deliver—that you will do everything humanly possible to help him* keep his job while he undergoes the prescribed treatment for his condition.

Addiction can happen to anyone, and as a manager, the way you handle this problem will greatly affect employee morale and the team spirit you are trying to foster.

The irony of it is that a manager who is himself a recovering alcoholic or drug abuser does not have to be taught compassion toward his fellow men or women.

GUIDELINES FOR THE NEW SELF-MANAGERS INCREASINGLY WORKING AT HOME TODAY

The statistics are there. Link Resources did a work-at-home survey in 1991 and found that over 39 million people did all or part of their paid work at home that year (*The New York Times,* May 24, 1992), and the numbers have risen ever since. The spirit of entrepreneurship has provided America with some of its brightest economic news, as well as some unbelievably good new products and innovative, marketable, much-needed services.

The pluses of working at home are undeniable, including, of course, the fact that it provides parents with the opportunity to be with their children. Family bonding is invaluable in a home office situation, but for a single woman parent, working at home may be the only way she can cope financially with her situation.

Becoming attached to the family computer allows the user total freedom in finding information, executing work tasks, and enlarging a network of unseen "computer pals" with whom communication is natural, easy-going, and often very amusing.

Affirmative Actions for the Entrepreneur with a Home Office

- *Don't allow your children to take advantage of your presence in the home.* A strict, disciplined work schedule may be necessary in order to have the business survive. Carefully explain the rules governing your work schedule to the children, post the rules in the house, and refer to them every time the children take advantage of Mom in her work space. It's difficult to tell an eight-month-old crawling baby to stay silent in his playpen when he's smiling up at you from the floor, tugging on your foot, beckoning you to play. But discipline is key for a working person at home, and it's part of the entrepreneurial spirit to find the options that will enable you to stick to a schedule that will not cheat on the children. Everyone finds his or her own way.
- *It is important for an entrepreneur (or any professional) working at home to live healthily.* You should "think nutrition and exercise," but also the importance of sleep.
  - *Take your body measurements every month,* and post them in a conspicuous place so you can easily compare body shape, as well as weight, of this month versus last. If sitting all day at your computer is giving you a thickened waist and pear-shaped hips, take action. Diet and exercise should be given priority. Here's a way to break the social isolation: Find someone else in your neighborhood who works at home, chained to a computer, and do your exercises together at the same hour each day.
  - *Join a local health club not only for health, but also to make friends.* Get out of the house regularly for a workout or for jogging or walking or the pursuit

of your favorite sport—your brain is working overtime, coping with the business at home, but your body needs exercise, too. You'll meet some people exercising who may have your same work schedule and who may become new friends.

○ *Get to know your neighborhood well,* so you can swap babysitting chores with neighbors. This will enable you to get out of the house, even for something as important as a professional meeting or useful seminar—another example of breaking the isolation.

○ If you are chained to a computer, *make sure the chair you sit upon is ergonomically correct for you.* (The purchase of the proper chair adapted for your height, weight, and the tasks you perform is well worth any extra expense.) If your body is comfortable and relaxed, your brain works better, your attitude toward your children is better, and you are a delight, instead of a drudge, to talk with on the telephone (including to your customers).

○ *Do some research in healthy cookbooks to find menus and recipes you could easily concoct* in your own kitchen. (Beware of snacking on junk food.) Be creative in what you cook, enjoy the taste of it, and then you'll have the courage to ask one or two people over for a quick lunch, tea, or dinner. You need to see people, and working in your kitchen can be an excellent release from too much computer concentration.

Keep Up Your Professional Look
(*See also* Chapter 9, "Dressing for Business")

Your daily at-home attire will probably be casual, but don't carry that over into your trips to client conferences and offices. A good-looking contemporary haircut and two knock-'em-dead outfits to wear to those meetings will enhance your professional image (and your business clothes will last a lot longer than if you wore them to work every day).

Don't Become Out of Touch with the Real World Outside the Home

• Read the daily newspaper more thoroughly than before.
• Keep up with your corporation's (or former corporation's) activities. Call old friends there and ask for the news. Read your company's employee newsletter. Watch for news of it in the financial journals. Subscribe to the important trade journals in your field.
• Don't watch daytime TV when you have a free moment during the day. Use any free time you may have to read some good books instead.
• Remember your childhood school days, and plan a schedule of an occasional field trip, such as to the city museum, the aquarium, the public library, and so on.

- Even if you don't have the time, need, or money to be interested in fashion, interior design, sports, music, or in whatever field you considered yourself an expert when you worked in an office, keep up on it. Subscribe to leading magazines in all of the fields in which you used to be up to speed, or arrange to read them at your public library. Working out of your home should enhance, rather than lessen, your knowledge of what's going on in your former field of interest. In other words, stay alive, interesting, and fun to be around.

- No matter how busy you are, there's always time to work in some kind of volunteer contribution (*see also* "The Company Encourages Volunteerism Among Employees," Chapter 16). Nothing will make you feel better about yourself; nothing will get you out in your community more visibly; nothing will more successfully offset the feeling of alienation working by oneself at home sometimes brings. If you have small children at home, volunteerism may have to wait, but you can always be doing research on what is most needed in your community, and looking forward to the day when your schedule will allow you to contribute your skills toward solving one of society's problems.

6

When The Executive Hires or Fires—Or Is in the Reverse Situation

I*t's no fun to lose a job; it's no fun to tell someone he has lost a job. It's a time for giving support to people who may feel totally down because of what has happened to his or her career; it's a time to help friends with new ideas of where to look, who to go see, what new avenues of job activities there might be to explore. It's a time for a person who may be floundering to get his or her act together. We should all help one another.*

PRESENTING YOURSELF FOR AN INTERVIEW

The rules for a job interview are the same for an experienced manager as they are for a college graduate:

- Be on time for the interview.
- While you're waiting in the reception area:
  - Read everything you can on the company that is available. Hopefully you have already located an annual report well ahead of this interview and know *everything in it*.
  - Be friendly and nice to the receptionist. She may be an invaluable aide.

- Take several copies of your resumé with you (and make certain they're spanking clean ones—no coffee or grease spots from the breakfast table).
- When you meet the person interviewing you for the first time, put out your hand and say his name. (Even if you know the corporate culture to be a very informal one, if you haven't met the interviewer, say, "Mr. Mathews, it is very good of you to see me," *not* "Hello, Tom, you're nice to see me.")
- Don't take a seat until the interviewer motions you to sit down.
- *Listen*, first and foremost. What do they need? Why did they grant you an interview? *Is* there a job extant, or are they merely thinking about staffing possibilities for the future? It is more important to know *what the interviewer is saying* than to articulate *what you want to say*.
- Whatever you do, don't tell the interviewer you don't know what you want to do with your life and suggest that he could tell you about his company." He doesn't have time to brief you on the company nor the inclination to talk someone into wanting the job. He *expects* you to want the job—passionately.
- Know your strengths and skills, and bring them forth at the right moment (not prematurely or awkwardly). There's a fine line between self-confidence and braggadocio. You can kill your chances if you cross that line.
- Find out if there are other candidates in mind for the job for which you are being interviewed. This is intelligence that might be very useful in competing for the position.
- Don't sound disappointed if the job in question is not the one you hoped it would be. Give it your best shot. It might turn out to be more interesting for you than the one you heard about.
- Be ready to relocate if that's what they want. If you need the job and they will pay the moving expenses, it may mean a great step up for you. If you're not ready to relocate, and it's the only job opening they have, listen very politely to the description of the job. It might well be worth your taking the risk, so don't just pass up the interview by leaving. Ask for a little time to think about it—but not too much—if they make an offer and you have any doubts.
- If you left a company for a negative reason, mention it simply, as a statement of fact, and briefly, but don't try to get the interviewer's sympathy. Don't be a whiner; there is nothing that will turn off the other person faster than to have you complain unendingly how unfairly you were treated.
- In fact, don't make any negative comments whatsoever about your previous place of employment. Talk only of its positive aspects. Rather than saying, "Company X is run by a bunch of jerks who don't know what they're doing," say, "Company X is a leader in their field of technology, and I was privileged to be in a great spot to learn it from the inside."
- Tell the person you're talking to that you:
  - Have the greatest respect for the company and would be very proud to join their team

- Are a very hard worker
- Are enthusiastic about the company's future
- *Want to get the job*. Don't waffle about it or act indecisively.

- The wrap-up is always a nice letter, written or typed on good-quality stationery:
  - If you get the job, write a long, earnest letter of thanks, with the promise that you'll fulfill the company's expectations and more.
  - If you were merely interviewed and never really had a chance, write a short, grateful letter thanking the interviewer for having seen and even considered you.
  - If you are told you lost out at the end to someone else, write a careful letter of thanks to the interviewer, and add something like, "Whoever succeeded in dazzling you so much that he or she got the job is one lucky person." You never know: At the last moment, the winner might not be able to take the job, and if your nice, friendly, grateful letter is sitting on the human resources official's desk, the next telephone call may be to you.

WHEN YOU HAVE TO LET SOMEONE GO FOR ECONOMIC REASONS

When you have to let someone go for just cause, such as stealing, selling drugs, and blatant nonperformance of duties, it is an unpleasant, difficult task. But when you fire someone who has become a colleague and friend because of downsizing and economic conditions, it can be heart-wrenching.

Be prepared when you give him or her the news. Do some research and have at your fingertips all of the policies that will go into effect at the time of separation from the company, such as:

- Number of weeks notice that must be given
- Possible severance pay
- An outplacement service
- The use of a desk, phone and receptionist for a period of so many weeks, or at least an answering machine to take calls
- The continuation of medical coverage for a specified length of time, etc.

Do the firing when you know his or her spouse will be at home when the executive returns there from your discussion. Experts constantly argue over whether the bad news should be given on a Monday or a Friday. What matters a great deal more is that when you give the bad news, devote sufficient time to it, to help the employee recover from the initial, terrible shock and to properly comfort and console him. A friend of mine was caught in the downsizing of a well-known company. He had worked for it his entire life after graduation from college, for twenty-three years, and he was let go by the CEO who called over his shoulder to him as he left the office Friday night, his golf bag slung over his shoulder. The conversation took about forty-five seconds of the CEO's time. The fact that his long-time employee was supporting a wife, both his aged parents, and educating four children, embarrassed the CEO. His solution to the problem of his own distress was to let his vice-president go in as painless a manner as possible—for himself.

Choose a morning when you know the executive you must let go does not have a lunch date. Go to his office late in the morning and make sure no one overhears you transmitting the bad news. Then take him out to lunch and have him go straight home afterward for the day. Even if he was worried over bad sales and profits, he probably was not accepting of the fact that it could happen to him.

As his or her supervisor, you should follow up:

- Make certain that everything possible is being done for him by the Human Resources department of the firm.
- Make telephone calls on his behalf to people who might advise him, steer him in the right direction, even possibly hire him
- Write him a letter of glowing reference that leaves no doubt whatsoever in the reader's mind that he was a valuable member of the organization and not let go for nonperformance of duty. Make it a personal, friendly letter that shows he was close to senior management, respected, and admired. Make it a letter that he will want to send to prospective employers. Your praise on the record will greatly help his search for a new position.
- Invite him and his family to dinner. Buck them all up. Make it clear how much talent their husband and father has and reassure them that all his friends in the organization are doing their best to think of companies for him to contact. Hopefully, if you have to let trusted employees go, you know how to do it in a way in which their esteem and self-respect are preserved, and in a way that will cause them always to look upon the company with affection.
- Keep in touch with him. Call him every couple of months, if you hear he has not yet found a position. Keep on advising and helping.

WHEN YOU HAVE BEEN THE ONE LET GO

A long period of joblessness for someone accustomed to being employed all of his or her adult life can be a lonely, stressful, really terrible episode to live through, but it does not have to be. The first thing you have to do is leave your office with a positive attitude, so that you will always be remembered that way. Who knows, the management might change tomorrow and you might be asked back. *Some action options you might consider*:

- Tell your office friends the bad news, separately and in private, as soon as you hear it. You will want them to have the facts straight, so they will have the proper information to dispel rumors. You will want them to know how much you have appreciated the working relationship with them. At this point in your life, you need every friend you have. It is no time to stand back and be shy.
- Realize that unemployment has been widespread. People are not automatically going to discriminate against you or think you are inept. It's important to show the world (and yourself) how resilient you are.
- Do everything you can for your secretary or assistant. Speak to Personnel about finding her another good job within the organization, be enthusiastic about her talents, and write a wonderful letter of recommendation for her, to be kept in her file but which can also be used by her to look for a job outside the company.
- Write a letter to your CEO, with a copy to Personnel, putting on the record how highly you regard the company, and how much you enjoyed being a member of the team. Even if that is not true, you will want to leave behind you the sweet smell of success instead of rancor. You can always point out the positive things you learned, the good experiences you had, and the major contributions you made to the company. Show what a professional you are, instead of telling off the CEO, which may be your inclination.
- Go on record with a hand-written note of appreciation to every important colleague and associate inside or outside your office who was nice to you over the past few years. For example:

Dear Mort,

    Although being caught in the downsizing of the company is very painful, I want you to know that one of the nicest aspects of my years with Aristel was having known and worked with you, a real professional. I'll miss our joint efforts on making projects like Equi an unqualified success, but I'll also miss our arguments over the NBA championships. Perhaps in the future, wisdom will come to you and you'll realize the Bullets are really superior to the Pistons.

    I hope our paths will cross and criss-cross often. You've been a real pal. I never thought I would tell a Pistons fan that I'd miss him, but I will. And, of course, if any career ideas for me should come to you in the middle of the night, this is one time I give you permission to call me at that hour.

    My very best to Margie and the kids.

- Purchase the latest and the best guide to management recruiters that exists. This kind of book lists recruiting firms that work on retainers or on a contingency basis. You will wish to contact some of them.
- Never let up on accuracy and neatness in your letters, no matter how tired or bored you may be writing them. Never send out anything sloppy that pertains to you, even if you feel a certain mailing is just a longshot.
- Take someone to lunch who will introduce you to his or her good friend, a leading executive recruiter. Your goal is to end up in that firm's computerized data bank.

- Write an accurate, honest resumé. There are stiff penalties for people who do not tell the truth. You could get fired later from the company that hired you. If you said you worked with one company for a year, and it was only six months, or if you falsely claimed to have attended a prestigious college or to have earned an MBA, such deceptiveness will seriously harm your reputation with the executive recruiters and personnel people.
- Customize your resumé (easy to do on a computer), so that it will seem targeted each time to the type of business enterprise considering you for employment.
- Ask some friends outside your industry to take a good look at your resumé to critique it and help make it more compelling.
- Think positively about going into an entirely different line of work, including an entrepreneurship. A complete change can be the most energizing step you could take.
- Call up the branch heads of your professional organizations in other parts of the country that are not as hard hit by the economy as your area. Ask them if they think you should visit their city. ("I'm just testing the waters out your way, since I have a great deal of experience correlating to the area's main industry and would enjoy coming out there.") Fax your resumé to each person you talk to, complete with a note of "thanks for any suggestions you might have."
- Contact your alma mater's placement service bureau, and keep them supplied with all of your various market-targeted resumés, not just one.
- If you were an overpressured, hyperactive executive in your last position, take one to two hours a day now to smell the roses, or use that daily hour of precious free time to better yourself or make yourself happy. (Learn gourmet cooking? Study French? Take drawing lessons? Take a course in business letter writing? Read the collected works of Shakespeare?)
- Eat healthy food and follow an energetic exercise regimen. Now is the time to get in shape. You have the time, and if you look better, you'll feel better and present a more affirmative picture to a prospective employer.
- Call up your old pals and former contacts all over the country to touch base and see if they know of any job activity in their part of the world. The sound of the human voice is very compelling to many people, and a follow-up letter or fax, containing excellent information on yourself, is a good reinforcement of that telephone call.
- Write a letter of thanks *immediately* after someone has done you a favor in your job search (*see also* "Thanking the Person Who Arranged for You to Have an Interview," Chapter 7). When you write at once, your mind is fresher with details of what transpired and your language will therefore be more vivid.
- Don't sound "down"—or drag others down with you. No one wants to have a depressed "moper" around. Keep up your energy and keep that sparkling personality polished brightly; retain your sense of humor, so that people will want you around and be eager to help you.

- Accept every dinner invitation for yourself (and your spouse, if you have one). You need cheering up, but you also need the exchange of ideas with other people. The sound of energy being expended on your behalf around someone's dinner table should be music to your ears.
- Don't stop entertaining. Even if you have to cut out all the frills of entertaining because of a reduced standard of living, invite people to your home, treat them well with hospitality and the warmth of caring, and you will *all* benefit. (Consider lunch or cocktails at your house instead of an elaborate dinner; a bite after a film or tennis game or an outing at a local event.)
- Look upon your frustrating time of job-hunting as a blessing in disguise as far as your family is concerned. You can be of immeasurable help to your spouse and get to know your children during real quality time that you never had before. It's important not to depress them with any negative feelings you may have yourself. Your family is your most precious asset.
- Realize that this may be a golden opportunity to go after that advanced degree you always wanted and knew you should have for your career's sake. Perhaps you can get a temporary job (of lesser importance and compensation than you would wish) that will tide you over while you attend night school. Besides, you may learn many new things on that job, even if it's just a polishing of your people skills.
- Realize that this may be the opportunity you've always wanted to learn a musical instrument. If you wanted to learn the guitar, for example, you might swap services with a guitar teacher (perhaps handle his children's car pool or take care of his lawn in exchange for weekly lessons).
- Realize, too, that you may never really have appreciated your city's architecture, museums, and parks. Often the things in a city that are free are its most exceptional assets. It's very stimulating to do something like take out a couple of books on Greek and Roman sculpture from the public library and then spend time in the museum in the Greek and Roman sculpture wing. The interplay of new cultural knowledge, of reading and seeing, can be a real pleasure in your life.
- When you and that new position finally mesh together, notify every person whose help you sought. It's not only polite, it's efficient. Even something like your university placement service should know the good news and stop giving your name to interested employers, and, of course, your college alumni magazine should carry the news of your new job in your class notes.

Be proud of yourself that you have not only survived a long and gruelling unemployment period, but perhaps have become a more important member of your own family, grown professionally, learned new skills, added to your resumé, and increased your self-worth. In the future you will probably show much more compassion and understanding of others who have just gone through what you have, and who have successfully survived.

HUNTING FOR A NEW JOB WHILE
YOU ARE STILL EMPLOYED

You might (or should) feel a certain amount of guilt when you decide to search for a job elsewhere while you are still employed. It's probably important to feel this guilt, because then you will cause your present company the least amount of harm. (Remember, your company is still paying you; you should deal with the situation in the best possible way.) Two suggestions:

- *Make appointments only on your lunch hour, after hours, or on weekends.* If an appointment starts to take much longer than you anticipated and you are supposed to be back at your office, be frank with the person interviewing you: "I feel very bad about this, but I'm overdue at my office. I hope you will let me return to finish this conversation. I'm needed back at my office." The interviewer will respect you rather than drop you for consideration for the new job. (If he doesn't, you should not want to work there anyway.)
- *Make calls concerning your job move on a pay phone on your lunch hour, away from your office.* Don't let anyone think you are using company time and money for your own job search.

AS YOU TAKE YOUR LEAVE

When you are offered the new job, be frank with the person in the new company about your responsibilities to your present employer, assuming you feel any sense of obligation to him. You might say to your new boss at this point: "When my boss hears that I am leaving and going to the competition, he will probably throw me out right then and there. He may ask me to empty my desk and leave. I hope that doesn't happen. I want to leave in an orderly, responsible way. I want to be able to say to my boss, 'I will find a good person to take over this job and I'll train him or her. If it takes three or four weeks to accomplish this, my new office will wait for me.' I don't want to leave them in the lurch."

That would be the best of situations. If your present boss becomes furious when you tell him you're leaving and accuses you of a lack of loyalty and makes other accusations, say calmly to him, "I'm really sorry you feel this way. I have loved this job. I admire this company and the people who work for it. I have been offered a much better opportunity, and for my own good, I must follow it, but I will always be grateful for what I've learned here, for the opportunities you have given me, and for the friendships made here."

If you know you are going to leave, tactfully, with no one being aware of it, copy your Rolodex and any of your own personal, important files after hours. Do this before you inform your boss of your impending departure. He may want you to leave at once, which would not give you the time to take your own personal files. It's wise to be prepared, and to have these materials already safe at home. It would be unethical to permanently remove materials that will be necessary to the next person who sits at your desk or to take anything that is really the company's and not your own files.

That's why you should leave your Rolodex there to be of help to your successor, along with anything else that would ease that person's path.

PART II

THE PERSON-TO-PERSON SIDE OF BUSINESS LIFE

7

Executive Communications

Human communication is in a strange state today. People don't talk, write, telephone, or listen to one another in a very human manner anymore. Modern electronic gadgets keep us away from one another, even while allowing us instant communication. The sound of another person's voice is no longer necessary to bring us together. Some people often don't talk face to face or even ear to ear—their communication is by means of messages left on and responded to by answering machines.

It is ironic that in our business lives the more relentlessly we pursue the latest technology, the more tongue-tied we become when sitting next to a stranger at a business dinner. The faster our fingers hit the keys to move the cursor along, the slower we react on a human level when we have offended someone, or when we should offer a special thanks.

A good manager reminds his employees of their duties to others on a human level. He shows them what to do—even how to write that letter or what words to use when calling on someone. The boss is, after all, ultimately responsible for the atmosphere in his group's working environment. The goal: a happy workplace.

In this chapter our discussions regarding executive communication are divided into the following sections:

- The importance of your voice
- The art of conversation
- Telephone manners

- Electronic uses and abuses
- Letter writing
- Memos
- Greeting cards

WHEN YOU SPEAK

Your Voice: How You Sound to the Outside World

A pleasant sounding voice is a great asset in business and social life: People want to listen to what you have to say. The only advantage to an unpleasant voice is that voice problems are often easily corrected.

Record yourself on tape. Listen carefully to that voice. Ask your family members or very close friends to listen, too, and to point out what *they* hear that needs correcting. You may think the reason your colleagues don't understand you easily is that you talk too fast; the people listening to your tape may point out something of which you have been totally unaware—like slurring words or other aspects of poor diction. Record yourself reading a paragraph from the morning newspaper, read a page from your company's annual report (that's real work—making your voice sound alive and exciting while reading an annual report!), or record your end of a telephone conversation (never record someone else, of course, without his or her express permission to do so).

Listening to a tape of your own voice is akin to looking at your reflection in the mirror in a harsh, cold light. In business you want to sound authoritative, educated, in charge—but also friendly and approachable. The balance is important.

It's not only your own voice that is important; it's the voice of your assistant who answers your telephone, or the voice of the office receptionist, who might answer several telephones. If an unpleasant sounding or badly accented voice answers your telephone, you should tactfully suggest that person get help on improving it. In our global economy employees with strong foreign accents who handle the telephone need this kind of assistance, if they are to work at top efficiency. The words *I didn't understand him* should never have to be heard in your division. If the company does not pay for speech improvement, you should become creative in seeking a way to pay for it, including urging the employee to pay what he can manage, too. After all, the voice answering your telephone and speaking for you reflects *your* executive image.

YOUR VOICE IS GOOD IF:	YOUR VOICE NEEDS IMPROVING IF:
It is easy to understand and your diction is clear.	It is difficult to understand and your words are not properly enunciated.
It reflects proper breathing. Short breaths from the diaphram, for example, give good oxygen support.	It is breathy, denoting indecision and a lack of ease.

YOUR VOICE IS GOOD IF:	YOUR VOICE NEEDS IMPROVING IF:
You have a low, comfortable pitch—that of a secure person.	Your pitch is too high, making you sound immature or overly nervous.
You have a clear tone, which lends authority to what you are saying.	Your tone is harsh and sounds strident and unreasonable.
You sound well-paced, not too fast nor too slow. Voice monotony should be avoided at all costs.	You displease the listener, either because you go too fast to be understood or too slow to be interesting.
You have a warm, intimate, vital quality.	You sound cold, uncaring, tired.
It expresses emotion—such as sympathy and enthusiasm.	Your tone is flat and seemingly unmoved by anything.
You speak without a regional accent, or if you have one, it is subtle and harmonious.	You have a strong regional accent that distracts and detracts from the content of the message.

The Relationship Between Voice and Vocabulary

If you think of another executive as having a good voice, you may or may not be aware that his choice of words also influences how you regard the sound of his voice. A good vocabulary helps a person to make good conversation and to communicate well; it also affects the quality of the voice affirmatively.

The English language has many beautiful sounds. An executive who uses a word like *mellifluous*, for example, must make an effort to pronounce it properly. It is a beautiful word, evoking a pleasant image. An enriched vocabulary sounds good to the ear and lends attractiveness to a voice. A person who uses distinguished words properly sounds distinguished and makes you *want to listen*.

A Cultivated Voice Implies a Cultivated Vocabulary

Contrary to what some people believe, a cultivated voice is not one with a phony "Eastern Establishment" accent. Someone who affects that kind of accent (partly British accent, partly muffled sounds and unfinished words) obviously feels insecure about his background. Locust Valley, Long Island, a place dotted with great estates and very rich people, has supplied the name people in the East have given this phony accent: Locust Valley Lockjaw. (Fortunately, very few people in Locust Valley speak that way.)

In reality a cultivated voice is:

- *Without a strong regional accent*, as noted
- One in which *only good grammar* is used

- Noted for the *absence of foul language*. I have heard construction men and miners use much better language than is heard today in many posh executive suites. Recently graduated MBAs seem to think it's perfectly all right to say "shit" or use "fucked up" every time they are slightly annoyed at anything. It's not perfectly all right. It tarnishes the image of their company and it's word pollution at its worst.
- One in which *pejorative nicknames are never used* when referring to people of other nationalities or religions. People who use ugly, loathsome terms like *dago*, *coon*, and *kike* are practicing an insidious form of bigotry and discrimination. Their word usage will completely shatter any image they might have had of refinement, culture, or education.
- One in which *all words are properly enunciated*
- One that does not tediously feature *repetitious phrases* (for example: "Know what I mean?" "Isn't that so?" or just "You know?")
- One in which *common slang is absent*. For example, starting every sentence with "Like" is totally ungrammatical. So is "I'm *into* aerobics" or "I'm *into* cooking." Things should be called by their proper names. Liquor is liquor, not "booze." Money is money, not "bucks" or "moola." A woman is a woman, not a "broad."

One particularly annoying speech habit of young people is finishing every statement that is not a question with "okay." This repetitious "okay" has become a conversational tic in our language today; it is not part of cultivated speech.

Speaking in Public

A great number of people in this world feel that speaking in public is one of the most terrifying experiences there is. (It is the number-one psychological fear.) It's tough enough in college or graduate school to get up on your feet and address the class, but the worst clutching moment occurs when you must do it in the conference room at your company or firm, when you feel your entire career may be at stake.

As someone who has risen to her feet all through her life, on occasions that have ranged from memorizing and reciting the Declaration of Independence before the eighth-grade assembly, to spending seven hours in one day lecturing on good corporate behavior to two hundred electrical engineers, I've learned good lessons the hard way. Here are some of my tips and some of Lily Lodge's, a speech consultant in New York who has worked on my training programs.

- *Get sleep the night before*. The larynx should be well rested.
- *Make sure you're appropriately dressed*. If you're worried about being overdressed, or too informally or sloppily dressed, you won't be able to devote the proper time to thinking about what you're saying.
- *If it's possible to mingle for a few minutes with your audience beforehand, do it*.

Shake a few hands, tell people you're looking forward to speaking to them and that you hope you're going to "give them something good to remember." Warm up your voice while you meet people, and show them how friendly you are. I always put on a big smile and tell people around the lectern just before I speak, "Now, remember, please, to applaud and not boo, promise?"

- *Fight anxiety by willing yourself to relax mentally, emotionally, and physically.* Expect the unexpected to happen, but don't be afraid of it. Know that you can handle it and keep an even keel.
- *Watch your posture.* Stand relaxed, but not flopped over the lectern like a rag doll. Don't stand in a rigid fashion, either. (I remember one of my Burlington Industries colleagues telling me at a practice session before my big speech that I looked like the Tin Woodsman from "The Wizard of Oz."
- *Take great care, of course, with the content of your speech.* State the theme of your remarks up front, in the introduction. Give solutions and new ideas in the body of the speech. Try to use a rich vocabulary and lace humor into your remarks as often as possible. (You don't want to bore your audience—ever.) Be aware of your stress points, dramatize them, and then let your voice become lower and quieter for contrast.
- *Know your material to perfection.* Be so well practiced, you can give your remarks by heart. (The more you go over your presentation, including just before falling asleep the night before), the fewer times it will be necessary to look down at your notes. Practice your remarks in front of a mirror at home, which will set you up with the toughest audience you could summon—you.
- *Don't eat just before you speak.* Dairy products, particularly, might constrict your throat with mucus.
- *Just before you start, psych yourself up.* Tell yourself you're terrific, your material is first class, you're a veritable Demosthenes in delivery, and that no one could make the presentation more effectively than you.
- *Relax.* If you're waiting offstage to be called to make your presentation (and the one who is speaking before you is finishing), *consciously slow down your breathing, yawn a few times (it relaxes the jaw and eases tension), and laugh, too*—if you can possibly find a reason for doing it. Your jaw will be nice and flexible.
- *As you begin speaking, look over your audience, still smiling, and then take a couple of deep, reassuring breaths.* You haven't said anything yet, but your audience will be thinking that there's a very agreeable smile on your face. They will surmise that you know something pleasant that they will want to know, too.
- *Make your first words something light.* Elicit some welcome laughter in the room.
- *As you talk, keep sweeping your eyes over the entire room.* Encompass everyone in it. Then find a friendly, pleasant face in the group and keep returning to it every so often, like a homing pigeon. It will be a comfort.
- *Keep listening to the sound of your voice in the room as it comes over the microphone.* Move closer or farther away from the mike as necessary.

- *Remember to use any trick of body language you can muster to help you sway your audience.* For example:

  ◦ *Think of your hands as artful persuaders* as you continue to emphasize your speaking points. Don't, however, keep moving your hands all over the place like the wings of an agitated bird, because your audience will feel equally unsettled.

  ◦ *Watch your spectacles,* if you wear them, to keep from nervously putting them on and off, or twirling them in your fingers, which will ultimately make nervous wrecks of the audience.

  ◦ *Control any other nervous hand habits you might have,* such as playing with a strand of hair, or worse, constantly pushing your hair back off your face where it has fallen.

    Speaking of hands, when I'm waiting in the wings offstage in an auditorium, prior to facing a big audience, I hold my arms down by my sides and shake my hands from the wrists very briskly, like swimmers do before a race. This exercise expels the tension in the hands—in fact, in the entire body. (If possible, don't let anyone see you doing this, because it makes you look like a blithering idiot.)

  ◦ *Stand upright, without clutching the lectern,* and without leaning on it in desperation, as if it were a life preserver. If you are much taller than the lectern, don't become too comfortable and relaxed, leaning hunched over on it, because your rear end will rise whalelike behind you—not a lovely sight.

- *Smile a lot.* The more you smile, including laughing at yourself when you make an amusing remark or an embarrassing gaffe, the more relaxed and accommodating your audience will become.

- *Keep a glass of water (not ice water) close at hand.* Sip it if your throat becomes constricted, but learn to sip only when there's a natural pause in the proceedings, such as when people are laughing at one of your witty remarks, or if there is a break in the proceedings, as when the lights are brought up at the end of a slide show or when a report is being passed around to the meeting participants.

- *Make absolutely certain your equipment has been thoroughly checked.* You shouldn't have to worry about projector bulbs not working, the carousel remote sticking, or other audio-visual horrors. If there's a glitch in your audio-visuals (and I am a veteran of every disaster in using microphones and projectors ever documented in history), keep your audience amused while whatever it is that doesn't work is being fixed. Tell them a joke. "Has anyone heard the story about ——?" "Would anyone in the audience like to learn some new swear words in Swahili that no one around you will understand, so they won't be shocked by what you're saying?" "Can you imagine how I felt when the projector wouldn't even turn on for my lecture on interior design that was based entirely on eighty-four slides? Have you ever tried to describe eighty-four colored slides?"

Once, at a Milwaukee country club, I gave a lecture—based on slides—in the ballroom, where the draperies had been sent to the cleaners. (The draperies, of course, kept the room darkened so the audience could see the slides on the screen.) On the day of my lecture, however, the sun shone on sparkling, white snow outside the windows of the room. The ballroom was so bright, it looked as though ten Hollywood kleig lights had been illuminated inside. Naturally, no one in the audience could see any part of a projected slide. Nothing. I had to change the subject of my entire lecture on the spot and talk without notes for forty-five minutes. I chose as my new subject, ''Embarrassing Situations and How to Survive Them.''

When your props fail you during your presentation, pretend you're out on a storm-tossed sea, praying that the boat will keep upright until help arrives. You *will* survive.

Getting Help from Professionals

There are large national communications consulting firms in major cities that will work on your presentation and its content. Communispond, Inc., at 485 Lexington Avenue, New York, NY 10017, is one.

Some large public relations companies, such as Hill and Knowlton, Inc., have in-house teaching facilities in several locations around the country. Look in your telephone books to see if any are in your locality, or check their offices in New York. Local public relations agencies (listed in the Yellow Pages) may offer this service in your area.

Two nationally known experts who specialize in preparing people for public speaking and television appearances are in New York City. Lilyan Wilder, a communications authority and speech consultant, has for thirty years been training corporate executives and many notables in their public presentations, among them Oprah Winfrey, former President Bush, and Apple Computer's John Sculley. She can be reached at (212) 988-2258. Dorothy Sarnoff is another speech and presentations expert who has trained legions of famous authors, corporate executives, and celebrities at her Speech Dynamics headquarters, at 111 West 57th Street, New York, NY 10019. A company like Jack Hilton, Inc., at 230 Park Avenue, New York, NY 10169, teaches senior management to handle tough, antagonistic questions from TV interviewers and the press.

Also bear in mind:

- Communications experts who teach at local colleges or universities often accept private clients.
- Look in the Yellow Pages under the listings ''Public Speaking Instruction'' and ''Speech and Language Pathologists'' for further listings.

Just don't forget that a good voice establishes trust and can calm or soothe people, or conversely, motivate and incite them into action. *A great voice is a great tool in business.*

THE ART OF CONVERSATION

Children used to learn how to converse from their parents, grandparents, uncles, and aunts, sitting around the dinner table. Now there are other distractions and entertainments. There are always earphones to put on, television screens to watch, and computer keys to stroke. The tender game of conversation is seldom played in an active family.

I really admire one CEO who, greatly concerned with the ever-decreasing communication skills of his young executives, confines his young "new hires" for three days in a room without televisions, radios, telephones, or reading material. They are all strangers to one another, but by the end of three eight-hour days, they either have learned to express themselves, learned about one another, and have become friends, or they are asked to leave the company because of communications problems.

The CEO has not had to fire anyone yet. Three days seem to force the imprisoned men and women to find ways to talk and develop a mindset to work well together to help achieve the company's goals, and even to become good friends. As the CEO expresses it, "They discovered something new—the power of words, and the joy of trust that comes from communicating."

The question of conversational skills is simple and complex at the same time, as illustrated in the following material.

Listening Is an Art

The ability to *listen* is an art, not just a skill, because it is the foundation of all good conversation—and also of good communication with one's bosses.

- One of the keys of diplomacy is to *act interested in what people are saying around you, even if you're not.* It's very rude to show you are bored or disinterested; for centuries people have managed to hide their boredom for the sake of making and keeping friends.
- When you treat the speaker with respect, even if you are not enthralled with the subject, *you will learn something from it*; you will grow in wisdom and articulation skills.
- Senior executives lament that today's average young person doesn't listen—that orders are given, complicated instructions are transmitted, but the person to whom the directions are given is day-dreaming or concentrating on his own agenda. There are too many conversations between boss and employee like this one:

    BOSS: But I told you about that, remember?
    EMPLOYEE: No, honestly, this is the first time I've heard of it!

BOSS: How can you say that, when we discussed it last Wednesday at the end of the meeting? You even promised you would get back to me by Friday.

EMPLOYEE: I'm sorry, but I honestly think you had this conversation with someone else, not me.

- People who do not listen carefully to instructions miss nuances and signals that could result in the loss of millions of business dollars—or their jobs.

You Are Listening Well When:

- You subjugate your impressions of how someone looks and the nature of his surroundings *to what he is saying.*
- You remember all major points of the conversation, particularly any action that is your responsibility.
- You ask intelligent questions at the end of the meeting or discussion.
- You *make your listening time also a learning time.*

Good Body Language Is Part of Good Conversation

Body language is a personal thing. It tells a lot about a person's character, such as whether he is making an effort when he's talking to you, whether he shows respect for others to whom he is talking, and whether he pays proper attention to someone else's ideas.

Think about your own body language. Be conscious of it. For example:

- *When you meet someone, don't stand too close.* (Remember the angry expression, "Stay out of my face!") An uncomfortable closeness is very annoying to the other person, so keep your physical distance, or he'll have to keep backing off from you. A minimum of two feet away from the other person will do it.
- *Never back someone into the wall* where he thinks you have imprisoned him so you can talk to him. Always allow space around a person—symbolic of the other person's freedom to move around, to get away from you if he wishes.
- *When you are in a conversational group, your body language will either be pleasant and polite or rude and negative.*

Some of the ways in which your body will tell the other person you are listening intently are these:

- *You sit attentively in your chair.* If you slump down on your backbone, your legs straight out in front of you, your body is saying, "I don't care what you're saying, and frankly, you bore me."
- You're neither a sprawler in your chair when you're talking to someone (like a loose, limp rag doll), nor are you one who sits terribly rigid and unmoving, like a Gothic statue.

- *You watch the face of the person speaking* and do not let your eyes roam randomly around the room. It's polite to give the person speaking your full attention, in a "do unto others as you would have others do unto you" kind of philosophy.
- *You keep your legs still*, not continuously shifting your position or crossing and uncrossing your knees. The latter body language signifies either aching joints or the fact that you can hardly wait to get away. Letting your knee bounce up and down continuously also denotes boredom with the present company, which is the way you may feel, but you should certainly disguise that fact.
- *You watch how you sit* if you are a woman in business. Men and women in (and out of) business should watch how they sit—but it is particularly important for women executives to sit with their knees together, and to watch their posture if they're wearing short, tight skirts. A woman who is not sitting properly is signalling the wrong kind of body language to the men who are present, and often she is not even aware of how she is sitting. (A woman on a stage *really* has to watch how she is sitting for the sake of her image.)

Sharpening Conversational Skills

Basically, a good conversationalist is:

- Well-informed and an active reader of books, magazines, and newspapers
- Polite
- Interested in others
- Enthusiastic and alive

If you have the above qualities, you are going to be someone with whom everyone wants to spend time, because good conversationalists:

- Make other people feel good
- Give them ideas and hope
- Make the time pass very pleasantly

Good conversationalists react to what is being said and what is going on around them, rather than remaining passive and letting everything "just happen."

Good Conversationalists:

- *Can talk on a broad range of subjects*, even bluff well on subjects they know nothing about
- *Show interest in what other people are doing, how they are doing, and where they are heading*
- *Are able to make a fast switch*, from business to world politics or from ecological concerns to a new opera being performed
- *Know how to tailor their topics* to the interests of the people with whom they are speaking

- *Don't interrupt.* It is extremely rude to stop someone in the middle of a discourse, even if he has been dragging on interminably. Wait for a propitious moment, and then break into the conversation, launching another topic.
- *Speak from experience and knowledge,* not careless conjecture
- *Look people straight in the eye when talking to them.* Eye contact is important in any situation. If you don't look directly at the person you're talking to, it could mean that you're hiding something, or looking for someone more important to talk to.
- *Refrain from correcting in public another person's facts, grammar, or pronunciation.* Real friends help by pointing out in private repeated errors that may make a colleague or friend look inarticulate or uneducated.
- *Show genuine interest in good news about colleagues,* and help spread that good news
- *Know how to question a stranger in a friendly, rather than a prying manner.* It's all right to ask someone how many plants his company has in foreign countries; it's not all right to ask if he's one of the people being considered to take over the job of the CEO, who's retiring shortly.
- *Accept compliments gracefully, rather than refuse them.* If someone gives another person credit for something he did not do, he should, of course, set the record straight; but if someone praises his performance, he should not deny it but thank the complimenter for the kind words.
- *Know how to pay compliments gracefully,* which means with sincerity and good timing and without exaggeration and false praise. You can always make a compliment less embarrassing to the recipient if you inject a note of humor into it: "Tony has done such an excellent job lately of writing the CEO's speeches, as well as his message to shareholders for the annual report, the rumor is that he's been tapped to write all the thank-you notes for the chairman's daughter's wedding!"
- *Know when to talk business and when not to.* People who can only talk about office matters are usually unmitigated bores. A good conversationalist really contributes to a business discussion with peers, associates, and clients, but also really contributes to discussions with people not associated with his business life.
- *Are always armed with many interesting topics—other than themselves—to discuss.* If they feel passionately about something and are leading the conversation, they know when and how to jump off the subject quickly and turn to another subject—just any other subject.
- Don't burst someone's balloon in front of other people. If someone is passionately defending a point of view, it is indefensibly rude to disagree disagreeably. You can always respond negatively without animosity. "There are two schools of thought on that subject, of course." Hold your fire until you see that person in private.
- *Address everyone within the group, not just one or two people.* It is rude to have the floor and then to single out someone to talk to, instead of the whole group that

happens to be present. It's exclusionary. A good conversationalist catches the eye of each person in the group on a rotating basis while talking, so that everyone feels like a partner in the conversation.

· *Know how to make a shy person feel part of the group.* If he notices someone off to the side, without anyone to speak to, he will ask that person a question and bring him into the group by introducing him and asking his opinion on some matter.

· *Know what to do if they sense they are boring people.* If they notice some of their listeners becoming glassy-eyed and beginning to fidget in their chairs, they immediately extricate themselves from their subject and toss the ball into someone else's court. "Now, that's enough on the presidential election. Let's talk about something more exciting. Grace, is your new puppy thriving? Any new tricks?" Even though his audience knows he is joshing, they also know he realizes it's time to talk of things other than politics.

· *Are nice enough to step in to fill an embarrassing void in conversation.* If that uncomfortable period develops when everyone suddenly stops talking and no one can think of anything to say, the person who rescues the group is a real hero. Learn a super joke to tell or riddle to solve. For years I've tried this: "I'll give five dollars to anyone here who can recite all fifty state capitols in five minutes." Several people will try to do it (few can within the time limit), but the tension is broken, the awkwardness of the situation is diffused, everyone laughs, and conversation begins again.

· *Have a sense of humor.* Without it, there is no hope for good conversation or good personal rapport.

I remember the advice of Clare Boothe Luce, my former boss at the embassy in Rome, to one of my young friends who had confessed to the ambassador that she had no sense of humor. "How do I go about getting one?" she asked.

"Pretend you are your favorite comic," Ambassador Luce replied. "Write down ten things a day that have happened to you or things that you have witnessed—ten each day for an entire week. Then concentrate on each incident and find something humorous about it, something that could be perceived as funny, something you can poke fun at. What would your favorite comic have done, playing off each of the occurrences you described in your list? If you really know his work, your mind will start to operate like his." She paused for a second and said, "And if that doesn't work, you can always just sit home and not partake of life."

When You Can't Think of Anything to Say

This is a truly common dilemma—when you're with an uncommunicative person you have just met or don't know well, and you can't think of anything to say. Some people solve the problem by always letting the other person worry about it. "Make the other person bear the responsibility for bringing up a new topic of conversation that will get the chatter going again'' is their motto. That is a selfish, defensive attitude, one that I'm positive the readers of this book do not have.

If you and your conversational partner are in that ''good-lord-what-do-we-talk-about-now?'' mode, just remember that if you sat down to count them, you could really come up with several thousand possible topics. Your own experience and what you see around you are an infinitessimal part of the range of subjects. All you have to come up with, when you're in a bind, is one topic, not several thousand. For example:

- *Make the person to whom you're speaking talk about himself.* The best way to get any conversation going is to turn the spotlight on the other person, and to remain fascinated by anything he or she might say:

  - ''I read all the editorials this morning, but what do *you* think about the government's position on the most recent economic news?''
  - ''Why are we so fortunate as to have you visiting here? Are you receiving an honorary degree from the university or something?'' (Guaranteed to please the other person, as he laughingly denies such an honor.)
  - ''Please forgive me, I should know, but what is it that you do? You're obviously important.'' (This should be said in a half-joking fashion with a broad grin on your face, so the other person won't consider you to be an insincere, boot-licking flatterer.)

    I will never forget the night I sat on a stranger's left at a charity dinner held in honor of a famous business tycoon and philanthropist at the Waldorf Astoria in New York. My dinner partner knew who I was, having consulted, he said, my etiquette books on occasion. He professed to being a fan. I became even more curious, so I asked him what kind of work he did. A natural question. ''I'm a professional award collector,'' he laughed. He was also the evening's honoree. (I recovered my composure by the time the third speech honoring him was finished.)

- *If you know the newcomer you're talking to has a family and is not divorced*, you can always ask, ''Did you have a hard time finding a place to live when you moved here? How about the school situation for your children?'' Pepper your dinner conversation with questions as to how he or she has been settling in to the new environment. Offer help and advice, and above all, be sympathetic to the problems the family may be having. All that sympathy will make you a fast new friend, one who will be easy to talk to for a long time to come, not just at the meal at hand.

  While you're on the subject of where the newcomer is going to live in your city, you can bring into the conversation three or four others sitting around you: ''Gwen, George, and Henry, this is Valerie Johnson, who has just moved here from Tampa, and she's wondering what neighborhood she should move into. She has three boys in grade school, and she's looked at houses in Kenmore, Dundee, and Hollow Acres. What advice would you like to give her?'' Suddenly, Valerie

Johnson will feel welcomed in this community, because four people are advising her on her real estate problems. She can call them tomorrow if she wishes to ask for further guidance and assistance.

· *You can always sympathize with someone who travels a lot.* "It's hard to travel so much, isn't it, with a family at home? I really enjoyed all the travel when I first began a sales job, but now I find it's tougher and tougher being away while our children are growing up without me."

  A show of sympathy will always make your dinner partner feel good, and he or she will like you for it.

· *You can always fill a conversational void by telling your dinner partner you like the way your host's table looks.* Perhaps the flowers are exceptionally beautiful, or the food is distinguished, or the guests are an interesting group. (Under no circumstance is it a good idea to knock the host's party, even if it much deserves it, and even if you can be very amusing in the process. Criticism is a downer, and it will probably get back to the host.)

How to Make Small Talk

It's ironic that something so frivolous-sounding as small talk is so important in establishing warm personal relationships in business. The dictionary defines it as "light conversation or chit-chat." Small talk is unimportant conversation that is like a prologue to the opening act of a serious business dialog.

Small talk is what you make when you are getting to know the other person before a business meeting seriously begins, or before the substantive discussions begin at lunch. The executive who is incapable of light conversation, who must jump aggressively into the business part of the meeting without any relaxed repartee beforehand, is considered boorish, overly eager, and insensitive to people.

Your dinner guest, who may have been trading on the floor all day, might very well wish to discuss what's happening to the local hockey team before you barrage him with your new financial scheme. Your boss, who is exhausted from traveling all day, may wish to hear some unserious gossip on the way home from the airport at midnight rather than the financial statements you are carrying in your briefcase.

Small talk is made for about ten minutes at lunch before talking business, and for about thirty minutes prior to the serious discussions at dinner. *Small talk ends and the business discussion begins according to the desired timetable of the host of the meal.* The guest has no right to launch into the business points; he must wait for the host to lead the way. When two couples are dining together and two of the spouses have a joint business interest, it often happens that when the time comes for the business part of the discussions, the two spouses not affiliated with the business are able to carry on their own quiet conversation.

Small talk may center on anything and everything: a discussion of the day's news stories, for example, or a talented comic who is hot, possible Olympic contenders, the newest laptop computer, or a diet that everyone claims really works.

If you are having lunch with a new client or customer and are not feeling all that secure about it, do some research. Find out what his or her main interests are. (Reading that person's biography usually tells you what you need to know.) Then you can launch into small talk by hitting on one of those subjects.

I have a friend who is a world-class expert on small talk. She talks animatedly and enthusiastically on any subject, to the point where her business lunches are often 80 percent small talk and only 20 percent business. She has now solved her problem of too much inconsequential talk. When she hosts client lunches today, she sets the alarm on her wristwatch; the warning buzz signals her to turn to business subjects.

Conversational Subjects to Avoid

There are subjects that a good conversationalist avoids, because controversy does not make friends nor does it help create a happy, relaxed atmosphere. Stay away from these topics:

- *Matters concerning money.* Money questions are much too personal to ask. For example:

  - How much your new fur coat cost at a retail price versus what you paid for it wholesale
  - What price you sold your house for versus your asking price
  - How much salary anyone makes, including benefits
  - How much in debt you or anyone else is
  - How much alimony someone has to pay
  - The horrendous cost of braces, plastic surgery, installing a new bathroom in your house, or sending your mother-in-law off on a cruise
  - The price anyone paid for his wife's new diamond bracelet, purchased because of a guilty conscience

- *Your health.* Anyone lucky enough to be in great health should answer the question, "How are you?" with a smile and a hearty "Great! How are you?"

  If you have contracted a serious illness, reply noncommittedly, "All right, how are you?" If someone asks how you are at a business meeting or a social affair, they don't want to hear that you have just been diagnosed as having the HIV virus, that you're facing a pacemaker insert, that you have just had a miscarriage, or that you have come down with skin cancer. If you really have something serious, word will get out in time, and people will offer their support and friendship. A discussion of a serious illness in public will not help anything.

  I know a man who would have become the CEO of his successful, mid-sized company, had he not been such a hypochondriac all his life. He was a dynamo, very smart, but he had the terrible habit of answering people with the truth when they asked, in passing, "How are you?" What they wanted from him was, "Fine, thanks, how are you?'' What they got from him was a litany of every detail in his life, from ingrown toenails to conjunctivitis and from a minor skin rash to a stuffed-up right sinus. I learned a lot from this executive—namely, never talk about your health.

- *Other people's health.* If a friend of yours returns to work after a serious illness, operation, or accident, you should always greet him with kindness and solicitude. Tell him in private that if he needs anything, you are there. Then start talking about what's going on in the office. Help this person slip back into his office routine. Don't make a permanent invalid out of him by constantly reminding him—and everyone else—of the serious nature of his problem.
- *Controversial subjects when the players are emotionally involved and have deep feelings:* politics, religion, abortion, homophobia, and nuclear energy.
- *Lugubrious subjects:* death, destruction, torture, starvation, abuse, etc. When people have gathered for a social occasion, or when colleagues are making small talk, waiting for the meeting to start, your job as ''conversation boss'' is to launch topics that will make people sit up, bright-eyed and awake, glad to be alive and involved in the world.
- *Rumor and gossip—stories that have been started but never substantiated.* Never go to bed at night wondering if you were a conversational gun in the slandering of a person's character or the endangerment of his future. (It's real leadership when you take over the conversation at a time like that and say, ''Listen, we don't know that story is at all true; there is no proof. It may be pure conjecture.''
- *Trite and overworked subjects.* Some subjects, like celebrities' marital and financial scandals, are so overworked in the media that the person who brings them up as a conversational topic seems boorish and totally lacking in imagination to others present. It's commendable when you launch a topic, such as current events, with which everyone is familiar and to which any and all can contribute. Beware of choosing something that has already been picked over and exhausted.
- *Your children.* Your offspring are endlessly fascinating to you, your family, and your good friends. To business acquaintances, they are an obligatory point of conversation that for the sake of politeness should be addressed only once during the meal. If you have no real sense of time, don't trust yourself. Pull out a stopwatch and set it when you begin to discuss them. Don't talk about them for longer than five minutes, no matter how exciting their latest news might be. (Of course, if you happen to be the parents of an incoming president of the United States, the time limit for talking about one's child is different.)

Talking in Business-Social Situations

The Cocktail Party

This kind of event is inevitably noisy, punctuated by interruptions, and is a terrible place for a substantive discussion. If you try to talk serious business with someone, that person may dislike you for trying to accomplish the impossible when he or she would rather be socializing and having fun. If you see the potential for a fruitful discussion or a continuation of an exchange of ideas, discreetly hand your business card to the person, and whisper in his or her ear, "I will call you this week to make an appointment to continue this conversation."

The Tradition of Switching Conversation Partners at Large Dinners or Lunches

Since the early nineteenth century, the great hosts of Europe and members of the diplomatic corps have solved the problem of a guest's being "stuck" throughout an entire meal by inaugurating a system in which guests switch conversational partners as each new course is brought in. The system assures that a guest gives equal time to the person on his left and on his right during the meal.

When a corporate host gives a large party and pays no heed to how the conversation is going around the table, there are inevitably awkward results, with certain guests left with no one to talk to for a long period of time. What usually happens then is that the guest left alone begins talking across the table to another guest left alone, and a shouting match over the din ensues. When a host sees this, he should straighten out the conversational traffic and jokingly direct the partner of the guest left alone to please turn in the right direction.

To illustrate, consider a dinner for eighteen given by Mary Smith, a manufacturer's representative, and her husband for Mary Smith's top customers. When the guests are seated, the soup course is brought out, and Mary, as the host, turns instinctively to the guest of honor on her right (her biggest customer). Conversational pairings should then continue to form to the right on around the table. When the meat course is brought in, Mary turns to her guest on her left, and everyone on around the table switches accordingly. And so it goes with each course.

The Host Is in Charge of the Conversation at His or Her Corporate Party Table

Corporations are constantly "taking tables" and hosting guests at large industry or charity events. So that goodwill is fostered, so that everyone enjoys themselves, and so that the goals for giving the party are attained, social rules should be observed. It's very important, for example, for the host to make certain that everyone at his or her table knows who everyone else is. The host should have a list of the table names in advance of the social event; he should know their companies and titles. He should introduce each person flawlessly to the entire table, even if he has never met them before and is simply acting as a company host at one of the tables. If a guest has a difficult foreign name, he should find out in advance how to pronounce it properly, and he should practice it and do it perfectly. (Details like this denote a company with class.)

The host is in charge of the conversational flow at his table. He should make certain that:

- *Everyone gets the opportunity to contribute to the conversation if they wish.* This may mean cutting someone off who has been hogging the conversation and then asking an eager guest, "Now what do you think about that, Sam? And, Ms. Williams, I'd like to hear your opinion on that, too."
- *The topic is changed if it has been exhausted.* Turn to something new if the subject at hand has run out of energy or if it is inappropriate for the occasion or if there are too many people present who know nothing about it or if someone is getting upset with the subject, or simply if there is something that would be more enticing to talk about at that particular moment.

The host has the power *and the social duty* to keep the conversation aloft and flowing with ease. It may require his interrupting at times to point out something of great interest or to deflect possible hostility in conflicting opinions or to inform someone of what the others are talking about. The host who manages the overall table conversation with deftness is the keystone of the good time had by everyone at that table.

TELEPHONE MANNERS

The telephone is a singular instrument of communication, capable of creating an entire range of emotions in human beings. It is the messenger of information. It brings good news, bad news, surprises, disappointments and everything from sharp personal criticisms to dreamy words of love.

In business someone who knows how to manage people knows how to use the telephone as part of his or her inventory of good management techniques. In telephonic communications it's important never to lose sight of the human equation.

In the early days of its existence, the telephone was handled with great formality. People watched their manners, feeling intimidated lest they make a mistake that could be heard by a critical ear in a far off place. Today we take it for granted and don't worry what kind of noise we are transmitting to the other person's ear—including the sounds of full-blown sneezes, coughs, chewing, grunts, and even soda being slurped through a straw. The beauty of the English language seems far removed from today's telephone jargon. Perhaps it's because we are so electronically spoiled.

The first sound heard by the public when trying to reach your company is the voice of the person answering the call or, if they're unlucky, a voice initiating them into your company's voice mail system. (I say "unlucky" because so many businesses do not have their voice-mail act together, and for someone calling the company, it can be a totally frustrating experience.)

The voice (and it could very possibly be your own) answering your telephone should:

- *Convey the necessary information* (the name of the corporation, for example).

- *Have a warm and welcoming tone* (we're not talking about a sexy voice here, but a live, vibrant one).
- *Speak distinctly.* (If the voice presently answering your telephone is difficult to understand, you should either send that person to a voice coach or put him or her in another job.)
- *Sound interested in why the caller is calling* and eager to accommodate the caller's needs. (This gift is growing rarer these days; the answering voice of today often sounds as though the caller had awakened it from a sound sleep to which it can hardly wait to return.)

Management Should Take an Interest in What the Public Hears When Calling the Company
(See also "The First Person to Project the Company's Image: The Receptionist," Chapter 2)

The CEO and other senior officers should call their company every once in a while, masquerading as anonymous members of the public, in order to see how the public is treated. Major reasons for calling a business are:

- To reach an employee or seek information on an employee
- To elicit information on the company
- To place, change, or cancel an order
- To seek information on the company's products or services
- To find out about the price and availability of the company's products or services
- To get a job with the company
- To complain about an employee or product
- To commend an employee or product
- To inquire about the company's possible support of a charity
- To request a copy of the annual report
- To iron out family personnel matters
- To complain about the corporation's stand on issues

How to Answer Your Telephone

How You Should Answer Your Telephone

RIGHT WAY	WRONG WAY
"Ed Anderson speaking"	"Ed speaking," or "Ed, here" *(too abrupt and informal)*
"Contract sales, extension 305"	"Extension 305" or "Sales" *(not enough information)*

How Your Secretary Should Answer Your Telephone

RIGHT WAY	WRONG WAY
"Mr. Anderson's office"	"Ed's office" (*too informal*)
"Ed Anderson's office"	"Anderson's wire" (*too abrupt*)
"Mr. Anderson's extension"	

Nicknames used in business, particularly on the telephone, can destroy any semblance of dignity in that office. Two totally different impressions are made by a secretary when she answers her boss's telephone:

"Geegee Hart's Office, Debbie Sue speaking."

or

"Henry Hart's Office, Ms. Arnold speaking."

A wise manager lists every reason a person would call the company's main switchboard and writes out (and continually updates) the appropriate responses, including those for the most difficult of situations. I will never forget calling a major corporation seeking some basic information about the public funeral services being planned for the CEO, who had tragically died of a heart attack the morning before. I had a little speech ready for the operator: "I know how awful you all must feel, and I extend my sympathies to each and every one of you." Instead the conversation went like this:

LB: I'm calling about the death of Mr. X.
THE OPERATOR: What? Mr. X is dead? I didn't know.

She was nonplussed, without an idea of what to do next. End of conversation. The only worse treatment of my call would have been a confrontation with the company's voice-mail system, in which I would have been presented with numerous options and numbered buttons to press, all going nowhere.

How to Advise People Who Answer Your Office Telephones

You should instruct—call it "train"—whoever answers your telephones. Employees need help with their telephone manners. They are not psychic. They need reminding about the proper way to handle the public; they should keep their telephone skills freshly sharpened. (There are also usually more than a few executives who could use the same kind of assistance.)

The boss should not only check up on the job the staff is doing with the telephones, but should also praise them—and reward them—for doing a great job, when it's merited. The way a company handles its phones establishes an attitude in the public's eye. The company can be perceived as a high-class operation or a schlock one based on its telephone manners alone. Here are some points of instruction:

- *Put enthusiasm into his voice* when answering any call for the boss. Regardless of how that person may be feeling that day, he should play-act and disguise any negative factors that may be bothering him, whether it's a common cold or an uncommon depression.
- *Answer after the first ring.* There are times when this is impossible, but if the caller has to wait for more than four rings it means poor staff management.
- *Show unfailing politeness and patience*, even under great stress. If this becomes the office work ethic, then employees will feel like real heroes at the end of the day.
- *Inform the caller that the person he is calling is out* (if that's the case) before *asking the caller his name.* Whether you, the boss, are in or out of the office, the secretary should say, right after she hears the caller ask for you, whether or not you are available. For instance:

> SECRETARY: Mr. Smith's office.
> CALLER: Is Mr. Smith there?
> SECRETARY: No, I'm sorry, Mr. Smith is not in the office. (*Or, "Mr. Smith is not available."*) May I ask who's calling?

The above is a much better scenario than the following one:

> SECRETARY: Mr. Smith's office.
> CALLER: Is Mr. Smith there?
> SECRETARY: Who's calling, please?
> CALLER: Jerry Seiden.
> SECRETARY: I'm sorry, Mr. Smith is not in the office. Is there any message?

In the second scenario Jerry Seiden probably concludes that he was given the brush-off when the secretary heard who he was. He feels unnecessarily snubbed.

- *Act as though he is glad the person called.* "Thank you for inquiring" should be said in a pleasant voice, even if he would prefer to wring the caller's neck.
- *Transfer the caller intelligently.* In other words, put even a cold call through to someone who really can handle the situation. A caller's animosity ratio rises with each person or machine he is forced to speak to without having his query answered.

How to Take and Leave Messages

Managers who don't receive their messages swiftly and accurately can lose clients and customers. The company's reputation can be damaged. Teach the entire staff the following:

- *There should be an ample-sized pad and a pencil (with lead in it, or a pen with ink in it) permanently placed near every telephone* so that a proper message can be taken. People should be taught to keep fresh pads and writing instruments in reserve, so that no message is lost.
- *There should be a central area that everyone knows about for posting messages.* It might be a bulletin board; it might be a spindle on the reception desk; it might be anywhere that is predetermined and to which everyone has easy access. If someone takes a message for you in another part of your corporate offices you should not miss it on your return. Messages left around haphazardly often end up on the floor, in a wastebasket, stuck in a venetian blind, or used as a bookmark in a telephone book.
- *When a person calls, the caller's name, telephone number, extension, and area code should be recorded.* The date and time of call should be posted—terribly important in these days of widespread, sudden business travel. The text of a message crammed with facts should be written down slowly and read back to the caller to check for accuracy.
- *It's wise to have your message written on a pad with a carbon copy behind the original*, because it's *very* helpful to have a backup if a message gets lost.

When Leaving Messages

- When you are giving a message on the telephone to someone who will then relay it to someone else, keep it simple and short. The person taking the message is not going to want or be able to take down a lengthy treatise. The only time in all my office life I ever heard of someone amenable to taking a long message was when a lawyer at lunchtime took a message (for a senior partner) that filled two pages of his legal pad. No one else was in the office. The call came from a woman to whom the senior partner in the firm had been proposing unsuccessfully for three years, much to the amusement of the entire office staff. The woman, now in a telephone booth at Kennedy Airport and on her way to Budapest, asked the lawyer taking the message to write down a quote from a piece of poetry by way of saying she had decided to marry the senior partner. The compassionate notetaker (a bit of a romantic himself) said he really didn't mind writing it all down, "considering the circumstances."
- Never leave a vague or mysterious message. People hate to find a scrawled message that says, "Nancy called, sorry not to reach you, has something absolutely earth-shaking to tell you," or "Jim Martin called you, said you'll never GUESS what has happened!"
- Never take a message for an office colleague when the caller says, "Just tell him 'Sam called.' " "Sam who?" you would ask. "He'll know," could be the exasperating answer. Don't let the caller get away with leaving such an unbusinesslike message. Make the caller give you a return number and full name.

How to Leave Messages That Get Returned

It's important for you or your secretary to leave the right kind of message—the kind that people respond to.

Keep your message short. Don't drag it out. Give the nuts and bolts of why you called, and why it is essential to both your interests for the other person to call back. "I called to give you a brief wrap-up of my meeting with Thayer. I convinced him to renew our contract, but he has put some restrictions on us. Please call me tomorrow, Tuesday morning, for the full report. I leave for Phoenix at noon."

You have given the facts and the reason it is to the other person's advantage to return your call.

Your Own Executive Telephone Manners

It's not enough to instruct the staff members who answer your telephone to do it with grace and efficiency. *You yourself should have impeccable telephone manners.*

- *Watch your speech volume.* Don't get too close to the mouthpiece and sound loud; you don't want people backing away from the receiver. Don't speak too softly, either; you don't want people straining in order to hear you.
- *Speed in returning your own calls is absolutely paramount.* Every call should be returned within the same day, but certainly within two days' time. If you are out of town and can't return a call, or if you don't wish to return a call, ask whoever handles your telephone when you are away to explain your time problems:

    "Mr. Lewis won't be back in town until the nineteenth. Is there anything I can do for you?"

    or

    "Mr. Lewis is out of town, but calls concerning his projects are being taken by Mr. Scott Taylor. Please hold and I'll see if he is in his office and can talk to you now."

- *If you have placed a call and you're disconnected*, you should place the call again, regardless of whose fault it was that the call was disconnected.
- *If you make a call and obviously have the wrong number, don't just hang up*, making a most unpleasant, jarring sound in the ear of the person you have just inconvenienced. Make a quick, sincere apology: "I'm *very* sorry. I called the wrong number. Excuse me, please." Then hang up. The other person won't hate the world for the rest of the day if you have apologized.
- *Call a busy person at a time that would be convenient for him, not you.* If you reach someone directly on the telephone in his office, always ask, "Is this a good time to talk to you?" If it isn't, you can reschedule a new time. He may be on a deadline or have people in his office or be engaged in any number of activities that take priority over your call. Without a secretary, he may be there when you

call, but he may be under pressure with other commitments. This is why it's so important for you to ask, "Is this a good time to talk?"

- *Make your call short and sweet.* One never knows how busy the other person may be, so take it for granted that he's pressured. Don't waste his time. Keep your conversation friendly, brisk, and conclusive. Finish what you set out to do in as short a time as possible, and sign off. If you handle your telephone in this manner, other people will always be glad to receive your calls in the office.

- *Be careful of background noises when you are on the telephone*, i.e., a TV blaring, people talking near you, or the sound of your jaw crunching as you eat your sandwich. Eating and drinking noises made into the speaker of the telephone are magnified and are very off-putting to the person on the other end of the line. (I have a friend who is ready with a question every time someone chews in his ear on the telephone: "Umm, sounds good. Nachos or Triscuits?")

- *Concentrate on what the other person is saying; in other words, listen.* You can dispatch the other person much more quickly if you do. If you half-listen to the other person while you read the *Wall Street Journal*, work on the *New York Times* crossword puzzle, or read a report on your desk, you will miss important aspects of the call. The other person cannot help but notice your flagging interest, and the call will begin to drag and take much longer than it should. Move your voice along briskly at a nice rhythmic pace, and the business at hand will be finished more quickly and more satisfactorily.

- *Don't interrupt the conversation* by suddenly turning to carry on a conversation with someone else in your office. Hearing you give instructions to your secretary or to a staff person when you're supposed to be giving your call your undivided attention is very unnerving to the person you're talking to.

- Likewise, *when people have an appointment with you in your office, it is very rude and inefficient to keep taking other people's calls* from the outside.

- *If you make a call to someone in a distant city and you have a favor to ask—or if you're trying to sell him on an idea—make sure that if he has to return your call, the call will be at your cost, not his.* In other words, if you are in New York and call someone who is not in his office in San Francisco, don't ask for that person to return your call; that's an expense *you* should be bearing. Ask when he will be available and call him back then. Or leave a message strongly requesting that he call you back *collect*, if you're in the AT&T system. (No one should feel cheap calling someone back collect when the original caller has requested you to do so.) A small business owner cannot afford to spend money on the long-distance calls of people who are soliciting something.

- *Be polite to cold-callers.* Telemarketing is such big business, there is little possibility you can escape the unknown voice that calls you at home or at the office, trying to sell you everything from insurance to a timeshare in a Florida condo. The people who call may upset you, but they are bashed and berated unnecessarily by the public for making those calls. Often they are young people, starting their careers, and barking at them is just plain mean. When someone cold-calls me trying to sell me something I do not want, I take over the conversation:

"Look, I don't need any brokerage services or stock advice. I am well taken care of in this department, but I appreciate your calling. You have such a nice voice, you have handled yourself very well with me, and you're obviously bright. I can't help but wish you luck. Hope you make a lot of sales!" Then I hang up. I have cut the caller off, but he or she will hopefully be smiling at the cut-off because of my praise, instead of feeling like locking himself in a closed garage with the car motor running!

How to End Your Telephone Conversations

Leave the other person feeling good. Forget clichés like "Have a nice day." Use your imagination. For instance:

- "Nice talking to you—and continue to keep the Braves in the winning column, will you?"
- If your business colleague has a son he keeps talking about who is a good athlete, say something like: "Well, I hope the next time we speak, your son will have won a place on the Olympic team."
- If it's time for you to invite the other person to lunch: "I'll call you next week to set a date for lunch, Julie. I heard about a great Thai restaurant close to your office."
- If it's someone you have recently met but would like to know better: "I enjoyed hearing your reactions to that, Terry. You obviously know a lot about the subject. Thanks for passing it on, and I'll call you for lunch soon."
- If your caller has been sick, say something like: "Well, feel better. You sound fine, and I hope the old pep returns right away."
- If your caller sounds low in spirit: "Nice talking to you, Nick. Remember, to-morrow's another day, the sun will shine, and you'll have good reason to smile."

Ending on an upbeat note is a lot better (for morale *and* business) than ending a call in a dirgelike fashion: "Well, I guess we'd better go. It's late and the weather's really lousy and I've got to get home before it gets even worse."

Other Telephone Techniques Managers Should Know

- *An executive should place his own calls if he is not in senior management.* You make an error of deference when you, a young executive, have your secretary place a call to a senior executive in another office. You have no idea how off-putting it is to someone in business when a young whippersnapper's secretary calls him, gets him on the line, and then makes him wait until she can get her own boss on the line.

- *Overscreening is totally pretentious.* The public is understandably vexed when a secretary asks a caller his height, weight, title, income, social security number, and shoe size (or so it seems!) before she'll let him talk to her boss. (The question I personally hate the most is, "Does he know what this is in reference to?" I find it particularly irritating when it was her boss who called me in the first place and I am merely returning his call.)

  The most important and distinguished CEOs I know do not have intensive call-screening by their secretaries. The secretaries go as far as this:

  "May I have your name and company?"

  "Will you also be good enough to tell me what this is in reference to?"

  The secretary to a less important executive should simply ask the caller's name and company. Her boss should know how to get rid of unimportant calls fast.

  If the boss is particularly busy, he should have his calls held until he has finished with the project at hand:

  "I'm sorry, Mr. Atkinson. Mr. Stanton is working on the annual report and can't take any calls until he is finished, which might not be until tomorrow morning. Could you possibly call him then, or could I transfer you to someone else, if you need to talk to someone at once?"

- *Wrongly transferred calls cause bad will and lost business.* Nothing angers a caller more than to have the person who takes his call send him off into outer space, where he hangs like a helpless satellite. When your staff transfers a call out of your office (and out of your responsibility):

  - She should know who should handle this call. That means she not only understands the company and people's jobs, but that she has been trained as to who does what in the company.
  - She should warn the person to whom she is transferring the call. If he is not there, she should send the call to another person, first explaining the situation and why she is transferring it to the party.
  - When she finally makes the call transfer, the caller should know the name of the person who will now take his call, that person's division, and the telephone extension (in case the caller is cut off during the transfer).

The Right Way for a Secretary to Announce Her Boss' Calls

Since we are in the age of fast communication, secretaries and executives, too, can save the business world a lot of time and fuss if they *communicate completely* when making a call to another company. Since the secretary to the person you are calling may have to ask a lot of questions before she will put you through, why not answer those questions before she asks them? In other words, when you place a call, give the *who, what, why,* and *how* right off the bat:

> SECRETARY: Ms. Atkins' office.
> CALLER: Martin Jeckworth returning Ms. Atkins' call.

When the secretary announces her boss is returning the other person's boss' call, it saves time. No questions need be asked. Or, in the case where the secretary doesn't know the person calling:

> CALLER: This is Marian Watkins, account executive of Schroeder & Wilson Advertising Agency, calling Ms. Atkins about her letter to me of January 7.

In one breath, the caller has told the secretary who she is and why she is calling; the secretary needs no further information from the caller.

When You Participate in a Conference Call

The conference call enables diverse groups of people located in many different places to meet almost as if in one another's presence. It has helped senior management make urgent decisions, gain a consensus of opinion about those decisions, and agree upon a course of action. The senior executive who calls the conference sits close to the microphone at a table in the board or conference room with other staff members. People in other offices around the country (or world) sit close to the microphone on the table in their offices, too. If people have trouble hearing, because of static or another kind of interference, everyone who speaks should say it *loud and clear.*

Some Conference-Call Etiquette Tips

- *Be where you said you'd be five minutes before the conference call is scheduled to begin.* Punctuality is key, because so many people are involved, and the conference call can't start until all the players are in place. The operator usually calls all participants alphabetically and asks them to stay on the line. (With my name beginning with "BA," I am always one of the first to be called and must wait anywhere from fifteen minutes to what seems like an hour until the operator has everyone on line.) Be patient, and prepare yourself to wait out this delay by having some work or required reading on your desk.
- *Remember to identify yourself each time you speak,* for the benefit of the people not in the room. "Rusty Jackson here. I think we should be very cautious at this point . . ."
- *Remember to turn the microphone toward you* when you contribute. Otherwise, your words will be lost.
- *Try to sound upbeat when you speak*—enthusiastic and knowledgeable. Remember, all those people out there are listening to you but can't see you. If

you sound like you're at a funeral, their perception of you will be equally lugubrious.

- *Don't interrupt when someone else is speaking*. Things become a jumble of unintelligible sounds when two people talk against one another.
- *Don't lower your voice to make sarcastic comments* or tell a joke that cannot be heard clearly by the others on the call. It's just plain rude—and bad business procedure.
- *Hold down the noise in the room*. Any undue rattling of paper or chairs scraping on the floor is magnified on a conference call. The sound of a telephone constantly ringing in someone's office—and not being answered—is another unsettling interruption.
- *When the conference is over, thank whoever is running it*. Don't just silently disappear into the night. Offer a quick, friendly signoff: "Good meeting, Greg. Thanks, and have a good weekend, everyone!"

Putting People on Hold

You and your secretary should avoid leaving anyone on hold for longer than fifteen seconds—and even then, you should apologize for having done it at all.

Train your secretary to say, if you are on another call, "I'm sorry, Mr. Smyth is on the other line. May I have him call you back?" Don't have her say automatically, "Mr. Smyth is on the other line. Would you like me to put you on hold?" Most people despise being left on hold. A minute becomes two hours in their minds.

When you are on the telephone, your secretary should be trained not to interrupt with another incoming call. There are, of course, certain incoming calls that might take priority over the one you're on, such as the CEO who wants to speak to you, or a doctor you have been waiting to hear from, or an important overseas station-to-station call or a pressing personal call from a family member. When your secretary has to interrupt your conversation with someone else because of a priority call, remember to get back to that person *immediately* after you finish with the second call.

Call-Waiting

Many people (I am one) have an aversion to call-waiting. It is usually meant for home telephone use, but since a lot of business is conducted on home telephones after hours, call-waiting serves a useful purpose, particularly if teenagers in a household have the lines tied up with their own calls.

However, let it be noted, if someone summons you from the shower to answer his call, and then you hear his call-waiting signal, you will be left hanging in mid-air, perhaps dripping bath water all over the bedroom carpet, while he talks with his other caller. Even if the person who has called you leaves you for a mere ten seconds to answer the other call (and he should *never* leave you for longer than that), you will probably feel put out.

For People Who Work at Home

If you have many business calls to cope with in your home, give your spouse and children their own line. Handle your business line in a brisk, efficient manner, so that you yourself won't need call-waiting. Make it a habit to keep your calls short, so that if someone trying to reach you gets a busy signal, he knows he can call back in five or ten minutes and your line will be free.

Otherwise, put in a second line that is attached to an answering machine. In this way, if you are talking to someone and another call comes in for you, the new call will jump to the line where the answering machine will pick it up. When you have finished with the first caller, you should, of course, immediately return the second person's call.

Answering Machines

Whether you're on the calling or receiving end, the answering machine now has an etiquette of its own.

When Leaving Messages

- Don't leave a message that rambles on beyond the pertinent information.
- *Don't leave a message that does not give enough information.* Your message should include:

    Whom you're calling
    Who you are—first *and* last name, please, and company name and title, if the machine owner does not know you
    The date you're calling and the hour
    The reason for your call (in a short sentence, such as "I'm calling to check on lunch today," or "I'm calling re the Burlow matter")
    Your telephone number (area code, number, and extension). Even if the person you're calling telephones you every week, help him out. Provide your number, so he doesn't have to search for it.

- *Don't assume that the answering machine of the person you are calling is in perfect working order.* Never leave an extremely important message on a person's answering machine without following up with the person's secretary or the person himself, to make sure he received it.
- *Don't leave mysterious, teasing, or ambiguous messages* that you might find amusing but which could be confusing to the person you have called. If someone who didn't understand your message fully can't reach you to clear it up, the result could be harmful to you both, like the time a friend of mine left a message on her partner's machine at home (before she flew off for two weeks to go up the Amazon River), jokingly implying that their PR firm had

just lost its biggest client. She was only teasing. Her partner, unable to reach her, not knowing it was a joke, immediately called on the client in person, emotionally pleading to keep the account. The personal embarrassment she suffered when she found that the account was not even up for review was considerable, all because of an unclear, supposedly witty reference in a message left on an answering machine!

When Receiving Messages

Don't use an answering machine that allows people to leave only very short messages. It's aggravating and expensive to have to make repeated calls to a machine with an overly short message time on the tape.

Some Rules for Recording Your Machine's Answering Message

The voice on your answering machine or voice mail should sound businesslike and warm at the same time. Give a good listen to what you have recorded. In order to record at your best on your answering machine, sit up straight, lift your voice, put enthusiasm into it, and act alive. *Re-record your message if you find anything wrong with the way you come across.* Keep trying until it is perfect. Your message may go something like this:

> "Lina Norstad's office. At the signal please leave your name, number, a message, and the date and time of your call. Someone will contact you as soon as possible."

(You don't have to say you're out; it's obvious you can't come to the telephone.)

Optionally, you can give people more information, which is a friendlier, less formal approach:

> "William Eaton here. I will return to the office at 5 P.M. today, Thursday, in case you wish to call me then. Otherwise, leave a message when you hear the signal."

Try not to make jokes, play weird music, or be flip in your recorded message. The CEO or the Japanese ambassador may be calling. It's better to have your answering machine ready for a person who might be very important to the advancement of your career than to take it for granted that a pal is going to be calling you for nonserious business.

Voice Mail

Voice mail, an extension of the answering machine, is a very efficient means of communication for large corporations, but it can also be heartless, cold, and annoying beyond belief when no human operator is involved. Many people spend what feels like hours trying to reach someone on the telephone whose extension they do not know.

When the caller tries to leave a message, following directions by pressing the multi-options buttons, they wander fruitlessly from one option to another, never connecting with a human being to talk to or leave a message with. They ultimately end up with a cut-off dial tone.

When a company's voice-mail system works in this manner (and the caller will usually let you know in no uncertain terms when it does), the company should call in experts and rework the system to make it more functional and user-friendly for the caller.

Handling Calls of Complaint
(*See also* "Fielding Letters of Complaint," later in this chapter)

In the matter of complaints, the person calling to complain has a responsibility, too. He is supposed to have manners as well as the person who must cope with his complaint. An unreasonable, overly argumentative, rude person who takes out his displeasure on the person handling his call makes a grave mistake. He will be far less successful in getting the error corrected than if he were in control of himself.

- *When a caller's complaint is justified,* soothe him, apologize with sincerity, and tell him you are going to investigate the matter at once. (Examples of justified complaints: when your law firm lets an important filing date for a client pass by without taking action; when your tailor is late with the custom-made tuxedo you were supposed to wear as guest speaker at an industry banquet; when your travel agency mixes up tickets; or when the products ordered by a customer on an emergency basis from your company do not arrive, even after you had sworn the deilvery date would be honored.)
- *Give the caller every courtesy and sign of compassion.* Allow him to "get it all out on the telephone." Take it on the chin, listen sympathetically, and tell him you are writing down all major points he makes. Then promise action.
- *Follow up* on your promise. This might consist of:
  - Informing everyone involved of the slip-up
  - Having another person in the company call to explain and apologize (the same day)
  - Making sure someone has done something to correct the problem
  - Writing the aggrieved party immediately to explain remedial actions taken
- *If there is no merit to the caller's anger,* tell him soothingly and politely that he must put his reason for calling in writing so that his complaint "may be studied by the proper authorities." Often, by the time the person does decide to write, his anger may have cooled. In any case, the person handling the complaint call should write a short memo on the subject and forward it to the person in the company who will receive the complaint letter, if one is ever written. Nothing makes the public angrier than to call a company and be ignored.

- *If the caller is abusive and uses foul language,* write down the words he used and the names he called you, in case you might ever need this information later for legal reasons. Then explain very slowly,

> "Mr. Jones, I cannot continue talking to you if you continue using this abusive language."

If he persists,

> "Mr. Jones, I am telling you one more time, I cannot continue listening when you are so abusive."

If he still persists, then you should say,

> "Mr. Jones, this is the end of our conversation"

and hang up. Make a thorough memo for the record of what transpired and send it to the head of Human Resources or Personnel.

When You Have Bad News to Impart

Don't put off communicating bad news. Do it *now,* no matter how uncomfortable you are as the bearer of bad news. The longer you delay this mission, the harder it will be on the one who has to hear the news. Speak with kindness and sympathy in your voice.

> "Alicia, we had to let Rick go. We terminated his employment this afternoon, and I wanted you to know about it, so that you will be ready to help him when he gets home tonight. I know what a blow this is to Rick, you, and the family . . ."

> "Jeff, I'm really sorry to be making this call. I wanted to be able to call and say you got the job, but Personnel just made the final decision to hire another fellow. All three of you were such top candidates. I'm really sorry you lost out, because you have such great qualities, you're such a nice person," etc.

> "Sue, I'd give anything in the world not to be making this call. Jim had an accident on the job this morning, they've taken him to Columbia Hospital, and I'd like to pick you up in ten minutes to take you over there to be with him. I really can't give you any details about his condition, because they're still examining him. Hold on tight. They're doing everything for him that is humanly possible to do. Are you going to be all right until I get there?"

Dealing with an Answering Service

If you use an answering service in your business, the first thing to remember is that the service is only as good as the instructions you give the service personnel and, second, that the people handling your calls are human beings who deserve to be treated like human beings. Answering services do slip up occasionally, particularly at very busy times when all of the clients are receiving calls at once. This is when callers are put on hold for too long and when messages occasionally are taken inaccurately. Losing your temper at your service personnel will not rectify a mistake already made. Usually the answering service gives you good service, and cares about the success of your business. Treat all of the people who work there with kindness and consideration, and you will see results in the way they treat you, even though they may never lay eyes on you.

The people I know who receive the best service from their answering services are those who know all of the people at the service by name and who acknowledge their importance by sending them boxes of candy or fruit at Christmas time.

ELECTRONIC MANNERS

There is a new code of electronic manners in using telephones, beepers, computers, faxes, and so on. You will be appreciated for your good electronic manners if you remember what follows.

Cellular Phones

No one should intrude on anyone's privacy by talking on a cellular telephone in a restaurant, during a concert, in the middle of a hot love scene at the movies, or during a church service.

When you use a cellular telephone on an airplane, you should not drone on endlessly, interfering with everyone around you. A loud voice dictating a long letter to a secretary inflight on a cellular phone, for example, is like the sound of nails scratching on glass to many of those sitting around the caller. The caller has to keep his voice at a high decibel in order to compensate for the noise of the engines. The result is that many of his fellow passengers would like to open the nearest emergency exit—just for him!

Laptop Computers

When you are working on your laptop computer on a plane, don't use your seat and half the seat of the person next to you for your laptop and all your papers. Also, if you are on a six-hour flight between coasts, tapping the keys continuously through the entire trip can drive your seatmates absolutely mad. I remember one man on a flight from New York to Los Angeles, angry at his traveling companion, an earnest but slow laptop typist. He suddenly burst out in a rage: "Can't you type any faster?" he asked. "You are going so slowly, I'd be glad to type whatever it is for you, so you can turn the damn thing off and I can go to sleep!"

Beepers

Don't turn on your beeper (unless you're a doctor on call) in auditoriums, opera halls, and other places where people are enjoying a performance. Just imagine what the din would be like if you were wearing a new German *piepser* (beeper) wristwatch, with a built-in pager that allows you to receive distinct signals from as many as four callers at once. Hopefully, if you possess such a watch, you will switch it off in public, putting the gadget into silent mode. Your incoming calls can be stored for later retrieval.

Faxes

Be a gentleperson with your fax. Don't fax long, unannounced, and usually unwelcomed material to others. Call the would-be recipient's office first and ask if it's all right to transmit material during a certain period. Always explain clearly what it is you are faxing. Other fax manners:

- If you must send someone a long fax that is liable to tie up his fax line, call ahead to make sure you're doing this at a convenient time for him. He may prefer the document be mailed.
- Whatever you do in your business, never allow your company to gain the reputation of being junk faxers. A junk faxer ties up the recipient's line and fax machine and wastes expensive paper. The sender of these faxes becomes the enemy, not exactly a propitious environment in which to make sales or do business!
- If you want to stop junk faxes coming into your office, write a nice polite letter to each source, making it quite clear that you do not wish to receive any more. After this strong rejection, be sure to end by wishing them well.
- You might also invest in a machine that automatically and selectively blocks transmission from about fifty junk fax offenders.
- A fax may be seen by many people in an office, so don't send anything personal or sensitive via fax.
- Faxes should not be used for all communications. Write your personal notes (such as a letter of thanks, congratulations, or condolence) on good stationery by hand or send printed cards. What potential guest will look forward to a social event when he receives your invitation on a slippery piece of cheap paper expelled from a fax machine?

Speakerphones

Watch your use of the *speakerphone*. It is considered an odious contraption by many people. Some executives I know refuse to talk to someone who has put them on the speakerphone. The echoing in your ear, the strange sound of the voice coming at you, and the unpleasant feeling that four people in that person's office are also listening in on your conversation can make you feel ill at ease, or worse, compromised.

The solution is for the executive not to use his speakerphone unless he is on a conference call with several people participating. If you feel ill at ease with another person's speakerphone, ask him *nicely* to turn it off.

Electronic Ethics

The swift efficiency of the computer world in which we live does not grant us license to substitute rudeness for manners. One person, for example, used electronic messaging to denounce his company with a furious, foul-language message—the result of having discovered that the kickstand of his motor scooter had been damaged in the parking lot. His rude outburst of anger through electronic mail was "like a guy who can't control his temper, starting a fight with all comers in a bar." People have been known to hide behind their personal computers to engage in racial remarks, gay-bashing, character assassination, and subtle or not-so-subtle innuendoes against usually innocent victims.

Before punching those keys and composing our electronic messages we should stop and *think about the repercussions of what we're doing.* E-mail, for example, is open to anyone's perusal, even if the communication is addressed to one person only. Since privacy is very doubtful, we should ask ourselves:

· Have I said what I really *meant* to say? Am I clear? No doubt as to the meaning?
· Have I used distasteful language: either incorrect grammar or misspelled or profane words, which will make anyone on the receiving end perceive me in a negative way?
· Have I harmed someone in my message, either by joking about an accusation or insinuating something that isn't true? Have I started a false rumor with my attempt at humor?
· Have I done a good turn for someone in my electronic messaging, such as tucking in a compliment for someone's good work? A pat on the back to a peer or an employee? Just as electronic mail has the potential for harm, it also has the potential for great good. The brain behind the fingers at work on the keyboard can be programmed positively just as easily as negatively.

Making Electronic Mail More Human

Much as electronic mail, or E-mail, as it's commonly called, is becoming more common in the workplace, being with other *people* is still important to most of us. If you are regularly in computer touch with a person or with a group, make a point of calling each of them on the telephone. Listen carefully and make note of the sound of their voices, so that when you are talking back and forth on your screens, you can remember their voice tones and "hear" them. If you have the video-telephone system whereby you and the person with whom your computer is hooked up can talk to each other while looking at one another on a screen, the problem is solved. You know what your computer communicator looks like. But if you don't have that technology, in your own words jokingly inform your E-mail correspondent, "We have never met and we probably never will, but I have decided to become more human this year. Since we talk all the time, I wanted to call up to say "Hello," so we can hear the sound of one another's voices." (You naturally would not do this with a person who is not a regular on your monitor, nor would you try such a folksy approach with someone far senior to yourself.) It's flattering to be called by someone who likes the way you "sound" on your computer and wants to know more about you.

Considerate Round-the-Clock Electronic Communications

Yes, we can communicate twenty-four hours a day with business associates, friends, even strangers. However, what is easy and convenient for one person might be very inconvenient and annoying for another. Here are some "consideration principles" to consider:

- *It's a given that you call someone at home only if absolutely necessary and at a decent hour.* If you are calling Europe, Japan, even another time zone within the United States, keep the time difference in mind. It may be six o'clock in the evening your time, but when it's midnight the other person's time, it is a real imposition for him to receive your call then.
- *Don't send your fax messages at an hour that will interrupt the peace of the recipient at home.* If you send unwanted, unsolicited, or unexpected fax material to another person's home fax, you are tying up his machine and using up his expensive fax paper. *You will make a business enemy out of him, rather than a friend.* He might have his fax located near or in the bedroom, and there is nothing less welcome to a person attempting to sleep than the sound of the fax machine humming away in the stillness of the night! (One young executive complained that he had to keep his home fax operating all night for emergency reasons, but that it greatly interfered with his love life with his wife.)
- *Don't call someone in his car unless it is really important.* Keep your conversations brief when you do. People cannot drive with full attention when they are on the telephone at the same time. (Driving time is also thinking time, listening time, and can even be learning time, when an educational cassette is being played.) If your business call can wait until the other person has reached his office, it is preferable to call at that time.
- *Don't beep someone at home unless it is urgent business.* A person's at-home and family time are precious and not to be interrupted for business except in cases of the utmost urgency.

Antidotes to an Overdose of Technology

A clarion call is sounding for management in the workplace. The message is urgent: "Stop the erosion of kindness and caring in the workplace, and the substitution of technology for the human process."

Managers should consciously think along these lines:

- *Soften the hard edges of the environment* for employees. For example, paint the cafeteria in bright colors; soften the overhead lighting in the work areas; install acoustical paneling to deaden the noise; when new chairs are purchased, make them more comfortable.
- *Teach employees how to relax when they're not working.* Get an exercise instructor to show employees how to do breathing and stretching exercises; have someone from the public library give a lecture on the joys of reading great books; have someone lecture on the opening of a new music series in your area; ask a cooking instructor to come to the cafeteria to hold a demonstration one month, a garden instructor, a home repair expert, or decorator to come the next.
- *Toss out some fresh, new ideas on how the staff socialize with one another outside the office.* Find new team sports activities after work in which spouses and friends can also join; nurture special after-work activities such as a film society, a gourmet club, a fitness group, and other family activities. You can even start "The Learn Chess Well Enough to Compete in a Tournament Society" and the "Learn All the New Dances in Spite of Your Spouse's Lack of Enthusiasm Society."
- *Encourage employees to improve themselves* (with academic courses, diet clinics, etc.). People often don't know where to go to find reputable resources like these; if they knew, they would spend more of their own money on the programs. When a company makes available brochures of the services of well-recommended, local, reputable "improve-yourself" organizations, it can be invaluable.
- *Make it easy for employees to join in volunteer activities* by posting all the opportunities available locally, including information on where to follow up or sign on.
- *Provide courses on how to be good conversationalists*, to make your staff the kind of people others want to have around them. We need more "hanging out" with one another—just talking, whether it's on company-owned park benches during lunch hour or in seminars and forums held by the company after work.

WRITING THE PERFECT BUSINESS LETTER

Business correspondence may touch on very personal matters, not just on making money. A considerate executive uses the mail to express friendship for his or her colleagues and associates in a human way. A letter is an important reaction to someone's good—or bad—news. A letter may be a means of refurbishing an old relationship that has grown musty. A letter of friendship pleases the recipient and may incidentally result in unexpected business, just because the writer has pleasantly brought himself once again to the recipient's mind.

Letters of friendship in the business world are exchanged between old friends, newer friends, and even people who meet only briefly for the first time. A letter takes only a few minutes to write and dispatch; its influence may be lasting.

This section of the book will take you step-by-step through the process of creating and handling any kind of letter that a manager may have to initiate, from the primarily corporate to the more personal.

Formal Business Letters

Every time you add a personal sentence or two to a formal business letter, you turn that letter into a personal-business letter. Every time you write a business letter that also touches on a personal subject, such as asking a personal favor of an executive, you are writing a personal-business letter. The volume of this kind of mail in the business world is massive.

Many times it's much easier to write what you feel or what you have to say than it is to tell it to a person face to face. In a world peppered with computer jargon and littered with business forms and form letters, a well-composed letter is like a ray of sunshine arriving on someone's desk. The person who sent it feels good about it; the person who receives it feels even more so. The writing of certain personal-business letters should be an automatic reflex for an executive. He should not need to be reminded to write these letters.

This section deals with the personal side of business letter writing. Not only is there structure, form, and etiquette inherent in this activity, but a good writer of personal letters uses the heart as well as the pen or computer to communicate the message. The information that follows covers the kind of letters that simultaneously please other people, perform an efficient function, and indirectly affect the image of the letter writer in his business milieu. It doesn't matter if he's running a farm, a factory, or a bank.

The range of this kind of business letter comprises everything from wishing someone well in his new business venture to explaining to the head of an advertising or PR agency why he didn't get the account and from writing a condolence letter to the office receptionist whose husband has just died to introducing a fellow executive to business friends in Rio de Janeiro.

The ability of a good letter to influence is considerable. I have seen many examples of this. A CEO passed around his organization a thank-you letter written by a young woman executive in his company who had attended a boiler-plate industry banquet as a guest at the company's table for twelve. No one else at the table had thought to thank the host afterward in writing. He circulated her letter as a subtle hint that his executives should send letters like that all the time—to outside clients and customers in particular. Writing a good letter that is personal in nature but that is business-related is not only the right thing to do, it is the *smart* thing to do.

Anyone who feels devoid of inspiration on the subject of letter writing has only to go to the public library and spend a bit of time perusing famous collections of letters to get his or her thoughts pouring. (A tip: Read all of Strunk and White's classic *Elements of Style*—Macmillan, third cloth and paper editions, 1979. It pays to know how to use the English language properly.)

The right kind of business letter is far more effective than a telephone call. A letter is on the record; its message is one that can be read to a large group, or individually copied to the group. A telephone call is heard by only one person and cannot be passed around for others to enjoy. One famous CEO is so astounded whenever he receives a nice thank-you note from a business associate or one of his customers that he often has it copied (without the writer's identity disclosed) and circulated throughout the entire staff of managers. He clips to each copy one of his small memo sheets, upon which he writes something like, "Are *we* impressing the world outside with nice thank-you notes the way I am impressed by this person's letter?"

A Letter Versus a Fax

A letter coming through the mail, delivered by hand or sent by a courier service, is more impressive than a faxed message.

IF YOU FAX YOUR MESSAGE:	IF YOU SEND A LETTER INSTEAD:
It is spectacularly swift, but often hurried in its composition.	There is often better preparation involved.
It is often unedited.	It is usually edited with care.
It is often printed on shiny, curling paper, unpleasant to the touch.	It is often typed or written on good quality stock, attractive from a tactile point of view.
It has no texture.	Not only does the stationery have texture, but if it is engraved, embossed, or thermograved, it is particularly pleasing to the eye and the touch.
It often has a messy looking transmittal sheet with numbers and abbreviations.	It usually has a handsome envelope, properly addressed.
It may be seen by everyone in office. Confidentiality is difficult to assure.	If in a sealed envelope, it is seen only by the recipient.

Some Points of Etiquette

- *The office letterhead is meant for business, not personal matters.* Members of senior management can, of course, selectively use their company letterhead for fund-raising for favorite causes, but it should be done with discretion in consultation with the top members of management or staff.

Others should be careful not to use company stationery for:

- Political or charitable fund-raising, particularly when it looks as though the company is officially behind this project
- Controversial letters of opinion to the media
- Personal money-making activities
- Matters concerning a lawsuit in which the company is not involved
- Purely personal matters (a condolence letter or a love letter, for example)

- *If you are involved in a project in which others also play leading roles, you should make copies for them* when you receive or send important communications regarding the project.
- *Don't send a copy of a letter in which you have cut off half the text or used white correcting fluid* to change what was originally there. The recipient immediately become suspicious, usually to an exaggerated degree. If you want merely a portion of a letter to be forwarded to someone, write that person your own letter (or fax) within which you state, "I think you'll be interested in what Andy has to say about the opening of our Budapest office:" You then have that paragraph typed with quote marks around it in your letter.
- *A hand-written letter is very compelling, whether it's on company letterhead or your own personal stationery.* A message of condolence, congratulations, goodbye, good luck, or encouragement is more memorable and much more personal when you write it by hand. But if your handwriting is ugly and difficult to read, have the letter typed.
- *Don't write or type on both sides of your office letterhead.*
- *It is permissible to write on both sides of your personal stationery, provided the paper is not too thin.* With correspondence cards, of course, there is no problem, because the stock is heavy. With transparent paper, however, the writing on one side of the paper will run into the writing on the other side, so that you cannot read it.
- If you are writing a letter by hand, use a black, navy, or dark brown pen. Fancy colored inks (fuchsia, lime green, etc.) look adorable in children's correspondence but very inappropriate in business correspondence.
- *If you don't have blank second sheets to use with your letterhead*, just use another piece of letterhead, and write "-2-" on the top of the second page.
- *If you are writing on a foldover note*, make the top side of the note your first page; if the note will be short, use the third page as the second and final page of your communication. If you have a long letter to write, make the top side your first page. Inside, write from the top down to the bottom of the interior double fold as your page two. Page three would be the back side, as you flip the note up and over from its inside position.

- *If you are writing a personal cover note of transmittal to be enclosed with an attached letter*, report, newspaper clipping, magazine article, script, etc., write the note, put it in its matching sealed envelope with the name of the recipient on the outside, then paper-clip it to the top left corner of any documents it accompanies. Then put the clipped material into a sufficiently large mailing envelope and affix a mailing label and postage to the outside envelope or wrapping.
- *If there's a time problem*, and you don't wish to risk the letter taking a week or longer to arrive at its U.S. destination, send it Priority Mail through the post office, or have it sent by one of the overnight courier companies. Of course, if time is a major factor, you should fax the letter.
- *Be sure that the addressee's name is spelled properly and that his proper title is included*. (Do *not* send anything addressed to John Doe; it should be "Mr. John Doe" or "Dr. Jane Doe" or "The Hon. John Doe" or "Jane Doe, Ph.D." or whatever designation the person is entitled to.) If you're not absolutely sure of the person's title, the spelling of his company or the address, call his office and obtain the correct information. It's well worth a telephone call in order to have your mail go out properly addressed (*see also* "Proper Forms of Address," Chapter 12).
- *Be sure that the letter is neatly typed (or hand-written*, as the case may be). Typos, cross-outs and misspellings are bad form and make the recipient think you just don't care about him. Letters awash in correction fluid are almost as bad.
- *Overfamiliarity in the salutation of a letter can get things off to a bad start*. Young executives in particular should be careful about first-naming people in salutations, especially international business colleagues, who already consider Americans excessively informal.

Some Guidelines for Salutations

The Circumstances	The Proper Salutation	Comment
You meet someone who is more or less a peer, and by the end of the meeting you are calling each other by your given names.	"Dear Joe"	
You have just met an executive and do not feel quite right about using his first name. Use both names in your salutations—a sign you do not wish to be stiff or overly formal.	"Dear Joe Williams"	Most likely he will respond using your given name—"Dear Alice"—a signal to you to use his given name in future correspondence. However, if he does not address you by your given name in his return letter, continue to call him by his last name.

The Circumstances	*The Proper Salutation*	*Comment*
You are a young executive who meets an older, senior one. Do not use "Dear Joe" as your salutation. That is too aggressive and overly informal.	"Dear Mr. Williams"	Even though he may respond with a "Dear Alice" you should continue to write him as "Dear Mr. Williams" until he requests that you use his given name.

Complimentary Closings

The only closing you need for a business letter is "Sincerely" or "Sincerely yours." "Very truly yours" sounds archaic to some. Some people are known for their signature sign-off phrases, sometimes foreign phrases: "Aff" for "Affectionately," "Saluti," "All the best," "A bientôt," "Ciao." But these are more suitable for your personal correspondence rather than for business.

If you are writing to the President or a high church official, you may appropriately use "Respectfully yours."

Signature Block

The typed signature block became customary in business correspondence because of the frequency of illegible signatures. (It is really problematical if the addressee of your letter doesn't know who in the company listed on the letterhead has sent him a letter.)

It's gross carelessness not to sign your typed letters, but it is common today. An unsigned letter is meaningless, a negative item. Don't let *any* communication leave your office unsigned.

You don't need to include your title (Mr., Mrs., or Ms.) in your signature block, but if you have a name that could be male or female (Clair, Sandy, Garrett, Casey), be sure to put "Mr." or "Mrs." or "Ms." as a title in front of your name in the signature block. People feel very chagrined if they unwittingly address a woman as "Dear Mr." or a man as "Dear Ms."

The Person Signing the Letter—A Point of Protocol

· If you are a junior executive, you should be careful not to ruffle feelings by sending unauthorized letters that have not been reviewed by a senior official in your company, particularly if a mid-manager or supervisor might get the impression you are cutting him or her out of the chain of command. If you feel there is some sensitivity on this subject, you should either show important memos and letters to your supervisor or, if your communication is a standard report and there are no senior managers' ego problems involved, you might only have to copy your supervisor. (A great way for a young executive to kill his career is to regularly send memos containing ideas or observations to senior management without his or her supervisors or mid-management being aware of it.)

- *As a point of protocol your important reports, letters, memos, and faxes to senior officials outside the company might preferably be signed by a senior official.* A junior person shouldn't just forward these communications. Your memo may be much more impressive if a vice-president signs it, rather than you. Ask the person to whom you report what is the proper thing to do. After all, people who are senior to you just may have sensitive information on the subject you're discussing with the outside person. A good team member has no pride of authorship in writing an important document. A communication with the outside should represent the best effort of the group.
- *Junior executives writing to their peers outside the company should, of course, sign their own communications.*

All the rules of etiquette concerning letters are based on plain common sense—and on the fact that letters have the power to carry along with them a good, strong impression of you and whoever you represent when they arrive at their destinations.

Informal Business Letters

Many letters exchanged by business executives today could as well be called letters of friendship, because they are really reactions to something of a nonbusiness nature. Their mission is to please in some manner.

- *A good informal business letter should be brief.* The shortest I ever received came from a supervisor who was trying to teach me to shorten my presentations. When I finally accomplished this feat, he sent a letter to my home address that was exceedingly brief, but I cherished every little word. The message was, "Dear Tish, That's it!"
- *A good informal business letter is thoughtful, honest, simple, and prompt.* Sometimes timing is more important than content.
- It is usually appropriate to *drop something informal and personal into your business letter right after the salutation*:

. . . It was very pleasant running into you at the game yesterday. You looked in great form, and it reminded me that I had never sent you the article I promised . . .

Or, in the last paragraph of the letter:

. . . I wish you, Serena, and the children a very happy Easter. After this winter we've had, I certainly hope you'll be in some warm and sunny place.

Or you may hand-write a personal note at the bottom of your letter.

- If you have something serious to impart, either enclose it on a separate piece of paper or send a separate letter containing just the business news. Your business letter can then be circulated throughout the recipient's office without any of your personal comments included in it.
- *A trace of humor and a trace of praise* of the recipient of the letter are two constant success factors in letter writing.

  . . . Next to the remaining Rockefeller brothers, you must be the most secure executive in the United States by now. Your success has been phenomenal!

- *Refrain from using foul language in a letter*, even if you think it will emphasize your main point. An unattractive word or expression always stands out in exaggerated form in print. It degrades the text.
- *Make sure that the first paragraph of the business part of the letter clearly reveals the purpose of the letter*. Don't make the recipient of the letter go on a scavenger hunt, trying to find the real point of your writing.
- *Before you write the letter, make a list of all the points that should be covered* in the letter, and let the list be a guide in the construction of your paragraphs, point by point. Here's a sample list:

  ○ Compliment your correspondent about his recent golf game.
  ○ Explain your new line of products and why they would be good for him.
  ○ Mention their exclusivity.
  ○ Explain when he could get delivery and how.
  ○ Refer to price.
  ○ Give him news of your classmates.
  ○ Sign off.

- *Don't exaggerate in order to persuade*. It lessens your credibility. It's all right to exaggerate your good wishes—"Here go a million good wishes for your new enterprise"—but it is not all right to say, "Everyone of your competitors has taken our new product line" if that isn't so.
- *Write simply*. Malcolm Forbes' advice was to "search out and annihilate all unnecessary words and sentences—even entire paragraphs." My brother, Mac Baldrige, created a furor when he had all of the Commerce Department's word processors programmed to reject trite, sometimes grammatically incorrect business jargon (e.g., *to prioritize, bottom line, impact* used as a verb, etc.) This was one of his first steps as Secretary of Commerce in the Reagan administration.
- *Write interestingly*. Read the advice of wordsmiths like *New York Times* columnist William Safire, so that you learn to use figures of speech correctly to add variety to your writing.
- *Carefully edit any important letter*. Rewrite it, if necessary, in order to make sure it is clear, that it fulfills its purpose, and that it contains no "distracting garbage." This applies to informal business letters as much as to formal ones.

The following are the kinds of letters that people in business should know how to write. Of course, everyone has his or her own style of writing. I am not trying to put my words into your mouth, but showing how I would write the letters. Note the form and tone; use your own words, keeping in mind what is and is not appropriate.

Letters to Congratulate or Mark Special Occasions

Be sure that you don't ruin a happy letter with bad news. When you are relaying good news or congratulations to someone, don't throw in negatives that could effectively destroy the cheer you meant to communicate. Avoid adding lines like "Did you know Spud is desperately ill and isn't going to make it?" or, "I think it's a shame Bill and Aggie are splitting on the eve of their fifteenth anniversary. They say that the kids are very upset."

Good News in a Colleague's Family

. . . You must be some proud father! The first thing that hit my eye in this morning's paper was the announcement that Rufus, Jr., has won the Stanford Alumni Club scholarship.

Your whole family must be celebrating. Even our family has declared a national holiday in honor of Rufus. Of course, he has done a lot on his own, but I think you will agree with me that his parents must take no little credit for his accomplishments. . . .

Congratulating Someone You Know Well

. . . Great news! You are climbing the ladder of success so fast that I'm dizzy looking up and trying to keep you in view. We're all celebrating for you.

Congratulating Someone You Don't Know Very Well

. . . Your new position is certainly a recognition of your contributions to this company during the past few years. No one is more deserving of the promotion and the added responsibilities it brings. We all wish you great luck.

Complimenting Someone on a Speech

. . . I was in the back of the ballroom today, so you probably didn't see me. Not only did you deliver your speech with a lot of punch, but what you had to say was important. I had no idea our Foreign Service career diplomats were in such need of support from us.

Congratulations on a first-rate job. I am ready to fire off cables to Congress!

Congratulating Someone on a Personal Triumph

. . . You won! All your old friends in this office really rejoiced when the final election results were announced and our favorite dark-horse colleague had won.

I wish I could have videotaped the reaction here at corporate headquarters. We'll miss you like crazy, but our loss is Washington's gain. Here's wishing you every success in your new life—but some fun in it, too. . . .

> If you don't have time for a letter, two lines are sufficient:

> Charlie,

> I was there.
> You wowed 'em. You're terrific!

Congratulating an Employee on an Important Anniversary of Service

. . . This may be a proud day for you, but it is one for us, too, in this company. You have worked twenty-five years with *Monarch*, and during all of them you have given of your talent and worked hard. People with your enthusiasm and dedication are what has made the company the success it is today. You are as important as the management that runs this company and the products we sell.

Congratulations. I am proud to have you on the team, and here's wishing you another happy, healthy, productive twenty-five years with us.

Acknowledging a Compliment
(*See also* "Compliments—The Best Way to Accept
and Give Them," Chapter 1)

If someone writes you or the company to say something nice about you, the company, its products, or its services, an answering note signed by you or by someone in senior management should be mailed within two weeks of receipt of the letter.

Make sure that the writer of the original letter knows that everyone mentioned in a complimentary way within the letter will have seen that part: "I have shown Ms. Hawkins your letter so that she could read the delightful comments you made about her. She is very pleased," or, "I have circulated your letter through the entire corporate communications division, and everyone is grateful for your kind words of praise."

You can always sign off your acknowledging letter with a phrase such as this: "It is certainly nice to come across something as pleasant as your letter in my large pile of austere business mail. It makes my job a lot easier."

Letters Pertaining to Favors

It is easier both to ask and decline a favor in writing, rather than face-to-face. When you put someone on the spot in person it can negatively affect your case.

Asking for a Favor

Opening paragraph: a personal message

. . . It was a great pleasure seeing you and Marge at the reunion. We're not growing older, just wiser, mellower, and much more exercised both in body and mind than we ever were at college.

Favor asked is stated clearly up front, as well as an acknowledgment that it might not be possible to grant the favor.

I have a big favor to ask, which may be out of the realm of possibility. (Text should follow, stating succinctly all the necessary information, including timetable, etc.)

Innocuous personal closing

Again, I understand perfectly if this is not an appropriate gesture I'm asking you to make. In any case, it was good to see you, I hope our paths will cross again before too long, and Jennie joins me in wishing you both the very best in the New Year. . . .

Declining a Favor

Inability to perform favor is mentioned up front.

. . . It's tough not to be able to grant a favor, but not to be able to help a really good friend is doubly difficult.

Short, clear explanation is given of why it did not work.

I immediately called Pete on receipt of your letter of January 3rd to see if I could get the deal back on the track again. (Etc.)

Exchange of wives' greetings. Letter ends with hope for another reunion and a promise to be of assistance in the future.

Marge sends you and Jen her love. We'll have to get together very soon and not wait for another class reunion. And I hope the next time you write, John, I'll be able to act with the speed of Superman. I had to let you down this time, but I hope that I can make it up to you in the future.

Thanking for a Favor, However Small

When someone does you a favor, it's wise to go on record immediately with your thanks, before you forget about it. If you become known as someone who jots a line to say thanks, you will also become known as someone who is thoughtful and well-mannered. People will be more inclined to extend you extra consideration, seeing that you value their willingness to be helpful and are ready to reciprocate.

The note takes very little effort—perhaps five minutes of your time from the moment you set pen to paper to the moment you throw it in the out-box. Only a few words are required.

. . . Your lending me your car this morning in the company garage when I couldn't start mine was a *lifesaver*. I made it to Aetna's headquarters on time for the meeting, and it was important that I be there on time.

I really owe you one. Thanks!

Thanking for a Meal

If someone buys you lunch, a short note of thanks is in order, whether you had lobster in an expensive seafood place or a fruit salad in a tearoom. Even if the person who took you to lunch was trying to negotiate a business deal with you or was paying you back for a favor rendered, you still have an obligation, manners-wise, to write a thank-you note.

The old tradition decreeing that it's the wife's sole responsibility to handle all thank-you notes no longer holds true in this era of supposed equality. For meals in which spouses are not present, the executive obviously thanks his host himself. For meals in which the couple is present and both people work, either spouse should write the thank-you note. It does not matter if the executive or his wife (or the executive or her husband) writes the host or hostess to say "Thank you" on behalf of the couple. What *does* matter is that the letter be written and sent within three or four days of the meal.

A Good Friend Takes You to an Informal Lunch

. . . Many thanks for the nice lunch yesterday. It was great catching up with you, and your new position sounds perfect. Congratulations on landing it!

I know it won't be so long before we lunch again. I'll call you in a few weeks to set a time and place. . . .

Someone Who's in Your Business Debt Takes You to Lunch

. . . Lunch was very pleasant yesterday. I'm glad you got our account, because the presentation you and your team made was better than anyone else's. I know we can expect great things from you.

A Colleague Invites You Home for Dinner

This requires a much more careful note.

. . . Amy and I enjoyed ourselves thoroughly last evening. What a superb dinner you gave us! Amy said she has never seen such pretty lilacs. I concentrated more on the lemon souffle for dessert. We particularly enjoyed meeting those attractive children of yours.

One of the nice results of having been transferred here are the new friends we have made and the warm welcome we have experienced. We both want to thank you very much for last night. . . .

Thanking Management for Gifts

Corporate America seems to think it is entitled to free gifts of products, tickets to evening charity events, tickets to the company box at the opera or the baseball game. Many executives consider these as regular perks to which they have every right. As a result, when a thank-you letter is written to senior managers, they usually pass it around, partly in pleasure, partly in shock at having received it! Here are some sample letters management would enjoy receiving:

For a Gift Marking a Major Occasion

	When the Executive Writes	When the Executive's Spouse Writes
Mention what the gift is, how pleased you are, and how you are going to use it.	. . . Rowena and I are delighted with the handsome leather frame you and Mrs. Winfield sent us for our wedding. It is ideal for our big colored wedding picture. The fact that our joint initials and the wedding date are embossed on the frame makes it all the more special.	. . . Malcolm and I consider your wedding present one of the greatest we have received. The frame with its gold tooling is the perfect size for our formal wedding portrait, and it looks very impressive on the hall table. In fact, when you open the door to our apartment, it's the first thing you see.
Explain why it is so useful.	You could not have chosen anything that was more needed, since we do not possess one frame! And even if we had looked hard, we never could have found one as handsome as the one you had made for us. I hope we can get our apartment in shape so that one day you will come visit and see how we are using your wedding present.	I hope it won't be too long before we can have guests. I have a job to do first in bringing order out of chaos, but I did want you to know how much your beautiful wedding present means to us. I look forward to meeting you both.
Express the hope that the giver will come to call one day to be able to see how well it looks.		

For the Annual Christmas Gift

. . . Our whole family greatly enjoyed the plump, juicy turkey at our traditional Christmas lunch. The company gift has become a much-loved tradition in our family, so I thank you and the officers of the company on behalf of my family for a most welcome holiday gesture. . . .

For Free Tickets to the Game

. . . You are most definitely the hero of the entire family, particularly since the Cubs' victory yesterday was such a spectacular one. Our seats were excellent; for the first time the kids were able to identify the players by their forms and faces, not just by their numbers. It was a day of great excitement.

Helen, Toby, and Warren join me in thanking you for a very special gift. . . .

For Tickets to the Benefit

. . . Your benefit tickets were well used by us last night. Roland James, our dates, and I represented the company last night at the Premio D'Oro dinner at the Remington.

The operatic solos were absolutely magnificent. The dinner was excellent (and so were the wines), and we got to meet the Mayor and his wife. We also did a lot of dancing.

Thank you for giving us the company tickets. We had a great time—and the cause was certainly a worthy one, too.

For a Corporate Giveaway, However Small

. . . The new *Treatco* calendar has just arrived, once again in time to mark all of my business appointments, and my New Year's resolutions, too.

Thank you. I look forward to this nifty calendar each year. Always keep me on your mailing list, and have a wonderful New Year yourself!

For a Gift of a New Product

. . . The new water gadget is first-rate. We immediately hooked it up to our faucet and it works! It was easy to install, it is easy to use, and it does a very effective job. I'm sure your company has a winner with this one. Thanks so much for remembering us this Christmas, and for letting us be one of the lucky ones to try out the new product.

Have a wonderful holiday, and good luck with the launch!

Thanking a Colleague for a Personal Gift

If a colleague gives you a gift—for a reason or just for friendship's sake—you should not just thank him on the spot or on the telephone. Write him a note. Tell him how or when you are going to use it:

> . . . The Swiss chocolate you brought back from Zurich has turned not only me but my entire staff into chocoholics. The box was so enormous I had to share it with them, although I am now rather sorry I did. There are furtive glances and footsteps creeping into my office during the entire day, as they try to snitch some more.
>
> I marvel at how nice you are to have lugged that huge box back on the plane. I guess you knew that, next to winning the state lottery, I love the taste of chocolate best!

For an Inappropriate Gift

There are times in life when we might receive a very inappropriate gift from a business acquaintance—such as something for your garage when you don't have one, or a sprinkler for a lawn you don't have. It's better to thank the person and *not* return the gift. (Give it to a good friend.)

The following is a sample letter from a recovering alcoholic to a person who sent a case of liquor:

> . . . It was a pleasant surprise to receive the nice gift from you and the company this holiday season. I appreciate the thought and send you and your family every good wish for the holidays. . . .

The case was delivered next day to the museum's fund-raising auction.

Politely Refusing a Gift

At times you may be in the position of not wishing to accept a gift from another executive. Great tact is called for in returning the gift. That is, after all, a very tough rejection for the sender. Phrase your response in a positive tone.

> . . . You were so kind to think of me this Christmas. Your gift was much too generous, however. There is a strict company policy governing the acceptance of gifts, and everyone of us has to comply. I must therefore return your wonderful present. I know how much thought you put into obtaining it.
>
> Thanks for the thought, and I wish you a healthy, happy, successful New Year.

Writing to a Journalist After an Interview

Following your appearance on a television or radio interview show, either the show's producer or the interviewer deserves a note of thanks for having given you the opportunity to communicate your message. The rare people who do write to thank the media are always remembered.

Thanking a Broadcast Journalist

. . . You were very kind to invite me to appear on the "Afternoon Show." You and Elena Enriquez make an excellent interview team, and you handled my subject with great intelligence and taste.

I appreciate your letting me give my side of the story. The fact that you are successful was proven by the number of people who told me that they saw the program the day I was your guest, and that they watch it regularly.

I enjoyed being your guest. Thank you.

Thanking a Print Media Journalist

. . . Your story was on target and very well written. I congratulate you for presenting the subject in an accurate, interesting, even humorous manner. The occasional negatives you mentioned were fair. Thank you!

Thanking When You Have Been Treated Unfairly

. . . I appreciate the fact that you took so much time and effort to profile this company in your story. However, in fairness to me, your readers, and the public, I must point out some grossly inaccurate statements that were made: (List them.)

I have the greatest respect for you as a journalist, so I hope that with this revelation of inaccuracies, you will be able to publish some kind of retraction. I thank you for anything you might be able to do. . . .

Letters of Encouragement

A letter written to someone who has just come through a very difficult time always means a great deal to the recipient. A colleague may just have been through a very messy court case, have returned from a tough rehabilitation program, or finished a long hospital stay. A note of encouragement is really appreciated.

If you know the person well, include a warm, personal compliment.

. . . Welcome back to us. You were missed for many reasons. First, because you're such a wonderful person, and second, because you're so good at what you do, no one around here can begin to replace you. We've all been sailing at half mast.

You have no idea how nice it is to have you "home" again.

An Executive Thanking His Staff for a Job Well Done

. . . Your group should feel proud of a job beautifully done and a thoroughly professional performance. The hard work and the polish clearly showed.

I hope you will express my personal thanks to everyone who pitched in to make our presentation a success; save a big vote of thanks for yourself, will you?

Letter to Consolidate a Contact

You meet someone interesting who will be coming to your city on a business trip. You feel you would like to maintain the contact and develop a friendly, closer relationship.

. . . Just a quick line to say how much I enjoyed meeting you at the conference and exchanging experiences in this crazy business of ours. Let me know well in advance of your next trip to St. Louis. My wife and I will take you to dinner and show you this town's culinary distinctions.

> All the best to you,

Retirement Letters
(*See also* "When an Executive Retires," Chapter 17)

The occasion of retirement calls for an intricate exchange of letters, many of which are put in the retiree's scrapbook and handed down to posterity:

- Letter from the retiree to his or her superior, expressing his love for the company and his sadness at leaving
- Letter from the retiree's supervisor to the retiree, expressing everyone's sadness to see such a valued team member depart
- Letter from the retiree to his successor, wishing happiness and success in the job
- Letters from the retiree's personal friends, wishing him well
- Letters from the retiree to everyone who wrote him or sent him a gift

Here are some examples:

From a Retiring Employee to the CEO

. . . AXCO's observance of my retirement was one of the nicest things that ever happened to me. The reception in the Executive Dining Room came as a total surprise. I still can't believe so many people turned out to honor me.

The handsome leather scrapbook will be the perfect sentimental reminder of all my years of service. It will take me a long time to place all of my pictures, clippings, and mementos in the book. I look forward to the task.

This letter is a very small expression of my gratitude to everyone responsible for making my retirement such a special occasion. My memories of this company and of everyone connected with it will be cherished for as long as I live. . . .

From a Retiring Senior Manager to the CEO

. . . It's hard for me to realize, much less accept the truth: that the time has come to go. I keep telling myself that retiring from this company is not retiring from life, and yet it is difficult to separate the two in my mind.

I have enjoyed my eighteen years with Aquarius for so many reasons, it would take me a book to list them all. Mainly, I will miss the people around here, all working enthusiastically for a common cause under your leadership. I will miss the feeling of camaraderie, the joy of watching the efficient interaction of our divisions on major projects, and the total satisfaction of a feeling of individual accomplishment.

This company is the best. Its management is the best. Its employees are the best. Its customers are the best. I will miss it every day of my life. . . .

The CEO's Response to the Above Letter

. . . If your retirement is difficult for you to accept, let me assure you that it is *impossible* for me to accept! You were the backbone of your group. I wonder if we'll know how to grow another one. I hope you will think of us, floundering and wondering which way to turn while you're pondering your next shot on the tenth hole.

You deserve to be on that golf course, and Ruth deserves to have you with her after all those years of spending all your time working your way through our problems. Her gain is our loss. I hope you'll always remember that.

Your sad friends bid you farewell.

From a Personal Friend to the Retiree

. . . The time has come to sleep that extra hour in the morning and not worry about whether the ice scraper for the windshield is in the glove compartment—and not panic when Miss Sidwell's word processor goes on the blink. Now you can finally read all those books on growing herbs you've never had time to read. In fact, you can start actually growing those herbs instead of just talking about them!

It's a big change in your life, sure, but it also means your friends like me will have more of a chance to see you, so as far as I'm concerned, it's a change for the better. . . .

If you don't know the person well, however, leave it at a simple statement that reflects a sincere sentiment without hyperbole:

. . . Good luck in your new life. You will be missed by all of us . . .

Letters for Difficult Circumstances

Condolence Letter
(*See also* "When an Executive Dies," Chapter 17)

Never hesitate to write a condolence letter, whether you are a very junior or a very senior member of management and whether the person who has lost someone in death is a very junior staff member or a very senior member of management. The two examples below may seem opposites in a way. One letter is from an executive to a young receptionist whose mother has just died. His letter is circumspect but warm. The other letter is from one executive to another who is a very close friend, on the occasion of the friend's wife's death. The same guidelines apply to both.

	To an employee who has lost a member of her family	*To a colleague who has lost his wife*
Explain how badly you feel about the news.	... Elsa has just told me the terrible news, and I want you and your family to know how sorry I am that you lost your mother.	... I don't know what to say, except that my heart is breaking for you.
Praise the person who has died. If you have some personal anecdote about the deceased, mention it.	I have heard from several sources that she was a wonderful woman and we all knew how close you were. These will probably be among the toughest days of your life.	Ginny was, quite simply, "the best of the best." Wife, mother, real estate agent, volunteer, she did everything with a careful, loving hand. The last time I saw her I marveled at her juggling abilities as she sold a client an apartment and three dozen Girl Scout cookies for little Ginny at the same time!
Make a concrete offer to be of help.	Your friends in this division are all thinking of you and wishing there was something we could do to help in this time of your terrible loss. Please call on us — for anything. . . .	We are all wandering around the office in a state of shock. We are actually suffering for you and waiting for your telephone call to press us into service. We are ready to answer phones, cook your meals, and handle any detail that needs handling for the funeral.

Letter of Sympathy When There Is Bad News

. . . I just heard the awful news that Ginny lost the baby today. What a terrible blow for you two to have such an occasion for joy turn into such an occasion for sorrow. I know it won't change anything, but you ought to know that all of your colleagues here are grieving right along with you.

When Someone Loses a Job

Your letter should take a positive approach. Talk about action in locating the new job. Don't just commiserate.

. . . I just heard the bad news. It may be devastating to you right now, but think about all that talent and experience you have amassed. You'll probably find something you like a great deal more, and in a company where your talents will be fully appreciated.

To me you are a winner. This is a temporary setback only. Why don't you call me to tell me when you and Jean can come for dinner, so we can talk about your future in a leisurely fashion? I've got some ideas, and I'm sure you do, too. . . .

Letter of Apology
(*See also* "Knowing How to Apologize," Chapter 1)

Apologies rarely come easy. It's always uncomfortable facing up to the fact that you've inconvenienced, embarrassed, or offended someone. You'd just as soon forget it. The difficulty is that not acknowledging your failing or error in a given situation is only likely to result in ill feelings hardening against you. Biting the bullet and expressing your sincere regret, on the other hand, will often regain you whatever goodwill you might otherwise have forfeited.

Here's a sample apology for a particularly inappropriate behavior. Note that a lack of intention to give offense is not really an adequate excuse. The apology here is for an unintentional racial slur delivered in front of a person of the race mentioned (*see also* "Apologizing for a Racial Slur," Chapter 5).

. . . This is probably the hardest letter I have ever had to write, because I've never been so wrong or acted in such a shameful way.

My remark this morning was reprehensible, uncalled for, and totally unforgiveable. But I'm asking you to forgive me anyway. I hurt you, but I hope you will show me all of the mercy I seem to lack myself.

I promise never again to think, much less express, a remark like that. I hope you are big enough to forget my lamentable behavior.

Letters Informing Someone Why He Didn't Get the Job or an Agency Why It didn't Get the Account

Serious contenders for an executive position go through a very harrowing experience of interviews, telephone calls, and endless waiting to hear if they will be chosen. So does the team of an advertising or PR agency, an architectural firm, or any kind of service agency going after a contract or an account. Sometimes, even though polite inquiries are made, nothing is heard for months. When leading contenders hear via "the grapevine" that someone else got the job or, even worse, when they read about it in the newspaper, it is a very debilitating kind of rejection. Corporate America is very tough about getting everyone to submit proposals and make their pitches promptly and in great detail. Unfortunately, corporate America is also very careless about thanking people and letting the contenders know when they do *not* have the job or the account.

There is a tremendous selfishness among companies in the way in which they handle people who are competing for their business. It takes very little time to make a telephone call to each "also ran" to inform them of a decision (the very day the decision is made). *It should be followed up with a letter*, with as much face-saving for the recipient and his team as possible, since people often don't retain what is said to them on the telephone in times of emotion.

To Someone Who Didn't Get the Job

Someone else got the job.

Reasons why someone else won out.

...As I told you on the telephone today, the position for which you were being seriously considered was given to another lawyer, a women with over fifteen years experience in our field of entertainment. We decided that this aspect of her background gave her a distinct advantage over the other highly qualified candidates.

Compliment the person's self-presentation.

I am particularly sorry in your case, because your credentials are excellent and you presented yourself in a very fine manner. We were all impressed by you and would like to keep you in mind in case you are interested in future job openings.

Wish the person luck and thank him.

I'm sorry things didn't work out the way we thought they would. I hope your search for a position as legal counsel will be successful right away. My associates and I thank you and wish you all the best for the future.

To an Agency That Didn't Get the Account

Another agency got the job.

Reasons why the other agency won out

...As we discussed on the telephone today, the chairman selected Agency X to handle the account. He had a very difficult decision to make, and in the end selected the other agency because of its strong international experience in the marketing field.

Compliment the agency's presentation.

We all know you would have done a great job, and we appreciate the amount of agency time and creative work that went into your proposal. The content of the presentation was excellent, the creative ideas were impressive, and your efficient approach to company planning was invaluable in giving us new insight.

Thank the agency and wish them good luck.

I have a feeling this is not the last time we will be approaching a project together. Please thank the team who put together your presentation, and I send you my best personal wishes for a successful year ahead.

Letters of Reference and Recommendation

When you are asked to write a letter of recommendation for a business colleague, keep the following in mind:

- *Write the letter immediately after you have agreed to do it,* preferably within twenty-four hours. Otherwise you may forget it, or you may do it in such a big rush your letter will be counterproductive.
- *Include the person's resumé or curriculum vitae* so that you won't have to waste precious letter space going into the details of his or her background.
- *Before composing the letter, write down a list of the person's affirmative points;* be sure to cover them in the letter.
- If you're writing to the board of an apartment house in which your colleague is trying to purchase an apartment, *remember to mention your colleague's "fiscal reliability."*
- If you have had a figurative gun put in your back, and you have to write a recommendation for someone when you do not wish to, *you can write a lukewarm letter* that sends immediate caution signals to the recipient (*see also* "Lukewarm Recommendation for Membership in a Club," later in this chapter).
- When you have sent a reference letter for a friend, *don't send* him a copy of your letter unless it is dripping in hyperbole. Do, however, send him a note saying that you dutifully sent off an enthusiastic reference letter in his behalf, and tell him the date you sent it.
- Remember to include all necessary information in your letters of reference:
  - The person's full name
  - The person's business title and business address
  - The person's home address, if pertinent
  - The names of family members and children's ages, if pertinent
  - The name of the seconder or others providing endorsement letters, if proposing someone for membership
  - Any athletic prowess, if proposing someone for a club with athletic facilities

Introducing Someone Moving to Another City

. . . Joe Doakes and his family are moving to Akron next week, where he will be opening a new office for his company, The Academy Marketing Group, of which he is a founding partner. His office address is 1300 Lake Street, Akron 00000, and his telephone number is 000-0000. Joe tells me they were fortunate enough recently to find "the perfect house," which they have purchased, at 34 Shoreacres Road, 00000.

You will notice in the enclosed biography that Joe has gone very fast in his career for a forty-year-old. His wife, Jeannie, is very bright and attractive, and so are the children, Joe Jr. (16) and Clare (12). They are not only close personal friends but Joe is an important investor in one of my new projects, so I would greatly appreciate anything you might do to smooth the way for them. I have asked Joe to call you some time next week.

We arc all well. My last two will be out of college in a year, thank the Lord. Susy and I send you and Michele a great deal of affection. . . .

Recommendation for Membership in a Club

. . . It is an honor to propose the John Boyton Wright family for membership in the Rolling Hills Club. The following information is submitted for the consideration of the Membership Committee:

John Wright, aged 38, has recently moved to Tennessee with his wife, Gloria, and their three children—Amy (12), Russell (10), and Nils (7). John is vice-president of the Erie Cement Company and has been transferred here to establish a Tennessee headquarters. He and his wife are both graduates of the University of California at Berkeley. The family presently holds memberships to the Erie Country and Downtown Athletic clubs.

John is a first-rate tennis player and was captain of the Berkeley squash team. Gloria is an excellent tennis player herself. She has headed the women's board of the largest hospital in her area for the past five years.

All three children are budding athletes, and the entire family is attractive, bright, and full of charm. The Wrights have also assured me that they would use the club facilities for entertaining—something which John, in his new position, will have to do frequently.

In the attached business biography of John Wright, you will find his addresses and telephone numbers.

Seconding and supporting letters are being written by George Humphries, Janet Wilkerson, Tim Wright, Dick Jones, and Neil Gallo.

I am honored to propose the Wright family for membership in the Rolling Hills Club. . . .

Lukewarm Recommendation for Membership in a Club

. . . In response to a specific request, I am addressing this letter to the Membership Committee of the Hopeful Executives Club on behalf of a colleague, John Doe, who is very anxious to join.

I have known John casually for several years, and have enclosed his biography, which will furnish the important details of his background.

I would be happy to discuss with anyone on the committee his qualifications and his suitability for membership. . . .

Recommendation for Membership in a Professional Organization

To the Chairman of the Membership Committee of Women's Forum:

. . . The purpose of this letter is to propose for membership in the Women's Forum Ms. Jane Marston, vice-president of Cable Network CYC Sports.

I have known Jane for fourteen years and have watched her career flourish as her accomplishments have multiplied. Her attached biography details her numerous awards in the television field, as well as her membership on the boards of several nonprofit institutions. She has made outstanding contributions in the field of drug abuse, and has a reputation for being a person in the communications industry who cares about her community and *does something about it*.

Jane is a wife and mother of two. She has managed to juggle her family and a distinguished career with a sense of expert balance. I know of no one who would make a more suitable member of the Forum, and I hope the Membership Committee will look kindly on this proposal for membership. . . .

Reference for an Executive Who Has Been Let Go

When you must let an executive go for reasons other than incompetency or theft, give him a good letter of reference by a senior member of management. A letter of reference addressed to "To Whom It May Concern" would contain the following:

To Whom It May Concern:

Dates she worked for the company and in what capacity

Ms. Anne Garrison worked for Atkins & Boyd from September 1, 1990, to September 1, 1999, starting as an executive secretary and functioning as an account super-

Give reason for the termination.

visor since 1995. Due to a reorganization of the executive staff and company-wide budget cuts, we are forced to terminate her services.

Explain what she accomplished and what her special skills are.

During her four years here she proved to be a loyal, bright, resourceful member of the executive staff. Her rapid promotion from secretary to account supervisor was well merited. She "learned" the company quickly, was interested in the company's goals, and helped us work toward them. She has strong people skills and is also adept at outlining projects and in writing proposals for new business.

She has a very creative mind and is able to articulate creative ideas in a practical fashion. She is a good writer and a good team member. I recommend her highly as a hard-working, able person.

Offer to talk to any prospective employer.

I would be glad to answer any questions on Ms. Garrison's service with this company.

Letters of Resignation

In most cases of resignation, it's wise for the person resigning to go on record with as affirmative a letter as he or she can muster. Whether you resign by choice or by force, your letter will remain in the files, to be seen in the future by people who may have some influence over your life.

From a Contented Executive

Gives reason for resignation

... It is with great regret that I submit my resignation from Seafarb as of February 9, 1998, after eight very happy and productive years of service. The reason for this decision is a personal one—my wife's deteriorating health. Her doctors advise an immediate move to a warmer, drier climate and her health is a top priority in my life.

Compliments management and employees

I have watched with pride Seafarb's growth from a company with $2 million to one with an excess of $9 million in sales. In these past months I have often reflected on what I am going to miss most in leaving this company, and the answer is always the same: the people. I'm going to miss not only management but also the employees, who have given me friendship and support during these wonderful years.

I wish you and every member of the Seafarb team a briliant, happy future....

From an Unhappy Executive

It's important that an executive's file not reflect an overly bitter and rancorous departure. You don't want a record of hard feelings to haunt you afterward.

An explanation of what the executive is unhappy about is in order. However, that should be given without any derogatory statements about staff or the company.

My resignation from Seafarb is submitted as of August 15, 1998, after six years as assistant vice-president and vice-president of the firm.

Explains why he is resigning

My resignation is submitted in protest over lack of senior management support for the much-needed plan you assigned me to devise for tightening up the management functions of this company. I have attached a copy of my final report to be filed with this letter. The report represents several arduous years of research and planning, so it was particularly difficult to accept the fact that I was not allowed to finish the job I was hired to do—and one that is desperately needed for the good of this company.

Mentions proudly what he accomplished

I am proud of the fact that during my six years I managed to effect a dramatic increase in both gross sales and net profit margins within my division.

Ends with an "up" note, wishing the company well

I have enjoyed knowing the many fine people in this company. Seafarb is a first-rate organization, and I wish it well for the future. . . .

Letters of Acceptance and Regret for an Invitation to Join the Board of a Nonprofit Institution

Letter Accepting

. . . Your invitation to join the Board of Trustees of the Melton Illiteracy Institute is a great honor, one I accept with pleasure.

I have watched the enormous strides the Institute has made in the community and throughout our state in combatting the growing problem of illiteracy. Under the leadership of Dr. Melton, I hope to be able to join you in contributing to the activities of the Institute. I will also search for ways in which my corporation can be of assistance in your work.

I am looking forward to working with you, Dr. Melton, and the staff of the Melton Illiteracy Institute. . . .

Letter Regretting

. . . With great regret I must decline your invitation to join the Board of Trustees of the Melton Illiteracy Institute.

I have long admired the excellent work carried on in combatting illiteracy by the fine people of your Institute. Your program has commanded national attention—and admiration.

The reason I must decline this honor is that I am already overextended with two other board positions. I am also overseeing changes in my company at the present time and must decrease, rather than increase, my outside activities.

I will certainly remain a steadfast supporter of the Institute, and I hope you will call on me for advice and help with contacts at any time.

All good wishes for a very successful year in your wonderful work. . . .

NOTE: If a donation check accompanies a letter of regret, the blow to the institution will be lessened.

Letter Declining to Endorse or Praise Something for Commercial Purposes

You can acknowledge having received something without endorsing it in any way.

. . . Thank you so much for sending me Daisy Mendendorf's new book. It looks very impressive, and I will enjoy perusing it the minute there's time in my hectic schedule for such pleasant relaxation. . . .

———————————————— or ————————————————

. . . How very nice of you to send me a sample of your latest product. I will certainly try it when time permits. Thank you for thinking of me. . . .

Letters of Complaint

Composing a Letter of Complaint

It takes time and reflection to write a really effective letter of complaint. When you first write it, don't mail it, because it probably reveals your anger too. Look at it again objectively the next day, tighten it up (including the grammar), and remove any vestige of emotional tone. Remember that a lot of people might be shown your letter. Remain polite. Action is usually taken faster in response to a letter written with a cool hand than to one written with a sense of hysteria.

Sample Letter of Complaint

Dear Mr. Jones:

The invitations printed by your company have arrived, exactly two weeks behind schedule.

We engaged your company to print a very important invitation for this company's 50th anniversary dinner. You were given a great deal of information on exactly how we wanted these invitations to look. I enclose a memo to me from our Director of Special Events, Mr. Ronald Smith, detailing the many errors in printing, layout, and color separation. The invitations delivered to us are unacceptable and certainly not in keeping with the image of this company.

This leaves us in serious difficulties. Since we cannot mail these invitations and cannot wait for new ones to be made, we will have to send Mailgrams to our guest list—an expensive but unavoidable step.

I would like to suggest that we meet as soon as possible to discuss the mutually agreeable steps we must take to reach an agreement on the settlement of your bill and of the expenses your actions forced us to incur. I know that your company has a long history in this community, as has ours, so I am certain we will be able to settle this matter equitably.

Sincerely,

cc: R. A. Smith   Helene Jenkins, Executive Vice-President

Fielding Letters of Complaint

(See also "Handling Calls of Complaint," earlier in this chapter)

The President of the United States, desiring to know what's on his constituents' minds, as part of his official function periodically checks on the thousands of letters addressed to him weekly at the White House. Heads of corporations should care equally about the nature of the complaint mail arriving in their company's mail room—not just to see what the complaints are but also to check on how they are being answered and what follow-up action is being taken.

When management attends well to complaints abut the company's services or products, it can often save the company millions of dollars. (It is also an executive's responsibility to write a careful letter of complaint when outside services his company uses prove inferior.)

Some companies receive thousands of letters of complaint every year. These are answered by form letters as much as possible but they do not look like form letters.

A computerized word processor that can automatically respond to any letter makes the logistics of answering mail fairly easy. The original of the response letter would be marked with the names and titles of the other executives within the company who should receive a copy of the complaint and the response. The recipient thus knows that many people will now be aware of his problem with the company. It's impressive and very good for the ego of the writer of the complaint letter.

The facet of advanced technology that must never be forgotten is the human side. No system can invent true kindness and thoughtfulness, so word processors can't be good guys automatically. A human being has to program them that way and an added sentence by hand at the conclusion of the letter might make all the difference.

Even if a letter is impolite, the company answer should "keep its cool." The task of responding to critical mail in a small company should be given to someone who is gifted with words—and tact.

In general, a substantive letter of complaint should be answered within two weeks' time. If it is a small matter, the letter may be answered within a month's time. Keep in mind that the longer you wait to answer a letter of complaint, the more furious the writer may become. It is best to defuse a potentially unpleasant situation as soon as possible.

Letter in Response to Receipt of a Complaint

Dear Ms. Jenkins:

Your letter, which just reached me by messenger, deserves an equally rapid reply by messenger.

I agree that the invitations that reached you today were two weeks late, but you failed to mention that your own staff did not return the signed, approved design dummy until eight days after we had submitted it, nor did Mr. Smith, the Director of Special Events, release the printer's proofs until ten days after their delivery, so we are hardly responsible for the delay in delivering the invitations.

The person in my company whom I appointed to direct this rush job for you has answered, point by point, the objections raised in the memo you enclosed from your Mr. Smith, and I think you will find them clearly answered, one by one.

I am leaving the city in one hour on an emergency trip, but upon my return in two days, I will come to your office at a mutually agreeable time to discuss the entire matter.

I am very sorry that you are unable to use the invitations we printed, but I also feel that a fair study of the matter would show us not to be entirely responsible for your displeasure with our services. I look forward to discussing this with you in person.

> Sincerely,
>
> Henry Jones, Vice-President
> Speed Printing Services

Letters of Acknowledgment and Thanks
(*See also* "Knowing How to Say 'Thank You,'" Chapter 1)

A handwritten or typed note of thanks is effective, shows thought, and is permanently on the record. The recipient usually reacts with a feeling that all of the trouble or expense he went to has been worth it.

There are thank-you notes and thank-you notes, of course, as, for example, these two versions of a letter thanking a vendor for a holiday business gift:

Dear Agnes:

The basket of fruit has arrived. We are all enjoying it and want to thank you for your generosity.

or

Dear Agnes:

The Felden Advertising Agency fruit basket just arrived, was placed in our reception area, has already had its beautiful wrapping removed, and is being attacked as of this minute by the many eager pairs of hands in this office. I'm sure the infusion of Vitamin C is going to make us all healthier, if not wealthier, and certainly more energetic. My staff and I are grateful to you.

You have brought us all the Christmas spirit. Many thanks!

Helpful Hints on Thank-You Notes

- It's never too late. Don't think, that as the weeks go by, you are off the hook because time has passed. Write that thank-you note for a gift or a favor even if months—years—have gone by. Just be a lot more apologetic about the delay.
- Don't ruin a thank-you note by sneaking in a request for a favor. Don't thank someone for his dinner in a great restaurant by adding a postscript: "By the way, if you can get me those Detroit Pistons tickets, I'd really appreciate it."
- Say "thank you" only once. You don't want to fill space in your letters with thanks said over and over, which then becomes trite and phony.
- A form thank-you letter that doesn't even mention what the gift was is, in my opinion, a lot worse than no acknowledgment at all:

  Dear Gates,
  > I really appreciated your thoughtful gesture, and I send you all best wishes for the New Year.

- It's gracious to mention everyone connected with a gift, not just the one person to whom you may be writing. "I hope you'll tell Gretchen how much I appreciate the role she obviously played in getting those golf clubs into my eager hands." Or else, "Please express my thanks to everyone who signed the card and who contributed to the present. I wish I could tell each one of you how much your generosity means to me."

Thanking a Colleague Who Defends You

. . . I heard what happened in the boardroom this morning—that you stood up for me on my Wallace report, regardless of the others' objections to my premise.

If you hadn't moved quickly and eloquently in my defense, my position in this company might have been put in serious jeopardy. Someday I hope I can return this act of friendship. I am most definitely in your debt.

Thanking Those Who Volunteer on a Major Project

There are many industry-wide projects that require one person to supervise others in the same business but not in the same company who volunteer their services. It may be a benefit for charity, a sports tournament staged for the good of the employees, social events at an industry meeting, or something similar. It is important for the person managing the event to write thank-you letters—the next day—to the manager of any division (or company) that donated its time and talent:

. . . Our awards banquet would never have taken place if you and your staff hadn't pitched in to save the night for me. Your group provided me with brains and brawn, all sorely needed. I will never be able to thank you enough.

My staff and I really enjoyed working with you, because, quite miraculously, everyone's good nature, sense of humor, and imagination never stopped functioning, in spite of all the crises. You were my great White Knights, come to the rescue.

I owe you several lunches, Mike. I'll be in touch. . . .

Thanking for a Job Interview

A letter to the person who interviews you should go out no later than twenty-four hours after seeing her; if you are a "hot prospect," have it delivered by hand.

. . . You were very nice to see me today in the middle of such a full schedule. It was profitable for me to listen to your comments on the direction of J. H. Cutter & Sons. I hope I will be seriously considered as a candidate for the position we discussed, because I feel I have the necessary experience, incentive, and drive to do a great job for the company in that slot.

The atmosphere in your offices, the company's widespread reputation for quality products, and the obvious dedication of everyone I met there make me even more enthusiastic at the prospect of joining the company.

I will wait to hear from you with a great sense of hope.

Thanking the Person Who Arranged for You to Have an Interview

. . . Mr. Reinhardt and I, thanks to your miraculous intervention, spent over an hour today discussing the position at J. H. Cutter. It is a job I want *very much*, not just a little.

It was your call that did the trick in getting me in to see him. It was because of your call that he did not settle on another person whom he had "on hold" for the slot. I am now playing the waiting game, hoping to hear affirmatively. If I do get the position, I'm going to invite you to a victory celebration worthy of my esteem for you — which means it will be *some* celebration!

HANDLING AN EXECUTIVE'S MAIL IN HIS OR HER ABSENCE

When an executive is away from the office for a period of time, a large amount of mail inevitably accumulates. Coping with it upon the return of the executive adds to the increased pressure of handling other deferred duties that also require attention. Yet it is a very important part of good manners to attend to all correspondence promptly. It is therefore advisable for a secretary or staff assistant to acknowledge all the executive's incoming mail as it arrives, immediately answering what can be answered or explaining why there will be a delay in a response to something requiring his personal attention.

Here is an example of the kind of interim response that will afford the executive a temporary reprieve in answering the writer:

> . . . I am acknowledging on Mr. Hendrick's behalf your letter to him of June 8. He is away for a few days; your letter will be brought to his attention as soon as he returns.

If the staff member knows the writer of the letter well, the tone could be more informal:

> . . . I am acknowledging on Mr. Hendrick's behalf your letter to him of June 8. He's fishing in Canada for two weeks and is evidently having a "good-catching time." I know he'll get in touch with you as soon as possible when he returns.

In this case, Mr. Hendrick's secretary obviously knows both boss and correspondent well enough that news of the fishing trip can freely be shared with him.

If an executive is ill, the secretary should refrain from mentioning that in answers to his mail, unless the illness is well known and has already been acknowledged by the company. Rumors fly with unreasonable speed. Before the secretary knows it, the executive's illness will become industry gossip.

If the executive's illness is serious enough to be threatening and it is a known factor, the secretary should still be noncommittal in the letters sent in response to the executive's mail:

> . . . I know how much Ms. Jones will appreciate hearing from you. She will answer your letter as soon as she is feeling better.

Or, if the executive's condition is very serious:

> . . . Thank you for your prayers and for your concern. I know how pleased Ms. Jones will be to learn of your letter.

MEMOS

How you write memos provides a clue to your style of management as well as to your personality. A good memo can serve offensive or defensive purposes. It gives you the opportunity to capsulize or summarize everything important in a lengthy meeting or presentation. A good memo reveals your sense of humor, if you have one, and it certainly reflects your writing ability. What the memo is about should be immediately apparent and clearly expressed—and what response, if any, is expected. For example, if you write a memo intended to prompt action somewhere and your memo indicates

- Who is to do what
- What should occur
- To whom it should occur
- By when it should occur

then you have written a useful memo.

A new executive in the company should be shown by Personnel or Human Resources (or a well-trained staff member) what the procedures are in writing and distributing memoranda within the organization.

These are some general guidelines to remember:

- A manager may criticize an employee in a memo, but it is preferable not to criticize one's fellow executives in a memo. Those criticisms are better made verbally than put on the record, where they might appear overly harsh or even unfair.
- It's wise not to complain about how much work something required. Management is not interested in the problems you encountered, but in the results, listed simply and explicitly.
- If you've seriously delayed taking action and someone is waiting to hear the results, memo that person about the delay, stating the reason for the delay and providing a new timetable. A memo is an efficient way to update another executive.
- If circumstances provide you an opportunity to praise someone, do so in a memo. This shows you are a secure and fair person and the object of your praise will not likely soon forget it: "Anderson really clinched the deal in those last few moments." "Jenkins was brilliant in shooting down their objections." "Agnes came forward with the compromise that saved us." "Henry softened him up perceptibly beforehand."
- Don't be known as a person who "manages by memo." Some individuals find it difficult to confront others in person; they hide behind the printed word rather than talk to a colleague or subordinate. A memo cannot replace a face-to-face meeting.
- A touch of humor is almost always a welcome relief, but don't let it distract the recipient from the real purpose of the memo.
- Don't write a flurry of memos just to justify your presence in a job. Generating a flood of unnecessary paper is criminal in any business office.
- Although a memo is a brief form of communication, good manners are still important. Phrases such as "Thank you very much for . . . ," "I would really appreciate it if . . . ," and "I'm sorry to have caused all of this extra work" are as necessary in a memo as they are in a formal letter.
- When you must criticize someone in a memo, say something nice before you say something that the recipient will not be pleased to hear. End the memo with a "thanks"; it softens the blow.

> . . . The presentation went well this morning for the most part. However, I had the feeling that the budgetary aspect could have been explained much more clearly, succinctly, and even interestingly. Perhaps more new audio-visuals would help. I hope you will give this your priority attention before the Florida presentation. Show me the changes as soon as possible, and thanks very much.

The Form of a Memo

There should be a definite policy on the form of interoffice memos sent by company people. For example:

July 2, 1999

MEMO TO: Harriet Coe (Marketing)
FROM: Daniel Jefferson (Personnel)

Copy everyone who should be copied.

cc: John Harrison (Marketing)
      Anthony Mendes (Personnel)

Put the message in the first paragraph . . . Praise is always welcome.

Your request for an additional staff member has been granted. Frankly, you prepared a terrific case for needing this person.

Sign off not too abruptly.

Proceed right away to find someone suitable. I look forward to talking to him or her when you have final candidates.

/s/ David Schellkopf
VP, Marketing

Communicating by Memo with a Person Whose Name You Don't Know

We are used to writing "Dear Sir," "Dear Madam," or "Gentlemen" when communicating with someone whose name and gender we do not know. There are three options for avoiding addressing a memo to someone by a title that does not correspond to his or her gender.

Straight Memo Form

MEMO TO: Name of company to whom you're writing
                 Address of company
                 City, state, and ZIP
ATT: Section or Division
RE: Subject to be discussed

(Text of memorandum follows.)

Your signature and title

Simplified Letter Style

Name of company
Address of company
City, state, and ZIP
ATT: Section or Division

(Text of memorandum follows.)

Your signature and title

Memo-Letter Style

> Name of company
> Address of company
> City, state, and ZIP
>
> Ladies and Gentlemen:
>
> (Text of memorandum follows.)
>
> Your signature and title

CHRISTMAS, HOLIDAY, AND GREETING CARDS

Greeting and studio cards are great, wonderful fun, or else they're sweet, sentimental, and create tears. They can also be raunchy, even downright dirty—but those are *never* appropriate in the business world. If you send a pornographic, supposedly funny card to a business friend, it has your name on it, the recipient may show it around. There it will be, a dirty card with your name on it, and people who see it will associate your name with dirt forever more.

Sending the right card denotes effort on your part as the sender who must find the right place and buy the cards and select the appropriate ones when faced with a sea of choices.

Holiday Card Etiquette (including Hanukkah cards)

- *Send to Christian friends cards that show religious scenes*, such as the Nativity scene or Christmas angels. Reproductions of great religious paintings are particularly appropriate, and the message inside would contain a wish for something like a "joyous, blessed Christmas." Also appropriate are cards with Christmas trees, wreaths, Santas, sleighs, candy canes, Christmas bells, and all the festive, decorative joy of the holiday season.
- *Send to Jewish, Arab, Moslem, Hindu, or Buddhist friends greeting cards that wish everyone a "Happy New Year"* or "Seasons Greetings" or any other non-religious statement of good wishes. Many Jewish people also like cards for Hanukkah, which celebrates an ancient Jewish military victory and is observed by lighting a candelabrum with nine candles, called a menorah. The eight days of this celebration, usually close to Christmas, is the period in which Hanukkah cards (or gifts) are sent to Jewish colleagues and friends.
- *Mail your greeting cards preferably any time between Thanksgiving and Christmas*. If you are out of the country and can't get your cards out on time, mail them anyway, whenever you can, with a note inside, "Sorry, this is so tardy, but I was in Hong Kong when I should have been home writing my greeting cards!" One lawyer friend of mine gets his Christmas cards to all of his clients and friends into

the mail "in time for Easter," and since we all expect his cards in the spring, we would probably be disappointed if they came before December 25.

- *Buy some pretty holiday stamps from the post office* instead of sending your cards through the office postage meter system. A stamped envelope is much more personal and attractive than a metered one.
- *Many people enclose a family newsletter in their greeting cards every December.* If you are in the habit of composing a family roundup each year, filled with all the news of what colleges your children are applying for, which child had his appendix out, which tennis tournament your wife won, and the fact that daughter Mary Lou is studying *haiku* poetry while still job-hunting, remember to enclose that bit of family history *only* inside greeting cards to close personal friends. Some of your business associates may fall into that category, but many of them do not.

  Do not include the grim details of bad news that occurred during the year, such as lengthy descriptions of illnesses and family misfortunes in these notes. Keep them as cheerful and upbeat as possible.
- *If your company sends out Christmas cards, it is very important that everyone in your division personalizes and signs every one of their cards.* "Personalizing" means that each person who sends a card to a colleague, client, customer, director, support staff, friend, etc., writes something on the card, below the corporate name. The sender's name, for one thing—and not just "Joe," but the full name, because there are many *Joe*s in the world.

  A few words should be written before the sender's signature, as simple as "Have a great Christmas!" or "Hope your New Year brings you great health and the tennis forehand you're aiming for," or "Hope next year is going to be terrific for you!" or "I hope your family will be all together this Christmas, as ours will be," or whatever you want to say.
- I don't like it when a corporation broadcasts its largesse and boldly mentions on the company card: "A donation has been made in your name to the Such-and-such charity." I think that is back-patting and not in the Christmas spirit. It is much better to make a handsome donation to the charity and forget about advertising it.
- *Company greeting cards may be signed:*

  . . . with both husband's and wife's names ("Jack and Gretchen Thurston," or, if the recipient knows Gretchen a lot better than Jack, she would sign the family card "Gretchen and Jack Thurston.")

  . . . or by just one person, if the recipient is a business colleague of the sender and has never met the spouse. (In this case, only Jack Thurston would sign the card.) A woman executive whose business colleagues have never met her husband and children, but who talks about her family to her customers, can always send her cards signed, "Gretchen Thurston and her family," a nice touch.
- *Company greeting cards should not contain little color snapshots of the executive's children.* Save that custom for family and close friends.

Greeting Cards for Someone Who is Seriously Ill
(*See also* "Gifts for Someone Who Is Ill or Injured," Chapter 11)

You should be very sensitive to the kind of get-well card you send someone. I remember so well when a colleague of mine was in Sloan Kettering Hospital, recovering nicely from a serious cancer operation, when she received a card from a mutual friend. The sender of the card had obviously not read it, but had probably dispatched someone from his office to buy a get-well card, and he had just signed it peremptorily. The card was "In Loving Sympathy" for the dead and featured a beautiful bouquet of white embossed roses on the cover, with a gushing text of comfort inside.

My hospitalized friend wrote him a note in return: "George, I am coming along fine, but I have put back your beautiful card in its envelope so it can be given someday to my progeny when I die, probably several decades from now. The sympathy card was much too beautiful to waste."

Be sure to write something personal inside the get-well card you select for an office colleague; the card's text alone won't say what you want it to say. Walk the fine line of appropriateness, too. Choose a card that is cheerful and makes you feel good, too. Refrain from selecting something dripping with saccharine sweetness or a card that attempts humor by sexual innuendo. Someone hurting in a hospital or a sick bed usually is not ready for an overdose of sugar—or smut.

If your friend is dying, send a cheerful get-well card anyway, every day, if you can't come to see him or be admitted to his bedside. You are sending yourself each day when you do that. There's always news to tell, something upbeat to write about inside the card. Your card is like a soft touch on his sleeve, to say you're thinking about him.

It's all called communication, and when a friend is ill, that's the time to communicate like you've never done it before.

8

The Executive Stationery Wardrobe: Why Everything You Send Out with Your Name on It Matters

When you write a letter or send an announcement or invitation through the mail or by messenger—or even hand someone your business card—you are communicating the essence and image of yourself and your business.

When you work for a large company, you communicate graphically with the outside world using the tools supplied by your company. It's their logo on the stationery, not yours. It's their taste in graphic design, quality of paper, and colors used. However, if your company's graphic design program for visual communication is considered to be inferior by the majority of people with whom you work, you should act. Any level of management has a duty to bring this problem to the top. Many times I have observed junior managers who have heard negative comments on the outside about the corporate graphics, and have successfully brought these criticisms to senior managers' attention. Inevitably, as a follow-up, corrective action has been taken.

Even if you work for a large company, your own taste comes into play with the private stationery you purchase to use in writing to business colleagues, friends, and contacts. Your letter paper and correspondence cards reinforce who you are and what role you play in the business world.

This chapter is written with three goals in mind:

1. *To make the reader aware of the importance of equipping employees with useful, well-designed corporate stationery*
2. *To help professionals, entrepreneurs, and small business owners understand the role well-designed stationery plays in the transaction of business and in the shaping of their images*
3. *To help people understand that regardless of the stationery made available to them by the company for their daily business or professional lives,* they need their own *effective, good-quality social stationery*

STATIONERY PROTOCOL

- *Fold your letter properly* before inserting it into the envelope. Part of the overall image of a company can be destroyed by something as small as the sloppy folding of the company's letters into envelopes. Unless there is an unusual design scheme, this is the classic way of folding a piece of paper and inserting it into a horizontal envelope:

  1. Fold the bottom edge of the page up to a line approximately one-third of the way down from the top.
  2. Then take the top edge and fold it down to meet the bottom edge of the bottom fold, thus dividing the page into even thirds, giving a shape that should slide easily from right to left into the back side of the envelope when that is held vertically toward you.
  3. If you are inserting a more square piece of paper (like a card or a foldover note) into an envelope, slip it right-side-up into the envelope and facing the back so that when the message is pulled out, it can be read at once without even turning it.

- *Always put your telephone and fax numbers on your letterhead.* It can be expensive, time-consuming, and maddening to have to call information long distance to seek out a phone number; it makes it that much harder for someone to respond to you.
- *Coordinate your stationery.* Order envelopes that fit your letterhead snugly. When you send out bills with an enclosed envelope for payment, be sure to make the envelope big enough to hold the average-sized check. Don't ever send out a communication without a matching envelope.
- It also looks tacky when the second sheet of a long letter does not match the first. In other words, if you order letterhead that is ecru-colored and you do not order

CORRECT WAY TO FOLD AND INSERT STATIONERY

plain second sheets in the same stock, you will find yourself sending a letter with a second sheet of white bond, instead of ecru stock. If you run out of matching second sheets, always pen a note of apology at the bottom of that page (''Sorry about the stationery mismatch!'').

- *If the information on your good stationery changes (the address, telephone number, etc.)* order new stationery and use the old as *scratch paper*. It's alright to type the correct information over it for a month, but after that, your new stationery should have arrived. It looks really tacky to send letters on corrected letterheads that are many months old.

- *Insist upon envelopes with a good gummy product on the back flap that seals it tight.* When you have to put cellophane tape over the back flap to make it secure, it destroys any esthetics the stationery might have.

- *Keep your stationery clean.* An open box left on the shelf collects dust very quickly and the paper shows soil easily.

- *Make certain that all of the text on your letterhead is large enough so as to be easy to read—without a magnifying glass.*

YOUR CORPORATE IDENTITY AND YOUR STATIONERY

Raymond Loewy, with his designs for the Studebaker car, Lucky Strike cigarette package, and airplane interiors, was the pioneer genius in the '40s and '50s in the new field of graphic design. Walter Paepcke, head of The Container Corporation in Chicago and founder of The Aspen Institute, spent a fortune educating American business on the importance of graphic and industrial design. He was ahead of almost everyone else in saying that the way a company visually presents itself and its products to its public means good—or poor—profits. By the 1960s a whole generation of accomplished graphic designers was flourishing and had become an integral part of their companies' business successes. There was Paul Rand's corporate identity program for IBM, for example, in which the layout of the memo sheets and business forms used by employees and the "Exit" signs in the buildings received the same attention given to the giant logo signs over plants and offices throughout America. Firms like Lippincott & Margulies, Chermayeff & Geismar, and Anspach Grossman Portugal, Inc., showed industry that good corporate design sells, uplifts, and motivates. Designers like Milton Green and Massimo Vignelli and postmodern architects like Robert Stern, Robert Venturi, and Michael Graves designed building interiors, calendars, coffee pots, letterheads, flatware, paper clips, and soda cans. The visual became as important as the mechanical. Corporations began to spend millions in one year changing their logos and corporate identities, some with the aid of such corporate identity firms as Pentagram, Riegel and Gale, Sandor Associates, and Cross Associates.

The small business owner must care about his own graphics, too. If you can't afford a renowned design firm like The Pushpin Group in New York to do your logo you should at least have the graphic look of your stationery, the sign on the door of your company (store or firm), and the sign on the panel of your mini-van identically neat, clear, unified, and reflective of the image you want for your business.

You make your own design decisions, but the chart below shows some of the most popular decisions of people in business:

	A Conservative Business	*A Contemporary Look*	*A Fashion Image*
	(Banks, pharmaceutical companies, insurance companies, stockbrokers, lawyers, doctors, accountants, textbook publishers, etc.)	(Automotive, computer, and home furnishings industries; design firms; ad agencies and communications companies; health clubs; restaurants, etc.)	(Retailing, textile industry, men and women's apparel, hair salons, cosmetic and fragrance industry, etc.)
Paper	Good quality paper; no texture interest	Good quality paper; heightened texture interest	Good quality paper with or without texture interest
Colors	White or ecru paper; black lettering	Smoky colors (gray, tan, olive green, etc.) with deeper colors of lettering	Unusual colors or color contrasts (for example, pink paper with fuchsia border or aqua paper with navy lettering)

A Conservative Business	A Contemporary Look	A Fashion Image
Traditional typeface, such as antique	Very contemporary lettering, often unusual	Wide range of typefaces used; the fashion is in the color

THE ENTREPRENEUR'S FIRST STATIONERY

If you're starting out in business or in a profession, you should retain a good, professional, freelance graphic designer (sometimes there is a good one on staff at a major printing house but most often there is not) to work on your logo and the design of your letterheads. He or she will then work with the printer on your stationery production, which is complicated, an art in itself.

You can find a graphic designer through word of mouth, or by checking on the work of the graphic designers listed in the Yellow Pages, or various graphic designer directories, available in bookstores and at the library. Once you have designed and approved the logo, and the layout sketches have been made, if you are a complete novice in the field of design ask two other people of taste look them over and agree with you that they are "terrific." After all, your image and that of your business are at stake! At all costs, you want to avoid making a mistake in printing your first stationery—it is too costly for most beginners to bear.

There are three decisions to make in ordering stationery:

1. *The kinds of pieces to order*

- Letterheads
- Note paper—an abbreviated form of the letterhead which can include your name only
- Envelopes for letterhead
- Envelopes for notes
- Invoices
- Business cards
- Mailing labels to put on large envelopes
- Correspondence cards

Think of the needs of your particular type of business before you order. A good stationer will show you the plethora of items available that can help make your business life easier and more efficient.

2. *Esthetics*

    Quality, weight, and color of stock

    Layout, logo, and entire design concept

    Typeface selection

3. *Lettering reproduction process*

    Printing. A flat image reproduction

    Thermography. A heat process that causes ink to rise slightly, giving it an engraved feel

    Engraving. A luxurious, top-of-the-line way to go. This process used to be terribly expensive but is less so today because—instead of steel dies—plates are used which are photographically reproduced. The recipient can tell a letterhead is engraved by the feel of it, as well as the beauty of it. The process makes an indentation on the back side of the paper. Only fine quality stock can be used.

        In most companies only senior management is permitted the luxury of engraved stationery, but a good number of professionals and small business owners like myself use engraved stationery most of the time because of the pleasure it gives to us—as well as the recipients of our communications.

    Other methods. Many companies have their letterheads and business cards printed, but combine the printing with either an engraved or an embossed logo to give it a very rich look. Logos often used to be blind embossed (textured, all in white), but since these are impossible to photocopy or fax, they are rarely used. In addition to engraved logos, embossed ones are popular, and often are foil-stamped in rich colors.

YOUR STATIONERY WARDROBE

Classic, Conservative Design

    The imaginary Frederick K. Baxter, chairman of Packard Industries, uses only engraved stationery, with black lettering on white paper, in the classic manner. His stationery elements include:

1. The regular office letterhead is 8½″ × 11″ (matching #10 envelopes). His staff uses the same stock—but printed instead of engraved.
2. He also uses a smaller letterhead for more personal letters (6½″ × 8″).
3. His business cards are 3½″ × 2″.
4. His memo pads (which may be of any size) are 5″ × 7½″.
5. His correspondence cards, which are used for personal notes and invitations, are 6½″ × 4½″.

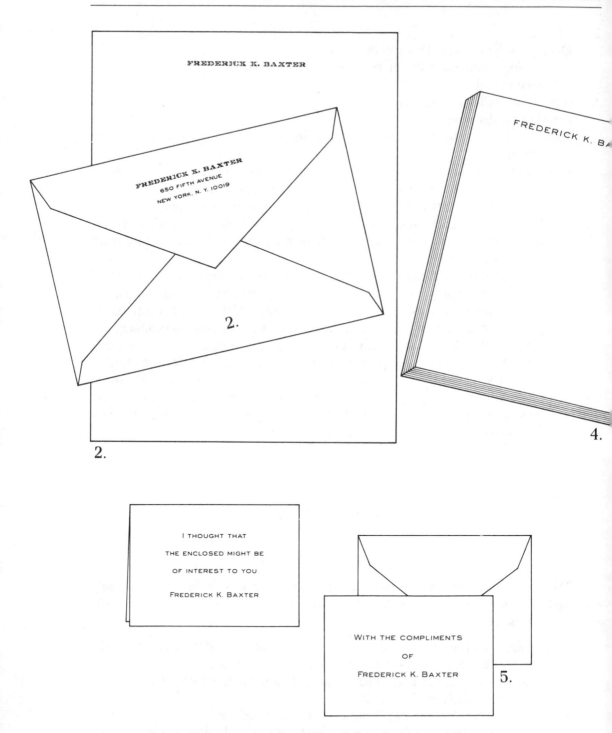

FREDERICK K. BAXTER

FREDERICK K. BAXTER
650 FIFTH AVENUE
NEW YORK, N. Y. 10019

2.

2.

FREDERICK K. B

4.

I THOUGHT THAT

THE ENCLOSED MIGHT BE

OF INTEREST TO YOU

FREDERICK K. BAXTER

WITH THE COMPLIMENTS

OF

FREDERICK K. BAXTER

5.

A STATIONERY WARDROBE FOR THE SUCCESSFUL EXECUTIVE

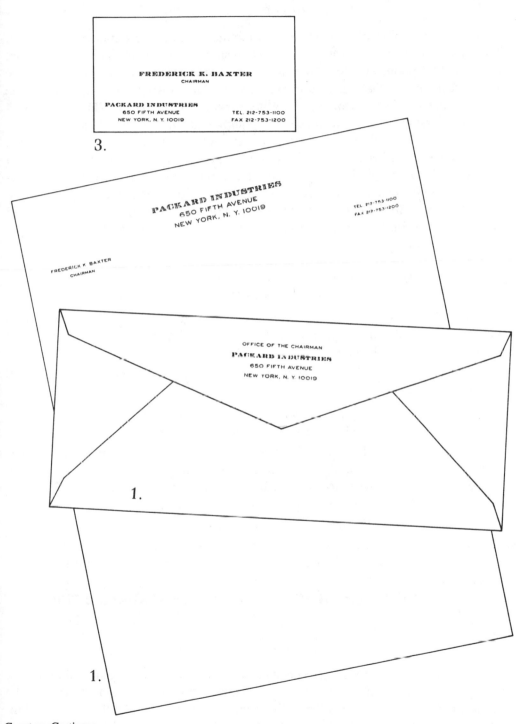

Courtesy Cartier

Less Conservative Design

Other people in business like to have color and dash in their stationery wardrobes. Bill Daniels in Denver, for example, uses white stock with green printing of his name, address, and telephone number—to match the ¼"-wide green stripe that runs down the left side of the page of all his stationery. A woman in the fragrance business has the shadow silhouette of her perfume bottle watermarked into the paper, which is always a pale pink parchment. Her word processing equipment prints in dark blue on her pale pink paper (the same colors as those used in her packaging). A Scotsman in Michigan has the insides of all his envelopes lined with paper printed with his family tartan in color. A lawyer whose middle name is Key has a tiny key printed in the upper right-hand corner of his personal stationery, because he says it brings him and everyone else good luck. A man in the photography business writes all his correspondence by hand in white ink on all-black paper, because, as he says, "it reminds people of the business I'm in."

Women Executives Often Need Stationery for Personal Use

In addition to the same office stationery items ordered by Frederick Packard, a woman may need additional pieces for personal use at home. She might order, for example, one of the following:

  · *Correspondence cards* with matching envelopes with *her home address* engraved in color at the top

245 EAST SIXTIETH STREET
NEW YORK, NY 10034

  · *Foldover notes*, used in place of correspondence cards for thank-yous, invitations, etc., with her given, family, and married names on the top fold, as, for example, Genevieve Taylor, who works under her maiden name but who has the following notes made for use in her life as Mrs. Gustave Woodworth:

Genevieve Taylor Woodworth

  · Correspondence cards with both spouses' names, for use at home for social purposes, such as informal invitations and thank-you notes, are helpful if the wife has retained her own name.

JOHN RIGHTER SCHULTZ AND MARIAN ATKINS SALTER

Business Cards

The first really important graphic statement for most of us is our business card. Today's young entrepreneur and professional orders his or her business cards at the first flush of business. I've seen the cards of many entrepreneurs, including an eighth-grader in the plant seed business, a golf caddy, a college student who acts as a mime, a senior citizen who dog-sits when people go on trips, and a handicapped woman who has a flourishing seasonal home business sewing name tapes on the clothing and possessions of young people who go away to school or to camp.

Most of us remember our first business cards and how proud we were of them. Mine came from Tiffany & Company, the famous New York jeweler, when I began as the store's first director of publicity and public relations. I remember how proud I was of how beautiful my engraved card looked. The store's name was engraved boldly in the center; almost hidden in one corner was my name and title in tiny lettering. When I remarked about this to the president, Walter Hoving, half seriously and half in jest, Mr. Hoving addressed me sternly. "When you work for Tiffany," he said with a trace of a smile on his face, "the only thing that matters is the company. The individual is secondary." He taught me a good lesson that day, as he did every day during the four years I worked under him.

Your business card and how you handle it is a very personal part of executive communication. It's like a handshake that you leave behind you. You should give your card to someone in such a way as to make him *want* to remember you and *want* to get in touch with you.

There are three main uses for business cards:

- To give to someone to remind him who you are, where you are, and how to reach you
- To use as a forwarding agent when clipped to something like a photograph, the annual report, a clipping from a newspaper or magazine, or anything you promised to send to a particular person or you know someone would enjoy receiving
- To use as an enclosure for a present or flowers

A handsome card, properly presented, makes a tremendous impression. We should know when to present our cards, when to take the initiative; we should know how to exchange cards gracefully when someone else has taken the initiative.

Business Card Etiquette

It is particularly important for a young executive to learn how to present his or her card properly, so as to avoid being "pushy" or appearing maladroit.

- *Do not force your card on a senior executive you meet.* Wait until he or she asks for yours.
- *Don't offer your card early in the conversation to anyone who is a complete stranger* and whom you meet by accident (for example, when sitting next to a person on a plane or at the lunch counter). Your overeagerness may be based on nothing more than youthful enthusiasm and may irritate your neighbor. (In addition, there is a possibility that if you knew the truth about the stranger, you would not want him to have your name, company name, and address!)
- *Don't scatter your card about in a large group of strangers.* People will immediately begin to think you're trying to sell them something, and they'll freeze you

out. Learn to be very selective about the people to whom you give your card. Also remember that at a business–social gathering the best way to do it is so that others are not aware you are giving someone your card. It should be a private exchange between just the two of you, not a conspicuous gesture made in public, and particularly not at someone's private dinner.

- When you attend a meeting outside your office with people whom you do not know, *wait for the signals that may be given*. Let *someone else* begin the exchanging of cards among those who do not know each other. Often cards will be exchanged at the beginning of the meeting, sometimes at the conclusion. However, if you are giving a presentation, you have every right to distribute your cards in advance to those near you, so that they will know exactly who you are before you stand up to speak.
- *It is much better not to give out a business card than to give one that is defective, out-of-date, or soiled*. Carry your cards in your wallet or in a card case to keep them protected and fresh. If your remaining cards are not spit-and-polish perfect, throw them out. Apologize to people you meet for a sudden depletion of your cards, and then write the necessary information on a piece of clean paper to give those who wish it.
- *Women as well as men should carry business cards in the evening at social events* in case a good business target of opportunity presents itself.
- No matter whether you are dining in a fast food restaurant, at a black-tie dinner in a hotel, or in someone's home, *cards should never be brought out during a meal*. People should be discreet about talking business when they are having cocktails or dining either at someone's home or in a restaurant when the event has been billed primarily as social, rather than business-related.
- *The most important part of business card etiquette is knowing when and how to personalize your card*. "Personalizing" your card entails putting a slash through your name and writing something personal with a pen on the front (or on the back, if there is insufficient room on the front). For example:
  - If you send flowers to your dinner hosts at their home, you would write on the back of your card something like, "Thank you for a perfectly wonderful evening. I enjoyed every second." You would sign with your first name only.
  - If you are sending something, you would write something like, "This might be of interest to you. All the best," followed by your first-name signature.
  - If you are introducing someone who has an appointment with a colleague of yours, attach your card to his resumé or brochure or whatever: "Know you'll enjoy talking with Ken," followed by your first-name signature.

The Design of the Business Card

A business card is part of a large corporation's unified graphics program. A junior executive's cards, like his stationery, are usually printed until he ascends the corporate ladder to a height where engraved cards are supplied. If you work for a large company, your card will be of a standard design used by all the executives. You will have no options.

For the entrepreneur or professional, self-expression is possible, and there are certainly many imaginative designs representing small businesses in circulation. Anyone in a quality-image business should keep in mind that a well-designed card on quality stock denotes a person of taste and importance. When you "think cheap" without any good design advice on your cards, you may very well look cheap to those who are left with your card to remember you by. A person who looks on your card as lacking professionalism may not want to do business with you.

Istvan G. Bokanyi
President

CGZ Incorporated
1834 Twelfth Avenue
New York, NY 13001

Tel (212) 947-6230
Fax (212) 947-6236

Budapest Office
Tel 011-361-482-7354
Fax 011-361-482-3746

THE ARTFUL PIRATE'S COVE

Victoria R. Negley
1435 Updike Drive
Alexandria, VA 12354
Tel (102) 238-6487
Fax (102) 238-7632
Car (102) 354-4937

TWO PROFESSIONALLY DESIGNED BUSINESS CARDS

Whether you wish to have a conservative business card or an illustrative one, let a graphics designer do the job for you.

A Hungarian export-import trading company president, Istvan Bokanyi, wanted a contemporary, conservative look to his card, featuring his company logo, and appropriate to his dealings with banks and government officials.

Victoria Negley, on the other hand, the owner of a gift shop in Virginia, wanted people to remember her pirate logo, which appears on the sign that hangs over her shop, on her shopping bags, invoices, stationery, and on the door of the mini-van she uses for deliveries. The dashing pirate-dominated business card helps people remember the name of her shop, The Artful Pirate's Cove. (The characters are fictitious, their cards designed by The Pushpin Group, Inc., New York City.)

The standard size of a business card is 3½" × 2" or variations thereof. Cards may be made in unusual shapes to represent certain types of businesses. (I have seen clever cards in the shape of a hamburger, automobile, French poodle, and typewriter.) If you have cards of this nature made for you, remember that what you gain in cleverness, you may lose in one respect: People cannot easily put an odd-shaped card in their wallets or card cases. Some people involved in the arts cleverly use unorthodox sizes to make their cards memorable.

The stock of the card may have a shiny or dull matte finish; it may be thick or thin but must be strong enough not to tear when fingered or when extracted from a card case. Managers often use both printed and engraved cards, the former to use in mass mailings and the latter to use for VIP business. The colors of the business card should, of course, match the colors of the company's stationery.

The information contained on the card should include the following:

- *The logo, trademark, or company symbol.* A small-business person may work with a graphics artist to find a symbol representing his or her work, such as a bouquet of flowers for a florist, a market basket full of vegetables for a food consultant, a calculator with printed figures issuing from it for an accountant, a camera with printing in the lenses for a photographer, a mug full of cosmetic brushes for a person in the beauty business, a dressmaker's dummy with a scarf wrapped around its neck for a dressmaker.
- *The text*, including the following:
  - Name
  - Title (if pertinent)
  - Company name
  - Business address
  - Telephone number
  - Fax number
  - Address of other offices in the country (if pertinent)

Some people who work out of their homes as well as out of an office include their home telephone and fax number along with their business number.

Proper Procedures on the Design of the Card

  - If you own more than one business, it is preferable to have separate cards for each business.
  - If you have offices in several places, you may certainly include this information on the card.
  - Unless you have a professional title such as M.D., Colonel, Ph.D., etc., do not use a title (Mr., Miss, Ms.) on your card. The exception to this rule is when you have a name that could be male or female (Duane, Clair, Marion,

Cameron, etc.). In this case you would be wise to put a Mr. or Ms. in front of your name.

◦ If everyone knows you by your nickname, include it with your formal name: "Marianne ("Buffy") Endicott, Vice-President."

Business Cards Abroad

(*See also* Chapter 10, "Doing International Business—
Profitably and Politely")

If you do a considerable amount of business in a foreign country, you should have your cards printed in English on one side and in the country's language on the other. Some European business people print extra information on their cards, such as the type of products manufactured, the number of employees and gross revenues. This kind of business card is a mini press release of sorts.

The classic European business card is often larger than ours (3″ × 4½″), leaving space at the bottom to jot a note if necessary.

The Japanese relentlessly present their cards to the people whom they meet in the business world, but they do it with grace, even to the point of showing deference to someone they consider more important. In this case they present the card in the fingers of both hands, bowing simultaneously. We tend to give ours abruptly and without much thought to protocol, gracefulness, or appropriateness.

Business Announcement Cards

Business news may be communicated through a telephone call, a fax, a letter, or the mailing of a business announcement card. A letter is, of course, the most personal way of imparting news; it also permits the inclusion of supporting material—brochures, press releases, newspaper clippings, etc. However, for a widespread mailing, it is expensive and cumbersome to send letters. For a large mailing, the best device is the printed, thermographed, or engraved business announcement card. A business announcement card reaches out in shorthand to a maximum audience of clients, customers, colleagues, associates, VIPs, potential customers, and friends.

It should be kept in mind that:

- The announcement card and envelope reflect the image of the company, just as its stationery does. Therefore, both should be of a good quality stock and thoughtfully designed.
- The card should not be so bulky in size that its weight exceeds the minimum first-class postage requirement (or it will entail an unnecessary added expense).
- The names and addresses on the envelopes should be either typed, printed by a word processor, or hand-written—*not* done on labels!
- There should be enough, but not too much, communicated on the announcement. If the recipient is confused by the purpose of the announcement, the desired effect will be lost.

- If you wish, jot a short note on an announcement card to personalize it. In fact, it is a good idea to do so.
- A printed announcement card is the least expensive way to communicate; an engraved announcement card is formal and more expensive but it creates an atmosphere of ''something special.''
- If your company sends out many announcements on a continuing basis, like an insurance company announcing its new representatives, it's a good idea to keep in stock white cards or folded notes that contain the company logo already engraved or embossed and the announcement message already engraved or printed. Then the name of the person, his address, and telephone number can be filled in by hand.

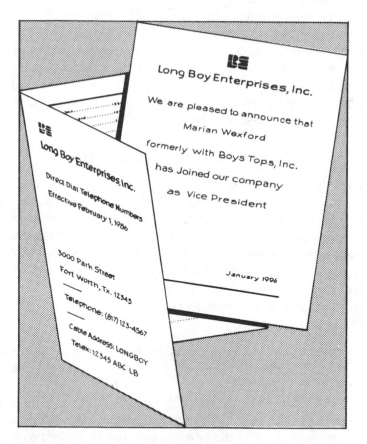

This particular announcement card serves two purposes:

- It announces the company's new direct dialing numbers and lists personnel alphabetically inside.
- It announces the appointment of a new company officer.

- When you receive a business announcement in the mail, you are not obliged to acknowledge its receipt. However, if you are a personal friend of the subject of the announcement, it's very nice to send him or her a short hand-written, or even typed, acknowledgment conveying your congratulations and best wishes. This is a simple gesture and rarely forgotten.

The Design: Formal Versus Informal

As with a company's stationery, business announcement cards should accurately reflect the company's image. The use of the same logo and typeface as well as colors of stock and printing helps reinforce the corporate identity; this holds true for a small business as well as a large one.

The wording of the business announcement should be carefully proofed before it is printed — a little mistake becomes a major error on a small card.

There are formal and informal ways of wording an announcement, as the following examples attest. The nature of the business governs which type of announcement should be sent:

Announcing a New Company

Formally

JOAN McINTOSH LEE
RONALD SCHULTZ
ANNOUNCE THE FORMATION OF
LECTON INC.
A MARKET RESEARCH FIRM
SPECIALIZING IN
FOOD SERVICES
3422 Contrad Street
Fargo, South Dakota 00000
Tel: (000) 000-0000
Fax: (000) 000-0000

Informally

TIM MCCOY
HAS OPENED
TIM'S TINKER TOYS
A CHILDREN'S TOY AND BOOK EMPORIUM
AT 4TH AND HOWARD
MINNEAPOLIS
Tel: (000) 000-0000
Fax: (000) 000-0000
Bring this card for a 20% discount on your first purchase.

Announcing a New Branch

Formally

KENYON, ATKINS & REYNOLDS
ANNOUNCES
THE OPENING OF THEIR FOURTH TEXAS OFFICE
3314 SOUTHWEST FREEWAY
DALLAS 00000
UNDER THE MANAGEMENT OF
MR. ALLAN E. ELKINS
VICE-PRESIDENT
DECEMBER 1, 1996
Tel: (000) 000-0000
Fax: (000) 000-0000

Informally

HI-JINKS PREMIUM DESIGNS
145 Broadway, Newark, NJ 00000
IS SUCH A GREAT SUCCESS
WE ARE OPENING
TWO NEW BRANCH OFFICES

124 First St.	314 Palisades, 14-F
Naples, FL 00000	Canton, OH 00000
Tel: (000) 000-0000	Tel: (000) 000-0000
Fax: (000) 000-0000	Fax: (000) 000-0000
Anne Cox, Manager	Ed Reed, Manager

A Change of Address (in a party invitation)

PLEASE JOIN IN CELEBRATING OUR MOVE
TO NEW OFFICES
MORGAN, LYMAN & BORNEMOUTH, P.C.
1345 SEAVIEW AVENUE
ATLANTIC CITY, NJ 00000
WEDNESDAY, MARCH 27TH
COCKTAILS—5:00 TO 7:00 P.M.
RSVP: (000) 000-0000
Fax: (000) 000-0000

A Group Departure for Another Firm

(Included in this mailing would be a separate card listing each lawyer and his or her direct-dial number.)

WE ARE PLEASED TO ANNOUNCE THAT,
HAVING TERMINATED OUR RELATIONSHIP WITH
GORDON, REEVES & HOLLYWORTH,
WE WILL CONTINUE THE PRACTICE OF LAW
UNDER THE NAME
GOODWIN, O'MEARA AND KRAFT
WITH OFFICES AT 345 DECATUR PLACE
LINCOLN, NEBRASKA 00000
September 1, 1996   Tel: (000) 000-0000
Fax: (000) 000-0000

A Move of Offices

JONATHON P. FILLMAN ASSOCIATES
PUBLIC RELATIONS COUNSELORS
ANNOUNCES THE LOCATION OF
THEIR NEW OFFICES AT
et cetera

or

JONATHON P. FILLMAN ASSOCIATES
PUBLIC RELATIONS COUNSELORS
WISHES TO ANNOUNCE A MOVE TO
A NEW LOCATION AT
1415 STATE AVENUE
ATLANTA, GEORGIA 00000
MARCH 1, 1996   Tel: (000) 000-0000
Fax: (000) 000-0000

or

JONATHON P. FILLMAN ASSOCIATES
PUBLIC RELATIONS COUNSELORS
ANNOUNCES THAT THE COMPANY HAS
MOVED TO A NEW ADDRESS AT
et cetera

A New Officer of the Company or Firm

COMPANY XYZ
IS PLEASED TO ANNOUNCE THAT
JOANNA S. BARKHORN
HAS BEEN NAMED EXECUTIVE VICE-PRESIDENT
JUNE FIRST

123 LA SALLE STREET
CHICAGO, IL 00000
Tel: (000) 000-0000
Fax: (000) 000-0000

or

COMPANY XYZ
WE TAKE PLEASURE IN ANNOUNCING
THE APPOINTMENT OF
JOANNA S. BARKHORN
AS EXECUTIVE VICE-PRESIDENT

123 LA SALLE STREET
CHICAGO, IL 00000
Tel: (000) 000-0000
Fax: (000) 000-0000

A New Division Within the Company

GEORGE LANOS, PRESIDENT
ANTIOCHTEK, INC.
TAKES PLEASURE IN ANNOUNCING
A NEW LINE OF PRODUCTS
''LUMINOSO''
LAMPS, LIGHTING FIXTURES, AND ACCESSORIES

Harold Wenzel, General Manager
''Luminoso'' Division
134 EAST ERIE
DETROIT, MI 00000
Tel: (000) 000-0000
Fax: (000) 000-0000

The Departure of a Partner for Government Service

AMES, CUTTER, McILHERNEY & JONES
ANNOUNCES THE WITHDRAWAL FROM
THE PARTNERSHIP
OF MARIO A. ANTONINI
TO BECOME
AMBASSADOR OF THE UNITED STATES OF AMERICA
TO THE REPUBLIC OF ITALY
APRIL 1, 1996
141 WATER STREET
MILWAUKEE, WI 00000
Tel: (000) 000-0000
Fax: (000) 000-0000

A Return to the Firm

(The partners and counsels of the firm would be listed on the inside page of a double-fold announcement; or, if the announcement is on a single card, the partners would be listed on the back side.)

THE PARTNERS OF
MANNING, BABCOCK, WEISS, GREEN, KOE AND STAIR
240 UNION STREET
SAN FRANCISCO, CA 00000
ARE PLEASED TO ANNOUNCE
THAT
THE HONORABLE WILLIAM A. GELLHORN
FORMERLY OF THE UNITED STATES SENATE
HAS REJOINED THE FIRM
AS OF
JUNE FIRST
NINETEEN HUNDRED NINETY-SIX

A Change in Senior Management

(For example, a senior officer retires but remains with the company in some capacity.)

PETER M. FINNERTY
CHAIRMAN OF THE BOARD AND CHIEF EXECUTIVE OFFICER
A. L. JOHNSON ASSOCIATES, INCORPORATED
IS PLEASED TO ANNOUNCE THE ELECTION OF
WILLIAM S. PEASE
AS
CHAIRMAN EMERITUS
MAY 1996

or

A. R. JONES
PRESIDENT, A.R.J. MANAGEMENT SERVICES, INC.
ANNOUNCES THE RETIREMENT OF
JOHN J. FINN
AND HIS APPOINTMENT AS
CONSULTANT TO THE COMPANY
2000 HUNTS POINT
BOULDER, COLORADO 00000
Tel: (000) 000-0000
Fax: (000) 000-0000

The Resumption of a Maiden Name

MARY BRIGHTON GRISWOLD, PH.D.
HAS RESUMED HER
MAIDEN NAME
MARY LOUISE BRIGHTON, PH.D.

A Company Name Change

EDMUND A. SINCLAIRE, PRESIDENT
THE SINCLAIRE ADVERTISING AGENCY
ANNOUNCES
THAT AS OF JULY 1, 1996
THE FIRM'S NAME WILL BE CHANGED TO
THE SINCLAIRE GROUP
331 MAIN
BATON ROUGE, LOUISIANA 00000
Tel: (000) 000-0000
Fax: (000) 000-0000

A Change of Name and Company

ANNE DAVIS
ANNOUNCES
THAT SHE WILL NOW BE KNOWN AS ANNE WELDON
AND THAT HER COMPANY
WILL NOW BE KNOWN AS
ANNE WELDON AND ASSOCIATES
1034 STANTON DRIVE
AUSTIN, TEXAS 00000
Tel: (000) 000-0000
Fax: (000) 000-0000

An Addition to a (Medical) Practice

SEYMOUR R. GRATIAN, D.D.S.
DIPLOMATE, AMERICAN BOARD OF PERIODONTOLOGY
ANNOUNCES WITH PLEASURE THE ASSOCIATION OF
PHILIP B. YORK, D.M.D.
IN THE PRACTICE OF PERIODONTICS
3422 STATE STREET   Tel: (000) 000-0000
DES MOINES, IOWA 00000   Fax: (000) 000-0000

Promotions

WE ARE PLEASED TO ANNOUNCE
THAT THE FOLLOWING HAVE BEEN ELECTED
SENIOR VICE-PRESIDENTS
ANGELA H. NIZZI   DANIEL R. KOCH
AND
THAT THE FOLLOWING HAVE BEEN ELECTED
VICE-PRESIDENTS
RAYMOND P. BONE   CARLOS J. LIAS
SUZANNE CHURCH   C. AUSTIN OLLMAN
NICHOLAS DAMORTH   PLATO POULOS
MORTON LEE & CO.
320 HUDSON STREET   MEMPHIS, TN 00000
OCTOBER 24, 1996

A Career Change

Formally

MARIANNE LINDSAY, A.S.I.D.
FORMERLY WITH THE INTERIOR DESIGN STAFF OF
MARSHALL FIELD & CO.
WISHES TO ANNOUNCE
THE OPENING OF HER OWN OFFICES

LINDSAY DESIGN CONSULTANTS

DESIGN CONSULTING BY THE HOUR
OR ON A PROJECT BASIS

1740 NORTH STATE STREET   Tel: (000) 000-0000
APT. 12-B CHICAGO, IL 00000 Fax: (000) 000-0000

Informally

RICK SONDHEIM
FORMERLY OF "ROCKLAND"
HAS OPENED HIS OWN RESTAURANT
"FOOTLIGHTS"
AND GIVES A SPECIAL WELCOME TO FRIENDS
345 Mohegan Avenue
Providence, RI
Tel: (000) 000-0000
Fax: (000) 000-0000

A Simple Announcement of a Merger

THE MERGER
OF TURNER REAL ESTATE
AND
BRENT PROPERTIES
HAS BEEN FINALIZED
THE COMPANY WILL NOW BE KNOWN AS
TURNER-BRENT PROPERTIES, INC.
1415 LAKESIDE
UTICA, NEW YORK 00000
Tel: (000) 000-0000
Fax: (000) 000-0000

A Complicated Announcement of a Merger

When two companies such as two law firms, merge, all four sides of a double-fold announcement are used.

Side one (the cover):	The announcement of the two firms having merged, the date of the merger, and the new name of the firm
Side two (left inside cover):	The name and address of one of the merging firms, the year it was founded; the number of lawyers "engaged in the general practice of domestic and international law"; the list of law specialties (such as "corporate," "labor," "banking," "real estate," etc.)
Side three (right-hand inside page):	The same information as on side two, but for the other firm involved in the merger
Side four (backside of announcement):	A list of the members of both firms and of the "of counsel" lawyers for both locations if two offices will be retained

9

Dressing for Business

It's sad, but it's a fact of life. No matter how talented a person may be, a man can show up at a black-tie industry dinner wearing a red damask dinner jacket and ruin his future with his company; a woman executive can do the same thing to herself if she shows up at a corporate meeting dressed in inappropriate frills and flounces, looking like a figure on a wedding cake. Clothes "may make the man," but they make the woman, too—or they may unmake them. There's equality between the sexes in the seriousness of business apparel blunders.

If you are a young person starting a new job, you may have to take out a loan to invest in the appropriate wardrobe. It's worth it. First, look around your new offices. Notice every element of how people dress. Ask questions. Take notes and be extra observant.

Two members of the audience at one of my business manners workshop groups let me have their on-site notes. One woman wrote: "The women here wear low heels—no one in high heels. Guess they're sensible because of the length of corridors around here. No long earrings, no glitter . . . Lots of scarves . . . Big handbags—guess they stuff them with important papers. Skirts are worn at the knee . . . As many dresses as skirts and tops. Hardly any suits . . . those I've seen have soft shoulders, soft silhouettes . . . Hardly any severely tailored items . . . No pants here . . . lots of long tunic jackets, printed silk skirts."

The young man's list read, "Lots of white shirts . . . Must ask if pastels are "out" around here . . . Ties are wide but run gamut in designs, some pretty wild. Must ask about that, too . . . Dark blue, light gray or dark gray suits mostly, but better-dressed brass seem to like faint striped and herringbone patterns . . . Everything understated . . . Fringed loafers everywhere, mostly dark brown . . . Some tassled loafers, some old-fashioned wingtips . . . No argyle-patterned socks—very *conservative navy, gray, or black lisle socks everywhere . . . Big brass wears shirts with French cuffs and cufflinks, but the rest don't . . . On Fridays sports jackets allowed, thank God. Some are conservative brown tweeds, some pretty wild patterns in muted colors . . . Asked about bow ties, told not even to try for a year—the old man doesn't like them."*

WHEN YOU'RE BUYING CLOTHES FOR THE OFFICE, ASK YOURSELF SOME QUESTIONS

To most people, the way employees look at work sends a very powerful message about the company itself (*see also* "The Importance of Proper Dress When Doing Business Abroad," Chapter 10). Before you buy something to wear on your job, ask yourself these questions:

- Is this appropriate for the kind of job I have?
- Is it a fad or will it hold up as a basic fashion idea for two or more seasons?
- Can I afford it?
- Does it fit properly? Is it okay for my kind of figure (or physique)?
- Is it *comfortable*?
- Is it the right thing to wear *this* season, in *this* climate?
- Is the fabric of really good quality?

WHO CAN HELP YOU?

- The best advice comes from someone in your office, in your line of work, who has a good eye, dresses well himself or herself, and is generally regarded by everyone as someone with excellent taste. Perhaps you can get that person to go shopping with you; arrange as payment to barter a service he or she may want from you. (Lunch in an excellent restaurant might do it.)
- Consult the fashion magazines like *Gentlemen's Quarterly* and *Esquire* for men and *Vogue* and *Glamour* for women. Read these magazines with selective caution. They are, after all, reporting advanced, extreme fashion to amuse and shock, as well as basic, good fashion to help you know what to wear to the office.
- Consult the fashion directors and personal shoppers at the department or specialty stores where you shop. Deal with them openly and honestly; say, "I don't have enough money to make a mistake. I must buy just the right look for my office. Is this too *avant garde*?" Or "Does this make me look fat?" Or "In your opinion is this too gaudy for the workplace?"

- There are freelance fashion, wardrobe, and image consultants (found by word of mouth or through the Yellow Pages). They charge by the hour—or by half-day— and will take you to all the right stores to guide you on your purchases (and they often help you buy at discount).

TO REMEMBER

- Some fashions are not meant to be followed, even if touted as the latest look by a fashion magazine—if they are ludicrous and unsuitable for your lifestyle. (Examples: a see-through black chiffon dress with no underwear; or a man's suit with wildly exaggerated shoulder pads.)
- Never dress in clothes that are too tight. They make a thin person look gaunt and a large person twice as heavy.
- A man should never wear short socks to the office. They are disastrously short if, when he sits down, his bare leg shows between the top of his socks and the bottom of his trousers. He should wear socks to the knee, or at least up over the calf.
- In summer a woman with bare legs and painted toes in the office is asking to be considered as someone who is not really serious about her career. A man who does not wear socks with his loafers in summer looks fine in his leisure moments, but not in the office. I will never forget Henry Luce's conversation with one of his Time-Life reporters one summer when the young man showed up wearing loafers but no socks to the office in Rome. It went as follows:

    "You may need money to buy soap to wash your socks. Or maybe you need money to buy socks. Whatever the problem, I'll sign the authorization to give you the money to solve it!"
- One should never be phony. If you're not from ranch country in the West or Southwest, it's better to stay away from the affectations of a Stetson, cowboy boots, a fake or purchased rodeo prize buckle, and a string tie.
- In a non-Southern climate, after Labor Day, it's time to put away your white shoes and accessories until the following Memorial Day.
- If you wear a double-breasted suit jacket, keep it buttoned. It looks awkward hanging open, like a gate that needs closing.
- If you work for a conservative company and have removed your suit jacket to be comfortable in your own office but are called into a senior executive's office, put your jacket on again. It's a mark of politeness and deference that is appreciated by the person you have come to see.

A MALE EXECUTIVE'S WARDROBE
IN A CONSERVATIVE OFFICE

A man who is seriously launched into a career in a conservative business (the law, finance, insurance, banking) and who works in a large city and travels a lot—particularly to foreign countries—needs a lot of clothes and the right clothes. The following is a suggested wardrobe that can be added to as time goes on and as the executive's income allows:

- 3 winter suits (perhaps a dark blue or pinstripe, a dark gray flannel, and a conservative glen plaid pattern)
- 3 summer suits (perhaps a tan and a navy poplin, and a lightweight dark worsted suit). In a very hot climate, he would need fewer winter suits and more lightweight ones, including something like a seersucker suit.
- 1 lightweight navy blazer, to be worn in any climate
- 1 tweed sports jacket
- 2 pairs of odd trousers, one of which would be gray flannel
- 3 pairs of casual trousers (jeans, chinos, corduroys)
- 3 pullover sweaters
- 12 pairs daytime socks (long length, please) plus 4 pairs athletic socks
- 1 topcoat or overcoat, depending on the climate
- 1 raincoat
- 12 business dress shirts (Buy shirts that are the fashion, whether button-down or with plain pointed collars; if you want to try a natty look, buy some shirts that are patterned or solid-colored with contrasting white collars and cuffs.)
- 8 sports shirts (polo, for example)
- 12 ties
- 3 belts or suspenders
- 2 pairs good-quality daytime shoes (brown and black)
- 2 pairs casual shoes (moccasins, loafers, boat shoes)
- 1 pair athletic shoes (2 pairs if he's a serious athlete)
- 2 pairs winter-weight pajamas; 2 pairs summer-weight pajamas
- 14 sets of underwear (be prepared to use two sets per day if evening activities are involved).
- 1 dressing gown and pair of bedroom slippers for travel
- Action sports clothes for special sports (jogging, tennis, skiing, etc.)
- Sweat pants and top
- Hiking, work, or snow boots (if necessary)

Attending Black-Tie Events

- 1 lightweight all-black dinner suit
- 2 white (plain or pleated, *not* ruffled) evening dress shirts
- 1 black bow tie
- 1 pair black suspenders or braces
- 1 pair evening shoes (either lace-up black patent, or patent pumps with grosgrain bows or shiny black loafers worn with thin black dress socks)
- 1 pair cufflinks for your dress shirt (studs can come later)

Your Suits

- It's far better to buy fewer suits but of a higher quality fabric and fit, because they will always look good.
- Remember to get suits altered every time your body perceptibly changes in size.
- Follow the style of the moment (whether it's double, single-breasted, or no vents on the back of the jacket; pleated or unpleated trousers; tailored shoulder or soft shoulder construction), but don't worry if you are not totally of the moment. Watch your jacket lapels, however. If wide lapels have been back in fashion for five years and you're still wearing narrow ones, consider investing in some new suits, or consider having a tailor narrow the lapels.
- If you are not slim, you are better off in dark solid suits, rather than bold patterns and conspicuous colors. Also, a single-breasted suit is much more slimming to the figure than a double-breasted one.
- Your suits will last longer and hang better on you if you hang them up on a heavy hanger—or put your pants in a pants presser—after brushing the suit every night.

Your Ties and Shirts

- Make sure they are spotless (watch stains from salad dressing, soup, and pasta sauce in particular).
- If you are a large or tall man, buy ties that are extra long (available in big men's stores).
- If all your ties are narrow and wide ties are suddenly in, buy some new wide ties, but pack your narrow ties in tissue paper and lay them away in a box; they will come back in style.
- If all your ties are wide, and narrow ones are "in," you can have your ties cut down to the fashionable narrow width.
- Never buy a tie without the suit and the shirt you will wear it with in mind. These three items of clothing shuld be color- and pattern-coordinated. If you are unsure of your color sense, find a savvy salesman to help you mix and match your purchases deftly.
- *Know who you are.* Flashy, loud patterns on ties may be in, but if you're not that kind of person, don't try to buy them. Stick to the tried and true stripes and small patterns. A mauve shirt with a solid deep lavender silk tie may look great on one of your colleagues who happens to be wearing a vanilla-colored poplin summer suit, but that same shirt-and-tie combination might look ludicrous on you (unless you're prepared to run out and buy a vanilla-colored poplin summer suit, too!). Also, when it comes to mixing patterns—for instance, a striped shirt with a differently striped tie and a houndstooth-patterned suit—be certain you're doing it correctly and tastefully. (My husband, for example, has an innate feel for pattern

and color mixing; when our son tries it, he becomes a walking fashion disaster, proving that this kind of taste is not genetic.)

- *Caveat on the subject of your undershirt*: If you are ever going to open the top button of your shirt and leave your collar open, don't wear a high neck T-shirt that will show beneath your open shirt. (Open collar plus underwear plus chest hair showing is not sexy, only sloppy!)
- On the subject of your *frayed shirt collars and cuffs*: They are a real turn-off. Have someone who knows how to sew turn them inside out; otherwise, you would do well to reduce your entertainment budget and spend the money on some new shirts.
- A navy, dark brown, dark green, or black shirt—particularly when worn without a tie—belongs in the creative world, not in the financial or business world.
- The shirt cuff should extend about an inch below the sleeve of the jacket.
- The fit of your shirt at the neck is most important; it should be snug but not choke you.
- Don't wear short-sleeved dress shirts—to many people they are tacky. You can always roll up your sleeves when you remove your jacket in the summer.

Your Shoes

- An executive's feet are always in view at some point, so shoes should be of good quality, well shined, in good condition, and preferably conservative in style.
- Shoes should be brushed and polished daily, with shoe trees put in them at night, to keep their shapes.
- Shoes should be resoled and reheeled regularly.
- Conservative shoes may be:

  - Black or brown
  - Laced oxfords
  - Wing tips
  - Cap toes
  - Leather loafers
  - Other types of leather slip-ons

- Colored leather shoes or half-boot shoes on young executives in a conservative office cause considerable wincing among senior managers.

Your Socks

Here are some combination suggestions:

COLOR OF SOCKS	APPROPRIATELY WORN WITH
White	White suits in summer
White sweat socks	Athletic shoes, boat shoes and loafers in leisure activities
Black, navy, or dark gray	Business suits
Brown	Brown or khaki suits
Pastels	Summer suits of poplin, khaki, and seersucker (for sharp dressers)
Bright colored and argyle	Blazer or sports jacket with gray flannels, or with corduroys or khakis for leisure wear only
Black sheer	Black-tie suits

HATS AND CAPS

Until 1960, a man's hat was an integral part of his attire (just look at newspaper photos of crowds in street scenes), and a woman's hat was an integral part of her fashion scheme. She would buy several each year. The great women hat designers were the queen bees of the fashion world.

A woman kept her hat on when she went to a restaurant, to church, shopping, the movies, and cocktail parties, and often she kept it on in a friend's home if she went there for lunch or to play bridge.

President and Mrs. John F. Kennedy probably did more for the destruction of the vogue of wearing hats than any other single factor. The President stopped wearing them from the day of his Inauguration, and Jackie Kennedy wore a hat only for the most formal of state visit arrivals and departures. The world copied the handsome young couple, and ever since, the bareheaded look has been a symbol of youth and high fashion. The glorious-looking top hat for the well-dressed man going to a formal party is gone too; white tie and tails are as rare as Viennese waltzes in America.

The baseball cap with its visor is now worn everywhere by some men. But it is not yet acceptable when worn in conservative places of business.

If men knew how handsome they looked in the old-fashioned felt fedoras, they might bring them back into style for winter wear. Today you see some fur hats, tweed caps, and wool helmets that protect male heads from the cold; they serve no esthetic purpose, but give protection from the elements.

The only point of hat etiquette for a man today is that he is supposed to remove his hat in restaurants, theaters, churches, and people's homes. The romance of a man's doffing his hat with a flourish is gone—probably forever.

Women's Hats

Hats go in and out of vogue with women for these reasons:

- Some women look simply wonderful in hats, and they know it.
- The right hat can "finish" a woman's costume perfectly.
- A hat can cover her hair (and disguise the fact that she missed an appointment with the hairdresser).
- A hat shades the sensitive skin of her face from the sun.

A woman would be wise to own a classic hat, like a beret, which never goes out of style but which helps with hair problems and adds a flourish to her costume.

A woman does not keep her hat on in her own office, but if she visits someone else's office (outside of her own place of business) she would keep it on throughout the entire meeting if she wishes.

Summer Straw and Cloth Hats for Men and Women

In warm climates through the years both men and women in cities have worn— and continue to wear—unisex Panama hats and straw boaters. (Women sport wide-brimmed straw beach styles as well.) These are often enlivened with variations of colored hatbands (or printed scarves used as hatbands by the women).

Growing more common are floppy-brimmed colored canvas hats, formerly worn only by boating aficionados and tennis players as sun shields. They look great for the world of sports, but are inappropriate for the office.

FASHION AND THE WOMAN EXECUTIVE

When women entered the executive ranks with a vengeance in the 1970s, they seemed to think they had to dress in as masculine a way as possible, in order to command the attention and respect of their male colleagues.

They soon found out otherwise. The severely man-tailored navy or black suit or pantsuit, worn with a man's white shirt and a necktie, scarf, or string tie, did not make their male colleagues comfortable—just the opposite. By 1980, bright-colored blouses, soft-shouldered suits, dresses, and skirts with coordinating tops came into fashion in the workplace.

The executive woman should keep the following in mind when shopping for herself in a conservative workplace.

- *Buy with quality—not quantity—in mind.* Good fabrics are essential.
- *Accessories are all-important.* Shoes, handbag, jewelry, hosiery, scarf—everything a woman executive adds to her basic dress or suit is integral to the general impression she gives.
- She should know what colors look good on her and buy those, whenever possible. She should know which colors clash.
- She should move around and sit down in front of a full-length mirror whenever she tries on garments, so that she can see what happens to the skirt when she moves or sits.
- *She should follow fashion, but not blindly.* If the magazines are touting something only a young, pencil-slim model can wear, she should take along a frank friend, who will steer her away from something that looks really bad on her. If she doesn't have such a friend, she should ask a store fashion consultant to square with her and edit her selection with honesty.

A Woman Executive and Her Decolletage

A woman may run around her house topless, wearing only a bikini bottom, and it's no one's business but her own. The amount of skin she displays in the office and at business-social events is another matter. Whether she's at a corporate party at a staid bank or at the industry convention in Las Vegas, modesty in dressing should be as important to her as the contents of her briefcase.

This means that she wears her little black dress cut high enough not to show cleavage, that she wears a dress that is not Marilyn Monroe–tight or with a hemline that does not rise to the crotch when she sits down in it. She should want to be as attractive as it is possible for her to be, with a unified look: Her hair, makeup, jewelry, and clothes should blend—nothing distracting, but everything refined, understated, perfect.

A Woman Executive in Shorts, Culottes, and Pants

Women who have the bodies for shorts look great in long walking shorts, but personally, I feel that if they look that good in walking shorts in the office, they would look that much better in a skirt.

Well-cut culottes—the divided skirt—are very appropriate for business. Well-cut pants in a good fabric are appropriate, provided, again in my personal opinion, that the woman who wears them is slim. When a woman has well-padded hips and thighs, the flesh obviously spreads on the chair when she sits down in slim pants, and she looks far heavier than she actually is. A loose A-line or pleated skirt masks much of that excess flesh.

When women complain that they don't like to be dictated to, that they are free to wear what they please, I say yes, that is all true. I am simply stating a philosophy, after almost half a century of observation in the workplace, that a woman *and* a man are perceived of favorably by everyone with whom they work when they make themselves as attractive-looking as they can.

I remember overhearing a top American diplomat describing a French businesswoman one night: "She looked terrific, she smelled so good, and she was in a plain black cover-up dress. All you saw was her face. Mysterious. Chic, sexy. Everyone in the room wanted to talk to her."

Suggestions for a Woman Executive's Wardrobe

- 3 daytime suits
- 4 dresses (alternatively skirts with coordinated tops, making "costumes")
- 2 pantsuits (optional)
- 1 "little black dress," classic in style, to wear to evening functions (cocktail parties and restaurant dinners, for example). This kind of dress changes its look with gold jewelry, sparkling jewelry, or scarves
- 4 blouses in different colors and patterns, to coordinate with the suits
- 2 sporty skirts
- 3 fine quality pullover sweaters, including 1 cardigan
- 1 winter coat
- 1 lightweight coat
- 1 raincoat
- 4 scarves
- 2 daytime handbags (black plus brown or navy) big enough to hold everything
- 1 small dressy bag (to wear to evening functions)
- 3 pairs shoes for office (two low-heeled, one mid-heeled)
- 1 pair dressy shoes for evening (higher heels, perhaps—pumps or sandals in suede, peau de soie, or satin)
- 1 pair athletic shoes
- 3 pairs athletic socks
- Shoes and clothing for sports
- 2 bathing suits
- Sweats
- 3 pairs summer slacks
- 2 pairs winter slacks
- 1 pair rain/snow boots
- 10 pairs pantyhose
- 4 bras; 2 athletic bras
- 8 pairs of panties
- 4 nightgowns or pairs of pajamas
- 1 dressing gown
- 1 pair bedroom slippers

Attending Black-Tie Events

A man's evening uniform is set in stone. A woman has to make many more choices.

- *If it's a "Black Tie Optional" party* (a terrible custom in our society; but check the invitation), she should wear a short dress or evening suit of a dressy fabric (silk, crepe, brocade), or she can get away with a silk dress that she wears with a jacket also made of a dressy material, such as silk or satin. She can add a pair of glittery earrings, and she's all set.
- *If it's a "Dinner Dance" or "Dinner with Dancing,"* she would feel better in a long dress. The two looks to stay far away from in any case for an evening of dancing are:

  - *The Scarlett O'Hara look*, with long white gloves (a no-no in business) and a huge bouffant skirt puffed out by many petticoats, or (horrors!) by a hoop under the skirt. I remember the advice of my old boss, Ambassador Clare Boothe Luce, when she answered a young woman's question about what to buy for an evening dress, "Just remember to buy a dress that does not take up too much room. You should *always* be able to seat three in the back seat of a New York cab."
  - *The "sultry vixen" look,* which is a dress so low cut a man doesn't have to fantasize what your bosom looks like—he can see it! This kind of dress is guaranteed to destroy any attempts at the kind of conversation you would want to have with management to advance your career. When a woman is an exhibitionist with her body at a business event, she is either stupid or is consciously trying to sabotage her career.

    Evening accessories are important for black-tie events. The well-dressed woman has the following, which are easy to pack and take with her to business meetings in other cities:

    - A long silk crepe sheath (wearable in warm or cold climes)
    - A silk, crepe, or satin jacket
    - A pair of black satin pumps, or sandals
    - A small dressy black satin bag
    - Jewelry—pearls and glitter earrings, or a glittery necklace with a pair of small earrings, or a pair of small earrings with a pair of glitter bracelets (in other words, two items of jewelry are enough, and please leave your watch with its leather wristband at home)

Accessories

- *If your legs aren't great*, don't draw attention to them with hosiery that is patterned or in wild colors. Neutral tones are best.

- *Shoes and handbags should coordinate* (i.e., black bag with black shoes, navy with navy, etc.). Women who travel a great deal learn to carry only black accessories with them, so that packing is easier and luggage is lighter to carry.
- *Any jewelry is wrong* if it distracts from a woman's professionalism (too big, too noisy, too sparkling). The clanking of a woman's dripping earrings against her cheeks as she moves her head completely destroys the concentration of others doing business with her. (Also, some women don't seem to understand that sequins and rhinestones are for evening, not for sunlight hours.)

  A woman should never wear too much at one time. Her watch, two rings, and either a bracelet or a brooch or a necklace are enough adornment for the office.
- *Handbags are very important.*

  ○ They should be polished, clean, unscruffy. (Do whatever needs doing, whether it's saddle-soaping leather, polishing brass handles or chains, brushing suede, etc.)
  ○ They should never be left on tables (whether it's in the conference room or on the table in a restaurant).
  ○ They should be roomy, to accomplish their task; i.e., storing the plethora of equipment that needs to be carried. Consequently, the interior should be cleaned out often (particularly straggly paper tissues and ticket stubs), and items should be properly stored inside in their special places, so that a woman "will not have to keep grappling and foraging in her bag like a frenzied animal for whatever she needs."*

- *Running shoes* should *not* be worn in the office, even if you're a candidate for the local marathon. Carry your regular shoes to the office if you're walking in your athletic shoes.
- *Head scarves* to hide hair that has been put up in pincurls or rollers are a no-no!

Makeup

The cliche "Less is more" certainly holds true concerning makeup in today's environment. A business woman's makeup is perfect if those around her are unaware she has applied it. In other words, it should be blended and harmonious, with nothing exaggerated or conspicuous.

The makeup disasters that upset people the most are:

- Long flashy-colored fingernails (how about the woman who paints each nail a different color?)
- False eyelashes

---

*This is how I have been described, vis-à-vis my handbag.

- Too much mascara
- Eye shadow (should only be applied in the evening)

A woman's makeup in the office need consist of nothing more than:

- A moisturizer
- A foundation that matches her skin tone
- Powder
- Blusher
- A thin eyeliner (and light application of mascara, if she wears it)
- Lipstick (negative on purple, blackish tones)

Makeup Application Etiquette

It's the kiss of death for a woman to apply makeup in front of business colleagues of either sex. She should repair to the ladies' room for this. Makeup should *never* be applied in the office, in a restaurant, or even in a car in the presence of other business colleagues.

Fragrance

People around you should hardly be aware of your fragrance. I remember a famous Parisienne, Mary Louise Bousquet, telling me when I was twenty-one and on my first job at the American Embassy in Paris, "Teesh," she said through the haze of the smoke from her gold Cartier cigarette holder, "zees perfume, it is too much." Then she proceeded to tell me I was wearing enough of Guerlain's L'Heure Bleue to take care of a freight train. "You must be *subtile*," she emphasized, "so zat zee men around you want you to be near them, and they don't quite know why."

It was a good enough explanation for me. I have used the strong perfume sparingly ever since.

Remember to:

- *Buy good perfume and cologne.* The cheap stuff is as offensive as a cheap cigar.
- *Apply it in private.* It's as personal as getting dressed, and should not be done in public.
- *Be careful in applying it,* so as not to cause a rash on ultra-sensitive, allergic skin and so as not to damage the delicate fabric of your clothing.

CASUAL DRESS, OR "CASUAL DAY"

In my original *Guide to Executive Manners,* the discussion of casual dress applied only to what a man or woman executive would wear at a resort or on a country weekend or at informal meetings at a sales conference.

Today, the concept of dressing casually (also aptly referred to as "dressing down") has advanced swiftly in many parts of the business world. But not everywhere. The financial world is still conservative in its dress code. When people entrust their money to an institution or company, they want those employees to reek of old-fashioned values and conservatism. Some of the old-line law firms have allowed casual dressing in their offices only to the extent that lawyers may now travel through the corridor outside their office in shirtsleeves, instead of having to don their jackets the second they peer from behind their closed doors.

Many companies have begun the trend of casual dressing by adopting Fridays as dress-down days. Corporations like Alcoa and Ameritech have gone further, and since 1992 have allowed their people to dress casually every day of the week. A basically conservative corporation like Pittsburgh Plate Glass stepped gingerly into the situation in 1992 by allowing its employees to dress casually as a special celebration. For example, in honor or "Worldwide Quality Day," employees were told they were having a "casual day."

It's a Question of Good Judgment

In the casual environment, executives who will be meeting conservative customers and clients should have enough judgment to know how to dress on that particular day — hopefully in a business suit or dress. They should know that if they are spending two days in another city working on a set where a commercial is being filmed, they don't have to abandon their jeans, T-shirts, sweaters, and running shoes, but that if they are meeting new corporate clients at their headquarters, the men should wear their best tailored suits, and the women, dresses with jackets. Executives are supposed to have enough sense to know that when they are going to receive distinguished clients on a certain day, they should go to their offices dressed in formal day business attire (suits and dresses), or at least be able to change into that attire.

Today architects and interior designers are faced with the problem of including bigger closets in their plans for offices today. Until the 1980s, only an occasional coat closet for employee apparel was necessary; today they must plan for areas to accommodate workout suits, changes of underwear, footwear, toiletries, hanging business suits and dresses, and numerous overstuffed gym bags. One senior manager told me that a lot of time is lost because too often an executive brings to the office a business suit (and accessories) to change into for an important appointment downtown in the afternoon, but then realizes he has forgotten to pack something like the proper shoes. Much valuable time can be wasted in the search for the errant item.

The Psychology of Dressing Down

Part of the psychology behind the corporate philosophy toward casual dressing is that it's more democratic. Some companies make their men and women employees wear identical shirts with the company logo on one side and the person's name tag on the other. In these instances, the uniform is the same for the CEO as for the messenger and is reminiscent of Chairman Mao's dictates several decades ago on the stern fashion of identical pantsuits to be worn by men and women in the People's Republic of China. Many senior managers look upon casual dressing as a low-risk morale booster and a perceived employee benefit.

There are many people, including me, on the other side of this question who feel that leaders should dress like leaders and should be people whom others look up to and aspire to emulate.

Dressing Casually but Properly

There is a certain amount of propriety involved in casual dressing. This kind of attire and good grooming go hand in hand. When all your comfortable items of clothing are not sparkling clean, the visual result can be very negative. Dressing casually in *most* offices does *not* mean that the following are acceptable:

- Jeans with holes in the knees
- Dirty jeans or slacks of any kind
- Soiled, torn sneakers (some large companies will not permit sneakers, running, or basketball shoes at all)
- Scruffy moccasins or boat shoes worn down at the heels
- Loafers or any kind of leather footwear that have not seen the benefits of a polishing kit for a long time
- Bare feet (especially those with dirty toenails) in sandals
- Athletic shoes with cleats (wrecks the floor covering)
- Dirty socks or ones with holes
- A T-shirt that really is an undershirt or a T-shirt with artwork and a printed message advocating sex, violence, or racism
- A halter top or bare midriff on women
- Camouflage or any kind of combat military surplus apparel
- Baseball cap or any other kind of hat, except as noted elsewhere in this chapter.
- Aberrations or mockery of formal business attire, such as suspenders, a tie with a T-shirt, or a business suit worn with athletic shoes.
- Sweat suits
- Shorts

The Well-Dressed Casual Look for Men

These are the elements that create this look:

- A jacket (or cardigan sweater) worn with trousers or pants that coordinate in some way, even if the coordination is a strong color contrast

- A polo or sports shirt, long- or short-sleeved
- A regular business shirt, open at the neck
- A sweater—turtle neck, crew neck, or V-neck
- Polished loafers or docksiders in good condition

One thirty-five-year-old management consultant I know works for a dress-casual company. He always appears dressed in something like gray flannel trousers, highly polished dark brown brogues, a wonderful tweed sports jacket, pastel-colored shirt, necktie, and coordinating silk handkerchief in his left breast pocket. He receives a lot of kidding from his colleagues, but they look on him with admiration and have always referred to him as "the well-dressed member of the staff."

GROOMING

No matter how much money your clothes cost, an omission or error in grooming can sabotage the entire effect. If you have trouble paying attention to small details, post a grooming checklist in your home, somewhere such as on the bathroom mirror. Before you leave home in the morning, run down the list and check yourself, point by point, so that when people see you, they will see nothing out of place—nothing to harm the overall harmonious effect.

HEAD-TO-TOE MORNING GROOMING CHECKLIST

	For a Man	For a Woman	For Men and Women

Head	Well-shaven
	After-shave applied
	Beard and/or mustache
	  well trimmed
		Makeup carefully applied
		Eyebrows plucked
		Jewelry polished and
		  clean
		If wearing a scarf, it is
		  unspotted and
		  pressed
			Hair well brushed, well
			  combed, well cut,
			  clean
			Face well washed
			Ears clean
			Neck washed

Body	Clean shirt
	Collar and cuffs checked
	  for fraying
	Spotless well-tied tie
		Fragrance applied spar-
		  ingly
		No makeup smears on
		  clothing
		Slip does not show
			Body well washed
			Deodorant applied
			Underwear fresh
			Clothes spot-free and
			  well pressed
			No buttons missing
			Clean handkerchief
			Check for dandruff
			  "fallout"

	For a Man	For a Woman	For Men and Women
Hands		Nail polish in perfect condition Hand lotion applied	Hands washed Nails clean and in good shape Rings clean and free from soap film Watchband in good shape
Legs and Feet	Clean socks pulled up high Laces on shoes or tassels on loafers in good shape	Pantyhose run-free If seamed, seams are straight	Shoes well-polished and free of scuff marks Shoe heels in good condition
Handbag and/or Briefcase			Leather clean and polished Hardware polished
Gloves			Clean

HAIR

When someone looks at you, one of the first things they notice is your hair. Your hairstyle can be in fashion without being flamboyant. A man with long hair looks as though he is fighting the establishment instead of working for it.

Beards and mustaches come and go in fashion. Many senior exectives do not like them but suffer in silence over their middle managers' tonsorial peculiarities. There is something nicely nondistracting about the direct gaze of a man who is clean-shaven and whose facial characteristics are clearly visible instead of being hidden by hair. Again, it is important to distinguish between a creative or intellectual environment, such as teaching and writing (in which an abundance of facial hair is fashionable), and a conservative business environment (in which facial hair is considered distracting).

A woman with long straight hair down her back, "flower child" style, may give the impression she is clinging obsessively to her youth. A woman who frizzes her hair all over and wears it "tangled jungle vines" style may look to others like an over-size scouring pad. A woman who teases her hair to the maximum should realize that the style is passé and improper for the office. A woman should be remembered for what is *inside* her head, not what is growing on top of it!

Here are some other hair grooming points for women to consider:

- *Keep your hair neatly combed or brushed at all times,* but don't fix it in front of others and certainly never ever in a restaurant.
- Don't overdose your colleagues with the fumes from your hairspray.
- Make an unbreakable promise to yourself *never* to be seen in public in hair curlers.
- *Keep your hands off your hair.* Constantly stroking the ends of your hair or pushing it back from your face are nervous, very distracting habits. It is particularly important not to touch your hair in a restaurant. I will never forget lunching with a lawyer in a restaurant in full view of a young woman constantly combing through her long hair with her fingers. The lawyer mentioned that there was something unappetizingly analogous between what she was doing and what he was trying to do, eat his way through a plate of thin spaghetti with a fork.

Dyeing Your Hair

- It is very rude to ask someone if he or she dyes his or her hair. It's too personal a question. (Most people in the business world who do it do so because they think looking young is essential to succeed.)
- If you yourself are young, without gray hair, and you decide to dye your hair a memorable color (such as when a brunette goes to white-blond with Madonna-like speed), get ready to be talked about. It's your right to dye your hair overnight any color you please, but be prepared for criticism of your choice, simply because anything conspicuous and distracting takes others' minds off what you *do* and directs it toward how you *look*. If you do anything very gradually, even turn your hair to a shade of fuschia-orange, people will eventually be able to adjust to it.

    A bad grooming error: The person who dyes his or her hair a completely different color but goes around with the strongly contrasting roots showing all the time.

Wigs and Hairpieces

- It is also rude to ask a person if he or she is wearing a hairpiece, toupee, or wig. Many people who wear these are embarrassed, possibly even suffering from a physical ailment, so the right thing to do is not to mention this.
- If a man who wears a toupee were to do a little market study among his friends and associates, he would probably find that people much prefer him without it rather than with it. In any case, he should never invest in a cheap one, or one that is not dyed to match his own hair, for such a hairpiece is very unsettling to the beholder, who usually remains mesmerized by it.
- A woman executive who wears a wig for whatever reason would be wise to select one for work that is in a conservative style and of a color most like her own.

Through the years in the workplace, I have noticed how important the way a person dresses is to his or her career. But fashion should not consume us. It should enhance us, not distract us from the real purpose of our jobs: to do the best we can, to be happy, and not incidentally, to make money for the company and ourselves.

A wonderful old salt of a CEO, who worked well into his late seventies running his corporation, said in answer to a fashion question from a *Women's Wear Daily* reporter, "Hell, I couldn't care less how my executives dress—as long as they've found a good dry cleaner, use a good deodorant, and put their shoes back on before they remove their feet from under the table."

10

Doing International Business—Profitably and Politely

$\mathbf{I}$f you are a young executive beginning your career, you will very possibly make some trips abroad on business, and you will even more possibly be responsible for hosting and assisting foreign colleagues who come to this country on business. Whether you're dealing with someone from another country on his turf or on yours, the same principle applies: If one of you makes an obvious effort to be accommodating, sympathetic, and kind, business will transpire, deals will be made, and profits and goals will be realized.

An American tourist abroad is very conspicuous, because our country is one of the richest as well as one of the youngest in the world, and because television has brought knowledge of our purported lifestyles to every corner of the globe ("purported" because the soaps and talk shows hardly portray American life as it really is). An American on business abroad is even more conspicuous. He or she is on duty, so to speak, in the service of business, and every step is analyzed by the visitor's host, every movement is fraught with seeming negotiating significance. When an American tourist makes a scene in the hotel lobby over the inadequacy of his accomodations, he is the center of everyone's focus; when an American businessperson makes a scene at the conference table, his foreign counterparts are usually shocked, ready to believe the worst, and quite unforgiving.

Many of us approach our travels abroad with the idea that we are very nice people (true) and that we should measure other people's niceness using ourselves

229

as the standard (not necessarily true). The main lesson I learned after years of living, traveling, and working overseas is that people everywhere are basically likable—if you have a mindset to like them. When moving to another country to live and work, tell yourself you will like the people, you will learn the language, and you will enjoy everything the country offers—and you will.

Even if you generalize that the inhabitants of some countries are more fun loving and good humored or more open and frank or more amenable to compromise than others, the individuals whom you will come to know (more than from just a vantage point across a negotiating table) are for the most part nice human beings. They are, like you, anxious to please and to succeed in your mutual business mission, and in the best possible atmosphere. They share your desire to make some money and would enjoy establishing firm friendships with you and your company as much as you would with them. Internationals want you to trust them, and they do not welcome any subterfuge that would make you appear untrustworthy. Once you have scaled the sometimes lofty heights of cold, stiff formality that may mark the beginning of a relationship between strangers from different cultures and experiences, the enjoyment of sharing common ground—of finding interests and feelings in common—is really invigorating.

You suddenly feel very different from when you were working back home at the office. You are having a good time, laughing, analyzing, arguing, and building for the future with people who are totally different, who even speak another tongue. Yet you are agreeing on matters and planning for the future together. Even when you disagree with one another, as long as there is respect and trust, rejection is never final and lasting. It's exhilarating to be able to say to American colleagues, when an international business person's name is mentioned, "Hans? He's a great guy. He's a real friend." "Yuko? She's terrific, one of the smartest women in Japan. I know her well."

It is quite wondrous to see how CNN has helped to bring this world together. Before the advent of international news unfolding live in homes, pubs, airports, hotel lobbies, and sports bars abroad, people would ask those Americans who were living in their country endless questions about American politics and our system of government. Now they can watch the President's press conferences, the hearings on the Hill and the United Nations sessions, and often they are better informed than the visiting American in their country.

If only we were as well informed about other countries' governments and mores as they are about ours. Our instruction on history and geography lags behind most of the countries of the world. It is another responsibility of business in America to upgrade teaching in these fields, so that we will perform better as global citizens in other markets.

Hopefully this chapter will make executives aware of the kind of homework they should do when they either go abroad to do business, live abroad to work for their companies, or receive international colleagues who come on business trips to the United States. It would take another volume as large as this to tell you everything you need to know about working in another country, so what you are getting here is a snapshot of the differences you will encounter, and how to handle them, in traveling abroad. A manager dealing with a foreign country should research the daily life, customs, and modus operandi of those areas thoroughly before traveling to them.

Once again, the key is the spirit of giving, not just taking, mentioned in so many other places in this book. The person who makes the effort wins. It's that simple.

The head of a company that does a great deal of work with the French told me he had just fired one of his brightest young managers, because the young executive could not accept the fact that his managerial style did not work in Europe. He recounted how early one Monday morning the young manager found a sales report from the office in Lyons on his desk, which reported much lower sales for the previous month. The American fired off an immediate fax, bristling with disappointment and anger, using clipped phrases such as "Those sales figures entirely unacceptable." Everyone in the Lyons operation was harshly castigated in the fax, which caused backlash in the French office. There was a good explanation for the sales drop.

The head of the French office had said in his report, "Jim, I will explain in detail the reasons for the drop on Monday morning when I reach you on the telephone." The American manager had not given his French colleague a chance to explain the one-time loss taken in closing a plant that was no longer cost-efficient. Jim's boss said, "Jim should have called Armand and begun the conversation with, "We haven't talked in a long time. How was your weekend? How's Denise?" Then, with both people having begun the conversation for sixty seconds in a pleasant way, Jim could have said, "Can you explain the sales report I found on my desk this morning, Armand? It looks pretty bad." The explanation would then have been offered, as well as a constructive criticism from the American side about Armand's manner of reporting the loss. Business would then have continued to proceed productively on both sides of the Atlantic.

Business makes ambassadors without portfolio of every single person going to another country for his or her company. When we are in someone else's country, we are sometimes considered a foreign, intrusive element. It puts us at a disadvantage, one that requires harder work and greater effort on our part. I remember Ambassador Clare Boothe Luce's sage advice in Rome to an American manufacturer who was hot under the collar because of the actions of his Italian counterpart in an export-import deal. "What steps should I take to tell these guys what bad news they *are, Ambassador Luce? What should I do with this terrible anger I have?" "Sit on it," was her three-word reply. End of conversation.*

THE IMPORTANCE OF SPEAKING FOREIGN LANGUAGES

No one can emphasize enough how important it is to know the language of the country in which you will be living. In using a foreign language in your work, you'll find yourself in possession of a skill that puts you well ahead of others. You will be translating letters, communicating with important foreign visitors, and in general filling a great need within your company. It will make you look very good. When you are in a foreign country people automatically warm to you when they find you have learned to speak their language, whether you're dealing with the concierge of your hotel (who usually speaks seven languages) or with a foreign peer on the other side of the desk. When you know another person's language, you can sense the nuances of his behavior (very important in business dealings); you can also enjoy his country's theater, films, books and newspapers, even television shows. You'll be tuned into the local gossip; you'll be a participant in lively exchanges of conversation instead of a perplexed spectator. You'll be able to bargain in shops, understand jokes, recognize political prejudices, and become a much more fascinating person yourself in the process.

Someone else may be more computer literate than you, but if you know a foreign language and he doesn't, his computer knowledge will not help him abroad when his car breaks down or when he loses his passport or has to find an emergency dental clinic. He'll need *you* at that point.

Part of the secret of learning a foreign language is learning to laugh at your own bad mistakes. Hundreds of Americans have refused second helpings during large meals in France by saying, *"Non, merci, je suis pleine"* (thinking that to mean "I am full"; instead it translates to "I am pregnant"). The American woman who says *"Je suis pleine"* is quite forgivable; a corporation that makes a major blunder in translation of an ad is less so.

When One Is Unfamiliar with a Foreign Language

- Being gracious and efficient go hand in hand. That is why it is wise to have your business card printed in the other language on the back. *Offer your colleague your card with the side containing his language showing.*
- If your international colleague does not have a good command of English, *have your business letters translated into his language*, so there will be no misunderstandings.

- If you are hosting international guests at a company dinner, *provide them with a program or agenda in their language.*
- *Make sure that each American to whom you introduce your visiting international guests is properly presented to them.* Introduce the person and then also give the name of the American's company, for example what the company does, and his primary responsibilities.
- If no interpreter is present and your international guest is not completely fluent in English, stop every so often during a meeting and make a précis as close as you can in his language of what has been going on. Let him ask questions. Speak slowly and clearly, so that he will have at least a summary grasp of what is transpiring.
- Never use profane language or tell dirty stories in front of an international visitor. Even if you think you know him well, he may be really offended by these actions. Even if he uses cusswords on occasion in his own office at home, he probably never would do so in front of people from another country with whom he is trying to build business relationships.

Efficient and Kind Handling of the Interpreter

If you are going abroad, make certain that an excellent interpreter has been engaged for you in that country. It could mean the success or failure of your trip.

- Brief your interpreter beforehand and make sure that he understands the purpose of the meeting and the nature of your own company's business. Tell him what your goal is in having the meeting or the company social event. Make sure you have selected a person who is familiar with the jargon used in your field, particularly if you are in a scientific or technological field.
- If you're in a meeting with an interpreter present, always look at the person who is doing the talking, even when his remarks are being translated into English for you. The interpreter is not the executive, only his representative.
- Help out the interpreter. Use short sentences with short words. If you use proper names, pronounce them slowly; spell them, in fact. Don't tell jokes, because they are rarely meaningful when translated into another language, and may sound just plain silly. Keep asking, "Are there any questions? Do you fully understand what I just said?"
- Don't be afraid to stop your discourse and have a little chat with the interpreter if you have a delicate, difficult point to get across that has many meanings, subtleties, and shadings. Make certain the interpreter understands perfectly all those nuances you wish to communicate to your business colleague.
- If two people in need of an interpreter are not of high official rank, the interpreter should be seated between them at the table and be treated as courteously as every other guest. He or she should be trained to sit in an unobtrusive position and to lean back at the table when whispering into either person's ear. The two protago-

nists should always be able to see each other clearly and be able to communicate with body language, even though the interpreter is sitting between them.

- Treat your interpreter with kindness. I have seen some pretty thoughtless handling of interpreters in my business career. I have seen interpreters spend an entire evening working, exhausted from hours of concentration, without ever being offered a drink or something to eat. On the other hand, I have seen interpreters not properly briefed about the dress code beforehand, with the result that they arrive unsuitably attired and very conspicuous. If your guests are formal in the way they dress, tell your interpreters to wear jackets and ties or, for the women, dresses instead of pants. If it is a black-tie event, instruct them to come in evening clothes.
- If the event is a top-level one, such as a dinner meeting between heads of major corporations or one including high-ranking officials and diplomats, the interpreter should sit in a small chair placed between the two main protagonists but slightly in back of their chairs, so that he or she can translate but the two protagonists will still be sitting close together. In this case the translator does not eat the meal but remains quietly poised to translate the two languages being spoken. (*Be sure to have any interpreters you retain given a meal before or after their work stint.*)

HOW TO FIND INFORMATION ON A FOREIGN CULTURE

- *Ask the librarian for the latest, recommended books* on the country in question, including history and travel books that emphasize customs and books on international negotiating styles. One of my favorite books of informational tidbits on all the major countries is by Roger E. Axtell, *Do's and Taboos Around the World*, published by John Wiley & Sons, New York. The third edition was published in April 1993.
- *Ask someone who has recent first-hand knowledge.* A family you know may just have returned from living in a country to which you will be traveling on business; you can debrief them easily on the dress and customs of the country. (Don't think that the information given to you by a tourist who was in that country for a week is going to do the trick!)
- If you live out in the country or in a small town and don't have access to a good library, *call the country's consulate in the largest city near to you.* Just tell the operator who answers at the consulate that you have some questions about dress and customs in that country. If there is no consulate in the area, *call the embassy of that country in Washington, DC, and ask to speak to the Cultural Attache.* If there is none, ask to speak to the *secretary of the Ambassador* (usually a treasure trove of information and almost always, very protocol-conscious). A word of caution here: Sometimes ambassadors from other countries have American secretaries, so be sure that the person whose information you are relying on has been in that country or is from that country, and not from Chevy Chase, Maryland!

- *The national tourist agencies and the international airlines' ticket offices* also usually have excellent pamphlets, brochures, and book recommendations which will give you some needed answers.
- *The Commerce Department in Washington, DC*, has a lot of available information on international business matters, since their primary mission is to increase American exports. Call the Trade Information Center (202-482-0543) for region-specific help. There are separate offices dealing with the Eastern European region, Russia, Mexico, Latin America, and other countries. Ask for the "FETs" (Foreign Economic Trends) and "CMPs" (Country Market Plans) for your region of interest.
- *The State Department offers short "Background Notes" without charge to people traveling abroad on business, as well as much more detailed "Post Reports,"* written by State Department staff posted in those countries. The Post Reports are useful for business people moving to those particular countries, and they include information on everything from whether you can bring in your own automobile and what kind of schools your children can attend, to the kind of medical services the country offers and what kind of electrical transformers you should bring so your appliances will work. Call 202-647-1105 to find out if the information you want is available and how much it will cost. (Each Post Report costs from about $3 to $15, according to its length.) Send the request for that country, plus the check for the proper amount made out to the Department of State. Address the envelope to OIS/PS/PR, Room B847A, Department of State, 2020 C St. NW, Washington, DC 20520.

The more knowledgeable you are about a country when you travel to it, the less chance there is of offending someone in that country, and the more opportunity there is to engage in enthusiastic, upbeat conversation with whomever you happen to meet. We Americans have a reputation for not being curious enough about other countries and for not caring enough to inform ourselves. *Your arsenal of knowledge will be a great asset to you in someone else's country.*

CROSS-CULTURAL TRAINING FOR FAMILIES MOVING OVERSEAS

In today's world, it makes good economic sense for a corporation to care about the adjustments made by its executives and their families who are posted to other countries. It's not only their morale that is at stake, but their performance on the job and their happiness as well. The issue is not only whether they have managed to adjust to their new lives, but also whether they have learned to live as *good global citizens*. A good global citizen is not only an excellent manager but also a skilled negotiator and therefore a profit-maker. A good global citizen knows how to earn the trust of the people in whose country he is a guest. Such skills are the secret of good business relationships and ones that carry an executive far beyond just being a good member of the corporate family back home.

It only takes one untrained, unfeeling person abroad on a ten-day business trip to destroy good business relationships that previously may have been fostered between two companies.

Texaco, Inc., now has a training program for executives that is jokingly referred to outside as "Texaco's Couth Course." Developed by Carl Davidson, vice-president and secretary, the course began as instruction on how to eat one's way gracefully through a meal. The subject matter then broadened to include how to entertain in the home, how to be a great guest and host, what kind of stationery to use, and the art of polite conversation. Texaco often brings in managers from the company's offices in Latin America and West Africa for this training, too, because although customs differ from country to country, there is a basic underlying protocol and gracefulness that remains constant no matter where one travels.

A good example of the globalization of American companies is Dupont. As its senior management saw more of its managerial families moving overseas in an accelerating international market, a former engineer with valuable experience in Asia, Florence Garvin, was moved into the position of "Manager of International Human Resource Development." She develops innovative programs to teach company executives how to adjust to their new countries, and is justifiably proud of the fact that there have been hardly any "failed families" in the program, particularly in Asia and the Pacific rim. She also trains executives in how to treat international guests when they visit the United States, aimed not only in making them comfortable, but in helping them accomplish their business goals with greater speed and success.

Many American business people are overwhelmed by the exigencies of international protocol, so Florence Garvin's work plan is simple and direct. She makes herself a double column checklist for each executive, in which she asks herself the questions, "What will this executive need to know about this country, either as a visitor or as a host?" and "Where can I find the answers?"

As a result, Dupont executives do business with internationals armed with essential information in their pockets for each country they will visit and for each guest they will host in the United States. One of the questions researched on a high-ranking visiting international figure (for whom a gift would be appropriate) is the possibility of donating something to the person's favorite charity. On the occasion of the visit of Prince Henri of Luxembourg, Dupont made a gift of wheelchairs in His Royal Highness' name to his foundation for handicapped children in Luxembourg, which made the people of that country particularly happy, and created good will for Dupont.

Cross-Cultural Training Centers

It costs a lot to train a manager and send him or her and the family abroad. According to Gary Lloyd, director of the Business Council for International Understanding Institute (BCIU) at the American University in Washington, if the cultural adjustment does not work out, and if the family returns to the United States because of an inability to adapt to their new country, it can cost the corporation as much as $2 million or more. It makes the cost of training seem insignificant in comparison.

Cross-cultural training has therefore become big business in this country. There are waiting lists for programs offered by the BCIU in Washington; the Key Man Course at the Thunderbird School in Phoenix, Arizona; and the Monterey Institute of International Studies in Monterey, California. There are also individual consultants who do this type of training. Cross-cultural training is not inexpensive.

A three-day program at BCIU, for example, can cost $12,000 per family, as of this writing, and a fourteen-day program up to $16,000, taught by a battery of country-specific resource experts. (It includes forty hours of face-to-face language instruction by native speakers.) There are special programs for teens and young children from the age of five, too, because if they cannot cope in the new country to which they are posted their parents will have an even tougher time.

The David M. Kennedy Center for International Studies at Brigham Young University in Provo, Utah, produces "Culturgrams" on many countries in the world. The International Society for Intercultural Education, Training and Research (SIETAR International) is also important in the field. Affiliated with Georgetown University in Washington, it is an association of professionals who work in intercultural education, getting the message out through nonpolitical avenues.

One of the goals of this kind of education is to reduce the number of marketing gaffes made in this country, such as those written about by David Ricks in his book, *Big Business Blunders: Mistakes in Multinational Marketing*. There was the telephone company, for example, that made a telephone commercial for Latin Americans, in which the wife says to her husband, "Run downstairs and phone Mary. Tell her we'll be a little late." The cultural errors were that Latin wives do not order their husbands around, and almost no Latin would feel it necessary to telephone to say he would be late, since it is expected. Then there was the toothpaste promoted in Southeast Asia as a product to whiten the teeth. The ad, however, ran in a region where the local people deliberately chewed betel nut to stain their teeth. In another ad, which was translated from the American text, the ad was supposed to read, "When I used this shirt, I felt good," but in the translation it became, "Until I used this shirt, I felt good." Then there was the case of the Chevrolet company's bafflement at not being able to market this country's popular Nova in Latin countries. The reason? "*No va*" in Spanish means "no go!"

Establishing an atmosphere of trust and compatability—which takes time for impatient Americans—before the negotiating can begin is a learned art.

CITIZENS EMERGENCY CENTER TRAVEL ADVISORIES

The U.S. Government cares about its citizens traveling overseas, so don't hesitate to take advantage of their services. If your business takes you to a country where there are concerns about disease, civil disorder, military action or a natural disaster, or even if you have a question about a foreign visa, use a touch-tone phone to call the Citizens Emergency Center in the State Department in Washington, DC (202-647-5225). Voice mail will escort you through a series of options that will give you information on as many as three countries in one region per phone call. The information you hear on a particular country comes from State Department officials posted in that area. You'll receive the telephone numbers of the U.S. consulates in that country, for one thing — something you should have in your possession at all times while traveling abroad. If you wish, an advisory on a particular country will be mailed to you. With your personal computer and modem, you can be connected to the CA (Citizens Advisory) Electronic Bulletin Board (call 202-647-9225).

You can also call the Citizens Emergency Center if you need information on an American abroad who may be in distress (sick, in jail, etc.). In an extreme emergency or Sundays and holidays, when the Center is closed, call the government operator in Washington at 202-647-1512 and ask to be connected to the duty officer at the Citizens Emergency Center.

GENERAL ADVICE FOR DOING BUSINESS WITH PEOPLE FROM OTHER COUNTRIES

When You Are Going There

- *Learn ten phrases in the country's language*; for example:
  - Hello.
  - Goodbye.
  - Please.
  - Delighted to meet you; happy to have met you.
  - I'm sorry.
  - This is delicious food.
  - I am having a great time.
  - I hope you are well.
  - Please come visit us.
  - Thank you so much.
  - No, thank you.
  - This is such a delightful country.
  - My company makes such-and-such (or does such-and-such).
  - We are a big (or small) company.
  - That is very impressive.

- *Learn some facts about the country before you go*. For example, before venturing forth into another culture, you might want to know:
  - How the government is constructed
  - Who the leaders are (the top four names)
  - What the national religion is, if there is one
  - What dietary laws prevail
  - What day in the week is their day of rest (and therefore no appointments are made)
  - Their national holidays
  - The names of their great museums and cathedrals, temples or mosques, and their leading universities
  - Their major agricultural products
  - Their leading exports
  - The names of their super-celebrities—whether it's a Nobel Prize winner, a scientist or professor, a great musician, athlete, or rock star

- *Bring suitable gifts for everyone* (*see also* "International Gift-Giving," later in this chapter). This requires planning ahead, finding out how many gifts you will need, and for whom. The visiting executive should bring a gift of some kind to the people responsible for inviting him in the first place and also for staff members who work hard on making his visit a success. Don't spend a lot of money on these gifts. You usually can't go wrong if you purchase things that are uniquely American. One friend of mine, doing business in Korea, brought the fourteen year-old son of his leading customer a Chicago Bulls sweatshirt, cementing relations with the boy's father probably forever. Another friend brought a tape player and some Michael Jackson tapes to the cook (and her children) in New Delhi who took care of him when he rented a house there on business for a month. (The owner of the house saw him in New York a year later and reported that his photograph is on display in the cook's room in the compound behind the house, framed, and with a votive candle that burns in front of it each night.)

    Don't forget the senior person's secretary, too, who perhaps went beyond the call of duty to assist you; or the interpreter who stayed with you for two weeks, day and night; or the helpful driver who served you during the entire visit. Ship the gifts to your overseas headquarters ahead of time, if at all possible, to be held for your arrival, so you won't have to worry about them as baggage. Buy, wrap and mark the contents of about ten *more* gifts than you think you'll need (and that will probably just be the correct number!).

- Bring your good stationery and *write thank-you notes all over the place*. Thank someone for seeing you in her office or showing you around her company. Thank someone who took you to lunch or dinner. Thank anyone who gave you a gift of any kind. It may not be in the culture of the country in which you're doing business to write thank-you notes, but they will be impressed by your letters. A note almost forces the recipient to like you and to be aware of your exquisite manners.

- *Never criticize the regime in power* in the country you are visiting, even if you think the people you're with are unsympathetic to the government. Just don't discuss it. It is not wise to register a bitter protest against the ruling party and leaders, because it may come back to haunt you. It is also unwise in another country to criticize severely whoever is running the government in the United States. This kind of vehemence embarrasses an international colleague. He may not know how to react to your comments and might therefore feel uncomfortable.

Don't Forget:

- To have your medical shots taken care of well in advance of your departure date
- To make certain your passport and visas are in order
- To be prepared for your electrical equipment *not* to work in foreign electrical outlets, no matter how many transformers you carry with you.
- To double-check all hotel reservations the night before you are scheduled to arrive there.
- To have with you at all times a foreign language dictionary for every country you will visit
- To treat your passport as though it were the crown jewels, because if you lose it, you will have more complications in your life than the Queen of England would have if the crown jewels disappeared from the Tower of London

When Your Business Colleague Is Coming Here from a Foreign Country

- Have some treats awaiting your international visitor and his or her spouse in their hotel rooms; for example, any or all of the following:
  - Their favorite brand of tea or coffee, sodas, beer and wine
  - Crackers and cheese
  - Something for a sweet tooth (chocolates, a tin of cookies, etc.)
  - Bottled water
  - Bowl of fresh fruit (plates, fruit knives, and napkins)
  - Flowering plant
  - English–foreign language dictionary
  - Tourist guide to your city
  - List of telephone numbers (home and office) and those of other people involved with the international traveler's visit—to use if he or she has questions or if there is some emergency
  - Annotated schedule (with everything carefully explained, with all the names of the people involved, their titles, etc.)
  - Suggested sports schedule for the visitor to play or to be a spectator (if you know he is a sports buff)
  - Suggested separate daytime schedule for the spouse

- Never over-schedule your visitor. Let him get to bed early the first night. Give him a very leisurely next day, to cope with possible jet lag. Do not wear him out—and if he has a cold after making that long flight, make sure that a doctor sees him and prescribes medicine for his condition.
- If you're entertaining an international colleague at dinner, invite a couple from your city who speak his language and who will make him feel at ease and help spark up the conversation.
- At departure time give your international guests a list of the names of everyone they were entertained by, with addresses. Hopefully they will write their American hosts thank-you notes.
- Your final gesture of hospitality will be the mailing of photographs, properly captioned, that were taken of them during their American visit (perhaps even in a nice little photo album). This will be a permanent reminder of the spirit of American hospitality, which will mold their perceptions of this country in an affirmative way, perhaps forever.

STANDING UP FOR YOUR COUNTRY ABROAD

Having lived so many years abroad, I personally feel there is nothing more thrilling than seeing an American in another country stick up for his or her country with intelligence, passion, and knowledge. It also helps if a sense of humor is mixed in there, somewhere, too, because if a person makes his case with a light touch, the people being preached to do not mind it as much.

I have seen U.S. ambassadors and senior government officials answering sharp political criticisms with aplomb during toasts at formal dinners in several countries; I have also observed with equal pride an American student at a self-serve gas pump in Florence, brilliantly answering an attack on American politics from a car full of anti-Americans who had also stopped for *benzina*. I witnessed an incredible debate in a hotel dining room in Avignon, France, between a member of France's communist intelligentsia and a woman from Florida who owned a McDonald's franchise outlet. These people all shared the same things: a love of country, a knowledge of history and politics, the gift of articulation, and the courage to stand up and defend.

Americans in the business community are under just as much scrutiny as the American diplomats in that country. So you must think before you express an opinion in another country. What may sound fine at home may be interpreted very differently away from home. If you are a totally committed Democrat in a Republican administration, or vice versa, learn to temper your attacks on the party in power in your country in the presence of your foreign friends. If you keep your emotions in check and make calm, fair criticisms, everyone around you will feel comfortable. If you explode with rage about your country's president and make exaggerated accusations, you can make those in your presence feel uneasy and upset about what's happening in our country.

You should watch your accusations, too, about the party in power in the country in which you're posted. Negative remarks about that country's head of state, no matter how justified, can hurt the feelings of that country's nationals. Remember that outsiders who criticize the regime are often resented and distrusted. You can make others turn against you and your company by attacks on the government of their country—even if they don't like the government themselves. Most serious of all, your negative remarks may get your foreign friends into trouble. When a political argument goes unchecked and becomes very heated, your wisest move is to attempt to change the subject or, failing that, to withdraw quietly from the group.

If the United States is harshly attacked by your host country's nationals in your presence, stand up for it in a calm, firm way, correcting any inaccuracies or falsehoods being bandied about.

You can't very well defend your country if you do not keep current on what is happening within it, so you should keep yourself well informed by reading periodicals, books, magazines, and newspapers on foreign policy and current events. Most American embassies have a library and information service (called USIS) where you can have access to American foreign policy statements. Arrange to have a copy of the daily State Department news briefing material routinely given to the local journalists picked up or mailed to you, so that you will be able to defend your country's foreign policy with intelligence. An American abroad, even if he doesn't agree with his country's foreign policy, should make sure he knows what it is.

Our crime rate, the sensational murders, hostage-taking shootouts, rapes and drug-related crises, make people from other countries feel our country is a floating time bomb. We should be able in conversation to set our international friends straight on this point. We are a big country with more press coverage of negative incidents than any other country, and yet we are also a wonderful country with so many plus factors! Learn to turn the conversation away from the favorite international sport of "United States–bashing." Learn to change people's perceptions of even the cities that seem to get all the bad press: New York, Los Angeles, Miami, and Washington.

Talk about our splendid hospitals and great universities, with their research labs working on breakthroughs that help mankind every day in the fields of health and science. Talk about the strides we are making in solving the world's problems in education and communication. Talk about the arts in America which, in spite of cutbacks and other fluctuations caused by hard times, are more alive and exciting today than in any other country in the world.

We also have more things to do and see per square mile than any place in the world. We should encourage tourism to the United States, and talk with enthusiasm about the great places to visit. Every American abroad has an opportunity to help our economy through tourism. If you think I sound like an American who became used to hearing her country criticized and who learned to react with speed, you are absolutely correct.

INTERNATIONAL GIFT-GIVING
(*See also* Chapter 11, "Giving the Perfect Business Gift")

In general, gifts are an integral part of the business scene in this country, but often they are even more important in other countries.

The first rule of gift-giving to an international visitor is not to give a bulky present that the recipient might have trouble carting home. If you do give something oversized, let the recipient unwrap it, then take it right back to have it shipped to him by your company.

Choose something in good taste. If you are not all that certain of your taste or knowledge of the gift market for executives in other countries with differing cultural values, have someone on staff who is more knowledgeable about such matters select the gifts. Or retain a professional gift consultant (check the telephone directory or inquire at any fine store) to do the job of coming up with suggestions, and seeing the gift through from ordering to engraving, wrapping, and shipping. A well-chosen gift showing some obvious research encourages a feeling of trust in the recipient's mind.

- If you are not familiar with the gift-giving customs of a country, ask the advice of someone knowledgeable, such as:

  - A business colleague who is familiar with the culture of that country
  - An official in the local consulate of that country
  - A business person from that country now living in the United States

- Your gift should never be too costly, or the recipient will consider it a bribe. While your intention was to please someone, you will have done just the opposite.
- Your gift should be tastefully wrapped—presentation is very important in other countries.
- The most flattering gift is one that has been secretly researched by talking to the recipient's secretary or associate to find out his interests. You might bring a welcome addition to his stamp collection or start a subscription for him to a publication for horse breeders; you might add to his porcelain collection or bring a gadget for his new automobile.
- A gift relating to his profession is always meaningful. For example, you might find an antique lawyer's sign for an attorney or an old book written by a journalist to give to someone in the media.
- A gift relating to both countries is particularly precious. For example, for a French colleague, you might find a reproduction of a map used by Lafayette in the American Revolution or an antique box painted with the head of that great French gift to America, the Statue of Liberty.
- A gift dominated by an oversized corporate logo will seem like an advertisement, not a present.
- Your foreign colleague will appreciate something bought in your own country more than a gift bought in his.

- You should be reticent about giving gifts to people you do not know well. Don't bring a gift to your first meeting, for example, or you might give the recipient the impression that you are pressing too hard to close the deal.
- If your gift is sharp or pointed (such as a bar knife or letter opener), send or present it with a cork placed on the sharp point. This will counteract any vestige of the old supersititon that a gift with a sharp point is meant to be driven into the recipient's heart. (You can explain the cork on your gift enclosure card.)

Ideas for Gifts

- With the exception of the Islamic countries, *a gift of liquor* is always a popular one. Until rather recently, it was considered unbecoming of a female executive to bring liquor to a male executive, but that is changing now. Always find out the kind of spirits the recipient drinks before shopping for it.
- *The latest American gadget* is usually cherished by a foreigner. If you decide on an electrical item, be sure to find out what the import tax will be and arrange to pay for it. It might be necessary to include an adapter to change the current and voltage to the other country's standards. If the wall plug is different in the other country, leave it to the recipient to take care of the adjustment.
- If your business associate abroad is fluent in English, *a best-selling book on American foreign policy,* on the President and his cabinet, or on American business practices will be of interest.
- *Pen and pencil sets* are always popular and appropriate. If they bear the corporate logo, it should be small in size. Remember to include refills as part of the gift (if they are needed).
- A box of *fine stationery* is always a welcome gift. (For a man, choose a conservative color, such as white, gray, or tan.)
- A gift involving *music* (tapes or compact disks of classical music, American jazz, folk, country, or rock) is usually a good idea for any age.
- *Food,* well-packed in tins or sealed containers, is a good family present—nuts, candy, cookies, gourmet crackers, preserves, etc.
- *A gift of clothing* is often very welcome (but *know* the size, don't guess at it).

  - Blue jeans and all Western wear (bolo neckties, belts, hats, etc.)
  - American-made sweaters and sweatshirts
  - Running shoes
  - Ski caps (with American ski organizations and team names)
  - T-shirts with amusing sayings or representing famous American sports teams
  - Designer-name accessories (scarves, ties, belts, etc.)

Gifts for Children

It is not necessary to bring gifts for the children of an international colleague when you visit, unless you have been with this family and have become close to them.

When a baby has just been born to an international colleague, I personally find it difficult to receive him in this country or to visit him in his without a present for the newborn. It is politic, of course, when presenting a baby present, to bring something small, like a box of candy, to the other children in the family, so they do not feel neglected.

A handsome but expensive gift for an infant might be a sterling silver mug engraved with the baby's name or initials and birth date. However, I was there when a very expensive ($500) silver mug bombed as a present because it was engraved with an oversized corporate logo that far outshone the baby's initials. The beautiful present was regarded as a commercial statement. Less expensive gifts in silver are a spoon, rattle, food pusher, or bar-bell teether. Linens for the crib make nice gifts, as do colorful mobiles to place in the nursery, stuffed animals, amusing night lights, and books for a baby (such as pop-up fairy tales or touch-and-feel books).

Toys made in America are popular presents, particularly those that are the big fad in the States at the present moment. Whether it's the latest recording, doll, or space toy, the word seems to pass around among children very quickly between one country and another.

Teenage girls who are allowed to wear makeup always appreciate gifts of American cosmetics (choose lighter colors), skin care products, and nail polish. They also like the latest American fads in belts, handbags, scarves, and costume jewelry.

Female Executives Giving Gifts

An American woman executive should refrain from giving gifts to her foreign colleagues until she knows them fairly well, simply because the position of women in most other countries is far less advanced than in our own. She should wait until a foreign colleague first gives *her* a gift (unless she knows him extremely well, or unless she is the honoree of a party he is giving).

If she has met the wife of a foreign colleague, she may certainly bring her a small gift when she goes to that country on business, for that is something easy for a male executive to accept. Cosmetics, nylons, a designer perfume, or costume jewelry make great gifts to a woman whom you have met previously. Travel cases, a good looking tote, and an umbrella make suitable gifts from one woman executive to another, even if they have *not* met previously.

If a woman knows her foreign colleagues well, she must still be careful to refrain from giving anything of a personal nature (such as a bathrobe). A clock, except in China, makes a suitable gift for a man; so does any kind of desk accessory. One woman I know scored a big success when she sent each of her foreign colleagues a handsome

American leather picture frame after her return to the United States. Her gift card suggested that the frame be used to hold a family photo. That suggestion immediately made her gift a suitable one, not an overly personal one directed at the man alone.

A woman executive who brings gifts of food is also on sure grounds in the art of gift giving abroad.

A Special Gift for a Foreign Guest Speaker

When you sponsor a program that features a foreigner as guest speaker, you should give that person a memento commemorating the occasion. If the speaker is not receiving an honorarium, you might give him a piece of luggage or a briefcase, something of good quality made in America. If your speaker is receiving an honorarium, it is still a nice gesture to send him a small gift, such as a book. You might enclose your business card or a correspondence card with this kind of message: "Your address was unanimously well received. It was substantive and well-delivered. Thank you from all of us."

What to Give a Colleague Who Is Going Abroad

Along with all of the helpful kinds of gifts there are on the market to assist a traveler in coping with a foreign currency and a foreign language, one of the best gifts you can give a colleague is the kind of *standard medical kit* that some companies provide for their executives. Finding a pharmacy in a foreign city is difficult enough; finding one open on an emergency basis in the night or on a weekend (or on one of the constantly occurring national holidays) is impossible. The Chase Manhattan Bank's medical kit for its executives, to give an example, contains items like aspirin, a decongestant inhaler, throat lozenges, a gentle laxative, an antacid, and small bandages. These are all over-the-counter items; when one needs such an item in a foreign country, it is very nice to find it stashed away in a compact kit, a gift from a friend.

Give a small dictionary to a person going to another country on business. These are also helpful:

- An inflatable neck pillow for long plane flights
- Three new paperback books in *his* favorite genre
- A money guide for foreign exchange
- Twenty dollars worth of change in the currency he will need at the airport when he lands

Some Things You Should Know About Giving Flowers

Flowers have a different etiquette in various parts of the world. Check local customs before you proceed. If you are in another country, ask a local florist for advice on the right thing to send.

YOUR FREE TIME ON YOUR BUSINESS TRIPS

Maybe you won't have any free time on your trips out of the country. Hopefully, that will not be the case. Try to arrive on a Friday in Western Europe, for example, so that you can check into your client's office and then have the weekend free to explore, to visit the great museums, take a boat ride, attend a soccer game, take in an opera or concert, wander through the village square, the marketplace, the cathedrals.

A woman traveling alone in a foreign country should make friends with the concierge of her hotel, so that he can book tables for her in great local restaurants for dinner (places that are also safe), and so that he can arrange transportation for her. All she has to do in return is give him a tip ($25, for example), and write a letter of recommendation on his behalf to the general manager of the hotel.

If men and women are traveling abroad on a business trip, male executives should be very careful to include female executives on their evening excursions. It is not easy being a woman in a foreign country in a strange hotel; it takes a lot of courage to go to a good restaurant alone, but it is also very boring, night after night, to have dinner in the hotel restaurant or in one's room. Even two women executives traveling together in a foreign land cannot go to many places in the evening without male escorts (hopefully colleagues, certainly not hired escorts!) accompanying them. One can deduce therefore that it's rude of men to leave their female colleagues behind at night in a foreign country.

You can say I'm being sexist with this advice, but having lived so many years abroad, I can testify to the inadvisability of a lone woman, or of even two women, going by themselves to have dinner in a famous restaurant when they do not know the territory, when they do not speak the language, and when they do not have a car and driver picking them up. A male colleague should at least inquire what plans his female traveling companion has for dinner. "Wouldn't you like to join me?" are the pleasantest words that women can hear.

Those are a host of escapades I've managed to survive in my life, such as the time I was arrested many years ago for having crossed illegally into the Soviet Zone of Vienna from the American Zone. I talked so fast, about so many things, the Soviet intelligence officers could not keep up with my English. The sight of a 6'1" young, female American, acting in a hyper (some would say hysterical) manner, threw them completely. Nothing in their Soviet intelligence training had prepared them to deal with someone like me, and so they let me go. Later, when working at the American Embassy in Rome, I became separated from a group of fellow diplomats in the toughest part of Naples. A very big man (he looked like a wrestler) stepped in front of me in a dark, narrow alley and pressed a knife at my throat. I do not know what prompted my reaction, but it was immediate. I put my raised hand up in front of his face, in a Pope-like gesture and shouted with full lung power my favorite saint's name. "Sant' Antonio, Sant' Antonio!" I cried to the skies. The thug menacing me was so surprised—in fact, shocked by my reaction—that he quickly turned and rushed away. St. Anthony had done it again.

I was in Yugoslavia on a business trip with a male colleague, and when we went to a Yugoslav's home for an after-dinner drink, I was given a glass of the famous local homemade plum brandy (slivovitz). Our host was very proud of this slivovitz, which had been "maturing" in the sun on his window ledge for weeks. I had had nothing to drink all day except water, so I drank the small glass of liqueur with zest. It was more than strong. I lost consciousness for several hours. It was rather comforting later to realize that my male colleague had stayed by me through the entire incident.

Then there was the time my car broke down on a lonely, narrow, unpaved French road at one in the morning, and the only vehicle that came by for two hours was an ancient truck. I was not only his passenger for forty kilometers in the cab of his truck, but he insisted I spend the night at his house, where I slept in the double bed with his wife while he slept on the floor. There was no other option he and his wife would give me. I was their guest, therefore I must occupy half the bed.

These incidents (and there have been so many in my life) are very funny to recall, but I recount them only to show that when you travel abroad on business, unexpected things happen. You can be in danger, but you can live by your wits (with the help of your guardian angel), too. You can also have glorious escapades that become woven into the tapestry of your life, forever reminding you that life back home in the old routine can sometimes be exceedingly dull!

AMERICAN HABITS THAT DISPLEASE PEOPLE FROM OTHER COUNTRIES

- *The most common complaint heard against Americans is our lack of punctuality.* With the exception of the Arab and Latin worlds, most cultures prize punctuality above anything else. We should be more sensitive to that fact.
- *The French don't like our insistence on serious breakfast meetings* for the purpose of intense business discussions. The morning coffee hour, with *croissants*, *confiture*, and newspapers read quietly at leisure is an important ritual in the French people's day. Our frenzied, early-morning activities are considered barbaric to many Western Europeans.
- *We should not take our international colleagues away from their families at nighttime.* We should get our business done during the day and make our own plans for dinner, unless we are invited by our hosts to join them.
- *Most countries do not like an overly long cocktail hour before dinner.* When internationals ask their guests for dinner at eight, everyone usually is at table and eating forty-five minutes later. But when guests at an American host's dinner are invited at seven, they sometimes don't sit down until nine or nine-thirty (to accommodate the hearty drinkers and the late arrivals). As a result, the visiting guests are tired, grumpy, and disenchanted by our brand of hospitality.
- *People from other countries would not think of criticizing our food.* They may not like certain dishes, but they would not comment on it. *When in their countries we aim our sermons at them on low-fat, no-beef, no-sugar, and roughage*, it is a

complete turn-off. People from other countries usually either praise our food or make no comment at all; we should do the same in their countries. Food is simply not a subject for discussion in negative terms.

- *It is never justifiable for us to give sermons to internationals on the fact that they should give up smoking for health reasons.* Several business people from other countries have mentioned this objection with no small amount of passion.

- *We should not repeatedly correct our international colleagues' mistakes in English, unless specifically asked to do so.* A person struggling in a foreign language is exhausted enough from the effort made without having every single error drawn to his attention. It's discouraging. At the same time, if someone from another country wants to try out his English on you, it is gracious of you to cooperate, even though you may speak his language expertly or an interpreter is present.

- Americans tend to discuss business deals in terms of American dollars as if it were the only currency in the world, and such things as measurements in feet and inches as though it were the only system. *If you are doing business in another country, you should talk to your colleagues in terms of their currency and their measurement system.* You should talk about litres of gas, not gallons; meters of fabric, not yards. In other words, when we are in their country we should learn the everyday language of their culture, not force our own on them.

- *The American who continually makes unfavorable comparisons between the host country and the United States* is both a boor and a bore. For example:

FOREIGN HOST	AMERICAN GUEST
"And here is our famous university."	"Oh, our state universities are *much* bigger than that."
"This is our newly automated system, of which we are very proud."	"Heavens! We had that eight years ago. We've gone way beyond that."

- *Americans who have not kept up with essential political changes in the host country* seem overly naive and uninformed. For instance, it would be a mistake to refer to the German Democratic Republic in the eastern part of the country, or to the Soviet Union, neither of which is in existence today, or to talk about Czechoslovakia instead of the Czech Republic or the Slovak Republic.

We are often criticized, too, for our lack of understanding the diversity of other cultures and our proclivity for generalization. As an Arab-Christian friend of mine once told me after hearing me make hasty, inaccurate statements about his part of the world, "If I did not consider you such a great friend, I would not tell you this. When you are in other lands, Letitia, talk animatedly about the subjects you know best, including American values and mores. But when you are not absolutely certain of your material, it is far wiser not to comment, but to use that time listening to authoritative sources in order to absorb knowledge, and therefore *to learn*."

No Teasing About Sacred Matters, Not Even in Jest

We Americans tend to fool around and joke a lot with one another. Some of the best ethnic, racist, and religious jokes we tell are about ourselves. In other words, they come from the very people who belong to those particular groups. But in other countries, this kind of humor often is misunderstood. Other nationalities don't toss around the jokes with the same abandonment that we do about "Once there were a Christian, a Jew, and a Muslim who died on the same day and went up to see God about entering the next life, etc."

Make it a rule never to joke about religions or sacred traditions when in another country—no matter how close you think you are to your foreign colleagues, no matter how comfortable you feel with them, and no matter how much you think you look at things identically. You don't—and you can get into serious trouble with your brand of humor, whether it's the obvious or the subtle kind.

It is considered in the worst possible taste in all corners of the world, for example, to make fun of:

- The Bible—the sacred writings of the Christian religion, comprising the Old and New Testaments
- The Koran—the sacred text of Islam, the word of God, as given to Mohammed
- The Torah—the entire body of Jewish religious literature, law and teaching in the Old Testament and the Talmud.

THE IMPORTANCE OF PROPER DRESS
WHEN DOING BUSINESS ABROAD

It is important to ask the question, "What clothing should one take when doing business abroad?" well *before* packing for a trip. Find out what your schedule will be, what the mean temperature is, and what social or sportive occasions will require special clothing. An American entrepreneur who never changes out of his chinos, boat shoes, and polo shirt will have a rude awakening in another country where *no one* will be dressed the way he is.

"But this is the way I always dress" doesn't hold much significance in another culture. The way you're comfortable and your particular lifestyle is not what matters. You are supposed to blend into the environment around you in that foreign country. What you wear is terribly important, because you represent a foreigner in that country. You also represent your country, as an American man or woman; as a business person; and last but certainly not least, as a representative of your company. That's a lot of representing!

Of course, the primary questions are who you are and where you are going. An engineer going to check on construction in Afghanistan is one thing. A lawyer going to represent a client in Jidda is another. A woman lawyer going alone to represent a client in Jidda is still another matter. A woman lawyer going alone to Saudi Arabia to represent a client does not have to worry about what's in her suitcase. No one will do business with her, anyway!

White is the symbol of mourning in the Far East. Therefore, even in the summer heat, leave your white suits or dresses at home. If your winter coat is white, leave that at home, too. Being conspicuous or inappropriate will not help your business appearance.

Loud colors are also too conspicuous. An American man wearing a loud Hawaiian-type print shirt over slacks is ridiculed behind his back as he walks down the street (people are too polite to do this to his face). A woman of a certain age wearing a bright pink or lime green polyester pant suit is also the object of amazement. If you're on the beach in Cannes or Acapulco, it's fine to wear a postage stamp instead of a swimming suit if you've got the figure for it. But in the rest of the world, when you are representing your firm on business, remember that dignity is a treasured asset and that you can easily lose it by wearing loud, conspicuous, or overly bare clothing. As for American men who travel abroad in the summer wearing only jeans and sleeveless undershirts, showing off their muscles and chests, it's too bad they are not made aware of the revulsion they cause. No one reading this book dresses like that in public, but it should be kept in mind that a person dressed that way while doing business in Whitefish, Montana, or in London, England, draws the same negative reaction.

You may be asked to remove your shoes before entering some homes and temples or mosques around the world, particularly in Asia. Therefore, make certain your hose are in good condition (or carry a pair of clean athletic socks in your briefcase and put those on over your own socks or stockings.)

In many Scandinavian and Western European countries, black-tie events in the evening are common. It may not be on your schedule when you leave the United States, but it might suddenly be put on your schedule. Be prepared, and take a dinner suit or evening dress with you.

In the evening, Filipino men wear sheer embroidered or pleated, short-sleeved or long-sleeved shirts, called *barongs*. They are cool, comfortable, and decorative, but when an American woman shows up at an evening party wearing it over pants, the Filipinos are uncomfortable. They would never mention it, but it is not proper for a woman to wear a man's dress in their country. They would much rather she wear one of the Filipino women's long dresses, with large butterfly-sleeves.

Men all over the world should pack that dark, formal suit and take black shoes and socks, dress shirts, and ties. If they are going abroad to check on an engineering job or an installation project where they will be working in the field, of course they should wear the same work clothes that they do at home. They will still need that dark suit, however, for dinner, whether they go to a restaurant or someone's home. The same holds true for Asian countries. In an office, in a restaurant, in someone's home (if you are lucky enough to find yourself in someone's home in Japan, for example, a rarity in itself), a dark suit and shoes are *de rigueur*.

In Israel men go jacketless and tieless all the time. Informality is the way of life, but in Arab countries, it is much more formal. As one Saudi explained it to me, "During a business appointment, in really severe heat, we manage to remove our jackets; in absolutely unbearable, record heat, we take off our ties, too."

The lesson to remember is, Go dressed in a way that might seem formal to you. Let your hosts suggest that you make yourself more comfortable. That is more impressive than if you just decide yourself that you will make yourself more comfortable.

SOME REGIONS WHERE CUSTOMS ARE MARKEDLY DIFFERENT FROM THE WESTERN WORLD

Much of the protocol that you will follow to get along easily in Western Europe and Latin America is now so similar to our American manners that you will encounter few problems. But there are regions of the world where customs differ markedly, and the material that follows gives special attention to what you need to know to feel comfortable in those areas when you do business.

Africa

This is a continent that is as complicated, mysterious, and multi-faceted as it is giant in size. One can only generalize about its various countries on occasion. Anyone going to an African country should study its individual history, economic development, and customs thoroughly. For example:

· South Africa is oriented toward the British and the Dutch cultures.
· The northern nationals are united in the Arabic language, Islamic religion, and dress code. They abstain from alcohol, and a businessman who brings along his wife on a business trip will have to leave her in the hotel during a business dinner—or perhaps the African's wife will invite her home to dinner if she is proud of her house.
· The French-speaking countries, such as Senégal and the *Côte d'Ivoire* (Ivory Coast), are more formal than the rest of the continent. They have French social customs, such as kissing a friend on both cheeks in greeting. They dress up more than their neighbors (including in black tie and evening dresses for formal occasions), and they cherish good French wines and cuisine.

Business Manners

You can not rush into business deals with Africans. First, there has to be an atmosphere of trust established. They like to take a great deal of time in making small talk before getting down to business.

Social Customs

- Africans shake hands constantly; it is an important part of their culture. They hold a handshake much longer than we westerners, but they are also careful not to give too strong a handshake. It is light, warm, and friendly.
- They tend not to observe what RSVP means and, as a result, are frequent no-shows at meetings and social engagements they have accepted. It is wise to keep calling their offices to reconfirm several times, if you are going to be their hosts. If a man has accepted for himself and his wife, you should also reconfirm this fact more than once.

Gifts

- Non-Muslims appreciate alcohol as a gift, but find out the favored brand.
- Don't bring jeans or any other items of apparel that are too hot to wear in this part of the world. Do bring T-shirts, baseball caps, jackets, and lightweight athletic uniforms marked with the names of world-famous teams and African-American athletes.
- Food is a welcome gift, but remember that chocolates tend to melt in this country. A box of gourmet canned soups or cookies (in a well-insulated tin), for example, are a hit.
- American movies to play on their VCRs are received with wild enthusiasm (the cassette tapes and CDs do not play on their equipment, but there are many places in Africa where American-made videotapes, audiotapes, and film can be converted to play on their local systems). Africans love rock, reggae, soul music, rap, and folk music.
- The greatest gift an American can bring back from Africa to his African-American friends are examples of the native clothing, headwraps, embroideries, local textiles, handicrafts, and folk art. A businessman or -woman who goes from the States to Africa should bring a large suitcase full of small items, such as wallets, amusing or sporty watches, and, of course, toys and black dolls.

The Arab World

The Arab world is multi-faceted, with different degrees of strictness in the adherence to religious customs. A very generous people, they are easily offended, so until you come to know your Arab colleague very well, don't tease him or make him the butt of a joke.

Business Manners

- Punctuality is not prized in this part of the world. As the Ambassador from the United Arab Emirates explained to me one day, ''When the train service came to

England, the English began looking up all the time at the big clocks in the stations, in order to be on time for their trains. We have not had such conditioning in our country.'' Be prepared, therefore, to wait for an hour or two when you think you have an appointment at a specific hour. (A Japanese businessman, who is typical of his countrymen and always five minutes ahead of time, told me that when he goes to the Arab world on business, he has a hard time adjusting to their lack of punctuality.)

· When you call on an Arab, you will be served very strong, delicious, hot coffee (or mint tea, perhaps). Coffee was first served in the world in Yemen several thousand years ago. There are five degrees of sweetness of Muslim coffee, the sweetest being that served in Turkey. Take only small sips from your small cup, because you will be served this coffee throughout the day and night.

· Arab businessmen admit that although they are not good letter writers themselves (''We are more verbal, face-to-face,'' as one diplomat described it), they are greatly impressed by and appreciative of an informal, warm American thank-you note—whether for business favor, a gift or being taken out to a meal.

· If you would like to give your visiting Arab business colleague tremendous pleasure, take him to participate in an outdoor sport—such as hunting or fishing. (Naturally, you would ask him first if he is experienced in these sports, but most often he will be.)

· Never schedule a business trip to the Arab countries during Ramadan (the annual month of fasting and prayer from sunup to sunset which occurs usually in March or April).

Women Traveling on Business in Arab Countries

The self-contained, independent American businesswoman has to bite her tongue on many an occasion when doing business in an Arab country. Not so in the less strict Gulf countries, such as Kuwait and Oman, but in Saudi Arabia, she will be unable to travel by herself. She would have to be accompanied by a man from her office; he would do the talking, and she would be allowed to be present, but nothing more. In fact, in the evening, she would either dine (and very well, too) with the wives of her business contacts or have dinner by herself in the hotel.

Social Customs

· Never use swear words or mention God.
· When sitting, do not expose the soles of your shoes to your Arab colleagues, because it is considered offensive.
· Do everything with your right hand (holding, offering, or receiving materials). (The left hand is for handling toilet paper!) If you are left-handed and are writing something, explain that you cannot help it.

- Do not point at or beckon to an Arab, because those are gestures they use themselves for summoning their dogs.
- When Arabs of the same sex greet one another, if they are good friends, they kiss one another on both cheeks.
- Arab men walk around the streets holding hands with their male acquaintances, a custom that is really different from most American street behavior.

Women's Dress in Countries with Muslim Populations

These countries include Indonesia, Iran, Pakistan, Iraq, Syria, Azerbaijan, Jordan, Tajikistan, Turkmenistan, the Maldives, Libya, and the Arabian Peninsula. In these lands some women are forced (perhaps it is more correct to say women prefer) to cover themselves. These are the countries that remind us how free and easy the lives of American women are by comparison. In order to protect themselves from sexual harassment, more and more Muslim women are now covering themselves and wearing the veil to earn the respect and protection it gives them. This is particularly noticeable in a country like Egypt, where Muslim extremism is on the rise and where formerly one saw women everywhere in western dress. Now many wrap themselves in public once again in the *chador*—the traditional garment of Muslim women, consisting of a long, usually black or drab-colored cloth that covers the entire body from head to toe, as well as all or part of the face. Some Muslim women will appear in public in a baggy kind of raincoat with a large head scarf. The clothing represents more than modesty: It is a trademark of the Islamic Revolution of 1979.

Quite obviously, an American woman on business in strict Muslim countries should dress in a very modest, covered-up manner, too (not in pants, however). To make fun of a woman's native garb or to wonder aloud how she can bear the discomfort or heat of the traditional dress is to be completely insensitive and offensive. An American woman writer-producer producer for documentary films, knowing that rich Saudi women have a passion for French and Italian designer apparel, appeared in Riyadh on a business trip in the latest designer mini-skirts, and there was plenty of decolletage on view for her first evening event. She scandalized the Saudis, whose wives she never met (and who wear their French clothes only in the privacy of their own homes or abroad). Her foreign hosts finally told her that she and her male entourage would be better off returning to Los Angeles. "You will be happier there," someone overheard a Saudi say very politely. Her entire film project was derailed, thanks to a total lack of sensitivity.

An American woman on business in any of the Arab and Muslim worlds would do well to dress always in her most covered-up clothing. A jacket or a long-sleeved sweater will cover up a short-sleeved or sleeveless dress. Skirts should be worn long, with the knee well covered and certainly no shorter than calf-length. A woman should never sit down and cross one leg over the other, shortening her skirt even more, and *no one of either sex* should sit in a manner where the soles of the shoes face the other people in the room. A woman in pants, sitting with one foot resting on the other knee, in a relaxed male pose, really draws negative attention.

A businesswoman should be familiar with the strict rules of dress in countries like Saudi Arabia, but she should also understand that these rules are much less strict in countries like Jordan and the Gulf states. As the ambassador from the United Arab Emirates explained it, the states on the sea have for many centuries been sea traders, which helped the people see and learn about the world. Consequently, many cultural Muslim standards are less strict there. An American woman can even go over to one of the Gulf states on a business trip by herself; in other Arab countries, she must be accompanied by a man who presumably is the senior business person present and who speaks for her (even if he occupies a much less senior position than she does). It's the culture. Don't fight it, respect it.

Conversation

- Most Saudi businessmen have been educated in English and American schools, and therefore speak English well, but if you learn a few Arabic words, they will be flattered and delighted.
- If you allude to the ancient history of this part of the world, and show knowledge of their many contributions to art and culture, you will be a much appreciated guest.
- Avoid the subject of Israel, just as you would avoid the subject of the Arab world if you were visiting an Israeli.
- The Arabs are fascinated by our political system. They tend to be well read on the subject and enjoy hearing Americans discuss local politics.
- The Arabs are big soccer fans; it is an international sport they discuss with enthusiasm.
- Do not ask prying questions abut their wives and children, particularly in Saudi Arabia, for they consider their families a personal matter. If you have met an Arab's wife from one of the less strict countries on the Gulf, because she had accompanied him to the United States on a business trip, that is another matter entirely.
- An American woman would do well to stay off the subject of the women's movement, and should certainly never criticize the lack of liberty of the Arab woman. I remember once, when my seatmate from New York to Los Angeles was a Saudi, and we talked the entire way across the continent. As we were about to debark from the plane, I teasingly said, "I hope I will be able to chat with your wife when she comes over to America someday." He replied, "It will never happen. She goes nowhere without me. She would be sitting next to me on the plane or she would be home."

  "But you have been so interested in my lifestyle," I protested. "You've asked me so many questions about my career, my role as a corporate director, my independent lifestyle."

"Asked questions, yes," he said gently. "I was truly interested during these past hours. It is fascinating to meet people like you when I travel."

"But it's not the kind of life for your wife," I said with a certain amount of irony.

"It's very definitely not for my wife," he said assuredly. "She would not like your life and your independence. I take care of everything for her. She is content." He smiled, secure in his convictions, and I was quite certain that his wife was happy, well taken care of, and secure in her home with her children. One of the great lessons of life learned in travel is that cultural differences change the absolutes, and that what causes indigestion in one stomach is an exquisite gourmet feast in another.

Gifts

- Don't praise any personal possession of an Arab too enthusiastically, or he may feel compelled to give it to you at once. (This can be most embarrassing for everyone if it's an oriental rug!)
- In a business gift exchange in an Arab country, your contact should give you a gift first.
- The Arabs tend to give elaborate presents, and your return gifts should be equally elaborate.
- Do not give alcohol, of course, to anyone in a strict Muslim country, like Saudi Arabia.
- Do not bring the gift of food to an Arab, for he might think you were casting aspersions on the quality of his food that will be served to you.
- A gift from a status store (such as a silver box from Tiffany's, a crystal bowl from Steuben, a pair of cufflinks from Neiman Marcus, etc.) is greatly appreciated.

Germany

Germany is a conservative, serious, "correct" country. We should handle ourselves in a more formal manner here than in many other Western European countries. As an example of the formality of relationships, even good friends do not borrow from one another. (I watched an American engineer make a major gaffe one time in Frankfurt when he asked to borrow a German colleague's car for two hours when it was not being used by its owner.) We should also be sensitive to the current economic problems brought about by the unification of East and West Germany.

Business Manners

- Respect your colleague's title and do not first-name him until he does it first to you. Instead address him or her politely according to his or her degree or profession. For example, an architect would be addressed as "Herr Architekt Ritter," a university graduate would be "Herr Doktor Muller," a woman graduate "Frau Doktor Schmidt."

- Never call a German at home on business, and most certainly not in the evening.
- Learn about the region in which the offices and plants of your German business associates are located. Study the history and the art of the area. Show you have done your homework. For example, if you are in Hanover, bring up the fact that this city has the reputation for being the center of the most pure-sounding High German spoken in the world. If there is a conversational lapse with your colleague, ask him how did the Royal House of Hanover become the Royal House of the British monarchs?

Social Customs

- Answer your own telephone simply by stating your last name (male or female).
- Punctuality is prized.
- Handshakes are expected between business colleagues, but not between friends. Never leave one hand in a pocket while you are shaking hands with the other.
- A man walks on the left side of a woman in this country.
- Avoid negative political discussions in conversations and reminiscences of World War II.
- Do not use slang in a pejorative sense. If you get angry at a driver, policeman, or anyone else and yell that this person is a dimwit, a stupid baboon, or much worse, the other person may seek a translation and you will end up with a large fine to pay.
- In making conversation, talk admiringly about the things for which Germans are justifiably very proud: music, cathedrals, wines, and engineering know-how, particularly in automobiles.

Dining Manners

Your host should drink first from his wineglass. He will raise a toast to the health of his guests ("Zum Wohl!" or more informally, "Prost!").

Gifts

- A very welcome gift would be four bottles of excellent American wines, which are almost impossible to find in Germany. They are interested in our growing wine industry, just as they are proud of their own fine wines.
- If you are invited to a German's home for drinks or dinner, it is very polite to arrive bearing flowers (not red roses, however, since they are only for lovers in this country). Unwrap your flowers before handing them over to your host.

- A gift related to the game of soccer is always welcome, because that is a national passion.
- Handsome desk accessories make welcome gifts. Do not bring gifts lavished with your corporate logo, however.

India

India is an increasingly important resource for the United States in the global economy picture. It is a fascinating country to visit on a business trip, because the colors, the sights, the sounds, the odors, and the movement of people are more intense than any other country in the world. The population is Hindu, Muslim, and Sikh.

The heat is a problem here. Try *not* to schedule a business trip to India from May through August, for the weather then is unbearably hot and monsoonal.

Business Manners

- English is spoken everywhere, even if Hindi is the national language. You will not need an interpreter. Even contracts are couched in the legal language used by English and American courts of law. However, speak slowly and distinctly, so that your Indian counterpart can understand you clearly.
- An Indian woman is pleased when an American businessman demonstrates chivalrous behavior toward her, such as helping her with her coat, rising when she enters the room, and so on.

Social Customs

- The traditional social greeting, almost reverential, called the *namaste*, is made by putting your two sets of fingertips together in a prayerful gesture, at about chest height. Bow your head slightly at the same time.
- Indians now shake hands, too. Some women are hesitant to shake hands with men, so if an Indian woman does not extend her hand in order to shake yours, give her a *namaste* greeting.

Dress

- Indian men wear lightweight suits, often without a tie, because of the heat. When it is really hot, jackets and ties are not worn. Only a very conservative, traditional businessman (whose small business has been handed down from generation to generation) still wears the traditional *kurta* (shirt) and *churidar* (cotton pants that wrap around the leg).
- A red dot on a woman's forehead is the sign that she is a married woman.
- An Indian Hindu woman wears the colorful, diaphanous *sari* on business or on social occasions. However, she usually prefers to wear a more practical,

and much warmer, garment for travel and work: loose pants (the *salwaar*) and a long tunic top (the *kameez*). This ethnic costume comes from the North, the Punjab, and is therefore favored by Pakistani as well as Indian women.

- American women would do well to leave their hemlines at the knee or below and to dress modestly. This is a traditional country, even if the women with whom you will deal are well educated, well read, and free to engage in business pursuits.

Conversation

- You will please your colleagues very much if you can talk about their history and art (which implies you have done some studying before your trip).
- Indians are also immensely proud of their beautiful palaces and gardens, and are disappointed if a business guest has not tried to see some of the great places of beauty (Agra, site of the Taj Mahal; Benares; Jaipur; etc.)
- It is undiplomatic to bring up the clashes of the religious sects—Hindus, Muslims and Sikhs. It is a source of sadness, but also sometimes of heated emotions and anger. Stay away from the subject of the country's poverty, or the amount of U.S. aid received.
- The smartest move an American businesswoman can make is to bring photographs of her family to dinner, and to be ready to talk about how she juggles career, family, cooking, and maintenance of the home. An American businessman who goes to India without his wife, but who has met his Hindu host before, would be wise to bring the family photograph, too. This is a very family-oriented country.

Dining Manners

- If your business contacts are Muslim, very probably the Muslim wives will be left at home, although not always.
- If you have a delicate stomach, watch out for the very spicy Indian food, particularly for food full of "chilis." Your host will not be offended if you say, "I would appreciate our going to a restaurant where the food will not be too spicy." If you are going to someone's house for dinner, you can say ahead of time, "I may not partake of your very spicy food, but don't worry, I will be happy to fill up on yoghurt and rice [present at most meals]." By the way, drink only bottled water (and use it for brushing your teeth, also).
- Remember, Indian Muslims do not eat pork, and Indian Hindus do not eat beef, for strong religious reasons.

Gifts

- Do not give a Hindu anything made of cowhide, as I almost did in my White House days, when I had navy blue leather frames custom-made as the state gifts for sixty-eight Hindu officials, each containing a doubly-signed photograph of President and Mrs. John F. Kennedy. The Presidential seal was stamped in gold on the top but, unfortunately, the frames had been made from cowhide, and the cow is sacred in the official state religion. My gaffe was discovered at the last minute, before it was too late. We gave the Hindu officials silver frames instead.
- Do not give an Indian Muslim anything made with pigskin. It is an insult to his religion.
- Hindus relish the gift of Scotch (probably left over from the days of British imperialism). It is inappropriate for an American businesswoman to give her Hindu colleague a gift of liquor. (She can present it, however, with the gift enclosure card of one of the men back home in her U.S. office.)
- Do not give Muslims liquor as a gift, even if Indian Muslims have been known to take a drink of Scotch.
- When you meet an Indian colleague for the first time, it is appropriate to bring him a small, inexpensive gift, such as an insulated box of chocolates or a tin of American cookies. They also love American souvenirs, such as a cookie tin with the White House painted on it, or a presidential election souvenir plate, or a George Washington-at-Mount-Vernon paperweight.
- If you go to a colleague's home for dinner, buy a sizable amount of cut flowers from one of the flower stalls on the street to present to the lady of the house.
- Always bring presents for your Indian colleagues' children, since children are the focus of everyone's lives. Dolls are appropriate, and whatever children's toys are the vogue. Also popular: children's jackets and rainwear.
- The best gifts for an Indian businesswoman or the wife of an Indian business colleague are cosmetics and perfume. They are inordinately expensive in India. (Remember to select dark shades and vivid lipsticks, in keeping with the colors of the Indian woman's skin.)
- You may have Indian customs problems with a major gift like a fax, so it is best not to try. You can probably bring in small electronics without much trouble (remember always to buy the dual voltage kind, so they will not have to be used with transformers).
- Popular gifts suitable for either sex:
  - Umbrellas
  - Tote bags
  - Carry-on suitcases for airplane travel
  - Inexpensive novelty watches
  - Small calculators
  - Briefcases
  - Sweaters

Japan

Business Manners

The Japanese are incredibly polite, and will do anything not to offend you. They have a hard time saying ''no'' to you in public, because they are so eager to please. Sometimes they agree to something in a meeting when what they have really done is say ''no'' to you. Other times they say ''no'' to you at the end of lengthy meetings, but they might contact you a year later, to say ''yes,'' and then they want the business to be transacted *at once*.

The business card is of utmost importance in the transaction of business. Here are some tips:

- Be prepared to dispense a hundred of your cards per week on a business trip to Japan.
- Have your business cards printed in Japanese on one side, as they do with English on their cards.
- Learn how to present your card to the other person with grace, as the Japanese do: Hand it with the Japanese side showing, face up, so that he can read it as you present it.
- Give a slight bow as you offer your card. He will give you his card held with the thumb and forefinger of both hands, as a mark of respect. You would honor him to do likewise.
- Read and digest the information on his card after he gives it to you, don't just pocket it.

Never hold a negotiation or any kind of important business meeting in your offices without supplying a good interpreter for your Japanese colleague. He will be suspicious of you if you have not taken care of this point properly.

Social Customs

- Noisy, raucous behavior is negative and conspicuous in this courteous country.
- Do not hug or kiss your Japanese colleagues. Modern Japanese now shake hands with Americans with ease, but this is not a culture in which people touch one another in public.
- If you would really like to please your Japanese colleagues, greet them with a bow and a smile.

  - A junior person stops first and bows to someone more senior.
  - The senior person returns the bow. If the junior person looks up and finds that the senior has not finished bowing to him, he should quickly return to the bow position. In other words, out of respect, the junior person bows first to a very senior person and emerges from the bow last.

- *For a standing bow of great respect*, bend forward at a 30-degree angle. Lower your hands, palms down, down the sides or down the fronts of your thighs, almost to the knees. Pause, then lift your head.
- Westerners should first learn to make a light bow, at a 15-degree angle, with hands at the sides of the thighs, and counting to three before reassuming an upright position.
- When you are in Japan, you will probably find a junior Japanese employee making a deep bow to you at the beginning of the business day, and then light ones every time thereafter when you cross paths during the day.
- As an international guest, the Japanese will expect you to precede them walking down the hall, going into a room, elevator, automobile, and so on.

Visiting in Someone's Home

- Shoes are usually removed before visiting someone's home or a sacred shrine. You may or may not be given slippers to wear. (Be sure your hose are in good condition!) Shoes are removed for the sake of cleanliness, but also to protect the delicate tatami mats. If you remove your shoes inside the house, place them neatly together facing the door, and when you leave, take off the slippers given to you, and align them neatly, too, facing the inside of the house.
- Sit in a kneeling position on the tatami mat (if you are able to). A man sits with one big toe on top of the other behind him. A woman should sit with knees close together and with hands clasped lightly in front of her. If you're not in good enough shape to do this, sit on the floor with your legs angled to one side.
- If you are offered a hot, moist towel, use it on your hands. If it is very hot weather, your host will urge you to use it on your face, neck, and arms. After using it, refold it and replace it in the container before you.
- You will probably be offered tea and cakes during your visit. Stay no longer than about an hour or an hour and a half, even if urged to stay longer (your hosts are just being polite).
- If there are older relatives in the room when you visit a Japanese home, be sure to give them goodbye greetings before leaving.

If you entertain Japanese visitors in your home in America (which is the nicest gesture you could make toward them), do as you would do with American guests. However, remember to show respect for seniority and age, including showing deference to your own parents or older relatives who might happen to be present.

Dress

- Do not wear an all-white dress or suit, the color of mourning.
- Leave your flashy, loud-colored clothing at home.

- Men should wear dark suits so as not to be conspicuous; the tie can be lively in color and pattern, but not comically so.
- A woman on business should not wear skirts that are too short or dresses that are too décolleté. (Evidently the Japanese think it's all right for a business-man's wife to dress in a sexy dress on a special occasion, but not a woman on a business mission, and I have to agree with them!)

Dining Manners

- It is considered bad manners to eat food in the street.
- Most entertaining in Japan is done in expensive restaurants.
- As the guest of honor, if there is a *tokonoma* (an alcove) you will be seated there, with your host and hostess sitting together at the opposite end of the table. If you are the host in the restaurant, seat your honored guests in the *tokonoma*.
- You will probably be served rice and soup and from three to five entree platters, from which you serve yourself small amounts.
- If you are the host, make sure to pour sake into the tiny cup of your senior, honored guest first, and then into your other guests' cups, and last, into your own.
- You will find your empty rice bowl on your left (remove the cover and place it face up next to the bowl. Do the same thing with the cover of the soup bowl which is on the right.) The server will come with a tray upon which you place your rice bowl with both hands. The server will return it filled with rice, and you remove it from the tray with both hands and place it on the table to the left. Now eat a couple of mouthfuls, holding the rice in your left hand and the chopsticks in your right.
- Now take some sips of soup, holding it in your left hand and praising it to your host (which is the gracious thing to do). Keep the bowl under your chin to keep from spilling.
- Now you would take alternating mouthfuls of rice and the entrees, as well as sips of soup, for the rest of the meal.
- If there are pickles on the table, save them for last, as they are strong in taste and could ruin the subtlety of the other dishes you are sampling.
- An old tradition that is often ignored by young Japanese is that if you do not wish more rice, you clean your bowl, but that if you would like some more, you would leave a few grains in the bottom of the bowl.
- You will make a big hit if you learn to begin the meal by saying, "*Itadaki-masu*" ("I shall now begin eating") and end it by saying to your hosts, "*Gochisosama*" ("I have eaten well").

Chopsticks Etiquette
(*See also* "How to Eat with Chopsticks," Chapter 3)

- Ask for Western flatware if you do not handle chopsticks with expertise.
- Never leave your chopsticks in the bowl between bites. They should be placed neatly, side by side, on the chopsticks rest provided.
- *Tipping.* In all probability a service charge of 10 percent has been added to your bill. If you wish to tip more, because the staff performed so beautifully, put yen in an envelope, give it to the head waiter as you depart, and he will distribute it among the staff.

Japanese Weddings

You might be invited to the wedding of two Japanese in the United States, which will combine modern American and traditional Japanese wedding etiquette. When a Japanese marries an American or another non-Japanese, the wedding usually follows Western traditions. It is a very great honor to be invited to a wedding reception in Japan. Send a gift a few days before the wedding—something for their new home (American glassware, plates, and linen place mats with napkins, for example, make a big hit).

It is customary for the sender of the wedding gift to receive from the parents of the bride, within a few days or weeks, a modest gift in return.

Japanese Funerals

- When a Japanese colleague or a member of his family dies, you would send from the United States a telegram of condolence.
- You would also arrange to have your office in Japan or an acquaintance in Japan send the proper flowers to the family.
- If a Japanese colleague dies when you are in Japan, you would immediately call upon the family, bringing flowers and a gift of yen in a special funeral envelope.
- You might be invited to attend a special "farewell ceremony," held before the private funeral service (which is for the family only). On this occasion, enter the room where the coffin is, bow to the close friends of the deceased lined up on the left of the coffin, then bow to the coffin and pray, then bow to the family and "chief mourner" who are lined up on the right side.
- *If you visit a shrine*, imitate the actions of your host, which may involve the washing of your hands, making a bow in front of the shrine, and so on.

Gifts

In Japan the entire tradition of gifts is steeped in ancient traditions.

- The two main gift-giving exchange periods with business contacts take place in December (*Oseibo*) and July (*Ochugen*). Many Japanese businessmen are trying to suppress this expensive, time-wasting custom, however, for practical reasons.

- The Japanese take great pains in their wrapping of gifts for the recipient. There will be color in the wrapping, instead of a funeral all-white scheme. The folding of the paper will be a work of art in itself. A gift with an outer silk scarf wrapping (a *furoshiki*) is the sign of an important gift for an esteemed colleague.
- The Japanese always unwraps his gift from you with great patience and care, so he can then rewrap it to perfection. An American should try to do the same. It is a mark of politeness.
- When you receive a gift, give a small bow of appreciation and thank the donor. Then write him or her a thank-you note within the week.
- If you are visiting Japan, always let your Japanese colleague give you a gift before you give him one. You would make him lose face otherwise.
- You should give your Japanese host a reciprocal gift after you have received yours, but always give a more modest one than the one he gave you.
- Never give a Japanese a gift in front of others unless you have something for everyone in the room. Gift-giving is a private, intimate ritual.
- Favorite gifts for the Japanese:

    ◦ Liquor (the kind and the brand that he drinks)
    ◦ A gift of art and culture—an art book from an American museum, CDs or tapes of American symphonic orchestras (if he likes classical music), CDs or tapes of American rock or folk music (if you know he likes this)
    ◦ Good quality, somber-colored neckties for men
    ◦ Silk scarves and good handbags for women
    ◦ A piece of art, sculpture, weaving, or ceramic by an American artist
    ◦ Cowboys-and-Indians outfits for the children

Korea

An ancient land, populated by one ethnic family speaking one language, the people of Korea are believed to have descended from several Mongol tribes that migrated from Central Asia into the Korean peninsula during prehistoric times. In spite of its troubles with its communist brother in the northern half, the country has managed to become one of the leading industrial countries in the world.

Business Manners

- The international visitor who can speak a bit about the country's history will endear himself to his or her Korean business colleague.
- Business cards are exchanged at the beginning of any discussion.
- Small talk then takes place, so the Korean can get to know his international colleagues on a personal basis. Koreans are interested in the family lives and the education of the American visitors. (They also enjoy receiving Christmas cards

from America that contain snapshots of the family.) This conversational period also allows the interpreter present to learn the cadence and rhythm of the Americans present at the meeting, and to become so accustomed to their voices, he or she will have less difficulty in translating them correctly.

Social Customs

- There are no dietary restrictions in Korea. The population is about one-third Buddhist, one-third Christian, and one-third (as a diplomat ruefully explained it), "nothing."
- Alcohol can be drunk by everyone.
- Koreans smoke to excess, but now health scares are beginning to take effect. There are no-smoking sections in restaurants and in some offices now.
- If an American businessman comes without his wife, he will probably dine with his Korean host and then go to a nightclub afterward to see the dancing and to judge the "physical fitness" of the Korean hostesses and showgirls. If he comes with his wife, his Korean host will bring along his wife for a sedate dinner in a restaurant.

Dress

People in business tend to dress in somber, dark colors, although the younger men have started to wear light gray suits, for example, which is considered modern thinking. The older businessmen will still be in their dark suits.

Before you go to Korea on business, write to the Korean Embassy, 2370 Massachusetts Avenue N.W., Washington, DC 20008, for a copy of their small but exceedingly helpful book, *Facts About Korea*.

Dining Manners

- The guest of honor begins eating first, so if you are in a quandary, just take a sip from your bowl of soup, and you will be doing the right thing.
- An American who is on a return visit to Korea will greatly please his hosts if he mentions a Korean dish he particularly liked and was hoping to enjoy again, such as *Ttokkuk*, a famous rice cake soup (made with beaten egg, ground beef, green onions, and toasted seaweed).
- When you arrive at a restaurant for dinner, there will be a bowl of soup and a bowl of rice at your place. The other items on the menu will be in many dishes all over the table. It is communal eating; everyone at the table will serve himself and herself from the platters. Take small portions of whatever you wish, and eat it mouthful by mouthful. Do not pile up bits of food on top of the rice in your rice bowl (which is considered very rude). Just pick a

morsel of food with your chopsticks or spoon, eat it and then pick a morsel from another dish.

- ○ You will be given chopsticks and a spoon, but, as in countries like Japan and China, you will be given Western eating utensils, if you prefer them.

Gifts

- · When you first visit your colleague in Korea (or when he comes to visit you in the United States for the first time), give him a small present, such as a pen, keychain, or a tie printed with your company's corporate logo.
- · When you first visit his home in Seoul, bring him fresh fruit and cookies or, the traditional first gift, a set of candles. Give any number of candles except four, because four is an unlucky number, associated with death.
- · On your next trip to Korea, bring him a bottle of Scotch or Bourbon, and a box of chocolates for his wife and children.
- · On your third trip, bring him three or five bottles of American wine (never four!), which is highly prized because it is unobtainable in Korea.
- · You will receive a gift from your Korean colleague in return each time, of the same value as yours to him.
- · If you know your Korean colleague well, if your relationship is going extremely well, you would symbolize the success in the relationship by the gifts for your colleague's spouse and children. Bring a variety of gifts, however modest, with you when you come on business. It is much easier to present them there than to have to send them from the United States.
- · You might well be invited to your Korean colleague's home for dinner, instead of a restaurant, particularly if a family event is being celebrated—a baby's first birthday, a parent's sixtieth birthday, or perhaps a housewarming for a new home.
- · *If your Korean colleague brings you a very special gift for your wife, such as a beautiful* Hanbok (a long, full, traditional garment with embroidery) in a magnificent color, made to her measurements, you will know that you are a beloved special friend. Your business relationship could not be closer.

A sidebar here: a Korean businessman once brought his American counterpart a beautiful Korean doll, dressed in a *hanbok*, authentic from the top of her carefully dressed black hair to her cotton socks and straw boat-shaped shoes. The doll was encased in a glass display box. The American was so touched by the gift, he brought back his Korean colleague on his next trip to Seoul a Barbie doll. She came complete with long blond hair and a wardrobe trunkful of clothes, including a tennis dress and a bikini.

The People's Republic of China

It makes business sense for American business men and women to learn how to deal politely with the people of China. The country is very important to us for its offshore manufacturing capabilities, and with its vast population has the potential of becoming an important destination for our products.

Business Manners

- Exchange business cards early in your meeting with Chinese business people. It is imperative that your card be printed in Chinese on its reverse side.
- Remember that the family name is given first on the Chinese card. In other words, you would address Wang Fuming as Mr. Wang, not Mr. Fuming.
- Make small talk for ten minutes or so before talking business.
- You will probably be served tea at every appointment. Accept it with a slight bow, and enjoy the beautiful porcelain cup and saucer. If you don't like tea, pretend to take a few sips. If you do like tea, ask questions about the type of tea you are drinking, where it comes from. It will honor your host.
- The Chinese will not talk business without the presence of a skilled interpreter. You would be helping matters by writing out in advance any difficult names or technological processes to which you will be referring in the discussions, so that the interpreter can study them before you negotiate. I remember witnessing an American-Chinese discussion involving very complex scientific data. Both the Chinese and the American executives had their own translators, and it was fascinating to see first one interpreter perplexed, then the other. The two interpreters would then hold a rapid discussion between the two of them in low voices to get matters straightened out on all overly-technical points
- The Chinese are slow to make business decisions. Their deliberations are often painful to impatient Americans, but patience is an Asian virtue worth developing.

Social Customs

- Noisy, conspicuous behavior is frowned upon.
- Punctuality is not just polite, it is a necessity. So allow extra time between meetings for the probable traffic jams that will occur.
- Dress modestly and in dark colors. Do not wear all white, the color of mourning.
- Do not embrace, hug, or pat a Chinese. They do not welcome body contact with people who are not family or close friends.
- It is important to instruct yourself, before you come to China, about the structure of the Communist government and the country's history in this century. But also learn something about the great dynasties, too, and the culture—the art of porcelain-making that began in China, for example, and the silks, jade, and other examples of fine art that are on view in all the great museums of the world.
- Do not bring up in conversation Tiananmen Square or any political problems between our two countries.
- Tipping is prohibited. There is a service charge already on the bills. (If you feel you must leave something extra, put the money in an envelope, give it to a hotel

official privately, and ask him to distribute it.) Personally thank everyone who served you in your hotel, and if you write a letter to the manager praising the staff and service, you will never be forgotten.

· Any thank-you notes to your Chinese colleagues (and they are potently effective when you do write them) are best translated into Chinese. You would send the letter in English with an accompanying translation.

· As a Westerner, you will be much stared at and smiled at. It's important to smile back. If you are in a rural area and the people, who are fascinated by foreigners, applaud you, applaud back.

Dining Manners

○ You will never be taken to a restaurant that does not have Western flatware for the asking. If you can manage chopsticks deftly, however, your Chinese colleagues will be pleased.

○ As an official business guest, you will be given a banquet. There are four categories of banquets, and before you leave China, you should give a return one of the same calibre (to host a more lavish one would embarrass your hosts).

○ Arrive very punctually at the banquet, and leave the minute everyone has eaten, for the guest of honor must leave first.

○ Early in the meal, your host will probably toast you. Fifteen minutes or so later, toast him back.

○ During the meal, the host may rise with his plate in his hand, walk over to you, and place a choice morsel of food on your plate, because he thinks you are more worthy of it than he.

○ In South China an all-male group would go to a bar after the banquet is finished.

Gifts

· Traditionally, the Chinese Communist government has discouraged the practice of its people accepting gifts from foreigners. Today, even though this tough rule is relaxing, it is still more appropriate to give a handsome, expensive gift not to your individual Chinese business colleague, but to his company or export group or some kind of professional organization to which he belongs.

· Your Chinese contact would appreciate a gift of liquor, but be sure to check with the travel agency handling your tickets to see how many bottles you are allowed to bring with you at that moment in time. If you are bringing a gift of liquor to a business organization, you might be allowed to bring in more bottles.

· If your contact likes classical music, the gift of the latest CDs would be greatly appreciated.

- Give gifts in pairs, not odd numbers (give four porcelain mugs, never three or five, for example; give ten flowers, never nine).
- Do not give a Chinese a clock, for it is strongly associated with death.
- A set of very fine, crafted chopsticks is a beautiful gift; a set of cheap, commercial ones with an American-Chinese company logo printed on them as an ad would be an amusing diversion for a Chinese. He would never use them but would have fun showing them around.
- If you have your contact's shoe size (have him send you a drawing of his foot to ascertain his size), a pair of American running shoes or sneakers would please him greatly.

11

Giving the Perfect Business Gift

Gifts touch the full range of our emotions, no matter how blasé or enthusiastic we may be about receiving them.

Gifts—whether business or personal—can cement relationships in the most wonderfully warm, personal way; conversely, they can completely decimate relationships when they are given as a payback (never fine enough), as a bribe (usually loathsome from every point of view), or as an apology for a wrong that has been committed.

SOME GENERAL GUIDELINES

- *The best kind of gift is chosen specifically with the recipient in mind.* (The enclosure card might read: "Hey, amigo, you've always complained you don't have a mini-computerized agenda like mine, so now you do!"
- *The best kind of gift is unexpected.* (The enclosure card: "I know how you love the Bears—as much as I do. I won this pair of tickets at a charity auction, and since I'm going to be out of town at a marketing meeting that week, I'm giving them to you. Cheer them on for me!")
- *The best kind of gift is a true gesture of friendship.* ("A little bird told me you were collecting jade amulets. I saw this when I was in Hong Kong last spring, thought of you instantly, and decided to give it to you at Christmas.")
- *The best kind of gift shows a sense of humor.* ("Since you and I have been arguing over one another's taste in ties for ten years, I have decided to give you the ulti-

mate tie this Christmas, to prove to you, once and for all, that my taste is better than yours!'')
- *The best kind of gift shows great research and thought.* (''Your secretary told me that the one missing link from your collection of eighteenth-century maps is Portugal, so I put my bloodhounds on it and came up with this one. I hope it will round out your collection.'')
- *The best kind of gift is one that does not exceed your budget.* It is unsuitable to spend more than the company can afford, or a sum that will anger shareholders. The days of incredible largesse are past, probably forever. Whether you are researching a corporate giveaway to send to 5,000 customers, or a present for the chairman of the executive committee who is stepping down, look long and hard, and you will find the right gift in your price range.

GET HELP WHEN YOU NEED IT: THE GIFT CONSULTANT

If you have potential crises looming on the horizon—a really complicated holiday gift project ahead, a plant or new office headquarters opening, an immense anniversary celebration year approaching—and you have no one on staff who is trained in the gift business, *use a gift consultant.* He or she will save you money by shopping the right sources, negotiating the price to its lowest point or knowing how to purchase at discount, perhaps designing something that only your company will have, staying within your budget, and getting the items properly wrapped and properly shipped *on time.* The gift business is complicated and demanding. Most companies do not have the trained hired hands on deck to do it successfully. Save yourself money, time, and ulcers. Use a professional.

There are corporate gift consultants in almost all big department stores and luxury gift stores who will steer you through their merchandise and arrange for a corporate discount. Otherwise, find a gift consultant by word of mouth or by checking the Yellow Pages telephone book.

THE REASONS WHY YOU SEND SOMEONE A GIFT

- To thank a business associate for an introduction to someone he or she knows, whether it resulted in a benefit to you or not
- To thank someone who gave a lunch or dinner in your honor
- To thank a couple who had you for dinner at their house
- To wish *close* business colleagues well when they:

  · Get married
  · Have a baby

- Come through a serious illness or operation
- Celebrate an important wedding anniversary

- To thank someone who gave you information that helped you land business
- To thank someone who treated you to the theater, a sporting event, or any major outing
- To thank the people who helped you in your work in the nonprofit sector
- To congratulate a person on the occasion of a major promotion
- To commend someone who has just won an award or trophy or has been elected to a high office
- To encourage someone you manage who has overcome a big obstacle in his life (conquered stuttering, achieved a needed weight loss, mastered a foreign language used in your international business dealings, etc.)
- To cheer up someone who has had a major illness or undergone surgery
- To help someone do his or her job better (an electronic gadget; a foreign language course, etc.)

WHEN YOU DO NOT WISH PEOPLE TO BRING GIFTS TO A PARTY IN YOUR HONOR

In my opinion, when hosts put "Please no gifts" on their invitations to birthday celebrations, anniversaries, and the like, the negative phrase jumps out right in the recipient's face, and ruins the look of the invitation. That word *no* is a strong negative, and doesn't belong on an invitation. It is preferable, in my opinion, if the advice is passed around by word of mouth. Any person in the office handling RSVPs, for example, should be trained to say at the conclusion of every telephone conversation with someone who has called to accept the invitation, "Oh, and by the way, Mr. Host would appreciate everyone attending *without* bringing or sending a gift. He feels his guests *are* the gifts."

Regardless of whether or not guests bring gifts to the party, presents should not be unwrapped, nor the donor thanked, during the event. Gifts should be set aside, opened after guests have gone, and donors thanked by letter.

BUSINESS GIFT IDEAS
(See also "International Gift-Giving," Chapter 10)

Giveaways

The company's promotional items, used by salesmen to give to customers and potential customers, and used generally by everyone in the marketing and sales force as a public relations tool of goodwill, should never be shoddily designed or manufactured. Even if it is a $1 item, a giveaway should never be allowed to detract from the company's first-class image.

Promotional items, ranging in cost from fifty cents to $50 each can be tastefully manufactured in the following categories:

Balloons
Bar glasses
Baseball jackets
Beach towels
Belt buckles
Books
Boxes or baskets
Brushes
Bumper stickers
Business card cases
Buttons
Calendars
Calculators
Calorie counters
Cameras
Caps
Carving knives
Combination locks
Combs
Cosmetic cases
Credit card cases
Cufflinks
Cutting boards
Decorative file
    folders
Diaries
Electronic address
    "books"

Expense account
    notebooks
First aid kits
Flashlights
Frisbees
Game sets
Garment bags
Golf balls
Golf shirts
Handkerchiefs
Highway emergency
    kits
His/her aprons
Jewelry items for
    women
Keychains
Legal pads in covers
Manicure kits
Map cases
Measuring tapes
Memo pads
Mugs
Neckties
Paper napkins
Paperweights
Pen and pencil sets
Penknives
Picture frames
Plastic rainhats

Playing cards
Pocket dictionaries
Ponchos
Posters
Puzzles
Racquet covers
Radios
Scarves
Scissors
Self-stick notepads
Sewing kits
Shoebags
Shoeshine kits
Ski hats
Stick pins
Stop watches
Sweat bands
Sweatshirts
Tennis balls
Tennis hats
Tennis towels
Thermometers
Thermos bottles
Tie clips
T-shirts
Umbrellas
Yardsticks
Zippered sports totes

The Corporate Logo Gift

When offering gifts bearing your company logo—such as golf balls, tennis balls, calendars and agendas, and umbrellas—the corporate logo should be small and unobtrusive. This is especially true for those items that will be part of one's personal life, like those that sit on a desk or nightstand or are kept in a handbag or briefcase. People usually don't mind using an umbrella printed with a large handsome logo or a pen with a tiny logo on the clip, but they are not going to keep their engagements in a leather agenda, the front of which is adorned with a huge commercial logo of a firm other than their own.

Keep the logo small. Emboss it on the underside of the leather notepad. Incise it on the backside of the clock. Engrave it in a tiny size on the keychain disk. Stamp it unobtrusively on the bottom of the silk scarf or on the underside of the leather wallet. The more unreadable or unnoticed it is, the more that item will be used by recipients who do not work for the company. In other words, don't waste corporate funds on over-commercialized gifts that you want people to use and enjoy.

Electronic Gifts

For young people who are in the early years of their careers, electronic gadgets make wonderful presents: cellular telephones, answering machines, palm-size computers, computer notebooks, agendas with calculators.

A kind grandparent or godparent who gives a young person a laptop computer with or without a printer will be entrenched, probably forever, as the favorite relative of all time.

Sending Flowers

Flowers are an easy-to-send, quick-to-arrive gift. They may be ordered by telephone; you can either send your card to the florist, or you can dictate your message by telephone to the florist. Flowers are telegraphed throughout the world. They are an international symbol of greeting, celebration, and gratitude. An executive who goes abroad to any country should remember that he should send flowers before or after any meal at which he is an honored guest *in someone's home.*

In this country, flowers were traditionally sent by couples, by a woman to another woman, or by a man to a woman, but never by a woman to a man. In this new era of equality, that qualification has disappeared. Women should send flowers to men for the very same reasons they receive them themselves. Generally, if a woman is sending flowers to thank a male executive for a favor or to congratulate him, she would send them to his office. If she has been a dinner guest in his home, she would send them to his home. If she sends them home to a couple, the flowers should be sent to both husband and wife.

It is always better to send flowers either on the morning of the party or the day after. If you arrive at the door with flowers in hand, your host will have to stop his or her activities in order to find the proper vase, to arrange them and to put them in the proper spot—an unwelcome interruption for the host.

If you are wondering whether to send an arrangement or cut flowers to someone, here is a good rule: *Send an arrangement to a person's office but cut flowers to his or her home.*

To an executive who is ill in the hospital, send a plant that requires little care. Flowers that need maintenance are neglected in busy hospitals. Send flowers when the patient is back home, recuperating from the hospital stay.

Important: When sending holiday plants and flowers to people's homes, check first with the recipients' offices to make sure they will be in residence when the floral offerings arrive. It is very depressing, if one is returning home from Christmas vacation, to find dead plants or flowers awaiting one at the front entrance or in the hallway.

Food as a Business Gift

Food is a wonderful gift. It is shared by the recipient with the others in his family or office, so it has a widespread influence. It is a gift that leaves a fleeting but pleasurable kind of memory behind it.

Gourmet food shops and mail order catalogs today make it possible for foods of all kinds to be shipped and handled properly, so that they arrive at their destination in good condition.

If the region in which you live is noted for a certain food (for example, peaches from Oregon, grapefruit and oranges from Florida and Texas, pecans from Georgia, cheese from Wisconsin, etc.) your gift to those in other regions is always a welcome one.

POPULAR GIFTS OF FOOD	EXPENSIVE GIFTS OF FOOD
Baked goods: cakes, cookies, breads	Beluga caviar
Candy	Fresh-killed wild game and fowl
Cheeses	Fresh lobsters flown in
Crackers	Frozen steaks flown in
Exotic teas and coffees	Gourmet food packages in reusable
Fresh fruit	containers
Frozen casseroles (for local use)	Imported pâtés
Gourmet soups in tins	Smoked delicacies
Jams and jellies	Smoked salmon from Scotland
Nuts	Special ice creams and sauces (for
Pure maple syrup	local use)

Liquor and Wine as Business Gifts

A gift of liquor or wine requires reflection. It's very easy to call up a retailer and have him deliver a case of good vodka to someone as a gift. But if that person is a Scotch drinker, he is going to shrug his shoulders and say to himself. "Oh, well, some day I'll have a cocktail party and use it up," or "This will please my vodka-drinking friends when they come by." How much greater an effect this gift would have had if a case of Scotch had arrived! The recipient would have known that the donor had remembered or had researched what he liked to drink. And, of course, if the male recipient of the gift is a Scotch drinker and his wife drinks gin, what an impact a case of half

Scotch, half gin would have! All that is required is a telephone call to the executive's secretary to learn the liquor preferences of the executive and his or her spouse.

Wine as a gift has a broad range of appeal, because if the recipient doesn't drink wine himself, he probably serves it at home to guests, whether during the cocktail hour or at the dinner table. You do not need to know the subtleties of your recipient's preferences—i.e., whether he prefers a Burgundy to a Bordeaux or vice versa—because wine is a gift meant to be shared, and a good bottle is appreciated by anyone who drinks wine, particularly in tandem with good food.

If you arrive at someone's home for dinner with a bottle or two of wine in hand, say immediately to your host, "Here's something to put away and enjoy on a *future* occasion." By party time, any good host has his wine selected and perhaps already opened and "breathing." Actually it's nicer if your gift of wine is delivered the day *after* the dinner, with your thank-you note attached.

Champagne is a luxurious symbol of celebration, rejoicing, and special occasions. Many people feel as do I, that if you can't afford a good imported champagne, or a fine American sparkling wine, don't buy it; buy a bottle of wine instead as your gift.

Good cognac (brandy) and after-dinner liqueurs are welcome presents. Don't send a gift of liqueur, however, to someone who rarely entertains at home; it will sit on the shelf for years gathering dust.

Remember never to send a gift of alcohol to someone who is not of legal drinking age, and naturally never to someone who doesn't drink, even if you think he will use it for entertaining others. Never send alcohol to a person's office, always to his home address.

In deciding how much to send a business contact, here is a general guide:

- As a gift of friendship or to say thank you for a meal in someone's home or in a restaurant, any of the following:

  - One or two bottles of a modest wine
  - A bottle of liquor
  - A bottle of sherry, aperitif, or liqueur

- A more significant gift for someone's birthday or anniversary:

  - A bottle of good champagne
  - Two bottles of good liquor

- An important gift (when you and your family have spent the weekend):

  - A case of champagne
  - A case of good wine
  - A case of good liquor
  - A bottle of rare wine, brandy, or port

Bar Accessories

These make great presents. Look around your business friend's bar in his home or office to notice what he needs. The wine bottle opener may be old and tarnished; he may be missing a bar knife. If the glasses are of different patterns, it is a sign that a set of a dozen bar glasses would be useful.

Here are some gift ideas:

- Small serving tray (with a rim to keep glasses from sliding off)
- Bar pitcher (a small one, to hold water)
- Ice bucket (the gift recipient can usually use a new one!)
- Ice tongs
- Bar knife and cutting board (for slicing lemon peel, sectioning limes, etc.)
- Coasters (for glasses)
- Cocktail napkins in paper or in fabric
- Wine cooler
- Wine bottle coasters (to put on the dining table for protection)
- Bar glasses and other glasses needed for a party:
  - Old-fashioneds
  - Highball glasses
  - All-purpose wineglasses
  - Champagne flutes
  - Sherry-liqueur glasses
  - Brandy snifters
  - Beer mugs

If you are buying glasses as a gift, purchase a minimum of six or eight.

For Special People and Special Occasions

For the New Executive

Card case
Desk caddy (for paper clips, rubber bands,
    tape, etc.)
Dictionary-thesaurus set
If executive begins career in another city, a
    year's subscription to his hometown
    newspaper
Latest book on management techniques
Leather desk calendar

Leather scrapbook
Membership in a health club
Pen and pencil set
Pen set for desk
Pocket calculator
Pocket calendar
Subscription to an important financial
    newspaper or magazine
The ultimate gift: the briefcase

For the Traveler

Expandable tote
First aid kit
Folding umbrella
Good face soap in plastic container
Luggage tags with name and address
Magnified folding cosmetic/shaving mirror
Palmtop PC
Piece of needed luggage (to match or in
    keeping with his existing pieces)

Portable exercise equipment
Portable smoke detector (could save his life)
Sewing kit
Shoe bags
Toilet kit for man; cosmetics kit for woman
Travel iron

For the International Traveler

Address book for foreign addresses
Battery-operated hairdryer
Battery-operated radio-alarm clock
Diary for trip notes
Foreign dictionary

List of world holidays
Money exchange calculator
Rolls of film (to fit his camera)
Wallet-passport case
Watch with time told on different continents

For a Colleague's Newly Decorated Office

Antique container for pens and pencils
Ashtrays
Bar glass sets (if senior executive has bar)
Bookends
Crystal jar containing hard candies
Desk or wall clock
Desk set with matching wastebasket (match
    the basic colors of the office)
Gift certificate to a lithograph-print store

Large standing plant in handsome container
Leather telephone directory cover
Letter opener
Magazine rack
Picture frame
Thermos set with glasses and tray
Wall mirror (if secretary or executive's
    spouse says it would be useful)

EXCHANGING GIFTS IN THE OFFICE
SHOULD BE DISCOURAGED

Employees should be discouraged from giving one another gifts inside the office, because when it is allowed, the office landscape becomes littered with gifts and wrapping paper, business papers are misplaced, work time is lost, and people are distracted.

It is also unfair because the popular employees are hidden behind a sea of gifts on their desks while the desks of others who do not have many friends are uncluttered.

Holiday gifts are best sent to each person's home, or exchanged after work or in a restaurant or somehow away from the office landscape. Then no one will be gossiping about who got what, or who got nothing at all!

COMPANY POLICY PROHIBITING
THE ACCEPTANCE OF GIFTS

Senior managers in some companies insist that all employees adhere to the company's policy forbidding the acceptance of any gift above a specified, modest value. (In other words, you're allowed to accept a plastic wallet-size calendar but not an azalea plant!) Some companies have "ethics awareness" programs for employees where the subject of gifts is discussed in detail; others make new employees sign a conflict-of-interest agreement that spells out gift policies. In copying federal agencies' strict rules governing gift acceptance, some companies will not even permit their people to be taken to lunch or dinner by a customer, based on the philosophy that one of their employees who is even slightly beholden to an outside source might allow that other person advantages in the transaction of business. Regardless of how you may feel about another company's strict policy, it is better for all concerned to know about it and to follow it. It is most embarrassing for the person who may be forced to return your small Christmas present, for example—embarrassing for him, but also for you.

If your company has any kind of limitations on the type or monetary value of gifts they accept, including lunches and dinners, articulate it carefully in personnel notices, and remind all employees again before the holiday season begins.

If your company deals with other corporations who have strict gift policies, be sure you have this information in your gift files, so gift returns won't be necessary.

A CEO made a profound statement on this subject one time, in an employee-management meeting:

"I don't have to give the men and women of this company a lecture on bribery. You all know what's right and what's wrong. You're intelligent people whom management trusts. You wouldn't have been hired otherwise. Therefore, I'm rescinding my predecessor's tough policy on gift acceptance. You can accept anything of minor value, and I'm not going to tell you what is minor or major. I'm not going to have you getting out your calculators to determine if the dollars involved in an object you've just unwrapped means you have to send it back. I'm expecting you to ask your consciences, not a calculator.

"And don't send me a Christmas present, by the way, because then I'd *know* you have a bad conscience!"

AT HOLIDAY TIME

The Company Policy Toward Employees and Gifts

A senior manager's holiday gift list is important. It can also get out of hand. There are two comforting factors to remember:

1. *Just because someone gives you a present does not mean you must give him or her one in return*. If that person was not on your original gift list, forget it.

The person who gives you a present when you had not planned to give him one may be thanking you for some special kindness or favor over the past year, one that you may even have forgotten about. (If you are *giving* someone a gift for a special reason, *explain why* in your gift enclosure card, so he won't feel obliged to rush out to buy a gift in kind. Your enclosure card might read: "This remembrance for the holiday season is just to say that I will never forget how you helped us out last spring when our office suffered so much damage from the big storm.")

2. *If profits are down and the company is downsizing, make a policy concerning gift giving on the executive level.* Send a nice holiday greeting to the customers who usually are recipients of your largesse at Christmas and communicate why they won't be receiving a gift. A greeting card containing a hand-written note would be appropriate:

Dear Angela,

     This hasn't been the kind of year that allows us to open up Santa's bag, but we want you to know how much we appreciate your fine support over the past months. We treasure our business relationship with you and look forward to better times a year from now. Thank you, especially for your friendship. Have a wonderful New Year.''

Bonuses are given for performance and are earned, even if they are distributed during the holiday season, so they are not considered gifts. Companies differ quite dramatically in the way they approach holiday gift giving, depending on how good their business is, the practices in the various regions where the company has offices or plants, and the type of industry.

Here are the options in Christmas gift giving:

- To have no company policy whatsoever
- To prohibit any gift giving
- To give each employee a food package, a transistor radio, a Christmas turkey, or something of this nature
- To give employees a gift catalog from which they order an item of their choice or receive the equivalent (such as $25) in cash
- To consider the company Christmas party as the gift
- To consider the company Christmas card, signed by the CEO, as the gift
- To distribute gifts to the needy instead of giving employee gifts

The decision management makes on this subject is an important one, in that it is related to employee morale and to how well the company is doing. Certainly it is an individual decision. What is good for one company may not be good for another.

Your Own Holiday Gift Policy

Your Secretary

If your secretary has worked for you a year or less, you might give her a small impersonal gift, such as a Christmas plant or a food basket.

- If she has worked for you from two to four years, give her a gift certificate to a favorite store for $25.
- If she's been with you for five to ten years, spend $50 to $100 on her.
- If you are successful and your secretary has been with you, serving as your right arm for many years, helping you climb the ladder of success, she deserves a generous reward at holiday time. You might think of giving a gift of company stock each year; you might send two tickets for a week's cruise. Or you might give her a handsome gold watch, or pay off the remaining small mortgage on the family's apartment or home. Probably nothing you can give in the way of a material reward will properly recompense for all that she has done for you through the years.
- If a secretary is shared by two or three people, which is often the case these days, the bosses should decide on a gift and each should contribute an equal share. A gift certificate to the kind of store she loves is probably a good idea for this present.
- Remember, the enclosure card—thanking your secretary for putting up with you—is as important as the gift.

Do not expect a gift from your secretary, although if she is close to you, you will probably receive one. She should certainly not buy anything expensive, but perhaps she saw some new fishing flies that would delight her boss, an ardent fisherwoman, or perhaps she knows when her boss's sweet tooth would be soothed by a box of favorite southern pralines. It would be inappropriate for her to spend a lot of money on her boss' gift. A holiday card with a warm message of gratitude inside is the very best gift of all, even something as simple as, "I feel fortunate to be working for you. Thank you for your many kindnesses this past year."

A secretary who has worked for a long time for one person usually knows her boss' family almost as well as her own. In this case, a book for each family member or a nice box of Christmas cookies for everyone is a nice gesture.

Ideas for Personal Holiday Gifts for Those in Your Professional Life

- Compact disks
- Gift baskets of food
- Gift certificates to an art studio or a bookstore
- Hard-to-get tickets to a game of his or her favorite sport or performing arts

The recipients for these gifts are:

- The manager of the executive dining room
- The driver of your company car
- Your corporate jet pilot
- Your foreign language teacher
- Your personal trainer

Christmas Tipping

Tips or gifts of money may be made in cash or by check, always tucked into a greeting card.

- The maitre d'hotel at your favorite restaurant ($25)
- The head of your garage at home where you keep your personal car (give him $100 to distribute to the other men and himself, but make it $200 if you have an exceptionally fine or large car that requires special care, or if you keep two cars in that garage)
- Donate $100 to the employees Christmas fund in every private club of which you are a member, but $200 if you use the club facilities and entertain there constantly.

A Gift of Money for People Who Serve You at Home

Remember those who deserve a Christmas card with a ten- or twenty-dollar bill tucked inside, including:

- The postman (one or more of them). If you have a normal amount of mail delivered at home, $10 each is fine. If you have a great deal of mail, give each one $20.
- If you have a private garbage service, give each person $10.
- The delivery person from your grocers ($10)
- Your dry cleaning and laundry delivery person ($10)
- Your newspaper delivery people (give each one $10)

A Gift of Money Plus a Personal Gift

- A woman who goes to a posh hairdressing salon weekly might give the following:
  - $50 and a gift, like a sweater, to her hairstylist
  - $20 and a gift, like a pair of earrings, to her manicurist
  - $10 and a gift, like a box of candy, to her shampoo person
  - Costume jewelry or scarves to the receptionists

In a modest establishment she would give much less, and there would be fewer employees to give to.

- A man who visits a hairstylist each week would give tips of money only, from $10 to $50, according to what each person in that establishment does for him.
- A man or woman who visits the hair salon or barber only on occasion might give the shop owner or the person who always takes care of him a tip of from $10 to $20 tucked into a holiday greeting card.
- The babysitter who comes to your home five days a week might receive something like a week's extra wages in cash and a gift she may really need, such a new jacket, a good handbag, even new tires for her car. Your child(ren) should also give her a gift, perhaps something made in school.
- If you are fortunate enough to have a housekeeper who comes to your home five times a week, she might receive a week's extra wages and a personal gift, too, along with a gift from your children.
- The occasional babysitter and cleaning person might receive a gift of $20 and a small personal item, like a scarf or pair of gloves.

Keeping an Updated Gift List

It's important to keep an updated computerized list of every gift given by the company, whether it's a giveaway, a present for customers, a gift for certain VIPs, or personal gifts of friendship from senior managers to their colleagues on the outside. It's important to be able to have a good overall view of what has been purchased, how much has been spent, and exactly who have been the beneficiaries of the company's holiday spirit.

The computerized list must be changed when people die, get divorced, remarry, change companies, or retire. I remember one senior member of management whose wife was murdered—with the story naturally well-known in the press—and who was absolutely furious when for years after the terrible event, several of his colleagues' companies sent him gifts and greeting cards addressed each time to him and his wife. One fellow executive would even pen a note, using the widower's and his late wife's given names with the coziest of familiarities.

Keeping good records keeps mistakes from happening, but it also keeps errors from happening such as sending the same thing this year that you sent two years ago, except that the gift two years ago was of much nicer quality.

PAYING FOR GIFTS

Many companies have a standard gift for employees at Christmas, a standard gift for customers or clients, and inexpensive promotional items used mostly as giveaways. Obviously all of these are paid for by the company.

Beyond this kind of gift giving, there is great diversity in company policies about gifts. Some companies pay for all of the gifts given individually by all members of top management to the business community. Others pay for special gifts given by all executives, provided justification has been furnished and written approval has been received in advance. Most executives, however, frequently face a decision on whether giving a gift to someone connected in business is worth the outlay of personal funds. It is much like giving a gift to a personal friend. (The government allows a tax deduction on a business gift only up to $25 in cost, which helps curb excessive gift giving practices.)

Most senior executives will agree that it is on occasion worthwhile for an executive to pay for a small gift to a business associate from his own pocket, provided the timing is right, the reason is justified, and the choice of gift is propitious.

How Much Should You Spend?

Gifts presented by junior executives and mid-managers to their clients cost around $40 on the average.

Gifts presented by mid- to upper-managers might cost $45–$60. Senior executives might spend from $50 to $150 for top customers and close friends in the business world.

Gifts costing more than $150 are only for very important and rare occasions.

THE MANNER OF PRESENTING THE GIFT

The manner in which a gift is made is extremely important. It should be presented to show that the donor has high esteem for the recipient *and* for the gift.

- *A gift should be presented in person,* if possible. When you hand a present to the recipient, it assumes added importance and meaning because of the impact of your voice, expression, and perhaps even your handshake or mini-embrace as you present it.
- *It should be beautifully wrapped.* Nothing is more of a downer than receiving a gift that is sloppily presented. I remember seeing the fallen expression on an executive's face when he was handed an expensive crystal bowl that had been beautifully wrapped but had been tucked inside a food chain's plastic shopping bag. The entire effect was ruined.

  Many U.S. presidents have used as their gift-wrapping a wonderfully handsome white paper, blind-embossed in a repeat pattern with the President's official seal. Gold and white ribbons are used with the paper, and the effect is stunning. Any business could have its own paper made and blind-embossed with its logo or symbol, a handsome way to display the company's imprimatur.
- *One should take pains with the enclosure card.* Enclosing your business card

without a signature and a personal message is a cold and impersonal way to send a gift. It conveys the feeling the donor never saw the present or had anything to do with its dispatch. If you use your business card as an enclosure, put a slash through your name and write your given name in ink. Add a sentence on the front or back of the card, such as "Hope you can use this." Or, if you're sending a wedding present to colleagues, write something like "With best wishes to Susan and Jerry for a wonderful life ahead."

Always use a piece of good notepaper or one of your correspondence cards, if you have this kind of stationery, for your enclosure card message. It's much nicer than your business card.

Be thoughtful about what you write on your card. A card enclosed with a dozen grapefruit that says, "Thanks for giving me the business, and I look forward to more," certainly does not have the impact of a card that says, "We've been having a long tough winter, you've been working too hard, so you deserve a little extra Vitamin C!"

If you're sending a gift to a married couple and you have forgotten the first name of the spouse, just write on your card, "To the Bradfords, with best wishes for . . ."

Enclose your gift card in an envelope, whether matching or not.

A gift worth giving is a gift worth presenting well. As the French say, in respect to a gift or a dinner: *"Il faut bien présenter les choses . . ."*

GIVING AND RETURNING THE INAPPROPRIATE GIFT

The giving and acceptance of gifts is not an easy art. An inappropriate gift that is too expensive, too inexpensive, too personal, or just in bad taste may cause embarrassment, even distress to the recipient. But it may have even worse repercussions on the sender. Danger signals are in order:

- When an executive gives a lavish gift such as jewelry or furs to his secretary
- When a gift is related to a smutty joke and is supposed to be amusing but falls flat when presented. (Such gifts are in particularly poor taste during the Christmas season.)
- When a gift has not been researched, with the result that an executive gives a car accessory to an executive who does not own a car, liquor is sent to someone who doesn't drink, clothing of the wrong size is sent as a gift, or a piece of sports equipment is sent to a nonplayer
- When a gift with obvious sexual overtones is presented

Any gift with sexual or with bribery connotations should be returned immediately to the sender because if the recipient keeps the gift for a few days, the donor will consider it accepted. I remember a pretty young secretary who received from her boss on her first Christmas an 18-carat-gold ankle bracelet. The boss' card read: "I'd like to see this wrapped around that beautiful ankle of yours.'' She rewrapped it and put it on his desk right away with her own note attached: ''And I'd like to see this wrapped tight around that beautiful little neck of yours.'' (The good part of this story is that she kept her job and he never bothered her again.)

If you receive something you know you shouldn't keep, return it at once. Retain a copy of the note you send back with it, including the date and the manner in which it was sent back. (This is obviously for self-protection.) It is not necessary to explain *why* you are returning the gift. It is enough to write, ''I do not find it appropriate to accept this gift, so I am returning it at once.''

ACCEPTING AND ACKNOWLEDGING A GIFT

Part of good manners is knowing how to accept a gift with grace. This means putting a big smile on your face, even when you open the package and find a neon orange scarf that you would hesitate even to hang on a clothesline, for fear of ruining your image. It means saying ''How *very* nice'' with enthusiasm when someone has given you a leather desk calendar and you already own four of them. It means being warm and gracious about a gift of an office dictionary with the name of the company in large letters all over the leather binding. Little white lies are in order at this time, and kindness decrees that you say you like something even when you don't.

If you feel that company products you receive are inferior, do not praise them in your thank-you note. Instead, simply thank the donor ''for being so nice to remember us this holiday season.'' But if you really liked the company products, let the donor know with as much enthusiasm as you can generate. It will please him immensely.

By the way, a thank-you note for a gift should be sent no later than two weeks after its receipt. However, don't use a missed deadline as an excuse for putting it off permanently. It's *never* too late for that note.

WHEN YOU HAVE BEEN SOMEONE'S GUEST FOR DINNER

If you have been a guest in someone's home for a lunch or dinner, do one of the following:

- Send flowers a day beforehand, so they can be on view in the living room or on the dining room table.
- Send flowers the day afterward, to say ''thank you.''
- Bring one or two bottles of wine or a bottle of champagne with you.
- Send a gift of food after the party—like gourmet nuts, special cheese, or a basket of fruit.

Don't do any of the following:

- Arrive at the front door with flowers in hand (as noted), because your hosts will be too busy to find a proper vase or a place to display them to their best advantage.
- Say to your host, "This wine is for tonight." (Your host will already have opened the wine for tonight.) Say instead, "These are for you to put away and to open on another festive occasion."
- Send perishable food to your hosts, unless you have ascertained there will be someone home to refrigerate at once anything vulnerable to spoilage. (Have you ever seen a chocolate cheesecake that has been sitting in the boiling sun on a back-door step for an entire day?)

From a Houseguest to a Host

Any food gifts are appreciated by a host, particularly frozen casseroles or cooked ham, turkey, or roast beef. Warn the host you are bringing this food, so the host can decide whether to serve it to the household over the weekend, or freeze it and save it for another time. The following are also nice to bring along with you:

- Books of interest to your host, or good novels to keep houseguests occupied in case of bad weather
- Sports equipment: cans of tennis balls, boxes of golf balls, or balls for whatever game is being played
- Compact disks and tapes (Find out from your host's spouse or secretary what kind of equipment is in the house.)
- Movies to play on the VCR
- Kitchen accessories, to help make the meals easier to prepare and serve
- Serving items you have noticed were missing or in poor condition (ice bucket, trays, dessert plates, beer steins, barbecue implements, etc.)
- Towels for the bathrooms; towels for the beach (never enough)
- Big canvas tote-bags or carryalls
- Large-size dinner napkins and cocktail napkins of paper, personalized with hosts' names or the name of the house
- Nice smelling things for the house: room spray, potpourri, guest soaps, cologne
- Portable radio hooked into the meteorological service
- Handsome stationery—and pens; whimsical notepads and mugs of pens and pencils
- A striking bulletin board with chalk, so the hosts can inform their guests of what is going on and who is charged with doing what
- Presents for the host's children, to keep them occupied

BIRTHDAY PRESENTS IN THE BUSINESS WORLD

Birthday gifts normally are not given in the business world, but if someone attains a very senior age (still working at seventy-five, for example) it is a gracious gesture to mark such an impressive rite of passage. I personally think that a person at an advanced age has everything he or she needs, but to give a gift *in honor of* is the nicest kind of all. I have known companies that have purchased books for libraries that couldn't afford the books in honor of a colleague's special birthday; one company sent fifty children from the inner city to the circus in New York as a birthday present to an octogenarian vice-chairman of the board. His great joy was sharing the day with the children and having his photograph taken with them.

Birthday Cards

If you send a birthday card to any level of colleague—in or outside of your company—it will give that person great pleasure. It's a good idea to buy a large batch of birthday cards (the noninsulting, nonsexual kind, please!) and to send them out every time an important colleague, friend, customer, or client has a birthday. In order to do that, you must have a "tickler" file system set up, which alerts you to the days you should mail cards.

PRESENTS MARKING EMPLOYEES' SERVICE ANNIVERSARIES

It's a tremendous morale booster to an employee to be able to look forward to a small gift marking his or her anniversary with the company, beginning in the fifth year and recurring every five or ten years thereafter. It's important for management to recognize loyalty.

An example of a fifth anniversary gift is a small leather address book marked with the employee's name, the name of the company, and the words *Fifth Anniversary* in gold lettering on the cover.

For the tenth anniversary, a gold tie tack for the men and small gold stickpin for the women, engraved with a tiny company logo, is an appropriate gift.

For a fifteenth anniversary, a good watch. For the twenty-fifth anniversary (silver) the employees might receive handsome sterling silver boxes, suitably engraved.

For the Jade Anniversary (thirty-fifth), the employee might receive a piece of jewelry with jade, or a clock with a jade on the base. By the fiftieth anniversary, the company should have something like a very fine 18-carat-gold watch or bracelet to give its employees. If the employees make it to their sixtieth anniversary, they deserve something with diamonds (and can will it to a grandchild)!

WEDDING GIFTS

A company often pays for a wedding present sent to a major client or customer. Sometimes, the relationship between a younger executive and his customer is such that the young executive will pay for a wedding present out of his own pocket, rather than not send one because the company won't pay for it. The symbol of friendship counts when it comes to something as important as a wedding.

Some people are ingenious at finding gifts that look expensive even though they are not. If you travel abroad on business, you can pick up unusual items that are amusing or practical or just plain beautiful, and no one in the United States can possibly guess their value. Some people know how to haunt the thrift shops and small antique shops to find items under $50. It is important to include with your gift its provenance (the approximate date and country of origin of the object) if the shop owner can supply it. Others haunt the big sales in the stores and buy china and crystal gifts at greatly reduced prices. If you store these things, you will have them at the ready when it comes time to send a gift.

One executive I know attends the post-Christmas sales in the fine stores and buys greatly marked-down pieces of fine English bone china (small boxes, serving bowls, cachepots, creamer and sugar bowl, etc.). He has each one wrapped as a gift, ready to go with his card, for special events like weddings.

A Company's Wedding Gift for VIPs and Their Senior Executives

Some companies have a standard wedding present for senior managers and VIPs, and a less expensive gift for mid- and junior-managers for their weddings. The following are examples of both:

EXPENSIVE ($150 OR OVER)	LESS EXPENSIVE (UP TO $50)
Antique wood tea caddy	Dozen glasses (six wine, six water)
Dozen dessert plates	Large crystal pitcher, with etched
Mantlepiece clock	monogram on the side
Small engraved Tiffany silver box	Porcelain salad bowl
Sterling letter opener	Porcelain wine bottle coaster
Steuben crystal bowl	Serving tray
	Six white dessert plates

GIFTS FOR A BABY

If an important client or customer who is personally close to you has a baby, a gift is in order, whether your company will pay for it or not. Leave your company logo off anything in sterling silver that you have engraved. A baby's gift should be personal, and not commercial in any sense.

The "top of the line" gift would be something in sterling silver, engraved with the baby's name or initials and date of birth. As a gift for her best customer, one manager had Tiffany's engrave a replica of the baby's birth announcement on the lid of a silver box. The following are some popular items, in sterling:

- Mug (very expensive)
- Porringer (incredibly expensive)
- Spoon, or spoon and fork set
- Rattle
- Small picture frame to hold baby's photo
- Small box for the baby's dresser

In porcelain:

- Set of baby feeding dishes
- China mug
- Porcelain-handled baby fork and spoon
- Porcelain frame for baby's picture

Also:

- Baby's first book: one of the children's classics, in a fine edition, to start his or her first library
- Baby blanket or quilt
- Little girl's first piece of jewelry: gold bracelet or gold chain with her saint's medal

GIFTS FOR SOMEONE WHO IS ILL OR INJURED
(*See also* "Greeting Cards for Someone Who Is Seriously Ill," Chapter 7)

- A plant, particularly a flowering one, that will require little care and watering
- An amusing soft sculpture that may become a "mascot"
- An audio tape made of the person's colleagues back in the office, giving all the gossip and news
- A book on tape
- A book of amusing cartoons
- Music tapes
- Stationery with which the patient can write thank-you notes for all his or her gifts; include with it a good pen and a roll of stamps!
- Wonderfully scented things like room spray, cologne, and bath soap
- Bedjacket or shawl for a lady; bathrobe for a man

GIFTS FOR THE RETIREE
(*See also* "When an Executive Retires," Chapter 17)

The gift a company chooses for a retiring executive should logically depend upon his length of service and rank achieved. Some companies give standard items, such as clocks and gold watches (inscribed with the dates of the person's service to the company) for important anniversaries and retirements. Other companies become very creative for their distinguished retirees' gifts. A few ideas:

- Give something related to the person's activities in retirement, such as new fishing equipment for someone who says he'll now be "gone fishin' " or a gift of art supplies for someone who claims he will now be "painting in earnest."
- Have a photograph taken of him in the office, with all of his staff and colleagues clustered around him; have the photo enlarged and framed, with an incised brass plaque on the frame.
- Have a handsome leather scrapbook made of career-related photographs, news articles, and memorabilia (which could be a wonderful surprise if the retiree's spouse becomes actively involved in the project). The cover of the scrapbook should contain a gold embossed inscription.
- Present the retiree and spouse with round-trip air or steamship tickets to a very desirable place. (Expense money should be included in the envelope for any retiree who could not otherwise afford the trip.)
- Ask the retiree's colleagues to participate in a kind of *Festschrift* (German for a "festival of writings"). Colleagues would write about their illustrious colleague, his career, and his ideas; they would include some ideas and predictions of their own. The collection of essays and tributes would then be loosely bound into a handsome cover for the retiree to savor and enjoy in the coming years.
- Find an attractive antique — such as a pair of decanters in a mahogany carrier, with a brass plaque added to the base and engraved with his name and dates of service.
- Commission an artist to paint the CEO's portrait or a sculptor to do a bust of him.

Before the recession these generous gifts were common for a beloved retiree. Today, the money to do it often is not there. Hopefully, the days of generosity will return.

A GIFT OF ART

For someone you know who is an art lover, who lives or works surrounded by his collection at home or at the office, a gift of art is the most pleasing one you could offer.

Consider a hypothetical case: You wish to give something to Alice Wainwright, an executive who has gone above and beyond the call of duty to help you out on some matter. You know she loves art and so you decide to limit your pursuit to this field.

Her office is decorated with blond woods and sand colors in an informal Western style. A target of opportunity suddenly presents itself when you find yourself in Santa Fe on business. While browsing around a charming little local art gallery, you see something you really like and can afford. The scenario goes like this:

Think of her office. Is the art already there small or large in scale? In recalling what she already has on the walls, you can learn about her size preferences. You should also think about how the frame on the picture you like will look in her office. (If she's a fan of the Southwest, a gold-leaf baroque frame will probably not look right, but a simple, contemporary one probably will.)

Ask the gallery for any available printed material on the artist, even a simple bio sheet, which should list the museums or galleries that have exhibited the artist. Alice will want all the information on the artist you can find.

Ask your Santa Fe contacts about the reputation of the gallery. Only after having heard it is exemplary do you return to make the deal.

Purchase the painting and arrange for its air shipment to the recipient (insured, of course) but only after receiving a written guarantee that the picture could be exchanged for something of equal value if the recipient does not like it.

Gift Certificates to Art Galleries

A gift certificate—from anything from a modest lithograph shop or museum gift shop to an art gallery—can be the way to go if you plan to buy art as a gift. I have seen too many ghastly examples of the following: "Go to the Such-and-Such store and buy whatever you want as my gift. Just choose it and have them send the bill to me."

That never works. The recipient is either so intimidated by the fear of spending too much that he will select an inferior picture or sculpture that he will hate for the rest of his life, or he will select something he really likes and worry for the rest of his life that he has overstepped the bounds of propriety in spending so much. *A gift certificate is a much better idea.*

If You Are Contemplating a Serious Gift of Art for a Colleague

In this instance, *use an art consultant* to save you from making a mistake. A professional will help you with your selection and will usually save you money as well, by dealing with the artist or gallery in a much more seasoned manner than you could. A word-of-mouth recommendation from a satisfied corporate executive is probably the best way to find the right consultant.

Commissioning a Portrait

Probably one of the greatest ways to honor someone who is retiring or who has presented an institution with a new building, or who has bettered the lives of those using the institution with a major gift is to commission a portrait of her, a painting, a sculptured bust, or a photographic portrait by a renowned photographer.

Fine, reputable portrait artists and sculptors are often represented by groups of business people (like Portrait Brokers of America, Inc., headquartered in Birmingham, Alabama; Portraits South in Raleigh, North Carolina; and Portraits Inc. in New York). These companies have representatives in major cities all around the United States who are out covering the business and social worlds, promoting their portrait painters and sculptors.

The portrait of an illustrious person should be on view in the institution to which he has given so much time or talent or money, but a copy should be made for the family, too, to hand down through future generations.

There are good artists who will do a pastel or water color portrait for $1,000. Established artists like William Draper and John Sanden of New York City might charge up to $75,000 to do a portrait (including a copy, which must be made separately, requiring the artist to go through the entire process again). A portrait artist *di moda* like Aaron Schickler (whose portraits of Jacqueline Kennedy and Nancy Reagan hang in the White House) can charge upwards of $100,000.

Clyde Smith of Cos Cob, Connecticut, paints in an impressionistic manner only from life, never from photographs. He does individual portraits with equal skill of men executives in pinstriped suits in their offices and of their wives in satin ballgowns at home, but his favorite commissions are "conversation pieces" of an entire family group—caught in a relaxed, intimate moment as though one were looking into the living room through a window. The conversation piece portrait makes a fascinating addition to the corporate headquarters lobby or some other public area when it shows several senior members of management, for example, conferring in a relaxed moment in one of their offices. Clyde Smith's way of charging for conversation pieces is amusing in itself: as of this writing, $10,000 for the first eight figures, and $500 for every figure after that. Animals are free! (He should have been born in eighteenth-century America, so he could have been commissioned to do the ultimate business conversation piece of all time: the signers of the Declaration of Independence.)

Alexandra E. Whitney, of New York, is an acclaimed sculptor of bronze portrait busts (for a price of around $15,000 as of this writing). She likes to oversee the installation of her pieces, particularly their illumination, which should be soft overhead lighting. The gift of a portrait of a distinguished person should not stop with the surrender of the artwork by the artist; it should be seen through to its final presentation, with a proper pedestal or base for a sculpture, and with a small plaque affixed to the frame of the painting or the base of the sculpture, engraved with the executive's name, dates of birth and death, date of retirement, or whatever is appropriate. The proper lighting of a picture, and its placement on a particular wall should be supervised by a professional.

Some photographers will charge $1,000 for a portrait sitting of an executive; others might charge $25,000. It's a question of the fame (and perhaps notoriety) of the photographer.

Other Commissioned Works

One does not hear much these days about "great commissioned works," but in the 1950s and 1960s corporate and individual works of art were commissioned by a person or a company for the good of the public. One hopes there will be a revival, as the economy improves. Among these contributions:

- Fountains and sculptured works in public areas
- Small parks in busy, usually dirty city areas (they used to be called "vest-pocket parks") which give so much pleasure and refreshment to tired, stressed-out urban citizens
- Concerts and ballets. Not only must the people who produce and perform in the event be paid, but the orchestra and hall must be hired, and rehearsal time must be paid for as well.
- Murals painted inside and outside of buildings and stained glass windows for institutions, churches, and synagogues.

The manager who pens a note to go with his gift of appreciation ("You can't imagine how much I've depended on you these past weeks") is the executive who can motivate his troops to follow him anywhere, anytime.

Granted, a successful gift should be well thought out, well timed, well researched. But if it *comes from the heart*, the intellectual part of the exercise doesn't matter that much. Everyone knows when he or she opens that box if the heart was involved.

PART III

THE PROTOCOL OF BUSINESS LIFE

12

Business Protocol

Many people think only heads of state and diplomats need to understand the intricate world of sometimes unfathomable rules and regulations called protocol. Dictionaries define "protocol" as "customs and regulations concerning etiquette, precedence and diplomatic formalities."

If you put a congressman in an unimportant seat at your company's dinner party, you'll hear from him. If you address a woman judge in a letter as "Mrs. George Smith" instead of "Judge Anne Smith," you'll feel the long-distance heat waves of her ire. If you are a thirty-year-old executive and ask your secretary to place a call to the sixty-eight-year-old CEO of another company (which means that when he comes on the line, he'll be talking to your secretary, not to you), you have breached protocol and he will consider you a loser. If you introduce a colonel in the U.S. Army as a captain, you will hear a complaint. If you make the CEO's wife drive in from the airport with someone's secretary in that person's own small, cramped car, while the rest of the entourage is transported to the event in chauffeur-driven limousines, you'll hear from everyone. If someone does not wait her turn but suddenly breaks into the movie ticket office queue in front of you, she has breached protocol. It was not her turn, it was not her right to get in front of you.

Rank should be understood, and adhered to. The privileges of rank, except in royal birth, are earned. If you've labored hard in your life and worked up to a certain level of achievement and power, you deserve to have small signs of appreciation of that fact demonstrated to you in public life.

Rank is as different, for example, in the hierarchy of the Catholic Church in the Vatican as it is in the military. It is as different in the hierarchy of the foreign service as it is in the complex corporate management structure. However, all these systems have one thing in common: Some people outrank others and deserve different degrees of deference.

Rank and deference sound un-American in a way, as though an artificial imposition of titles was more important than people's true value and worth, but that is not the case. Adhering to protocol, understanding and obeying its rules, brings order to the workplace and to society. There is even an aspect of kindness in protocol, as, for example, when a younger person defers to age and gives a frail, older person his seat on the bus; or when you acknowledge in your remarks to a crowd of people someone present who thinks everyone has forgotten about him ("There is a very renowned former government official in this room tonight: John Cabot Perry, former Lieutenant Governor of the State of Nebraska. Stand up, John, so everyone can welcome you"); or when you give your old schoolteacher the place of honor on your right at a formal dinner, and you announce in your welcoming address to the other guests at the table that "the most important person here tonight is the person who got me through school when no one else thought it was going to happen."

If no one in your community knew "who goes first" in any aspect of daily life, there would be chaos. Observing protocol makes things work better. For you, the executive, understanding it will make you feel more secure about how you handle yourself. That is a worthy end in itself.

This book—and this chapter in particular—will guide you through the process.

DEFERENCE: THE BASIS OF PROTOCOL

You show deference when you help an elderly person into a car. You showed it as a child when you were taught to wait until your parents began eating before you did. You show deference when you stand up in an auditorium when the President of the United States enters to give a speech, and you show it when you slow down a revolving door that is turning too fast for the stranger ahead of you who is on crutches. You are deferring to his condition.

Many of the charming vestiges of deference in children have disappeared, such as when little girls curtsied to their elders. I still emphasize deference strongly in my lectures to corporate America, because senior management wants it, even if we have the world's most relaxed, informal corporate culture. Management wants employees to understand deference and do it naturally without anyone having to command it.

The person who shows deference when it is the right time to do so is definitely a leader with an important asset. Even if everyone in the company today calls one another by a first name, the CEO likes it when a young executive rushes ahead to hold the door for the retired chairman of the board, or when his executives stand back and wait for him to enter the dining room first, instead of knocking him down in their haste to enter.

I always love to watch the Ceremonial Protocol section of the State Department at work on state visits, when foreign leaders come to visit the President and the First Lady in Washington. From the minute the foreign guests arrive at Andrews Air Force base from their countries, the Protocol staff and the First Lady's staff are on their toes, showing the visitors which way to pass; they clear the way through crowds for the visitors, they line them up in order of importance in order to be introduced, and show the visitors a thousand little courtesies. It all works. There are no embarrassing delays as hosts and guests attempt to figure out what to do. Instead there are graceful motions of the arms as the protocol experts gently suggest "This way, please." It is like watching a beautiful ballet. And it all makes sense. The movements are designed to make the occasion efficient and attractive to the crowds watching, as well as pleasing to the VIP guests. It's not only the State Department that has this asset of protocol know-how. Many of America's large corporations have officers on staff who know their protocol and who teach the people around them how to show deference when important people are guests. There is nothing artificial and foppish about it. It is rather a plain and simple recognition of hard work, quality, and achievement.

I remember explaining what deference was to a group of young MBA graduates who had just begun working in a large food company. "We don't go for that kind of stuff in this company," a young man interjected with feeling. "The emphasis here is on informality and democracy, the exact opposites of deference."

I talked him down on the point, explaining how humane and kind deference is, particularly when applied to older people, or even those who aren't necessarily elderly but who have worked very hard all their lives, slugging their way up the corporate ladder to senior positions. People deserve an earned reward, and deference is one. It's very pleasing for such notable people to have others open doors for them. They feel in command when they sit at the head of the table as the host, or to the right of the host as an honored guest. It is justice, not just an ego trip, when they are introduced properly, with their full titles, and *are treated with respect*. That really is what deference is all about.

After I had explained all this to the young MBA executive who had challenged me, he smiled and said, "I see the logic of it. And besides, you're the teacher, and you're a lot older than I. I guess I have to defer to *you*."

You Are Showing Deference When:

- You let a senior officer precede you into a room.
- You raise your hand at a meeting and catch the meeting chairman's eye and his nod of approval before you speak.
- You don't begin eating until the host or the guest of honor has begun.
- You introduce your guests to your boss first.
- You hold open a door for visitors and with a sweep of your hand usher them through it.

- You take the less important, only uncomfortable seat in the room or on the plane or in the car, in deference to senior management or guests.
- You stand up to greet or say "Goodbye" to the visitor who enters your office.
- You arrange a visitor's transportation for him; you handle checking or fetching his coat and hold it for him, and hold an umbrella as you walk him to his car.
- You stop to let a car from a side street (that has been trying unsuccessfully to get into the main street) get in ahead of you. This is deference at its very best—kindness to a stranger in trouble.

HOW TO SEAT GUESTS AT A TABLE ACCORDING TO RANK AND COMPANY POSITION
(*See also* "Seating at a Large Party," Chapter 14)

It's commendable to know the basics of seating your guests around the dinner table: the sexes seated alternatively, husbands and wives separated (even at separate tables). *However*, if you have guests of rank and executives who are senior in their companies attending your function, they should be placed in proper positions around the tables, *according to their importance—not their gender*. Every manager should know how to seat his or her guests at a table *according to the priorities of protocol*. This system was worked out for the sake of efficiency well over a century ago (Louis XIV even worked on it at Versailles). It is standard procedure with all of the countries of the Western world, and has been copied by many other cultures in other parts of the world when foreign visitors are present.

Being sensitive to rank may well require your making telephone calls to some of your guests' offices to check on their titles in the table of organization; it may require doing some research elsewhere, as in reference books that list official titles. When everyone sits down at the table and is aware that the seating has been done properly, officially ranked guests are impressed, honored, and pleased. So are prominent civic and business leaders. So are the officers of *your* company.

When you properly seat the people in your own company, according to who is senior in position to whom, your colleagues will be pleased. When you do the seating haphazardly, without reference to who outranks whom, to who is more important than whom, you may think you're "just being democratic about the whole thing, our company doesn't care about stuff like this." Your ranked guests will probably feel otherwise, even if they never mention it. When guests are not seated properly, your company will lose prestige with everyone in that room who knows anything about protocol, including honored guests.

For a business meal (all official, not a purely social occasion), the seats are ranked in order of importance *with no reference to gender*, in the following manner:

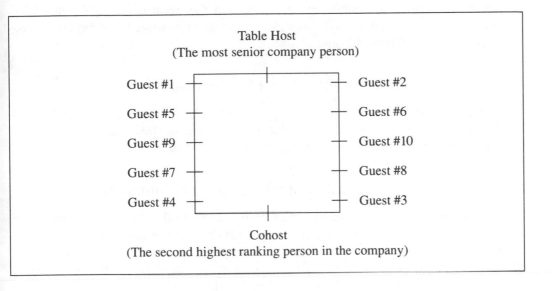

Table Host
(The most senior company person)

Guest #1	Guest #2
Guest #5	Guest #6
Guest #9	Guest #10
Guest #7	Guest #8
Guest #4	Guest #3

Cohost
(The second highest ranking person in the company)

The First Priority: Your Officially Ranked Guests

A person with *official rank* (someone who holds a high elective or appointed office) must always occupy the place of honor. He or she becomes Guest #1 on the chart above), flanking the host or cohost (or host's spouse).

For a meal with spouses, each person's spouse assumes the rank of his or her mate and is given a "high seat" accordingly. In other words, if the mayor and his wife come to your CEO's lunch, he would probably be the highest-ranked person there. The seating would therefore be as follows:

Mr. Ackerman
Host

Mr. Smith
Cohost

(If the Mayor is a woman, at a gathering with both sexes, she would sit on the CEO's right and her husband would sit to the right of the CEO's wife.)

I would be rich if I had been paid a quarter over the years for every CEO who has complained to me about having to sit during a long meal between two wives who had nothing to say to him about business, and vice versa. I have always replied, "It's your fault for having organized a meal with spouses. If you want just to talk business, make it a business-associates-only lunch or dinner. If you invite spouses, it won't hurt you to spend a little time in general conversation with the guest of honor's wife. Who knows, you might impress her with your charm and be responsible some day for getting a great deal of new business from her husband.''

When You Have a Foreign Guest

One important fact for business people to remember is that a foreign guest (and spouse) would always be seated in the places of honor at the table, unless, of course, the President of the United States happens to be sitting there, too.

A Guest's Elevated Standing in Your Community

Someone in high rank in the hierarchy of his company should be assured of a high seat, too. A Catholic Cardinal or an Episcopalian Bishop, for example, would be seated close to the host. The commanding officer of the military base, the superintendent of the school system, the president of the local university—these are all people of prominence in the community, and should be offered highly placed seats.

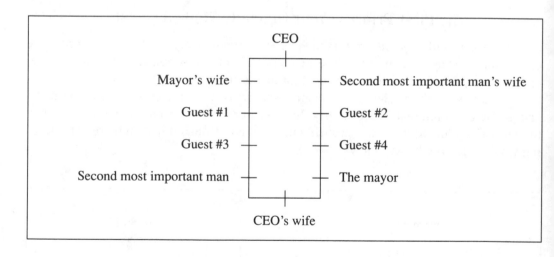

Your Own Company Colleagues and Business Colleagues from Other Companies

These guests should be seated according to their place on the table of organization. The table of organization differs from one company to another, but here is a typical one as to rank within the organization:

· The chairman and Chief Executive Officer (if the president is also the CEO, he would rank first and the chairman second)
· The president (may also be CEO or COO)

- The Chief Operating Officer (COO) (if there's a vice-chairman, he or she would rank next to the COO)
- The Chief Financial Officer (CFO)
- Executive vice-presidents (which usually include any or all of the following: the general counsel, the chief administrative office (CAO); the chief information officer (CIO); and executive vice-presidents of the commercial divisions)
- Senior vice-presidents or group vice-presidents, many of which are general managers
- Assistant vice-presidents (usually found in the financial services or the creative services industries)

In a Law or an Accounting Firm

The managing director ranks first. The senior vice-presidents follow and, informally, they are ranked according to the size of their billings.

In the Health Care Business

There are two parts:

- Corporate (the management of hospital centers is the same as in the corporations listed above, except that the CEO may be called the executive director)
- The Medical Ladder:
  - Chief administrator
  - Academic deans (if a university is involved)
  - Department heads

If you already know who reports to whom, you'll be able to figure out how the individuals are ranked within their companies.

If you are doubtful as to who outranks whom in any kind of business or profession, call and ask the executive secretary to the CEO or ask the Public Affairs Department. They may not know either, but at least, they will be galvanized into finding out for you!

At a certain moment, having seated the VIPs at your table, you can continue *seating your tables according to whatever works well* and will make the meal pleasant and amusing. If it is a social occasion, with both sexes in attendance, you might seat a beloved elder in the group next to a pretty young woman (or a dowager next to a handsome young man). You would seat someone who has just returned from South Africa next to a South African student; you would seat your son who has just begun law school next to a lawyer; you would seat a very fashionable young woman next to a visiting dress designer from New York; and a visiting art gallery director next to your town's most distinguished woman artist.

Although the best meal with both sexes present is one where there is an equal number of each, never be distressed if you have too many men or too many women. Great conversations do occur between people of the same sex.

Your Guide to Official Ranking of U.S. Officials and Diplomats

The official ranking for U.S. officials that follows shows who takes precedence over whom. The White House and State Department work together on compiling this list, which is fraught with potential dynamite; i.e., grumblings from newly appointed White House appointees and such who don't like the way they've been ranked. Each president changes things around just a bit, mostly by creating new positions within the administration or by downgrading one appointment while upgrading another. If you're hosting a very important function with many officials in attendance, you should check with the State Department to make sure you have the very latest ranking. The following list was in use in the early part of 1993, but is bound to change with the increase in duties and importance of the First Lady's White House staff.

Official Rankings for U.S. Officials

- President of the United States
- Vice-President of the United States
- Speaker of the House of Representatives
- Chief Justice of the United States
- Former Presidents of the United States
- Secretary of State
- Secretary General of the United Nations
- Ambassadors of foreign powers
- Widows of former Presidents of the United States
- Associate Justices of the Supreme Court of the United States
- Cabinet Members:
    - Secretary of the Treasury
    - Secretary of Defense
    - Attorney General
    - Secretary of the Interior
    - Secretary of Agriculture
    - Secretary of Commerce
    - Secretary of Labor
    - Secretary of Health and Human Services
    - Secretary of Housing and Urban Development
    - Secretary of Transportation
    - Secretary of Energy
    - Secretary of Education
    - Secretary of Veterans' Affairs

- Administrator, Environmental Protection Agency
- Director, Office of Management and Budget
- U.S. Trade Representative
- Senate (Senators are ranked with each other according to length of continuous service)
- Governors of states (when outside own state)
- Former Vice-Presidents of the United States
- House of Representatives (ranked according to their state's date of admission to the Union)
- Governor of Puerto Rico
- Chief of Staff for the President
- National Security Advisor
- Assistants to the President
- Charge d'Affaires of foreign powers
- Under-Secretaries and Deputy Secretaries of the Executive Departments (number-two official)
- Director of the Central Intelligence Agency
- Administrator, Agency for International Development
- Director, U.S. Arms Control and Disarmament Agency
- Director, U.S. Information Agency
- Secretaries of the Army, Navy, and Air Force
- Chairman, Board of Governors of the Federal Reserve System
- Chairman, Council on Environmental Quality
- Chairman, Joint Chiefs of Staff
- Chief of Staff of the Army, Navy, and Air Force (ranked according to date of appointment)
- Commandant of the Marine Corps
- Commandant of the Coast Guard
- Secretary General, Organization of American States
- Representatives to the Organization of American States
- Administrator, General Services Administration
- Administrator, National Aeronautics and Space Administration
- Director, Office of Personnel Management
- Director of Action
- Chief of Protocol
- Assistant Secretaries of the Executive Departments
- Members of the Council of Economic Advisors
- Active of designate U.S. ambassadors and ministers (career rank, when in the United States; when they are in their foreign country posts, they are given much higher rank)
- Mayor of the District of Columbia (when in own city, follows assistant secretaries)
- Under-Secretaries of the Army, Navy, and Air Force
- (4-star) Generals and Admirals

- Assistant Secretaries of the Army, Navy, and Air Force
- (3-star) Lieutenant Generals and Vice-Admirals
- Former U.S. ambassadors to foreign countries
- Ministers of foreign powers (serving in embassies, not accredited)
- Deputy Chief of Protocol
- Deputy Assistant Secretaries of the Executive
- Counselors of embassies of legations of foreign powers
- Assistant Chiefs of Protocol
- (2-star) Major Generals and Rear Admirals
- (1-star) Brigadier Generals and Commodores

Researching Your Official Guest's Rank

- If you have questions regarding *senior appointed or elected officials or foreign dignitaries* who will attend your function, call the Office of Protocol, Department of State (Ceremonial Section), 202-647-1735, to find out who outranks (and is therefore seated ahead of) whom.
- *To find out the official ranking for U.S. officials,* consult the list that begins on page 306.
- *To determine the ranking of members of Congress,* remember that:

  ○ U.S. senators outrank members of the House of Representatives.
  ○ If more than one U.S. senator will be attending your function, the one with the longest length of uninterrupted service in the Senate ranks first.
  ○ If you have more than one congressman, the one with the longest uninterrupted service in the House ranks first. If you have two congressmen with the same length of service, *the one from the state first admitted to the Union ranks first.*

  If you don't have any information on their length of service, consult the most recent *Congressional Directory* (available in every public library) or contact the Government Printing Office, Washington, DC 20401.

  Of course, a member of Congress who holds a top office in either body (the Majority or Minority Leader, for example) would outrank his or her fellow legislators.

- *For a listing of diplomats and their spouses, obtain from the Department of State (Publication 7894) the latest "Diplomatic List,"* which is regularly updated and can be purchased from the Superintendent of Documents, U.S. Government Printing Office, Washington, DC 20402.

  Another helpful book is *The Complete Handbook of Diplomatic Official and Social Usage,* by Mary Jane McCaffree and Pauline Innis, published by Devon, and available in paperback at major bookstores.

- *If you need help with your United Nations ranking of ambassadors*, call the United Nations in New York (212-963-1234) and ask for the Office of Protocol.

· *If officers in the military services are attending your function*, their rank and title are known. Since an army captain outranks a second lieutenant, he or she would sit ahead of the second lieutenant at the table (the spouses are accorded the same rank as their mates). It becomes more complicated if you have high-ranking officers in different services, and you don't know how they rank vis-a-vis one another. If you have a general and an admiral of equal rank in their service attending your function, *find out which one achieved that rank first, and give that person the higher seat.*

For questions on military rank, consult *Service Etiquette* by Oretha Swartz, a book published by the Naval Institute Press (1-800-233-8764).

For questions on the rank of White House staff, cabinet members, government agency heads, and the diplomatic corps, consult *The Social List of Washington* (otherwise known as "The Green Book"), Box 29, Kensington MD 20895.

When Both Husband and Wife Have Official Ranks or Titles

A wife shares her husband's official rank—and vice versa—unless there is an equally high-ranked official of the same sex as the spouse of a high-ranked individual.

The highest-ranked cabinet officer, for example, is the Secretary of State. If the Secretary of State were a woman, her husband would occupy a very senior male-occupied seat at the table. However, if another male cabinet officer, like the Secretary of the Treasury, were also present at the dinner, even though he is outranked by the Secretary of State, he would occupy a seat ahead of the Secretary of State's husband. This kind of dilemma occurs rarely and always at a large affair, involving several tables.

The problem is solved when the two cabinet officers are placed at different tables as ranking guests, and spouses are put at different tables, too, in high positions, so that no one feels slighted. (Once, in Paris, at the embassy, we had so much international top brass in our 160-member guest list, we were frantic worrying that top-ranking guests would feel they were not being seated high up enough. So we changed from sixteen tables of ten each to twenty tables of eight each, thus giving us more tables at which to place more ranking guests to the right and left of the table host.)

When Spouses Are Not Present

One does not have to worry about seating guests man-woman-man-woman. The host is surrounded by the number one ranked man or woman guest on his or her right and the number two ranked guest on his or her left. Seated on the cohost's right is the third ranked person, while the fourth-most-important person is seated on his or her left. There is no preoccupation about separating the sexes. The seats in the middle of both sides are for guests of "lesser importance." As long as you give each guest his or her

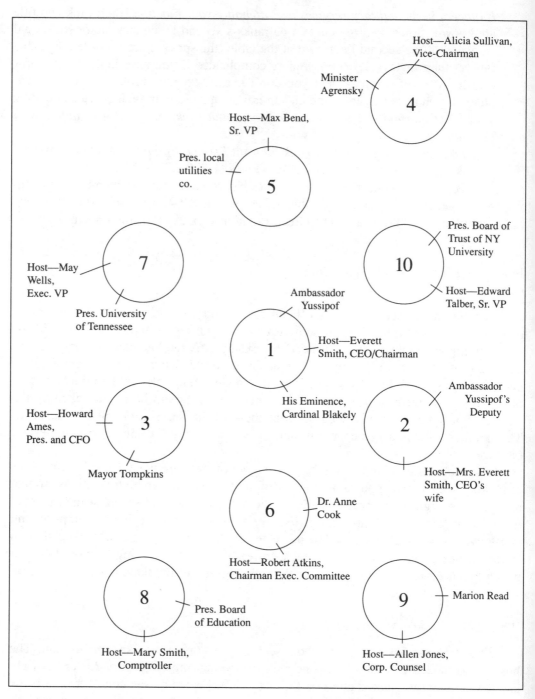

Table Plan for Luncheon for 100 Guests, With Place Cards for Hosts and Honored Guests Only

proper title on the place card, no one will be miffed (for example, "Senator Johnson," "Ambassador Griffith," "Colonel Adams," etc.). Fortunately, most officials sitting in the seats in the middle of the table don't have a clue as to how seating by rank works, beyond the fact that they're not sitting on either side of the host.

Seating at Round Tables

The same system works for a round table, except that you don't need a cohost at a round table. If you do have four important guests, it's easier to have a cohost. Mark the host's and cohost's place cards, for the edification of the guests seated at that table:

If the guests don't know who anyone is, forget about doing the place cards "properly" (i.e., with last names only). In this case, for clarity, include the host's and cohost's first names on their place cards.

Open Seating

Open seating is sloppy and unwieldy, but sometimes made necessary by the reluctance of many guests today to reply promptly or *at all* to business invitations. Since the host company cannot tell who's coming and who's not to the big luncheon in the hotel ballroom, guests fill in the round tables as they arrive. To have order instead of chaos, each table should have a senior company host with his place card in place, and each VIP whom you know is coming to your function should also have an assigned seat with a place card to the right or left of the company host at a table. The VIP guest should be watched over with the greatest spirit of hospitality. Each honored guest's table host should not only see to it that the VIP is guided safely to his or her particular table and place card, but he should also see to it that all introductions are properly handled at the whole table.

The corporate hosts should have in their hands numbered table charts, with the name of the host and honored guest(s) at each table, as in the following imaginary luncheon for an ambassador from an eastern European country visiting the company on a trade mission.

THE PROTOCOL OF LARGE CIVIC-SOCIAL FUNCTIONS

When a large corporation hosts a lunch or dinner on an important civic occasion (a national holiday, a major anniversary, a "Welcome home" ceremony for returning heroes, etc.) it may be appropriate to pull out all the patriotic stops, complete with bands, flag, and the national anthem.

The order of procedure at a banquet once all the guests and dais guests are seated is the following:

- The posting of the colors (if that is to take place). Everyone rises.
- The Pledge of Allegiance (rarely done anymore)
- The singing of the "Star Spangled Banner" (which may now be sung in A-flat, much easier to sing than in B-flat, the key in which the national anthem was written)
- The clergyman's invocation

The Invocation

When there is an invocation, the master of ceremonies for the event should prompt the audience: "Please rise and remain standing for the invocation, to be delivered by Reverend John Madison Barr, pastor of the Church of St. John." No one should talk, eat, or drink at this moment, but remain silent, with head bowed. If the ceremony is out of doors and any men present happen to be wearing hats, they should remove them during the invocation.

Even if a clergyman considers it an honor to his ministry to be asked to deliver the invocation, the corporate host may wish to send him a small, unsolicited check immediately following the event, enclosed in a letter of thanks for coming. The host might write something like "This small check is only a symbol of the esteem in which our company holds your ministry." A business person might make his check for $50 to enclose in the letter to the clergy person; the CEO of a major corporation might write a company check for $250 to $500. It depends upon the size of the town and the resources of the company involved.

If the event is held in an out-of-the-way place, transportation to and from the event should be provided for the clergyman or woman, and he or she should be given a seat of honor at the meal.

The National Anthem

When the "Star Spangled Banner" is played, everyone should remain standing at attention (and most properly of all, with the right hand over the heart). Military personnel stand at salute. It helps, if the national anthem will be sung, to provide background music for support, such as a piano. Otherwise, the singing of it can sound more like a funeral dirge than a patriotic song, unless you are lucky enough to have an opera star standing at your microphone!

Displaying the Flag

If you are going to display a group of flags at a meeting, banquet, or any event sponsored by your company, remember that the flag of the United States of America is always accorded the place of honor, positioned on its own right. The flag should be on the speaker's right, the audience's left; the other flags (state, corporate, etc.) should be positioned to the left of the speaker.

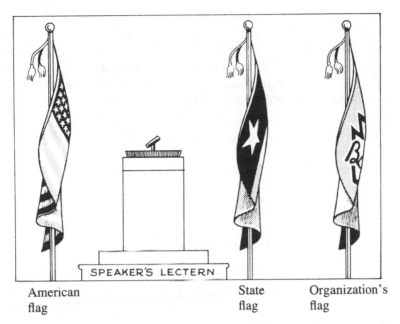

American   State   Organization's
flag   flag   flag

DISPLAYING THE FLAG AT A MEETING, BANQUET, OR PRIVATE EVENT

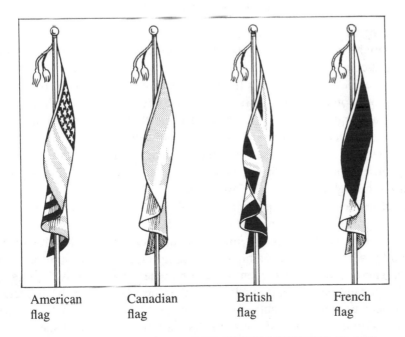

American   Canadian   British   French
flag   flag   flag   flag

DISPLAYING THE FLAG WITH OTHER NATIONAL FLAGS

When a group of domestic flags are on display, the United States flag should be in the center, on some kind of a platform, raised above the others or to its own right. When flags of other countries are displayed, all flags should be of the same size, on separate poles of the same height, and displayed in a straight line. The U.S. flag should always be to its own right (the audience's left) as in the illustration here.

The flag should never be used to cover a ceiling or a lectern, or to drape a platform. Use bunting of red, white, and blue stripes (with a blue stripe on top) for those purposes. A flag may not be used properly to cover a car or any vehicle (except when firmly attached to a staff).

For detailed information on flag etiquette, contact The National Flag Foundation, Flag Plaza, Pittsburgh, PA 15219.

TOASTING

To be able to make toasts effortlessly is an art, a graceful talent, a skill, and an important business tool. To know how to toast is to know how to establish a wonderful atmosphere for an event, to raise it up above the mediocre, and to give pleasure not only to the object of the toast, but to the entire group. A good toast can make a drab evening into a very special one. An accomplished toaster therefore has a terrific asset in his or her arsenal of tools.

Who Does the Toasting?

The host of the event is supposed to make the first toast (and sometimes only one is necessary) to the honored guest at the meal or cocktail party. However, if no one has made a toast, a courageous guest may make the first and only toast, either to the host, or to the guest of honor. Sometimes the host does not make a move, because he finds the social custom bordering on torture. I know one prominent CEO who, because he is painfully shy about public speaking, does the same thing at every event he hosts. He rises and says, "Welcome, everyone, and a special welcome to our distinguished visitor." With that, he raises his glass and then sits down and doesn't open his mouth publicly again. He makes sure that some clever members of his staff make memorable toasts later on through the meal. It all works out.

Men and women have an equal right (or call it responsibility) to toast the guest of honor. The spouse of the host or guest of honor should certainly not feel compelled to make a toast, but a host member of management (male or female) should not let an occasion go by when food and or liquor are being consumed without a toast having been made. There have been frequent occasions where an executive's wife gives the toast, simply because she does it much better than he does. There have been frequent occasions where a woman executive's husband takes over the toasting duties at his wife's business dinners, simply because he does it much better than she.

Why Make a Toast?

The reasons are manifold:

- To welcome a new colleague
- To bid goodbye to a colleague
- To launch a new business, product, or service
- To welcome an important visitor

Who Gets Toasted at Your Table?

- Your foreign guests ("Señor Alvarez, we are delighted that you are with us this week. Your factories in Spain have become very important to us, and we are counting on even stronger, more fruitful future collaborations. It has been a joy for us here at our Atlanta headquarters to work with such a dynamic and *simpatico* partner. Ladies and gentlemen, a toast to Juan Carlos Alvarez! *Salud!*")
- Any official sitting on your right ("We are honored to have the Lieutenant Governor of the state of Maine, Mr. Johnston North, with us today. He has made time in his busy schedule to be here for the opening of the new plant. John North has become a national leader in environmental causes, and that is why his recognition of our conservation efforts tied into the plant is so important. I would suspect that the Governor and John are also interested in the fact that the plant will create many new jobs in this area. Welcome, John, and I ask everyone in this room to join me in toasting our illustrious Lieutenant Governor!")
- An old friend, or a relative passing through town
- The leading protagonist in a business deal you've just made (or hope to make)
- Someone celebrating a birthday, anniversary, promotion, etc. ("I think a toast is in order to Gerry Sundlun, who after fifteen years of telling me I should promote her to comptroller of this company has finally won out. The only mistake I have made with this company, Gerry, is not to have made you comptroller fifteen years ago. To Gerry, congratulations!")
- A friend or colleague who is leaving the company or the city
- A new friend or colleague who is arriving ("PECPORT is fortunate to have a terrific young lawyer joining us as our new legal counsel. He's going to have his work cut out for him with this company, but he works out every day and he's physically fit, so he can take it. He's also rumored to have even more brains than brawn. We welcome you, Jim. You'll like this company, I promise, and we're going to like you. To Jim Heatherton!")
- Any important person in your life, such as your doctor, clergyman, favorite teacher, etc.
- Someone elderly sitting at your table, such as a visiting grandmother or a favorite octegenarian ("I would like to raise a toast to my very favorite beautiful, brainy,

Dallas woman. I think we're just plain lucky to have her grace us with her presence today. To Ida May Renshaw!'')

- Someone retiring from the company. That could be anyone from the CEO to the head of the mailroom with forty years of service. (You would list all of the achievements of the person retiring, and wish him well in the next chapter of his life. You would tell a couple of short, funny stories about him and give him a gift just before you raise your glass.)

- Anyone who deserves a special word of thanks from you. (''Marian has single-handedly raised the employee contributions this year to our city hospital fund drive. She is a go-getter, an irresistible force. She deserves all our thanks, so let's raise our glasses to the miraculous Marian!'')

One of the best toasts I ever heard was made at a very stuffy, boring dinner held in a private New York club. Voices were low and tired, the atmosphere seemed to be heavy and gray. Then, at the beginning of the dessert course, a close friend of our CEO host arose, having secretly ordered champagne to be served to all the guests at the beginning of the final course. With a full glass in hand he announced, ''Before we lose the real purpose of this evening, I would like to remind all of you that in a joint venture with his wife, our host this very evening has produced the most magnificent product of his entire career with this company. It is indeed the most perfect, unblemished, fully functioning, magnificently designed product end to end: a baby girl named Denise.'' We all gasped, laughed, and stood to toast our host and the baby. The man who made the toast added a final note, ''And, John, you'll be glad to know I charged the champagne to your private account. I knew that would be the way you wanted it.'' To great laughter, he sat down, the party was made, congratulations flew to our host, excitement rose in the air, and none of us will ever forget that evening, a meal that had begun as the ultimate in boring dinners.

At What Point in the Meal Should a Toast Be Made?

- *At the beginning of the meal*, which is a Scandinavian *skal* custom. First the host gets his guests' attention and then says a quick but warm word of welcome. If there is someone sitting in the guest of honor's seat, he would mention why that person is today's guest of honor. (''We're so honored to have my old pal Ben Sylvester here tonight, a man who is proceeding like a cannonball in this political campaign, a candidate who has the credentials and the ability to win, and who, once he will have won, will make the best mayor this city's ever had. To Ben! On to victory, old buddy!'')

- *Halfway through the meal*. The host would get his guests' attention and turn to the foreign guest sitting on his right. ''We are delighted to have you here, Ingenieur Montclair. Our joint venture in the world of chemicals and petrocarbons will bond us together stronger than the English Channel tunnel. We are pleased you have come to visit us, we are delighted to be working with such a great company

as the Petrochimique France-Atlantique, and I would like to have everyone raise a toast to you, Ingenieur Montclair, and to the entire management of your company. *Bienvenu à Cleveland!''*
- *At the conclusion of the meal.* In this case, the tip-off is the presence of champagne glasses at the table settings. Once champagne is poured before or during dessert and everyone has some in his or her glass, the host should rise and offer a toast to the guest of honor.
- *At a cocktail reception, a toast is usually made along with remarks at the high peak of the traffic*, at about 6:30 for a 5:30–7:30 cocktail party, for example.

When You Give a Toast

- *Look around the table before you toast. People should have liquid in their glasses*, preferably something like wine or champagne, but toasting with water is all right these days, too. It is the symbolism of the good wishes and the wit or wisdom of the toast that counts, not the liquid in the glass.
- *As host, you would face the person you are toasting*, make your remarks, and at the conclusion, look straight into the person's eyes, raise your glass high in a salute, say, ''To Arthur,'' and sip from your glass, still keeping your eyes on his (or hers). Then you put your glass down on the table. Everyone else, except the toastee, will immediately follow suit, saying ''To Arthur'' and then taking a sip. If it was a specially gracious toast, it's also nice for the guests to murmur ''That was really nice,'' or ''Good job, Harry,''
- *If you are the one being toasted, you do not take a drink with the others*. That would mean you were toasting yourself. Instead, just smile, say ''Thanks, Regina,'' and keep your hands off your glass. It's your moment to be honored.
- *If you do not have any wine or champagne in your glass*, you may certainly join in someone else's toast holding a glass filled with water, soda, or fruit juice.
- *Don't preempt your host's toast.* It should be his or her right to make the first one. In other words, wait to see if someone else is going to do the honors before you seize the initiative. If it looks like no one else will, and you want to make one, whisper to your host, ''Would you mind if I made a toast?''

  In 90 percent of the cases, your host will be delighted that you've taken over the chore of making the evening special. Usually, he will show his pleasure. But I myself have felt the rejection of the other 10 percent of the cases, in which the host replies brusquely, ''I wish you wouldn't.'' (It can be a painful moment, but don't let it ruin the event.)
- *The best toast is one minute in length.* A substantive, important toast lasts from three to five minutes. Any toast longer than that loses its impact, like a punctured balloon, falling to Earth. Mark Twain said that, except for his own, no toast should last longer than sixty seconds, but ''thirty seconds is really long enough to say anything worth saying.''

- *The more people you honor and include in your toast* (all out-of-town visitors, for example, not just one), the more happiness you will spread around the table.
- *If you must tap the rim of a glass to get peoples' attention, do it gently*, very gently. Countless numbers of glasses are broken and their contents spilled every year all over the world by people tapping their glasses too harshly.
- Some people have the feeling it is obligatory to clink glasses with everyone once a toast has been made. This, too, is hard on the glassware. *Toasts do not require clinks!*
- *Never give a toast after drinking too much.* You are not in control, and although people may laugh as you forget things or slur your words, you may very well railroad a promising career. If you are someone who tends to over-indulge in alcohol, remember to raise your toast as host at the beginning of the meal (and after a very short cocktail hour!). If you are not the host, let *others* do the honors.
- *If you are making a welcome toast to a table of ten or more people, stand up to give your toast.* If your table is small, you may certainly remain seated. No one else at the table who makes a toast need stand, but if it's a large table or a room with several tables in it, it is wise to stand and speak as loud as you can. Everyone should be able to share in what usually is fun to hear.
- *If you're at a large party, make sure the object of your toast is present.* I will never forget Jacqueline and Aristotle Onassis' fifth wedding anniversary dinner at New York's El Morocco. I stood in the glaring spotlight of the totally dark nightclub, addressing the microphone, because I could not see anything. I gave what I considered to be a clever, romantic, sentimental toast. When I called for "everyone to join me in toasting Jackie and Ari," people called out to me from the dark corners of the room: "Tish, they're both out of the room!" I was toasting two empty seats at separate tables (Jackie was in the ladies' room, Ari was settling the bill at the office). It was not one of my better moments.

Returning a Toast

If you are the one who has been toasted, as an honored guest, you should either return the toast as soon as your host has finished hers to you, or you should return it before or during dessert. Never wait until the end of the meal, when it looks like an act of desperation as people make moves to stand up and leave the table.

Your return toast should be memorably short. (You can outdo your host in wit and charm, but never try to outdo her in length.) If you are shy, all you have to say is "Anne and Jeff, you have given us all a great dinner tonight. I thank you for your hospitality, and I'm sure everyone here would like to join me in thanking our wonderful hosts. To Anne and Jeff!"

The Very Short Toast as an Automatic Sign of Welcome

If you have a guest sitting by your desk, about to join you for a lunch of sandwiches and sodas, you can always, just as you are both about to eat, say "Here's to you" as you lift your glass of soda. If you're at an athletic event and about to consume beer and a hot dog, raise the beer bottle to your guest and say, "Glad to have you here." One-word toasts like "*skol*" or "*salud*" have become international symbols of welcome.

Foreign visitors are pleased if you toast them in their language. If you have a Japanese visitor, before your first sip, you might say "*Kanpai*"; to a Chinese visitor, "*Kanpei*"; to an Italian, "cin cin"; or to a French person, "A votre santé." But do find out ahead of time how to pronounce these toasts!

When Sentimentality Is Appropriate

At his wedding anniversary dinner, the CEO arose, went to stand behind his wife's chair, put his hand on her shoulder, looked around at all twenty-four faces at the table and simply asked a question of his guests, "Why do you suppose *anyone* was allowed to be born worthy enough to spend his life alongside a talented, amusing, beautiful, exceptional woman like this?" Then he raised his glass to her. He had said enough. It was not the kind of toast a CEO would give to his guest of honor, but I noticed many of his peers were impressed.

The Best Toast Ever Made (at least in my book)

At a dinner given for Nobel Prize winners in the State Dining Room of the White House, President Kennedy rose and said, "I think this is the most extraordinary collection of talent, of human knowledge, ever gathered at the White House, with the possible exception of when Thomas Jefferson dined here alone."

PROPER FORMS OF ADDRESS
(*See also* "Official Rankings for U.S. Officials," earlier in this chapter)

There is so much informality in the workplace today that in many offices, time is wasted, business is lost, confusion reigns, and goodwill is destroyed because of a total disregard in written or electronic communications of how people wish to be addressed, what their titles are, and how their names are spelled.

When you realize that much of today's mail is simply sent out addressed to "Joe Doakes" and "D. Smithers," it's miraculous that people even bother to open their mail. When the correspondent doesn't bother to take the time to find out a person's sex, much less proper title, there's a feeling in the recipient's mind that the communication doesn't really matter. "After all," I heard an executive say the other day, in defense of informality, "we all use just first names and not titles around here."

The executive's attitude may represent the philosophy of some people in management today, but it does not represent the majority. It is a question of educating senior managers and employees alike on the importance of proper forms of address. They help *profits*.

"Jr.," "Sr.," "2nd," "3rd," and So On

A "Jr." after a surname signifies that the person has the exact same name as his father. If father and son live in the same city, they do well to use "Jr." and "Sr." both, so that people will be less confused with mis-identifying them.

After the father's death, the son generally retains the "Jr." for a few more years, then drops it, because the confusion between the two men no longer exists.

When "Jr." gives his son the exact same name, the son uses "III" or "3rd" after his surname.

A child named after his uncle or grandfather becomes "II" or "2nd." When a female child is named after her grandfather, she also becomes "2nd"; I know two women, a "Sidney" and an "Allen," who are "2nd" in honor of their illustrious grandfathers, but I do not yet know any women named after their aunts and grandmothers who are "2nd!"

The Use of "Ms."

In past books on manners, I always had to write a ringing defense of the use of "Ms." in office communication. In this book, it is no longer necessary. "Ms." is here to stay as a title for a woman who wishes to use it in conjunction with her given and family names; that is, until something much better and more efficient comes along.

Professional Titles

No title is used before a name when a professional title follows it. For example, an architect who uses "A.I.A." (American Institute of Architects) proudly after his name, would not be addressed as: "Mr. Gerald Wainwright, A.I.A." Rather, he would be addressed as "Gerald Wainwright, A.I.A." Some other examples are: a doctor—Roscoe Abrams, M.D.; an American Society of Interior Designers member—Susan Porcher, A.S.I.D.; a lawyer—Jonathon Jerne, Esq.; a nurse—Esther Hernandez, R.N.; a nun—Gwendolyn O'Reilly, R.S.C.J.; a Doctor of Jurisprudence—Jacob Breckinridge, J.D.

The Use of "Doctor" for a Ph.D.

People with Ph.D.s, who are in academia or in research laboratories or involved professionally in the field in which they received their advance degrees, may certainly be addressed as ''Dr.'' and certainly written to with ''Ph.D.'' after their names.

However, many believe that people who are not in their technological or teaching fields at work today look slightly pretentious if they insist on being called ''Dr.'' Pretentious or not, it is a matter of choice.

Addressing Invitations to Couples

You should write each person's name on one line:

Mr. and Mrs. Amos Jay Winthrop

If he has a title and a very long name, you would use the second line for the wife's name, indenting three spaces from the left in this manner:

The Honorable Stanislaw Rutherford Jersiekiwicz
and Mrs. Jersiekiwicz

When you're writing an invitation to a couple, disregard the professional initials after their names. For example, James Smith, M.D. would be addressed as ''Dr. and Mrs. James Smith,'' not ''Dr. James Smith, M.D. and Mrs. Smith.'' ''Edward Welles, Esq.'' would be addressed as ''Mr. and Mrs. Edward Welles.''

When Both Husband and Wife are Doctors

Address their invitation as:

The Doctors Richardson

or

Dr. Samuel Richardson and Dr. Anne Richardson

When a Woman Has Kept Her Own Name

Her husband's name would come first on the envelope and, if possible, both their names would be placed on one line:

Mr. Joseph Schultz and Ms. Anne Merrure

When They Are Living Together Unmarried

Their names would be placed on separate lines, above their mutual address, and they would be listed alphabetically on the envelope:

Mr. Anthony Hawthorne
Ms. Margaret Kinkaide

When the Wife Outranks Her Husband

If she outranks her husband, her name comes first:

Major Grace Renshaw and Lieutenant Gregory Renshaw

If she has retained her maiden name, she still comes first:

Major Grace Milliken and Lieutenant Gregory Renshaw

Addressing People as "Sir" and "Ma'am"

Generations of young people in both the social and business worlds, particularly in the South and Southwest, were brought up to begin or end every conversation with an elder with a "Sir" or "Ma'am."

Using "Sir" and "Ma'am" titles by the nonmilitary makes many people uncomfortable, since they feel it smacks of servility.

There are certainly many occasions in the upper strata of government and business worlds, when a staff member, male or female, will use "Sir" in conversation with the senior man: "Sir, I believe you forgot this memo . . ." or "You can count on me, sir, to do that." The title is an appropriate mark of deference in *these* cases when used for people of great importance.

Young people accustomed to saying "Sir" or "Ma'am" constantly, to members of mid-management as well as senior management, would do well to train themselves when they go north and west to substitute "Yes, Mr. Jones," "No, Ms. Pinchot," or just "Yes" and "No" or "Thanks," as the case may be. This will make the young Southerner's contemporaries and supervisors feel more at ease.

When to Use a First Name

In the best of worlds, young executives in business are taught always to call people senior to them in age and position by their family names, with a title in front. It is up to the senior executive to say, "Alice, enough of my last name. From now on, call me Rick."

That's in the best of worlds. *A younger or new executive waits to be told when to address an older person by his first name.*

Even in a totally informal corporate culture, the CEO always secretly hopes that the young executives will understand the nuances of life enough to know that they should not greet the seventy-five-year-old widow of a former chairman of the board with a "Hi ya, Gert!" but will instead say, "Mrs. Wilkins, it's a pleasure, yes, and an honor, to see you here again."

"The Honorable"—A Title of Respect in America

"The Honorable" in front of a person's name is a title held for life by a person who holds or has held high office at the federal, state, or city levels. However, there is a nuance that must be remembered: A person who is addressed by others as "The Honorable" should not put the title on his own business cards, his own personal letterhead, or on the invitations he extends. If, for example, an ex-official is now a partner in a law firm, on the firm's stationery his name would be listed with the other partners with "The Honorable" before it, but if it is his stationery alone, his name should not bear that honorific. In other words, it is a distinction bestowed by someone else on a person, not by the person on himself.

How to Address an Envelope Using "The Honorable"

	To a Woman	To a Man
Use three lines for the title	The Honorable Julia Rosen Treasurer of the State of Maine Address	The Honorable George Voutas United States Senate Address

Indent three spaces for spouse's name when addressing invitation.	The Honorable Julia Rosen and
	    Mr. Geoffrey Rosen
	Address
		The Honorable George Voutas and
		    Mrs. Voutas
		Address

When someone is no longer in office, "the Honorable" is still used (name and title on one line).	The Honorable Julia Rosen Address	The Honorable George Voutas Address

Addressing invitation to couple when official is no longer in office	Mr. Geoffrey Rosen and the
	    Honorable Julia Rosen
	Address
	(The wife's names goes after her
	    husband's when she is no
	    longer in office.)
		The Honorable and Mrs. George
		    Voutas
		Address
		(When a person is no longer in
		    office, it is permissible to use
		    the abbreviation "The Hon.,"
		    as in:
		        The Hon. and Mrs.
		        George Voutas)

NOTE: When a woman who has held a high official position remarries and changes her name, she still retains the right to "The Honorable" (or informally "The Hon.") before her given name.

If you're wondering whether or not to give a person "The Hon." when you're writing to him or her, go ahead and use it. It always pleases the person to whom you have given the title.

When Highly Ranked People Are No Longer in Office

Officially, when a person is no longer in office, he or she has lost the rank and privileges of that office. However, courtesy, sentiment, kindness (or whatever you wish to call it) dictates that we call the person by the old title. Once a governor, always a governor. Once an ambassador, mayor, judge, senator, always one. It pleases the person very much, so it's nice to call, write, and introduce a former official by his or her former title.

When a U.S. President Is No Longer in Office

A president always retains the title as a courtesy, but once out of office, he is no longer addressed as "*The* President of the United States." He is simply "President Reagan" or "President Bush." Their wives are no longer addressed simply as "Mrs. Reagan" or "Mrs. Bush" in a letter. They are now Mrs. Ronald Reagan or Mrs. George Bush. A joint invitation reads: "President and Mrs. Ronald Reagan" instead of in the days when he was president, when their joint invitation read: "The President and Mrs. Reagan."

The following charts are comprised of a combination of proper forms of address material that is new, or excerpted from my original *Complete Guide to Executive Manners* and from my *Complete Guide to the New Manners for the '90s.*

Addressing Government Officials: A Sampling

Personage	Making Introductions/ Addressing Envelopes	Letter Salutation	Speaking To	Place Card
The President	The President The White House Address (Abroad he is introduced as "The President of the United States of America.")	Dear Mr. President:	Mr. President	The President
The First Lady	Mrs. Madison (She is the only official woman always addressed out of respect as "Mrs. Madison," without a given name.) *A Social invitation would be addressed to:* The President and Mrs. Madison	Dear Mrs. Madison	Mrs. Madison	Mrs. Madison
The Vice-President	The Vice-President The White House Address *A social invitation would be addressed to:* The Vice-President and Mrs. Adams	Dear Mr. Vice-President:	Mr. Vice-President	The Vice-President
Vice-President's Wife	Mrs. John Adams Address	Dear Mrs. Adams:	Mrs. Adams	Mrs. Adams
Speaker of the House	The Honorable Michael Duncan Speaker of the House *or, socially:* The Speaker of the House and Mrs. Duncan	Dear Mr. Speaker:	Mr. Speaker	The Speaker of the House

Personage	*Making Introductions/ Addressing Envelopes*	*Letter Salutation*	*Speaking To*	*Place Card*
Chief Justice	The Chief Justice The Supreme Court Address *or, socially:* The Chief Justice and Mrs. Warner	Dear Mr. Chief Justice:	Mr. Chief Justice	The Chief Justice
Associate Justice	Justice Zissu The Supreme Court *or, socially:* Justice Zissu and Mrs. Zissu	Dear Justice: *or* Dear Justice Zissu	Justice *or* Justice Zissu	Justice Zissu
Cabinet Member	The Honorable Desmond Palmer Secretary of Labor Address *or, socially:* The Secretary of Labor and Mrs. Palmer	Dear Mr. Secretary	Mr. Secretary *or* Secretary Palmer	The Secretary of Labor
Under-Secretary of Labor	The Honorable Otto Norgren Under Secretary of Labor *or, socially:* The Under-Secretary of Labor and Mrs. Norgren	Dear Mr. Under Secretary:	Mr. Under Secretary *(subsequently* Sir)	The Under Secretary of Labor
Attorney General	The Honorable Edward R. Warden Attorney General of the United States *or, socially:* The Attorney General and Mrs. Warden	Dear Mr. Attorney General:	Mr. Attorney General *(subsequently* Sir)	The Attorney General
Director of Central Intelligence	The Honorable Agnes L. Schmidt Director of Central Intelligence Address *or, socially:* The Director of Central Intelligence and Mr. Helmut Schmidt	Dear Director:	Madam Director	The Director of Central Intelligence
U.S. Senator	The Honorable Frederick H. Lee United States Senate Address *or, socially:* Senator and Mrs. Frederick H. Lee	Dear Senator Lee:	Senator *or* Senator Lee	Senator Lee
U.S. Representative	The Honorable Sarah Thune House of Representatives Address *or, socially:* The Honorable Sarah Thune and Mr. Christopher Thune	Dear Ms. Thune:	Ms. Thune	The Honorable Sarah Thune *or* Ms. Thune

Personage	Making Introductions/ Addressing Envelopes	Letter Salutation	Speaking To	Place Card
American Ambassador Abroad	The Honorable David R. Luce American Embassy Address *or, socially:* The Honorable David R. Luce and Mrs. Luce	Dear Ambassador Luce: *or* Dear Mr. Ambassador:	Ambassador Luce	Ambassador Luce
Governor	The Honorable Francis L. Fine Governor of Florida Address *or, socially:* Governor and Mrs. Francis L. Fine	Dear Governor: *or* Dear Governor Fine:	Governor *or* Governor Fine	The Governor of Florida
State Senator	The Honorable Jorge Morales *or, socially:* State Senator Jorge Morales and Mrs. Morales	Dear Senator Morales	Senator Morales	The Honorable Jorge Morales
Mayor	The Honorable Stanley Breck, Jr. Mayor of Providence *or, socially:* Mayor and Mrs. Stanley Breck, Jr.	Dear Mr. Mayor: *or* Dear Mayor Breck:	Mayor Breck	The Mayor of Providence
Judge	The Honorable Robert Quinlan Judge, Appellate Division Supreme Court of the State of New York *or, socially:* Judge and Mrs. Robert Quinlan	Dear Judge Quinlan:	Judge Quinlan	Judge Quinlan

Addressing Spouses of Officially Ranked People

	Addressing Envelopes	Letter Salutation	Speaking To	Place Card
The Standard: When a Wife Uses Her Husband's Name	The Secretary of Commerce and Mrs. Pott	Dear Mrs. Pott:	Mrs. Pott	Mrs. Pott
When She Keeps Her Own Professional Name	The Hon. Ralph Pott and Ms. Grace Wells	Dear Ms. Wells:	Ms. Wells	Ms. Wells
When a Man Is Married to a Woman with High Rank	Senator Mary S. Reed and Mr. Philip Reed	Dear Mr. Reed:	Mr. Reed	Mr. Reed

		Letter		
	Addressing Envelopes	*Salutation*	*Speaking To*	*Place Card*
When Both Husband and Wife Have High Rank	The Hon. Frank Giles and Major Anne Giles	Dear Deputy Director Giles:	Deputy Director Giles	Deputy Director Giles

Addressing a Military Man or Woman

The Army, Air Force, and Marine Corps have the following commissioned officers according to rank:

General

Lieutenant General

Major General

Brigadier General

Colonel

Lieutenant Colonel

Major

Captain

First Lieutenant

Second Lieutenant

The Navy and Coast Guard have the following:

Admiral

Vice-Admiral

Rear Admiral

Captain

Commander

Lieutenant Commander

Lieutenant

Lieutenant, Junior Grade

Ensign

NOTE: All officers in the Navy and Coast Guard are addressed as ''Mr.'' up through the rank of lieutenant commander. A woman officer is addressed ''Ms.'' or ''Miss,'' never ''Mrs.''

A captain in the Navy or Coast Guard has a higher rank than a captain in the Army, Air Force, or Marine Corps.

A warrant officer's rank lies between that of a commissioned and a noncommissioned officer.

Examples of Military Rank	*Making Introductions/ Addressing Envelopes*	*Letter Salutation*	*Speaking To*	*Place Card*
First lieutenant	First Lieutenant Richard Dix, USMC *or, socially:* First Lieutenant and Mrs. Richard Dix	Dear Lieutenant Dix:	Lieutenant Dix, *or,* Lieutenant	Lieutenant Dix

Examples of Military Rank	Making Introductions/ Addressing Envelopes	Letter Salutation	Speaking To	Place Card
Captain in the Navy	Captain Joseph Piteo, USN *or, socially:* Captain and Mrs. Joseph Piteo	Dear Captain Piteo:	Captain Piteo, *or,* Captain	Captain Piteo
Lieutenant colonel	Lieutenant Colonel Frank Haig, USMC *or, socially:* Lieutenant Colonel and Mrs. Frank Haig	Dear Colonel Haig:	Colonel Haig, *or,* Colonel	Colonel Haig
Chief warrant officer	Chief Warrant Officer Jane Turner *or, socially:* Chief Warrant Officer Jane Turner and Mr. Anthony Turner	Dear Chief Warrant Officer Turner: *or, informally:* Dear Ms. Turner:	Chief Warrant Officer Turner *or, informally:* Ms. Turner	Ms. Turner
Noncommissioned officers in Army, Air Force, and Marine Corps	Master Sergeant Tony Tatum *or, socially:* Master Sergeant and Mrs. Tony Tatum	Dear Sergeant Tatum:	Sergeant Tatum	Mr. Tatum
(Follow same form for any rating, including Sergeant Major, Sergeant First Class, Platoon Sergeant, Corporal, Specialist (classes 4 to 9), Private First Class, etc.)				
Enlisted person in Navy	SN Robert Peltz Address of his command *or, socially:* Seaman and Mrs. Robert Peltz	Dear Seaman Peltz:	Seaman Peltz	Seaman Peltz
Retired officer in Army or Air Force	Major Robert Orr, USAF Retired Address *or, socially:* Major and Mrs. Robert Orr	Dear Major Orr:	Major Orr	Major Orr
Retired officer in Navy or Coast Guard*	Rear Admiral Spencer Davis, USN Retired Address *or, socially:* Rear Admiral and Mrs. Spencer Davis	Dear Admiral Davis:	Admiral Davis	Admiral Davis

*Only Navy and Coast Guard officers with rank of commander and above retain their titles after retirement; officers in the Reserve do not.

Examples of Military Rank	Making Introductions/ Addressing Envelopes	Letter Salutation	Speaking To	Place Card
Cadet at West Point (same for Air Force Academy, with address change)	Cadet Mark Boland, U.S. Army Company __, Corps of Cadets United States Military Academy West Point, NY 10996	Dear Mr. Boland: *or,* Dear Cadet Boland:	Mr. Boland	Mr. Boland
Midshipman at U.S. Naval Academy; Cadet at U.S. Coast Guard Academy	Midshipman Joan Doan U.S. Naval Academy *or* Cadet Stephen Cole United States Coast Guard Academy	Dear Ms. (*or* Miss) Doan: Dear Mr. Cole:	Ms. *or* Miss Doan Mr. Cole	Ms. Doan

NOTE: Try to put the name of husband and wife on one line on the invitation envelope. For example:

> Captain and Mrs. Robert Smith
> (address beneath)

If the names are too long for your envelope, indent the spouse's name three spaces on the second line. For example:

> Captain
>   and Mrs. Jerome Alexander Gallipuccio
> (address beneath)

The limitations of space in this and the following charts do not permit us to give the address lines in preferred form.

Addressing Religious Officials

In closing a letter to a very high religious official, use "Respectfully yours," or use "Sincerely" or "Sincerely yours."

Protestant Clergy

Official	Making Introductions/ Addressing Envelopes	Letter Salutation	Speaking To/ Place Card
Clergyman with Doctor's degree	The Reverend Dr. Amos E. Long *or, socially:* The Reverend Dr. Amos E. Long and Mrs. Long	Dear Dr. Long:	Dr. Long
Clergywoman without Doctor's degree	The Reverend Anne Smith *or, socially:* The Reverend Anne Smith and Mr. Peter Smith	Dear Ms. or Miss Smith:	Ms. or Miss Smith
Presiding Bishop of the Episcopal Church in the United States	The Right Reverend James Gard, Presiding Bishop *or, socially:* The Right Reverend James Gard and Mrs. Gard	Dear Bishop Gard:	Bishop Gard

Official	Making Introductions/ Addressing Envelopes	Letter Salutation	Speaking To/ Place Card
Bishop of the Episcopal Church	The Right Reverend David Webb Bishop of Washington *or, socially:* The Right Reverend David Webb and Mrs. Webb	Dear Bishop Webb:	Bishop Webb
Methodist Bishop	The Reverend Michael Forest Methodist Bishop *or, socially:* The Reverend Michael Forest and Mrs. Forest	Dear Bishop Forest:	Bishop Forest
Dean	The Very Reverend Angus Dunn *or,* The Very Reverend Angus Dunn Dean of St. John's *or, socially:* The Very Reverend Angus Dunn and Mrs. Dunn	Dear Dean Dunn:	Dean Dunn
Archdeacon	The Venerable Stewart G. Dodd Archdeacon of Boston *or, socially:* The Venerable Stewart G. Dodd and Mrs. Dodd	Dear Archdeacon Dodd:	Archdeacon Dodd
Canon	The Reverend Randolph Tate Canon of St. Andrew's *or, socially:* The Reverend Randolph Tate and Mrs. Tate	Dear Canon Tate:	Canon Tate

Notes on Protestant clergy:
- Clergy with degrees optionally use the initials of their degrees after their names. For example: The Right Reverend James Gard, or The Right Reverend James Gard, D.D., LL.D.
- A member of the Episcopal clergy who is not in a religious order may call himself "Father." In writing him, you do not use his Christian name, but rather his surname: "The Reverend Father Stimson."
- A Protestant minister who retires remains "The Reverend So-and-so." If he or she resigns, that person normally becomes "Mr." or "Ms."

Mormon Clergy

Official	Making Introductions/ Addressing Envelopes	Letter Salutation	Speaking To/ Place Card
Mormon Bishop	Mr. Timothy Blake Church of Jesus Christ of Latter-day Saints *or, socially:* Mr. and Mrs. Timothy Blake	Dear Mr. Blake:	Mr. Blake

Roman Catholic Hierarchy

Official	Making Introductions/ Addressing Envelopes	Letter Salutation	Speaking To/ Place Card
The Pope	His Holiness, the Pope *or* His Holiness, Pope Augustus III	Your Holiness:	*Speaking to*: Your Holiness
The Apostolic Delegate in Washington (the Pope's representative)	His Excellency The Most Reverend Bishop of (City) The Apostolic Delegate Address	Your Excellency	Your Excellency/His Excellency the Apostolic Delegate
Cardinal	His Eminence, Joseph Cardinal Sheehan Archbishop of St. Louis	Your Eminence: *or*, Dear Cardinal Sheehan:	Your Eminence/ Cardinal Sheehan
Bishop and Archbishop	The Most Reverend Paul Murphy, Bishop (Archbishop) of Chicago	Your Excellency: *or*, Dear Bishop Murphy:	Excellency/Bishop Murphy
Monsignor	The Right Reverend Julius Cuneo	Dear Monsignor Cuneo:	Monsignor Cuneo
Priest	The Reverend Father James Orr Church rectory address	Dear Father Orr:	Father Orr
Brother	Brother David Maxwell	Dear Brother David: *or*, Dear Brother Maxwell:	Brother David *or* Brother Maxwell
Nun	Joan Reynolds, R.S.C.J. *or*, Sister Mary Annunciata	Dear Sister:	Sister Reynolds *or* Sister Mary Annunciata

Eastern Orthodox Communion

Official	Making Introductions/ Addressing Envelopes	Salutation	Speaking To
Patriarch	His Holiness, the Ecumenical Patriarch of Constantinople	Your Holiness:	Your Holiness
Bishop and priest	Same as Roman Catholic Church		
Archimandrite	The Very Reverend Gregory Costos	Reverend Sir:	Father Costos

Jewish Faith

Official	Making Introductions/ Addressing Envelopes	Letter Salutation	Speaking To	Place Card
Rabbi	Rabbi Melvin Schwartz Address *or, socially:* Rabbi and Mrs. Melvin Schwartz	Dear Rabbi Schwartz:	Rabbi *or* Rabbi Schwartz	Rabbi Schwartz
Cantor	Cantor Samuel Stein Address *or, socially:* Cantor and Mrs. Samuel Stein	Dear Cantor Stein:	Cantor Stein	Cantor Stein

Military Chaplains

Making Introductions/ Addressing Envelopes	Letter Salutation	Speaking To	Place Card
Major John Martin, Chaplain Address	Dear Major Martin: *or*, Dear Chaplain: *or, for a Catholic Chaplain:* Dear Father Martin: *or, for a Jewish Chaplain,* Dear Rabbi Martin:	Chaplain *or* Major Martin	Major Martin *or, for Catholic,* Father Martin *or, for Jewish,* Rabbi Martin

Addressing U.S. Ambassadors to Other Countries

An American Ambassador credited to a foreign country is addressed in person as "Mr. Ambassador." He is introduced to others as "Ambassador Bruceton." If you are introducing him before his speech, you would say, "And now I present the Ambassador of the United States to Italy, The Honorable Perry Bruceton."

The envelope of a letter addressed to him would read:

> The Honorable Perry H. Bruceton
> United States Ambassador to the Republic of Italy
> American Embassy (Use the appropriate APO or FPO address)
> Rome, Italy

For a salutation, you would write: "Dear Mr. Ambassador:"

If you were sending the ambassador and his wife an invitation, you would address the envelope:

> The American Ambassador
>   and Mrs. Perry H. Bruceton
> American Embassy, etc.

His place card would read: "The American Ambassador," if he is at his foreign post; otherwise, if in America, "Ambassador Bruceton." His wife's card would always read,"Mrs. Bruceton."

Addressing Foreign Ambassadors to the United States

An Ambassador to the United States resides in Washington and outranks the ambassadors to the United Nations in New York. He or she is the official representative from his government to our government. Since many ambassadors travel constantly throughout the United States, it is very possible that you will cross paths with one in your business life.

In talking to an ambassador, you would address him or her as "Mr. Ambassador" or "Madame Ambassador." An ambassador's wife is referred to as "The Ambassadress" when speaking of her, but in addressing her, you would say simply "Madame" or "Madame Richaud." (The husband of a woman ambassador has no honorary title. He is simply "Mr. Smith" or "Monsieur Blanchard.")

In writing to an Ambassador, you would say: "Dear Mr. Ambassador:" in the salutation. The envelope would be addressed to:

> His Excellency
> Herve Richaud
> Ambassador of France to the United States
> Embassy of the Republic of France
> Washington, DC 20007

If you are sending an invitation to him and his wife, you would write

> His Excellency
> Herve Richaud
>   and Madame Richaud
> Embassy of the Republic of France
> Washington, DC 20007

In introducing him, you would say, "His Excellency Herve Richaud, the Ambassador of the Republic of France to the United States."

Writing and Speaking to Officials of Foreign Republics

When you communicate with officials of a foreign republic, follow the style given in this chart for the country of France:

Official	Making Introductions/ Addressing Envelopes	Letter Salutation	Speaking To	Place Card
President of the Republic	His Excellency Henri Vaudoyer President of the Republic of France Address *or, socially:* The President of France and Madame Vaudoyer	Dear Mr. President:	Mr. President	The President of the Republic of France
Prime Minister of the Republic of France	His Excellency Jean de l'Abeille Prime Minister of the Republic of France *or, socially:* The Prime Minister of France and Madame de l'Abeille	Dear Mr. Prime Minister:	Mr. Prime Minister	The Prime Minister of the Republic of France
Minister of Foreign Affairs of the Republic of France	Her Excellency Jeanne d'Arcy Minister of Foreign Affairs *or, socially:* The Minister of Foreign Affairs and Monsieur Pierre d'Arcy	Dear Madame Minister:	Madame Minister	The Minister of Foreign Affairs of the Republic of France

Western European Titles

The king or queen of any foreign country is addressed as "Your Majesty," and referred to as "His Majesty" or "Her Majesty" respectively.

The prince consort to the queen is referred to as "His Royal Highness" and is addressed as "Your Royal Highness."

When royal titles still exist in a country that is not a monarchy, even though these titles are meaningless, they are still treated with respect by the people in that country. Western Europe has a long history and a love of tradition, and therefore people who have inherited defunct but legitimate titles may use the royal crest on their stationery, engraved on their silver flatware, etc.

In order of rank, the titles are these:

· Prince and princess (Call them by their title and surname, not their given names, when introducing them; in conversation call them "Prince" and "Princess.")
· Duke and duchess (Call them by their title and surname, not their given name, when introducing them; in conversation, call them "Duke" or "Duchess.")
· Marquess and marchioness (*marquis* and *marquise* in France; *marchese* and *marchesa* in Italy; *marques* and *marquesa* in Spain)
· Viscount and viscountess
· Count and countess
· Baron and baroness

You would write an invitation to them in the following manner: "Count and Countess Philippe de Beaumont." If one of the couple is titled and the other is not, use the title for the one who holds it: "Signor Emmanuele Capriccio and Contessa Eleanora Capriccio."

Many Western Europeans do not use their titles when doing business in the United States, but when you write to them in their country and when you are visiting in their country, you should use their titles.

Writing and Speaking to the Royal Family of Great Britain

Protocol for the royal family is carefully adhered to in Great Britain and in certain parts of the Commonwealth. Even though we Americans are far removed from a philosophical attachment to the monarchy, we have traditionally paid respect to it. American women do not curtsey to the Queen when being presented to her, but making a slight dip of the head while shaking hands with the Queen is a nice gesture. An American who shows a lack of respect for the Queen and her family is displaying the worst kind of manners, and no corporation in this country should tolerate that kind of behavior here or in Great Britain.

- One does not write directly to a member of any nation's royal family directly, but always through a channel. In the case of the British royal family, address your letter to "The Private Secretary to . . ." and then add:

  - Her Majesty, the Queen
  - His Royal Highness, Prince Philip, The Duke of Edinburgh
  - Her Majesty Queen Elizabeth, the Queen Mother (one friend of mine wrote to "Her Majesty the Queen Mum" and received a polite letter in return from her secretary)
  - His Royal Highness, The Prince Charles, Prince of Wales
  - Her Royal Highness, The Princess of Wales (as of this writing)
  - His Royal Highness, The Duke of York
  - His Royal Highness, The Prince Edward
  - Her Royal Highness, The Princess Anne (Mrs. Timothy Lawrence)
  - Her Royal Highness, The Princess Margaret, Countess of Snowden

- Introductions are made and place cards read as listed above.
- The Queen and the Queen Mother are addressed as "Your Majesty," and in subsequent conversation, you would say "Ma'am."
- The other members of the royal family are addressed as "Your Royal Highness," and subsequently are addressed as "Sir" or "Ma'am."

Making Conversation With a Royal

When you are presented to the Queen or any member of the immediate family, you do not speak first. The royal speaks first, saying something as exciting as, "How do you do? It's nice to meet you." You would reply with something equally stimulating: "It is an honor to meet you, Your Majesty."

The conversation might proceed as follows:

THE ROYAL: Did someone say you were from Chicago?

YOUR RESPONSE: Yes, Ma'am. We think we live in a fine city.

THE ROYAL: The Art Institute is one of the finest museums I have ever visited.

YOUR RESPONSE: I'm so happy you have seen it, Ma'am. We are very proud of our museum.

THE ROYAL: I hope to return there some day. If you see your Mayor (Mayor Daley, I believe), give him my best wishes.

At this, Her Majesty would turn away to speak to the next person in line, and thus would end your conversation with Her Majesty the Queen—longer than most people have in their lifetimes.

Writing and Speaking to the Peerage

Peer	Making Introductions/ Addressing Envelopes	Letter Salutation	Speaking To	Place Card
A nonroyal duke	The Duke of Oakford *or* The Duke and Duchess of Oakford	Dear Duke: Dear Duchess	Duke Duchess	The Duke of Oakford The Duchess of Oakford
	(The English often address a duke and duchess as ''Your Grace'' and speak of them as ''His Grace the Duke of . . .'' but Americans are not expected to follow this procedure.)			
Duke's eldest son and daughter-in-law	The Marquess of Chester *or, socially:* The Marquess and Marchioness of Chester	Dear Lord Chester: Dear Lady Chester:	Lord Chester Lady Chester	Lord Chester Lady Chester
Marquess's eldest son; Earl's wife, a countess	The Earl of Meads *or, socially:* The Earl and Countess of Meads	Dear Lord Meads: Dear Lady Meads:	Lord Meads Lady Meads	Lord Meads Lady Meads
Viscount, eldest son of an earl	Viscount Brentwood *or, socially:* Viscount and Viscountess Brentwood	Dear Viscount Brentwood: Dear Lady Brentwood:	Lord Brentwood Lady Brentwood	Viscount Brentwood Viscountess Brentwood
Baron Baroness	The Lord Lyndhurst *or, socially:* Lord and Lady Lyndhurst	Dear Lord Lyndhurst: Dear Lady Lyndhurst	Lord Lyndhurst Lady Lyndhurst	Lord Lyndhurst Lady Lyndhurst
Baronet	Sir Albert Northrop, Bt. *or, socially:* Sir Albert and Lady Northrop	Dear Sir Albert: Dear Lady Northrop:	Sir Albert Northrop Lady Northrop	Sir Albert Northrop Lady Northrop

Canadian Officials

	Making Introductions/ Addressing Envelopes	Letter Salutation	Speaking To	Place Card
Governor General	His Excellency Eric C. Johnson *or, socially:* Their Excellencies Governor General and Mrs. Johnson	Dear Governor General	Governor General	The Governor General of Canada
Lieutenant Governor of Canada	His Honour The Honourable Gerald L. Dowd Lieutenant Governor *or, socially:* Lieutenant Governor and Mrs. Dowd	Dear Lieutenant Governor:	Lieutenant Governor Dowd	The Lieutenant Governor of Canada
Prime Minister of Canada	The Right Honourable Andrew C. Fitch, P.C., M.P. Prime Minister of Canada *or, socially:* The Prime Minister and Mrs. Fitch	Dear Mr. Prime Minister:	Prime Minister Fitch	The Prime Minister of Canada

	Making Introductions/ Addressing Envelopes	Letter Salutation	Speaking To	Place Card
Premier of a province of Canada	The Honourable Carolyn Cadré Premier of the Province of Quebec *or, socially:* The Honourable Carolyn Cadré and Mr. Jacques Cadré	Dear Madame Premier:	Premier Code	The Premier of Quebec
Member of Senate	The Honourable Laura Flynn The Senate, Ottawa *or, socially:* The Honourable Laura Flynn and Mr. Lesley Flynn	Dear Senator Flynn:	Senator	The Honourable Laura Flynn
Member of House of Commons	Samuel Morris, Esq., M.P. House of Commons *or, socially:* Mr. and Mrs. Samuel Morris	Dear Mr. Morris:	Mr. Morris	Samuel Morris, Esq., M.P.
Mayor of a city or town	His Worship Mayor Kenneth Woods City Hall *or, socially:* His Worship Mayor Kenneth Woods and Mrs. Woods	Dear Mr. Mayor:	Mr. Mayor	The Mayor of Toronto
Chief Justice	The Right Honourable Roger C. Bolton, Chief Justice of Canada *or, socially:* The Right Honourable Roger C. Bolton and Mrs. Bolton	Dear Mr. Chief Justice:	Chief Justice Bolton	The Chief Justice of Canada

NOTE: Since people in Great Britain and the Commonwealth spell it *Honourable*, with the *u*, it is a nice touch to address them with their own spelling.

Writing and Speaking to Officials at the United Nations

Unlike the diplomatic corps accredited to Washington, DC, the United Nations diplomats change in rank and precedence on a rotating basis (which means that length of service in the job or importance of the country has little to do with who outranks whom).

Official	Making Introductions/ Addressing Envelopes	Letter Salutation	Speaking To	Place Card
The Secretary General	Her Excellency Françoise d'Estain Secretary General of the United Nations	Dear Madame Secretary General:	Madame Secretary General (Madame d'Estain, *subsequently*)	The Secretary General of the United Nations

Official	Making Introductions/ Addressing Envelopes	Letter Salutation	Speaking To	Place Card
A foreign UN ambassador	His Excellency Koto Matsumada Ambassador of Japan Permanent Mission of Japan to the United Nations	Dear Mr. Ambassador:	Mr. Ambassador (Sir, *subsequently*)	Ambassador Matsumada
The United States Representative to the United Nations	The Honorable Henry Gregory United States Representative to the United Nations	Dear Mr. Ambassador:	Mr. Ambassador (Sir, *subsequently*)	Ambassador Gregory

Invitations to UN ambassadors and their spouses are addressed to their residence as follows:

His Excellency Koto Matsumada and Madame Matsumada

or

Her Excellency Françoise d'Estain and Monsieur Eric d'Estain

Addressing Foreign Professionals

We should accord foreign professionals their titles when addressing them. For example, in Italy, if you have finished university and earned your degree, you are called "Dottore" (for a man) or "Dottoressa" (for a woman) as the title before your surname for the rest of your life. In writing a letter, you may abbreviate the title to "Dott." in front of either his or her surname—"Dott. Cavalchini." We Americans should use this title if we have any correspondence on personal or business matters with an Italian who merits this honorific.

In many countries a man or woman who has earned a professional degree is thereafter addressed by the title of that profession (and not necessarily by his or her name) for the rest of that person's life. For example, in France, in speaking to a person, you would address a lawyer formally as "Monsieur l'Avocat" (Mr. Lawyer) or a woman ambassador as "Madame l'Ambassadeur." In Italy you would say "Signor Avvocato," and you would call your architect "Signor Architetto." In Germany, instead of calling the CEO of the company "Herr Schmidt," you'd call him "Herr Direktor"; an engineer would be addressed as "Herr Ingenieur," and so on. (It makes life very easy for people who can't remember names; all they have to remember is a professional title!)

Once an American becomes involved at length with a foreigner in a country where a professional title is important—whether it's a business or a social matter—the polite thing to do is to use his or her title in addressing that person. Learn the foreign pronunciation, learn how to write the title in the foreign tongue. Your foreign colleague will be pleased and respect you more because of it.

Addressing Women in Foreign Countries

The great thing about using the diplomatically accepted title (French spelling, however) "Madame," is that you can use it as the title for any spouse of a European, Asian, African, or South American official. (Not so for people with royal titles, however.) If you don't know the generic title for "Mrs." in a foreign language or even a woman's husband's given name, just put a "Madame" in front of the last name. (For example: Madame Mitsumoto, Madame Moerner, Madame Balmain, and Madame Agryopoulos.) It's a nice acceptable title (a French diplomatic word) that lets you off the hook around the world from knowing more information.

An even greater thing about "Madame" is that you can call a woman that just by itself, and never mention any other name when you see her, if you have forgotten her various names. "Ah, Madame, it is such wonderful news about your husband!" or "Goodbye, Madame, I hope to see you soon again." (You can't do that in English. "Ah, Mrs.," would not work at all.)

American married women who use their husbands' names are known socially by their husbands' names. It's "Mrs. John Regan," not "Mrs. Prudence Regan." In Western European countries, a woman is known by her title, her given and her married name. When you write her, address the envelope to "Madame Hermine Blanche" with the address below (not to "Madame Henri Blanche"). In Germany you would write to "Frau Elsa Hoffmanstal," not to "Frau Erik Hoffmanstal."

Young people entering the business world often wonder about all the trappings of protocol they see around them—the place cards done just so at a business lunch, an official introduced to people in the office with his full name and title, managers standing up when important visitors walk into the conference room. In time they come to appreciate protocol as a grand scheme that causes things to move along smoothly and helps to bring order out of chaos.

13

Running and Attending Meetings and Conferences, from Inter-Office to International

Mericans attend more meetings than people in any country in the world. Many in the business community say that 75 percent of those held are unnecessary, and some are even counter-productive to accomplishing agreed-upon goals. However, no matter how much any one company may suffer from meeting overkill, meetings bring us together to allow us to learn from one another, understand better what the company is trying to achieve, observe what the brass is up to, and engage in human interaction.

WHY MEETINGS ARE HELD

Even if American businesses do spend more money on getting together and having meetings than any other society in the world, there's a good reason for it. We are the most diversified of all melting pots in this global economy, so we need the coming together, the joining of forces, and the sharing of experience and information that meetings provide. There's another reason for all these meetings, too. We often enjoy them!

The person who calls a meeting in the first place may be motivated by any of the following reasons:

- *The manager needs to know what is going on down the line.*
- *The manager needs to pep up the staff* and instill some spark and enthusiasm into their work.
- *The manager has some new staff members whom he wishes to introduce* to everyone in the division, but whom she also wishes to observe in group interaction, to see how they do.
- *There are new ideas, products, or plans that need to be presented or communicated* fully, carefully, and accurately.
- *There is trouble brewing within the division*, and the chair needs to find out what it is, how bad it is, and who is involved.
- *The chair needs to shape up a working group that has become slack and careless* or who aren't trying hard enough.
- *The chair wants to thank some people* who have done a splendid job on a project.
- It is a regularly scheduled meeting to bring everyone up to date and/or bring up new business.

You, as a participant in a meeting, on the other hand, should welcome it as a chance to:

- Show that you have something to offer. If you are shy, a meeting gives you the chance to change others' perception of you by putting forth useful or imaginative ideas.
- See colleagues in action and observe how they relate to one another. A meeting can be an excellent training lab.
- Get to know senior managers better and make them aware of your potential.

A meeting may be called for any number of reasons, but it will not be productive unless the need to call it is properly communicated and unless everyone leaves it understanding the signals and the lines of responsibility and takes appropriate action as a result.

Behavior in an office meeting should not differ from behavior at meetings outside the office, and that includes conventions, sales meetings, conferences, and seminars in which each of us represents our company to the community at large. Of course, since we are on show in public—a different kind of show from that in our offices—we should not only demonstrate the same consideration we do in our office meetings but make an even greater effort. Social animals that we are, the more we practice, the more automatic the correct responses become, and the easier and the more natural good manners become.

The manners of the individual attending a meeting are important; those of the organizers who stage the event are equally so. The whole feeling—the ambiance—of a large meeting really depends upon the professionalism, efficiency, creativity, and caring attitude of those in charge.

A large gathering can be a warm, personal experience for its participants. I have, for example, the warmest of memories of a three-day seminar I attended in the Montreux Palace Hotel in Switzerland for a major financial services company (at which I was one of the speakers). All attendees were sent several mailings of material before our departure so that we arrived in Montreux thoroughly briefed on the company's program, the country, the history of the hotel, and options for what we could do in our free time. Our suitcases were tagged with large bright-colored tags, which made them readily identifiable in airports. When we checked into the hotel, we each found a beautiful packet of Swiss postcards, all stamped with Swiss air mail stamps, ready for us to send back home. Each night a little gift was left in our rooms by the meeting manager. One night it was a small box of chocolates, another night an embroidered Swiss handerchief, another night a basket of fresh fruit.

Since this was an international meeting, protocol was strictly followed; every dinner was properly seated; all Swiss and American business people and government officials were properly introduced to each other, with names and titles correctly given. Every little detail was "just right," because a great deal of advance planning had gone into it. The meeting manager had beautiful manners; he was very conscious of the image his company was trying to project, particularly since so many thousands of dollars were being spent on its projection.

However, even if your meeting is in Room R-4 on your office floor rather than at the Montreux Palace in Switzerland, remember the old saying: It *is* the little things that count!

THE EFFECTIVE MEETING CHAIRMAN

The chairman is supposed to include, among his or her managerial skills, a knowledge of the protocol of conducting meetings. *Robert's Rules of Order*, by H. M. Robert (published by Fleming Revell, available in paperback as well as hard cover, and in every library in America), is the acknowledged classic on the order of meetings.

The *polite* meeting chairman:

- *Is thoughtful about when he schedules the meeting*, knowing that most people are at their best and freshest in the morning. He does not schedule meetings on Friday afternoons, when people are trying to get away for the weekend. He does not schedule them on the eve of important holidays, when out-of-town participants will have difficulty returning to their home cities. He does not carelessly schedule meetings on important religious holidays.
- *Informs participants as far ahead as possible of the date*—two weeks ahead of an in-house meeting, if possible, and four weeks ahead for participants who have to travel from other cities.

- *Is apologetic if circumstances force him to call a meeting without a proper lead time*, because he realizes he may have greatly inconvenienced the people who must attend.
- *Invites people to his meetings on a selective, carefully thought out basis*, realizing that only those who *must* attend should be invited. He is aware that many meetings do not have to be called at all. He includes those who have direct responsibility for the business at hand, as well as those in training who would find it useful to be there. He invites people from other areas of the company whose expertise will be needed, so that he will never have to say to himself, "I *should* have asked so-and-so to attend today." However, he keeps remembering that valuable management resources must not be wastefully tied up in meetings.
- *Distributes the agenda well in advance*, to give invitees the time to think about the subjects at hand, as well as pertinent materials the participants must read *before* the meeting.
- *Determines how long to wait for missing people before starting*. One executive I know will not wait one minute beyond the scheduled hour for *anyone*, including the CEO. When he begins the meeting, he starts a tape recorder and makes anyone who is tardy stay behind afterward to hear what he missed. (The tape also records permanently the embarrassment of the latecomer.)
- *Introduces all newcomers to the group in a complimentary manner* and introduces the others to the newcomers with their names, titles, and responsibilities.
- *Shows the younger executives that he is approachable and human*, not only by his sense of humor but by allowing the younger people (or newcomers or visitors) the opportunity to show what they know and to contribute to the discussion. In other words, he orchestrates the proceedings in a way that permits them to establish their knowledge and expertise before their peers. He asks the newcomers easy questions.
- *Is aware of any tension and nonverbal communication that flows in a hostile way around the room* and talks it over afterward with anyone involved. Sometimes, of course, there is open hostility, which must be dealt with on the spot. I will never forget being present in a meeting of two sharply opposed factions. The chairman, a senior executive, had trouble keeping order as managers argued vehemently on two sides. Finally he rose from his chair and walked over to the light switch on the wall. Suddenly fifteen emotionally upset executives were plunged into total darkness. There was no sound in the room; it was as though a cool wet blanket had been wrapped around a steaming room interior. A few seconds later, the chairman switched on the light. It worked. The discussion continued in a calm, rational way; the disagreement was settled, and the meeting came to a close.
- *Keeps one eye on the clock and one on the agenda* and thereby avoids delays caused by people rambling and talking off the subject
- *Does not smoke if smoking is not permitted in that room*

- *Handles the "meeting hogger" with agility.* Shuts off with kindness and firmness the person who tries to dominate the meeting.
- *Sees that the meeting place is comfortable*—that it is:

  - Clean
  - Well lit
  - Aired out (stale air makes stale minds)
  - Cool in temperature
  - Equipped with comfortable seating
  - Equipped with ice water and glasses
  - Equipped with pads and pencils

- *Calls a seventh-inning stretch for participants* every hour and a half of a very long meeting, to allow them to stretch their muscles, talk to colleagues, make telephone calls, etc.
- *Gives credit to everyone* who gave presentations but also to everyone who helped prepare the meeting, including those who prepared any graphs, slides, and/or audiovisual presentations that were used.
- *Sets the date for the next meeting of the group* and makes certain that everyone present knows exactly what followup he individually is responsible for.

THE EFFECTIVE MEETING PARTICIPANT

The protocol for proper behavior of the meeting attendant suggests:

- *He arrives on time*, even several minutes before the meeting is scheduled to begin.
- If he's on new turf of his own or on someone else's turf, *he introduces himself* in a friendly, informal manner to anyone also waiting. If he is the outsider, he explains to the others who he is and why he's there. This is also the time for him to hand out his business card, if the executives with whom he is talking ask him questions about himself and his company.
- As a newcomer, *he does not take a seat* until someone who knows why he is there motions for him to "take a seat anywhere," or perhaps to "sit over there, next to Ann Smith." It would be bad politics to plunk himself down next to the meeting chairman. The seats to the right and left of the chairman are for that person's peers or honored guests.
- If the meeting is delayed for some reason (such as the late arrival of the chairman), he should turn to someone on either side and launch into a conversational topic (unless that person is studying the papers in front of him). He might ask a question about current events ("What did you think of the incredible upsets in yesterday's primaries?") or perhaps bring up the meeting itself ("I'm anxious to know the presentation of the new campaign, because I hear it's a great one.").

- *He arrives prepared for the meeting* with all his homework carefully done.
- *He has rehearsed his own remarks well if he is to do a presentation, and has asked the manager to let him try out any audiovisual and electrical equipment* needed for an audiovisual presentation, to make sure it works properly. In other words, *he is ready.*
- *He receives permission from the chair before using a tape recorder.*
- *He makes careful notes of the discussion and the criticisms* that are put forth on his own ideas and makes careful notes, too, of his own criticisms of others' ideas.
- *He doesn't slump in his seat*, an action that denotes boredom, which is the exact opposite of the impression he should be trying to create.
- *He does not doodle*, another very distracting gesture. (True, U.S. presidents have been known to doodle in cabinet meetings; when the junior executive gets to be President of the United States, he can doodle, too.) He also refrains from other "conference table tics," such as bending paper clips into endless combinations or rolling bits of paper into tiny balls.
- *He avoids interrupting whoever has the floor*, instead making a note of what he wanted to say at that moment. Particularly in the case of large, formal meetings, he awaits a timely moment in which to interject his comments. He obtains recognition to speak by calling out the name of the chairman and half-raising his hand, as though he were in school getting the teacher's attention. The chair will then nod in his direction or call out his name, signifying he may now have the floor.
- *He resists the temptation to monopolize the proceedings* at any point, even if he is qualified to do so. (He remembers how his classmates felt about the student who perpetually had his hand up first every time the teacher asked a question.)
- *He has the courage to ask for clarification* of an unclear point. Probably there are several others in the room just as confused as he is. He knows that there is wisdom in admitting one does not understand, rather than trying to bluff through it.
- *He is relaxed about showing his positive emotions but careful to control any display of negative emotions if in violent disagreement* with something that has just been said. There are degrees of showing disapproval; "violent" disapproval is rude. He can evince his disagreement by shaking his head and making a quiet comment after the other person has finished speaking. If the chair does not call upon him to elucidate further, he should keep quiet and voice his opinions only after the meeting.
- *He uses the editorial "we" instead of "I"* when talking to the group. "We" signifies he is part of a team; "I" sounds egocentric, as if he refuses to grant credit to the others working on a project (even if their role is very small).
- If shyness overcomes him when he has something to say, he knows *he can put his thoughts in a memo* sent to the chairman and to whoever else present at the meeting should receive it.
- *He thinks before he speaks* and presents his comments in an organized fashion. He sticks to the subject, in order not to waste everyone's time.

- *He uses a glass for canned or bottled drinks*, if glasses have been made available. He also discreetly conceals the empty can, paper cup, paper napkin, or any litter about him.
- *He thanks the chairman of the meeting as he leaves* the room.
- *He returns to his office and immediately makes notes of what he personally must do as a follow-up to the meeting.* He also marks the date of the next meeting of the group in his agenda.

GET THE MOST OUT OF THE MEETINGS YOU ATTEND

If you are going to a meeting out of town, look upon it as an opportunity to advance your career—and as a privilege. The proper mental attitude will make it possible for you to come away with some excellent information, with new ideas, and with fresh contacts to rely upon in the future for assistance, idea-sharing and, yes, friendships.

- *Prepare yourself.* Read each and every page of the sometime endless materials in your meeting kit. They all serve a purpose.
- *Ask every person* with whom you have a good conversation or whom you find *simpatico* for a business card and write down the necessary information about them and your meeting.
- *Make notes of everything of interest you hear* in the meeting sessions. Organize those notes when you get home and make a synopsis of what you learned and refer to them every so often.
- *Use the meals offered to sit down with strangers*, and thus make new friends. You will find new information and ideas often more nourishing than the food being served.
- *Show what beautiful manners you have.* The minute you return home, get out that note paper. Write or type a letter:
  - To thank and praise the meeting planner who did such a great job, together with his or her staff, in organizing the meeting
  - To the CEO, telling him how much your group appreciated the chance to attend the meeting, and how much you all profited from it (it will probably be the only letter he receives, so he'll remember you forever)
  - To congratulate any speakers at the meeting who were immensely effective. Those words of praise are really appreciated.
  - To thank the manager of the hotel or meeting facility, if you were greatly impressed with the operation, and particularly if you were helped out in special ways. Since the only mail the general manager usually receives consists of rude complaint letters, you will be remembered.
- *Drop a short note to any new friend you made,* saying you hope your mutual paths will cross in the near future, and wishing your new friend well. It's amazing how

these new friendships really do flourish, and how often people do see one another again in different cities.

Think Before Speaking

A young executive often has a tendency to project creative ideas at meetings based more on enthusiasm than on substance, feasibility, and logic. I am grateful to Ely Callaway, who was once my boss as president of Burlington Industries, at that time the world's largest textile company. He chaired a meeting that I attended in my new capacity as the company's first woman senior executive and first Director of Consumer Affairs. At one point in the crowded conference room I seized the floor and became inflamed with the passion of my own remarks. Ely very quietly slipped me a note, which I managed to glance at while on my feet still talking. "Tish," it read, "enough is *enough*." He had sent me a signal to stop, for my own good. I finished quickly and sat down, my cheeks flaming red.

He explained afterward that I had not been communicating properly to the group. I did not have the *sense* of the group. When I thanked him for tipping me off, he urged me to have a little more patience. He explained that a newcomer first has to gain the respect of old-timers before suddenly interjecting a whole stream of new ideas. "Prove first that you're a professional," he advised, "before trying to change the world." Then he chuckled and said, "But, Tish, you gave quite a performance!"

GOOD MANNERS AT ROUTINE MEETINGS OUTSIDE THE OFFICE

Both junior and senior executives' actions are conspicuous when they attend meetings outside their own offices. As a visitor, an executive is very much on parade.

- If he is a casual dresser, *on the day of the meeting he should dress up, and conservatively.*
- *He should arrive on time.*
- *He should not ask to use the telephone* of anyone present, nor should he ask anyone's secretary to make a call for him or run an errand for him during the meetings. (He should have done all of that previously, using a pay telephone if necessary.)
- If no one in the host group introduces him before the meeting, *he should extend his hand to those near him and give his name and company.* He should also introduce himself to the meeting chairman when the latter arrives. In this way the meeting will begin on a friendly note.
- *He should wait to sit down* until someone has waved him into a seat or until the chairman has asked everyone to be seated.

- It is the host's duty to offer the group refreshment, like coffee, tea or soda, but *if nothing is offered, the visitor should not request anything.*
- *An absence of ashtrays in the room is a sign that he should not ask to smoke.*
- *It is wise for him to hand his business card to the person taking the notes of the meeting,* so that the note-taker will know his name and affiliation immediately when he contributes to the discussion.
- *He should make a special effort to remain alert and look interested* throughout the meeting, even if he is acutely bored.
- *He should personally thank the meeting chairman for his hospitality* at the meeting's conclusion.

MEETING MANNERS AWAY FROM HOME

A company shows its class, or lack of it, by the way it organizes and invites people to events under its sponsorship, whether it's a lecture, workshop program, or seminar. Those attending these meetings, conferences, and seminars also show their class, or lack of it, in their behavior, by the way in which they interact and by the way in which they follow both the prescribed rules of the meeting and all the subtle "unsaid" rules. The latter involve attitudes toward noise, litter, tardiness, lack of cooperation, and generally selfish behavior. For example, a conference or meeting is no place to drink to excess and to use drugs, or to smoke, if it is not permitted. The use of controlled substances (including pot) or an excess of alcohol may lead to the damage of hotel property as well as physical damage to the person; it may also completely sabotage the objectives and goals set by the meeting's sponsors.

The company minds its manners by having a staff that is meticulous in its planning and production of the meeting; the attendees show their manners by their behavior during the meeting. But a third factor also comes into play in the making of a successful event—the attitude and performance of the facility's management staff. If all three factors are well in place, the meeting will be a sure-fire success.

When Spouses or Dates Come Along

If spouses or dates are present, and if the meeting will last three days or longer, it is very wise for the sponsoring organization to schedule special activities for them. In a resort situation, with sports available, it is only necessary to organize one activity, preferably early in the morning. A good speaker is always a plus; exercise classes and sports tournaments for women are usually successful (male spouses are usually excused from an activity, if they wish to be, when they are very pronouncedly in the minority). The days of "the little woman" programs, doing such things as making lace valentines together, are gone; women today, even if they do not work outside the home, are usually involved in major projects and do not enjoy being patronized by a silly program.

If a fashion show luncheon is planned, it had better be a good one—fast-paced and with the fashion part of the program done quickly and very professionally.

What is important for the spouse is to be allowed to sit in on as many sessions as possible, particularly when the guest speaker is someone with an important message. Also, it is usually extremely important to an executive's career to have his or her spouse understand the company's business and its problems and to be able to speak knowledgeably about it and offer support—as well as good ideas whenever those would prove helpful.

A spouse who remains aloof from the rest of the crowd is not doing his or her partner any good at all; the executive becomes the innocent victim of a snobby spouse who acts "too good for the rest of them," a situation hardly likely to help in one's career. I have a good piece of advice for the spouse who is bored by conventions and meetings and consequently does not wish to participate with enthusiasm: Stay home.

As for "friends" who join executives (their apartment mates, lovers, or just dates), they have a responsibility, too: to act in a discreet fashion and to play the game along with everyone else. No one should be discriminated against at meetings in which spouses participate just because they are single. When recreation and entertaining are a major part of the agenda, a single person should be allowed to bring a date, but both people should watch their comportment.

A LARGE MEETING AT CORPORATE HEADQUARTERS

Holding a meeting or event in corporate headquarters, whether yours or your client's, is simple in comparison to holding one at a conference center or hotel. When the meeting is in another city and attended by a large number of people, sometimes from other companies based in other cities, then the logistical planning for the sponsor becomes very complicated.

A first-class company should hold its meetings in first-class facilities. A facility that is close by and easy to reach may not be worth the convenience; one that is "really cheap" may be a total waste of money rather than a saving of it.

A meeting out of town is usually worth the planned expense, because changing the scene instigates fresh ideas. If the attendees are well taken care of, they usually regard attendance at the meeting as a cherished executive perk.

The Person in Charge

The CEO's executive secretary or an administrative staff person can make the arrangements for small meetings held on company premises or in other cities. When a large, complicated meeting is to be organized, either at company headquarters or in another city, if there is no special events person on staff, it may be time for the CEO to retain the professional services of an outside company that specializes in developing an entire scenario for the meeting, including dealing with the hotels, negotiating with the airlines, setting up the programs, the banquets and the entertainment, deciding on the menus and the decor, making arrangements for office and audiovisual equipment needed at the meeting, running the sports programs and, as one wag expressed it, "holding hands and wiping noses."

Large corporations often have a meeting planner (or meeting manager) on staff, whether they use outside professionals or not. This person, sometimes referred to as the Coordinator for Special Events, has the full-time responsibility for arranging the company's meetings, entertainment events, and seminars and conferences—both on home base and around the world.

The person directly in charge of the meeting may take care of the physical atmosphere, but the desired psychological atmosphere at the meeting and the statement of objectives to be achieved are the responsibilities of senior management.

THE ANNUAL SHAREHOLDERS' MEETING: A COMPANY'S MOST IMPORTANT LARGE MEETING

The annual meeting of a publicly held corporation is traditionally held when the year-end accounting is complete, when the directors are voted back into their seats on the board (or not, as the case may be), and when the stockholders have the opportunity to propose changes and to criticize, question, or applaud management's decisions during the preceding year.

Even the CEO of a small company should look upon his or her annual meeting as an important opportunity to communicate in person with the company's most important audience: its owners, the shareholders. The meeting is an opportunity to present management as a strong, competent, no-nonsense group of executives worthy of shareholder's trust, as well as their money.

Sometimes when a company has a big story to tell, a little "show biz" is called for—perhaps photographic blow-ups in the entrance to the meeting, a short film, a slide presentation, or even a fashion show (if the business is related to fashion). An effective graphic or audiovisual presentation impresses stockholders and influences their support of company plans *if* it is well done.

Time and Place of the Annual Meeting

The annual meeting is held once a year by law, often in the spring, within a reasonable time after the close of the fiscal year. It may be held at any hour, but the most popular time for a publicly held company is in the morning or early afternoon, in order to allow the press sufficient time to write a thorough story before the newspaper goes to press with the next day's news. The company's charter or by-laws set the place, date, and time for the meeting. All stockholders are invited to attend this meeting.

Many companies with stock plans for the employees give those employees time off to attend the meeting. After all, they are shareholders, too.

The meeting may be held *anywhere*—in the headquarters office or in a factory, ice skating rink, hotel ballroom, or football stadium.

Many companies take their "show on the road," away from their corporate city headquarters and into an area where they have plants, subsidiaries, or just a large aggregate of retired shareholders. Attendance is always high in cities where there is a large proportion of retired stockholders.

The company should make very certain that its image is projected well when it goes on the road, that it demonstrates away from home that it is an efficient, well-run organization. It should also be ready to prove that it has a strong social conscience, which can be demonstrated in its handouts, displays, and speeches from the podium.

Communicating the Details

The CEO of a publicly held company must send out a notice of the annual meeting to all shareholders a minimum of three to four weeks beforehand to allow for a good response on proxy returns. (The president of a privately held company obviously is not as limited as the CEO of a publicly held one. The head of a private company can change the date of his annual meeting simply by telephoning his board—usually close friends and family members—and arranging another time.)

Accompanying the notice of the meeting is the proxy statement (a disclosure document announcing where and when the meeting will be held and what proposals will be voted on), plus a proxy voting card for the stockholders who will not be at the meeting. Everyone should fill out and mail back the proxy voting cards at once. When there are written comments on these voting cards, management should note them with care, for they often reveal which way the wind is blowing in terms of feeling toward management. The proxies can also hint trouble that might occur at the annual meeting, such as demonstrations by dissident factions against company policies.

A successful corporation is a responsive corporation. It listens to the voice of its shareholders.

If the place where the annual meeting will be held is difficult to locate, it is wise to include a map with the proxy material. Some companies also include a program of the meeting; some even give the lunch menu if this meal will be served free to shareholders!

Mailing the Annual Report

A corporation's annual report must be mailed in advance of the meeting. (It is sometimes sent along with the notice of the meeting.) There is usually tremendous deadline pressure on the staff charged with the responsibility for producing the report, professionals on both the inside and on the outside. Last-minute changes are inevitable.

The CEO should be compassionate about these pressures on the staff. Gestures such as arranging to have a catered dinner brought in for the late workers and sending them home late at night in taxis, if they don't have cars, are very much appreciated by everyone working on the report.

Another person who deserves consideration at this time is the corporate secretary, whose job involves tremendous responsibilities. The annual report must reflect that he or she is fully conversant with the laws of the state in which the corporation is incorporated, with the requirements of the stock exchange listing the company's securities, with the board of directors' standing resolutions pertaining to the annual meeting, with the company's by-laws.

Ensuring Security and Comfort

Security is a prime factor in selecting the place for a large corporation's annual meeting. The company should assure that only stockholders and invited press are admitted. Mailing tickets to stockholders when they request them is one method of controlling the situation. It is better to have two registration areas for a large meeting when admission tickets are used—one for stockholders who brought their tickets and one for those who forgot or who didn't bother to write in. It takes time to check their identification and find them on the stockholders' list. Someone from the legal staff should be standing by at the ''No Tickets'' desk, as well as company representatives who are gifted with an extra dose of patience and good manners. (Those who must be turned away from the meeting must be treated very diplomatically.) The company should use its most gregarious and well-mannered people to greet the shareholders, collect ballots, help register, and perform other duties at the meeting.

The quality of the lighting, ventilation, bathroom, and first-aid facilities are other important factors to consider when staging the annual meeting. The sound system is paramount. Nothing makes a stockholder more hostile than not to be able to hear what is going on. That is also why company spokesmen should speak up clearly when they are at the microphone. Directors who offer resolutions to be voted upon should turn toward the audience and address them in a clear, well-projected voice, so that everyone hears every word of the resolution.

If the group is not too large, it is very hospitable of the corporation to offer attendees coffee and muffins before a morning annual meeting—and sodas before an afternoon meeting.

Keeping Order

The days have long since gone when publicly held corporations looked upon the annual meeting as a mere cut-and-dried series of approvals of the CEO's motions. The combative forces of social trauma seem to have joined the corporation permanently and refuse to evaporate either in good times or in bad.

Therefore, corporations cannot remain aloof from the social needs and aspirations of the public. Issues such as the handling of minorities, investments in controversial countries, and environmental considerations will always be raised in this era. When questions are properly asked, a company must be responsive, not antagonistic. The annual meeting is not a time for fuzzy deception. The CEO should be up-front; he and the stockholders should respect each other's views.

Most corporations now place a time limit (five minutes) on shareholders' speeches. If the company officers are well organized and professional about the way they handle the meeting, it will be orderly. Questions may have had to be submitted beforehand with the returned proxy statements, thus providing the CEO with enough time to ready himself with the proper answers. If a shareholder is unruly and unreasonable, peer pressure in the meeting generally disciplines him far better than the chairman could.

Sometimes a little creativity helps if the economic climate is hurting the company's and the stockholders' pocketbooks. One chief executive officer who has a good sense of humor concluded a particularly lugubrious, bad-news annual meeting with a smiling last word to the shareholders as they rose to leave: "I certainly don't want anyone here leaving this hall without feeling that our company smells like a rose." With that, the corporate staff pulled out great bouquets of fresh roses from beneath the check-in tables and handed each person a very sweet-smelling flower.

It must have worked, for they all came out smiling.

Shareholders' Manners at Meetings

Sometimes bad manners are demonstrated by shareholders at annual meetings. Corporations have begun to let meeting participants know what constitutes good behavior by distributing the rules with the agenda, as in these "Meeting Guidelines" given to every shareholder at First Chicago Corporation's 1993 annual meeting:

"Meeting Guidelines

1. Stockholders and proxyholders should not address the meeting until recognized by the Chairman. Questions or comments relating to an item of business should be raised only when the Chairman calls for discussion on the related item of business. Other questions or comments may be raised during the general questions or comments session. Please step to the aisle and use the microphone when speaking.
2. Courtesy and respect for the rights of others are standards for behavior during the meeting. We request the cooperation and understanding of all attendees in the conduct of a fair business meeting.
3. Your cooperation in assisting us to meet the [attached] timetable . . . will be appreciated. In fairness to others, each stockholder or proxyholder will be limited to one comment or question and then, if time permits, may speak a second time after all other waiting speakers have had their turn. The Chairman may impose time limitations if he deems it necessary."

The Agenda

Most annual meetings follow a general pattern. The chief executive officer introduces himself, calls the meeting to order, and after introducing the company officers and directors, he gives a kind of "president's report," highlighting the main events of the past year.

A typed or printed copy of the agenda should be placed on the chair of each person before the meeting.

The following is a sample of a typical agenda:

AGENDA

ANNUAL STOCKHOLDERS' MEETING

(Date and time)

(Location, city, state)

1. Meeting called to order
2. Introduction of directors, directors emeriti, officers, and others
3. Notice of Meeting
4. Roll of stockholders present or represented by proxies
5. Motion re affidavit of transfer agent pertaining to mailing of Annual Report, combined Notice of Meeting and Proxy Statement, and Proxy, and a copy of each, together with affidavit, made a part of the minutes of the meeting
6. Convene meeting, quorum present
7. Corporate secretary to read minutes of previous year's annual stockholders' meeting
8. Motion to be made (by a director) to dispense with reading of the minutes of previous year's annual stockholders' meeting
9. CEO's report
10. Viewing of film on new product
11. Inspectors of elections to be appointed
12. Directors to be elected after ballots are counted
13. Proposed acquisition to be voted on
14. Proposed ratification and approval to be voted to the company's auditors for the forthcoming fiscal year
15. Any other business to be discussed
16. Questions
17. Adjournment

THE BOARD OF DIRECTORS MEETING

(See also "The Serious Business of Joining a Nonprofit Board," Chapter 16)

This kind of meeting should take top priority in a Chief Executive Officer's life, because he is answerable to the shareholders through this group of people. Service on a board of directors is often most desirable, both for the inside directors (whose presences signify that they are the company's leaders) and for the outside directors (for whom this service is an honor, a challenge, and sometimes financially very attractive, because of the fees).

Because of stricter Federal laws, and the rash of shareholder suits against boards of directors, outside directors are no longer the rubber-stampers of the CEO's desires they once were, when they would automatically back the CEO. In former days the Chief Executive Officer would stack the board with his personal friends, so there would be no trouble in getting his recommendations approved. Today there usually are more outside directors than inside ones. They are often offered as likely board candidates to the nominating committee of the board by executive search firms. The boards try to become balanced in the makeup, talent, and experience of the outside directors and, as a result, discussions are more lively and protests are more easily registered. Senior management finds itself so closely scrutinized in its performance, that, as one beleaguered CEO described it, "At the conclusion of each board meeting these days, I feel as though I have added another notch to my belt. But I also feel my scalp hanging dangerously close to someone else's belt, too."

Accountability is a serious word these days. Management's accountability to the board really means the board's accountability to the shareholders. To serve on a board's committee is a very responsible assignment. Each member must show up on time, well prepared, ready to concentrate. The days of relaxed camaraderie and secrecy in these committee meetings have disappeared. Because of "full disclosure" commands today, all a shareholder has to do is attend the annual meeting and read the proxy statements carefully to find out what is going on and then make herself or himself heard.

The Importance of Good Communication Among Board Members

A productive board is a well-informed one; necessary materials should be sent out and studied by directors well *before* the meeting. If management understands the importance of advance communication and has put the material into each director's hands in advance, the work process should flow smoothly, and the directors will feel better about handling their responsibilities toward the company.

The following summarizes the contents of a typical monthly packet sent by the corporate secretary to each outside director four or five days in advance of a board meeting.

- A full agenda of the upcoming meeting, as well as the announcement of the date, time, and place for it
- The standard report material (most importantly, the financial reports)
- The full minutes of the preceding board meeting (which, if read and found to be without error, can then be quickly approved at the board meeting)
- Special presentations dealing with policy, procedure, budgets, and/or committee reports

- The full minutes of committee meetings (except for those committees that meet the same morning, in which case there will be an oral report by the committee chairman at some point during the meeting)

When a Director Attends His First Meeting

When an outside director arrives for his first meeting, there should be extensive introductions made. The new director should be introduced personally to everyone in the immediate executive office, but it's productive and courteous if, after the meeting, the CEO also takes him around as much of the company as can be covered within a hour's time for brief introductions.

The new director's photograph and biography should be published in the house organ so that everyone at every level will know about the newest management team member.

It is imperative that new directors know how the company functions, how it markets itself, how the divisions interrelate, and how its products or services reach the consumer, starting from an idea or perhaps a drawing board sketch through to a sale or a finished contract. A tour of the corporate offices and of a plant or factory operation, even if it requires a trip to other cities, should be planned at the outset of a new outside director's term. The knowledge gained from this kind of tour is as important to a board newcomer as being able to read the balance sheet properly. But it is also important for the morale of the employees on the line (often very interested shareholders) to meet and talk to outside directors.

For the outside directors' benefit (but also for the benefit of those inside directors who are isolated in their positions) it is helpful if the CEO regularly schedules at board meetings a brief appearance of the various division heads and their senior managers. A board member who comes to know the executive and his or her division personally, who understands what that division does, who can pick up the telephone and find out information on that person's division directly is going to make much better decisions for the company.

The Director's Manners

- A director of a conservative business should always be neatly, properly dressed. There is no question but that when men wear business suits and ties, and women directors are smartly attired in dresses or suits, the whole table looks business-like, disciplined, serious.
- Directors should not interrupt one another during the meeting. If there is a traffic jam of people wanting to express opinions on a controversial subject (things can become heated), they should use the hand-held-up attention-getting technique, and speak only when the chairman nods approval at them to do so. I have watched heads of companies hog the conversation and not let other directors speak at meet-

ings, with the result that the other directors uniformly lose respect for the one whose arrogance causes him to think only his opinion is important.

·   Each director should treat the staff with respect and should not order them around as if they were their private secretaries. Usually when board meeting time comes around, senior management runs on overload, with too many projects to finish and too much work to do in getting things ready and in making sure reports and the agenda are sent beforehand to directors. They are under pressure. But the working staff is under even greater pressure, not only in printing out and duplicating reports and compiling all the elements of the directors' books, but in making hotel reservations, providing transportation, in planning the meals, in making sure the board room is in shape.

It is essential that directors do not make additional demands on the corporate staff and that they thank the staff members over and over for their courtesy and help before and during the meeting.

I will never forget the wonderful executive assistant to a CEO who was mistreated with overwork and a lack of appreciation for years. She finally could stand it no longer. The week before a board meeting, she announced she was leaving in two or three weeks, whenever a proper replacement was found. The upcoming board meeting was a particularly rough and tough one. One director, famous for treating the secretaries like his slaves, approached her when she was particularly pressured, trying to juggle all of the tasks the CEO had just asked her to perform. The director calmly handed her a list of ten people in different offices around the country. He didn't know their telephone numbers but "you can ask information." He added in a harsh, commanding voice, "Get each one for me on the telephone, in the order of their names on this list." She was ready for him. She had amassed a quantity of quarters. She grabbed his hand and slowly counted out ten quarters, placing them in his palm. "Here," she said, "as you can see, every phone in this office is stacked up with calls to make for our management. I'm leaving the company shortly, but I've been dying to tell this to you for three years. There's a public telephone just outside this door. Here are the quarters. Go make the calls yourself." The other members of the support staff within earshot of this little scene applauded when he rushed through the door, scarlet with rage, on his way to find the pay phone.

On the other hand, there are directors like one I know who sits on six boards. Every year the executive assistants and corporate secretaries of all six of his boards receive a Christmas present and a short note of appreciation from him.

The Group Photograph of the Board

Many companies take a group photograph of the board (using professional photographers skilled at taking these photographs) to be published in annual reports.

It is a nice gesture from senior management when each member of the board receives the latest color photograph, matted and framed, as a holiday gift.

THE ANNUAL SALES CONFERENCE

One common type of "away" meeting is a company's annual national sales meeting, which provides an excellent forum in which management can observe executives' interactions with both their peers and their seniors. The purpose of such a sales conference may be to present a new line of products or to motivate the sales force to push harder with the old line. In either case, this coming together serves as the perfect time in which to pep up the attendees, to recognize their individual contributions during the past year, and to provide fresh assistance and ideas for attaining the company goals. The atmosphere at a good sales meeting inspires the staff, raises everyone's morale, and provides them with a lot of new and helpful information at the same time. It's a time for motivating, learning, explaining, questioning, planning, renewing old friendships, getting to know senior management better, and incidentally having a good time. It's a time for senior managers to be more available and friendly than circumstances permit them to be at the home office. But along with all the camaraderie, management's aim for the meeting should be inserted clearly, concisely, and *often* throughout the proceedings.

It helps, too, when the meeting is run in a warm, personal way with an occasional touch of humor. I remember being in a ballroom at a company's final banquet meeting one night, in the middle of 350 people who were all fired up watching a slide film with an accompanying musical sound track. The film consisted of clever candid photographs taken of the participants at the previous year's meeting. There were some very funny shots; everyone laughed, hooted, and applauded all the way through, particularly at the end when all five screens used in the presentation showed different views of a popular sales manager fast asleep in his chair, his head down on the table, during the CEO's final banquet speech.

The head of a company usually judges this kind of conference a success if:

- The objectives of motivating the sales force were achieved.
- The executives understood the new technology presented in the training sessions and are eager to begin working with it.
- Everyone received a nice pat on the back.
- Those who had fallen short during the past year were encouraged and are now willing to try harder.
- Those who had excelled were properly recognized and felt sufficiently rewarded.
- Everyone perfectly understands the plans and the new products and is eager to get going.
- All participants came away with increased respect for the company.
- Everyone had a good time.

For a more intimate kind of meeting, a company can plan:

- A weekend in a cozy country inn
- A chartered cruise for a conference at sea

- A meeting in a ski resort in the mountains, even if many participants don't ski
- A meeting in a health spa, where participants can take advantage of the facilities and special menus to any extent they choose

Conference Centers for Training and Planning Sessions

The conference center is a favorite kind of facility to use as a three-day think tank, or for a full week of executive training or motivation sessions. It is typically set away from the noise and distraction of the city, with its own restaurants offering simple, good food. There is no partying allowed, no music or distracting noise. The participants go to classes, attend workshops, have rap sessions, think, and study. These places are sometimes austere, so that seminar participants stick to their homework and conversational exchanges. Some conference centers have no athletic facilities, but meeting participants usually can jog along beautiful, scenic routes; other centers are equipped with elaborate sports equipment in their gyms, and their own racquetball and tennis courts.

A tyical conference center is the Tarrytown House Executive Conference Center in Tarrytown, New York (914-591-8200). Business groups fill its 148 rooms very quietly during the week, but the facility turns into a lively family weekend getaway on Friday nights, with children enjoying the one-lane bowling alley, indoor and outdoor pools, gym, and tennis courts.

The Allen Center, under the auspices of the Kellogg School of Business, Northwestern University, in Evanston, Illinois (708-864-9270) is nationally renowned as a meeting and training facility. Companies are allowed to book up to 150 available bedrooms with baths. The bedrooms are also used by students working on their Kellogg Executive Masters Program in open enrollment seminars. The Allen Center has full audiovisual capabilities that can be utilized by visitors for their presentations or for vidcotaping parts of their meetings. There are several classrooms and a new 200-seat auditorium. The meetings can be catered with anything the corporation wishes to serve its guests. Cocktails are served in the evening, and there are televisions in the main lounges, but not in the bedrooms. It is a serious, no-nonsense meeting place in an academic environment, but meeting participants are given sports passes and can use Northwestern's sports facilities any time. The really great thing about the Allen Center is that companies have the option of having the Kellogg School custom-design and run the training meetings for them, either for a week's duration or a four-week's duration. Participants work from 8 A.M. until 9 P.M. on a very rigorous schedule. They are allowed one free afternoon a week, during which they are supposed to engage in sports, but many say they just go to bed that afternoon, because they're so exhausted from the nonstop stimulation of the programs.

The Fuqua School at Duke University has a similar well-known facility and there are others in formation. It makes a lot of sense to spread the expertise of the academic world to the corporate world, and vice versa.

Meeting Planners International

Meeting Planners International (1950 Stemmons Freeway, Suite 5018, Dallas TX 75207-3109; 214-712-7700) is a professional trade association of over 11,000 people in the meeting business. It publishes an important, helpful monthly magazine, free to members, called "The Meeting Manager," and offers educational opportunities and advice. There are some very helpful trade publications, too, including "Meeting News," "Successful Meetings," "Meetings and Conventions," "Association Meetings," "Association Trends," and "Insurance Conference Planners."

VIDEOCONFERENCING

You might, at some point in your career, participate in an electronic meeting, or videoconference, which is an excellent diversified tool used by large companies for communicating a uniform message simultaneously to audiences in multiple locations. It is also used to enthuse all the people who will be selling an important new product around the country and for allowing a small group of managers to meet and discuss an urgent problem. In other words, if you can't bring everyone to your meeting at headquarters, you can bring the meeting to them. Even though senior management does most of the talking, this technology permits anyone within camera range to speak up. (You know you're being recorded on camera when the lens is aimed straight at you and a red light goes on.)

It's smart to be ready for the camera eye, even if it is only sweeping the room.

It's easy to look foolish in a videoconference. Conspicuous elements of attire are drastically magnified through a camera lens. A loud plaid suit will "scream" at the camera. A woman with spots of color in her makeup will find them looking clownlike on the monitor. A man who works in the Southwest and never wears a jacket or tie to work will suddenly realize that he must look overly casual to his counterparts in the north, who are sitting around the table uniformly clad in dark pinstripe suits.

Of course, any lapse in manners in a two-way audio-video conversation jumps right out from the screen. The person who interrupts too often, the person who raises his or her voice, the person caught making a sour face behind the back of the speaker, the person doodling in a bored manner: the camera catches and magnifies these actions almost mischievously. The camera also magnifies one's nervous mannerisms: studying the fingernails, stroking the hair, picking at fingernails, chewing on the stem of one's glasses, or—far worse—chewing gum.

The optimum impression of oneself glimpsed on a monitor is of a relaxed yet authoritative person, someone with a sense of humor. People who are unused to television are at first quite stiff and perhaps overly formal. Their voice may be forced or overly loud; their laugh may be very artificial. They may shift position constantly, which is quite distracting to viewers. After viewing themselves in replays and after practicing being relaxed, those same people find they can look good and act well on camera.

This kind of meeting—although very quick to arrange and useful in the business of efficient communication—will never replace the importance of traveling to a place and meeting face to face with one's colleagues, competitors, or leaders in the field. Nothing replaces the synergism of being together under one roof, developing new friendships, learning new things, and just experiencing a different place.

CHOOSING A CONFERENCE OR SEMINAR LOCATION

The target group usually dictates what type of facility is used. Your company may wish:

- To offer employees an incentive vacation-meeting situation, where the top producers and their spouses, perhaps even children, are given a nice week's vacation (such as beaching it in California or Florida, taking in the shows at Las Vegas, skiing at Aspen, and chatting up Mickey Mouse in Orlando). Part of the time, of course, the employees are in business-related meetings, qualifying the event as a business expenditure.
- To hold a serious think-tank kind of meeting over a weekend in a suburban motel that has good meeting rooms and none of the at-home distractions
- To hold a national sales meeting in a large centrally located facility, where the importance of the size of the exhibition space in the public areas of the hotel far outweighs the niceness of the bedrooms and the excellence of the food and service
- To entertain top customers at a posh recreational spot, such as The Greenbriar in West Virginia or The Homestead in Virginia, or any other first-class facility. You can easily contact the national sales managers of the top hotels (such as the Ritz Carlton, the Four Seasons, the J. W. Marriotts, etc.). One call will enable you to access information on their meeting facilities in hotels in cities and resort areas all over the United States.

When You Are Booking a Facility for Your Company

- Remember to keep a record of every conversation you have with the management of the facility you have chosen.
- Be fair and square with the facility. Come right out with your budget total and billing requirements, and they will work with you to make your desires fit within their possibilities. Smart negotiations are the answer, and the more open each party is, the more successful the result.
- If you're booking a new, unfamiliar facility for your meeting, be sure to check with another company that has been there within the last couple of months. The environment of meeting places can change so quickly that you need a very recent evaluation.

- After you have used a facility for your meeting, it is really important for you to give them feedback on exactly how good a job you thought they did. They can't possibly improve their services if they don't hear your comments. Criticize every droopy salad, unclean table, untidy meeting room, or surly facility employee. They need to hear the minuses, loud and clear, and of course, it is only decent to let them hear any justified praise. The letter you write them, commending their considerate handling of your group will make them feel good, will help the people involved get promotions and will assure you of a twenty-four-karat-gold welcome upon your return.

I once wrote the manager of a well-known hotel a lengthy letter of fair but detailed criticisms after a meeting I ran there for one of my consulting companies. Four years later we were back, and I was no longer in charge of the meeting, attending only as a participant. An envelope was sent to my room the morning we were all checking out. Inside was a copy of my own letter of criticisms from four years previously. The manager clipped a one-line typed question to the letter: "How did we do this time?"

He was smart, he was wise, and he received six red roses from me before I departed the hotel that morning.

Negotiating for the Site and Services

Often senior management has no idea of how important the job of the meeting planner or meeting manager is. A good manager proficient in the art of negotiating can save his company hundreds of thousands of dollars in meeting expenses. This person needs experience on the job. He needs to keep himself constantly informed; he needs to gain information through the networking possibilities offered by the various meeting managers' associations. Before any written confirmation is made reserving a conference site, or before an entertainment contract or a deal on group fares on the airlines is concluded, a meeting manager has to go through a delicate series of negotiations. He is truly performing an important management function.

A good planner does not settle for the first price quoted on anything. He either tries to get the price down, or he tries to get additional services added for the price quoted. He should negotiate group rates on:

- Meeting rooms charges
- Room rates (perhaps getting lower prices on smaller rooms or rooms without views or rooms next to noisy areas)
- The entertainment (for example, obtaining a special price should one orchestra play for four functions during the meeting)
- Banquet facilities (for example, getting special prices if the Grand Ballroom will be used for lunch and two dinners consecutively)
- Use of the recreational facilities
- Gratuities paid as a percentage of the total cost

- Remember that if the host company promises to pay all meeting-related charges in cash (saving the facility the fat percentage paid to credit card organizations), a great cost savings will be realized by the host. There is no shame in trying to get the best possible price for the company that is hosting the meeting. It is just smart business.
- Remember to have the hotel, resort, and all suppliers *confirm in writing* the agreed-upon prices for everything, from the room rates right down to the last pitcher of ice water brought into the meeting room.
- Another point to have confirmed in writing beforehand: the agreed-upon times of delivery for all products and services

Tips and Gratuities
(See also "Tipping at a First-Class,
Big-City Hotel," Chapter 4)

Some planners find it economically advantageous if each attendee tips as services are rendered and then is later reimbursed by his home office. If this is the plan, each attendee should receive a memo in advance of his departure for the meeting explaining the tipping system, so that he will be properly prepared.

If a meeting planner decides to provide "blanket gratuities" for his group, he will pay anywhere from 15 to 22 percent of the total facility charge (minus bar tips, always paid for by the attendee himself). The planner should make sure that the tips go to the right people by specifying to the hotel manager those members of the staff who were particularly helpful and under great stress (such as beleaguered telephone operators, the maître d'hotel in the dining room, and the main bellmen). Unfortunately, some unscrupulous hotel managers take the gratuities and hide them in the hotel's monthly profit statement rather than pass them on to the staff.

If service was excellent, a corporation should tip very generously as an investment in the future, so that when it returns to that facility it will be greeted with open arms.

If service is poor, it's the meeting planner's job to demand from the facility management that an immediate improvement be made. (Threatening to omit the gratuity payments usually works.) As an extra reward, on the last day of the meeting some planners carry with them envelopes containing $10 and $20 bills to give those who worked extra hard to give the group good service.

The worst thing that can be said about a company when it leaves its meeting facility is "Those people are cheap." Courteous treatment should be expected by a paying customer, but it should also be rewarded!

THE MEETING PLANNER'S NOTEBOOK

The consummate tool for anyone in charge of meetings is his or her notebook. The first thing one learns to do in this business, in order to survive, is to write it all down, including having all the questions written down before the necessity arises to ask them. The quality of the checklists, charts, and information—kept neatly filed and always updated—can spell the success or failure of any operation of this kind. The information contained in the meeting manager's notebook should cover everything from the kind of beds requested by the VIPs to the quality of the air-conditioning in the meeting rooms. For an in-house meeting, there are few pages required for the notebook, since the logistics of the conference room or auditorium are a given. However, when a meeting planner utilizes a facility outside company headquarters, the number of pages grows quickly.

A meeting, conference, or seminar is a success not only because it is well organized, but also because of the considerate attitude of the special events staff in charge, all of which reflects very positively on the company's image. Disorganized, sloppy individuals usually are not well mannered. They don't have time to be thoughtful and to think of others; they spend all their time trying to muddle through their responsibilities. The following pages represent the way one meeting manager who is admirably organized goes about managing his company's large events. He has different colored entry sheets for different types of meetings and events.

The meeting planner's notebook will include enough space for entering information in the following fifteen categories:

1. Basic information
2. Evaluation of the facility where the event will be held
3. Post-meeting evaluation of the facility
4. Invitations to the meeting
5. The budget
6. Transportation checklist
7. Room assignments
8. Inventory of supplies for the meeting
9. Flowers
10. Audio-visual checklist
11. Speakers and Entertainers
12. Meeting room floor plans
13. The menu
14. Thank-yous
15. Copy of final letter to the general manager of the facility

1. Basic Information

This section of the notebook lists:

· The title of the event
· The purpose of the event
· The date

- The place
- The sponsor of the event (such as a particular division of the company)
- The contact for the sponsoring division

2. Evaluation of the Facility

This section of the meeting planner's notebook is proof that you were aware of all the shortcomings of the site, and yet the favorable factors overcame the unfavorable ones. You might include on this page:

- The names, telephone and fax numbers of:
  - General manager
  - Assistant manager
  - Banquet and sales manager
  - Their secretaries

- The location's proximity to the airport and train station
- Parking facilities
- Probable weather conditions at time of meeting
- Negotiable prices of:
  - Meeting
  - Banquet
  - Double and single bedrooms
  - Suites and villas

- Number of inferior rooms (noisy, no view, etc.)
- Condition of facility when seen (bedrooms, suites, meeting rooms)
- Person who recommended the facility and reasons for the recommendation
- Condition and special offerings of the business center
- Availability of :
  - Secretarial help
  - Fax machines, printers
  - Copy machines
  - Mailing supplies and equipment
  - Backup stationery supplies

- Athletic facilities on premises or close by:
  - Rented bikes
  - Indoor pool
  - Outdoor pool
  - Squash courts
  - Paddle tennis

- ◦ Court tennis
- ◦ Ice skating
- ◦ Ping-pong tables
- ◦ Volleyball court
- ◦ 18-hole golf course
- ◦ Skiing (downhill, cross-country)
- ◦ Fishing
- ◦ Horseback riding
- ◦ Trail hiking
- ◦ Skeet shooting
- ◦ Sauna
- ◦ Fitness center
- ◦ Supervised programs
- ◦ Billiards
- ◦ Running track

- · Food and beverage quality
- · Condition of mini-bars
- · Quality of service
- · Quality of room service
- · Housekeeping services
- · Medical services available
- · Staff attitude
- · Shopping availability
- · Cultural activities
- · Availability and evaluation of restaurants
- · Banquet/meeting facilities:

  - ◦ Type
  - ◦ Name
  - ◦ Capacity
  - ◦ Location

3. Post-Meeting Evaluation of the Facility

An effective meeting manager fills out the post-meeting evaluation report immediately at the conclusion of the meeting, when all of the impressions are fresh. This page in your notebook will help in deciding whether to return to this facility in the future and also whether to recommend it to others.

In this section you would record your own impressions along with those of the staff more directly involved with each entry. Included would be opinions on:

- · Service at meals
- · Quality of food and beverages

- Baggage handling
- Telephone service and message capabilities
- The condition of:
  - The rooms and bathrooms
  - The grounds
  - The Hospitality Suite
  - The Press Room

- The availability of business equipment (computers, printers, faxes, and related supplies)
- Audiovisual capabilities
- Sports facilities, including trainers and pros
- Air quality, heating, and air conditioning
- Parking facilities efficiency
- Facility bus and shuttle service
- Front office cooperation
- Check-in, check-out efficiency

4. Invitations to the Meeting
(*See also* Chapter 15, "Invitations")

The obvious prelude to any large meeting hosted by a company is issuing strong, effective, can't-miss-this-event invitations. There must be a feeling of excitement in the look and the text of the invitation, which may be printed (or engraved, for very special occasions). When something is complicated to communicate, an explanatory letter may be the best invitation. The least attractive one, of course, is the faxed invitation—which, although it has a sense of urgency, also conveys a feeling of either "we waited too long to let people know about this event" or "we didn't feel the expense was justified in sending you a proper invitation."

Invitations to a one- to three-day meeting, requiring people to come from many different areas to the meeting place, should be extended from three to six months ahead (preferably the latter), to allow busy schedules to be cleared for that precious time slot.

The company might issue a "Save the Date" card six months before the event, and the actual invitations could then be mailed three months prior. By sending the Save the Date announcement, you have already put the recipients in a state of curiosity, even a bit of excitement about the upcoming, important affair that they should not miss.

A system of gathering the R.s.v.p.s* must be set up, and usually that means that within a month before a major meeting, someone from the host company sits on the telephone all day, every day, perhaps, calling everyone who has been invited, to see if they will be attending. Whether there's an enclosed R.S.V.P. card or a telephone num-

---

*"RSVP," "R.S.V.P.," and "R.s.v.p." are all correct.

ber for R.S.V.P.s supplied on the invitations, it is unfortunate that the need to respond means so little to managers today. (Personally, I do not like "Please reply by [a certain date]"—it sounds as though the host thinks the guests don't know enough to respond.)

It is important that the invitation itself list the important guest speakers, celebrities, and any honored guests. Their names should sell the event to the invitation list.

The Invitation page in the meeting book might contain the following notations:

- Who is responsible for design and text of invitation
- Name, address, and telephone number of printer or engraver
- Number ordered
- Delivery date
- Name of person to give final approval to proofs
- Person responsible for compiling guest list
- Who will address envelopes and by what method?
- Hand-stamped or metered postage? (If the invitations are extended by letter, many of these questions are irrelevant.)
- Date invitations to go into mail
- Person responsible for handling R.s.v.p.s

This section of the meeting planner's notebook should also include a comprehensive entry for each guest, including the following information:

- Guest's name
- Spouse's name
- Guest's title
- Name of Company or Organization
- Telephone Number

After each entry it would be noted whether the guest accepted, regretted or was still tentative.

5. The Budget

The budget section of the meeting planner's notebook should contain the estimated budget figures in one column and the actual cost report in another. Here are the headings for a typical meeting budget:

	Estimated Budget	Actual Costs
Accommodations Hotel rooms		
Transportation/Travel Airfare Limos/cars Van/buses Parking/valet service		

	Estimated Budget	*Actual Costs*

Catering
  Food
  Wine/cocktails
  Staff/labor
  Rentals
  Checkroom
  Gratuities		

Special Staff
  Security
  Porters
  Maintenance		

Decor
  Possible party designer
  Flowers, including table
    centerpieces
  Trees/plants
  Tent
  Dance floor
  Other		

Entertainment
  Sound equipment rental
  Lighting
  Musicians
  Piano rental
  Audio/visual equipment
  Technicians
  Speakers fees and
    transportation		

Photography/Press
  Photos to send guests
  Press photos and releases
  Press kits		

Printing
  Calligraphy costs
  Place cards
  Badges
  Menus/programs
  Invitations and R.s.v.p. cards
  Signs for all events
  Other		

Rental of Site		
Rental of Electronic and Other Business Equipment and Supplies		

	Estimated Budget	Actual Costs
Secretarial Help		
Gifts/Prizes		
Sports Activities		
Golf		
Greens fees		
Golf carts		
Pro fee		
Staff fee		
Caddies		
Golf balls		
Range balls		
Club rentals		
Locker room		
Gratuities		
Tennis		
Guest fees		
Pro fee		
Staff fee		
Courts		
Tennis balls		
Racquet rental		
Locker room		
Indoor courts		
Gratuities		
Contingency Fund		

6. Transportation Checklist

The travel plans of all meeting participants should be marked in the meeting planner's notebook, and distributed to everyone on staff. This section should include the names of officials as well as the lost-and-found baggage and security departments at the airport or railroad terminal. Each attendee's date and time of arrival and departure should be included, and whether the person needs picking up upon arrival at the terminal.

A *car rental* section should also be included in this checklist, listing the agency name and telephone, the contact person, the attendees requesting vehicles, and the car model (and license number) each person receives.

Also to be included in this part of the notebook are:

- *Buses* to be chartered (dates, times, capacity of each bus)
- *Limos* to be reserved (dates, hours, attendees authorized to use)

7. Room Assignments

The meeting planner needs in his or her notebook a chart showing the names of all attendees and staff people, as well as anyone connected with the special events taking place during the meeting (speakers, entertainers, etc.). The following information is needed for each participant:

- Hotel room number
- Type of accommodation (*S* for single, *D* for double. Specify also *TB* for twin beds, *ST* for suite, *V* for villa)
- Arrival and departure dates

8. Inventory of Supplies for the Meeting When the Facility Has No Business Center

A list of supplies needed for each room of the facility should be prepared in advance and included in the planner's notebook. Sometimes there will be a Business Center in the facility, but usually it is not fully equipped. When supplies are packed, they should be put in boxes marked with the room number. The list should be packed inside each box. The inventory list could include any or all of the following:

____ Computers, laser printers
____ Paper and supplies for the above
____ Duplicating machine
____ Paper and supplies for the above
____ Computer software
____ Blank tapes and cassettes
____ Calculator
____ Fax machines
____ Copies of the agenda
____ Extra copies of press material
____ Message pads
____ Pens and sharpened pencils
____ Pencil sharpeners
____ Paper clips
____ Staplers
____ Staple removers
____ Masking tape
____ Cellophane tape
____ Fed Ex envelopes and forms

____ Cord or string
____ Postage meter or stamps
____ Rubber bands
____ Scissors
____ Portable blackboards and chalk, or cork-boards and tacks
____ Staple gun
____ Company stationery
____ Steno pads
____ Jiffy bags (indicate sizes)
____ Rulers
____ File folders
____ Notebooks: lined and unlined fillers
____ Legal pads
____ Expense voucher forms; petty cash slips
____ White bond paper
____ Markers
____ Express mail envelopes and forms

9. Flowers

- Florist's name, telephone number
- Arrangements needed for:

- ○ Reception area
- ○ Hospitality Suite
- ○ VIP guests (including speakers' and entertainers' rooms)
- ○ Banquet centerpieces each night

- Table arrangements needed for:

  - ○ Main table
  - ○ Round tables
  - ○ Cocktail tables

- Arrangements for lunch tables
- Flowers for stage
- Flowering trees to mark receiving line
- Rented trees to enhance stage

10. Audiovisual Checklist

- Date of Event
- Place
- Division executive in charge of event
- Name of outside professional companies involved, name of contact to use, and telephone number
- Company personnel involved in staffing the event and in charge of lighting cues, room-darkening draperies, running the projectors
- Speakers, times of their programs
- House electrician on duty and telephone number
- Number of outlets
- Extension cords needed
- Video/TV monitors required
- TV taping equipment required (½" tape; ¾" tape)
- Number and types of projectors needed; empty carousels, extra bulbs and stands needed
- Electric pointers needed
- Screen requirements
- Lectern—to be placed:

  - ○ Needs logo shield
  - ○ Pitcher of ice water and glass

- Microphones: number of necklace or standing mikes needed
- Audio-taping through the microphone available if needed
- Easels required
- Blackboards, chalk, and erasers needed

11. Speakers and Entertainers

There are four ways in which to handle speakers that will make them love the host company forever:

- Schedule them lightly, so that they do not have to talk to too many people before their appearances or answer too many questions and risk straining their voices. They should be given a place in which to rest and time expressly for that—an hour before they should appear.
- Treat them graciously at all times, including introducing them properly.
- Express immediate appreciation for their efforts, ideally in a letter written by the CEO the day after the presentation, telling them how great it was, thanking them, and congratulating them on a job well done.
- *Pay them promptly.* This is very important. If there is an agent, the latter usually gets the money immediately, removes his percentage (often 10 percent) and then sends a check to the speaker for the rest. If there is no agent, the nice way to pay the speakers is to hand them an envelope with the check inside as they leave to catch a plane or train. Mention that out-of-pocket expenses will be reimbursed immediately upon receipt of a list of expenses and receipts.

The meeting manager needs an entire section of the notebook devoted to the speakers at the meetings and the meals, and to the entertainers also. (An entertainer can be anything from a ballroom dancer who is hired for an outdoor luau to teach the hula, to a top name on network television who's given a contract to sing a few songs after dinner.) Each of these performers deserves to be treated with professional consideration and kindness, no matter how much or how little they are compensated.

Along with the speaker's or performer's name, address, telephone number, and fax number, you will need the following information:

- Date of her or his performance at your meeting, and time frame
- Lecture bureau's or agent's name, address, telephone and fax numbers
- Program or speech title
- Length of program
- Mode of transportation. Arrival and departure times. Person responsible for tickets
- Type of accommodations at facility. Room number?
- Permission received to video- or audio-tape performance?
- Publicity: Who to be responsible? Will there be a press conference? Press kits made? A book signing?
- Special guests to be invited for speaker or entertainer?
- Will celebrity join meeting participants for any meals?
- Audiovisual support requirements
- Rehearsal time to be scheduled?
- Dressing room needed?
- Give him/her instructions on how to dress for the program.

- Date bio and publicity photos requested; date received
- Amount of fee and expenses, how and to whom to be paid
- Who will make the introduction for him or her?

12. Meeting Room Floor Plans

The meeting manager should make a rough sketch in the notebook of how he wants each room or area set up by the facilities manager for each use. He would sketch one room per page, with instructions, and give a copy of each to the facilities manager. Following is a hypothetical page from a meeting planner's notebook, showing the kind of rough sketch and information needed by the hotel staff to prepare a room for one group's morning seminar, to be followed by lunch on another floor.

February 22—Morning Session and Lunch for the Marketing Division

The Bristol Room—Mezzanine North
9:30 to 11:45 A.M.   Seminar with slides
       projected
       Electric pointer
       80 people seated auditorium
       style
       Projector and sceen
       Head table with 6 chairs
       Lectern at side

The Cheshire Library—off Lobby
12 to 2:00 P.M.   Lunch service for 100 people
       No head table
       10 tables for 10 people
       Lectern with mike
       Open bar
       Piano in corner

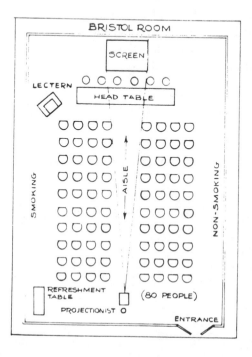

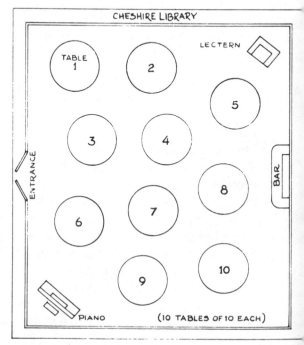

13. The Menu

There are two new trends in "meeting cuisine," as it has often been referred to ironically. First, the food does not have to be boring and monotonous; second, today's preferred food is much healthier food than it was in the '80s and earlier. It all depends on the meeting planner and how much he or she cares about the subject, because if the person in charge has the will to work hard with the food and beverage manager of any facility being used, the results will be good. When a synergy is established between the two, success is assured. Some things to remember:

- No matter how hard you work at it, no matter how much meticulous planning goes into your food ordering, not everyone will be pleased. There will always be gripers and complainers; it is endemic to meeting functions. Just forget about the complainers when they are in a very small minority; listen hard if they are in a majority.

To save time and have minimum service at your meeting meals:

- *Have the first course pre-set on the table* at each place, whether it is a buffet or a served meal.
- If you're really in a hurry for a served meal, *have the dessert pre-set, too*, the plates pushed up toward the center of the table (although I personally don't like this time-saving device, particularly since if my children were present at an event, they would eat the dessert as the first course.)
- *Never serve a salad as a separate course between the main course and the dessert.* It's a real time-waster. Pre-set the small salad plates to the left of the entree plate on the table.
- For a buffet, *set out the desserts on a special table of their own*, near the main buffet service, so that the guests can decide right then and there to eat lightly on the main course, in order to save room for dessert, or, to skip the dessert entirely and fill up on the entrees and vegetables instead.
- *The easiest desserts to serve are self-contained tartlets or eclairs or individual fruit desserts* (such as a small half-cantaloup filled with cut-up fresh fruit. Something that always pleases is a big basket overflowing with different kinds of cookies and brownies, to which each guest helps himself on one of the little plates stacked there on the dessert table.

The menu entries in a meeting planner's notebook for one day might look like this:

Breakfast: 60 people, buffet setup in Sun Patio
    Orange, grapefruit, or apple juice
    Melon slices
    Scrambled eggs and bacon
    Choice of dry cereals with fresh fruit, yoghurt, and honey toppings
    Rye toast, toasted English muffins, bran muffins (butter or margerine), and choice of jam
    Coffee, decaf, and tea

Skim or lowfat milk
Sugar or artificial sweetener
Mid-Morning Refreshments: 4 workshops of 20 each, in Meeting Rooms A, B, C, D
Coffee, decaf, tea, etc.
Tall glasses of sparkling water
Platters of cheese and fresh fruit cut into finger-food bites
Lunch: 125 people, seated in Baroque Room
Salad of strips of smoked chicken on bed of Boston lettuce, sweet-and-sour salad dressing
Tortellini with broccoli florets
Fresh strawberries with cookies
Hot or iced tea, coffee or decaf, etc.
Afternoon Refreshments: 4 workshops of 20 each, in Meeting Rooms A, B, C, D
Cups of hot beef consommé with wheat crackers
Platter of raw carrot and celery strips
Reception: 300 people, on Grand Terrace
Open bar, including red and white wine, beer, and lite beer
Melba rounds with hot crabmeat
Small rye sandwiches of fresh tomato, basil, olive oil, and mozzarella
Melon bits wrapped in prosciutto
Cold shrimp dipped in lemon juice, on toothpicks
An assortment of nuts
Dinner: 250 people, seated in the Grand Ballroom
Stracciatella soup
Roast lamb
Boiled new potatoes with butter and herbs
Mint sauce
Steamed baby carrots and peas
Mixed green salad
Mocha butterscotch parfait with small cookies
A California bordeaux wine
Coffee or decaf

14. Thank-You Notes

This page should be reserved for the meeting planner to write the name, title, and address of everyone connected with the event who did a good job and who deserves a letter of thanks, which in reality is also a letter of recommendation for that person. (Commendations of special employees are usually recorded in their files and can result in faster promotions and greater job security.)

On this page the meeting planner should write down not only the name of the person to be thanked and praised but also the date on which the letter was actually sent.

Prompt thank-you's can also lead to a warm welcome upon return to a meeting facility. The owners and staff of a hotel, conference center, or other meeting site judge a company by the behavior of its employees, but most particularly by the manners of the meeting manager and his staff.

15. Final Letter to the General Manager of the Facility

This page should contain a copy of the letter sent to the general manager of the facility, in which he or she is thanked and complimented, but in which constructive criticism is also offered. The recipient of this letter needs this information in order to do his job better and to make more companies return to his facility. Good criticism is the best favor you can pay the head of a facility.

MEETING REGISTRATION

The first thing the tired, perhaps irritable traveler sees when checking into a meeting or convention is the Registration Desk. Your most outgoing, cheerful staff people should be the official greeters, because the first impression a stressed-out participant receives of the meeting may last throughout.

In your meeting planning book, make a list of what will be needed in this area: a very pretty arrangement of flowers, desks, tables, cloths, chairs, computers for registration, name badges (including plenty of extras), markers, pads, pens, and a registration kit for each participant, which should include:

- Information sheets and brochures on the city
- Spouses' program
- Schedule of events (including list of speakers and their bios, times for golf, and use of the tennis courts)
- Dress requirements, if any
- List of attendees, their home office addresses and telephone numbers, and their room number at the meeting facility
- Emergency instructions (what to do in case of fire, how to call a doctor, name and number of an all-night pharmacy)
- Tourist information: famous museums, churches, etc.
- List of good restaurants close by
- List of good shopping areas
- Information on local churches and synagogues
- List of hairdressers for men and women
- Transportation arrangements
- Tipping and check-out instructions

Often the registration kit includes a product giveaway or gift (which might also be left in the guest's room). The gift might be something practical (like sunscreen lotion and sunglasses or a tote bag) or something to wear (like a T-shirt or hat), or something for sports (like golf or tennis balls, imprinted with the company name).

Badges

·   A badge should be worn high on one's upper right shoulder—the easiest viewing point for a right-handed person talking to the badge wearer.
·   Only professional titles need be included on these badges, such as "Dr.," "General," "Judge," "Ambassador," etc.
·   When meeting attendees are not known to one another and come from all over the country, put their company name and their city beneath their names.
·   If a spouse is well known to the company, her badge would read "Mary Howard." If she is unknown to the group, her badge should include her husband's name:

> Mary Howard
> (John N. Howard)

This is particularly important if the spouse uses her own name instead of her husband's family name:

> Betty Greco
> (Mrs. Roger Watkins)

·   If the host company has invited a large number of guests to join a conference, it is helpful to have the company badges marked "Host" at the top and the others marked "Guest."

THE HOSPITALITY SUITE

This is an important part of the company's public relations at a large event, when the company is vying for honors with its competition in a hotel or at a convention center during a trade show. The vendors, the customers, and the VIPs are all desirable guests. The hospitality suite is important, too, at a much smaller, all-company meeting, where participants need a place to go to relax, meet their colleagues, and talk over what's happening.

Proper organization of this space:

•   An aesthetically pleasing company logo sign or banner—and flowers—should be prominent as you enter the room.
•   The area should be cleaned three times a day, with special attention paid to the bathrooms. One hotel maid told me she has used up many bottles of cleaning detergents just in cleaning the telephones in the hospitality suites "because people eat sticky food and get it all over the receivers."
•   Have a fax, computer, printer, and copier on hand in a closed portion of the suite.
•   There should be extra telephones installed in this suite, along with extra message pads and pens.
•   There should be extra coat racks and umbrella stands, if the closet space is insufficient (it usually is).

- Have a supply of extra registration kits, badges, and press kits.
- There should be healthy refreshments available, including bottled waters, sodas, fruit juices, raw vegetables with dip, baked (not fried) fat-free crackers, healthy sandwiches, yogurts, fresh fruit, and—for any participant with an active sweet tooth—hard candies, brownies, and cookies. A samovar of hot consommé makes a big hit, as an alternative to the always-present coffee or tea. Some companies serve alcohol (beer, lite beer, and wine are the most consumed). Some companies do not serve any alcohol.
- There should be a first-aid drawer in one of the desks, containing anything from aspirin and small bandages to medicines for indigestion and diarrhea.
- If your company really wants to attract the crowds to your hospitality suite, have a podiatrist in residence in a small well-lit cubicle space (privacy supplied by drawn curtains). At large conventions, the two parts of the body that suffer the most are the stomach and the feet, and a podiatrist can literally regenerate an exhausted exhibitor, customer, or visitor to the trade show.
- Have a daily delivery of newspapers from the cities your customers primarily come from. They will drop by to read those papers and chat—of that you can be certain.
- A copy of the meeting planner's notebook should be kept in this room so that all the pertinent information is available at all times.

THE PRESS ROOM

If your meeting will make major news, and if the press will be in attendance, make things comfortable for them in their own area; they will be in a better mood when they write about your company or its products.

Have closet space—or at least coatracks—available. Install desks, chairs, and telephones for each journalist, with proper lighting in the area, whether from individual lamps or overhead ceiling light. Rent one or more fax machines, word processors, or computers with word processing software; have compatible laser printers on hand. Make it possible to use modems for transmitting their material.

Have plenty of paper, pencils, steno pads, and legal pads on hand, and one or more fast copy machines.

Stock a refrigerator with a plentiful supply of sodas, bottled water, and fruit juices. Keep a large coffee dispenser filled with fresh coffee and platters of Danish and muffins. Make sure there are a couple of sofas and occasional chairs in the space, so that journalists and photographers who just want to exchange information can do so in comfort.

Of course, there is the obligatory large table filled with the company's handouts: press kits, photos, copies of speeches, and background information.

14

Business Entertaining

Entertaining is an art and should be approached as such by businesses. Some senior managers don't realize that to be truly successful, entertainment requires the addition of heart—really caring about the well-being and enjoyment of your guests.

Entertaining in the nineties is no longer the runaway express train of frivolity it was in the eighties when everyone was making a lot of money, or thought they were about to. Funds for this activity should be considered an investment, with an expected return. The necessary budget planning must be done. Your entertainment plans should have realistic goals, which everyone within the organization should understand and be prepared to accomplish.

It's sad but true that a company can splash its money around ostentatiously and yet the event can fall flat on its face. The planning may have been sloppy: The food was too heavy; dinner was served too late and lasted too long; the music was so loud that no one could talk; the speeches were numerous, ponderous, and lacking in humor; no one was introduced properly and conversation did not flow at the tables; the entertainment was endless and boring; the number of bugs in the outdoor dining area was calamitous, since no one on staff had thought to bring insect repellent. Any one of a thousand details can railroad a party, and when that happens, the social event detracts from the company image, rather than enhances it. All of the effort and the cost of the party then goes into the debit column on the balance sheet.

On the other hand, someone who entertains with heart pays attention to details by making sure that the food is light and palatable, that the noise level is comfortable, that everyone is introduced in a flattering manner to one another, and that the small, caring details are attended to. There should be a surprise birthday cake for a guest whose birthday is that day; or when it rains, and the guests have to move through an unprotected area, there should be escorts with large golf umbrellas to *walk them dryly to their destination; and the meticulously clean restrooms should have good soaps and attractive guest towels awaiting the attendees.*

YOU ENTERTAIN MORE THAN YOU THINK

In hundreds of ways, large and small, the social side of business goes on all the time. In fact, it is one of the pleasures of working! When we think of entertainment, we think of the big splashy events with formal invitations, but when you offer someone coffee in your office, you are also entertaining. When you stop on the road with a client at a fast-food restaurant for a quick hamburger and you pick up the check, you are entertaining that customer. When you take him out for a game of golf, or take him to a show, or meet her for a quick conversation over a cup of tea or coffee, you are extending the hand of hospitality. Offering a person something to eat or drink, or amusing him or her in some way while you are transacting business is what entertaining is all about, and you engage in this activity for many reasons. No matter what your rank in the corporation, you entertain your colleagues in many ways, for different reasons:

* To get to know a person on a one-on-one basis
* To make new friends and business contacts
* To thank someone for a favor or service rendered
* To sell someone an idea, product, or service—or maybe even yourself
* To repay someone's hospitality
* To reinforce a relationship with an old customer
* To acquire some needed information
* To honor a person, an organization, or a company because there is reason to do so (an award or honor to present, an anniversary to celebrate, etc.)
* To extricate yourself from an embarrassing situation (such as accidentally having forgotten an appointment with someone). Taking the aggrieved person to lunch just might make it all right.
* To seek someone's advice and assistance on a project
* To assist a nonprofit organization in raising needed funds by hosting and paying the expenses for its event
* To help add polish to the company's image in the community

Just as a chef carefully measures the ingredients in his recipe, to ensure the success of his dish, so the person in charge of company entertaining—or the individual extending his own brand of hospitality on behalf of the company or firm—should measure the amount of good will generated by each event. Entertaining is too expensive not to be goal-oriented, but there's something terribly nice about the fact that one of the main goals of this activity is to make people feel good and to give them a good time.

This chapter treats the role of the entertainer and the guest almost equally, because in business one often switches from one role to the other. One of the benefits of being in business a long time is that as the years pass, one realizes that horrible crises in entertaining are always survivable, and usually very educational, and the same thing can be said for the faux pas one commits as a guest. "Live and learn" may be a tired cliché, but it makes me feel infinitely better to know it is true!

THE ART OF PLEASING PEOPLE

Those responsible for an event have to ask, Did it underline the corporate mission in a subtle, sophisticated, unobtrusive way? Did guests come away having had a stimulating, enjoyable time, but with a deeper respect for and understanding of the corporation and its goals?

When you really want to please present or future clients, invite them to:

- Lunch at a fine restaurant (1½ to 2 hours)
- A game of tennis, squash, or golf at your club, followed by a quick lunch (from an entire morning for the golf and lunch to an 1½ hours for tennis and lunch)
- Dinner with spouses or dates at a fine restaurant (2 to 3 hours)
- Tickets to a major sporting event (World Series, U.S. Open Tennis Championships, Superbowl, Masters Golf Tournament, Stanley Cup, NBA Finals, etc.), followed or preceded by a quick meal (4 hours)
- Tickets to a show, a play, an opera, preceded by a light supper (4 hours)
- An invitation to join your table for a prestigious political or charity fund-raiser dinner (3 hours)

The last five invitations are expensive, often time-consuming, but at the same time immensely flattering to a customer or client. When you indulge in this kind of entertaining, your guests know they are very special in your eyes.

AN IMAGINATIVE PLACE FOR YOUR PARTY

When a company chooses a really creative place to hold its party, instead of having it in "the same old place," the guests often remember that event for a long time to come. The unique and the unusual raises a party site above the pedestrian. In recent years, corporate functions have been held: in a circus tent, on an ocean liner's deck, in an old mill, among the fountains of an urban plaza, in a dance studio, on an old Indian mountain trail, on a squash court, at a roller rink, in a museum, on the opera stage, in a botanical garden, on a coal barge, on a TV sound stage, in a public library, on a football field, in an old schoolhouse.

One great corporate party was given in an empty airplane hangar that had been transformed by an interior designer with hundreds of yards of silver mylar fabric, which, when hit by stage lights and candlelight, reflected shimmering, magical shafts of silver everywhere in the giant space. Another caterer dressed his staff in Elizabethan costumes in a similarly decorated space to go with the Shakespearian theme of a corporate dinner.* Each waiter spouted lines from Shakespeare's plays to the guests of his table, and anyone who recognized the play from which he was quoting was given a rose. (The waiters were all unemployed actors, which helped.)

Another caterer, in preparation for a party given by a Florida condo developer, had her area's top divers secretly trained as waiters. As the guests were seated at tables around the giant swimming pool in the new condo complex, the group of young men and women diving waiters dove into the pool from the high boards—to taped music. Then they all swam in formation, rose out of the pool, donned identical white-toweled bathrobes, and to the sounds of enthusiastic applause and shouting, proceeded to serve the dinner.

You can't rent the White House, but if you want an inspired idea for a place in which to hold your party, there's help out there—in the form of publications—to tell you where you can rent unique places. For example:

- Hannelore Hahn of The Tenth House Enterprises (Box 810, Gracie Station, New York, NY 10028) publishes an annual *Directory of Public Places for Private Events and Private Places for Public Functions* (also on sale in New York bookstores for $24.95).

- Edna Greenbaum in New York publishes a book called *Protocol*, which helps company protocol officers and meeting planners of large and small companies by providing information and resources for corporate entertaining in the major cities of the United States and abroad ($39 from Protocol Directory, Inc., 101 West 12th Street, New York, NY 10011).

- The National Trust for Historic Preservation, headquartered at 1785 Mass. Ave. NW, Washington, DC 20036 (202-673-4000), oversees the preservation of landmarks dating from the seventeenth century and the protection of endangered buildings of great historic value. Any corporate invitation should be coveted to an affair held in or on the grounds of these famous properties, which range from rustic Western train stations to grand Federal houses in Washington, to adobe Southwestern dwellings, to Frank Lloyd Wright houses and extant examples of Miami's Art Deco buildings. When you are permitted to hold a function in one of these places, a corporate donation is made to the National Trust to help with their very high maintenance costs. (Inquire at the Trust headquarters, or at one of the regional offices of the National Trust in Philadelphia, Chicago, Denver, Fort Worth, Boston, Charleston, or San Francisco.)

*Parties such as this can be held in Washington at the Folger Shakespeare Theatre at the Folger Shakespeare Library—for a donation, of course.

- Of course, to many people, there is no more magnificent site for a top-ranked corporate function than on the lovely grounds of Mount Vernon, George Washington's eighteenth-century home in Virginia, overlooking the Potomac River. For the privilege of entertaining in this magical place, the sponsoring organization is first approved, all the rules are observed to the letter, and a handsome fee is donated by the corporation to the Mount Vernon Ladies' Association, for the upkeep of our first president's home.

ENTERTAINING YOUR COLLEAGUES

Inviting the Boss

In the world of business protocol, the invitation from a manager to his or her boss is always the stickiest wicket. If you grew up next door to the person who's now your boss, if you were in college together, or if you served in the Persian Gulf in the same fighter command, of course, there would be no problem. You would ask him to dinner whenever you wished, as he would you.

When special guests—your boss, for example—come to your home for dinner, the table setting becomes more complex than usual because the menu is, too. Crabmeat cocktail is the first course, followed by roast beef and Yorkshire pudding for the second, salad and cheese for the next, and strawberry shortcake for dessert. Both white and red wineglasses join the water glass for this kind of meal.

Most likely you don't have that familiarity with your superior at work, so it's better to hold off on the invitations until you have worked in that company a couple of years—and even then, only if you have close contact with your boss on a daily basis.

A new manager should not ask the boss to lunch. It should be the other way around. One can always visit the boss' office—after checking with his secretary or assistant—at a time convenient for him or her to ask questions and receive guidance. When you're new with the company, asking the boss to lunch looks pushy, puts him on the spot, and makes him uncomfortable. If a boss goes to lunch with you, he will feel pressured to accept the lunch invitation of every young executive in his department. He might also feel an obligation to ask the one who invited him to a return meal. There aren't enough lunches in a year to take care of all of this politeness.

If you have a special affinity for your boss and if you want him to see your new home, ask the boss and spouse to a cocktail party. That's the kind of invitation he can accept or reject with ease; there's no pressure in it. A meal is a different thing altogether.

Asking your boss to your wedding or a family celebration is pushy, too, unless you are very close friends.

When the Boss Invites You

If you are single, it may well be that if the boss and his wife invite you to their home for dinner, they need an extra man or woman. Therefore, the last thing in the world they want to hear from you is an acceptance to their nice invitation and the request to "bring along a date."

If your boss and spouse invite you often as a single person, and you are dating someone seriously, write a note in which you regret the dinner invitation for such-and-such a night, because you are now "seeing a special person," and the two of you have mutual plans for that evening. This tips off your boss you are no longer to be considered a single person "fill-in" at their dinners, and hopefully they will invite you and "the special person" as a couple soon. Don't count on it, however. A hostess friend of mine put it this way: "Any single man is a jewel on the social scene, provided he owns a pressed dinner jacket and can open his mouth and say one sentence every time a course is served."

Never ask to bring a date to any business meal, unless specifically told to or unless you find written on a formal invitation your name, followed by "and guest."

If the boss invites you (and your spouse) to a party, do not tell the other people in the office. They will feel hurt they weren't asked, and they may well resent you or wonder what you're doing to "kiss up" to the boss. Just keep it quiet.

Inviting Colleagues with and without
Spouses or Dates

- Invite someone with whom you have a strictly business relationship *to lunch in a restaurant*.
- Invite a business colleague with whom you now have a personal relationship, along with his or her spouse or date, *to dinner in a restaurant*.
- Invite a business colleague who has become a really good friend, with his or her spouse or friend, *to dinner in your home*, which is the most work for you but the greatest compliment of all.
- It is proper to invite a person to lunch during the week without his or her spouse, but not to a social dinner at night or on the weekend. It is improper to invite an executive to anything in the evening where other spouses (even only one) will be included, if that guest's spouse is not also included. An exception to this is, of course, if the one spouse present also works for the company and it is considered a working dinner.
- It is perfectly appropriate for a single or married woman to be invited to lunch alone with a single or married male executive; it is not appropriate, however, for two executives who are married to other people to have dinner alone. Even if their dinner engagement is totally innocent and only for business, it looks otherwise. Gossip can ruin many lives, so it is wise to play it safe. When people are on the road for their companies—in another city—their having dinner together is not cause for gossip, but on home turf it is.
- A woman manager should not feel timid about asking a male colleague to lunch. She might state up front that she wants to bend his ear about something or seek his advice. Once the lunch takes place, the only serious mistake she might make is to allow him to pay the check. (That would be unprofessional behavior if she had invited him to lunch.)
- If your out-of-town business colleague arrives with his or her spouse in tow, then invite that couple to dinner with your spouse. Do not make a dinner appointment with an out-of-town visitor that excludes that person's spouse.
- If someone has taken you to a business or socially oriented meal, you have not repaid the obligation by asking that person to have a drink with you. It's tit for tat, meal for meal.
- If a colleague invites you to lunch or dinner in a modest restaurant, do not reciprocate by inviting him to a splashy, expensive place. It will make him feel inferior. Pick the same kind of place your host did.
- If both spouses work and you are inviting another dual career couple to dinner, the husband or wife who knows the husband or wife of the other couple should extend the invitation. Let's say Bob is a partner in an accounting firm and his wife, Sally, is a lawyer for the Doodle Corp. Sally wants to invite a lawyer from an outside firm, Daniel, and his wife, to have dinner with her and Bob. She wants to get to know Daniel better, because of a big case coming up for her company on

which they will be working. She would call Daniel at his office and extend the invitation to him and his wife to join Bob and herself "a week from next Saturday at a great new Chinese restaurant we found." Daniel would RSVP to Sally, and although all four people will show up, it clearly is a pleasant business dinner involving the Doodle Corp.'s legal matters. After the dinner, Daniel would send a thank-you note to Sally, on behalf of himself and his wife, and in his note he would send his very best wishes and thanks to Bob. In this way, only the two laywers, not their spouses, are involved with the etiquette of arranging the dinner. It's the easiest, least confusing way to do it.

ENTERTAINING THE OUT-OF-TOWN BUSINESS GUEST

When you are entertaining a business colleague who has been on the road for a long time or who has just come a long distance to meet you, have pity on his physical condition. He may have had travel delays and problems; he may have had little sleep but a lot of stress. If so, don't make him go to a noisy, crowded cocktail party where he'll have to stand up and inhale smoke. Don't take him to a restaurant—no matter how great its reputation—where the two of you will have to stand waiting a long time, perhaps drinking at the bar, before your table is ready. Don't take an obviously exhausted person to a noisy restaurant, particularly a place with loud music, where it is difficult to think, much less talk.

However, if your out-of-town guest is young, full of energy, and obviously not tired, he or she may be greatly pleased by an invitation to dine in a place featuring music and lots of action. Ask your visitor on the telephone before he arrives to name his preference in restaurants. Ask him in advance what kind of food he particularly likes, and choose the place accordingly.

Beware of being overly creative. A lawyer friend of mine quite innocently put one of his visiting clients through a torturous evening in a small Japanese restaurant where diners either kneel or sit on the floor. The guest, who suffered badly from arthritis but was not about to admit it, went through the meal in agony. His host had hardly picked a winner for his guest's first night in town!

When someone passes through town, it's an opportunity to put your city's best culinary foot forward. However, never exceed your budget unnecessarily. No business deal was ever consummated solely because someone took someone else to lunch at the town's most expensive restaurant. (After all, major deals have been forged over food like pizza in places like the parking lot!)

If your company has put you on a modest entertaining budget, you can always invite a business acquaintance passing through town to "come and have a drink at home" with you (*see also* "When You Entertain at Home: The Most Flattering Invitation of Them All," later in this chapter). If you are busy for dinner, explain that and provide a good suggestion for a restaurant he might enjoy—on his own, of course.

Never be too proud to suggest to a business colleague that you go to a modest restaurant. When times are tough, expensive lunches are anachronistic. But the quality of food and service should still be taken into account. There are lots of modest restaurants proffering good food and friendly service. Don't treat a colleague to a noticeably inferior restaurant experience.

The Care of an Out-of-Town VIP Visitor

A visiting guest of honor, particularly one from another country, deserves very special treatment. An official or high-ranking individual, the head of a company, a visiting lecturer of great distinction—all come under the category of "VIP visitor."
Here are some things to remember:

- He or she should be met at the airport by someone of equal rank, such as a company vice-president. He will require help with his baggage and he usually arrives with many questions to answer.
- There should be welcoming flowers or a plant in the hotel room, liquor or wine of his choice (researched before his arrival), soda water, an ice bucket full of ice, and some soft drinks. There might be a basket of fresh fruit (with a plate, fruit fork, and fruit knife); perhaps also a small box of chocolates to satisfy the cravings of a sweet tooth.
- A personal note of welcome from the CEO or the highest ranking company person he will see during his visit should be awaiting him.
- The guest should be provided with a complete schedule of events for his stay. If he has a health problem (like a heart condition), his schedule should *not* be over-taxing. If he has come from another country, he will be very tired and probably jet-lagged; his schedule should be *very* easy the first day.
- If he does not know your city, provide him with a short history or a guidebook containing the important facts about the area.
- He should be asked if there is anyone he has met previously whom he would like to see during his stay.
- Comfortable transportation should be provided at all times.
- He should be provided with an adept interpreter if his command of English is inadequate.
- He should be given a *carefully annotated guest list* for every meeting and every business/social event, so that he will be well briefed on the cast of characters. Giving him a mere list of names is totally useless. His list should explain who the people are, what their businesses are, why they are important. Interesting information on their spouses should be included, too.
- When the VIP is escorted to each meeting and social event, he should be carefully introduced. If a reception is given in his honor, he should stand in a receiving line with his host.

• Whenever wine is served at a meal, the guest of honor should be given a toast before the meal is through (*see also* ''Toasting,'' Chapter 12).

COMPILING THE GUEST LIST

Entertaining requires a really logical sequence of events. First, you need a reason to give a party. Then you have to have a date and a place. You have to know what kind of refreshments you're going to have and who will serve it as well as cook it.

You obviously need a host to give the party, but the most important element of all is this: Who will attend?

Without the people, there is no party. I've seen parties where the food didn't arrive. I've seen parties where even the host didn't arrive. But who has seen a party without guests?

The Well-Blended Guest List

The blend is the secret—a mixture of ages and nationalities—of creating a great guest list. It works when you combine guests of totally diverse careers: a retired vice-chairman, a football coach, a minister, the president of the local ballet, a university professor, a lawyer, an ad agency account manager, and a poet. People enjoy meeting new people, learning about what they do, how others think. It is a major reason for going to a party in the first place.

The company's party planner logically maintains the files of the master list of guests—those who have been invited in the past, those who should be invited in the near future, and the ''glamour'' names of celebrities and officials who add lustre to the list. These names should be filed alphabetically, with special code letters put on each card by the person in charge of entertaining. For example:

IBF for *important business figure*   *CO* for *city official*
St for *staff*   *StO* for *state official*
GC for *good customer*   *V* for *vendors*
PC for *potential customer*   *NPS* for *nonprofit sector*
PR for *press**   *Soc* for *social figures*

Keep These Names on File Cards

Some corporations waste money and ruin the specialness of their invitations by inviting the same people every time. After a while, the whole event seems to sag like a tired horse. It's easy to avoid over-duplication of invitations by keeping accurate files on who came to dinner when. It's very important that these alphabetical lists (not only

*Your corporate entertaining events offer an excellent opportunity to make friends with the press. Caution: Make certain any guest deep in conversation with a reporter knows to whom he is speaking.

of people who came, but also of people who were invited and had to regret) be kept up to date, on file cards and in your computer. Being kept up to date means that information on each guest (such as a possible divorce, a spouse who dies, job and title changes) all are carefully noted on the individual's card.

Any special talent, such as a speaking knowledge of a foreign language, should be included on the card. A language talent, cross-referenced in the computer, would enable the host corporation to invite that person to sit between two non-English speaking dinner guests and carry on a good conversation. A typical file card would read

---

Williamson, Gregory, M.D., and Ms. Anne Gordon
3420 Portway, Galveston, TX 00000
Tel.: 000-000-0000
He's head of heart surgery, St. Francis Hosp.;
she's acct. exec. with Wellington PR Agency; has
kept her own name, speaks fluent French.
Both came to Red Cross dinner 6-24-96. She
came to French trade lunch 2-2-97.

ADVICE ON CUTTING YOUR ENTERTAINMENT BUDGET

If you overshoot your budget, it will have to be cut. There are several ways of doing that, and there are several ways *not* to do it.

WAYS TO CUT	WAYS NOT TO CUT
Cut the number of guests invited.	Don't cut all the young people off a guest list that is top-heavy with older, "big brass." The latter like to have some young, attractive faces around to add zip to the party.
Delete total luxuries like caviar, and cut the number of courses in the meal. You might omit the fish course and leave the soup; you might cut the salad-and-cheese separate course, and just add a small salad to the main course.	Don't cut the quality of the food you serve. It's better to serve only two courses at lunch and three at dinner, but to have them *delicious*.
If you have a white and a red wine on the menu, serve only one wine. If you have champagne on the menu with dessert, cut it.	Don't serve really cheap, poor-quality wine. It's better to give your guests only water.
Cut out the entertainment, if you must, or reduce the number of musicians or number of acts performing.	Don't replace a fine performer with one you've never heard of who comes "cheap." It's better to have *no* entertainment than *poor* entertainment.

WAYS TO CUT	WAYS NOT TO CUT
Cut down on the number of flowers in the centerpieces and substitute greenery instead. If you were planning on something very exotic and expensive as a floral scheme, change it to something simple but still beautiful.	Don't replace fresh flowers and greenery with plastic or any kind of fake stuff. It's better to have nothing at all on the tables.
If you are extensively over budget, delete the tent with its dance floor. Arrange for dancing in the area where dinner was served—indoors.	Don't replace live music with taped music for a formal dance. It is better not to have dancing.

WHEN A COMPANY-HOSTED EVENT MUST BE CANCELLED OR POSTPONED

There are many reasons why an event should or must be canceled, including a national disaster, the death of a member of the host's family, predictions of a hurricane, a blizzard that has made travel impossible, a widespread epidemic of the flu, etc. Even if a company had planned an event a year ahead, if it then suffered unexpectedly severe losses, it would be logical to cancel the function. In this era, probably the one time when everyone in the United States canceled everything for a week's time—so traumatized was our nation with shock and sadness—was when President Kennedy was assassinated.

Contractual Obligations in Cancelling an Event

A cancellation clause is inevitably built into all contracts with outside suppliers for an event, including the food and beverage service and the entertainment. (Unfortunately, the consumer protection laws governing cancellation differ from city to city.) If you inform the hotel, restaurant, or caterer several months prior to the event of your cancellation, and if they can book the space with someone else, in most cases there will be no penalty to pay. If a facility is unable to book the space on the night of your intended event, they may charge you a percentage (even a hefty one) of the total amount you had originally contracted for. It is important to read every word of a contract with a hotel, restaurant, or caterer before signing. The cancellation penalties will be spelled out, and you must be prepared to pay them.

Local union rules determine the number of days within which you can cancel (without penalty) for musicians and entertainers. These regulations vary from forty-eight hours notice to weeks. A proficient meeting planner on staff should know, or retain someone who does know, how to negotiate entertainers' contracts on matters such as the company's cancellation of their event. Sometimes it's the entertainer who will want to get out of the contract in order to accept a more lucrative engagement elsewhere. The entertainment contract should have tough language about this kind of cancellation, too, laying the responsibility on the entertainer instead of the company. Often an entertainer is legally held to 120 days advance notice on the cancellation.

Some Actions to Consider When Cancelling a Large Company Event

- If time is of the essence, put as many staff members as needed on the telephone to contact each guest personally, or at least a member of that guest's personal staff. (The telephone is a more personal, gracious conduit of a cancellation or postponement than a piece of fax paper.) The company staffer making the calls should write down the date and the time the call went through, as well as the name of the staff member who took the message and confirm the change in writing.
- If a guest cannot be reached by telephone, then fax a short but informative memo explaining that such-and-such an event on the specified date is being cancelled. Also explain *why*.
- If there is plenty of lead time, mail a printed card that announced the cancellation of the event and the reason why. If the event has been postponed and a new date already selected, provide the new date for the event, and mention that another invitation will be forthcoming. Be sure to have a telephone number in your company for confused guests to use when needing information, because people do become confused easily when dates are changed around.
- Always supply the reason for the cancellation. If you put on a card, in a letter, or in a fax the words "because of illness," you will be deluged with worried calls, wanting to know what's the matter. Have an operator ready to take all those calls and explain, "Mr. Jones has had a heart attack, but he is out of intensive care and coming along fine. No, thank you very much, but he is not taking telephone calls, and please, no flowers. You are very kind, but he just needs rest. I will let him know you have sent him your good wishes, and I assure you that he will appreciate it."

If the reason is a death "in the family," and there is time to have a card printed to cancel the event, the text might read:

Henry Fortsun
Chairman of Fortsun-Dominex
sincerely regrets that
due to the death of Mr. Bernard Sunton's wife
the dinner in Mr. Sunton's honor
March twelfth
will not take place

If the death occurs immediately before the scheduled event, fax the card to people's offices.

It is wise to have a company operator and all employees who cover the telephones prepared to handle the many calls that will come in to the company when the guests learn of the cancellation and the reason why. They will want to offer condolences, but also to learn when and how it happened.

Every letter of sympathy received after the company's cancellation of an event because of a death should be acknowledged by someone in the company ("on behalf of Mr. Miller, I wish to thank you, etc.").

· If the event is cancelled because of a fire at the plant, or a late shipment of the prototypes for a new product launch—whatever the reason, say what it is. Don't leave a veil of mystery enshrouding your company's activities. False gossip and rumor can really hurt.

THE COMPLETE GUIDE TO PLANNING AND RUNNING THE BIG CORPORATE EVENT

The person in charge of large corporate entertaining functions and special events should be equipped with a notebook containing all of the logistical requirements for a particular event. A large event is demanding and tough to organize, and one is constantly surprised by what does and does not happen. I remember when a young woman was sitting by my desk at the White House for career advice (her father, a senator, had sent her to me). I had just been told I had to reseat a dinner for 220 people, because all of the senior people had been changed at the last minute.

Our chef and his assistant had both just gone home, too sick with the flu to stand up, and I was trying to find two substitutes to replace them. The flowers throughout the entire reception room floor of the White House reeked of an incredibly smelly cheese, thanks to the French muralist, Bernard Lamotte, who was working on murals for President Kennedy's swimming pool, and who had kept his strong French blue cheese for two days of lunches in the fridge of the White House flower shop. The flowers had totally absorbed the cheese smell, and Mrs. Kennedy simply commanded, with a look of desperation (near asphyxiation, perhaps), "Do something."

The butler stood by my desk at the same time and said they would have to change all the linens on the tables in the Blue Room, because of wine stains and mildew all over them. They had not been used in years. Of course, we did not have any substitute linens for those tables, because they were never used under normal circumstances. (For a moment I contemplated ripping the blue and white sheets off the beds of the third floor guest bedrooms.)

The young lady watched all of this unfold before her eyes with astonishment. "Ooh," she cooed, "you must have *so much fun* doing this job!"

Whenever I think of unbelievably complicated entertaining logistics today, my mind inevitably turns toward the White House and the President, whether he entertains in his own house or elsewhere. When President Bush entertained 400 delegates to the

United Nations at the Metropolitan Museum of Art in New York one night, the Secret Service had to conduct a "sweep" of Museum premises before any guest was allowed to enter. The Secret Service men and their dogs scoured every nook and cranny of the giant property, searching for bombs, snipers, and would-be assassins. So when Chris Giftos, the talented Museum florist who was busy at the forty-some tables creating floral arrangements that would be worthy of such an important group of international emissaries, was ordered out of the building, he was stuck! He knew he could never finish his arrangements in time if he left during the security check, so he hid himself and three assistants in a broom closet until the search party had passed by. Then they sneaked out and finished their work in peace!

Even a party site like the staid Met must adapt to change and "go with the flow" if it is to hold many parties. After serious discussions of many of the successful corporate parties that had been held in the beloved fountain area in the center of the museum's restaurant, the fountain was removed. It's the kind of tough managerial decision that must be made when too many guests for too many years fell into the pool, had to be helped out, and had to be sent into the big kitchens to be dried off near the ovens.

Plan Your Event Like a Military Campaign

A successful party is the sum or many successful parts, and the person responsible for the event must accomplish (or see that others accomplish) the following duties:

- Oversee the design, production, and mailing of the *invitation*, and the compilation of the RSVPs.
- See to it that the proper *guest list* is drawn up, with all the approvals necessary having been obtained (which in a corporation, when several offices are involved, can be delicate and complicated).
- Coordinate with the banquet manager, head caterer, or whoever is in charge of the production of the party, including:

    ◦ Where the guests' cars can be parked (valet parking, if necessary)
    ◦ The menu for the food and drink
    ◦ The decor of the party place (party china, crystal, flatware, linens, table centerpieces, room decoration, floor covering, table favors, etc.)
    ◦ How the waiters will be dressed
    ◦ The logistical backstopping for the entertainment (sound system, lighting, dressing rooms needed, etc.)

- Select the *entertainment*: sign contracts, coordinate arrival time and transportation of entertainers, their housing, rehearsal times, etc.; produce program for entertainment, if this is appropriate; check sound and other logistical support on party night.
- Make the *seating charts*, get them approved, and check to see if proper protocol has been observed.

- Oversee the making of the *menus and place cards*.
- Organize the *check-in staff* (seated at tables and chairs at the entrance of the party) to check in arriving guests, give them their table cards or at least show them where they are to sit, and to make sure place cards are properly placed on the tables and guests ultimately properly seated.
- Organize the *receiving line*, if there is to be one, and make sure that introductions are properly handled and that corporate staff are all doing their hosting jobs enthusiastically.
- Make sure that *proper security* is in effect (if any important official or celebrity guests are present).
- *Handle the payment and tips*. If a good job was done by the hotel, restaurant, or catering staff (and it usually is), congratulate and thank all of the staff for a job well done. Hand out cash tips in envelopes to the top figures who worked the party. Pay the entire caterer's or hotel's bill before leaving, if required.
- Write *follow-up letters* thanking the banquet or catering staff, lauding their efforts (this kind of letter is invaluable for their getting other jobs) and detailing the aspects that were particularly well done. Write a similar letter to the entertainers, musicians, head of security, valet parkers, etc. It means so much!

The Party Planner Looks Above, Beyond, and Behind

The company whose entertaining operations are important to its business may manage those operations in any of several ways:

- There might be one staff person who coordinates senior management's entertaining as only one part of his or her job with the company. He or she might be part of the Human Resources or Administration divisions. (It is wise to have this person spend some time observing a large catering operation, to learn all of the many complicated facets of producing a party.)
- If entertaining is frequent, there should be someone on staff who handles these logistical details full-time. Large banks, for example, usually have a "Protocol Officer" handling such tasks.
- Large international corporations usually have an entire department devoted to the success of their business entertaining, knowing that it is cost-efficient to do so, and realizing how much is at stake in regard to the image they project in the community.
- A medium-size or small company would retain on an ad hoc basis a special events-planning company, or else a freelancer with a distinguished track record in staging these functions. The special events coordinator of a large corporation would also use these firms and freelancers for large projects—such as staging an industry meeting or sales conference in another city, or running an international conference at home or abroad, or producing an open house reception for two thousand people to inaugurate a new plant or celebrate a major anniversary.

The way to find a company specializing in special events planning is through word of mouth in your community. When you hear a great deal of complimentary chatter about an affair a company just staged in your city, call that company's PR department and ask for the name of the outside professionals used. Once you have the name (let's say the party planning company is called *"Fêtes d'Affaires"* ("Business Parties"), and after having had an informal chat with someone from the host company about the special event just past, ask that person, "What does your management *really* think of the job *Fêtes d'Affaires* did? Would you use them again?"

If any reservations about that firm were expressed, slight though they may have been, write them down. Reread your notes when you make the plans with that firm for your function. If a client of *Fêtes d'Affaires* raved about them but cautioned, "Their caterers are slow with the service, that's the only thing. We kept trying to hurry them up, to no avail," point this out clearly to the party planners you are hiring for your event. Insist that they guarantee to speed up the service for your party. (*Fêtes d'Affaires* may not be hiring enough waiters, to save themselves money.)

The special events coordinator, party planner, or party manager should have eyes in the back, front, and sides of his or her head. He should always be observing, eyes darting to all corners of the room, and to every part of the space being used. His ears should be open to catch any sounds of dissonance—a complaint, a criticism, a lament. He might see empty chairs at a table that must be removed; he may notice a table with only empty bottles of wine on it; he may sight a table with a wobbly leg that needs correcting; he might notice a table of people in the corner that have not yet been served their main course; he may see a late guest arriving, not knowing where to sit. He may see a waiter spilling red wine on a woman's dress; there might be a drunk and abusive guest with whom to cope. At any given moment during a large event, a drama may be unfolding, and the party planner is supposed to see it first and solve its negative aspects without anyone else noticing.

A party planner never sits down with the guests to enjoy the party. He or she is much too busy righting the wrongs (insignificant or ominous) that inevitably occur at social functions. In my long professional life as a social secretary at American embassies abroad, as a White House Social Secretary, and as the president of a public relations company, I have my own list of horror stories in running events. Now that they are past, I have reached a distinctly comforting conclusion: One always survives, no matter how serious the disaster. For example:

In retyping a copy of the list of names of guests who had accepted Ambassador David Bruce's dinner invitation at the American Embassy in Paris, I accidentally omitted the name of an important, temperamental, difficult woman guest. She arrived at the official residence at the appointed hour in a ballgown and jewels, only to find her name was not on the guest list and there was no room at the table for her.

Shortly after that incident, not knowing who was sleeping with whom in Paris, and having to seat men next to each other because of a rare surplus of male guests, I managed to seat a top government official at a dinner party in the seat next to his wife's lover. Everyone in Paris (except me) knew of the liaison.

In my days at the American Embassy in Rome, we expected three important U.S. senators and their wives as houseguests at the residence one weekend; we were also giving a seated dinner for forty-six in their honor, already over the absolute maximum number of guests we could serve in the house. We had only two guest rooms, plus Ambassador and Mr. Luce's suite of rooms. Six senatorial couples—a total of twelve people—arrived, all refusing to stay anywhere other than the Residence, each pair determined to stay "with the Luces." (A Roman prince helped us out by putting up eight of them at his fantastic palazzo down near the Forum, the only alternative that would suit the senatorial couples. It took me a year of special social favors to pay him back for that one.) Since there was no way to accommodate a dinner for over fifty in the house, we had to move the dinner party outside in the gardens, on a cold late autumn night, with the winds blowing and the guests wondering what kind of madness had touched the Luces to force their guests to eat out in the cold.

In my White House days, the fuses throughout one whole section of the East Wing of the mansion blew (due to an electric overload of stage lighting), in the middle of a Broadway show performance on our little stage—which was the after-dinner entertainment for an important state dinner. We were plunged into total darkness; the music stopped; the dancing chorus froze on stage; the Secret Service rushed to the doors of the ballroom, guns drawn, fearing a plot; and the guests were frightened and confused. The tension in the darkened ballroom was broken only when President John F. Kennedy whispered in the front row to the King of Morocco, his honored guest, "Your Majesty, this is all part of the show." (His Majesty, not understanding the plot of the musical *Brigadoon*, with its story of spirits from an earlier era and a cast dancing about in rolling fog on the stage, accepted the President's explanation.) The fuses were fixed in about three minutes—three hours to this party planner. (The buck always stops with the person in charge of the event, even when the culprit is an electrical failure.)

Perhaps one of my worst gaffes occurred when I organized a party for a thousand—an open house for a hotel—but my carefully designed invitation was so clever and so obtuse, no one who received it understood that it was really a party that the invitation was communicating. No one came.

At another event, neither of the two important guests of honor arrived, having succumbed to the old devil gin in their hotel rooms beforehand. Their speeches were the evening program, so the CEO announced into the microphone at dessert time that the two awards would be delivered tomorrow to the recipients, which meant that the dinner guests would be spared an award ceremony and a total of three very long substantive speeches. (I wrote these remarks for the CEO, who was in a catatonic state of anger at the missing honored guests and at me.) When the guests rose to give him a standing ovation after he said there would be no speeches (they all wanted to go home), he immediately patted himself on the back as being a "genius who knows how to roll with the punches."

Life goes on, and I was very fortunate, because my jobs did, too.

Putting Your Big Party Plan Together

If your company wishes to be immensely creative in its entertaining, and someone in the corporation (or the caterer) has a terrific, novel idea—ask yourself some important questions. Bear in mind that inexperience and attempting the impossible with an untrained staff can result in social disaster.

- Do you have the budget to fund this incredibly novel concept for a party?
- Do you have a truly creative party planner on staff?
- Is your caterer's staff agile, fast-moving, talented, and ready for such a project?
- Has your legal staff okayed your plans from the point of view of liability, security, fire laws, and insurance?
- Is your in-house public relations staff capable of insuring the proper kind of press coverage of your event? (If not, arrange for an outside firm to handle it on an ad hoc basis.)
- If the main creative thrust of your corporate party is an unusual place in which to hold it, and if you are satisfied that your caterer is up to this complicated task, ask yourself further questions:
  - Does the place in which you intend to hold the party conform to your corporate image? (Examples of nonconforming image parties would be the steel manufacturer who gave a party in a doll museum, and the expensive jeweler who gave a barn dance with ambience provided by a great deal of hay and red neckerchiefs, accompanied by the waft of manure as the all-encompassing fragrance for the evening)
  - will the climate be a negative factor at this time of the year? (Mountains are magnificent, for example, most of the year, but less so in the muds of April.)
  - will parking be a problem? Is public transportation possible? Will buses be required?
  - will the guests be comfortable in terms of seating, temperature, and space in which to circulate?
  - can the toilet facilities be made to function more than adequately?
  - are extra security measures necessary?

In short, even if the budget is feasible, make sure the company has enough lead time to host this unusual party. Is there enough in-house talent for supervising the various facets of the operation?

Think hard and work hard at devising the list of all the negatives for holding such an unusual event and see if you can overcome that list with smart planning. If you can, go for it. Give a party that will do your company proud, one which the guests will remember for the rest of their lives.

THE PARTY PLANNER'S NOTEBOOK

If you are the one managing complicated events, it's a good idea to have standard forms printed to fill in with information and to keep in your party notebook. The party planner should never be separated from his or her notebook. The planner or someone on staff should make a duplicate copy of changes in the notebook *every day*, so that if the worst should happen—the loss of the notebook—there would be another copy back in the office. The notebook sheets illustrated here that are to be filled out by the party planner from beginning to end of the event are the kind suitable for a large, rather lavish black-tie dinner, with dancing afterward in a separate tent. This kind of organizational recording can be downsized to a modest corporate dinner for six people in a restaurant. It's called "getting organized."

Your notebook will include the following 13 sections:

1. Basic Information (purpose of party, date, time, and place)
2. Budget
3. Guest List
4. Invitations
5. Caterer (food and beverages)
6. Florist
7. Tent for Dancing
8. Diagrams of Room Floor Plans
9. Party Decor
10. Party Protocol
11. Music and Entertainment
12. Press Coverage of the Event
13. Security Arrangements

1. Basic Information

Date and hour of party: _____

Place: _____

Purpose: _____

Type of party: _____

Dress: _____

Maximum number of guests allowable: _____

Staff members responsible (telephone extensions included):

_____

_____

_____

_____

_____

2. Budget

Approved by management: $_____ Contingency fund total: $_____

    Invitations:

        Design costs: $_____

        Production costs: $_____

        Mailing costs: $_____

        Freelancers to handle RSVPs: $_____

    Facility rental: $_____

    Caterer's total: $_____

        Food: $_____ Wines and liquor: $_____

        Personnel hired: $_____

        Rental of caterer's equipment: $_____ Coat-checking: $_____

        Total gratuities in caterer's bill: $_____ Tax: $_____

        Extra gratuities given in cash on party night: $_____

    Valet parker's total: $_____

    Musicians and entertainment: $_____

        Audiovisual—sound support systems: $_____

        Carpentry/construction costs for podium, lectern, stage, bandstand: $_____

    Florists total: $_____

    Photographers' costs: $_____ Extra prints for guests: $_____

        Cost of limos hired for VIP guests: $_____

        Extra security hired: $_____

3. Guest List

Total possible: _____

Division heads responsible for names:

        _____   Tel no.: _____

        _____   _____

        _____   _____

People invited:

Name	Title	Company	Address	Tel. no.	Accpt. or rgrt. and date of reply

Total Acceptances

4. Invitations

(Paste copy—or at least draft text—of invitation on this page.)
No. to be ordered: _____ _____

DESIGN
Designer's name: _____
        Address: _____ Tel. no.: _____
Date design approved: _____ Approver's name: _____
Deadline for finished artwork to be submitted: _____

PRINTING
Printer's name: _____
        Address: _____ Tel. no.: _____
Date finished proof to be delivered: _____ Approver's name: _____
Date finished job to be delivered: _____
Components of invitation:
    Double-fold invitation and envelope
    RSVP card and self-addressed envelope
    Map of location of party place

MAILING
    Supervisor of addressing, stuffing, stamping, and mailing:
    _____ Tel. no.: _____

Outside mailing house to be involved?
Company name: _____ Our contact: _____ Tel. no.: _____
Date materials delivered to our office or outside mailing house: _____
Date invitations mailed: _____

RSVPs
In-house or outside person in charge: _____ Tel. no.: _____

5. Caterer: Food and Beverages

(Paste copy of full menu of food and wines on this page.)
Caterer (or facility's banquet manager): _____
Address: _____ Tel. no.: _____
Lead contact: _____ Substitute contact: _____

	Food to be served	Liquor, wines, nonalcoholic drinks to be served
Cocktail Hour:	_____ _____ _____ _____	_____ _____ _____ _____
Dinner:	_____ _____ _____ _____ _____ _____	_____ _____ _____
After Dinner (in the tent):	_____ _____ _____ _____	_____ _____ _____ _____

Help hired:
No. in kitchen: _____ No. of waiters and waitresses: _____
No. of coat-checkers: _____ No. of valet parkers: _____
No. of restroom attendants: _____

Restrooms:
Suitable for guests? _____
Need guest soaps, guest towels? _____
Are portable facilities necessary? _____

6. Florist

Name: _____ Address: _____ Tel. No.: _____

FLOWERS AND GREENERY:
    Cocktail area: _____

    _____

    _____

    Dining area:
        Table centerpieces: No. needed: _____ Scheme: _____
        Head table or dais arrangements: _____
        Rented trees and plants to disguise the area:

        _____ _____ _____

        _____ _____ _____

    Tent:
        Tent poles decorated? _____
        Greenery around bandstand? _____
        Small arrangements needed on the little tables? _____
        If so, how many? _____

7. Tent for Dancing

Name of tent company: _____ Address: _____
Contact: _____ Tel. No.: _____
Shape: _____ Colors: _____ Dimensions: _____
Flooring: _____
Side flaps: _____
Heaters needed? _____ Air conditioners needed? _____
Date to be constructed: _____
Date to be dismantled: _____
Name of insurance company: _____ Tel. No.: _____
Person in charge of supplying umbrellas in case of rain for guests walking from
    dining area to tent: _____

8. Diagrams of Room Floor Plans

Always give the caterer or banquet manager a drawing of how you want the room set up. If you have rented a hotel room for your luncheon, for example, and the room is rectangular with windows along one wall, draw the rectangle with the door and windows marked, draw where the bar might best be placed and where the piano might be placed so as not to interfere with the meal service. Then draw your tables, where you want them placed, and you can then mark on your table seating plans the best seats

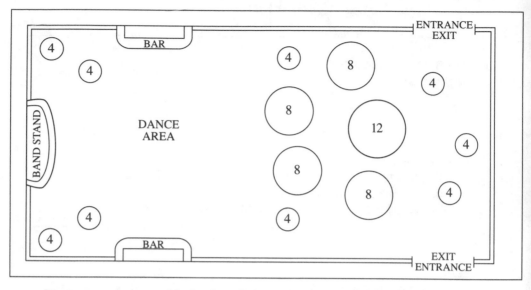

Room setup for tent with dancing. Only small tables will be needed, since guests will spend most of their time dancing.

in the room for the host, cohost, and honored guests to sit—those with a commanding view of the room, and away from the doors into the kitchen!

In the case of a large dinner with a tent for dancing afterward, make a picture for your caterer like the one above of exactly how you want the tables and chairs (for four, eight, or twelve people) to be placed around the dance floor. These tables, covered with cloths and perhaps centered with a hurricane lamp (surrounded with flowers at its base), will be used by guests for chatting and drinking when they're not dancing.

Of course, you can rely on the caterer to figure out the table placement himself, but I have never seen a large party yet where the party planner did not disagree with the caterer's decisions. This means that the poor, harried person in charge has to change it all at the last minute to suit the party planner, something that could have been avoided by the party planner's having made floor plans for each room.

9. Party Decor

(On occasion an outside "party designer" is retained, who will coordinate all of the party decor, including the floral decorations.)

Names of inhouse designer or outside consultant: _____

    Address: _____ Tel. no.: _____

    Overall party theme: _____

Flower designs:
       Entrance: _____ Receiving line area: _____
       Serving tables for cocktails: _____
       Dinner table centerpieces: _____ Head table: _____
       Tent area table centerpieces: _____ Tent poles: _____
Linens chosen: _____
Table favors: _____
Floor covering for tent: _____
Bandstand decorations: _____
Embellishments of restrooms: _____

10. Party Protocol

(Copy of seating for all the tables, including the dais, if there is one, to be attached to this section in the notebook.)

Staff needed to check in at door: _____
No. of tables needed: _____
Table cards? _____ In stock or to be ordered? _____
       No. needed: _____ Person responsible: _____
Seating charts to be made? _____ Blown up to what size? _____
       By whom? _____ On easel stands? _____
Place cards:
       No. needed: _____ In stock or to be ordered? _____
       Names to be: Handwritten: _____ Typed: _____
       Done in calligraphy: _____ Person responsible: _____
Menu cards:
       No. needed: _____ Handwritten: _____
       Typed: _____ Calligraphy and offset: _____
       Person responsible: _____
Person in charge of seating: _____ Tel. ext.: _____
Receiving line: Where? _____ Names (in order of standing in line):
               _____
               _____
               _____

Will there be an introducer? _____
       Name: _____ Ext.: _____
Names of staff "party workers"   _____   _____
       and extensions: _____   _____
                       _____   _____

No. of copies of guest list required: _____

11. Music and Entertainment

Music:
    a. *Cocktail hour* (jazz quartet on elevated platform with sound system)
        Name of group: _____
        Name of agent: _____ Address: _____
        Tel. no.: _____
    b. *During dinner in dining room*(string quartet)
        Name of group: _____ Agent: _____
        Address: _____ Tel. no.: _____
    c. *Dancing after dinner in tent*
        Orchestra: _____ Agent: _____
        Address: _____
        Tel. no.: _____ How many musicians: _____
        Singer's name: _____ Agent: _____
        Address: _____ Tel. no.: _____
Names of staff member in charge of their transportation, housing,
    and feeding: _____ Tel. no.: _____
Special needs (such as dressing room required, etc.):

_____

_____

_____

Scenario for dinner program
    Master of ceremonies: _____
        Address: _____ Tel. no.: _____
        _____ introduces _____
        _____ introduces _____
    etc.
Scenario for after-dinner program
    CEO and spouse take their two dinner partners and walk them from dining
        room to tent, upon signal from the maitre d'.
    CEO and spouse dance first dance with their honored guests, second dance
        with their second honored guests, third dance with each other.
Audiovisual support requirements
    Lecterns needed: _____ Podium: _____
    Name of company constructing bandstand: _____
        Contact: _____ Tel. no.: _____
    Lighting engineering firm: _____ Address: _____
        Contact: _____ Tel. no.: _____
    Sound equipment firm name: _____
        Contact: _____ Tel. no.: _____
    No. and type of microphones needed:
        At dinner: _____
        In the tent: _____

Taping:
    Of dinner speeches? _____
    Of remarks made in tent? _____
(It is an elegant gesture to send tapes of these remarks to the people who made them, as well as to the people being honored and talked about so flatteringly!)

12. Press Coverage of the Event

Staff person in charge of press for this event: _____
    Tel. no.: _____
Press invited to dinner (include media and tel. no.):
    1. _____
    2. _____
    3. _____
    4. _____
Press invited to tent after dinner:
    1. _____
    2. _____
    3. _____
    4. _____
Host company's photographers:
_____ Tel. no.: _____
_____ Tel. no.: _____
Videocam recorder operator: _____ Tel. no.: _____

13. Security Arrangements

Names of company's own people on duty:
    In uniform: _____ In black tie: _____
_____ Tel. no.: _____
_____ Tel. no.: _____
_____ Tel. no.: _____
Name of outside agency: _____
    Contact: _____ Tel. no.: _____
    Address: _____
    Names of people dispatched: _____
    _____

City/county police to be notified by company's security and requested to help route traffic around the party area:
    Date done: _____

SEATING AT A LARGE PARTY

The following information on seating can also be found in "How to Seat Guests at a Table According to Rank and Company Position," Chapter 12. It is, however, so important that I include it in a slightly different form here. Many people may go directly to special parts of this book for specific basic information, and at the risk of being redundant, I prefer to repeat rather than to leave a reader who is skipping parts she thinks not pertinent to her problem fail to find a solution to it.

The Dais

It is a distinct honor to be invited to sit on the dais. Such an invitation means you are either a person of great distinction or you are involved in a top-level capacity with the purpose of the function.

Spouses of those invited to sit on the dais are not included, except for the spouse of the main speaker, who may be invited to join the dais.

It is important that you communicate to anyone being asked to sit on the dais at a fund-raising benefit whether or not the invitee is supposed to pay for his or her dinner or lunch ticket. (The answer usually is yes, except for the speakers.) In your letter of invitation to a dais guest, indicate either, "We are enclosing a complimentary dinner ticket for your use" or "You may purchase your benefit ticket by filling out the enclosed card and mailing your check to . . ."

Organizing the Dais Group

Dais guests should be invited to convene in a special room (usually close to the ballroom or the area where the function is to be held) half an hour before the dais guests are supposed to march in formation into the ballroom. Company staff members should be present to greet them, show them where to check their coats, introduce them to the company hosts and guest of honor, make sure they are served refreshments, brief them on the scenario for the affair, and get them into their proper places in line before marching into the ballroom.

On rare occasions, there is a very large dais of from twenty to fifty people. In this case the dais is built in rows, like bleachers, usually on the ballroom stage.

When organizing a dais of this size, you would be wise to line up rows of chairs in the "dais convening room," to duplicate exactly the rising platforms in the ballroom. (The important guests will be placed on the lower levels of the ascending platforms.) Each chair should have a name tag. The dais guests should be lined up in the proper order in the convening room and, just before going into the ballroom, should sit in their assigned chairs so that they are ready to march to the dais in proper order. Unless this is perfectly organized, dais guests will wander forlornly back and forth trying to find their places. That is very undignified and does not reflect credit on the sponsoring hosts.

When everything in the ballroom is ready, the maître d'hôtel will signal the company official in charge of the dais group that it is time to assemble in proper order and to enter the ballroom. The maître d'hôtel then goes to the microphone in the ballroom and announces, "Ladies and gentlemen, the honored guests!"

The musicians should then begin to play something military and brisk, suitable for marching, so the dais guests enter at a quick pace to mount the steps to the stage and the dais platforms. The guests should applaud enthusiastically as the dais guests appear; there should be some staff members planted in the audience to applaud on cue, thus prompting the entire ballroom to begin applauding.

The music that heralds the dais guests is really important, whether it's a piano arpeggio, an accordion flourish, a roll of the drums, or even a trumpet flourish. (Dais guests who walk limply to their places at a large function without a musical introduction always look to me like a funeral procession!)

The Seating on the Dais

The most uncomfortable seat on a dais is the end one on either side. The person on each end is left without anyone to talk to during a great part of the meal. This problem can be solved simply by putting guests close to each other *in pairs*. In addition, no one should be seated behind the lectern, for he or she would be totally obscured from the audience. The guest of honor should sit on the right of the host; the second ranking guest should sit on the right of the second ranking corporate executive. At Company X's civic dinner, the dais might look like this:

Substitutions on the Dais

Never send a substitute for yourself on the dais. If a guest to be seated on the dais cannot attend the function at the last moment, he must have someone notify his dinner hosts, regardless of how busy he may be. It is the height of rudeness not to let the hosts know, because this means there will be an empty seat on the dais, which looks like a missing piano key.

It is not proper for a dais guest who cannot attend the function at the last minute to take upon himself the selection of a substitute to attend in his place. This is a decision for the host company to make, either to find a substitute or to remove his place from the dais.

Alternatives to the Dais

It is not all that interesting to sit on the dais once you've done it once or twice. In fact, it can be extremely boring to sit facing everyone under their constant gaze. There are alternatives. One alternative is to seat the honored guests and celebrities around the room, one at each table. (This can be done at large functions with many round tables.) The presence of a "star guest" pleases everyone at that particular table. The "star guest," of course, is seated to the right of the company host of that table. Another alternative is to seat the master of ceremonies and the honored guests together at a large round table on a raised platform in the center of the room. In this way, everyone's view of the VIPs is excellent.

When using either of these alternatives, the master of ceremonies or dinner chairman—whatever you wish to call him—should introduce each honored guest individually (speaking through a microphone). As each person is introduced, a spotlight beam should fall on him or her making that person visible to everyone in the room. He should stand when his name is read and remain standing while the master of ceremonies talks about him. The audience should applaud at the conclusion of the announcement of all the names.

Learn How to Seat According to Rank

(*See also* "How to Seat Guests at a Table According to Rank and Company Position," Chapter 12)

The number-one principle of seating by rank is, of course, to seat the most important person on the host's right and the next most important on his left, and to seat

Executive Host

Guest #1	Guest #2
Guest #5	Guest #6
Guest #4	Guest #3

Cohost

the third and fourth most important people on his cohost's right and left, as shown.

There are many more human elements that enter into the proper seating of a dinner, however, which have less to do with rank and more to do with giving honor to someone who deserves it. You would give a seat of honor, for example, as well as raise a toast to:

- A foreign guest
- Your houseguest
- An elderly person
- A person who had a distinguished career
- Someone who used to hold high office
- A person celebrating a birthday, anniversary, engagement, promotion, etc.
- Someone you sentimentally hold in high regard, like a beloved former high school teacher

How to Get Help in Ranking Your Guests
(*See also* "Researching Your Official Guest's Rank," Chapter 12)

It's better not to guess when you are seating people at a meal. It's better to make a telephone call or look in a book that shows you how people are ranked. When you do it right, officially ranked people are impressed and consider the host company to be a class act.

Military officers are quite offended when not given their proper rank in a seat at a dinner; so are ambassadors, judges, congressmen, and everyone else. They will say nothing if your company ignores their rank in seating the dinner party, but there may be good bit of parboiling going on inside them! If you have an ambassador, a mayor, a lady admiral, and the head of a government agency coming to your company's immense anniversary dinner, do some research before you place one tab in your seating chart.

How to Do the Seating

Seating a large meal used to be a fascinating puzzle, somewhat like being in a maze that made one feel victorious upon working one's way out of it. Today it is just one of corporate life's most thankless jobs, because of the bad manners of people who don't even bother to respond to invitations and those who accept the invitations but are no-shows.

Seating a meal, after all, with place cards to show people where they sit, is meant to bring a harmonious order to the proceedings. It's efficient. It takes the hassle out of the act of getting a crowd into a ballroom and into their seats. When people do not respect where they are supposed to sit, or when they are no-shows at a seated dinner they have accepted, chaos results.

Seating a large party properly is best done in the following manner:

- *Schedule yourself plenty of time for the task*, so you don't get flustered. A large function of a hundred or more can take many hours.
- One of the first things you must research, of course, is each person's rank or status. Once, in my consulting days, I was rushed and careless about researching who the guests were for a corporate luncheon I was managing. I mis-sat a revered former governor of the state. Having not recognized his name, I plunked him down "at the bottom" of the list and sat him between two secretaries who were allowed to attend their boss' luncheon only in the case of last minute no-shows. When the CEO saw what I had done and pointed it out to me in no uncertain terms, I went to the ex-governor, apologized, and begged him to let me reseat him. Nice fellow that he was, he said he was very happy where he was, and that he hadn't had the chance for forty years to sit between two beautiful young women. (That's what I call manners!)
- *Write the men's names on small slips of one color of paper, the women's on another.* You can use self-adhesive notes for this as well.

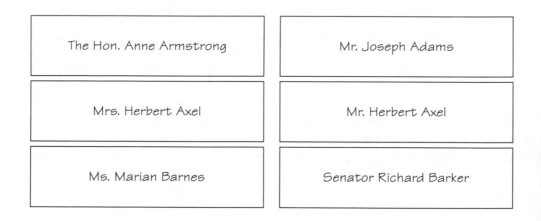

Put a piece of clear tape on the end of each name tab, so you can easily attach— and detach—the tabs on the sheets containing drawings of tables. You will want to seat an equal number of men and women at each table. Of course, if you have too many men, for example, you will want to distribute the lesser number of women equally among the tables, so you don't wind up with one whole table of men.

- *Make a drawing of each table on separate sheets of paper.* Number each table and write in the center space the number of guests who will sit at that table. For example, you might have in the ballroom for your dinner eight round tables of ten guests, one long rectangle of twenty-four guests and three round tables of eight each. Put little marks on the outline of each table to show where a person will sit, as shown.

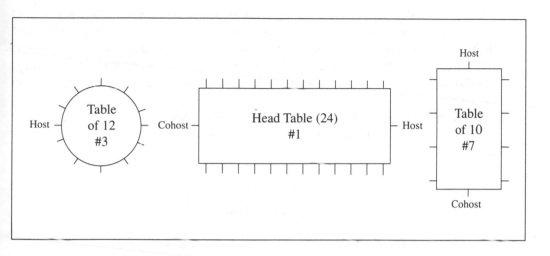

- Take each name and attach it to a seat, putting first a host (and a cohost, if there is one) at each table. Using tape permits you to keep changing the placement until the very last minute. Some party planners prefer using thumbtacks rather than tape.

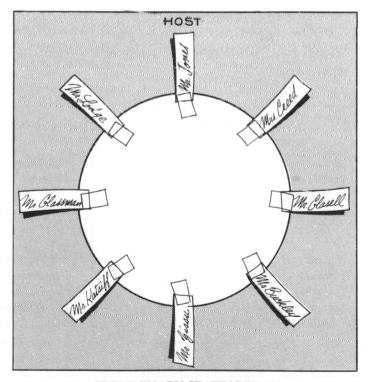

PRELIMINARY SEATING PLAN

- *Give each male host or cohost an important guest of the opposite sex on his right and left sides*; give each woman host or cohost an important man on her right and left. Then fill in the other seats at the table, man–woman–man–woman, if possible. If there is a great inequality in the numbers of men and women, don't worry. Good conversation and a good time do not depend just on an equal number of men and women at each table. Keep rank in mind, however, as you group people around the host and cohost at each table. The number-one-ranked guest must sit next to the highest-ranked host in the room (presumably the host company's CEO).

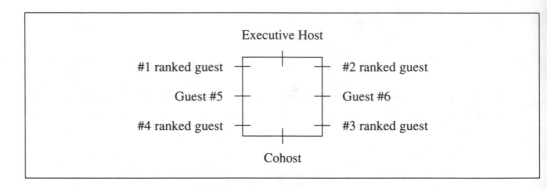

- *Normally a host and his or her spouse sit opposite one another at the table*, as illustrated below:

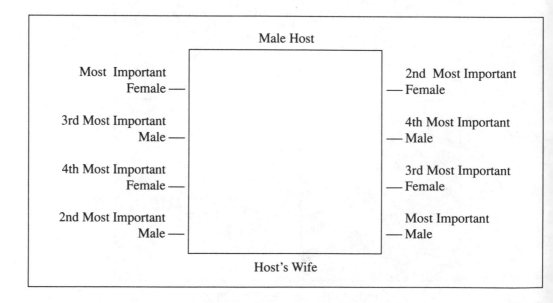

- *In tables that are quadruples of four* (i.e., tables of eight, twelve, sixteen, etc.), *the host and hostess, if there is an even number of male and female guests, can not sit opposite one another,* that is, if the alternating style of seating men and women is to be carried out. In the case of a table of a multiple of four, one spouse will sit around the corner from the bottom of the table.

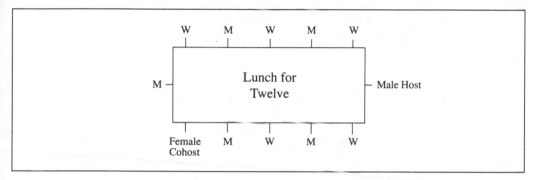

Of course, if the table is round, there is no table end to worry about, and therefore no problem of having one spouse sit around the corner.

Or you can put your host and hostess off-center, in the middle of the sides of a rectangular table (this is very European).

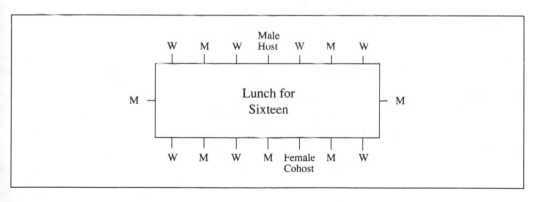

- *Don't put husbands and wives next to one another.* Don't even put them at the same table if you have more than one table.
- Try to put a *foreign guest who speaks no English next to someone who can communicate with him.*
- *Mix the old with the young.* It flatters both generations.
- Realize that after hours of hard work to get everything right, when it's party time tomorrow night, there will be many last-minute changes, and *you will have to do a large part of the seating all over again!*

Making the Door Lists

When it's party time, the seating has been finalized, with the last-minute changes incorporated into the table plans, run off many typed copies of the door list. This is the list of guests' names alphabetized, with a table number by each name. A copy of the list would go, of course, to all the senior hosts for this event, to the maitre d'hotel and any of his staff who will help seat guests, and, of course, to all the staff people sitting by the door and checking in the guests at a table as they arrive.

The arriving guest has his name checked off and the staff person smilingly tells him his table number.

Table Cards Are a Good Idea for a Large Function

Chances are good that when the staff person checking in the guests tells each person the number of his or her table, that person will have forgotten it by the time the guests proceed from the cocktail area into dinner an hour later. This is why table cards make sense: small, white single cards, rather like a place card, or alternately a fold-over "tent card" with the guest's name on the front and the table number inside. (In the case of a single table card, the table number is on the back.) These look very handsome when written in calligraphy, but they can also be written in black ink by hand (a fine hand, please) or, in the case of a luncheon, they may properly be typed. The table cards are lined up alphabetically on a large table at the entrance to the event. Each guest takes the appropriate card as he or she arrives, and then stashes it away in a jacket pocket or handbag, to refer to when needed later.

When the Guests Enter the Ballroom

By the time the guests have finished cocktails and go into dinner, the staff person can look down the list and see who is missing, who has not checked in. (Sometimes guests will drift by and not check in, so it is wise to wait until the middle of the first course before your staff person checks out the missing seats and has the waiter remove the place settings of the no-shows from the tables.)

The Party Planner Needs Copies of the Overall Table Plans

If you are running this event, you also need in your hands a copy of all the numbered tables showing exactly where each guest sits, such as in the illustration of a dinner given for the President of India by President and Mrs. Kennedy. This particular dinner had a rectangular head table for eighteen and ten additional tables seating ten each. Notice how the host's name is underlined at each table—valuable information for any trouble-spotters during the dinner.

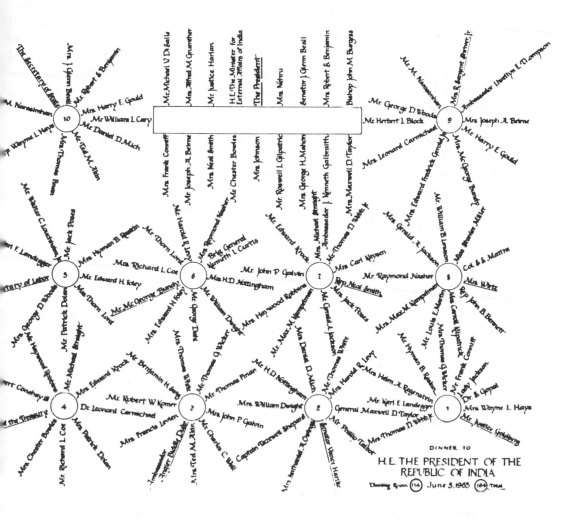

COMPLETE TABLE PLAN FOR A BIG KENNEDY WHITE HOUSE PARTY

Introducing Guests to the Hosts

When There Is No Receiving Line

When there are fewer than sixty guests, a receiving line doesn't make sense, but one or two staff members should see to it that every person who arrives is introduced to the host(s) of the affair. This is particularly important if the host does not know all of his guests personally.

The host should stay near the door of the room so that he is available to meet all his guests. It is a common tendency for a host to glimpse a good customer or close friend and go off in a corner for a lengthy conversation. This can ruin the party mood very quickly. At a party for fifty, for example, everyone in the room is aware of where the host is and to whom he is speaking and for how long. All of the guests should have more or less equal time, even if the host would much rather be off in a corner with an important person.

A staff person should remain at the door and make sure that each person entering the room is brought to the host. Once the guest has been introduced, the host or the staff person should call over a waiter or else direct the guest to the bar. The staff person should also introduce each newcomer to one or two people, so that the newcomer will be able to join a conversational group and not be left alone as a stranger, not knowing anyone and feeling like a typical wallflower.

When There Is a Receiving Line

A receiving line is a tremendous aid at a business-social function with more than sixty guests. If many of the guests do not personally know their host(s) or each other, a receiving line and badges will help identify people to each other and make conversation easier. Nothing is drearier than being wedged into a large room crowded with scores of unrecognizable faces and wondering who they all are. Guests who have no idea of who or where the hosts are soon begin not to care. The party is then cold, impersonal, and certainly off to a bad start.

- *The proper location must be found* for the receiving line, so that the traffic flow will not be obstructed and so that the majority of the other guests will be able to view the receiving line as the party progresses. (There is a natural curiosity about who is arriving; receiving-line watching is a corporate sport for some people.) The line should be formed inside the party area, near the entrance but not near a crowded passageway or a staircase that blocks the door. It should not be close to the food service and bar, which would cause an instant traffic jam.
- *The length of time the receiving line should stay in formation* depends upon the size of the party. For a cocktail party for five hundred of a two-hour duration, the hosts should stay in line for over an hour, so that almost every guest will have had the opportunity to shake hands with them. If the great majority of the guests have arrived within a short space of time, the line can break up and the hosts can circulate around the room.
- *The composition of the line is, of course, very important.* It should be as short as possible. For a strictly business party, spouses should not stand in line. However, if the guest of honor from another city or country is accompanied by his spouse, the corporate host's spouse should also stand in line with the two visitors.
- *If a female executive is part of the official receiving line,* the spouses of male

executives who are also in that receiving line should not expect to stand with their husbands. The female executive is there for a business, not a social reason.

- *If several corporate hosts' names were on the invitation,* it is preferable that they not all stand in the line together. It makes the process too long. The hosts should spell each other in groups of three or four, so that guests can pass by quickly. A party with a long, cumbersome receiving line quickly becomes a tiresome logjam, with guests impatient because they don't like waiting that long.

- *When a staff assistant sees the line bogged down,* he or she should step in at a certain point to break it up. This may mean a warning to the senior host: "The line is now out to the street. Do you think we might speed things up a bit?"

  If the party helper keeps a sense of humor and apologizes about pushing people quickly through the line, he won't be resented. He's only doing a job that has to be done, and everyone will benefit in the long run.

- *Drinking in a receiving line should be done very circumspectly if at all.* If you're standing in a receiving line, waiting to greet your guests, you should refrain from drinking in too obvious a manner. You might have a drink placed on a table behind you and swing around every so often to take a sip; you shouldn't hold a drink in your hand as the guests come by to shake your other hand.

  Guests shouldn't hold a drink, either, as they go through the line. If, however, the line is interminably long, a guest may either leave it, go get a drink, and then come back later into the line, holding his drink. However, by the time he reaches his hosts, he should have dispensed with the glass on a nearby table or on a passing waiter's tray.

When a Large Party Needs an "Introducer"

In the case of a large, official reception, with a cast of hundreds, a company person who is good at names and who is very knowledgeable about the guest list should act as the introducer for the occasion. This man or woman should be stationed at the beginning of the receiving line and be able to introduce the name and title of each guest properly and clearly to the first person standing in line. A host should not have to guess at his guests' names. When guests introduce themselves, often they do a poor job of it—they mumble their names, with the result that the host still doesn't know who they are. An introducer who voices the name and title of the person with a clear enunciation is a tremendous asset for the party and its host.

The introducer should greet each guest with a friendly smile and a handshake and then guide him toward the front of the line (if the guest is not already patiently waiting at the front of the line). The guest should supply (without having to be asked) his name and company name, which the introducer then repeats in a clear, well-enunciated manner to the first person in the receiving line: "Mr. Caldwell, may I present Janet Mc-Kenzie, our media buyer at the Spence Agency?" The introducer then turns to the woman guest: "Ms. McKenzie, this is Mr. Alexander Caldwell, our chairman." Mr. Caldwell and Ms. McKenzie then shake hands while the introducer returns to his station at the receiving line to bring another person forward. Mr. Caldwell, in the meantime, should turn to the person on his right in the line and introduce Ms. McKenzie to that person: "Charlie, this is Janet McKenzie, who does the media buying for our ad agency." Charlie would then shake her hand and give her his full name, followed by some little expression of welcome: "I'm really glad to meet you." Ms. McKenzie then passes on to the next person in line, putting out her hand to shake that person's hand, and this time she gives her own name and company: "Janet McKenzie, the Spence Agency." She gives her name and company name to each person on down the line, and each person in the receiving line in turn gives back his or her name as the handshake is consummated.

It's very flattering to be properly introduced at a corporate function. Perhaps it is so flattering because it happens so seldom!

Menus and Place Cards

Place cards are a necessity for a well-run meal of eight or more guests. Menu cards are a nicety, a wonderful touch that makes the meal and the occasion very special. When there are menus and place cards on the table, made of matching stock and each embossed or printed with the corporate logo at the top, the dinner springs to life as "an important affair."

Menu Cards

- It is nice to have one for each guest, but if you don't have enough, place a menu on the table between every two place settings.
- The menu card may be placed on top of the napkin that is placed on top of the plate, or it may be placed on the left side of the place setting (just to the left of the forks), or it may be placed flat on the table at the top center of each place setting, or it may lean up against the glasses at each place setting.

   In private homes, the host may have his own menu holders, which hold each menu upright. These are made of crystal, sterling silver, mother-of-pearl, or any decorative material. Often they are made with pedestal feet. I have seen them made of seashells, of gold discs (monogrammed with the host's initials), and even miniature houses made of calico.

- A light-colored stock is best. Menu cards thinly bordered in a color that matches the corporate logo at the top center are very handsome.
- 5" × 7" or 4" × 6" or any vertical rectangular size is appropriate.
- Black ink is best to use (easier to read in dim light).
- Menus may be:

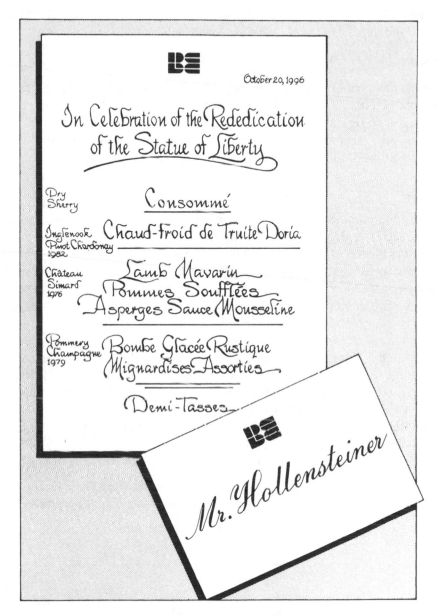

MENU AND PLACE CARD

- ○ Written by hand in calligraphy (one menu is hand-lettered by the calligrapher, and the rest are duplicated from the original by a printer)
- ○ Set in type by the printer and printed, even in calligraphy
- ○ Typed on an office computer (desktop publishing)
- ○ Written by hand (nice handwriting, please)

In the good old days, menus for grand dinners were always engraved. Then again, in the good old days, they didn't have air conditioning.

"Menu-ese"

- List the main courses you are serving. (Don't include rolls and butter, celery tray, chocolate truffles with dessert, and other incidentals. Stick to the simple name of courses to be served.)
- Try to make the food sound romantic: "Green beans with almonds" or "Green beans with fresh dill" sounds a lot better than just "Green beans."

Place Cards

- Usually the corporate logo or the host's initials or the party's decorative theme motif, such as a flag in July or a sprig of holly at Christmas time, is embossed or printed at the top of the place card (as it is on the menu cards).
- Properly speaking, only a person's title and last name are put on the card (as, for example: Mr. Jones, Ambassador Grant, Dr. Smith, Ms. Swanson, etc.). When there are two or more attendees with the same last name, the first names are added (as, for example: Mr. John Macomber, Mr. William Macomber).
- When no one knows anyone else at the function, it is preferable to put all first names on the place cards, to help out those guests like me, who can't remember a person's first name, having heard it only once. If your tablemate's first name is on the place card, you can call that person by his or her first name, thus cracking a lot of ice with a gentle blow.
- A present or former elected official or a person of rank must have his rank or at least "The Honorable" in front of his name.
- It is now permissible to write an official person's place card one of two ways:

Ambassador Lodge	or	The Honorable John Davis Lodge
Governor Harriman	or	The Honorable Averell Harriman

- If you have a long name and title to put on a place card, you can split up the title and name:

Major James *Hennessy-Frankworth*	or	*The Honorable* *Averell Harriman*

The Place Cards May Not Be Changed by Guests

It's unbelievably bad manners, but it's happening with greater frequency at both business and social meals. Certain guests who reach the tables first change the seating to please themselves. In other words, they give themselves "better" seats. This is not only rude, but it's cheating, and this kind of person deserves to be blackballed from any future invitations, no matter how important he or she may be. The host or the host's staff seats the meal to follow the rules of protocol and to please certain very special guests. A guest with his own agenda can ruin the host's intentions.

A SOUVENIR DINNER PROGRAM FOR GUESTS AT AN IMPRESSIVE EVENT

At times a dinner will be given to mark an extremely important event in the corporation's or firm's life, such as introducing the new CEO to the community, bidding goodbye to a retiring CEO, or the marking of the firm's 150th anniversary.

A dinner program is a very nice approach in this case. It becomes a souvenir of a special evening and makes the event more prestigious than it already is. It should be designed and written by the party planner and printed by the same printer who worked on the invitations for this event. The cover should be good quality stock, with perhaps the corporate logo bumped embossed on it. If the event is the retirement of the CEO, a more relaxed kind of program would be appropriate, such as one bearing an informal photograph of the retiring person.

A dinner program should contain:

- The logistics (time, date, place of the dinner)
- The reason for the event, and a written tribute to the person being honored (if it is in honor of someone)
- The program of events, including the names of the clergyman giving the invocation, the master of ceremonies, and any important dignitaries present (such as the Governor or Mayor)
- The names and titles of guests at the head table or on the dais
- Alphabetical listing of the other guests with table numbers
- The menu for the dinner
- A list of the speakers, in the order in which they will appear
- The name of any performers or musical groups, including the compositions played
- A history of the company or any special message it might have (other than a commercial one)
- Some information about the charity, if the event benefits one

A dinner program is a wonderful public relations vehicle. The company should mail a copy to every person who was invited to the event but could not attend. It should be mailed to all of the directors who were not present, and be given a widespread press mailing.

If one person in particular is being honored at this event, it is a nice gesture for the host company to mail a copy of the program to the alumni magazines of the honoree's schools, to be picked up by them for mention in a future issue, and thus spread the good word of the prominence of this alumnus(a).

THE ROLE OF THE COHOST OR SPOUSE
AT A LARGE EVENT

The cohost of a business function may be a peer or a subordinate; for a party that spouses attend, the cohost is the host's spouse. It is very important that every cohost, including spouses, be conversant with the company's operations and be able to discuss the company's business with intelligence and enthusiasm. The cohost is in charge of all of the guests at his or her end of the table. A cohost may also be the host of one entire table, when there is more than one table at the party.

- Just as the most important and the second-most-important guests sit to the right and left of the host, so their spouses sit to the right and left of the cohost. If there are no spouses at the meal, then the third and fourth most important guests on the guest list, regardless of sex, sit to the right and left of the cohost.
- In a business group of men, with only one woman executive present, she would not serve as cohost unless she is of sufficient rank to do so. If another man outranks her in the hierarchy of the company, he would be cohost to the person giving the party, and she would sit in a seat on the side of the table.
- If the company is hosting a lunch for 200 men and women guests, let us say, there might be 20 tables of 10 each. There would therefore have to be a total of 40 in the host and cohost category. You might have every senior member of management and his or her spouse in this category, plus members of the board of directors and outside consultants who know the company well, such as the head of the advertising agency and the senior partner of the company's law firm (*see also* ''Seating at a Large Party,'' elsewhere in this chapter).
- The host or cohost of a table should introduce everyone around to one another, keep the conversation going on upbeat topics and manage to provide the guests with information on the company's activities. He should also help out when anyone needs his assistance—such as an elderly guest who needs help in finding a taxi home, or a guest who has lost his glasses or another one who wants to know how she can get hold of an annual report.

THE IMPORTANCE OF THE MEAL SERVICE

One of a meeting or party planner's most important jobs is to make sure that not only the food but the service is first-class. You have only to say a couple of times to the caterer or banquet manager that your company cares very much how the waiting staff looks and presents themselves, and how they serve the meal to motivate them to do the best job they've ever done. (Be sure to congratulate them afterward with the same enthusiasm with which you exhorted them beforehand.)

I know one meeting planner in charge of all entertaining for her company who gives all the serving help a pep talk before the meal, and when it's over, she gives them a "Well done!" speech. As a result, for her, *they really try* to make it a successful event. She has told them that in her opinion they are the most important key to the entire evening. Her success in motivating them is unquestionable. She makes them proud of the job they are doing.

Some staffs are not well motivated by the meeting planner or supervisor of the restaurant, hotel dining room, or catering establishment. They are barked at to do things fast, to get going at any cost (and when as a result they "get going," soup often ends up on someone's jacket or dress). Some waiters are so pressured that they grab your fork from your hand in their eagerness to clear off a course. That kind of service gives everyone indigestion. It is the duty of the person supervising the party to keep an eye out for negative details such as this and to correct them by speaking to the head waiter.

The appearance of the waiters and waitresses will most definitely affect your guests' impressions of the meal service. The party manager should stress in his or her instructions to them:

- They should come to work bathed and having used a deodorant
- Their hands and fingernails should be very clean
- Uniforms should be spotlessly clean
- The men should be clean-shaven
- Their hair should be neat and clean
- Their shoes should be shined and unscruffy

If you are in a situation (such as using a group of college waiters for a function on their campus) where there are no uniforms available, have the men dress in solid black pants (jeans or any kind of trousers) and white long-sleeve shirts. Give them inexpensive black bow ties to wear. The women should wear solid black skirts of any length, with the same men's white long-sleeve shirts and bow ties. You may have to pay for the shirts as well as the bow ties, but they should invest in their own black pants or skirts (as a business expense for future waiting jobs).

Another important aspect of the service of a meal is the way the food is apportioned onto the plates. There should never be a wasteful amount—too much looks unappetizing. An overly skimpy portion is bad, too—it leaves the guest wondering why his host chose to stint on the food. The party planner should make sure that just the right amount of food is placed on each plate and that it looks attractive, perhaps with something small used to garnish the plate.

Money is saved on the number of waiters needed when the food is served onto plates in the kitchen, and then a plate is put before each guest. However, it is far more gracious, if the waiters are skilled enough, to have them serve each guest from a large platter (always serving from the left, of course). In this case the waiter holds a large serving spoon and fork pincerlike in one hand, while he holds the platter from beneath with the other hand. He lifts each guest's portion of food off the platter and places it neatly, even decoratively with the garnish, onto the guest's warm (or chilled) plate. A typical serving platter might contain something like (per person) two slices of beef, one potato puff, one grilled tomato, a stack of five small asparagus covered with a strip of red pimento, and one large stuffed mushroom.

Sauces should be served separately.

Points to Remember in the Service of a Buffet

- The most important point of all: *Have good, comfortable,* and *ample places to seat your guests.* Never make them eat standing up—a travesty of hospitality! You can always put up various sizes and shapes of tables to handle the crowd (I've seen tables put up for buffet parties in people's homes in hallways, bedrooms, dressing rooms, home offices, gyms, and saunas.)
- Make the serving tables attractive with flowers, fruit, dried flowers and leaves arrangements, or just decorative tureens. The tables should not look as though the food and plates were simply plunked down on them, or your guests will feel they're going through a cafeteria line
- Be sure to have pretty linens—long enough to cover the tables and any ugly table legs
- Have warm dinner plates (not burning hot, of course) for the guests to use.
- Provide extra-large napkins for your guests. Skimpy little ones (like those provided by hotels and caterers) are very unsatisfactory. A buffet meal requires a spacious napkin, because of all the moving around, people accidentally hitting one another, etc.
- Have oil or alcohol burners under the large serving dishes of food that should be kept hot. (Nothing is less appetizing than luke-warm buffet food.)
- Arrange your platters of food in a logical sequence as guests pass along the buffet, i.e., stack of plates first, then the rice perhaps, then the hot beef Burgundy (the sauce of which can be poured over the rice), then the vegetables, salad, and rolls
- To make things easy for your guests, have their napkins and eating utensils already set up at their places at the tables you have supplied.
- Have someone pour wine at the place where each of your guests is sitting. It is too difficult for your guests to balance plates of food, handbags, and wineglasses when going from the serving table to their eating places.
- Plates of dessert should be brought to your guests, if at all possible. It is very disconcerting and ruins conversation if guests have to get up from their seats, walk to a dessert buffet, stand in line, and then return, perhaps balancing three plates in their hands for themselves and others at their table. It breaks the rhythm of gaiety in the room.

ARRANGING A BUFFET TABLE CORRECTLY

A buffet table should be attractively arranged with fruit or flower decorations (and in this case, because it is for a birthday, balloons). Different shapes of serving pieces can add to the decorative appearance. Plates, eating implements, and napkins should be placed together. Drinks and beverages should, if possible, be placed on a separate table to one side.

- There are, of course, many buffets for which there are not enough waiters to serve people properly. People must do all of the serving themselves. This kind of party can still be great fun and very successful. If you are entertaining in your home, for example, you can put the main hot food platters on the dining room console; you can put the salad and rolls on another serving table; you can put the bottles of wine and wineglasses out in the hallway; the dessert service and coffee can be in an entirely different room of the house. All you have to do to make it work is communicate it to your guests. Keep reminding them that ''You'll find the salad over here,'' ''The wine is on the piano,'' ''Your fork and knife are rolled into a napkin; they're laid out on the dining room table.''

The Food You Serve at Your Parties

If you overhear a guest saying, "The food was *great!*" you know you have given a successful party. Food is the great comforter of mankind: the satisfier, the pleaser, the social binder. There's no excuse for not having good food at your business event (which also means you have *enough* food), but there is also no reason to strive for opulence in menus. Imagination and healthy food are what we all should be looking for in food planning.

The presence of imaginative food at your function results from your caring enough to step away from the tired and true (and perhaps boring) menus, and your chef's being capable enough to execute the new ideas. Take a fresh look at your menu plan for the next party. Tell the caterer you don't want any guest present to say, "Oh, I know who your caterer is," based on the fact that the caterer's food is always predictable, recognizable, and tastes the same for every party. If your dinner is in a restaurant, you don't want to overhear any guest saying, "I had this same menu last week."

Maybe you have some strong budget restrictions on what you may spend. That still should not affect the taste and the imagination of your menu. If you're the party planner, always be on watch for new ideas for foods that are not too complicated or expensive to prepare.

When you go to a really great restaurant, listen carefully to the menu recommendations of the maitre d' for ideas that you can pass on to your caterer for corporate events. I asked Alex von Bidder, general manager, and Julian Niccolini, banquet manager, of the legendary Four Seasons restaurant in New York, about some of their most popular dinner menus. Here is one they passed along that might readily be duplicated for an important event:

*Maryland crabcakes with a light mustard sauce
(served with a cold Chardonnay: Grgich Hills 1990)*

---

*Roast rack of lamb with nutted wild rice and green beans
(served with a Cabernet Sauvignon: Chateau Montelena 1987)*

Individual raspberry soufflés with a raspberry sauce

Save clippings from the food pages in newspapers; make a photocopy of a wonderful-sounding menu from a magazine; make notes of a delicious dish you had in a restaurant (which may have been something as simple as broiled chicken with a sprinkling of fresh herbs on the side and a pair of cherry tomatoes stuffed with roquefort cheese). You can pitch some new ideas to your executive dining room chef, or the caterer for the anniversary dinner, or the banquet chef at the hotel where you're giving a reception for 500, or the wonderful cook who comes in to do special business parties in your home. One day when you're perusing a magazine, you might notice on the food pages a recipe for rolled pork loin roast with basil and pistachio stuffing—easy to execute, comparatively inexpensive to make, and very delicious to behold on the platter. Pork is reasonable and not often seen on banquet menus as an entree. (It is not, of course, a dish to be served to observant Jewish people or those of the Moslem faith, to whom pork is forbidden, so you must be sure to instruct the waiters to offer an alternate main course to those who request it.)

In diplomatic life, religious observances that make certain food taboo must be taken into account. Today in our global economy, business hosts must be as sensitive to this subject as our White House and State Department party planners are. If you're unsure about what your international guest may not eat, telephone his embassy in Washington, ask for the ambassador's secretary, and she will tell you whether your menu is appropriate. Of course, one never knows. The State Department gave a large elaborate luncheon in honor of King Hussein of Jordan, with no alcohol served and with no pork products on the menu. The king pushed back his plate and asked the waiter to bring him a "hamburger, please."

You will find menu inspiration everywhere you look. Bookstores provide any kind of menu cookbook you could imagine today. If you are involved in corporate party planning you need a variety of those that most closely relate to your needs for regular reference.

When you leaf through them and find new dishes you wish to include in an upcoming event, make sure that the chef or caterer handling your event tries those dishes well in advance of your function. Put together a small group of people involved with the event whose food taste you trust, and have a sampling session. This will give your chef or caterer a chance to amend or substitute if there are any questions about a dish you plan to serve. Beyond that, your chef or caterer can steer your menu in original directions.

The Caterer's Imagination Is Essential

Caterers today seem to undertake any project anywhere; the phrase "it's impossible to do" is an irresistible challenge to many of them. New York caterer Sean Driscoll of "Glorious Food" for example, has been the power behind so many galas for celebrities, business moguls, and heads of state in glamorous places—everything from socialites' Park Avenue penthouses to the Egyptian Temple of Dendur in the Metropolitan Museum—his firm has become a major influence in how people of money entertain. I think Glorious Food probably outshines anything the royal staff of Louis XV could have produced at Court at Versailles, having staged in one normal day, for example, a breakfast at the jeweler Tiffany's, a luncheon in Central Park for 1,000, a museum exhibition opening dinner for 500, a cocktail party for 600 at an auction house, and several luncheons and dinners for private clients in their homes!

The corporate caterer at times must prove himself or herself to be heroic, such as the time a terrible downpour and cyclonic winds collapsed a big tent in a farm field on top of the guests, tables, and food. The caterer in this instance had his staff check the guests for injuries. Finding none, he and the corporate special events planner herded the soaked, surprised guests into a nearby barn. The catering staff then went into town and returned with amazing speed, armed with blankets, towels, and hot pizzas with cold beer and wine. The band managed to play some lively songs in spite of doused instruments, the pizzas were served to guests on the barn floor, and everyone said later that it was one of the best parties they had ever attended.

What You Serve Today

Although alcohol and food are the two traditional embellishments of entertaining (some might term them the necessities), the unwritten social rules for what, how, and when they are served have changed considerably in the last two decades. Today, because of diets and health preoccupations, menus have changed drastically, with brown grains and greenery having assumed priority over the fats and rich, creamy sauces. There is also much less consumption of hard liquor as the new millenium draws near, and less tolerance for over-indulgence in it.

Lunchtime today in a restaurant is often a completely nonalcoholic occasion, and business people often eat only one course and sometimes do not even take coffee at the end of the meal. This spare kind of business lunch is a far cry from the typical one of a couple of decades ago when the custom was one or two cocktails before lunch, plus a three-course meal, inevitably concluded by one or two cups of coffee. There are three advantages to this trend: It's healthier to eat this way; it's less expensive; and the meal can easily fit into a one-hour time span. (The restaurants are less pleased, of course.)

The Pursuit of Healthy Food in Menu Planning

America increases its health and diet consciousness every decade. A company that ignores this fact will be considered very out of date. There are many ways in which the food the company serves at its entertaining functions can be healthy, no matter where you entertain. For example,

- Always serve sauces on the side, so dieters and abstainers have an option. When a sauce contains alcohol, it should be labeled as such (''Brandy sauce,'' ''Cream sauce with Vodka''), so that anyone who needs to will know immediately not to take any of it.
- Offer your guests margarine as well as butter (put them in separate containers on the table).
- Have brown breads on your menus (rye, pumperknickel, whole wheat, etc.) in

rolls, bread, or breadsticks. Serve *baked* wheat *low-fat* crackers instead of fried buttery ones.
- Put more brown bread and rolls than white in your bread baskets.
- Use low-fat mayonnaise in making salads and sandwiches such as chicken salad, tuna salad, etc.
- Always have containers of low-fat yogurt on your buffets.
- Creamed foods (creamed chicken, Seafood Newburg) are "out" in these anti-cholesterol days.
- Give your guests a choice of a traditional dressing (house, roquefort, or oil vinaigrette) or a low-cal yogurt dressing.
- You can never have too many hot or cold pastas on a buffet. People love them and feel these carbohydrates are healthy for them.
- Keep away from too many fried foods at your parties.
- Soup should be clear, not creamed.
- Use olive oil as a base for your pasta sauce, instead of cream.
- Don't let the chef overcook the vegetables; ask that they be steamed. Don't let him or her smother them in any kind of rich sauce. A very small amount of olive oil and fresh herbs should make them delicious enough.
- Have large dishes of crudités on each table, so that people can fill up on ice-cold raw vegetables. You might have a double dip serving bowl that people pass around with the crudités—one side would contain a creamy dip, but the other, for the virtuous, would be filled with herbs and spices only, a totally noncaloric dip.
- Have all rich sauces (such as gravy or chocolate sauce) passed separately, so that anyone who wishes to can abstain.
- Have the waiters pass two desserts, from which the guests take their pick. One could be a sinfully caloric one, like chocolate mousse; the other a healthy one, such as fresh strawberries without cream. (Usually the guests take some of each, so that they feel half-virtuous, half-diet-negligent.)
- Give your guests a choice of coffee or decaf at the end of a dinner party, also a choice of sugar or artificial sweetener and light cream or milk.

The corporation that serves too many courses makes a social mistake. A light appetizer, an entree with vegetables, and dessert are all that is necessary. Endless individual courses of soup-and-fish-and-sorbet-and-meat-and-salad-and-dessert numb the senses, enlarge the waistline, and dull the enjoyment of the party, as well as drive the bill to astronomical proportions.

Vegetarians and Animal Activists

I consider it very rude for a vegetarian to complain about the presence of meat on the menu when a guest *in someone's home;* I personally feel in such a situation the guest should keep quiet but fill up on the vegetables and salad on the menu.

However, if you are a meeting planner dealing with a commercial facility, you should make it easy to anyone who objects to meat to order a vegetarian meal, or at least a fish dish as a substitute for meat. Instruct the banquet facility to have enough plates of alternate food to the main meat course so that no one will be unhappy. The vegetarian plate or the fish plate should be mentioned by the servers as they begin to offer food. Hotel banquet managers tell me they keep a plentiful supply of prepacked vegetarian and kosher dishes in their freezers which take forty minutes or so to bake, and less to microwave. As long as the banquet manager knows a few hours beforehand how many special meals will be needed for a function, the situation can be handled with ease.

Animal rights activists have been known to raise an enormous fuss over the presence of veal on the menu. As a result, some companies prefer to avoid the issue altogether, and will serve something like grilled or poached salmon as a main course. More companies, however, will take a stand and say that no one activist group is going to dictate to them what they are going to serve their guests.

For meeting planners who believe that everyone has the right to order a meat (or fowl), or optionally, fish, they should find out the numbers of people wanting fish versus meat at least five days beforehand (this is accomplished by having participants return a duplicated form on which they mark their preferences for specific dinners). I saw one large sit-where-you-please dinner where labeled flowers gave the cue as to what was to be served. In this case a yellow rose was placed at the top of the entree plate for fish eaters and a red rose was placed at the top of the plate for meat eaters. When the guests approached the tables, they sat down before the rose of their choice, and the waiters had an easy time of bringing the correct entree to each person. (Meat eaters are usually two to one at a dinner.)

Religious Dietary Laws Should Be Observed

- You never serve a Jewish person, or a Muslim, pork.
- You do not serve a Hindu any meat from the cow family.
- You do not even offer a Muslim food during the forty days of Ramadan fasting, between sunrise and sundown.
- If a Jewish guest tells you several days before your banquet that he wishes a kosher meal, arrange to have it served to him. (The waiter will have his name, and as he starts the service of that table, he will ask the person to identify himself or herself, much as they do on airplanes.)
- Be prepared for Catholics to refuse meat on Fridays during Lent.

Regional Specialties

When your company has an event in a special part of the country, it is nice to have regional specialties on the menu, at least for one dinner. In Atlanta, for example, you might serve a ''Southern dinner'' one night—barbecued baby back beef ribs, corn-bread, or baked ham—and Georgia pecan pie for dessert. (You should explain the history of the Southern dishes being served).

In Colorado, you might have a buffalo-and-venison dinner; in Albuquerque, a hot salsa-based dinner of Mexican specialties.

When You Are Doing a Banquet in Honor of Guests from Another Country

It helps to do some research when giving a dinner with an international flavor in honor of foreign guests. I will never forget the puzzled look at one function on the faces of guests from the People's Republic of China. In their honor, the corporate hosts devised a menu with chop suey as the main course, thinking that this famous Chinese dish would do them honor and alleviate their homesickness. The only problem was that chop suey is unknown in China.

I also remember a night when couscous was the featured specialty, in honor of visiting Moroccan businessmen. The only problem there was that this dish was more than the hotel kitchens could handle. The Moroccan guest of honor, with a very puzzled look on his face, asked his host, ''What is this dish we are eating? A new American specialty perhaps? It's hard to identify what it is, but it's most exotic and interesting!''

The moral of this story is that it is best to serve great American dishes to visitors from other countries at your meeting. You wouldn't serve a platter of hot dogs to Arabs, of course, but you could certainly serve some wonderful fried chicken, sweet potato soufflé, and American corn on the cob as only this country grows it.

More Tips on Menu Planning

- Never go over your budget. (If you see that you are going to, take action, such as substituting chicken for the pricy lamb chops, or apple tart for the luxurious cold fresh raspberry soufflé.)
- Choose what is fresh and in season (asparagus, for example, is relatively inexpensive and in season in the spring, but costly in the winter months).
- Don't load extra items onto the meal, bits of this and that. The price of the meal rises with every addition, whether it's green olives you want in the celery dish or croissants that ''would be nice'' when just hard rolls will do.
- Remember the season. Don't serve a hot, heavy—even though delicious—veal stew on a hot summer day, nor a fresh fruit salad in the northern part of America during January. (By the way, it's best not to serve canned fruit on top of shredded iceberg lettuce at a corporate party, and *most particularly* not when imbedded in a scoop of cottage cheese!)
- Balance your meal. You can almost never have an overabundance of vegetables and fruit, but it is wrong to be heavy-handed with the starches. A dinner starring

pasta and potatoes is not in balance; nor is a dinner of Beef Wellington (beef encased in pastry) with cherry tarts for dessert.

- If you serve fish as the entree, have the waiters ready to suggest to any guest who can't eat fish, "We can bring you a vegetable plate or a roast chicken platter, if you prefer."
- If you're a party planner, don't even try to do menus without consulting something like Julia Child's menu cookbook. The master of the kitchen tells us how to do anything from a VIP Lunch (champagne with black currant liqueur as an aperitif; filets of sole and mushrooms baked in choux pastry; watercress salad with endive and cucumbers; fresh pear sherbet) to an important formal dinner (artichoke scoops garnished with shellfish; roast rack of lamb with buttered new carrots, baked tomatoes stuffed with lamb and eggplant; scalloped potatoes with onions and cheese; fresh strawberries and rolled hazelnut wafers filled with lightly whipped cream).
- It is perfectly all right to use English, French, and Italian dishes or a combination thereof—and if you're serving a Moroccan dish, for example, give the Moroccan name for it. Here's a sample menu, mixing the languages:

Melon and Prosciutto

*

Ragout Touloussain in Vol au Vent

Haricots verts

Tomates Concassées

*

Tiramisù

Demitasses

Sometimes it's very difficult to list the menu completely in English and still have it sound terrific. "Pizza," an Italian word, sounds a lot better somehow than "cheese pie." *Blanquette de veau* as a major dish sounds better to me than "veal smothered in cream sauce." "*Spaghetti alla carbonara*" sounds more delicious than "Spaghetti with bacon, raw eggs, and cheese all mixed together."

- Wines are listed on the lower left bottom of the menu in the order in which they are served. They may also be listed on the left hand side of the menu together with the course each wine accompanies. (If there's only one wine, place it at the bottom left on the menu.)

ARIEL (logo)

June 3, 1998

Lunch

In honor of Marilyn Baum and

her fifty years of service with ARIEL

Iced melon balls with mint

Soave Bertani   *

Grilled lamb chops

Château Laville   Spinach tarts

Bertrou 1993   Tomatoes Provençal

*

Bombe Caramelle

Demitasses

A Completely American Menu Is Fine, Too

Americans have always looked to the White House for menu inspiration, particularly since the menus for all of the important functions are released to the press. Ever since the days of the earliest presidents, Washington and Adams, citizens have been writing the President and his wife for their recipes, too, and attempting to dine in a presidential style in their own homes.

President and Mrs. Clinton's first White House state dinner, on January 31, 1993, in honor of visiting state governors, featured an all-American menu, with two Virginia wines and an Oregon rosé. People all over the country have written to ask how to duplicate the menu of food and wines. They were:

First Course

Smoked marinated shrimp with a horseradish mango chutney sauce, accompanied by my Charlottesville friend Felicia Rogan's ''Oakencroft Virginia Chardonnay.''

Main Course

Roast tenderloin of beef in a port sauce, with a basket of baby vegetables (including Yukon gold potatoes with Vidalia onions).

Salad Course

A winter salad with hazelnut dressing and native goat cheese.

Dessert

Apple Sherbet Terrine with applejack mousse, topped with a hot cider sauce. Cookies were also passed.

An imaginative party planner might very possibly duplicate a famous party menu and include the information on the menu card at each guest's place. It makes the dinner very special.

Sample Menus for Sit-Down Meals
(*See also* "Cocktail Party Food," later in this chapter)

A party planner should keep menu files on separate kinds of parties: breakfasts, cocktail parties, cocktail buffets, lunches, teas, dinners, and evening receptions. When you are present at a party with an excellent menu, write it down. When you hear about one, write it down, and when you read one in a newspaper or magazine, copy it. For example:

Breakfast

Sit-down	*Buffet*
Two fruit juice selections	Two fruit juice selections
Plate with melon slices and wedge of lemon	Bowl of cut-up fresh fruit and pan of baked fruit
Plate of shirred eggs with sausage and bacon	Omelets (made to order, if possible); also, scrambled eggs
Bread basket: freshly-made rye toast, hot croissants, English and bran muffins	Bacon
Mimosas (champagne and orange juice)	Platter of Danish pastry and bran muffins
	Brown rice with herbs and sauteed vegetables

Lunch

Half an avocado stuffed with shrimp
Barbecued butterflied leg of lamb
Spinach in butter
Pineapple sherbet served in hollowed-out
  pineapples
Dentelle Cookies

Individual chicken pot pies
Mixed green salad with feta cheese and oil-
  vinaigrette dressing
Farfalle Pasta Primavera
Baked tomatoes
Orange Bavarian cream
Fresh fruit
Brownies

Dinner

Consommé Madrilène
Roast veal with roast chestnuts purée
Spinach salad with raspberry vinaigrette
  sauce
Tomatoes stuffed with tiny French green
  beans
Cold lemon soufflé, raspberry sauce

Slices of melon, figs, and prosciutto
Chinese lemon chicken
Fish mousse
Snow peas in butter
Herbed rice
Salad of endive, watercress, arugula, and
  roquefort dressing
Boston cream pie
Assortments of sherberts

Serving Coffee

In many American homes, people drink coffee with their meal, or certainly with their dessert. When entertaining, it is more proper to present it after the guests have been served their plates of dessert. In formal entertaining, coffee is served entirely separate from the meal: often away from the table, in another room of the house, in small demitasse cups with small silver spoons. If a guest takes his coffee black, the waiter does not offer him a demitasse spoon (it is only a bother when not in use).

Many restaurants and hotels do not have demitasse cups. It is perfectly all right to have the coffee served in regular-size coffee cups (they're really teacups, if one wants to be technical), with regular teaspoons.

If you're entertaining, after dinner give your guests a choice of:

- Coffee or decaffeinated coffee (served in two separate coffee pots)
- Milk or half-and-half (in separate small pitchers, of course)
- Sugar or artificial sweetener (the sugar in a sugar bowl with a small spoon, or else sugar lumps in a bowl with small tongs; the sweetener is served in its packets in a pretty crystal or silver bowl. Both sugar and artificial sweetener should be served on the same small tray.

Coffee may be served at the table, or in a room separate from the dining area. This allows guests to move around and talk to people they were not sitting next to at dinner. It allows for good, pleasant conversation; one can feel the party temperature rising in a room where people are mixing. (The old diplomatic custom of the men and their lit cigars staying behind at the dining room table when coffee was served, while the women had to retreat with their coffee to a bedroom is, thankfully, passé.)

Liqueurs and Brandy

At a formal dinner, sweet liqueurs and brandy are served last, after the coffee has been given to the guests, although they are offered less frequently these days. Waiters pass around with trays bearing the bottles of liqueurs and brandies, as well as a quantity of the appropriate glasses with which to serve them. Tall glasses of ice water should also be passed at this moment for guests who do not wish liqueurs or cognac.

A PARTY GIVEN FOR THE ARTS

A corporation often has the power to help a local writer, artist, or performer's career in a major sense of honoring that person with some kind of reception.

If a friend of the company or one of its own executives publishes a book, someone in management can give a cocktail party for bookstore owners, press, prominent citizens, and local librarians. If the company is helping a young local artist, it can host a cocktail party preview of that artist's show in the gallery or museum where the work is on display. The company might also put that artist's work on exhibit in its own lobby or somewhere else on the corporate premises.

The company might host a party following a musician's concert in their hometown; guests would be served a glass of wine and meet the performer. Again, the press would be invited (to help the musician but also to help the company image), and the affair would be a social event, a musical event, and a good public relations effort all in one.

A company might mount an exhibition in its offices of the work of the artist who executed the paintings illustrating that year's annual report. The originals of the artwork in the report would, of course, be included with other works by the artist—an excellent public relations idea.

The company's invitation to any such event should relate to the works being honored. For example, for a book party, the book jacket might be used for the invitation. An invitation to a party "in honor of the architects and designers of our new building" might incorporate reproductions of the original drawings or renderings of their work.

A BUSINESS TEA PARTY — WHY NOT?

It's nice to surprise people once in a while. People always remember a party that is different. A change of routine, an altered format, and a different party hour add a pleasant touch of the unusual to a social occasion. A tea party is one such different event. (Europeans, notably the British, have known this for centuries.)

The place where a tea party is held should be warm and attractive. The tea hour conjures up visions of a fireplace, a library, or a view onto a garden. A particularly pretty public room in a hotel or in a restored historic building is also appropriate for a gathering at the tea hour—at three-thirty or four o'clock in the afternoon (and lasting until five or five-thirty at the latest). After this hour, people expect cocktails.

There is something about taking a break in the late afternoon that is healthy and enjoyable. It is a tension reliever; a cup of tea really refreshes the spirit. I have organized corporate tea parties from coast to coast, and each one was a success—because of the novelty of it and because it was a moment of relaxation in the guests' supercharged schedules. After tea, one can return to work, if necessary (whereas it is very difficult to return to work after a function at which alcohol is served).

A tea party need take only an hour (or even forty-five minutes) out of one's schedule. If there are remarks to be made by the business host (such as at a press conference attended by others), the exact time of the remarks should be marked on the invitation (*see also* Chapter 15, "Invitations").

One way of serving tea is to set large silver tea (and coffee) urns on a large table that has been covered with a pretty cloth. Each guest approaches the table, picks up a cup, and is served individually. He serves himself from the food on the platters, and he also picks up his own tea food plate, napkin, spoon, and dessert fork. He then goes to sit down at one of the small cloth-covered tables scattered around, or he wanders around talking to various people, sipping his tea and eating the goodies while standing up.

The second way of serving tea is to have each guest served while seated at a small table. Waiters or waitresses bring each guest tea and pass the food. Each guest has a napkin and flatware awaiting him at his place at the table, as well as a teacup and saucer. There might be a bud vase in the center of each little table, with a blossom or two. A footed compote dish crammed with a variety of cookies and petits fours and perhaps a small dish of chocolates would also be placed on each table.

A tea menu might look something like this:

Tea
Coffee, decaf
Sparkling water
Small crustless bread sandwiches (egg salad, mushroom pâté, cream cheese and
    watercress, etc.)
Warm scones, biscuits, or muffins with butter and different jams and honey

Warm cheese straws
Hot cinnamon toast
Fresh strawberries and cream
Small cups of sherbet
Small cookies and cakes

A tea party should look very special. The silver should be gleaming. The napkins should be linen, not paper. The china should be pretty. The service of tea is a ritual, and the waiters or waitresses should be properly trained in it. An invitation "to have a proper cup of tea," as the English would say, is an intriguing idea to business people.

If just a small group is having tea, and it is at all possible, the tea should be brewed and served from a teapot. Tea bags ruin the romance of the ritual to me. However, a pretty china cup can do wonders for a tea bag! (Furnish a saucer near guests in which they can dispose of used tea bags.)

THE COMPANY'S CHRISTMAS PARTY

The office party has undergone radical changes within the last two decades. Too many corporations have witnessed what overconsumption of alcohol can entail—from embarrassing episodes between supervisor and employee to lawsuits of criminal negligence because of serious automobile accidents involving employees on their way home from the party.

Today's office parties at holiday time are pretty tame—and sometimes nonexistent. Some companies have abandoned the idea altogether. Here is what some companies are doing instead:

- A lunch or breakfast is given at the office (or plant) for employees and their families. Santa Claus or perhaps clowns may appear, to amuse the children. There may be a local high school jazz band playing and a local college's a capella choir to sing Christmas carols. Usually, there is a presentation of gifts collected and donated by the employees that will go to poor or abused children. I remember one very snowy December when the meeting planner who was organizing the corporation's holiday party for employees rented a huge old-fashioned horse-drawn sleigh. He piled it high with the employees' children's gifts for needy children. The driver of the sleigh was dressed like Santa. A van with a sound system that broadcast Christmas carols drove behind the sleigh. Motorcycle police escorted the sleigh and cleared traffic for it, as it made four stops at institutions for children. Christmas really came to that town that day, and what was beautiful was that there was nary a corporate logo, sign, nor company attribution attached to the sleigh as it passed through the snowy streets, to the delight of all passersby.

- If an evening party is held for employees where any kind of alcohol is served, the wise executive arranges for taxis to take people home, or for a designated driver to be in charge of every vehicle.
- Some companies go to a great deal of effort every year to have a Christmas party with funny skits, musical songs, and the showcasing of employee amateur talent. The company pays for the production costs (very minor) and for food and refreshment afterward.
- Some companies ask their employees each year, via a memo which goes through the office mail, to name their preference for:

  · Having the party
  · Receiving a half-day holiday for shopping instead
  · Donating the money that would have been spent on the party to charity

- Some corporations have abandoned the holiday party, because the climate is so bad in their part of the world in December, and the employees prefer to have it in the summer months, outdoors, and with their families in attendance. These picnics often include athletic competitions and games for all ages, as well as the awarding of trophies and prizes.

The Most Important Part of the Annual Employee Party: The Behavior of Host and Guest

It is imperative that members of senior management attend the party, en masse, and stay for a long time. Many top executives are bored by this party, consider it an annual pain in the neck, and their attitude ruins the enjoyment of the people who look up to them and who would welcome the chance to have informal conversations with them. Some senior managers think they are doing their duty by passing by for ten minutes. They are *not*.

The employees, on the other hand, should watch their behavior, too. The annual office party is not the time to hit hard on one's agenda while talking to a senior manager. It's not a time to "kiss up to" an executive, hoping to make a favorable impression, and it is certainly not a time for an employee to drink too much and then, with loosened inhibitions, strike forth with overly frank opinions or out-of-control behavior.

HAVING ENTERTAINMENT WHEN YOU ENTERTAIN

It makes for a warm, wonderful party if you have entertainment—and if the company budget will allow it.

"Good entertainment" means something appropriate for a particular group on a particular occasion.

When Not to Schedule Entertainment

· When you can't afford it
· When you can afford only unheard of amateurs
· When a friend or relative has volunteered to perform at the last moment
· When you have a small group, such as a dinner for eight, and it would interrupt the flow of good conversation

When to Schedule Entertainment

· When you can afford the price stated by the performer or his or her agent (you accept that fee and you do not haggle over it; otherwise you get someone else whose fee you know will be less)
· When you're worried about your dinner being very dull
· When you have a particularly long social event, with many people in attendance. For example, you might wish to book:

  ○ A jazz combo at the cocktail hour (not too loud, so that people can hear themselves talk)
  ○ Very soft music played in the background at dinner (to permit good, uninterrupted conversation)
  ○ A celebrity master-of-ceremonies for the dinner speeches and program, if appropriate
  ○ An orchestra for dance music after dinner
  ○ A solo performer to entertain guests after dinner

Retain an Entertainment Consultant for a Large Event

Find your entertainment consultant by word of mouth, recommended by other meeting planners and special events coordinators who have used that performer and found him or her absolutely necessary to the success of the event. This kind of person is up on all the fresh new faces in the entertainment world. He knows how to negotiate and when not to. He knows which stars are great to work with and very professional, and he'll tell you which ones aren't. He knows which famous comedians use tasteless material when they're away from the television cameras, and he knows how to scout your city's colleges and universities for musical talent in the music department.

An entertainment consultant can find bagpipers in kilts for an exhibition unveiling, clowns for the employees' Christmas party, a roller-skating troupe to perform in the parking lot for a remodeled factory opening or a Viennese waltz orchestra for a party celebrating the signing of a joint venture with an Austrian conglomerate.

When booking entertainers and musical groups yourself, refer to "Music and Entertainers," earlier in this chapter.

Things to Remember

- Keep the sound system down when musicians are performing but people are primarily talking, not dancing.
- Try to have variety in your background music if you have a long event planned—not just classical, but not just jazz or pop either.
- Never schedule any program after dinner that lasts longer than thirty minutes (if there are going to be speeches, hold them to ten minutes, so that the total time span of attention guests will have to maintain is forty minutes after dessert).
- Give your local artists, musicians, actors, and performers a break. Try them out, look at what they do, and use them, if you can, to build up the local talent.
- Try always to schedule a rehearsal for them (even if you have to pay extra for it), so they will be able to study the acoustics of the room, the lighting, etc.
- Make them confortable. Give them a room in which to dress, relax, and get ready. Feed them. Treat them with consideration. Pay them promptly. (Many of them are very hard-pressed financially.)
- Introduce them properly and enthusiastically before they perform, so that the guests know their names and have heard an enthusiastic introduction.

Be Tough with Your After-Dinner Speakers

Next to not having the caterer show up, the quickest way to ruin your beautiful dinner is to have too many speakers who talk too long.

Up to the moment the speeches begin, the guests have been having a wonderful time eating, drinking, making new friends, listening to the background music perhaps, laughing over a dinner partner's jokes, arguing over a beloved cause, and gossiping over the latest juicy scandals. Then come the speeches. Suddenly the balloon deflates, punctured in the second it takes for the introducer to say, "Ladies and gentlemen, . . ." One can hear the sound of the deflation as the evening descends to a lower threshhold and the space suddenly quiets. People shift positions in their chairs, the room temperature takes a nosedive, and the guests begin worrying about their transportation home, the weather conditions outside, the long wait at the coat-check place, the babysitter's departure schedule, or the vicissitudes of tomorrow's work schedule.

This is why the party manager should have a talk with the CEO to discuss various speaking disasters that have befallen *other companies' parties.* This is why the party manager should ask the CEO's (or whoever is hosting the party) permission to dictate the rules to the speakers and the master of ceremonies (never to the CEO, however).

The Role of the Master of Ceremonies

A master of ceremonies is necessary if the event includes a program of speakers as well as entertainment. Someone has to introduce the stars of the event, make statements that might seem too self-serving for the host to make, and keep things moving along in a lively manner for performers and audience alike. It is an honor to be asked to be the master of ceremonies at a function. It means that you have a sense of humor, know how to project your voice, and can handle audiences. It means that you have the gift of being able to "think fast on your feet," so that you react quickly in an emergency. (An "emergency" arises when the lead entertaining act has not arrived, when the main speaker falls ill and has to be taken home, or when the air-conditioning ceases to function and the microphones don't work!)

The master of ceremonies (who may be male or female) should be a fairly high-ranking executive or a person of distinction—and someone who knows enough to hold his alcohol consumption to a minimum on the day and evening of the event. The M.C.'s role includes the following:

- He introduces himself to the audience, even if he thinks everyone knows who he is. He reminds the audience why they are present on this occasion.
- He makes brief introductions. Since he has requested good biographical information on everyone in advance, his well-prepared introductions sparkle with clarity and wit.
- He puts the audience at ease. He handles everything with a light touch. Even a subject like cancer research does not have to be treated in a funereal manner. A good M.C. can always find a way to make people smile every so often and to keep their attention drawn to the podium. Also, the guest speaker usually makes a much better speech if he has been relaxed by an amusing, flattering introduction given by the M.C.
- He acts as timekeeper for the speaker(s). If the speaker has had too much to drink, the M.C. might have to cajole him to leave the podium, rather than have the audience continue to suffer through an embarrassing presentation.
- He fills in inadvertent brief gaps in the program. The M.C. should know how to ad-lib when stalling for time. For example, I remember a lunch when the M.C. announced a special performance, but when the drums rolled, the performers failed to appear. The M.C. quieted the audience's laughter and asked them to get out pencils and paper. Then he proceeded to give them his grandmother's "Spaghetti alla Carbonara" recipe, which he knew by heart. Three minutes later, before he was finished, the act signaled from the wings that they were now ready to go on stage. "Well, they're ready now," he said to the laughing audience. "Do you want the rest of the recipe first?" The audience, by now in a really good mood, roared back, "Yes, yes!" so he finished the recipe. None of us will ever forget that M.C.

- The perfect M.C. makes the audience feel they have profited from attending the function, and that they have also had a good time.

Advice to the Master of Ceremonies

- Be funny.
- No dirty jokes
- No poking fun at anyone present unless you know for certain that person can take it
- Introduce the speaker properly and distinctly, and get his or her name right (the wrong or improperly pronounced name of the speaker is a common mistake in introductions).
- Keep each speaker to his time limit, which is accomplished by:
  - Nudging him
  - Handing him a note on the lectern
  - Ringing the school bell in front of you, as previously threatened, so he knows he's already well past his limit

The Party Manager Makes a Few "Speakers' Rules"

He or she will:

- Hold after-dinner speakers who precede a twenty- or thirty-minute entertainment to a total of ten minutes of speech-making
- Schedule a distinguished solo speaker (when there is no additional entertainment) to twenty minutes (she'll take thirty)
- Schedule two speakers (when there is no entertainment) to ten minutes each (they'll each take fifteen)
- Follow a really terrible speaker, such as a CEO who has a poor delivery, but who loves speaking anyway (which is something to be lived with, alas) by someone who will make some light remarks—even a humorous or comic kind of speaker—so that the evening will end on an upnote

Give Your Speakers Good Logistical Support

- Don't have giant spotlights focused directly at a speaker's eyes. Have the lighting technician shift them away.
- Give him a choice of how he wants the house lights handled, up or down. (Some speakers want the house lights on in order to see their audience's faces; others do not.)

- Have a glass of fresh water (already poured, please) right within his grasp.
- Have a strong lectern, so that he can lean on it, and it won't wobble every time he does.
- If he has to climb up onto a high podium, give him a little stairway, so he can mount it gracefully. (That's not just nice, it's necessary for anyone with knee problems.)
- Check the sound system in all parts of the room more than once. Nothing is more aggravating to a speaker than to have members of the audience unable to hear.

If your guests know there will be a *short* speaking period, they will be truly attentive and quiet. They will also enjoy it more.

When You Have a Celebrity

When a very well-known celebrity is involved in a company function, you must be prepared for problems of security, over-zealous fans, and overly enthusiastic corporate peers who want to meet and chat with him or her. A star deserves to be treated with consideration, and given peace and quiet in a comfortable spot somewhere before performing. Here are some ways to help:

- Don't ask him to sign autographs for everyone, unless he expressly says he enjoys doing it. Many stars will simply not do it, on the basis of "if you sign an autograph for one, you have to do it for everyone, and I'll never get out of here." Also, autograph seekers are notoriously selfish about a celebrity's time, seeking not only the autograph but wanting to ask questions, bring home quotes, etc.
- Don't talk to him or allow anyone else to disturb him before he performs.
- When he has finished performing and tries to eat some dinner, protect him; let him eat. Then he can speak to his fans.
- Arrange for the photographers to have a session just for them. And after they get their photos, they should leave.
- If you make life comfortable for your celebrity performer, he will remember you and the company fondly, and he will come again.

WHEN SERVING OR CONSUMING ALCOHOL
(*See also* "The Corporate Cocktail Party," later in this chapter)

To Drink or Not to Drink

Job applicants who are invited to have lunch by their interviewers are constantly being advised by job counselors and friends not to drink at this meal, even when offered a cocktail or a glass of wine. However, when the host and everyone else at the table is drinking wine, my opinion is that the job applicant should feel free to have a glass, too, if he wants it, based on the theory that:

· The others at the table are taking it.
· He will take only one glass and not even momentarily consider a second one.
· He will not critique the wine or carry on about what an expert he is.

Young executives have always been urged to watch their drinking on the job in the presence of senior management and to look the other way, or to protect, those same senior managers when *they* over-indulge. Today, because of health and dieting, most people are drinking far less. Twenty-five years ago, if you asked for something non-alcoholic at a party, you were considered a wimp. It was a negative. Today, the presence of a nondrinker is normal, not a phenomenon. The days are gone when the host would argue with a guest, "Oh, but you *must* have a drink."

For those executives who are against serving alcohol on religious grounds, the best way to entertain is at breakfast, lunch, or tea, where guests really don't expect alcohol. Today it is perfectly appropriate to offer only fruit juices and sparkling water to guests at a business lunch before they sit down to the meal.

A host who does not drink but who does not object to alcohol on religious grounds should offer guests wine or a cocktail before the meal, and wine with the meal.

Although it is against the Muslim religion to consume alcohol, Arab and Muslim diplomats and businessmen will occasionally take a cocktail or wine in this country. Rather than not offer them liquor when you have offered it to your other guests, ask them quietly if they would prefer an alcoholic or a soft drink. On the few occasions that the answer is yes, serve it quietly, without making an issue of it.

In general, when Middle Easterners and Arabs will be present, always have more than one offering of fruit juice and soda on the tray of drinks being passed to guests.

Keep in Mind the Corporate Responsibility in Serving Alcohol

Today corporations that serve too much liquor for too long a time may be held responsible for allowing their staff and guests to over-indulge. "Getting smashed" is no longer the proof of a good party. Companies may be sued when their drunken guests cause driving accidents after leaving their parties, and party planners must be aware of this. The core of cautious planning for a company concerned about alcohol abuse is:

· Short cocktail parties (one and a half hours maximum)
· Short cocktail hours before meals (no longer than a half-hour)
· Slow refilling of wine glasses during the meal. (Waiters can be instructed not to fill anyone's glass more than once, and to serve a modest amount each time.)
· The removal of the car keys of any guest who has over-indulged (that guest may have arrived already inebriated, but the company could still be held responsible for an accident caused after leaving your event).

A guest who has over-indulged should be sent home by taxi or driven home by one of the staff people present. His car keys should be dropped off at his home or office then or later. I will never forget the woman host who herself delivered her drunken guest's keys to his apartment the next day. Because he was still trying to sleep it off when she came, she left the envelope with the keys on his bedside table. Included in the envelope was the name and telephone number of a friend of hers at the local Alcoholics Anonymous chapter. A couple of days later, he hit rock bottom and called the number that had been inserted in the envelope. He now claims that his dinner hostess helped save his life.

If you have to entertain an important customer or client with a drinking problem, keep your corporate responsibility in mind. You may know of a terrific new restaurant that doesn't even have its liquor license yet, and you can conveniently "forget" to have brought along the customary bottle of wine. Or take him to lunch in a place famous for its fast service, and plead a tight schedule, so that he does not order two or three drinks. Escort him around a private showing of a corporate exhibit and talk some business then. Meet him at 3:30 in the afternoon at a hotel that boasts of an attractive salon for serving tea. Play tennis or golf with him, but let him know that right after the game, you have another business appointment. This allows you, after showering and dressing, to take him safely back to his office or home. There are many ways, if you show a little ingenuity, in which you can see and entertain your alcoholic client, customer, or friend in a situation where drinking does not occur.

Helping Control Costs When You Serve Alcohol

The considerable expense of serving liquor can be kept to a minimum if the party planner is both careful and thorough. He or she should instruct the bartender "to control his free hand" while pouring from the bottles. There are about twenty-two drinks in a litre bottle of liquor. Bartenders should be requested to pour all drinks with a 1½-ounce jigger so that they will neither exaggerate the amount of liquor in each glass nor cheat on the amount.

Make sure the head bartender knows the exact hour at which the bar is to be shut off at the conclusion of your party; otherwise stragglers will keep running up your party cost, both for liquor and for overtime for the bartender.

If you're having a dinner party in a hotel, allocate from forty-five minutes to an hour for the cocktail hour before taking your guests in to dinner. The restaurant, hotel, or club management should be given firm orders before the event in order to hold to your schedule.

The most economical way to work with a hotel is to keep count of the bottles actually used and to pay by the bottle. Return the unopened bottles to the hotel's inventory. Bringing in your own liquor does not help keep costs down, since the hotel will charge you an expensive corkage fee for handling the glasses, providing the ice, mixers, and water, and for opening the bottle.

The *unlimited consumption plan* is one way of paying for the alcohol consumed in a large facility. With this system a corporate host pays a flat fee per guest, no matter how much or how little that guest consumes. For example, if the drinks cost $5 and you are figuring three per guest, you would pay a fee of $15 per guest, whether that guest has one drink or five.

If you are paying by the drink, it is impossible to guess what your budget will be without inquiring and negotiating. The price per cocktail can be anywhere from $4 to $8 (with an average of $6 in a first-class facility). The price of a drink depends upon where you are (an expensive city or a less costly small town) and what kind of liquor you serve (top quality or a lesser quality), plus the negotiating that may have occurred between the meeting planner and the banquet manager.

It is always a good idea to order more liquor than you think you need, because it's really embarrassing to run out of anything, whether it's vodka or white wine. I personally feel that it is better to invite fewer guests and to serve top quality brands than to try to economize by serving cheap liquor, which "makes *brutta figura*" ("presents an ugly face," as the Italians say) on behalf of the company.

The Cash Bar

One sees it everywhere today: the cash bar. It's logical that when the company treats them to dinner, managers pay for their own drinks in the evening after a sales conference or training seminar. It's logical when the chairman of a company-sponsored fund-raising benefit requests that guests use a cash bar before dinner. (This becomes necessary when the charity badly needs to make money off the dinner, and not lose all of the corporate donation by paying for over-indulging guests at the bar.)

A cash bar when a company invites guests to a social function, on or off its premises, is, in my opinion, chintzy. To have to pay for one's drink before a meal (whether it be a martini or a diet soda) completely ruins the atmosphere of gracious hospitality. However, since cash bars are even cropping up at weddings these days, perhaps it will take a stronger hold of us eventually.

The Service of Wine

The wine purist who drinks only a certain kind of wine with a certain kind of food (and only the best labels, at that) is no longer of much relevance in our business world.

We are drinking less and are much more pliable about wine etiquette than our grandfathers were. In the old days people rigidly drank white wine with fish and red wine with beef and fowl. Now there are so many exceptions to the rule that the rules seem to be disappearing. (Some people find white wine too acidic and therefore drink only red; others like the taste of white wine much more than red, and so stick to white throughout the meal.)

The Decanter: When You Give a Business Dinner at Home

In the old days you would sometimes put an inferior wine into an elegant decanter set upon the table, so that guests could not see the original bottle's label, but the main reasons for using decanters are twofold: they are very handsome adornments to the table, and it is easy for cohosts to serve their guests sitting near their respective ends of the table. A guest who would like to refill his own glass would ask the host, "Do you mind?" (The host is never supposed to mind!)

We are now told that the lead in an antique European crystal decanter may have a harmful chemical interaction with the wine kept in it for a long time. Therefore, if you are using antique crystal decanters on your dinner table, it is wise to store wine in them only for a day.

The best way to use a pair of decanters is to put one filled with red wine (at room temperature) at one end of the table, and a decanter filled white (chilled) at the other. Provide coasters for the wine bottles, so that any spillage won't harm the table linens.

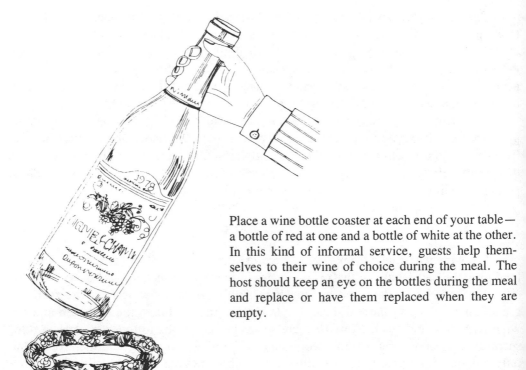

Place a wine bottle coaster at each end of your table—a bottle of red at one and a bottle of white at the other. In this kind of informal service, guests help themselves to their wine of choice during the meal. The host should keep an eye on the bottles during the meal and replace or have them replaced when they are empty.

When a Waiter or Waitress Serves the Wine

In restaurants today, and at parties at home, the waiter often passes around the table with a bottle of red and one of white in each hand, serving each guest his choice. Some guests stay with one wine through the entire meal. Others prefer to start with white, and to continue with red when the main course is served. Note: *A red wine should never be served in a glass which has just been used to drink white wine, and vice versa.* (In other words, a different wine means a different glass.)

Wine is poured into the guests' glasses immediately after the first course is served. (Sometimes, when an extraordinarily good wine is to be served, the host will save it and have it poured only with the entree—and sparingly, at that.) That kind of delay usually signals that this bottle is a very good one and should be given homage.

Serving from the guest's right, the waiter serves first the guest of honor on the host's (or hostess') right, and then continues on around the table counterclockwise. The last glass he pours is therefore the host's (or hostess').

He fills the white wineglass ⅔ full, the red wineglass ½ full. (The champagne glass is filled about ¾ full, with the bubbles rising to the top of the glass.)

The Wines at a Formal Dinner

Traditionally, at a grand dinner, the wine service proceeds as follows:

- Sherry is poured into a very small stemmed glass with the first course—to accompany a consommé, for example, or a cream of shrimp soup.
- White wine is served next in the smaller of the two wineglasses—to accompany the fish course.
- Red wine is served next in the largest of the wineglasses—to accompany meat or fowl.
- Red wine continues to be served during a salad and cheese course.
- Champagne is served in a fluted or tulip-shaped goblet at the beginning of the dessert course.

The Wines at an Informal Dinner

The host may serve:

- One red wine throughout the meal (the bottle should be opened ''to breathe'' at least thirty minutes before serving)
- One white wine throughout the meal (it should be well chilled, and kept cold by the waiter or host or hostess in an ice bucket or thermos winebottle holder)
- A white wine with the appetizer and a red wine with the main course
- A chilled sparkling rosé or a white sparkling wine throughout the meal
- In addition to the red or white wine, a chilled sweet dessert wine (like Sauterne) in white wineglasses

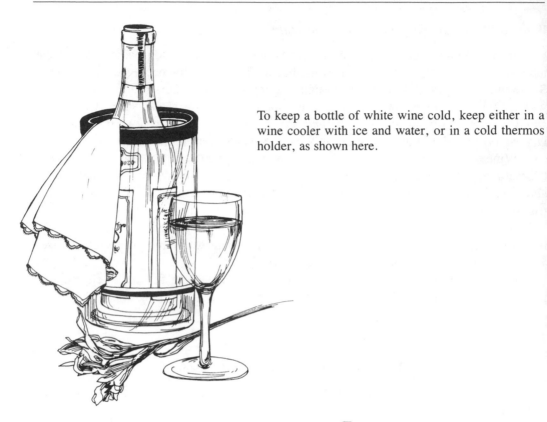

To keep a bottle of white wine cold, keep either in a wine cooler with ice and water, or in a cold thermos holder, as shown here.

At the end of a formal meal in your home, after the demitasses have been served, bring in (or have your server bring in) your prettiest tray set with bottles and decanters of port and liqueurs, plus small liqueur glasses and brandy snifters.

- In a celebratory mood, the queen of sparkling wines—champagne—either throughout the meal or with dessert

After-Dinner Drinks

- Sweet sherry in a small wineglass, or port or Madeira in a white wineglass may be served at the table after dessert has been consumed. They are sipped at room temperature.
- Sweet liqueurs such as Cointreau, Benedictine, Irish Cream, etc., are served in small stemmed glasses at room temperature. Crème de Menthe is served over shaved ice.
- Cognac, Armagnac, Grappa (Italian brandy) and Eaux-de-Vies (clear brandies made from distilled fruits) are served in brandy snifters. The guest holds the snifter by the bowl, thereby warming its contents, and swirls the brandy around a bit in the glass. Then he quietly inhales the aroma, hopefully with pleasure.

If You're Ordering Wine for Your Guests in a Restaurant

- Never go over your budget when ordering wine. Look at the price of what the wine steward or waiter may be recommending, and remember, you will probably be ordering more than one bottle, if you have more than one guest.
- If you're at lunch or dining in a modest restaurant, never be embarrassed to order house wine.
- Order the wine only after your guests have finished ordering their meal. If everyone has ordered meat, you are probably safe on ordering a bottle of red. If one of your guests has ordered fish and two have ordered meat, you might order a half-bottle of white and a bottle of red.
- Never be embarrassed to order separate glasses of wine (even house wine) if your guests are ordering different things and you know they're not big wine drinkers. If you're having poached salmon as your main course, for example, and your three guests are ordering meat or fowl entrees, order a glass of white wine for yourself and a bottle of red for your guests.

Tasting the Wine in a Fine Restaurant

The wine steward (the *sommelier*, or, as is sometimes the case, the maitre d'hotel or the captain):

- Brings the host the wine list
- Makes suggestions on what to order
- Takes the order
- When the bottle arrives, opens the wine, shows the host the bottle's label, and then hands him the cork.

- The host then pinches the cork to assure himself that it is not all dried out or wet and soggy (either condition is unfavorable to the condition of the wine in that bottle).
- The host next sniffs the cork, to make sure that it does not bear the aroma of wine gone bad (vinegary, in other words).
- The host returns the cork to the wine steward or lays it down on the table and gives his nod of approval.
- The wine steward now pours a small quantity of red wine into the glass of the host, who then sniffs the aroma, sips a bit, and nods his approval. If he is a wine expert, he swirls a bit around in his mouth in a quiet way (not like a morning gargle!) before swallowing it and giving his approval to the wine server. (This much attention is not given to a white wine, only to a red.)
- The wine is now served, first into the guests' glasses, and last, into the host's glass, to add to the small quantity of wine already there for tasting.
- On a rare occasion when the wine has indeed ''gone bad'' or ''turned,'' the host, having tasted it (and probably winced) should speak quietly to the wine server, who will then taste it himself. If it has indeed gone bad, another bottle will be brought at once to the table. (A good wine is very expensive, and no good restaurant wants to risk its reputation by serving an inferior wine at a superior price.) If the wine steward or maitre d'hotel thinks the bad taste is only in the host's imagination, a quiet respectful disagreement may ensue over the status of the wine.

I remember so well one night at a very expensive restaurant, when our young host, who didn't know what he was talking about, complained loudly about a very expensive wine he had ordered for us. (As we proceeded with the meal, more bottles of this vintage would be produced for his guests, and we were really looking forward to this wine.) The wine steward tasted it, pronounced it very fine indeed, but the host persisted in saying it had turned, and then loudly insisted his guests be served a bit of the wine, so we could taste the calamity for ourselves. Unfortunately, the wine tasted ''very fine'' to all five of his guests, who reluctantly sided with the wine steward. This situation was a very sticky wicket, but we simply could not back up our host. I doubt if our host will ever forgive us. Actually, we were embarrassed to have been put in that situation. It would have been preferable for him to battle it out privately with the wine steward, and not involve his guests at all.

At a dinner in his own home, the host does not first taste the wine and nod approval to the waiter, as he does in a restaurant. The wine to be served at home should be opened in the kitchen, tasted, approved of, and allowed to breathe at least thirty minutes before serving it.

The Proper Wineglass

The best kind of wineglass is a slender, thin-stemmed goblet, with a bowl wider than the rim of the glass, to allow the maximum aroma to waft up to the nostrils.

Very popular today is the all-purpose wineglass—neither large nor small—and suitable for red or white or a sparkling wine.

If you are going to own separate red and white wineglasses, they will be of two different sizes, often of the same pattern, but not necessarily so. (I, for example, use on my table a tall, round-bowl stemmed red wineglass with an antique, elaborately cut crystal white wineglass.)

If you're going to have several glasses at each place setting, make a grouping of them above the knife and spoon of your place setting. They do not have to be in a straight row. If you are using a sherry glass, place it on the outside right, but if not, put your white wineglass on the outside right, then the red wineglass to its left in the middle center, and the water glass would go at the upper left. The champagne glass, if

The table setup for an elaborate dinner of soup, fish, veal, and a chocolate ice-cream praline bombe for dessert. The white wineglass is correctly lined up on the far right, then the red, then the water glass, and last, but certainly not least, the champagne goblet at the rear. The dessert fork and spoon are placed horizontally above the plate.

there is one, would be placed to the rear of the grouping, like a graceful guard watching over the other glasses.

Serving Beer

More and more young people today are drinking beer with meals in fine restaurants, sometimes as a substitute for wine. Often, they drink beer and nothing else at discos and parties.

In order to accommodate this trend, if you entertain a great deal at home, you should have attractive glasses in which to serve the beer. Pilsner glasses, handsome steins (not the kind with commercial logos on them), and even oversized red wine goblets are suitable serving containers for beer. It looks tacky to serve it in plain tumblers, as you would water or soda.

When you're pouring beer into glasses in the kitchen, prior to serving them to your guests, pour it from the can or bottle into a tilted glass or stein, so the foam (or "head") is just right.

Beer Etiquette

- Do not put cans of bottles on the table at your lunches or dinners. Always serve beer in a tall glass (big enough to hold the entire serving of beer from its original container, and I'm not referring to a keg!). If you get into the habit of pouring beer into a glass when you're home alone, you'll automatically find a suitable glass in which to drink it whether you're a host or someone else's guest.
- Beer is served with hearty or simple food. It should not be ordered in a fine restaurant with a delicate fish, for example, or selected to accompany a rich gourmet dessert like *crème brûlée*. It goes well with corned beef, sandwiches, hamburgers, pizzas, Tex-Mex food, oriental food, as well as picnic and barbecue parties. If you're out for lunch with an executive and he orders a cocktail or wine before or during the meal, it is perfectly all right for you to say, "I would prefer a beer, please."
- It is pretentious to launch into a beer selection test with the waiter, as though you were querying him on his finest wine suggestions "from the cave" (pronounced k-aahv"). You may be an expert on the provenance of all foreign and domestic brews, but keep it to yourself when you are with others in a fine restaurant.
- Do not wander around a cocktail party clutching a beer bottle or can. Hold a glass instead, please!
- If you wish to serve beer and not wine at your business lunch, it is perfectly all right to do so, provided the menu is informal, the proper glasses are available, and the waiter is prepared to bring any guest who asks an alternative beverage, such as wine, iced tea, or coffee. In fact, if you have beer glasses on the table at your meal, you should say to your guests, "If anyone prefers something other than beer, just speak up. You can have whatever you like."

Entertaining a Recovering Alcoholic

Care should be taken in selecting the menu of recipes when a recovering alcoholic will be among your guests. Wines and liqueurs that burn off in the cooking process are harmless; wines and liqueurs poured at random over food might seriously upset the rehabilitation of the recovering alcoholic.

Examples of harmful things to do are pouring Kirsch over fresh raspberries or dousing a Crème Brûlée dessert with brandy. The correct way to handle the serving of a sauce containing alcohol is to pass it separately and to make sure that everyone knows it has alcohol in it. Don't pour vodka over fruit sherbert, for example. Pass the vodka separately in a small sauce pitcher and tell your guests what it is. The recovering alcoholic will not touch it. If it's already been splashed over his dessert, he might innocently consume it (which could result in a terrible setback in his fight against alcoholism).

When an associate returns from long difficult weeks spent in a recovering alcoholics program, he or she does not want to be treated differently from anyone else, nor made to feel conspicuous. However, when a recovering alcoholic wants to talk about his problem on a one-to-one basis, it's the time to listen with full attention. (A party is usually not the place for such a conversation.)

Too many times a host will greet a recovering alcoholic at the door of his or her home during a party and say something thoughtless like this: "You're not allowed to drink now, are you? What kind of soda do you want?"

The conversation should go like this instead: "What would you like to drink?" When you bring the soda or fruit juice or whatever it is (sometimes coffee) to this guest, it should be served in one of your prettiest glasses.

If an alcoholic says at your party, "I'd like a gin and tonic," give it to him without comment. It is, after all, the alcoholic's personal business to indicate what he or she wants.

The place setting of a recovering alcoholic guest should be the same as everyone else's at the table, including wineglasses. Do not turn his wineglass upside down (nor should any guest, for that matter, turn his own glass upside down when he comes to the table). When the wine is being poured, the universal sign of not wanting any served is to put the fingertips on the rim of the glass, a gesture that signifies either "None, thank you" or "No more, thank you." A recovering alcoholic may also allow his glass to be filled with wine and then not touch it through the entire meal (a true show of the strength of his willpower).

When toasting time occurs at a dinner party, the recovering alcoholic will take his water glass and toast along with the others or, if he's superstitious about toasting with water, as some people are, he might raise his arm in a gesture of holding a glass, a kind of salute.

One of the best toasts I ever heard was made by a recovering alcoholic at a dinner honoring the retiring chairman of the board of his company. He gave a brilliant four-minute speech that had everyone on their feet laughing and crying at the same time. No one noticed he was holding only a glass of water in his hand. That was irrelevant.

WHEN YOU ENTERTAIN OR ARE ENTERTAINED IN A RESTAURANT

Showing Courtesy Toward the Restaurant Owner

- *Never change your mind about going to a restaurant where you have made reservations without calling to let them know.* After all, they have held your table and turned away other paying customers on your behalf. When you don't show, they lose money. If you hope to be a regular customer this is the quickest way to lose your welcome. Always call to warn them you will not be able to make it, so they can give the table to other diners.
- *Be on time for your reservation.* Many popular places have two sittings, and they count on you being on time. If you show up at 8:30 for a 6:45 reservation, you deserve to be turned away; you will have cost the restaurant money by removing the possibility of two seatings at your table that night.
- *If the number of people in your party changes from the time you made the reservation, call to advise them of the new number.* The restaurant must move tables and chairs around to accommodate you, and this takes time. They need this information as soon as possible.

Restaurant Manners for the Host

- *On the morning of your lunch, make two telephone calls:*
  - To reconfirm your reservation with the restaurant
  - To reconfirm with your guest (who may not have recorded the proper information in his or her agenda)
- *Always arrive at the restaurant before your guests.* It's lonely and embarrassing for your guest to arrive punctually and be obliged to stand forlornly in a crowded restaurant foyer, wondering where you are and if he or she should wait outside, check a coat, go to the table, etc.
- *Make it clear, before you meet, that you are paying the bill.* As soon as you have issued the invitation and received an affirmative reply, take charge. Settle the time, place, and date. The entire warm mood of the occasion is ruined when people argue over the bill and grapple for it at the end of the meal in this manner:
  > "It's *my* lunch."
  > "No, it's *mine!*"
  > "I wanted to take *you* to lunch."
  > "No, I absolutely *insist*. It's *my* turn."

And on and on. If the invitation were properly communicated in the first place, the disagreement would never have had to take place.

- *If possible, invite your guest a week ahead*, so she or he won't consider themselves an unimportant person or a last-minute substitute for someone who had previously accepted.
- *If you are taking someone to a place with a strict dress code, communicate it before the date*, so your guest won't show up in embarrassingly inappropriate clothing.
- *If you have a serious time problem, inform your guest of this fact the minute you sit down.* Don't just fret over it silently; it will destroy your concentration. Your guest will help you get things going faster if he or she knows the pressure you're under.
- *Always give your guests the best seats at your table.* If there are two armchairs and two armless chairs, you and your company colleague (or your spouse) should take the armless ones. Let your guests sit facing the crowd of diners. It's all right for you to face a blank wall or a swinging door from the kitchen, but it's not all right for your guests. Give them the banquette seats against the walls, while you sit opposite. If you and your spouse invite another couple to dinner, seat the husband and wife on the banquette (not the two women side by side), while you and your spouse sit facing them, the wife host opposite the male guest and the husband host opposite the female guest.
- *An especially heavy or disabled guest should have an outside seat*, not a banquette, from which it is difficult to enter and exit.
- *Have your guest order first, and help her if she seems ill at ease with a foreign menu.* Show her the specialties, and point out the dishes you have sampled that were really delicious. If you're on a tight budget, recommend a couple of the lesser-priced dishes. She will catch on, without your having to say anything, and she will order in the modestly priced range of entrees.
- *Always make certain that your guest is served first.* Pass him the breadsticks first. See that the wine is poured into his glass before yours. If your guest's order was not properly filled, call the waiter and correct it. You are supposed to remember what each person at your table ordered and make sure they get it, exactly as ordered.

> "Waiter, I think this gentleman ordered lamb chops, not veal chops."

> "Waiter, this lady ordered her roast beef rare. You brought it well done."

- *Even if you do not drink, offer your guest a premeal drink as well as wine with the meal.* If your guest orders a cocktail or glass of wine before the meal, order a glass of mineral water or a soda to keep him company. You do not have to order a bottle of wine. Suggest that he order a glass of wine with his entrée, and if you see it quickly emptied, suggest that he have another.

- *It's a very good idea to preorder the meal, if you have a dozen or more guests.* The waste of time and the confusion caused by a large group ordering from menus is awkward and uncomfortable. Preorder easy, noncontroversial items: for the first course, the famous soup of the house or melon and prosciutto (instead of frogs legs) or for the main course, a grilled roast fowl (and not *osso bucco*).
- *If you are dining as couples with spouses who do not work with you, don't talk business all the time.* It's natural to discuss serious matters of mutual business interest, but half the conversation should be nonbusiness-oriented, in deference to the people at the table who are not involved in your affairs.
- *If you have an abnormally slow eater for a guest, who is holding up everyone's schedules, you must politely intervene,* and mention to him in a low voice that you hope he won't mind if you instruct the waiter to bring the next course, because of time constraints.
- *If you're disappointed by the food and the service, don't have it out with the waiter in front of your guest.* Just say, "This place is usually much better than it is today," and let it go at that. After your guest has left, you should tell the owner what happened, or write him a good letter. He needs to know what happened, so that he can improve his restaurant.
- *When it comes time to end the meal, you, as host, are supposed to give the signal.* It's a very simple act called "asking for the bill." It means—in any language—that the meal is over. You can quietly catch your waiter's or the maitre d's eye and signal that you are ready for the check. (If you disagree with the total figure and it's a complex matter, make some quick notes but don't haggle now, in front of your guests; pay the check and tell the head waiter or maitre d' on your way out that you will call him tomorrow about a discrepancy in your bill.)

    Once you have paid the bill and the waiter has returned your credit card, simply rise from the table and say, "It's been wonderful being with you." If there is a person on duty with the checked coats, tip that person a dollar for each person's coat and say goodbye to your guests out front.

Restaurant Manners for the Guest

- *Don't keep your host waiting for your answer.* Tell him yes or no at once in reply to his invitation, so he can make other arrangements if you cannot accept.
- *If you must cancel the lunch date or dinner, get your host personally on the telephone* to apologize and explain. Don't let something like this be handled between secretaries. Don't just leave a short message on his answering machine. It's also your responsibility to call your host and ask him to dine within two weeks. Don't wait for him to ask you again.
- *If your host doesn't show at the restaurant after twenty minutes of waiting,* call his office. If they don't know where he is, wait a maximum of forty minutes, then leave, having left a message with the head waiter. Leave a tip of $10 for the waiter

at your table, since you tied it up for practically the entire lunch hour. (Later that day or evening, the mystery probably will be solved as to who misunderstood what about your date.) You deserve a letter of apology if you were stood up, plus another date made quickly by your errant host.

- *Be on time.* It is as rude to keep your host waiting as it is for him to keep you waiting.
- *If you arrive first, go right to the table and sit down.* Don't order a drink, however, or put the napkin in your lap or eat a roll with butter or touch the place setting at all. It should look pristine clean when your host arrives. (The same should apply to your host, if he is the first to arrive at the table.)
- *If you arrive as a group at your restaurant table, don't just plunk yourself down in the chair of your choice.* Wait until your host seats you.
- *At a small lunch or dinner you should wait until the host begins eating,* unless he or she motions you to start right in.
- *You'd be wise to take only one drink before lunch or only one glass of wine* (not a drink plus a glass of wine) if you are trying to impress someone. Otherwise, he or she might surmise you have a problem with alcohol, even though that may not be the case. Everything in life is perception, and a person who takes only one alcoholic beverage shows he is in charge of himself.
- It's not up to you to dive quickly into the business at hand. *Your host is supposed to begin the business talk, but only after about ten minutes of small talk at lunch,* or a half hour at dinner. Small talk allows two people to get to know one another informally, and the relationship usually becomes easier, better. If you sit down and go at your host with your ideas with the force of a battering ram, you are not making an impression on him with your knowledge and intelligence; you are telling him you are overly aggressive, rude, and impatient (*see also* "How to Make Small Talk," Chapter 7).
- *Don't call the waiter over yourself* when you are someone's guest. The host is supposed to deal with the waiter. You should tell the host what you want or need, and he should then take care of it:

> "Waiter, please bring my guest another glass. This one is chipped."

- *Be careful of the dress code in the restaurant* where you will meet. Find out in advance from someone in your host's office if you must have a coat and tie where you are going. (If the dress code is strict, that means no jeans or running shoes.)
- *Don't upset the kitchen by ordering catsup or any other piquant, spicy sauce to pour from the bottle onto your meat entree,* unless you're confronting a hamburger in a fast-food place. Chefs in good restaurants supposedly season and sauce their main dishes to a delicate gourmet taste level, and bottled sauce on top of that in many cases would send them into despair.
- *Never complain about the restaurant or the service.* You don't have to gush with praise if the food was bad; just don't say anything at all.

- When you have been someone's guest, always write a thank-you note. It takes all of two minutes to write something like this:

Dear Al,

     The pleasure in catching up with all your activities today at that wonderful Henri's was matched only by the quality of their crabcakes. It was a great hour and a half we spent together. Thanks!

Restaurant Manners for Host *and* Guest

- *Watch the noise volume at your table.* A class act is always inconspicuous; raucous, boisterous laughter upsets the people around you. Women, in particular, with their higher-pitched voices, should be careful in restaurants.
- *Table-hopping* should be avoided like the plague. The waiters are the only ones who hate the table-hopper more than the other diners, for this creature obstructs the narrow passageways through which they have to travel loaded with plates and trays. He makes their jobs much more difficult.
- Almost as obnoxious is the *table-telephoner* who either asks for the telephone to be brought to his table the minute he sits down, or who whips out his own cellular phone and proceeds to talk on it through the entire meal. It's his way of saying to everyone within view, "Look at me, look at me!" The people dining around him wish to do anything but! There is no excuse for someone who utterly ignores his guests throughout the meal.
- If there's a mirror near you in the restaurant (on the wall, a mirrored pillar, etc.), avoid it as though it were hazardous to your health. *It's impossible to gaze at yourself in a mirror without self-grooming*—a swipe of the hand on the top of the hair, a pursing of lips to check the lipstick, a patting of the sideburns, a straightening of the tie while jutting out the chin—it's impossible not to do these things, which are seen by everyone in the restaurant, unless you block it from your vision. *As for women at a business meal applying makeup at the table*, the rule is *never, never, never*! Marie Antoinette used to spend thirty minutes at every meal repairing her face, but she was not trying to become a vice-president of her company. (For a purely *social* evening, I personally feel a woman who looks bad without her lipstick can give a quick pass of her lipstick tube to her mouth while looking into her compact mirror, at the end of the meal when no one is looking without anyone being aware she even did it.)
- A woman should not leave her handbag on the restaurant table. It should stay on her lap or beneath her seat. (If she is worried about having its contents stolen, she can always put it at the bottom of the back of her chair, and then sit against it. Her posture throughout the meal will be exemplary, for she will be sitting ramrod straight!)
- *If you are on a weight-loss diet, or if you have a food allergy, or if you cannot eat what has been put before you in the restaurant, say nothing.* There is no more

boring nor inner-directed conversation topic than one's diet. It is of no interest to anyone and is very self-absorbed. If you can't eat what you have been served, push it around and pretend to like it. If anyone notices you have not eaten, just say you're not very hungry. That takes one second to say.

· *Don't strew the restaurant table with papers, files, and work tools.* It upsets the peace of the diners around you, and makes it extremely difficult for the waiters to serve you. I saw two people at a posh restaurant in Atlanta one day, sitting at a table for two, both with their laptop computers on the table, madly copying into their files pertinent items from the business conversation they were having. I envisaged an exasperated waiter pouring chocolate sauce all over one laptop and raspberry sauce all over the other.

Why be petulant about such things? Because it upsets the procedures of the restaurant and enjoyment of the diners around them. Those two easily could have ordered pizzas at their desks.

Tipping When You Entertain in a Restaurant

Tipping is an integral part of the entertainment and service industries; more importantly, it is an essential part of the income of the people who wait on you and take care of you in the restaurant experience. Many advise that if the service was inferior, one does not have to tip a cent, but I am not of that school. I think that in case of bad service you should tip less than you normally do, and that you should explain in detail, in a quiet aside, at the end of the meal exactly why you are tipping less. The server really needs to know what he did wrong. I believe in giving the server the benefit of the doubt. Imagine that this has been a particularly tough day for him or her, with serious personal problems at home, which is why he has been less attentive than usual. It is wise, of course, not to lose your cool or to lash out at a waiter during the meal. It embarrasses your guests.

You are free not to tip at all, but please remember that the person you have chosen not to tip may be earning less than little that entire day because of your action. Furthermore, chances are good that at least part of the problem you experienced was totally beyond this person's control.

If the service was exceptionally good, tip more than you would have normally, thank and praise the people who served you, and commend them to the owner or the maitre d'hotel on your way out of the restaurant.

Here is a formula for tipping in a modest and an expensive, first-class restaurant.

MODEST RESTAURANT	EXPENSIVE RESTAURANT
Give the waiter (waitress) 15 percent of the bill minus tax.	Give 20 percent of the total bill minus tax in gratuities, split in the following manner: 12 percent to the waiter 8 percent to the captain

MODEST RESTAURANT	EXPENSIVE RESTAURANT
There won't be a wine steward. The wine will be part of the total bill. No maitre d'hotel, so no tip	From $3 to $5 extra for the wine steward, or 8 percent of total cost of the wines Give $10 to the maitre d' if he gave you a good table and took great care of you on a crowded room day.
No coat-check person, so no tip	$1 for each coat checked to the coat-checker person; $2 per person if a person leaves a lot of paraphernalia
No ladies' room attendant, so no tip.	$1 to the ladies' room attendant. Give her $5 if she sews on a button or cleans a spot on your dress, etc.
$1 to the waiter, if he goes outside to fetch you a cab.	$2 to $5 to the doorman for getting you a cab, depending on the weather
$1 tip to the garage attendant who brings your car to front of garage	$3 to the garage attendant who brings your car to the front of the restaurant

Tipping in a Fast-Food Take-out Place

You are not obliged to tip in a fast-food place like a self-service restaurant, a pizza parlor, or a deli. However, I personally feel that it is a very nice, and very just, action to tip anyone who has cheerfully gone to a great deal of trouble for you. Examples of those who take extra pains for you and still keep smiling: the pizza server who takes your order for ten different pizzas, hovers over them, gives you many extra napkins, extra plates, and cuts the slices for you in the box according to your stipulations; the sandwich-maker who makes six different sandwiches and packs six different beverages with "lots of extra ice" for you to bring back to your office. Give those people a dollar or two as a tip. They deserve it. So does the person who delivers to your office or home a quick fast-food order; and the young person who cleans up a great mess on your table at a place like McDonald's, after your children have smeared catsup all over the table, dropped French fries on the floor, and spilled milk all over the seats in the booths.

WHEN YOU ENTERTAIN IN THE EXECUTIVE DINING ROOM

Many executive dining rooms are pedestrian eating places, a notch above the employees' cafeteria. The decor and the food vie for mediocrity. But then again, some companies have absolutely smashing executive dining rooms, the *ne plus ultra* of a dining experience for a young manager. Some of these dining rooms are paragons of interior design—the work of renowned decorators and filled with exquisite antiques and antique reproductions, as well as carpets specially woven in Portugal and window treatments of which the cost is far too exaggerated for a shareholder to be made aware. When a designer has a free hand, he or she often has the china made with the corporate logo in the center. The crystal stemware also bears the corporate crest, and the linen napkins are embroidered with it. The placecards and menu cards are also embellished with the corporate logo, bumped-embossed.

Important clients and customers, distinguished colleagues and VIPs in the community are guests in this place. Often no liquor is served; sometimes wine is served before or during the meal. (I saw the CEO of a New York insurance company visibly flinch when a young executive asked the waiter in his dining room for a "cooler" with his lunch; the waiter blanched, and the young man realized what he had done and said, "I mean a glass of mineral water, of course.")

The food and the quality of service in the corporate headquarters dining room are supposed to be superior to the norm. The beauty of design of this area, however, can not mask the poor manners of any manager eating there. This place gives senior management a good insight into how a young manager conducts himself or herself at table, not only in terms of table manners, but also hosting abilities.

Corporate Dining Room Manners for the Junior Executive
(*See also* "The Executive at Ease at the Table," Chapter 3)

Those who are privileged to use or to be occasional hosts in the executive dining room are advised to remember the following:

· Eat slowly, quietly, and watch those table manners, because everyone else will be watching them, too!
· This is not a place for glad-handing, eye contact, or table-hopping. Each table host usually has his or her own important, discreet agenda in the executive dining room, so don't interrupt them with greetings. Don't scan the room, keep your eyes on your companions and your food. Don't stand by colleagues' tables, waiting to be introduced to their guests, whom you don't know. (This is particularly important if they are hosting some VIP.) They may not want anyone to know who their guests are. A complicated, sensitive deal may be in the making at their table.
· If wine is served, never take a second glass. The clients or senior executives present may suddenly see a flashing red light when they see you doing this.
· Never light up a cigarette, even if everyone else at your table is smoking. (You will show executives senior to you that you know enough not to smoke in a social situation, and that even if they break the rules of politeness, you will not do so.)
· Keep your voice low. Very confidential deals are made in this safe, protected (from the company's point of view) environment. You never want to act in a conspicuous manner in a place that is supposed to be calm, quiet, and soothing.

- This could be a golden opportunity to persuade a customer or client to pursue a more powerful business relationship with you. You are on your own well-mannered turf; it is a perfect place in which to negotiate.
- Do not plop files and charts on the table, which is very off-putting to the waiter and to the guest who is trying to enjoy his meal. You can't handle eating utensils, a plate of food, and a sheaf of papers at the same time. The way to handle this is to say, ''I have some very good background material on the project, which I can show you quickly back in my office after lunch. Five minutes will do it.''
- If your client was particularly pleased by the meal, pass on the praise to the chef, who usually hears only complaints. (Justified praise makes a person like his job and want to do even better.)

The company dining room can be used as an excellent public relations tool vis-a-vis the city's community organizations and major charities. During nonbusiness hours, the dining rooms can be loaned for meetings of the boards of directors of nonprofit organizations, or for fund-raising dinner parties, the expenses of which are borne by the company. There is an enormous amount of good will generated by this activity, provided the food and service are good, and the dining room itself is kept in pristine condition.

Little details are important in a successful executive dining room. There should be no dusty plastic plants and flowers (or even any nondusty ones), only fresh greenery and live flowering plants. The lighting should make people look good—men as well as women—in order to enhance the mood and atmosphere. The restrooms should constantly be kept clean.

I remember one lunch in a bank's dining room where the purpose of the meal was to close a deal. It fell through because the outside client said he was almost asphyxiated by the unbelievably strong smell of roach spray that permeated the room and, I'm afraid, our food. Once again, insensitivity shown by the host amazed and horrified the guest. The client said he did not have confidence in a bank where no one intervened or took action, and yet everyone at the table sat for two hours and suffered in what was, for him, an untenable situation.

WHEN YOU ENTERTAIN IN A PRIVATE CLUB

A club with attractive dining room facilities, a wonderfully trained staff, excellent food, and well-appointed private rooms for parties is a perfect place to hold business-social functions. It is the closest thing to a private party at home. However, entertaining in a club today can be like opening a Pandora's box of problems. Thanks to the women's movement (and the charges of sexual discrimination in membership), clubs have changed greatly in the past ten or fifteen years. Bastions of male tradition have now admitted women to their membership list. They have desegregated their dining rooms and sport facilities (not without a great deal of indignation from the men), and they have banished the special entrances and staircases women formerly had to use. I myself fought hard to banish those special entrances when the purpose of our meeting in the club happened to be a business one. Many times, as the only woman director of a particular corporate board, I would be relegated to a small back door with a narrow staircase, because I was female. My boards stopped doing that to me, because of my sarcastic comments, but also because they finally saw the lack of logic in it.

There are several categories of private clubs:

- Those with excellent sports and eating facilities
- Eating clubs only
- Clubs primarily of a business nature
- Social clubs where business functions are not allowed

The reason for disallowing *any* business to take place in this last category of clubs has to do with the delicacy of the tax-exempt status of those clubs. No money is made in these clubs, so as a result, you may not meet a business contact there for a drink, nor even sit in one of the public rooms with your briefcase open and with your files at hand—or any piece of paper, for that matter, which smacks of business. (Once a board member attacked me for working studiously on a piece of paper on my lap in the sitting room of a woman's club. It turned out to be a crossword puzzle. She was embarrassed for having accused me of such heinous business dealings, and I told her that to make up for her gaffe, she had to finish the crossword puzzle for me.)

In this purely social kind of club, the by-laws drawn up by the directors will not allow your company to pay for your annual dues nor even reimburse you for your business entertaining expenses. You must pay your dues and bills *personally*.

If you are hosting a business function and wish to have the press present, don't hold it in a private club. Some clubs will never allow any press coverage; others will lay so many restrictions on you, it is easier to climb Mount Kilimanjaro than to cope with them.

If you are having a large party in a club, deal with the banquet manager exactly as you do with a hotel banquet manager. You sign a contract after making your menu and beverage selections. Each club has its own rules as to how far ahead you must guarantee the number of guests and what cancellation fee you must pay if your party is cancelled.

The club manager will arrange for flowers for your party unless you wish to supply your own. (If the club is to supply them, be sure they are included in the estimated cost of the party which you are quoted.) For a seated lunch or dinner, if you send over your place cards (and menu cards if you're providing them) and a seating chart in advance, the maître d'hôtel will arrange everything for you on the tables.

Even though the club will add a 15 to 20 percent gratuity (as well as any tax) to your bill, you might wish to tip some of the staff separately. Some clubs forbid all tipping; if it is permitted, it should be done very privately, which isn't all that difficult to do. If your club does not allow tipping, you can always increase your yearly contribution to the employees' Christmas fund (a pool of money contributed by members on a voluntary basis and split up among all the staff).

When You Are Someone's Private Club Guest

- When you are asked to dine in someone's club as a purely social gesture (to have a good meal and a conversation), *be aware of the nature of your host's club;* don't try to buck its rules.
- *Ask your host what you should wear.* Some clubs demand whites for tennis and squash, some demand jackets and ties in the dining room, although they allow casual dress in the grill. Find out from your host what the drill is, so that you don't make an embarrassing mistake.
- *Dress conservatively,* which, for a woman, means no flashy sequins and bare midriffs in the evening. For men, it means no wild colored slacks with an even wilder striped shirt. In the evening, most clubs prefer their members and guests to dress in classic business attire, unless, of course, the occasion is a black-tie event.
- When you arrive at your host's club and she or he is not there, *wait quietly in the area shown to you by the doorman.* You are not supposed to wander around on your own tour of the premises.
- *Before you tip anyone*—caddy, coat-check person, locker room attendant—ask your host what the club policy is. Stick to it.
- Of course, *you may not pay for meals and drinks in cash* (in the majority of private clubs), so even if you would like to pick up the check for dinner, you may not. Pay back your host another time.

When the Circumstances Are Right
to Entertain in Someone Else's Club

- Don't ask someone if you can use his club for an event unless it is a business club that makes a profit on entertaining, and therefore welcomes the business.
- Don't ask someone you don't know *well* to sponsor your event. It is very forward to ask such a big favor of someone who isn't a friend. He may very well turn you down, particularly since most club rules require that your sponsor attend your party. Many business people will not do that.
- If there are already company members in that club and you wish to give a business function there, you are in luck. It should be relatively easy to make the arrangements. If your corporation is a constant user of those facilities, ask the member colleague you know best to sponsor you and your party.
- You have a serious responsibility in regard to your and your guests' behavior. Be careful that no one becomes drunk and disorderly or does anything that would bring down club disapproval on the person who sponsored you.
- A gratuities charge will be added to your bill. In most cases the bill for your party will be sent immediately to your sponsor, the club member who allowed you to entertain there. It is only polite to let the sponsor know that the minute the bill for your party arrives on his desk, he should send it to you, and you will reimburse him *immediately.* If your party was a great success, and the staff performed ex-

tremely well (and even if extra tipping is not permitted in that club), write out a check to the club's Employee Christmas Fund. Leave it at the front desk and tell the maitre d'hotel you have done so. Also write a letter to the club president, praising the banquet department of the club. (Such a letter will be copied and placed in the files of every employee who worked on your party; it really helps them.)

WHEN YOU ENTERTAIN WITH A SANDWICH AT YOUR DESK

It's a generous gesture to make under many circumstances, including those times when you have not finished your morning business with the person sitting by your desk, and you say, "You must be hungry, I know I am. How about a sandwich and something to drink for lunch?"

You may not have an executive dining room to which to take your guest, so someone in your office would send out for soup, sandwich and a beverage of choice for each person. Don't just plunk the deli's paper bags on your desk and litter the area with plastic cups, paper plates, and undersized paper napkins. If you dine at your desk more than rarely, bring some attractive tabletop items from home and keep them there for these lunch emergencies: large, soft paper napkins, china plates for whatever you're eating, crystal glasses for the beverages, china cups and saucers for the coffee, and silverplated or handsome stainless steel flatware. Keep some washed, peeled, raw vegetables in your office fridge, to decorate the plate on which your guest will be served sandwiches. (The *crudités* will also give him some much needed nutrition for the day.) Such details make all the difference in how much your business visitor will enjoy the meal. It shows you care.

WHEN YOU ENTERTAIN AT HOME: THE MOST FLATTERING INVITATION OF THEM ALL

Since there is so little entertaining at home these days, if you have the energy and the room, your home is the best place of all as the party site. People (constantly traveling business persons in particular) really enjoy being welcomed into the warm, personal atmosphere of a lovely house or apartment.

Entertaining at Home Requires Organization and Sensitivity

- If your house is difficult to reach, send each guest a clear map with instructions enclosed in the invitation.
- If you live out in the country and have a guest of honor, someone from out of

town or an elderly person coming to your party, arrange to have them picked up by a car service (or by another guest who knows how to find your house with ease).

- If people have traveled a long distance to see you, it's your obligation to feed your guests a meal, not just serve them cocktails and hors d'oeuvres.
- If there is a shortage of parking space at your home for a large group of guests hire the services of a valet parking company (or request your caterer to do it).
- Your house should have sufficient, comfortable seating space and eating space for the number of guests expected.
- Serve cocktails no more than an hour before dinner or thirty minutes before lunch.
- If your party is on a weekend in the country, make the dinner hour early enough (such as seven o'clock), to enable guests to travel homeward at a decent hour.
- There should be enough trained staff to serve the meal smoothly. Loving hands at home just won't do it. Hire a good caterer.
- *If you just have a colleague "dropping by" your home for dinner,* there is still another set of entertaining details to observe:

  - He or she deserves a proper meal, not just leftover spaghetti you happen to have in the fridge.
  - Arrange to have a choice of cocktail or soft drink on hand.
  - Set a proper table—no plastic plates or glasses, nor paper napkins.
  - He will probably ask to help; don't let him.
  - The small children of the house should be introduced, but should not be allowed to take advantage. An exhausted guest should not have to suffer through noisy, hyperactive children's scenes when she's supposed to be having a relaxing meal.

- If your house is inhabited by dogs and cats as well as people, ask any potential guest beforehand if he is allergic to animal fur before inviting him into the house. If your pets jump on people or crawl into their laps, confine them to another room for the duration of the occasion.

The Planning Aspects of an Important
Dinner at Home

A designated staff person is key to the production of a large, successful dinner (or lunch) in a senior manager's home. No matter how hard the spouse may work on this party, there should be someone from the office who rides herd on all the many details. This person may be an executive assistant or perhaps a staff person from Human Resources or Administration. Whoever is in charge should be resourceful, helpful (not dictatorial) to the spouse, and able to manage people (whether they are temperamental chefs, inebriated butlers, out-of-control guests, or no-show musicians). The staff party aid should have eyes in the back of her or his head, so as not to miss something that needs fixing somewhere. Among this person's duties would be the following:

- Supervise design, production, and mailing of invitations; help compile guest list
- If the spouse does not wish to participate in the planning, oversee the flowers and all coordinating activities with the caterer.
- If there are menu cards, place them at each guest's place; put the place cards in their proper places at the tables.
- Check in guests as they arrive and show them where to check their coats.
- Call to check on absent or tardy guests; handle all incoming telephone calls during the party.
- Coordinate the entertainers, if there are any, showing them where to dress, giving them refreshments, etc.
- Pay everyone at the conclusion of the party.

Key, also, of course, is the caterer, whose duties for this party at home include:

- Hire the necessary staff; prepare the food; prepare the bar (liquor may be provided by host or caterer); bring rental equipment for anything lacking in the house.
- Provide ice and cocktail napkins.
- Set up coatcheck facilities; employ and supervise the parking valet.
- Serve the meal after cocktails; serve after-dinner drinks.
- Clean up everything pertaining to party, including putting furniture back to where it was before the party.

What Kind of Service?

For your party at home, if you have up to 24 guests, it is much more efficient to have guests served at three or four round tables, which the caterer will supply. If you have more guests than this, make it a buffet, where guests can sit all over your house at any kind of table after serving themselves at one major food service area.

It is preferable to have the guests' wine (or beer) glasses already in place at the tables, as well as their napkins and flatware. It is difficult for a guest to juggle a plate, napkins, glass and flatware all at once.

The Spouse Cohosts an Important Dinner at Home

An executive's spouse is certainly a great asset (in fact, sometimes an essential ingredient) in a successful business lunch or dinner at home. As your co-host, your spouse:

- Is present at the door to greet guests as they arrive and help with their coats, umbrellas, etc.
- Helps create the ambience of warmth and welcome in the house from the minute the guests enter
- Helps introduce guests, which may require a constant reference to the guest list, tucked in one's pocket

- Helps keep the conversation flowing, so that there is no sad, drooping wallflower in your home
- Keeps an eye on the service to correct any problems
- Handles the incoming telephone calls, so as not to interrupt the host with the messages (unless necessary)
- Helps control the movement of guests from the cocktail area to the eating area
- Helps guests find their places at the table(s)
- Rises when the meal is over and leads guests away from the table and into another area (for coffee or for a presentation)
- Supervises the service of any beverage served after the meal, and stands at the door to say goodbye to guests

Cohosting in an Executive's Home Where There Is No Spouse

A widow or bachelor host may certainly ask another executive close to him or her in rank to cohost a large gathering at home. Remember, however, that the traditional role of cohost in a home is a wife's or husband's; therefore, a single woman executive does not appropriately cohost a man's dinner in his home. The guests might rightly or wrongly conclude that there's a relationship there. A cohost of the same sex is more appropriate in such a case.

The same goes for a single woman executive. She is better off having a married man, not a bachelor, as her cohost or, even more appropriate, another woman executive. Remember, too, that a single host giving a dinner in his or her home requires no cohost at all. But if it's a very large party (over 24 guests), a cohost is very useful in keeping conversations going and in spotting little things that need correcting.

When Your Guests Should But Won't Go Home

Your business and social dinner party at home was a terrific success, and now the guests won't go home. (Usually it is only one or two guests who won't go home.) If you have a high official guest in your home, he or she will leave by 11 P.M., according to protocol. The other guests can't leave until the guest of honor does.

If your guests came to a 7:00 o'clock dinner, they should leave by 10:30 or 11:00 at the latest, unless there is dancing or a closed circuit fight in Las Vegas you're all watching on TV, or something memorable going on.

If it is a normal weeknight dinner and there is nothing special going on, and it is is now 11:15 P.M. and you have a couple of sleepy looking guests who are consuming some totally unneeded additional drinks, it's time for action. Jump up from your chair with great cheerfulness and energy (it's important that your spouse know what you are doing and quickly mimic your fast rise from the chair). Say something in an exaggeratedly joking tone, in your own words, of course, such as, "We're all so important to the world of business—unfortunately we have to be bright and clear-eyed tomorrow—so I guess we all need to get some energy sleep. It's been a *wonderful* evening. Thanks so *very* much for making time to be with us!" Although your guests are being thrown out, they won't know it. They will jump up cheerfully, too, and take themselves home. (I've done it so many times, I know it works; no one has taken offense, and everyone has felt better the next day and thanked me.)

When You're a Guest in Someone Else's Home

Your manners really show when you are a guest in a private home.

- *Treat the staff graciously*, from the parking attendant on. Greet whoever greets you at the front door warmly. Of course, you don't have to do as I did, in my Rome embassy days, when I arrived at a black-tie dinner at Prince Nicolo Pignatelli's *palazzo*. At this point I had only met the prince and princess once, and had forgotten what he looked like. As I stepped through the great wooden palace door, I saw Nicolo and gave him an ebullient hug, saying, "It's so wonderful of you to have me tonight!" The man I hugged, distinguished-looking beyond belief in his black tie and dinner jacket, drew back blushing furiously and stammering. It was, of course, Prince Pignatelli's butler. I got over my embarrassment only later when the Prince, unable to control his laughter, told me that the butler was much worse off from the embarrassment than I was, and therefore I should forget the whole matter, except to empathize with the butler.
- *Don't be a snooper in the house*. It is in appallingly bad taste to open your host's medicine cabinets, go through your hostess' closets, and the like. One night I found one of my colleagues in a professional woman's organization going through every name and address in our hostess' address book, which was lying on her bedroom desk—a complete invasion of privacy. The very next night at a party a male colleague found one of his office peers trying on their host's jackets in his bedroom. When caught in the act of preening himself in front of the full-length mirror, the culprit dismissed it airily: "I was thinking of getting a suit from this tailor and was just seeing how his specially-cut shoulders feel."
- *Don't go on your own house tour*. If your hosts urge you to accompany them on a tour, or to "wander around by yourself," fine, but don't go off without authorization. That's snooping. By the way, one of the worst crimes you can commit is to open the nursery door for an unauthorized look at your host's baby.
- *Stay out of your host's kitchen*. You may want to see what kind of a range and refrigerator she has, or you may have heard your boss had just had her entire kitchen redesigned. Wait until you see it in a magazine; and let the party staff do their job.
- *Don't fool around with your host's property—and don't ever feed his dog*. What you give him could make him very sick. One CEO I know said he will never allow

another office party in his house after three overly enthusiastic cocktail guests poured cocktails into his prized aquarium, with the result that every fish in the tank died!

THE CORPORATE COCKTAIL PARTY
(*See also* "Cocktail Party Food," later in this chapter)

The good news is that the cocktail party presents the easiest and least expensive way of entertaining a large group of people. The bad news is that many guests don't consider a cocktail party sufficiently grand for them; also, this kind of party can still take a big chunk from the corporate budget. (In a small town a cocktail party may cost $25 per person, but in a place like a first-class New York hotel, it can cost $125 per person.)

Things to remember:

- Send the invitations three weeks in advance.
- Remember that on Friday nights, weekends, and the eve of major holidays, you'll lose many guests to other events.
- If you tell people where and how to park (on a small separate card), you will receive many more acceptances.
- Enclose a self-addressed RSVP card, but most people in big cities today, alas, will ignore it. Just study your guest list and figure that in a small city, 80 to 90 percent of those invited will show up, whereas in a big city, unless the party is unique, only about 50% will show up.

Be sure that at your party:

- You have enough bars for the crowd.
- You never overcrowd the room (if too many have accepted, or if you have enlarged the guest list, rent a larger room at the facility).
- You have enough helpers (company staff people to mingle with the guests).
- You have sufficient waiters to attend to the guests.
- There are small tables and chairs scattered around the fringes of the party space for guests to sit while they drink and chat with friends.
- Any music provided is good, and low enough to allow for conversation above the din.
- The bar is shut down one-half hour after the party was supposed to end, in order to discourage alcoholism and people staying far too late.

Cocktail Party Manners
(*See also* "When Serving or Consuming Alcohol," earlier in this chapter)

The guest has responsibilities, not only the host. There's no question about it: A group of well-behaved people have a much better time all around than badly behaved or simply unaware guests.

- *Reply within a week to your cocktail party invitation.* Go when you have said you would, and, if at the last minute, something comes up and you can not attend, be sure to call your host's office the next day to explain and apologize. (You don't have to talk to the host personally; just be sure his secretary took down the message and will relay it.) If you missed the party because you were called away on business, send a postcard from the city you traveled to, apologizing for not having been able to make it. It creates a wonderful impression.
- Don't bring a guest without first having called to see if it would be all right to do so. Give your guest's name to the host's office, so that his or her name will be on the door list.
- It's rude to arrive at 7:40 P.M. for a cocktail party scheduled for 6:30 to 8:00 P.M. Hosts and staff may feel they have to hang around with you past what was to have been the deadline on the party.
- Hold your iced drink in your left hand, even if it has a napkin around it. No one wants to shake a cold, wet hand.
- Pass up the gooey hors d'oeuvres. No one wants to have your greasy fingers touch his own in a handshake.
- Gluttony is very conspicuous and not exactly a plus factor in your image. In other words, if you're standing by the buffet table, don't remain there continuously chewing and grabbing at the shrimp and other goodies while others try to get close enough to obtain at least one.
- If you're smoking, be very careful of your ashes as well as the trail of your smoke, since parties are usually hostile environments for smokers.
- Circulate among the guests. Don't monopolize the host or celebrity guests, because others want to talk to them, too.
- Don't try to talk business to someone who is a captive prisoner at a cocktail party. Tell him you'll call him the next morning to set up an office appointment.
- Drink modestly. Everyone is on display at a cocktail party, no matter how crowded it is. Who was it who said, "Heroes are made in battles, but losers are made in cocktail gatherings?"
- To me, just about the tackiest thing a cocktail party guest can do is to roam around, beer bottle or can in hand, swigging from it at will, when a bar glass is close at hand. Here comes a sexist remark: I think it is even tackier when a woman does it than a man.
- The final gesture, the wrap-up of the party, should be your thank-you note to the host, written within the week. It can be short, hand-written or typed, but it should be well thought out, particularly since your thank-you note may be the only one the host receives.

The Staff Should Be Trained to Work the Cocktail Party

The executive and support staff should not look upon an invitation to a company party as an invitation to have a good time. Staff members are supposed to work, and to work so hard, they will be exhausted at the end of the party. I must confess that at most of the corporate entertaining events I have attended in the last five years, the executives and employees have stayed on the fringes, clustered like grapes, sipping their drinks together, laughing, chatting, and obviously having a good time with their own buddies. They seemed oblivious to the real purpose of the party: making the guests feel welcome, stimulated by the conversation, and making them aware of any news of the company that the company representatives might communicate to them. Instead, it is commonplace for the guests who don't know many people to wander around feeling estranged from the group and unconnected to what is happening. This adds up to a big waste of corporate money spent on giving the party.

A good staff party worker (and he or she should be present for no reason other than to work hard to accomplish the company's goals at this party) should step forward to greet every guest who arrives. She should make sure that each guest has met all the members of top management present and that the guest is introduced to anyone who happens to be walking by. She should make sure, before moving away from that guest, that he has others to talk to, and that he has been properly introduced to the group she is leaving him with.

The executive host should make sure that everyone is served or has access to the refreshments that are being offered. If it is a lunch or a dinner, she helps them find their seats at the table, introduces people at his table to one another, and keeps the conversation upbeat, peppy, and happy, in the true party spirit.

A good staff party worker is someone who really cares about the guests. He wants them to have a good time. He wants his company to put its best foot forward with this group of people. He wants to help his company shine in the public eye—and make more money—because of the success of this party.

It takes effort to do this. It takes caring.

Different Parties at the Cocktail Hour

People are sometimes confused when they receive an invitation to "cocktails," a "cocktail party," a "cocktail-buffet," or a "cocktail reception." The main difference between a cocktail party and a cocktail-buffet is that there is a great deal of food at the latter kind of party, removing the necessity for dinner plans afterward. A cocktail reception is the most formal of the three and is usually held later in the evening, and often with champagne served.

This chart explains some of the differences between these "sound-alike parties."

	COCKTAILS OR COCKTAIL PARTY	COCKTAIL-BUFFET	RECEPTION
Type of Event	Informal invitations are sent. People mostly stand up and circulate through the rooms. This may be an impromptu spur-of-the-moment party or a way to entertain a couple of hundred customers. It is the most common type of entertaining of a large group.	A more formal occasion. There should be a place to sit down to eat for the guests after they fill their plates at the buffet. Often some small tables and chairs are set up at random. This is a special event, not just a gathering of people. It could be an opening night party of an association meeting, a party to honor someone, or a chance to commemorate something.	The most formal. Usually for a distinguished guest of honor or for a special event, such as a party before or after a museum opening or a performing arts event, or for an anniversary. Champagne is always on the menu.
Hours	For 1½ to 2 hours, held usually in the evening, starting anywhere after 5 P.M. and ending by 8:30 P.M.	For a 2- or 3-hour duration, usually between 6 and 9 P.M.	Usually from 6 to 8 P.M. or, if after an event, from 10:30 to midnight.
Dress	Business dress	Business dress (Women can be very dressy)	Very dressy, business attire, often black tie
Food and Drink	Cocktails, wine, soft drinks; hot and cold hors d'oeuvres	Same as cocktail party, but there is a buffet table with more food and one or two hot dishes included. Guests may make dinner out of this buffet.	*Before dinner:* elaborate cocktail party food *After event:* late supper menu including desserts

Where to Have a Cocktail Party
(*See also* "An Imaginative Place for Your Party," earlier in this chapter)

The easiest place to host a cocktail party, cocktail-buffet, or cocktail reception is in a place like a hotel or club, where the establishment's staff is used to staging these functions and can advise you.

The nicest business, social or combination business-social cocktail party is one given in your home (*see also* "Entertaining at Home Requires Organization and Sensitivity," earlier in this chapter). Guests feel special when they are allowed into a person's house. It is a privilege, and there is an undeniable warmth and sense of pleasant informality in the air. The extra work you must go to to organize your house is worth it. Use all the rooms on the first floor. If guests tend to cluster and become stuck in one room, lead them into others, to open the traffic flow. Have bars and food at both ends of the first floor of your house (or out on the terrace or in the yard, if the weather is pleasant). A major mistake is to have the food and drink in one place only, because that guarantees one massive traffic jam in that area.

Do not hold an over-sized party in your house if parking is a serious problem for blocks around in the neighborhood; not even the world's best valet attendants can cope with that. I remember when an illustrious presidential assistant, known to be a rather dazzling international problem solver, held a cocktail party in his Georgetown home during the American Publishers Association convention in Washington. Traffic was blocked for two hours all around the busiest streets of this historic but crowded residential neighborhood. One angry Georgetowner, unable to move his car for more than an hour, abandoned it in the middle of the street. He put a sign on his windshield addressed to the party host: "_____, you caused this damnable situation. Now you go solve it." (His host wrote a sincere letter of apology, paid the police fine, had someone go to the police towing lot, claim the car, and drive it back to be parked in front of the owner's house.)

If you're having your cocktail party in a hotel, club, or similar facility, you will be dealing with the banquet manager or head of catering, which is much easier than organizing the party at home. Even so, there are details to be checked. Don't just order "flowers for the serving table"; state your preference or look at photographs of the kind they suggest. Don't just take it for granted that the linens covering the tables will be attractive; they very well might not be. In my many years of party managing, I have shamed many a hotel banquet department into buying new, fashion-colored linens, unfrayed and without holes in them.

Make your own checklist, to suit your requirements, based on this prototype:

Basic Equipment

- Bar tables and cloths to cover them (long ones, please—short ones look like window shades halfway down)
- A simple floral centerpiece for each table, unless, of course, your caterer has some design ingenuity and will make a centerpiece of fruits, vegetables, and cheeses.
- The right kind of bar glasses (don't use plastic unless you absolutely have to, such as if you are in a garden, on the beach, or on a boat)
- Small tables (these usually need cloths) and chairs for those who want to sit down if there isn't enough available seating space
- Coatracks with hangers (and someone to guard the coats and other possessions checked)
- A container for umbrellas, if it's raining
- Large and small trays for passing drinks and hors d'oeuvres

- Nice cocktail napkins. Cloth napkins are the nicest to use in your own home. Otherwise, purchase pretty paper ones from a party store. You might have them printed up with a special message if your party has a special theme or guest of honor.
- Colorful toothpicks to use for the hors d'oeuvres requiring them
- Ice, crushed or in cubes, delivered in large multigallon containers or paper sacks. Be sure to place the sacks in containers to catch the water that seeps through the bags when the ice melts.

What the Bartender Will Need

- Electric blender for special drinks
- Bar knife and small cutting board
- Angostura bitters
- Lemon squeezer and strainer
- Precut lemon and lime wedges or lemon peel "zests"
- Sugar bowl with spoon
- Cherries, olives, and cocktail onions
- Pitcher with long-handled stirring spoon
- Large water pitcher
- Cocktail shaker
- Measuring spoons
- 1½-ounce jigger
- Bar towels
- Large metal tub to keep beer and soft drinks on ice

Drink-Making for the Well-Stocked Bar

- A selection of nonalcoholic drinks
- Salt-free soda water, tonic water, and ginger ale (for mixers)
- Tomato juice (for Bloody Marys)
- Vodka
- Gin
- Dry vermouth
- Scotch
- Bourbon
- Blended or Irish whiskey
- Rum (dark or light)
- Wine (chilled white, also red)
- Full and lite beer (to be served always in glasses)
- A sweet aperitif (Dubonnet, red Cinzano, etc.)
- Sherry (sweet or dry)

Items Needed for a Minimally Stocked Bar

- Sparkling water and tonic water
- Soft drinks
- Scotch or Bourbon
- Vodka or gin
- White wine
- Full and lite beer

Guaranteed to Succeed: A Nonalcoholic Bar

A specially decorated serving area for those who are not drinking can be a very popular place. The following might be served here:

- Several soft drinks (some of them diet)
- Several brands of sparkling and mineral waters served with fruit slices
- A variety of fruit juices, each served in an attractive glass filled with shaved ice and with a piece of fruit floating in it (a strawberry, a small cluster of grapes, a piece of cantaloup, a cherry, a slice of peach, etc.)
- Sodas, frappés, and milkshakes featuring milk, fresh fruits, sherbets, and fruit juices mixed in blenders

The Number of Bars and Servers Needed

For a cocktail party, the bartender makes the drinks; the waiter or waitress takes the orders, delivers them to the guests, refills glasses, cleans ashtrays, passes hors d'oeuvres, and keeps the hors d'oeuvres trays replenished.

For a party of 50 to 60: One experienced, efficient bartender and waiter (or waitress) can handle 50 to 60 people, particularly if some of the guests step up to the bar to help themselves to the ice nearby and add their own water and mixers, which would also be handy.

For a party of 60 to 100: Two bartenders are needed and two waiters.

For a party of 100 to 200: Four bartenders and three waiters are needed.

If you don't have the space for the proper number of bars or serving areas, have the bartenders make the drinks in the kitchen or in an area away from the crowd. Then they can pass the drink orders in among the crowd.

If you have a giant overflow crowd, have the waiters pass through the crowd with a mixture of drink offerings on a tray—for example, scotch and water, vodka and tonic (in summer), white wine, a diet soda, and sparkling water.

Glasses

- Don't use delicate, stemmed glasses. They are too fragile, and the contents spill easily in a big crowd.
- Don't use plastic glasses indoors. They look tacky and drag down the party image.
- Usually two types of glasses will be sufficient for your party:

   ○ A highball shape (for soft drinks, soda water, mixed drinks, highballs, etc.)
   ○ An old-fashioned shape (for any kind of liquor served "on the rocks," for wine, or for any aperitif)

Cocktail Party Food

Since people are eating less today, the first thing to go in the prelunch cocktail hour is the luxurious assortment of hors d'oeuvres that used to be served. All you need to serve your guests before a lunch party today are some "munchies"—mixed nuts and cheese straws, for example.

The selection of hors d'oeuvres for a cocktail party, however, must be ample and attractive, for three reasons:

- Your guests will arrive hungry.
- Attractive platters of cocktail food are very pleasing to the eye, and greatly add to the festive spirit.
- People who stand around drinking perhaps more than they should while conversing need food to act as a blotter.

Typical Cocktail Party Menu

- "Munchies," available on tables throughout the room
- Healthy food: raw (or ever-so-lightly steamed) vegetables with a tasty but low-cholesterol dip
- Three hot hors d'oeuvres, such as

   ○ Grilled waterchestnuts wrapped in bacon (on toothpicks)
   ○ Grilled tenderloin cubes rolled in bourbon marmelade (on toothpicks)
   ○ Grilled swordfish squares in lemon mustard on crackers

- Three more cold hors d'oeuvres, such as:

   ○ Endives (the tips stuffed with Roquefort cheese)
   ○ Melon cubes wrapped in prosciutto on toothpicks
   ○ Small bacon, lettuce, and tomato sandwiches on toasted brioche slices, spread with scallion mayonnaise on rye

Typical Cocktail-Buffet Menu

- Giant platter of different kinds of crackers and different soft and hard cheeses
- Slices of roast herb-encrusted lamb, with a fig, apricot, and feta cheese chutney
- Slices of roast chicken, varied sliced breads, and a variety of spreads for the bread
- Platter of cold shrimp, generously sprinkled with lemon juice and herbs
- Bowl of *fusilli Primavera* (pasta spirals with vegetables in an herb and olive oil sauce, served hot or at room temperature)
- Large mixed green salad
- Hot veal stew with rice
- Mixed fresh fruit and brownies for dessert

Food to Have at the Cocktail Hour
When Times Are Good

- Fresh oysters and clams
- Fresh Russian caviar
- Fresh lobster bits
- Imported smoked salmon
- Crab claws
- Imported *Pâté de foie gras*

Menu For a Dessert-Buffet Reception

(You might host such a gathering after a corporate-sponsored art exhibition, a concert, or a movie premiere.)

- Wines (Krug Grande Cuvee Champagne; white and red wines)
- Apple tart with cinnamon ice cream
- Double chocolate mousse
- Fresh raspberries with zabaglione sauce
- *Oeufs à la Neige* (Floating Island)
- Pineapple sherbet (vodka on the side as a sauce)
- Assortment of *petits fours*
- Coconut cake with fresh peach ice cream
- Mixed fruit sorbets
- Pears poached in wine

SMOKING MANNERS

Many people today absolutely will not permit smoking in their presence. When people light up in public places, the nonsmokers may make a scene and a disturbance may result, with lost tempers and even screaming and yelling. The nonsmokers feel heart-and-lung-disease-threatened by smokers, and rightfully so; the smokers feel their very rights under the Constitution are being abrogated, and paranoia complexes abound. What people do in their own homes about smoking is their affair, but in public, it would be a much nicer world if people would step back, be cool, and make an effort to be reasonable in their confrontations over this habit (which to some is an addiction). I have a specific point of view in all this as a reformed smoker whose mandate is to give advice that will help us all live with one another. I have never seen an ugly confrontation yet that wasn't solvable by both parties suddenly becoming calm and reasonable, with the smoker backing off upon receipt of a kind, polite request to do so. If, for example, you are on an elevator and someone enters smoking, you can say calmly and pleasantly, "It would be nice if you would extinguish your cigarette, because of the Federal law banning smoking in elevators." How differently the smoker would react if you were to bark at him when he enters, "Put out that cigarette! Don't you know it's against the law?"

Most People Feel a Smoker Should:

- Never disobey laws governing smoking.
- Never disobey a company's policy about smoking on its premises.
- Never light up in anyone's office in a place of business where smoking is permitted, if there is no ashtray present (a sign that the occupant of that office does not smoke).
- Never smoke in someone's home without first receiving the approval of the host *and* the other guests present.
- Never smoke during the meal—ever. When the dessert is finished, this is the moment to light up for smokers who are permitted to smoke in that house.
- Never smoke in a restaurant, unless you are in a sectioned-off, approved smoking area, and in the presence of other smokers.
- Never force your nonsmoking guest to sit at a table in the restaurant in your preferred smoking area. In other words, when you are hosting a nonsmoker, it is much more courteous to suffer a little (or a lot, as the case may be) and sit with your guest in the nonsmoking area. A host should be ready to sacrifice for his guest. I remember seeing one deal sabotaged when the host, without even asking, made his guest sit in the smoking part of a café in an area that was crowded, hot, shrouded in smoke, and without ventilation. The guest was soon choking for air, gasping in disbelief that her host did not even notice her extreme discomfort as he puffed away. "When it got to the point where I could hardly see him through the

haze,'' the guest confided, ''I knew that our deal would not work. It was too bad, but I will not do business with someone that insensitive. He didn't have a clue as to how uncomfortable I was. I can't work with people like that.''

· Never light up in anyone's car, unless everyone in the car is a smoker.
· Never smoke in a nonsmoker's bathroom (and this includes bathrooms used by the public). The smoke hangs in the air sometimes for days.
· Never leave dirty ashtrays around. (The contents smell for hours and are very offensive to nonsmokers; go out to the kitchen and wash your ashtray, please.)
· Always be mindful of where your smoke is drifting. You might innocently be blowing it in someone's face. Change the direction of your seat, blow the smoke away from the other person with your hand, or perform any machinations necessary to redirect it away from the faces of others.

A Nonsmoker Should:

· Turn on full charm and sweetness if you are sitting next to someone (on a barstool, for example) whose smoke is upsetting you. You might put a smile in your voice and turn to the person, saying ''Would you mind terribly putting out your cigarette? I happen to be allergic to smoke, and unfortunately, there's no other seat available where I could move.'' When the person acquiesces, you would say, ''That's *really* nice of you. Thank you very much!'' This kind of scenario is a great deal better than snarling at your neighbor with a command: ''Put that thing out!'' Rudeness is guaranteed to get an angry reaction from the smoker, who might retaliate by blowing smoke in your face through the rest of the evening.
· Realize that as a host you no longer are required to put ashtrays on the coffee or dinner table (or anywhere else in the house, for that matter). If a guest asks your permission to smoke in your nonsmoking home, I think it's nice to give him permission—at the dinner table, after people have finished eating their dessert. Say to your other guests, ''I hope you won't mind if Jim smokes.'' (Open a window in your dining area for the comfort of the other guests.) Hand him an ashtray. If you don't own one, the saucer of a teacup will do. Like many hosts of my vintage, I own numerous ashtrays from my mother's and grandmother's collections of china and silver ones. In those eras, it was the custom to put an ashtray at every place setting on the table, as well as every table in the house.
· Inform your dinner guests in advance, if you are adamant about there being no smoking in your home, so that a smoker will not be unpleasantly surprised when she tries to light up. When you're extending the invitation by telephone, you might say, ''I hope you don't mind, but we don't smoke in our home.'' A heavy smoker would much rather forego your dinner invitation than have to survive an evening without being able to chainsmoke.

A nicotine addict (like any addict) deserves our compassion, rather than condemnation. We should make it possible for really heavy smokers to spend time with us, and yet absent themselves when they have to have a cigarette. It takes more effort to do things nicely and kindly, but it's worth it.

Hosts with ingenuity who don't allow smoking in their homes show smoking guests a patio or porch outside (with lanterns, ashtrays, comfortable chairs, and even flowers). "Go out there any time you feel the need," such a host would say to anyone who has to smoke. A New York friend, who lives in a small, modest apartment, yet who entertains constantly, dresses up the iron fire-escape outside her living room window for smokers. Smokers sit on cushions on the freshly cleaned steps; there are hurricane lamps and pots of geraniums to make everything more festive. She closes the window on the smokers, and when they are through, they tap on the window, and she lets them inside again. Her guests, part business, part social, rush to accept her invitations. (Another example of the subtlety of her entertaining capabilities is that there is a small bowl by her apartment front door, chock full of pamphlets and brochures, available to any guest, that are published by organizations claiming to help a person stop smoking.)

The Polite Cigar or Pipe Smoker

In nineteenth-century society, a good cigar was the mark of a "fine gentleman," although it was mostly smoked in the company of other men or a man's mistress. It was considered extremely sexy for a woman to use a cigar cutter to snip off the tip of a cigar, light it, drag on it to make sure it was properly lit, and hand it to her man. In late twentieth-century society, a cigar or a pipe is considered unacceptable in most social gatherings. The air in financial trading rooms may hang heavy with cigar smoke and no one thinks about it, but when that same smoke intrudes upon people's homes (absorbed by draperies and upholstery) and in restaurants and other public places, it is not at all welcome.

The smoking of cigars or pipes is looked upon as an inalienable right by some men (and occasionally by women, too, although many of the latter probably smoke cigars more to cause attention and public outrage than they do for love of the aroma).

If you are enjoying an expensive meal in a good restaurant, and the man at the table next to you has lit a cigar, you have some options for action:

- Ask him nicely and humbly if he would mind putting out his cigar, as it's affecting your taste enjoyment of the food. Be so charming and apologetic, he will find you hard to refuse.
- If that doesn't work, ask the restaurant owner if he would ask the gentleman to put out his cigar.
- If that doesn't work, ask the owner or maitre d'hotel to seat your party at another table, far from the cigar smoke

- If that doesn't work, because there are no free tables, eat your meal and leave, resolved never to give that restaurant your business again. It may be that the cigar smoker is that restaurant's biggest, most loyal customer, and they will do nothing to displease him. (In this case, you're out of luck.)

The polite cigar or pipe smoker:

- Would never light up in someone's home until after dinner is completely over, and only if the men are going into a room or a place outdoors away from the rest of the group. However, if someone comes to your house for a meal and takes a cigar from his pocket, preparing to smoke it, you have every right to protest gently, ''I would really appreciate your not smoking that in this house.''
- Would never smoke in a restaurant unless everyone at his table has finished eating and has agreed that he should go ahead with his cigar—*and* if the other diners nearby have finished their meals and are seated far away from him! This combination of circumstances rarely occurs, but I've seen it happen. I have also seen a man go over to the nearby tables when everyone had finished eating and ask them if they would mind if he lit his cigar. They, of course, were bowled over by the stranger's politeness, and even though they probably hated cigar smoke, they said, ''Go right ahead.''
- Takes his dirty ashtray into the bathroom or kitchen, disposes of the butts and ashes, and rinses the ashtray, so that the odor does not linger in that area.
- Always offers guests cigars before he lights up his own in his home or office.
- Never lights up in anyone else's office, unless that person is also smoking a cigar.
- Is conscious of ventilation at all times when he's smoking. To help the air circulation, he opens a fresh window near him or perhaps a door, unless the escaping smoke would displease people in the other rooms close by him.
- Never tries to smoke a cigar in the home of noncigar smokers, unless he can do it outdoors.
- Replaces a friend's supply of good cigars that he has smoked, because they are very expensive and he doesn't wish to be called a cigar-welcher.

Let's face it, cigar smoking is no longer part of socially acceptable behavior, but some people couldn't care less about that subject. It's their prerogative.

If your boss smokes cigars around your office and pollutes the air, what should you do about it?

Absolutely nothing. Someday you'll be the boss and can tell everyone they can't do it. Until then, say nothing, and do nothing, if you want to keep your job!

SOCIAL DRUG USE WHEN YOU ENTERTAIN
AT A BUSINESS FUNCTION

Many people begin to use drugs in social situations because they are ill at ease and want to feel "one with the group." They think, mistakenly, that drugs will relax them, make them come alive with good conversation, become attractive to the opposite sex, even to have better sex when there is the opportunity to have it. All of these reasons for taking drugs are fallacies.

Since drugs are one of the greatest scourges of mankind, there is a serious corporate responsibility to educate employees about its evils. There is also a responsibility for any employee of the company not to stay in a place where drugs are being used (including in one's own boss' home, at a party). It is ironic to see a social use of controlled substances that kill or maim or cause brain damage. That is certainly not the goal of entertaining!

If someone brings drugs into a function you are hosting, you, as host, are in control. It's not just a matter of your being able to stop it. You *must* stop it. It's the law. Just say, "Not in my house; I'm sorry you felt you had to bring that stuff. I'm going to have to ask you to leave."

15

Invitations

A *good invitation communicates every important aspect of an event and makes an affirmative public relations statement for the host. Whether or not it will be accepted, it has the power to create in the recipient feelings of goodwill toward the host company.*

THE WAYS IN WHICH INVITATIONS ARE EXTENDED

There are many options for extending invitations, ranging from the handsome and the classically correct to the fastest and the least impressive. Here are some of the most common forms in which invitations are extended:

- Through a telephone call
- On custom-made printed, engraved, or thermoengraved cards
- By letter, typed on your office letterhead
- By a note, hand-written on your personal stationery
- By formal engraved or printed invitational cards, with blank spaces which you fill in with the details, found at a good stationers. (Suitable printed invitations are also available in card shops, but avoid the "cutesie," over-designed ones, which aren't businesslike.)

Invitations may be delivered in any of the following ways:

- Locally by a messenger service (expensive but sometimes necessary as a time saver)
- Via express or priority mail or a next-day mailgram
- By an overnight courier, which is expensively impressive

- By a faxed letter of invitation (not very enticing)
- Via electronic mail, from one person's computer to another's (the coldest and most impersonal of them all)

JULIAN FORTESQUE INVITES GUESTS
TO AN IMPORTANT LUNCH

It's interesting to me how different invitations to the same event can come across as invitations to entirely different parties, depending on the way in which the guest is approached. Let's consider a hypothetical lunch host, Julian Fortesque, who is chairman of an international corporation, FATAinc/USA, the American branch of Franco-American Trade Agreements Inc. His colleague from Paris is coming to Washington, so he is going to give him a lunch for people involved in French–American trade. The lunch is very important to him. He wants to make a good impression on present and future clients, and he wants his French colleague to think he knows how to entertain with style and distinction, as befits their international corporation.

Let's say that one of Fortesque's guests is Robert Holstein, president of an Anglo-French chemical company.

- *He might telephone Robert Holstein,* get his acceptance over the telephone, and then send him a *"reminder" card* in the mail, so that Holstein can make sure the lunch is properly inscribed in his agenda on the correct date. Host Fortesque keeps a supply of engraved fill-in reminder cards ($3\frac{1}{2}'' \times 4\frac{3}{4}''$), which he has his secretary send to everyone who will be attending the lunch whom he has invited by telephone. It would look like this:

In honor of M. Georges Blanc
Directeur Générale FAT Ainc/France

To remind you that
Julian Fortesque
Chairman, FAT Ainc/USA, is
expecting you
for lunch
on Wednesday, October 20th
at 12:30 o'clock
Hotel Four Seasons
2800 Pennsylvania Avenue

- *He could write the invitation in an informal letter on his FATAinc. letterhead,* which he could also use for a fax or E-mail.

FATA

inc.

341 Park Avenue
New York, NY 10017

Fax: (212) 555-1234   Tel: (212) 555-1200

September 22, 1999

Mr. Robert Holstein
President, Holstein Chimique-US
2339 Massachusetts Avenue NW
Washington, DC 20008

Dear Robby:

You have heard me speak of my French colleague, Georges Blanc, president of the French FATAinc. He will be here from Paris next month, and I am rounding up a small group interested in hearing the latest on the European trade agreements from the French perspective. Please join us for lunch Wednesday, October 20th at 12:30 at the Hotel Four Seasons, 2800 Pennsylvania Avenue in Washington.

Just have someone call my office to let me know of your availability, and I do hope we'll have the pleasure of seeing you on the 20th. I think you'll find the discussions very interesting and pertinent.

Meilleurs voeux,

Julian Fortesque

- *He might write Robert Holstein a note on one of his correspondence cards,* inviting him to the lunch. Many executives keep their personal notepaper and corre-

---

JULIAN FORTESQUE

September 20, 1999

Robby,

My French colleague, Georges Blanc, who runs FATAinc in Paris, will be my guest at a small lunch for people interested in the French trade situation. The date: Wednesday, October 20. The time: 12:30. The place: Four Seasons Hotel on Pennsylvania Avenue.

Please join us—I think you'll enjoy it. Have your secretary call me.

Saluti,

Julian (202/555-4400)

---

spondence cards in their briefcases, so they can write notes by hand while waiting in airports or riding to appointments. A smart secretary keeps her boss' envelopes pre-stamped, so that once the boss has written the note, he can mail it wherever he is.

- *He might send to each guest one of his "fill-in invitations,"* of which he also keeps a supply in his office, if time permits him several weeks to send out invitations and receive RSVPs. These are engraved ecru stock cards with matching envelopes, of a larger size (i.e. 6" × 4½") than the engraved fill-in reminder cards:

In honor of:
Monsieur Georges Blanc
Directeur Générale
FAT Ainc/France

Julian Fortesque
Chairman, FAT Ainc/USA
requests the pleasure of your company
at lunch
on Wednesday, October 20th
at 12:30 o'clock
Hotel Four Seasons
2800 Pennsylvania Avenue
Washington

RSVP
202-555-1626

- Or he might send each guest a mailgram, as below:

WESTERN UNION MAILGRAM

```
1-002295K264 09/20/92 ICS IPMBNGZ CSP WHSA
2025551212 MGMS TDBN WASHINGTON DC 50 09-20
0424P EST
► ROBERT HOLSTEIN
2339 MASSACHUSETTS AVE NW
WASHINGTON DC 20008
```

WE HOPE YOU'LL BE ABLE TO JOIN US FOR LUNCH WEDNESDAY
OCTOBER 20, AT 12:30 AT HOTEL FOUR SEASONS, 2800
PENNSYLVANIA AVE. IN WASHINGTON IN HONOR GEORGES BLANC,
FRENCH PRESIDENT OF FATAINC (FRANCO AMERICAN TRADE
AGREEMENTS INC) IN PARIS. PLEASE RSVP 202/555-4400
JULIAN FORTESQUE
CHAIRMAN FATAINC/USA

16:24 EST

MGMCOMP

- If *Julian Fortesque is planning to invite a hundred or more* people to his lunch for Georges Blanc, he would have ecru or white *invitation cards printed or engraved* (5¼ × 7½″ size, or smaller), and they would look like this:

> *To meet Monsieur Georges Blanc*
> *Directeur Générale FATAinc./France*
>
>
> *Mr. Julian Fortesque*
> *Chairman of FATAinc./USA*
> *requests the pleasure of your company*
> *at lunch*
> *Wednesday, October twenty-second*
> *at 12:30 o'clock*
> *Hotel Four Seasons*
> *2800 Pennsylvania Avenue*
> *Washington, D.C.*
>
> *RSVP Card Enclosed*   *Valet Parking*

- *If Julian Fortesque's company were to make an important press announcement at this lunch,* or launch a new product or service, for example, or announce an award or a major competition, then the project of making an exciting invitation should be given to a graphic designer, who would undoubtedly substitute an imaginative design for a traditional one. The designer, of course, would keep in mind that no matter how exciting the action is at the lunch, the client should always want to retain those elusive qualities called taste and elegance.

THE GRACEFUL ART OF MOTIVATING SOMEONE TO ATTEND YOUR FUNCTION

A person will accept the invitation to your company's function for any number of psychological or business reasons:

- He or she is bored and has nothing else to do, perhaps even to the point of deciding with relief that accepting the invitation means that person won't have to cook dinner that night.
- She thinks she can meet people who will help her in her business, further her career and contacts.
- She thinks she can improve her social skills by watching people who are at ease in social situations and picking up some hints.
- He needs certain information and finds the group a wonderful research laboratory for his project.
- If she doesn't attend, some competitors who do attend might get ahead of her in the competitive races of business life.
- He feels the hosts will feel miffed if he doesn't show up at their party, and he wishes to remain in their favor. He also hopes that by attending their function, they will now come to his company's gatherings.
- He just wants to have a good time, be with people, and enjoy the group.

The invitation you extend will persuade your prospective guest either to come to your affair or skip it. A well-designed invitation thus sets the scene for a successful party. It's almost an assurance of success, just as the reverse is true of a poorly designed or poorly extended invitation (such as one that does not communicate all that it should; an invitation that contains errors, including in the address on the envelope of the recipient; or an invitation that arrives much too late).

All in all, the process of summoning a large number of guests by invitation is no small feat of logistics.

DESIGNING AND PRODUCING INVITATIONS

Invitations today are often designed via the "loving hands" method, by a manager who knows nothing about design, working with a printer who knows nothing about design. Management should see to it that a professional in the graphic arts oversees the design and the production of the invitations, from the first rough sketches through to the finished product, ready to be mailed. This requires constant coordination with designer and printers (or engravers, as the case may be) to take the various components of the invitation through production. There are often color separations to be checked and layers of approvals to be sought, including the last step: the signing off on the printer's proof.

Today there are too many printed pieces going out from companies that are full of errors in spelling, grammar, and punctuation. It doesn't matter whether the invitation is from a junior or a senior manager; mistakes are equally egregious. When a salesman, for example, sends out invitations to his traditional customers at the tradeshow "to a morning coffee to see our new products in Booth 4735," it sullies the complexion of the entire company if the text is pockmarked with errors. (One acquaintance of mine lost her job, but fortunately later was rehired, when she let 3,000 invitations go out in the mail with the CEO's name misspelled; her approval initials were on the printer's proof.) It's amazing how many serious mistakes are uncovered even when checking over the first *finished* invitation. One memorable error was in the mailing of 2,000 invitations by a major corporation with the wrong date for the ground-breaking ceremony for its new corporate headquarters, but even worse, the name of the company was misspelled. Otherwise, it was a great-looking invitation! (Fortunately, this was a disaster with which I was not associated.)

THE DESIGN DOES NOT HAVE TO BE BORING

There are ways of giving some punch to even the most conservative kind of printed invitation.

- You can change the colors of both the stock and lettering (for example, using navy lettering on pale blue stock, maroon on pale grey, brown on pale yellow, etc.).
- You can put a narrow border on the invitation, of the same color as the print, or of a contrasting color, if the lettering is black.
- You can have your envelopes lined with colored tissue, the same shade as the lettering on the invitations.
- Having your logo *embossed* on your invitations gives a very rich look.
- If you're in a creative world like retail, fashion, film, and beauty, you do not have to take the conservative route. Your invitation will get attention arriving in the mails if it is of a different size or shape, or if the color scheme is vibrant, or if it is made of an unusual material—something other than paper. (Invitations are printed on fabric, tree bark, rubber, cork, glass, balloons that show the invitation when they're blown up. Invitations are also recorded on audio cassettes!) Some companies have even done clever invitations in the form of jigsaw puzzles, which the prospective guest must assemble in order to read.

Be as imaginative as you wish. Just keep in mind the image of the company and the decorum of the event to which you will be inviting guests and make sure that the invitation represents you properly.

ADDRESSING THE ENVELOPES

Someone should be put in charge of addressing the envelopes, either on the computer, on the typewriter, or by an accomplished, neat hand (the latter method is the most personal and formal). It is really tacky is to affix printed adhesive address labels to the front of the envelopes. It is also sloppy and ugly to mail invitations to people without any titles before their names—in other words, to write simply "John Anderson" instead of "Mr. John Anderson."

STAMPING THE ENVELOPES

The office postage meter is an easy way to stamp your invitations, but it's also pedestrian and uninspiring. It shows that the host company doesn't much care. If you're giving a large business-social event and want to follow through on a first-class image in your invitation, have the envelopes postage-stamped neatly, in the upper right hand corners of the envelopes. The selection of the stamp is important, because using an appropriate one further enhances the design of the invitation. If your business is sports-related, for example, choose a stamp with a well-known athlete. If you are in the field of education, find a stamp honoring an educator or writer. If you are in women's cosmetics, a stamp of a famous woman in history or a flower would be appropriate.

STUFFING THE ENVELOPES

Someone should be assigned to oversee the stuffing of the various components of the invitation into the stamped envelopes. The RSVP card and envelope should be on top, sitting on the larger invitation, so that it will not be missed. If there are several pieces, such as an RSVP card and envelope, map, and special instructions, clip the various pieces together with an attractive paper clip, perhaps color-coordinated with the invitation design.

WHEN TO MAIL THE INVITATIONS

An invitation should be in the mail sufficiently far in advance of the event; for example:

- Three weeks before a cocktail party or a tea party (this gives the post office an entire week to get it to its destination)
- Four to six weeks before a breakfast, lunch, dinner party, or evening reception
- Six months before a major all-day or two-day meeting, to allow guests to clear their schedules for traveling to the destination

If you are expecting international participants:

- Send hold-the-date cards eight months ahead.
- Send invitations six months ahead.
- Send reminders to those who have accepted one month ahead.

A SAVE-THE-DATE COMMUNICATION

If you are planning a major event and want to make certain that the people your company really cares about attend the party, the smart thing to do is get the date into their agendas months ahead of time. Send a letter or a simple printed card through the mail to the entire guest list, explaining the nature of the upcoming function.

If it is a terribly important function and you want a large acceptance list and time is of an essence, send a fax message to your guests' offices, but realize that this method is not half as gracious as reserving the date by means of a communication through the mails.

One type of save-the-date (or hold-the-date) text:

> A Special Awards Dinner
> in honor of Paul Richards and Agatha Woodward
> will be given by
> The President and the Board of Trustees
> of Kenyon College
> Gambier, Ohio
> Friday, May twenty-third
> (Invitations to follow)

or, another kind:

> Please hold the date of
> Saturday, January 28th
> for a dinner given by the members
> of the senior management of
> ONTEL
> in honor of the retirement of
> Marilyn Van Santword
> Austin, Texas
> (Details will follow)

SOME SAMPLE INVITATIONS

The Classic Formal Invitation to a Formal Event

The classic formal invitation to a formal dinner or reception is a rarity these days. It is engraved or thermoengraved in black on an ecru or white good quality stock. The typeface is usually one of the traditional scripts commonly seen on formal wedding invitations. This kind of double-fold invitation is meant to symbolize the dignity and integrity of the host or the host organization or the importance of the guest of honor.

The invitation can be in the form of a large card or a double-fold invitation, like one for a wedding. The inside contents (cards containing a map, special instructions, or the RSVP card with its self-addressed envelope) match the engraving or thermoengraving on the invitation.

To a Formal Dinner

The following are two different kinds of formal invitation cards for the same dinner party. This kind of double-fold invitation is costly, quietly showy, and creates the advance impression that this will be a very special, important event:

Corporate Logo
(blind embossed)

In honour of
The Secretary of State
and Mrs. Doe
Mr. and Mrs. George Atwater Richardson
request the pleasure of the company of
Mr. and Mrs. Bowen Pitcairn
at dinner
on Tuesday, May twenty-sixth
Nineteen hundred and ninety-eight
at eight o'clock
The Carlyle Hotel
New York City

R.S.V.P.   *Black Tie*
2000 Causeway   *Dancing*
Miami Florida 00000
000-000-0000

This is a truly formal invitation, calling for a written reply, because no RSVP card is enclosed. The recipient is supposed to send a written acceptance or regret. The guests' names are handwritten.

Corporate Logo

In honour of
The Secretary of State
and Mrs. Doe
Mr. and Mrs. George Atwater Richardson
request the pleasure of
Mr. and Mrs. Bowen Pitcairn's
company at dinner
on Tuesday, May twenty-sixth
Nineteen hundred and ninety-eight
at eight o'clock
The Carlyle Hotel
New York City

RSVP Card Enclosed   *Black Tie*
Dancing

This is a bit less formal, because the invited couple's name is handwritten (not in calligraphy) before the word "company." Also, instead of a formal written reply, the guest is told on the invitation that there is an RSVP card contained within it. To us traditionalists, not having to write a formal reply to a formal invitation, rather than filling out a card, is a cop-out, but to the world in general, it just means that even very formal invitations are succumbing to "what is easiest is best."

To a Formal Reception

This kind of party is usually held at eight o'clock or later, often after something like a concert, opera, ballet, or art exhibit opening in a museum. Guests wear evening clothes and champagne is served with desserts (sometimes very elaborate ones, other times some simple cookies and an assortment of miniature petits fours). A single card, measuring anywhere from approximately 5″ × 7″ to 6¾″ × 9½″, would be appropriate for this kind of social function:

Atkist Corporate Logo

Cheldon Hampton Longworth
Chairman of the Board
requests the pleasure of your company
at a reception
following the premiere performance of
"Così Fan Tutte"
of the San Marino Opera Company
sponsored by the Atkist Bank
on Friday, January first
at eleven o'clock
Grand Foyer
Chelsey Opera House
Pittsburgh

RSVP Card Enclosed   *Black Tie*

When There Are Several Hosts Representing Several Companies

Logo

The Alliance for
Italo American Trade

In Honor of H. E. Dott Giuseppe Maroni
Minister of Foreign Trade for the
Republic of Italy
Giovanni Amarillo, The Buitoni Company
Icodoro Bosco, The Fante Group
Maria Cadoro, Cadoro Jewelry
Tomasso Dantini, Dantini Tessuti Importers
Pietro Pasquale, Fiat, New York

request the pleasure of your company
at cocktails
Tuesday, March 23rd
6 to 8 P.M.
The Rainbow Room
Rockefeller Center
New York City

RSVP
Mrs. Corloni
Società Azzurra
234 Park Avenue
New York, NY 00000
(212) 000-0000

When Two Married Doctors Entertain

Logo

Doctor Jonathon Smyth and Dr. Anne Sturgis Smyth

request the pleasure of your company

at

on

at

1240 Park Avenue

New York City

R.S.V.P

[Address of his office]

[Tel. no. of his secretary]

When a Senior Officer and His
or Her Spouse Entertain

When they entertain frequently at home, they use engraved fill-in invitations:

Logo

Mr. and Mrs. Henry Vaughan

request the pleasure of your company

at

on

at

1030 Fifth Avenue

New York City

R.S.V.P

[Address of his office]

[Tel. no. of his secretary]

When an Executive Entertains in Her Company's Dining Room

It is nice to have fill-in invitations for this purpose:

Logo

[space for host(s) name(s)]

request(s) the pleasure of your company

at lunch

on

at   o'clock

The Executive Dining Room
135 State Street
Denver, Colorado

RSVP   *Parking Facilities on*
000-0000   *Level B*
Ext.

When There Is a Retirement Party

LOGO

Marifé Espinosa
President of MUYGUAPA, INC.
invites you
to join the friends of
Antonio Garrigues
for a surprise party lunch
on the occasion of his retirement
Friday, October 7th at 1 P.M.
Casa Rosa Restaurant
13 Shore Road, Carmel

RSVP Card Enclosed

When the Company Hosts a Product Launch

Ada O'Connor, President
Herley's Imports
cordially invites you to
a dinner
in honor of Drury Scotch
Herley's newest import
Monday, November 17th
at 8 o'clock
Tavern on the Green
67th and Central Park West
New York City

RSVP Card Enclosed   *Black Tie*
or Kilts

Appleyard Cutlery Inc.
Logo

Manny and Marie Appleyard
invite you to a hearty feast

"Breakfast in Goteborg"

to view the new Swedish cutlery lines
Monday, January 25th
7 A.M. to 9 A.M.
etc.

When the Company Hosts a Two-Day Meeting
(*See also* "Invitations to the Meeting," Chapter 13)

The host for a major meeting, one lasting for two or three days, usually invites guests via an extensive letter, full of information as to the purpose of the meeting, who will be there, and a general outline of the program.

With this letter goes a detailed RSVP sheet, which is as important as the letter of invitation, because it shows the "buttoned-up" spirit of hospitality of the host company and casts an efficient, appealing light over the meeting. A sample RSVP sheet is as follows:

LOGO

Meeting: "Inter-Corporate Environmental Cooperation"
Intercontinental Hotel, New York City
September 3–4, 1997

I will participate ☐   I cannot participate ☐
My spouse will accompany me   Spouse's name (to be used on badge)
Yes ☐   No ☐   _____
I (we) will need transportation from airport to hotel _____
Arrival time Sept. 2 _____ Flight # _____ From _____
Airport name _____
I (we) will need departure transportation from hotel to airport ☐
Hour of departure _____ Flight # _____ Destination _____

MEETING PROGRAM:

		Myself	Spouse
September 2nd evening: Free			
Sept. 3	9 A.M. Working session at hotel	_____	_____
	12:30 Lunch at hotel	_____	_____
	Cocktails at United Nations 5:30 P.M.	_____	_____
	Dinner and address by Secretary of the		
	Interior at 8 P.M. The Four Seasons	_____	_____
Sept. 4	9 A.M. Working session at hotel	_____	_____
	12:30 P.M. Lunch and closing remarks		
	by the Mayor at Gracie Mansion	_____	_____

Check your preferences for items to be left in your hotel room:
Soda _____ Liquor _____ Type of fruit _____ Biscuits _____
Tea bags _____ Instant coffee _____ Choice of mineral water _____
Choice of daily newspaper _____ Other _____

THE TEN ELEMENTS OF AN INVITATION

Once you learn the proper form of an invitation, you will remember it all your life and can help your company word their invitations in a graceful, efficient way. Here are the numbered parts of a formal invitation:

Universal Bank Logo ——————— 1. The corporate symbol (may be placed at the top or the bottom)

2. Names of hosts ——— *Mr. and Mrs. Rufus Sean Gallagher*

request the pleasure of your company ——— 3. The phrase of invitation

at a reception and

4. The kind of —————————— *dinner*
  party

in honor of ——————— 5. Purpose of the party

H. E. Ambassador and Signora Roberto Caracciolo

on Friday, the twenty-second of May

nineteen hundred and ninety-eight ——— 6. The date

7. The hour ————————— *at eight o'clock*

3427 Sherman Oaks Drive ——— 8. The place

R.S.V.P.
Office of the Chairman
100 Empire Boulevard
Houston, Texas 00000
000-000-0000

Black Tie
The Ambassador will speak
at half after eight o'clock

9. Special instructions

10. Where to reply

---

1. The Corporate Symbol

This is generally placed at the top but may also be placed at the bottom or on the side, if the designer so chooses. The smaller the size and the less obtrusive, the better. It's best if there is no advertising text (like the company's favorite slogan) in the wording of the invitation, so that it doesn't look too commercial.

2. The Names of the Hosts

In a formal invitation the full name is spelled out. In an informal one, initials, even nicknames, may be used, if that is the commonly known name. If the Gallaghers were giving an informal cocktail party at home, their names as hosts might read, "Rufe and Margie Gallagher invite you to . . ."

It is important to remember that *people* invite you to a party, a company doesn't. There always should be a human being who does the inviting, or at least a group of people, like "The Board of Directors of Universal Bank cordially invite you to . . ."

When there are several hosts, the chairman/CEO and the president are the hosts, the senior person's name comes first:

Rufus S. Gallagher
Chairman and Chief Executive Officer
and
Neil K. Jacobs
President
request the pleasure of your company, etc.

If Neil, the president, is also the CEO, then his name would come first on the invitation:

Neil K. Jacobs
President and Chief Executive Officer
and
Rufus S. Gallagher
Chairman
request the pleasure of your company, etc.

If you have two hosts and wish both names on one line, the most senior person's name would be on the left of the invitation, the other host on the right:

Rufus S. Gallagher, Chairman   Neil K. Jacobs, President
request the pleasure of your company, etc.

If you have a large group of hosts of more or less the same rank, list them alphabetically—in two or three columns, if you wish—at the top of the invitation.

Don't list women with a confusing barrage of titles in front of their names. For example, don't put "Mrs. John Baker, Ms. Joan Titus, Mrs. Barbara Jones" at the top of your invitation. Put only a woman's given and last name (as is done for the men), so that there is a balance and symmetry to the list of hosts (or honorees or committee members) on an invitation, i.e., "Suzanne Baker, Joan Titus, Barbara Jones."

The exceptions to this rule (cases where titles must be used), are names preceded by "The Hon." Also a judge, a medical doctor, or an officer in the military—people whose titles are inextricably tied to their names.

3. The Phrasing of the Invitation

"Request(s) the pleasure of your company at" is the most formal style (unless you are inviting people to a wedding ceremony in a church, when it becomes even more formal: "Request(s) the honour of your presence at.")

Less formal are the phrases "invite(s) you to" or "cordially invite(s) you to." It is also permissible to omit an inviting phrase on an informal invitation:

Jane Stark

Lunch

Saturday, June 3rd

Noon

14 Star Drive, etc.

4. The Kind of Party

This is where communication on invitations often breaks down. We don't say what kind of party we're giving.

- "Cocktails" means drinks and light hors d'oeuvres.
- "Cocktail-buffet" means a longer-lasting party and enough food on the buffet to constitute dinner for most guests, who eat, mostly standing up, balancing plates and glasses.
- "Buffet supper" means cocktails followed by a large amount of food, which people serve themselves and then consume seated at a table somewhere (without place cards). One should never put just "Buffet" on an invitation. Put instead "Buffet lunch" or "Buffet supper."
- "Reception" is a more formal, protocol-conscious event than a cocktail party. It is held before dinner (with elaborate hors d'oeuvres) or after dinner (with champagne and a dessert service). An early-evening reception is not held for someone like your old college roommate; it's held to honor an important official or diplomat, such as the new president of an important college, or the president-general of the United Nations, who is in town.
- "Supper" is held after a ball or a large, important event. It is more formal than a "Buffet supper." People are usually in evening clothes. If you're invited to a formal dance, for example, it may say in the lower right hand corner of the invitation, "Supper at midnight," which means you will be served some hot dishes (Seafood Newburg; pasta; a salad, rolls; a variety of desserts; champagne or wine, or both).
- "Breakfast," "Lunch," or "Dinner" are self-evident.
- "Brunch" is very confusing to many people. Someone who has not eaten all day and who arrives at noon for a party expects lunch, not eggs and sausage and some

wilted broccoli. This party is staged anywhere from the hours of 11 A.M. to 2 P.M. (I'm for the lunch bunch, not the brunch bunch.)
- "Tea" is served in the afternoon and may consist of hot tea and coffee, or if it is hot weather, iced tea or cold drinks. The food is light: some tiny, crustless sandwiches and some sweet things like cookies or small tarts.

5. The Purpose of the Party

This is important. Corporate America often does not include the party purpose on their invitations, rendering them less effective. One company gave a party for a beloved retired executive but did not put his name on the invitation, with the result that few people came to the cocktail buffet in his honor. When people who had not accepted— but would have had they known who the honoree was—later discovered his identity, they were mortified and angry at the CEO. The latter's office received at least fifty letters of complaint. ("If only I had known this was a gathering in Jeff's honor, I would have been there. *Nothing* would have kept me away.")

Phrases to use in invitations to denote the purpose include:

- "To meet So-and-so"
- "To celebrate the occasion of" (the new plant opening, the successful completion of a fund-raising campaign, the attainment of a major sales goal, the opening of a new store, etc.)
- "To commemorate" (an anniversary, the establishment of a major new program, the completion of a new building, etc.)
- "To launch" (a new product or service)
- "In support of" (a nonprofit organization or program, a political candidate, etc.)
- "To congratulate" (someone who has received an outstanding honor or who has become a hero or who is leaving the company to assume a high political or appointed office
- "To announce" (a joint venture, management changes, etc.)

The purpose of the party should be in small-size print in the upper left-hand corner of the invitation or in the middle of the body of the invitation, shown respectively in the following examples:

In honor of Olympic Gold Medal Diver
Mary Cantwell

Rebecca Rawson
President, Siren Swimsuits, Inc.
invites you to
lunch
Monday, October 1st, etc.

Rebecca Rawson
President, Siren Swimsuits Inc.
invites you to
lunch
in honor of Mary Cantwell
Olympic Gold Medal diver
Monday, October 1st, etc.

6. The Date

The date is always written out in a formal invitation:

Saturday, the twentieth of January

But it is rendered in a simpler manner on the average invitation:

Saturday, January 20th

To use abbreviations for dates on invitations is tacky:

Sat. Jan 20

7. The Hour

In the most formal of invitations, it would be written in this manner:

six to half-past eight o'clock

In less formal invitations it would be:

six to eight-thirty o'clock

In the most informal and most commonly used way:

6:00 to 8:30 P.M.

8. The Place

If the party will be held in a major hotel ballroom in your town, you do not have to put the street address of the hotel or your city. If the hotel has many function rooms, however, always put the name of the room, such as "Salon A" or "The Embassy Suite," etc.

If your company has offices or plants in many different cities, you might be inviting customers or clients from different cities. In this case, always put the city on your invitation, and the street address, so that a guest will know in what city the party will take place, and a taxi or limo driver will be able to find it, once the guest reaches the city.

9. Special Instructions

These are usually placed on the bottom right (occasionally on the bottom left, too, below the RSVP information) of the invitation. Sometimes, these instructions are so complicated, they are printed on a separate card and inserted into the invitation.

Instructions That Are Useful

There are valid reasons for putting certain instructions on the invitation: to save telephone calls seeking information from the host's office, for one thing, but also:

- To impede gate-crashing, to discourage guests from inviting other people without permission, and to discourage sending an unwanted substitute:

  "Please present this invitation at the door."
  "Invitation not transferable."
  "Only those on the door list will be admitted."
  "Because of space limitations, we will be unable to accommodate guests of invited guests."
  "This invitation admits one only."
  "This invitation admits two."
  "This invitation is for your personal use only."

- To communicate the special arrangements that have been made for parking:

"Parking provided in Garage XYZ for guests"
"Valet Parking"

- To assist with transportation to and from the event:

"Map enclosed."
"Plane, train, and bus schedules enclosed."
"Chartered buses will leave from the Plaza Hotel every ten minutes between 4:30 P.M. and 5:30 P.M."
"Limousine pick-up service has been arranged at all commercial airports."
"Taxis will be provided for the return trip."

- To communicate weather arrangements:

"Rain date: June 26th"
"In case of inclement weather, call 000-000-0000, Ext. 000"
"In case of rain, the picnic will be held in the Auditorium"

- To communicate the clothing requirements:

"Black tie" (if guests are to wear evening clothes)
"Business attire" (men in suits and ties, women in dresses), which usually is not necessary to include
"Beach attire" (in case the company's party is by a pool or on the beach)
"Tennis and golf" (to signal that guests should bring the proper clothing for those activities)
"Jackets and ties required for men in the Club Dining Room"
"Dress warmly" (a warning that the affair will be held outside and it might be chilly)
"Boat shoes" (if the party will be held on a boat)

Communicating a Speech or Presentation

If there will be a speech or a special performance given during your business cocktail party, include that fact on the invitation, to assure the greatest number of guests being present at that particular time. For example, in the lower right-hand corner of your cocktail invitation, you might have:

"The Mayor of Kansas City will speak at 6:15 P.M."

If a special musical group will be performing after dinner, give that information on your invitation, too, to tip off your dinner guests to plan on staying late to listen to them:

"U-2 will perform at 10 P.M."

Communicating What Guests Will Be Doing, Other Than Eating

One host discovered, six months in advance, that his party was scheduled for the exact hours of the telecast of the Superbowl game. He could not change his own party plans for the hotel reception because of the rigid schedule of his very important foreign government official guest of honor. He therefore very wisely put on his invitation in the lower right-hand corner:

"Excellent Superbowl Viewing"

Everyone he invited accepted his invitation. A buffet lunch was served, and there were television sets in every corner of the suite of banquet rooms, with comfortable chairs and small tables (each one holding a huge, often refilled bowl of freshly popped popcorn). His royal guest was enchanted with the informality of the occasion, made some excellent business contacts, and learned about the magic of football.

10. Where to Reply

The R.S.V.P. request is handled in two ways:

- The letters "R.S.V.P." are in the bottom left-hand corner of the invitation on a very formal invitation, and one is supposed to know enough to write an immediate acceptance or regret by hand on good stationery.
- The letters "R.S.V.P." are in the bottom left-hand corner of the invitation, with the following printed below:

    - The name of a person and his or her telephone number
    - The name of a person and a fax number to respond to

- Most commonly used today: a printed (or engraved for the rare, very formal invitation) R.S.V.P. card and matching envelope, which are enclosed in the invitation.

ADMISSION TICKETS AND RESERVED-SEAT TICKETS SENT WHEN THE HOST RECEIVES AN AFFIRMATIVE REPLY

When a corporation sends invitations to a great gala performance, for example, in a place like the Los Angeles Center for the Performing Arts, Lincoln Center in New York, or any theater, admission tickets and/or reserved seat tickets will be necessary. (An "open seating performance," of course, requires only admission tickets for the main entrance.)

Numbered tickets of admission or reserved seat tickets should be mailed from the host corporation immediately upon receipt of a guest's affirmative reply. It is much easier to mail them in advance than to have huge crowds milling around a check-in desk in the front lobby. (One must always have this desk, of course, for last-minute ticket adjustments.) The host's office must keep a list of the guests who accepted the invitation and the numbers of their admission tickets or reserved seats, in case tickets are misplaced or forgotten.

A ticket of admission should contain:

- A number
- The corporate logo
- The date of the event
- The place of the event
- The time of the event
- Information, such as "Guests must be seated in the Auditorium by 8 P.M." or "This ticket is not transferable" or "Parking on Lower Level C," etc.

RSVP ETIQUETTE

It's a sad commentary on today's manners that business hosts have to use staff and precious office time to get on the telephones in order to call invited guests again and again, so that their responses to invitations can be solicited.

- Invitations should be responded to within a week of their receipt.
- If you have accepted a meal and can't go because of a last-minute emergency, call your host's office to relay the message that you are unable to attend. If it is after office hours and you can't get through to anyone in your host's office, call the place where the dinner will be held and relay the message to the restaurant owner or the hotel banquet manager or the maitre d'hotel. *Never* be an unexplained no-show for a seated meal, because your host will resent it, maybe forever.
- If you accepted a cocktail party or a buffet invitation and find at the last minute that you can't go, do something about it the next day. Either call your host's office to apologize and explain, or write her a note of apology. Usually hosts have no idea of the reason why guests who said they would come did not, and it certainly does not help the image of the guests in question, who are just plain rude.

"Acceptances Only" and "Regrets Only" Don't Work

These phrases don't work, so it's better not to use them. If you ask only those who are going to accept to respond to you, you will see that people just won't bother to respond. The same goes for "Regrets Only." People don't want to be tied down; they are usually loathe to make a commitment. It's called "social wiffle-waffling," which is a polite way of saying "hoping that something better will come along." Since there's an epidemic of this rudeness, don't think you can closely estimate the number of guests who will attend your cocktail party or buffet lunch, because many of those who have regretted will show up anyway, having changed their minds at the last minute and not bothering to let anyone know. Many of those who have accepted will be no-shows, again, not bothering to let anyone in the host organization know.

In large cities this situation makes it impossible to seat dinners and lunches (in smaller cities people are much more responsible and polite), or tell the banquet manager how many people are coming to the cocktail party. Be prepared for six of your seated guests not to show up at your dinner for eighty people, for example. Know that two or three won't show up at your lunch for twenty-four. If you are prepared for it to happen, you won't be thrown, you can quickly reseat the tables, remove the empty chairs, and make everyone at the tables with no-shows feel festive and happy again. As people become less considerate and ruder, you have to learn to adjust to them rather than retreat to your office to pout.

Make a calculated guess that two-thirds of your cocktail list will actually show up. If it's a rainy, stormy day, subtract as much as half from the list, and you'll probably have a fairly accurate head count.

"The Favor of a Reply is Requested"

Forget about using this phrase, along with a specific cut-off date, on your invitations. It doesn't work. It is difficult enough to get guests to check off an R.S.V.P. card.

Bringing an Uninvited Date or Escort to a Party

The only polite way to bring a date or escort to a party to which you've been invited is to call your host and ask if it would be all right—if there's room, in other words, and if you know it is a *big* party. (If a host is paying $250 for your dinner, as he does in a big-city fancy restaurant or hotel, he may not want to pay that price for a stranger's dinner alone.) Therefore, call and tell your host's office that you "understand perfectly if it is not convenient for you to come with an extra person."

Some companies, when they host cocktail parties or receptions, are happy to have single unaccompanied people come with dates. On their RSVP cards, therefore, they allow room for you to give the name of your guest:

LOGO

M. M. _____

Name of Guest _____

Accept(s) _____ *Regret(s)* _____ *Tel. No.* _____

Lunch, Monday, November 2nd

Metropolitan Club

Washington, DC

How a Secretary Replies for Her Boss

(*See also* "Handling an Executive's Mail in His or Her Absence," Chapter 7)

A secretary can:

· Telephone the host's office to reply for his or her boss
· Fill in and return the RSVP card
· Fax a letter of reply
· Write a formal acceptance or regret and mail it

A Formal Acceptance

Centered on a piece of good stationery would be this kind of reply to a dinner invitation for an executive and his wife (typed or preferably written by hand if the penmanship is beautiful):

> Mr. and Mrs. Thomas Wall
> accept with pleasure
> Dr. and Mrs. Alcott's
> kind invitation for
> Friday, the fourth of May

If the secretary is accepting for a woman executive and her husband, who use two different names, it would read:

> Mr. Thomas Wall and Ms. Duane Elliott
> accept with pleasure, etc.

If the secretary is regretting for the couple, the following would be written:

> Mr. and Mrs. Thomas Wall
> sincerely regret that
> due to their absence from the country
> they are unable to accept
> the kind invitation for
> Friday, the fourth of May

Often a letter of regret sent by mail or by fax is preferable to a formal regret when the person invited (or his or her secretary on his or her behalf) wants the host to understand the reasons for having to refuse the invitation. A warm, gracious letter makes the host feel good:

> . . . It sounds like a great party, George, and I'd give anything to be with you. Only the coincidence of having our Board of Directors dinner on the same night could force me to miss it. Good luck! I'd really like to hear you take on the SEC in your after-dinner speech that night!

When You Have Not Been Invited

No one's business career has been ruined by failing to be invited to a party. However, many careers have been ruined by overanxious people trying to get themselves invited to a particular party. A person who pushes his way into obtaining an invitation may be momentarily successful in reaching his goal, but in the long run his actions are usually self-destructive.

Investigate if you think it was only a clerical error that kept you from receiving an invitation. Ask a friend who was invited to inquire casually of the secretary of the host if your name was on the guest list. If it was not, don't try to put it there. Nothing makes a worse impression than an executive ''operating'' to get himself invited to a function where his presence is not a priority.

16

The Important Business of the Nonprofit World and the Duties of the Nonprofit Board

T*he business community of the United States has given birth to special new phrases in the world's dictionary: "social responsibility," "corporate support," and "corporate donations." This country started it all in the early twentieth century and we're still far out in front in leadership in the field. It is a position in which we can feel justifiable pride.*

A company that is considered "socially responsible" contributes from the company's own funds, and urges the employees to contribute from their funds toward:

- *Education*
- *Improvement in the lives of the sick, the needy, and the disabled*
- *The preservation and improvement of our environment*
- *Carrying out research for the benefit of mankind*
- *Developing cultural enrichment for the general public*

Of course, company actions for the common good are not based on sheer altruism alone. They are good for business. People like to buy goods and services from a company known for its social responsibility.

A COMPANY NEEDS A POLICY FOR ITS
CORPORATE SUPPORT ACTIVITIES

The hands seem to be stretched out from every corner. Lobbying is intense, and a company faced with many requests for donations needs a policy to refer to and a framework in which to give its money. Executives can become slightly paranoid — colleagues from other companies stop them on the golf course to request contributions for their pet causes; wives are hounded by other wives for corporate donations; there's pressure for financial support from the children's schools. Everyone seems to be running a fund drive or having a benefit. The cry for need comes from all sides. The public library is in a dismal state; the local animal shelter might have to close; the hearing-disabled center needs a new roof; the ballet troupe will have to disband without an immediate money transfusion; the chairman's son's Boy Scout troop has an exciting community project to fund.

The options for ensuring an orderly, manageable response:

- A large corporation may solve its donation problem by establishing a foundation to handle all funding requests. In this way the company executives can resist pressures to exert personally any influence they might otherwise bring to bear: "It's entirely in *their* hands." In other words, the negative response comes from elsewhere.
- A middle-size company may retain the services of a professional consultant to develop a plan for its corporate support policies, which includes what kind of letter to send in answer to requests for donations.
- Entrepreneurs and small businesses may establish a modest, general fund that enables the company each year to purchase benefit tickets and take one-eighth-of-a-page ads in benefit journals.
- A company's options for giving include these:

  - The same charity is benefited each year, and others learn not to ask. For example, if a company has committed itself to helping keep alive its local public television station, other charities learn not to ask that company for support. In talking to people on the telephone and in answering letters asking for donations the company says, "We feel we can be most effective in the nonprofit sector by focusing our support efforts on an organization that affects this whole community — our local public television station."
  - The same general field is benefited each year, but each time a different organization within the field receives the money.
  - A designated beneficiary receives a contribution for five successive years; then the company initiates a new five-year cycle with another institution.

A SOCIALLY RESPONSIBLE COMPANY SUPPORTS
THE SURROUNDING COMMUNITY

The community service area should not be overlooked when a company establishes its support policies. Some options:

- Pay the fees and expenses for a year or two of an established professional fund-raising organization to help an institution with its major fund drive. (Check out a prospective fund-raising organization with its other clients.)
- Give money outright as a contribution or as a matching grant.
- Support benefits by purchasing tickets.
- Pay all the expenses of a benefit, thus becoming "the corporate sponsor."
- Place institutional ads on a charity's behalf in the news media.
- Contribute company products to an organization.
- Organize programs for the public in health fields, such as getting donors to give blood, having people check for early cancer, or having them check their blood pressure regularly.
- Lend company premises for special meetings of nonprofit organizations.
- Lend executives to serve as trainers and advisers; give free legal, accounting, and public relations advice.
- Encourage employees to become volunteers, either working in the institutions or helping with fund-raising.
- Make a generous donation to a charity and note that on the back of the company holiday greeting card.
- Sponsor performing arts events; make art exhibitions possible in museums.
- Tour performing artists and art exhibits to other parts of the country.
- Contribute to faculty enrichment of colleges and universities.
- Give grants for research.
- Endow chairs and pay for lectures in the educational field.
- Assist in civic events, providing manpower and funds.
- Enable hospitals to purchase needed new equipment.
- Lend computer capabilities to organizations that cannot afford to have their own.
- Host a corporate dinner to benefit a charity, for which fellow executives from other companies buy tickets. During this event, usually held in a hotel, the CEO honoree is extolled to the skies for his civic endeavors. This kind of dinner can be a real money maker.

THE CHARITY BENEFIT WITH CORPORATE SPONSORSHIP

One of the most popular fund-raising techniques (and one of the biggest sources of revenue for the hotel industry, incidentally) is the charity benefit, primarily social in nature, but dependent in most cases on corporate funding to meet basic expenses. This party may be held in any of a number of places—on the institution's premises, in a mansion or on a historic property, or (and this is most common) in a hotel ballroom. A board of socially prominent women usually runs the event; if there is a "men's committee," its purpose is to sell tickets to the corporate sector. Tickets sell from $100 to $2,500. A great deal of very hard committee work goes on behind the scenes, and a great deal of money is spent to make the party perfect. One or more corporate sponsors are needed to pay for the basic expenses, which allows the benefit committee to turn over to the charity a check for the difference between the total revenues and any additional expenses, if any. In New York, as of this writing, a dinner dance for 350 guests in a well-known hotel might cost anywhere from $60,000 to $75,000 to produce. If tickets cost $500 per person, the gross would be $175,000, leaving the charity $100,000 after all the myriad expenses are paid.

Here's a look at what some of those expenses might entail:

- The design, printing, and postage for eye-catching invitations
- The services of someone to hand-address and stuff the invitations
- The services of a professional social secretary to handle the RSVPs, the mailing of tickets (if this is necessary), and the supervision of the check-in desk at the door of the party
- The banquet costs of the hotel, including liquor, wines, coat-checking facilities, gratuities, and tax
- The flowers and decoration of the ballroom, and possibly party designer
- The entertainment (together with the sound system and lighting related to it), including dance orchestra and "star" entertainer
- The printing of the ball program or journal
- The cost of retaining a professional publicity agency to handle the media and promote the event—an unnecessary expense if the benefit committee volunteers know how to handle publicity (but they often do *not*)
- The cost of extra security guards, parking valets, etc.

There is a strong public relations benefit for this kind of event, quite apart from the money raised. Someone important might hear about what the organization has been doing for mankind and take home a brochure describing the work of the institution— and often the sponsoring corporation's annual report as well!

The income derived from a charity benefit can come from any of these sources:

- The corporate sponsors' donations
- The proceeds from the sale of the tickets
- The proceeds from the sale of higher priced "Patrons Tickets"
- The profit from the sale of ads in the program journal distributed free to each guest
- The sale of raffle tickets for donated goods and services

Invitations to the Benefit

If a company is paying for a nonprofit institution's benefit invitations, it naturally should assure that the invitations are in keeping with the company's image—it should have final approval of the invitation before that goes to the printer.

An invitation should:

- Be well designed and not cheap looking—but not too lavish either
- Communicate clearly the charity being benefited
- Contain all the important logistical information in proper sequence (the who, what, where, etc.)
- Contain an efficient RSVP card and return envelope to use for ordering benefit tickets or for mailing in a contribution
- Give appropriate credit to the sponsoring company

The following are sample invitations extended for different types of community events.

This invitation shows how a corporation discreetly takes credit for underwriting a major cultural event:

Mr. David L. Reed
President of Maiden Products, Inc.
and Mrs. Reed
and
The Honorable Wolfgang Schwartzenberg
Consul General of Austria
request the pleasure of your company
at a special performance of
The Viennese Opera Company in Concert
Entirely underwritten by Maiden Products, Inc.
on Thursday, December second
at eight o'clock
San Diego Opera House
300 Market Street
RSVP Card Enclosed Black Tie
Tickets will be issued   A reception will be held
in order of receipt of   on stage following the
request   concert.

We regret that this invitation is not transferable.

A Fund-Raiser Conceived of and Hosted
by a Corporation

This hypothetical fund-raiser is a Saturday breakfast staged in the lobby of the corporate headquarters building, during which the closing ceremonies of the Summer Olympics are to be watched on television monitors placed throughout the lobby. The invitation reads as follows:

(Dalton Logo)

James Q. Sneed, President
and the employees of
The Dalton Corporation
hope you will join them at a breakfast
to benefit the **Utah Youth Clubs' Athletic Program**
on the occasion of the closing ceremonies
of the Summer Olympics
Saturday, August 20th
9 A.M. to 12 noon
Promenade and Lobby of the Dalton Tower
14 Regent Street
Salt Lake City

RSVP Card Enclosed

Catering and food service
courtesy of
the employees of Dalton

Program:
9 A.M. Telecast of the Closing
Olympic Ceremonies
10 A.M. Address by Governor
So-and-so
11 A.M. Performance by the
Mormon Choir
11:30 A.M. Performance by the
UYCAP Pentathlon Team

The RSVP card provided below has the Dalton president's name and address on the return envelope:

(Dalton Logo)

Thank you for your support of The Utah Youth Clubs programs

Breakfast and Olympics Wrapup

Saturday, August 22nd

9 A.M. to 12 noon

Dalton Tower

Number of reservations @ $100 _____

Names of your guests: _____   _____

_____   _____

Enclosed is my check for $_____

I regret I am unable to attend, but I wish to make a contribution.

Enclosed is my check for $_____

Name _____   _____

Address _____Tel: _____

Make checks payable to UYCAP

Contributions are tax deductible

AN INSTITUTION'S GOOD MANNERS TOWARD A SPONSORING CORPORATION

The nonprofit institution should demonstrate its own good manners toward the benefactor by remembering to:

- Keep the company informed of its activities when the information would be of obvious interest to the company
- Show appreciation for a gift regardless of its size
- Wait a suitable length of time before asking for another gift (six months to a year, depending on the size of the last gift)

- Assign either the executive director or the assistant director to attend institution-company meetings
- Credit the major corporate sponsor on all appropriate publications, press releases, etc. The sponsor of a benefit, for example, should be acknowledged in the invitations, press releases, program, and from the floor when the benefit chairman makes his or her remarks.
- Say "thank you" in creative ways. One CEO, reminiscing about his long and distinguished career, said the most memorable nonprofit experience in his life came as a result of his company donating a special hospital wing for children. Several months after it was opened, the president of the hospital presented him with a large scrapbook, its pages filled with letters, drawings, and poems made by the children patients in that hospital. It was a "gift of their gratitude." The CEO circulated it throughout his organization and printed excerpts from it in the company newsletter. (The corporation has been a firm supporter of the hospital ever since.)
- Record a major donation in a manner to be visible to the public, such as placing a plaque on the wall or carving an inscription in the stone facade of a building to which a company was a major contributor
- Thank the sponsoring corporation from the stage for a corporate-sponsored performance. I remember one moving evening when the entire cast of a Shakespearean drama assembled at the foot of the stage at the end of the play to shout "Thanks, Company X!", smiling and blowing kisses over the footlights at the executives in the front row. (In the newspaper the next day, a front-page photograph showed this scene; everyone agreed it was company money well spent!)
- Host a social event (not opulent) for the major donors. Appropriate *short* speeches of thanks should be made to the companies involved
- Give the donor or donor company a small memento of a major gift like a building—perhaps a framed architect's rendering in color of the new building, accompanied by a suitable inscription from the institution to the company
- Arrange a series of guided "familiarization tours" of a donated facility for the employees of the donor company, so that they will understand and appreciate their company's role in the project

A CORPORATION'S GOOD MANNERS TOWARD NONPROFIT INSTITUTIONS

Good manners should govern the way in which a corporation relates to any nonprofit institution it assists. The company should, for example:

- Make its donation in a philanthropic (derived from two Greek roots meaning "love of mankind") rather than totally self-serving manner. The company should refrain from repeating, "But what are *we* going to get out of it?" Nor should it expect an attitude of obsequious gratitude on the part of the institution benefited.

- Assign a well-mannered executive, senior enough in rank to serve as an effective company representative for the CEO. One of this person's responsibilities should be to keep the CEO advised of all activities involving the company and the nonprofit institution; another, to gain the maximum possible cooperation of his company in helping the institution.
- Treat the head of the institution with respect, not with a patronizing attitude.
- Make sure that all company tickets purchased for the institution's charity benefit are used. Empty places at any event are a strong negative. The tickets should be used by appropriately dressed company representatives or by important customers.
- Expect no more than four to six free tickets to benefits it sponsors. The purpose of the benefit is to raise money, and even though the corporate donation may be generous, the charity's purpose for staging the benefit is to *sell* tickets, not to give them away free.
- Not use a benefit as a forum for self-promotion. If the CEO makes some remarks to the assembled guests at the benefit, he should not use the occasion to give a long speech (three minutes is *plenty*), nor should he use his time to broadcast a commercial for company products or services. He should quickly thank the benefit committee, praise the charity, reaffirm his company's commitment to it, and sit down.
- Avoid interfering with the day-to-day activities of the institution. When a company sponsors a concert, for example, a company representative should not try to change the musical program. If the company is one of the sponsors of a new hospital wing, it should not try to interfere with the architect's plans (unless, of course, a serious error has been detected). The company should offer its expertise to the organization it is helping, but then let the organization's staff handle things on its own. There should be an atmosphere of trust in the working relationship between donor and recipient.

SUPPORT OF THE ARTS

The great art shows held in America's major museums would never come to pass without corporate generosity. Distinguished concerts and new ballets are sponsored by corporations; symphonic works are commissioned by them; sculptures, murals, and tapestries are commissioned by them for the lobbies and important public areas of buildings.

Companies that spend money for the better quality of life of their employees and the communities in which they live deserve to be lauded to the skies.

Not Only Giant Corporations Assist the Arts

You don't have to be Ford, Aetna, Mobil, or Exxon to support the arts. This is what a small company can do to encourage its employees' love of art:

- *Hang attractive art on the office walls*, perhaps in the form of good quality framed posters or prints, or perhaps works of art on loan from the local museum's inventory of rentable art. It is important that a committee of the employees, perhaps in conjunction with a decorator, be allowed to make the art selections that will dominate their office environment. Once the art is hung, the employees should be furnished with information on the various artists. Works of art make the employee's surroundings a better place; the employee becomes more knowledgeable about art in the process, and the art world prospers with the purchase of or the rental fees for the art.
- *Pay for part or all of the membership fees of the employees to the local museum*, thus encouraging more of them to use the museum's resources and to develop an interest in art.
- *Urge the employees to attend all of the major exhibits;* make it easy for them to go, even if it means helping with transportation or giving them a half hour extra time off. Make them proud of their local museums.
- *Make small contributions to the museum exhibitions*, thereby tying the company more closely to that institution.
- *Organize a small library of art history books somewhere in the office,* for the enjoyment and education of executives and employees alike.

Support of Music, Dance, and the Theater

A small company, or the branch office or plant of a corporation in a small town, can bring the arts to the people in that community, thereby creating the very best of goodwill for itself, and bringing untold enjoyment and jobs to the people who live there. For example, a regional business can sponsor a dance troupe or the concert of a local musician or composer. The company would provide a grant, which pays for hiring the hall and orchestra (for performance and rehearsal time), and for printing and mailing invitations to the "premiere performance" of the event. The whole town would thus have the opportunity to hear or see the local talent. The company's public relations department would handle the publicity for the event, and the company might pay for recording the work on cassette tapes. These tapes could then constitute the company's Christmas present sent to customers, VIPs and the press; and the tapes would also be very helpful to the advancement of the performer's career, — and they could raise funds toward the event when sold in the lobby or to music outlets. A new star in the classical music field might very well be born as a result of the company's generous support.

Sometimes a sum as (relatively) modest as $15,000 will pay for the production of a play given by a local group of actors. The sponsor would have to keep in mind that it will be a lot more expensive to do a play like Thornton Wilder's *Our Town*, using twenty-two actors, than a play like Neil Simon's *The Odd Couple*, which uses eight. The corporation's gift would pay for the following:

- Hiring a theatre or another place in which to hold the event
- The payment of scale wages to the actors* for the total of four weeks (three weeks of rehearsal and one week of performances, for instance)
- Hiring a lighting technician
- Paying a stage director
- Making or renting simple costumes
- Preparation of proper press kits
- Hiring the ushers and box office staff
- Printing tickets, programs, and promotional posters.

The result of the corporate gift is that local theater comes alive, the actors are inspired, and everyone has a good time. The town, now transformed into something of an arts center, begins to plan for its next play and a sponsor to pay for it, and the company that came up with the $15,000 is undoubtedly the hero of the year.

Don't Spoil the Image by Overspending

Nothing will work faster to destroy the good will created by a corporation's donation to a benefit than the rumor that too much money was spent on frills for the party, which makes it seem a Marie Antoinette let-them-eat-cake kind of affair. Both the benefit committee and the sponsoring company should work together to see that this does not happen. The company's donation should not be spent on lavish decorations, masses of flowers, extravagant invitations, wines, and chocolate truffles served after dessert.

I will never forget what were among the prettiest table decorations I have ever seen. The cloths for this dinner (held in May to raise money for a local school) were pale green cotton; they had been borrowed from a charity fund-raiser in another city. Clusters of lilies-of-the-valley, each tied with a tiny green ribbon, sat in a terra cotta pot in the center of each table. The chairman of the benefit announced on the microphone each guest at each table was expected to take home a cluster as a favor. (Wild applause as a result.) When I congratulated the chairman on the beauty of the decor, she announced that the best part of it was that it cost nothing. She had planned on running this benefit a year ahead, and specially grew the flowers in her back yard for

*Hiring a well-known professional actor to join the local thespians in their effort can create a bonanza of riches for the community. Such professionals can be contacted through agents such as Lily Lodge of the nonprofit organization Private and Public Theatre, Inc., in New York City (212-764-0543).

it. The white candles in votive cups were all donated by the committee, each member of whom had a large quantity of votive cups that were used for her own parties. The terra cotta pots were donated by a professional landscaper. Cost of the table decorations: nothing.

Tooting the Company's Horn

A company would be silly and wasteful not to take full credit for corporate sponsorship of the arts. A good strong public relations program is called for in almost all cases of corporate contributions. The company communicates the nature of its gift:

- In an institutional ad in the newspaper
- In the annual report
- In the program of a performance in the performing arts
- In the catalog of an exhibition it sponsors
- In the press releases of both the company and the institution
- In a brochure published for press, stockholders, employees, VIPs, customers, and clients
- In a tag-line of a sponsored public service television or radio spot: "This performance was made possible by a grant from _____."

INSTITUTIONAL ADVERTISING TO SUPPORT THE NONPROFIT SECTOR

A newspaper or magazine ad is very expensive, and when used to promote a nonprofit venture, many executives, not to mention the stockholders, wonder if it is worth it to them. No immediate profit-related results can be measured. No one can prove that any products were sold or that the value of the stock rose in response to an institutional ad's appearance. However, this kind of advertising can be a powerful communicator of a bright and shiny corporate image, as well as a reflection of a company's good citizenship.

An institutional ad powerfully promotes a museum, library, botanical garden, opera company, symphony, dance company, or theatrical group when it furnishes the dates and times of special shows, exhibits, and performances.

THE COMPANY ENCOURAGES VOLUNTEERISM AMONG EMPLOYEES

It starts at the top. The CEO should encourage his or her people to render volunteer service in the community—*not to the charity or cause of the boss's choice, but of the employee's choice*. The person doing the volunteering should be emotionally motivated to do the best job. When people pick charities close to their own hearts, they give it their all. Some people care about education more than anything, others about health care. A family member may have died of AIDS, and so that person may volunteer in an AIDS homecare program; a child may have multiple sclerosis, and so the parent signs up to raise money for research for that disease. The employee who is an amateur violinist may prefer to help the local symphony; another employee who had a wonderful, happy childhood may feel he should devote his efforts to underprivileged youths. A retired academician may prefer to help the Folger Shakespeare Library with its projects of bringing Shakespeare to school children; an executive who cares about the environment will want to help with endeavors linked to that concern.

YOU AS A VOLUNTEER

Almost all of us can be valuable assets as willing volunteers to a nonprofit organization. There is nothing better for your self-esteem than to have people waiting for you, needing you, and counting on your help. As an internal auditor of a financial institution confessed to me once, "I don't have what others consider a scintillating profession. People don't exactly grin at the mention of my name in this office, but every Monday, Wednesday and Friday nights I leave here to read from textbooks to visually handicapped students who are working for their graduate degrees in law and accounting. My students make me feel like I'm really something, a hero. I would *never* let them down. Last night one of them said to me, 'You know something? I hope some day that I end up in an office with someone like you as my boss. That would just be perfect.' I typed his comment on a card and attached it to my desk blotter."

If you are new in the community, your volunteer work will probably become an integral part of your life. It will allow you to make new friends outside your office, to settle into the rhythm of the town, and to become known as a caring and capable human being.

Here's how you can get started:

- *First, match what needs doing with your capabilities and your time.* Don't waste a volunteer agency's time by enthusiastically applying and then not delivering because it takes too much time.
- *Do some self-analysis.* Which part of the nonprofit sector are you most comfortable with? Working with children? Handicapped people? The elderly? The sick? The homeless? Single mothers? Welcoming and helping international students adapt? Acting as a docent in the evening when the museum is open late? Are you better at raising funds than working hands-on with people? Are you better at designing programs in the back office than executing them out front?
- *Know exactly how much time you can devote to the activity* you finally decide to undertake. In other words, don't make promises you can't keep. But don't ever

say, either, that you don't have enough time to help out in *any* capacity. I know so many people who seem to work twenty-four-hour days who always contribute. One successful woman lawyer with three children, who lost both her parents when they and she were young, devotes a quick visit every evening of her life to a home for indigent elderly people a block away from her offices. She is motivated by the fact that "I never would have wanted my parents to be in a home like this, abandoned, with no one coming to see them." She has a "flying squad" of anywhere from ten to twenty people who drop in after work every day at the home, just to make contact with the inhabitants. Sometimes they appear with a puppy for everyone's amusement. One person will play the piano for half an hour. They sometimes have sing-alongs. A younger executive will bring a tape recorder with the latest rock rhythms and put on a short dance demonstration. They bring the residents magazines, snacks, tell them jokes. The average visit lasts about fifteen minutes. They bring life and happiness into that community. What is more important is that the residents consider these volunteers real friends.

- Once you know the sector of volunteer help that would appeal to you most, *research all of the existing organizations and agencies in your town that deal with that kind of assistance.* For example, if you're motivated to help with the problem of alcoholism, you might become a valuable contributor to a support group. You can look up the local chapter of Alcoholics Anonymous, Al-Anon, and Alateen in the telephone book. If you're anxious to help children who are having a tough time getting through school, contact the Board of Education for volunteer groups that tutor in remedial reading. You can always suggest that your company "adopt" a public high school with a mentoring and tutoring program.

When you have finally chosen the group you would like to help:

- Find out if anyone in your company (such as someone in the human resources department) has had an association with the organization that might interest you, and investigate it.
- Go visit the place. You can always ask for a tour of the premises, to watch a volunteer program in action. "I'm doing a survey for my company on volunteer agencies in the city, so I hope you won't mind my dropping by at a time convenient to you."
- If you like what you see, make an appointment with the Executive Director or someone in a managerial position in the facility to discuss your trying out volunteering in a short-term basis. If you like what you see and what you do, you then can join and devote more time to the work or to raising funds for the group.

    I've noticed that the most successful volunteer work is often something the volunteer developed over time. For instance, something needed doing, but there was no one to get it done; the volunteer stepped in.

- Remember that the most important attribute of a volunteer is to *show up* when you're expected. A last-minute cancellation on your part could ruin a volunteer program that day and cause undue hardship. If you know some office-related project might arise on a certain day, arrange for a substitute to cover for you. Ask another volunteer to do this; then repay her by filling in for her in an emergency.

WHEN YOU HONOR A CEO WHO HAS PERSUADED HIS COMPANY TO HELP THE COMMUNITY

Some people are real heroes under pressure. One executive I know is always called by the local Red Cross when the blood supply for the Washington area hospitals becomes very low, because they can depend on him. He calls other executives into action and he himself rounds up close to a hundred donors within a couple of days. He is also the one who organized a squadron of drivers of four-wheel vehicles to work all day and night picking up and driving home patients to and from the local hospitals when the blizzard of 1993 struck. Whatever situation needs his help he reacts to, and through his example leads the way for many others to follow.

I have attended hundreds of boring "honoree" dinners, given in hotel ballrooms, where the "entertainment" is an overblown series of accolades of a CEO whose corporation has made some very nice donations to a particular charity. The charity receives the profits from the dinner, and it is, of course, most often a sell-out. Once their CEO is being praised in public, the corporation must fill every table in the ballroom with bodies: vendors, clients, ad agency personnel. The charity makes money, so even if the CEO is not the hero he's made out to be on the night of the dinner, the end justifies the means.

There was one such dinner at New York's Plaza Hotel several years ago that will stand out in my memory forever. The CEO was introduced by the emcee without one word of praise, obviously at his insistence. He went to the microphone, gave some very interesting news of recent advances made by the nonprofit organization being benefitted, and then he brought up to the stage five of his company people, ranging in rank from a senior vice president to the secretary in the nurse's office. He introduced each one to the audience and told what each had done in a considerable volunteer commitment to the charity involved. The story of their work was inspirational. When he finished telling it, he said, "This dinner tonight is not in honor of me. It's in honor of *them*. I'm so proud of them!"

Who said that a "corporate heart" is a contradiction in terms?

THE SERIOUS BUSINESS OF JOINING A NONPROFIT BOARD

A charity is like any business. Its board of directors—or trustees—must hire, oversee, and set the compensation of the president or executive director and other senior management people. The board must replace the executive director, too, if he's not doing a better-than-good-enough job. The trustees are charged with making certain that the financial health of the institution is assured, and that the funds are expended wisely, with no malfeasance involved, and that housekeeping matters (including insurance) are being handled properly. They must make certain that the proper mission statement (the goals of the institution) is drawn up and communicated to and followed by everyone involved. Usually a nonprofit board meets from twice to six times a year, and in times of crisis, much more often than that.

If you are asked to serve on the board of a nonprofit institution, it is a great honor, one not to be taken lightly. It does not matter if it's a large prestigious organization like the American Cancer Association, or something young and new, like a local day-care center for welfare mothers trying to find jobs. You must be prepared to make a *time and a financial commitment* to your organization. If you miss most of the board meetings, you are not only hurting the charity, you are permanently damaging your reputation in the community. Other trustees really resent a "name only, Mr. No-Show" fellow trustee.

Some men and women whose names are famous—even golden—in a certain region will be asked to accept board positions for the lustre they add, even if they rarely attend meetings. Some are conscientious and send a surrogate to each meeting, a trusted member of their staff who will report back to them what went on at the meeting. (This should be prearranged as being acceptable with the board.) The "golden name" will then call the executive director for a chat if she senses something is amiss; she will follow up with offers of support, either financial or emotional (the latter might entail knocking together the heads of some other board members or of the institution's management). A good board member always keeps himself or herself briefed on what is going on in the organization. The presence of these famous names on the board may lend credence to the institution; their sizeable annual donations also help compensate for their absences from meetings.

You should never lobby to get yourself on a board. Others are supposed to come after you. It is the kiss of death when someone who is upwardly mobile tries to insinuate himself or herself into a group for personal social gain.

The Trustee's Good Manners

- Always come to meetings.
- Arrive on time, and don't dash back to your office long before the meeting is over
- Do your homework before the meetings, so that the business at hand goes forward, instead of having to be stalled while you struggle to catch up on the agenda.
- Offer to help the head of the organization with contacts or access to special information.
- Notice when something is amiss (such as inadequate computer support) and seek to correct it.
- Talk proudly about the charity on the outside, thereby doing an important public relations job for it.

- Always buy at least two tickets to your charity's benefit, and many more if it is possible to do so without financial strain. The trustee who is a top executive of a large corporation is expected to "buy a table" (or more) as a corporate donation.
- Always thank the volunteers who work in that institution, including the people who organize the benefits.
- Always remember promises made at board meetings to take on specific responsibilities by taking good notes and following up with action.

The Financial Commitment of Trustees

Several charities are frank about what they consider a reasonable annual contribution from their trustees or directors. For a large prestigious city museum or hospital, a trustee might be asked to write a check for $200,000 (as an ad hoc gift toward a major, much-desired art acquisition or equipment for the clinic) with the same ease that a trustee of a small city's young people's club might be asked to come up with $300 as his share of emergency repairs to the clubhouse's boiler system. Everything is relative, according to what the trustee is worth and the size of the institution.

The average-size philanthropic board would expect its trustees to donate from $2,000 to $5,000 annually; the board of a large, prestigious one might be expected to give from $35,000 upward, and if they suddenly find themselves in reduced financial circumstances, are supposed to resign from the board. The real reason is money, but no one is crass enough to come out with it.

A Commitment of Hearts and Hands

Most *big* institutions have become very cold-blooded of late and often elect only those with access to the very big bucks—"even if these people have absolutely no social standing in the community," as one irate spurned socialite reported after campaigning hard but unsuccessfully to become a trustee. But other smaller philanthropic organizations gladly take on trustees who are enthusiastic, well liked in the community, and who give them a gift of their brains and heart. The well-proven theory behind their election is that these trustees will probably grow and prosper in their careers, and be able to give much larger sums one day. In the meantime, they earn their right to stay on the board by contributing their services. The lawyer who gives his time free, the accountant who does the organization's books at no charge, the public relations specialist who advises the charity's management on all press matters without charging; the special events coordinator who volunteers work on a group's benefit dinner: these donated specialized services really contribute to the organization's bottom line. They also publicize the talents of the professionals who have worked on a pro bono basis.

A word of caution here: *Sometimes the executive director of a nonprofit organization with board members who have special skills will take too much advantage of them.* In other words, executive directors sometimes unknowingly abuse their relationships with trustees. The chairman of the board should police this situation carefully. The trustees, after all, have to make a living and cannot be giving unfairly large hunks of their time month in and month out, just to supply their charity with their generous donations of services. A trustee who is not made of money cannot be asked to spend endless money on lunches at home or at a club for the benefit of the institution. The management of the nonprofit organization should be sensitive to the size of the wallets of the trustees.

Put a Young Person on Your Board

I am a great proponent of putting one or two young members on every board of trustees of a nonprofit institution. At first they probably will not be able to commit more than a modest amount of money a year, but:

- They will be yours for a long time, even lifelong supporters of the institution.
- They keep the board from becoming pompous and stuffy.
- They bring fresh, new ideas of how to manage the institution.
- They receive important managerial training in their nonprofit board jobs that will make them better executives.
- They represent the *future*, the most important constituency any non-profit organization has.

A PARTY FUND-RAISER GIVEN BY YOUNG EXECUTIVES

One of the great "giving" gestures a young executive can make is to be on the organizing end of a fund-raiser for charity, and to involve his and her contemporaries—even if the group consists of people in their twenties and early thirties who are "not exactly embellished with big bucks," as one described himself to me recently.

When young people, who are working very hard and have very little leisure time, make the time to organize a benefit party with their own hands, imaginations, and hearts, it inspires more people their own age to do likewise. A good example can imbue others with a sense of civic responsibility.

If you would like to give a fund-raiser, make a task plan:

- *You need a cause.* One group I know raises money for ad hoc projects for their local hospital, which desperately needs the funds. The hospital saved one of the young people's lives after a motorcycle accident.
- *You need something entertaining that will happen.* This group decided to give a party on Superbowl Sunday, when people like something to do. It has many possibilities for socializing.
- *You need someone to lend you a house or apartment*, or garden or tennis court— someplace to put a big partying crowd.

- *You need a committee* that will:

  · Get someone to donate the party place
  · Organize donated refreshments
  · Arrange the entertainment
  · Design, produce, address, and mail the invitations, paid for by a local business
  · Compile the guest list and keep track of the RSVPs
  · Be in charge of banking advance checks as they come in, and supervising the cash box on party night
  · Scout local merchants and service companies for donated prizes to be raffled off or given as prizes for some sort of competition
  · Organize local publicity on the event—whether it entails talking-it-up, inserting mentions in the suburban or neighborhood papers, getting publicity in the beneficiary hospital bulletin, or putting up posters in the offices of friends (who will hopefully attend and bring people from work)
  · Clean and decorate the party space, and clean up afterward
  · Organize the parking in some manner (Sunday is a good day for a party, because often there are free parking spaces in the neighborhood)

Several rented big-screen TVs, scattered through the party space (or donated house), are essential for a Superbowl party, so are chairs and floor pillows for comfortable seating. There should be a "serious viewing room," where people can watch with concentration and relative quiet. The food might consist of munching things, sandwiches, pizzas, Tex-Mex food, hot vegetable soup, pasta dishes, and a dessert buffet—anything goes, provided it's plentiful and the platters are kept refilled. Beer and lite beer, sodas, bottled water, and wine should be available. Former football stars who live in the area could be urged to attend the party as guests, to talk to the other guests about what's happening in the game, and to spin a few tales about the time they were in the pros or played in the Rose Bowl or whatever. They add great local color.

Since there are many people who are not interested in sitting transfixed during the entire game, there should be plenty of space for nongame watchers, including perhaps an area for "tea dancing" to taped music before the game (and during, too).

When guests leave, they would be handed a leaflet stating the purpose for which tonight's hospital benefit was held. For example, if the money will go toward a new piece of equipment, it would be described.

If you have 200 guests in attendance who have paid $35 a ticket, and if you get all the expenses donated, you can clear $7,000 for the hospital. Your guests will feel good, too, having contributed to charity when having a good time with friends. All of the organizers of the event will feel proud of their success in helping a local institution, and the companies that employ you and your fellow benefit-organizers will undoubtedly feel very glad that they hired you in the first place!

A CAVEAT ABOUT CORPORATE GIVING

There are shareholders who feel management has no right to spend profits on matters not directly relating to the company. There are some shareholders who feel that the business sector is not tough enough about holding the nonprofit sector properly accountable for the deployment of donated funds.

Fortunately, there are other shareholders who realize that the positive relationship between a company that is a giver to its community, instead of just being a taker, makes for a better quality of life for that community—and also a stronger company, with happier employees, operating in an environment of growth and hope, instead of stagnation.

The company that proudly maintains its stance of giver, and which encourages employees individually to do the same, is the one that *everyone* cheers on to greater success.

WHEN FRIENDS AND BUSINESS COLLEAGUES TAKE ADVANTAGE OF A SUCCESSFUL EXECUTIVE

It can be difficult, tedious, and embarrassing for a person to be perceived as a rich and successful executive, particularly one with a generous heart, when people quite obviously take advantage of him. It is triply difficult when the executive really does not have the financial assets people think he has. A man, for example, with a wife who is active in the social side of charities (i.e., organizing the big splashy benefit through which a nonprofit organization might raise a major part of its annual budget for operations) is expected to say "yes" every time one of his business or social acquaintances calls him to take a table to the annual dinner dance. In New York, Chicago, or Los Angeles, "taking a table" often means contributing $10,000 for the privilege, and then often no one wants to use the tickets.

Many executives I know use up the entire budget for this kind of corporate donation and then dig deep into their own pockets to pay for more of these benefits, thus depriving them of the opportunity to use those personal contributions for a cause they really care about. They begin to feel as though they are victims of a racket when people they hardly know confront them on the telephone in the middle of a very busy day and apply pressure ("I bought five seats at your wife's charity last year. Now you have to take two tables at mine.")

Many executives resent having to spend their charity donations in this manner ("so the wives can show off their designer ballgowns and get into the society pages"). Others resent having to shell out many thousands of dollars for dinners that honor another CEO, just because all the CEOs who know him or her feel forced to buy tables. It is an increasingly serious problem. My advice to these put-upon executives is to work out a corporate and a personal donation policy, and set up a foundation to handle them both, one for the company, and one for personal contributions. The executive might make a commitment to one or two aspects of the nonprofit world and stick to his guns. A small board of directors would then make wise decisions on which nonprofit organization receives which monies. Someone from the foundation would mail out the letter, under a signature other than the beleagured CEO's, that informs the person or group of the "yes" or "no" decision. The "no" decision can be logically explained because "in order to operate most effectively, our foundation is committed to the field of health (or education or the disabled or ecology or whatever), and therefore your request unfortunately does not fall within our contributions guidelines."

In setting up a private foundation, talk to your tax advisor in order to comply with government rules and regulations.

A company and its executives should be allowed to give money where they want to; they should not be coerced to back certain social events that have become ego-serving and, in the minds of many, very boring at the same time.

17

Celebrations and Rites of Passage

A*t its core business is a community of people—not offices, machines, products, and spread sheets, but human beings.*

Since the company often becomes an employee's family, it also becomes the employee's family's extended family, whether its purpose is to make waste disposal equipment or underwear, trade in the stock market, sue people in court, make sick people well, advertise their products, or grow crops to put on the table. Business is about people, and people have babies, get married, get sick, grow old, die, and engage in all kinds of other human activities. A happy, healthy place to work is one where the most senior people are aware of the human needs of those who work for them.

A COMPANY CELEBRATES ITS ANNIVERSARY

A company of any size should give top priority to the celebration of an important anniversary, because it's a perfect opportunity to remind the public, press, and employees of its accomplishments and future aspirations. The benefits of an effectively handled anniversary include:

- Better employee morale
- Increased employee motivation
- A more highly polished company image within the community
- Great visibility of the company's products or services
- *Increased sales*

The really important anniversaries are the tenth, twenty-fifth, fiftieth, seventy-fifth, hundredth, and every quarter thereafter. If a company has a good reason for celebrating an in-between anniversary (such as a need for public visibility or a stimulus to employee morale), it should certainly proceed. The first through fourth anniversaries do not require any attention by the public, but they should be noted in-house, if for no other reason than it celebrates the fact the company has survived and is still in business. (The CEO might place a large bouquet of flowers in the reception area and circulate a memo to the employees, reminding them of the anniversary date and thanking them "for their large share in the progress of this company.") The fifth anniversary, while not major in terms of public visibility, is well worth celebrating by the company and its clients.

Planning the Celebration

- Define the reason for the celebration.
- Establish a budget.
- *The most important aspect of planning your company anniversary is the person put in charge of it.* There should be one imaginative, creative person given overall responsibility, someone who knows the company and, of course, its people, extremely well.
- *The employees' participation is paramount.* Their own committee should be involved from the start. Ask for employee suggestions, too, in the house organ, and award prizes for the best ideas. This is key to this project's success.
- *Create a plan.* A small company's anniversary celebration probably requires a year's advance planning; a large corporation, five year's advance planning.
- *If you are having a large celebration, immediately involve both your ad agency and your public relations people.* The effectiveness of your efforts will shout with success or whimper with failure based on how you communicate your anniversary to the public.
- *Decide on with whom you will share the celebration.* You can involve all of the following in the festivities:
    - Your employees
    - Present or potential customers or clients
    - Vendors, freelance support staffs, etc.
    - The nonprofit, educational, and institutional leaders in your community
    - Colleagues involved with your international operations
    - City, state, and U.S. government officials you would like to impress
    - The media—trade, local, national, even international
    - Last, but certainly not least, your shareholders and the financial community

Playing Up Company Nostalgia

Have someone research the company files and the newspapers for material reflecting the feeling of the times when the company was founded (a reprint of the local newspaper the day of the company's opening would be very interesting). *Organize an exhibit of the past* (the first years of the company).

Seek out photos and artifacts that document the company's history. These can include:

- Pictures of the employees, showing how they dressed at work
- Photos of the old offices—what kind of desks they sat at, how the old board room looked, etc.
- Photos of company parties, sports events, and picnics
- Samples of old stationery
- A copy of the old menus from the cafeteria
- Vouchers and accounting sheets
- Advertisements

Even if the company is only a quarter-century old, employees and customers alike would enjoy seeing how people looked, dressed, cut their hair, and did their jobs in that era. Even photographs of the employee parking lot showing the kinds of cars people drove—and the trucks used by the company—would be of interest.

Planning a Unified Graphics Campaign
for the Anniversary Year

A very important anniversary deserves a special graphics design scheme to be used in all ads and on all printed materials for the entire anniversary year. This involves having a graphics designer come up with a symbol that can be printed on stationery letterheads and envelopes, invoices, napkins in the cafeteria, and press release letterheads, to keep reminding the public of the anniversary. (One company kicked off their anniversary year by distributing thousands of oversized, helium-filled balloons, printed with the new anniversary logo, for employees in the offices and plants to take home to their children and their children's friends. Those balloons blanketed the communities in which they were distributed; one saw the balloons tied to supermarket shopping carts, baby strollers, and briefcases.)

When Two Companies Have Merged,
It Is Worthy of Celebration

Sometimes a very old company merges with a young one. When the newly merged company has a fifth or tenth anniversary and is doing well, it is nice to look back into the past of the two formerly separate companies—not from the point of view of the officers of the companies, but from that of the employees.

I watched the thirty-minute musical comedy performed at a tenth-anniversary dinner hosted by what were formerly two small separate companies but was now one midsize, successful company. In the last scene of the show, staged in the hotel ballroom, two ballet dancers appeared, one in yellow tights, his head covered in a large paper reproduction of one of the old company's original logo. The other dancer, in red tights, had her head covered with the paper logo of the second former company. They danced an amorous *pas de deux,* ending it with an embrace and a kiss of the two logos, which caused much laughter. As they exited, out came a third dancer—this one with one yellow leg and one red leg, his head covered with a paper reproduction of the new company's joint logo. It was beautifully done, there was cheering, shouting, and stamping of feet as the merged company logo dancer pirouetted exuberantly off the stage. The feeling in the ballroom that night was wonderful, full of hope and good will. Here are some ideas for specific anniversaries.

Fifth Anniversary

- Forego the office Christmas party and host instead a punch, sandwiches, ice cream, and cake anniversary party for employees and their families. (They are, after all, most important. Have music or other types of entertainment and give everyone a small party favor (such as a small box of chocolates or a bag of cookies).
- Mail a press release about the events and the company history to media, customers, employees, and friends.

Tenth Anniversary

- Mail a comprehensive press kit to local, state, and national media, including separate feature stories with interesting photographs (meaning, not photos of the CEO sitting behind his desk!).
- Give a cocktail party buffet for customers, press, and prominent local figures.
- Take a half-page ad in the local newspapers, congratulating the company on its accomplishments and its civic record.

Twenty-Fifth or Fiftieth Anniversary

- Do a special anniversary feature in the company's annual report for the benefit of stockholders.
- Launch a full-scale publicity campaign, with press kits, news features, radio spots, and fascinating film cuts for TV news departments.
- Take a full-page ad commemorating the anniversary in the newspapers of every city where the company has offices and plants.

- Have souvenirs and promotional items produced (well-designed, useful objects, NOT junk) to commemorate the anniversary (scarves, ties, pocket calendars, key-chains, mini-flashlights, pens, etc.).
- Give a very special party for employees.
- Give a party for customers, VIPs, and press.
- Do something special for the community such as:

  - Fireworks display
  - Gift of new equipment for a local hospital
  - Purchase of special new books for the local library
  - Sponsor a concert or something in the performing arts

Naturally, a company celebrating its twenty-fifth would do something more modest than a company celebrating its fiftieth.

A Company's Traveling Road Show

The offices and plants of a large corporation, located in several parts of the country, deserve their own special anniversary celebrations. It would be wise to have a standard format for anniversary plans in each place. For example, there would be supplied:

- Anniversary graphics (for company stationery, labels, etc.)
- Press kits to supply to the local media
- Order blanks on which to order necessary number of anniversary souvenirs, books or cassettes, etc.
- Ad layouts for the local newspapers
- A "Party Planner," showing the how, what, where, when and why of a reception to be given locally, right down to details such as cocktail party food, flower decorations, musical groups to entertain, etc. The invitations can also be supplied by corporate headquarters (each local office has only to fill in the date, time, and address of the party place; the invitations would then be printed locally on the stock supplied by headquarters).
- Order blank for anniversary visuals to be put up in the office or plant lobby (photographic blow-ups of company history). One group of employees made a quilt for their company, telling the story of its history; this quilt was displayed in forty offices and plants during the anniversary year, and is now encased in glass and on permanent display in a museum of folk art.
- Instructions on how to book interviews with local media for senior managers when they come to town during the year
- Instructions on how to proceed with a gift for a local nonprofit institution as an anniversary gesture
- Sample letter of acknowledgment to anyone who writes a letter of praise or congratulations (you should be so lucky)

Major, Expansive Projects for a Company Celebrating an Anniversary of Fifty or More Years

- *Have a team develop a history of the company produced in book form.* For the book, you need a crack writer with a good research team (including a photo researcher). He or she should be given full liberty to make it witty and fun, not just a heavy corporate promotion. The book would be offered free to customers and clients, as well as press and city officials. If the company deals with a mass market, it could be offered for a modest price to the public through mail order advertisements.
- Produce a half-hour video cassette on the history of the company.

You will need a crack director and a freelance film company. They will make what seem like unreasonable demands budget- and time-wise; they will disrupt the daily flow of work as they move around with their cameras. If you hire them, back them to the hilt. Otherwise, the video will be wooden, boring, and destined for everyone's wastebaskets. The cassette should be offered to TV stations in short excerpts; it should be given free to customers and clients; it should be shown on a giant screen at a special party for customers and press.

Organizing a City Parade Commemorating the Anniversary

You need a creative trade show producer or director, plus a company specializing in parades. Be sure all of your employees have some sort of role in it. Stage it at a time that is approved by the mayor so as not to disrupt the commerce of the city. Top-level personal visits from management would be required to solicit the enthusiastic help of every city official whose department would be involved, from the police to the city sanitation department. The Board of Education is key, to allow the schools' marching bands, gymnastic teams, etc., to perform in the parade. It should not be commercial; it should be a tribute to city history and to the trades your company represents. Above all, it should be *fun,* and the public reaction should be very enthusiastic.

To launch all of your major anniversary celebration projects, you should budget generously for advertising announcements of the events, direct mail pieces to your specific audiences and press relations support. If you have a good story to tell, good people to do the telling, and the budget to communicate what's happening to the public, your company's anniversary will make history by itself.

WHEN AN EMPLOYEE MARRIES OR HAS A BABY

- *As an employee, you are not obligated to invite the boss and spouse to your wedding.* However, if you know the boss well, it is polite to send an invitation with a note attached, which says something like, "I know you probably don't have the time to come, but I wanted you to hear about this happy event directly from us." (If the boss has a busy travel schedule, you can write, "I know you will be in Europe the weekend of our wedding, but we wanted you to know about it anyway." Make it easy for the boss to decline. If he or she goes to your wedding, she will have to go to everyone's wedding.)

- *As the boss, you are not obligated to accept a wedding invitation you happen to receive,* particularly since it may set a bad precedent and it could mean you'll be spending all your time going to employees' parties.
- Save the company a lot of grief: Issue an imperial decree that *wedding and baby showers are to be held anywhere but in the office.* Employees who wish to band together for showers can do so at lunch away from company premises.

When an Employee Marries

If you are the boss and know the employee well, or if he has worked for you for a long time:

- Give the couple a small wedding present. It's wise to stock several pieces of the same item which would be given to all bridal couples in this "know well" category, so that there would be equal treatment for everyone. This gift might be anything from a leather-bound dictionary to a set of six water glasses.
- If the person being married is a very important customer, you might purchase a piece of sterling silver hollowware and have it engraved with the initials of the bride and groom and the date of their wedding. (I know a CEO who spent $1,500 at Tiffany's ten years ago and had his own initials engraved on the beautiful sterling box, instead of the bride's and groom's. They laugh about it to this day, but they still use it.)
- If you don't believe in giving wedding presents or if money is tight and prohibits generosity at this time, you might give the employee a day off as a gift.
- If you do not send a gift, send a note (three sentences will do it) to the pair before their wedding which they can then show to everyone there. Sample: "I'm sure this is the biggest day in your lives so far. I hope all the rest of your lives will be as happy and exhilarating. Good luck to you always, and congratulations for having found one another—a triumph in itself."

When an Employee Has a Baby

You are not obligated to send a baby gift to an employee. However, you should send a personal note of congratulations to the parents when you hear about the baby's birth or if you receive a birth announcement from your employee. Even a note by hand such as this one will be enthusiastically received by the parents:

Dear Ralph,

There are times in life when people really succeed in life, and from what I hear about Ralph, Jr., you and Sally have both outdone yourselves with your recent production. I hear he is the handsomest, sweetest, smartest baby ever born. Congratulations are in order to you both and to Ralph, Jr. I wish a long lifetime of happiness.

I will never forget the executive of a large company who heard that the assistant to the head of the company's food services (who was also the father of an illegitimate baby) was getting married to the mother of the baby. The CEO found out the baby's name and social security number and opened a savings account with $50 in the child's name. He sent a note to the baby's father and mother, stating that congratulations were in order on the occasion of their marriage, but that the real news was the blessed event, and he was therefore giving his wedding present to the baby. The story—a touching one—was told and retold among the company's employees for years to come.

CHRISTENINGS, BAR MITZVAHS, AND BAT MITZVAHS

As the head of the company, if you are invited by one of your employees to attend his or her baby's christening or, later in life, the child's First Communion, Confirmation, Bar or Bat Mitzvah, you are not under obligation to accept. Feel flattered that you were invited.

If you are very close to that employee and know the child, it would be nice if you sent a small gift, greeting card, or even *a note of congratulations* to commemorate the occasion, which means so much to the parents.

Employees who are invited by peers to their children's festivities should accept or reject the invitation as they wish, but if they accept, they should mark the occasion with a small gift or perhaps, in the case of a confirmation, a bouquet of flowers for the child. (One friend of mine does not bring a gift for the child to these celebrations—he brings two bottles of wine to the parents, claiming "they need a present much more than the child does.")

WHEN AN EMPLOYEE HAS A BIRTHDAY

Many managers perceptibly wince when employee birthdays are mentioned, and with just cause. When such celebrations within the office become a habit (and birthdays occur once a year in every employee's life, unfortunately), the situation can turn into a real personnel problem, for the following reasons:

- The employees complain about being solicited all the time by their peers for financial contributions to the birthday gift and/or the cake for their colleague.
- The managers complain about losing all that valuable work time while employees ooh and aah over the gifts, read aloud their birthday cards, and eat and sip sodas.

The people who clean the office at night complain about the mess, and the occupants of nearby desks often find sticky bits of birthday food stuck among the keys on their keyboards for days after.

If you are a senior manager and want to make a strong policy about birthdays in your office (and the same goes for wedding showers), do it. Simply issue a memo or announce in a personnel newsletter that henceforth all birthday celebrations and showers are appropriately held outside of office premises and on the employees' own time. Immediately after such an executive edict is published, it would be very smart of the CEO to state once again that the annual holiday office party will, of course, be held in December, and that *all* employees are invited to one last company blast of the year—the final, all-in-one birthday-wedding-baby-shower celebration. (It will show that the CEO's heart is in the right place.)

WHEN AN EXECUTIVE RETIRES
(*See also* "Retirement Letters," Chapter 7)

Retirement is common today among younger executives, those who are being cut from the ranks of management for economic reasons and given early retirement, and those who are not happy in their jobs and want to step back to think, reassess, and perhaps do something else. It is nice to be in the second category, that is, to have the financial resources that will allow a person to stop work and "smell the roses" for a bit.

When someone who has been with the company for a long time and who is truly beloved retires, there is a usually a groundswell of affection and nostalgia as the time comes for his or her departure. Whether this person is on the janitorial staff or the board of directors, the employees will want to be part of the ceremony. Some suggestions:

- *Some companies have a very handsome framed "Certificate of Service" scroll done in calligraphy*, so that the retiree can put it on his wall.
- *Senior management should fete an important retiree with a party* in a hotel, near the offices, or even in the employee cafeteria at the end of the day, so that anyone who wishes can attend. (The party site should be decorated with bunting, or perhaps some blow-ups of photos tracing the life of the retiree from childhood through adulthood.) The CEO should make a few remarks, and the person's entire family should be in attendance, standing alongside the retiree.
- *The retiree should be given a nice present* from the company at this party, something like a handsome desk set, for example, with a blotter holder, letter box, pen set, letter opener, etc.), with the person's initials and the corporate logo embossed on the leather. Other ideas are a set of golf clubs or another gift appropriate to her or his hobbies.

One man, a driver of the company's cars for thirty-eight years and a patriotic World War II veteran, was much loved by the entire corporation. When he received at his retirement party two flags to put in his home (each mounted on a metal staff with its holder)—one a flag of the United States and the other a corporate flag—the driver broke down and let a few tears flow. So did the CEO and just about everyone else in the room.

- If a special ceremony is held for the retiree, it is very nice to give:

  · A video cassette or an audiotape of the remarks made at the event
  · An album that contains the candid photos taken by a photographer at the ceremony

- *A photo of the retirement ceremony with a write-up should be included in the next edition of the company newsletter.*
- If the retiree is a member of senior management or a director, *the board of directors might pass a resolution wishing that person well on retirement.* The resolution is lettered on a scroll, then framed and sent to the retiree.

Obviously, everyone who retires does not merit this kind of special treatment, but people who have given themselves to the company for many years deserve to be royally feted when it comes time to leave.

Some Company-Sponsored Retirement Activities When Times Are Good

· The company may organize retired executives into consulting groups that provide professional advice for other small companies.
· The company may channel retirees into badly needed volunteer positions in hospitals, nursing homes, and schools (Honeywell, Inc. does this).
· The company may recruit retirees to join with professional staff members in visiting or telephoning elderly or ailing retirees (Levi Strauss does this).
· Certain companies encourage executives (soon to retire) to spend a day a week in community work at the beginning of their last year of work; by the final quarter of the year, they are working only one day a week and four days as a volunteer.
· Very few programs are as inspiring as the former Bell System's "Telephone Pioneers of America," many of whom are retirees. These skilled people use their retirement hours to help not only their local communities but mankind in general. The engineers use their retirement time to invent things that help people with problems—for example, making it possible for blind children to ride bikes and blind teenagers to play soccer and helping autistic children learn how to communicate by placing two-way radios in teddy bears, so the child thinks the teddy bear is talking to him. There are many other examples of good old-fashioned human compassion in this program.
· Many companies urge the retiree to seek further education; some companies, contribute financially to courses, both for the retiree and his or her spouse.

- Some companies make available the lifelong use of the company store or provide the opportunity to purchase the company's products at a discount.
- The company may invite the retiree annually to the Christmas party, as well as send him a birthday and/or holiday greeting card.
- The company may pay for his membership in the American Association of Retired Persons.

When You Are the Retiree

You might wish to communicate the fact that you are retiring by placing the information on a printed card (or even a postcard) to be mailed to everyone you know. It will also be useful in that it will supply your address and telephone number, so that people will know how to reach you. Your informal, humorous text could read something like this:

> . . . In spite of my youth and after only thirty-eight years with Reincol, I will be retiring as of June 28. In September, Anne and I will be moving to John's Island, Florida (here give your complete new address, telephone number, and fax). We welcome your visit, because we certainly don't want to lose touch with our old (or rather, young) friends.
>
> We're really going to miss you, and we wish you luck and happiness. Please wish the same for us.

If you are going to continue as a consultant or if you are moving to another company, communicate that fact on your card, giving your new office address and telephone number. It's important to keep open the communication lines with all the personal and business friends you have made.

A retiree should be sensitive to the number of times he returns to his old office. The tempation to keep showing up will be great, but he must learn to let go and to turn his energies toward other interests and different people.

The retiree should not criticize the efforts of his successor in public, regardless of how much he disagrees with the new style or regardless of the comparative success or failure of his successor's efforts.

The Retirement Speech

When a member of top management retires, at some point he or she may have to give a good-bye speech. It's nice if it is laced with humor and kept short. It also should show gratitude toward the people who have really been the key to the retiring executive's success and happiness, like his executive secretary and his spouse. The speech can later be printed in the company newsletter.

At the retirement ceremony of an important, senior officer of the company, the person who will assume his or her position should make a short, affectionate return speech directed at the retiree when he finishes his remarks. This is also the moment to present the retiree with the company's gift.

One retirement ceremony I will never forget was that of a CEO who used to play the piano every year at the company's Christmas party. It was a longstanding company joke, because he was so bad at it. The incoming CEO, with a grave face, announced that everyone in the company had grown concerned that the CEO's piano-playing performances through the years had grown steadily worse. Therefore, the employees and management had raised enough money to buy him as a retirement gift something he would now have the time to use: a small upright piano (which was wheeled onto the stage) and a year's worth of piano lessons. The retiring CEO quite obviously loved his gift, and sat right down to play some Christmas carols once more for the employees (even though it was July). He explained with the last notes of "Rudolph the Red-Nosed Reindeer" that he could hardly wait to learn how to play the piano properly, whereupon the new CEO made one last official presentation onstage: a pair of earplugs to the retiree's grateful wife.

The Junior Executive's Attitude Toward the Retiring Executive

Some young people, without really realizing it, act in a patronizing fashion toward the older executive who is nearing or at retirement age. Because this is often such a difficult period for retiring executives, the way in which younger executives treat them is very important. Retiring executives should not merely be shrugged off as "being on their way out." They should not be treated as though they don't count any more. Sometimes a panting eagerness is displayed by younger people impatient to move up in the hierarchy within an organization, and that eagerness may be shown openly around the older executives. (The junior executives should keep reminding themselves that it will not take long before they are in the same position.)

The intelligent younger executive, instead of dismissing a senior member of management who is about to retire, gets to know him. The imminent retiree has more time for visits and chats. The younger person, in seeking him out for his advice and his general sense of the state of the business, does him honor. But the younger person is also acquiring a tremendous amount of invaluable information he can use for the rest of his life. This is another case where being thoughtful and polite is the same as being very, very smart.

WHEN AN EXECUTIVE DIES

Although much of this chapter concerns protocol and compassion on the death and burial of a high-ranking executive or professional, most of the etiquette and helpful ideas can also be adapted to what you can do for a lower-ranked executive in a simpler manner on a much simpler budget. The tragic news of a colleague's death should trigger an instantaneous reaction of "How can I help?"

Any survivor deserves to be treated with dignity and kindness, and we should never forget that the preservation of a person's memory is of great importance not only to his family, but also to his friends and colleagues. It's all the same, whether it concerns a member of your family, someone of senior rank in your company, or one of your small company's employees. The company is the extended family; in times of sadness, it should show its humanity.

Tasks to Be Undertaken Immediately

Sometimes an executive will die unexpectedly in the office or on a business trip or during the business day, away from his or her home. In this case, the most senior person in the company should:

- Make sure the late executive's doctor has been notified.
- Contact the spouse and all members of the immediate family.
- Offer the comprehensive help of the company in this emergency and immediately arrange for all the jobs to be done that the spouse wishes to be done.
- Contact the lawyer of the deceased.
- Formally notify the employees, both in the corporate offices and all plants and officers elsewhere.
- Send a top-ranking person to the home of the deceased, to remain there as long as needed or desired.

Tasks to Be Undertaken in the Home of the Deceased

- Small children will need a relative or babysitter to care for them.
- Some able person should be in charge of the telephone. Messages must be relayed properly to everyone involved with funeral arrangements and condolences.
- Someone should notify by personal telephone call all relatives of the deceased. Any information already known on details of the funeral or memorial services should be relayed. Their arrival in town for the services should be coordinated, so that arrival and departure times are listed, room reservations are made, and transportation to and from the airport or station is arranged. The name and telephone number of the company person handling these details should be supplied.
- Incoming messages, flowers, gifts, telegrams, faxes, etc., should be carefully recorded in a notebook, for later acknowledgment by the spouse or the company.
- Food for the family should be arranged, either by making certain relatives or friends can take care of it, or by using a catering service to deliver the meals.
- An officer of the company should personally notify the board of directors and

major longtime customers or clients of the death of the executive; any known details of the funeral or memorial service plans should be relayed.

- Someone in the public relations or press office or Office of Information should:

  ◦ Place a paid *death notice* in the local press for two consecutive days. Some funeral homes will do this automatically for the spouse of the deceased. Whatever details as are available on the upcoming funeral would be included in the announcement, including information on when to call on the family at the funeral home (the wake). This is also the time to include the family's wishes: "In lieu of flowers, donations may be made to the American Heart Association" or whatever charity will benefit.

  ◦ Place a simple *ad announcement in the business section* of the local newspapers as well: "With profound sorrow we announce the death of our friend and our beloved Chairman and Chief Executive Officer Martin Edward Akerment on May 15, 1999." It would be signed: "The executives and employees of Communikare, Inc." (This could be one-quarter or one-eighth of a page in size). Optionally you could add to this ad-announcement: "Out of respect for his memory, our offices will be closed on Friday of this week."

  ◦ Deliver an accurate, well-written *obituary* (approved by the family) to all local news media and to the local wire services (from which it will be distributed nationally, if the person was indeed prominent).

- Instruct your company telephone operators (as well as people who handle incoming calls through voice mail) how to handle incoming calls from the press, business colleagues, stockholders, etc. It is most efficient if all incoming calls are routed initially to two operators, who can then send the calls elsewhere, if warranted. Be sure these people sound at least somber, instead of rude, when the public calls for information. I remember calling a company once the day after the CEO had been killed in a company jet crash. The memorable conversation went like this:

> ME [sounding very sympathetic]: I'm calling about the accident. You must all be terribly upset. I'm so sorry, I——
>
> OPERATOR [spoken in a bored voice]: Uh-huh, so where do I transfer this call?
>
> ME [fighting back the tears]: I just want to find out about the funeral services. He was a really good friend. I'm going out of town, and I wanted to arrange to be here——
>
> OPERATOR [interrupting]: I haven't heard anything from anyone about anything.
>
> ME [abashed]: So I guess I should call back.
>
> OPERATOR: Yeah.

Thus ends a conversation and one example of a disaster of public relations on a sad day in the history of that company.

The Obituary

An obituary of a person from a small town almost always appears in the local newspapers, if it is sent in. In large cities, only the obituaries of the most prominent citizens are published.

A company or firm should keep on file an *updated* biography and a *recent* black-and-white head shot of each senior executive. If a death occurs on a weekend when offices are closed, the executive's secretary or the duty officer should know how to locate a copy of the biography and photograph.

If the photograph sent to the newspapers with the obituary is more than two years old, it should be dated on the back. Be sure to include the name and telephone number of the person to contact for verification of the material.

The following list is a guideline for information that should be kept current on all senior executives:

- Name
- Address
- Place of birth
- Education, including degrees and honorary degrees
- Military service, if any
- Current title and important past career information
- Corporate directorships; nonprofit board memberships
- Any major awards received
- Titles and publishers of books, plays, films, etc.

When death occurs, the person in charge of distributing the obituary to the media should add these facts to the deceased's biography:

- Date, place, and cause of death
- Names and relationships of immediate survivors (spouse, children, parents, brothers and sisters)
- Details, if applicable, concerning funeral home hours, the funeral, or memorial services. If interment is private, it should be so stated. (Some newspapers do not want this information, some do.)
- Name and telephone number of person to contact for further information

The person assigned by the company to disseminate the obituary (usually the public relations officer) should send a copy by hand to the local and suburban newspapers, as well as to the local bureaus of the wire services. A copy should also go to the alumni class secretary of the late executive's schools and any boards on which he served at the time of his death.

In the case of a death of a prominent executive in the New York area, one would call the Metropolitan Desk of the *New York Times,* which might assign a reporter to the story. (*The Wall Street Journal* does not publish obituaries.) Most newspapers maintain a running file on prominent people in their area, so that when death occurs, ideally only a short updating of the bio is necessary. A local reporter usually makes every effort to place an obituary story in the next edition of his paper. However, if no one is available to answer his calls for information, a woefully short, inadequate story is apt to appear.

Writing the Obituary

The obituary of the very prominent, fictitious Martin Edward Akerment should be a joint effort of a family member of the deceased and a knowledgeable company person who knows the business details of the executive's life perhaps better than the family. It might look like this:

Martin Edward Akerment. Chairman and chief executive officer of Communikare, Inc., Denver, Colorado, died suddenly of a heart attack on May 15, 1999, in Washington, DC, while giving an address at a meeting of the International Association of Healthcare Givers. He was fifty-nine years old. A lifelong resident of Denver, he graduated from Deerfield Academy in Massachusetts in 1958 and from Dartmouth College in New Hampshire in 1962, where he was captain of the ski team. He was a member of the U.S. ski team at the Winter Olympics in 1963. He received a law degree from the University of Denver in 1972.

Mr. Akerment began his career in the healthcare field with the Préparerbien Company in Paris, France, in 1964 and after six years, he returned to America to get his law degree. He began working for Communikare, Inc., in 1978 as legal counsel. He became president of the corporation in 1985 and chairman and chief executive officer in 1990. He was to have retired in September of 1999.

At the time of his death, he was a director of Recherches France-États-Unis, the Pitcairn Corporation, the Maynard Company, and General Pharmaceutical. He was a member of the following nonprofit boards: The University of Denver, the Folger Shakespeare Library in Washington, the Alliance Francaise, and the Special Olympics. He is survived by his wife, the former Adrienne Leblois, two daughters, Suzanne Johnson of Denver and Denise Lecarre of New Orleans, and a son, Martin, Jr., of New York. He is also survived by three grandchildren.

On the Subject of Flowers for the Funeral

Flowers are appropriately sent to the funeral home from the company—or else to the church or to the grave site—whatever the family wishes. The only way to determine this is to ask a member of the family about their preference. Remember, too, that flowers are never sent to an Orthodox Jewish funeral. At a Catholic service, only the family's bouquet on the casket and perhaps one bouquet of flowers on the altar are permitted. Flowers sent to the funeral home are usually transported to the gravesite for the interment.

The envelope of the card accompanying your company's flowers would be addressed simply to: "The Funeral of Mr. Martin Akerment" and sent care of the funeral home. The white enclosure card, written in black ink, would say: "With the deepest sympathy from everyone at Communikare, Inc."

I have been to funerals where corporations have obviously tried to outdo one another with huge gaudy arrangements: clashing colors of gladiola shooting up to the sky like firecrackers, the kind you'd see in Las Vegas or that you'd put around the neck of a horse that has won every horse race that exists in that year. When a big arrangement of flowers is adorned with a huge gold lamé ribbon, printed with the corporate name in six-inch-high letters, it can provide onlookers with the only moment of hilarity in an otherwise solemn occasion.

If you have anything to do with the flowers your company sends to a funeral, make them simple and beautiful. Two dozen pale pink roses are perfect, and the most beautiful ones I ever saw were tall, simple sprays of tiny white orchids in a small white mother-of-pearl vase. (The widow had them sent to her home the day of the funeral and I saw them in her bedroom the next day. She said they were tasteful, beautiful and serene—the kind her husband would have sent her.)

The Funeral Home

If you are going to make a call on the family at the funeral home, be sure to arrive during the hours of the visitation. If you arrive too early, you could interrupt a planning session of the family; if you arrive too late, you could keep everyone waiting when they all want to leave and are ready to drop from exhaustion.

When you get to the place, sign the book that usually is very visible at the entrance to the funeral home. Do not bring flowers or gifts. Just get in line to greet the family, and introduce yourself to those you do not know. Explain how you knew the deceased. "Mrs. Garrett, I am in the Travel Department of the company. I made most of your husband's reservations for him. He was always so nice, even when I mixed up the tickets. We all loved him a lot. I want you to know that."

If you know the family well, you might very well be like me, a soggy mess by the time you reach the family in the receiving line, out of control and totally incapable of saying one word, but capable nonetheless of giving each family member a warm, silent hug that says it all. (If you don't know the family, when you greet them in the funeral home, a handshake will do. Forget the hug!)

The Funeral

The company should make it possible for everyone in the company who wants to attend the funeral of a beloved executive to be able to go (via chartered buses, if necessary). It may not be possible to arrange this for a celebrity executive's funeral because of a lack of space, in which case senior management should arrange for the company to hold its own memorial service on its premises for the deceased, for the employees and their families.

If the funeral is held in another city, the company should be well represented by a delegation from senior management.

The Interment

The ceremony of the lowering of the casket into the grave is an intensely personal one, and usually the family wants only the closest friends of the deceased to join them for this—and often only the family. The corporate executive who has been in charge of the funeral preparations should ask the widow if he may accompany her, but he should explain that he understands perfectly if she says she wishes only the family there. Then he must inform others of that wish.

How to Dress

People who attend funerals should wear somber clothing, nothing loud, flashy or overly bright. A man should wear his darkest suit and a dark tie; a woman, a dress or suit of a quiet color. In my opinion, a woman attending a church funeral in pants looks unsuitable, but many women will disagree with me.

Program for the Order of Service in a Church

It's a very nice touch when the late executive's family (or company, for that matter) provides for each person who attends a funeral or memorial service a little pamphlet printed on its cover with "The Order of Service for the Funeral of _____" or "A Service of Celebration and Thanksgiving for the Life of _____." Sometimes the church will order this, sometimes the undertaker, but many people prefer to have it printed, on good stock, themselves. The pamphlet would list:

- The years of the person's life
- The name and address of the church
- The name of the town
- The date and hour of the service
- The prayers (with their sources), the hymns (with their composers), and instructions to the congregation on when to stand, when to be seated, when to kneel, and when to join in the prayers and hymns
- The names of all the clergy in attendance, with their titles

The end of the order of the service text might include an invitation, such as "All are invited to greet the family in the Parish House" or "All are invited to lunch at the Oxnard home on 34th Street." The final page of a four-page program might contain a special prayer or a dignified photograph of the deceased in a thin black frame. It's a nice memento to take away, and keep, of the life of a person you loved or admired.

The Eulogy

In some churches the policy is that only the minister makes the eulogy for the deceased at the service. In others the honor lies only with the minister and perhaps a brother, sister, or child of the deceased. In some churches when a distinguished person's memorial service is held, there will be anywhere from one to five short eulogies given, by people who really want to and who are certain they will be composed during such a ritual. The procedure should be well orchestrated, with each person knowing exactly when in the service he or she is to go quickly up to the pulpit to say a few words. Each person is introduced before speaking, either by the clergy person or the previous speaker. These short eulogies are given separately, usually following a prayer or a hymn, and are made by anyone from a law partner of the deceased to his best friend since boyhood, and from one of his factory foremen to one of his college professors. Any eulogy should mention members of the immediate family, and should be:

- Brief
- Respectful, but it can also be amusing
- Anecdotal
- Descriptive of positive legacies left by the deceased

Reception Following the Memorial Service

Occasionally there is no spouse to host it, or occasionally the spouse is too upset to handle the logistics, so it is a gracious gesture on the corporation's part to step in to host a lunch or reception of some kind following the funeral or memorial service of their late distinguished executive.

In this case there would be a white invitation card, edged in black, (5½″ × 7¼″, for example) with the following kind of text engraved or thermoengraved, and sent to all the family, friends and business associates of the deceased.

You would not put an RSVP on this kind of invitation. You would simply prepare for a huge mob to attend. If you send out five hundred invitations, you will probably have four hundred people coming. You would have the club set up an open bar; champagne and hot and cold hors d'oeuvres would be served. You would have a buffet, too, for those who are making an early dinner of it. You would have little tables and chairs around the ballroom for the elderly to sit. Mostly people will mingle in the crowd, reminiscing, greeting old friends, as well as consoling the family and "celebrating" Helen Jelpnat's passage to a much happier, better world.

The cost of the invitations and the reception are appropriately borne by the corporation in this case. If the widow hosts the memorial service and reception by herself, the family would pay for the expenses.

The family of
Helen Milhart Jelpnat
and the officers and board of directors of
The Jelpnat Corporation
invite you to attend
a memorial service
in her loving memory
at four o'clock
Thursday, the twenty-sixth day of September
Nineteen hundred and ninety-nine
Saint Thomas More
Sixty-five East Eighty-ninth Street
New York
Reception to follow
The River Club
Fifty Second Street and the East River

Ushers and Pallbearers at Funerals and Memorial Services

Close friends and business associates of a very distinguished man or woman are sometimes invited by the family to serve as honorary pallbearers or ushers for the funeral or memorial service. (Only ushers are needed for a large memorial service, since the casket is not present in the church; the body had already been buried, or perhaps it was cremated.)

The ushers help seat people as at weddings, using a seating plan designating the areas in which certain people should sit (the family in the front pews on the right, for example, the pallbearers in the front pews on the left, people of official rank directly behind them, etc.). The ushers are often younger friends of the deceased, young executives from his or her company, or perhaps nephews, nieces, or godchildren. Traditionally they are men, but there is no reason to deny either sex from serving as usher or pallbearer.

In very important Christian funerals, from four to ten honorary *pallbearers* escort the casket in or out of the church preceding it in a procession of two by two. If the casket is already in place at the altar, the pallbearers march in just before the service begins and sit in the front pews at the left, opposite the family. These honorary pall-bearers do not handle the casket (the funeral home has experts who do that). Rather they are present to symbolize the distinction a great person has achieved in his or her life. Honorary pallbearers are people like heads of companies, presidents of museums, distinguished doctors, lawyers, educators. When a woman executive dies, there should be at least one female honorary pallbearer.

In the old days, pallbearers wore cutaways, and the ushers wore morning suits, but today either usher or pallbearer dresses in a dark suit and white shirt with either a black or a very conservative tie.

When there are no honorary pallbearers, the ushers march up two by two and sit in the front pews on the left just before the service begins. When there *are* pallbearers, the ushers, after finishing their ushering duties, sit in the back of the church.

It is a distinct honor to be asked by the family of the deceased to be an usher or honorary pallbearer. It is an honor one does not refuse unless there is a terribly good reason.

A Mass Card: A Gesture to a Catholic Family

If the executive who dies is a devout Catholic, it would be very appropriate for colleagues to send his or her family a mass card in lieu of flowers. The donor obtains a mass card from a priest in any parish, who then notes on the card the date and hour of the mass to be said for the deceased. The card and an envelope are then given to the donor, who either gives it or mails it to the family. Nuns in convents also have "novena cards," assuring the family of so many series of prayers said for the deceased in their convent.

Although no one is obligated to make a donation for a mass card or novena card, most people do (from $10 to $50, in cash or by check). They hand the donation in an envelope to the priest or nun. This kind of gesture is in lieu of flowers sent to the funeral.

When a special mass arranged by a friend is to be said in memory of the deceased executive, it is particularly nice if a member of the family can be present at that mass.

Special Observances for Families of Deceased Jewish Executives or Employees

When a Jewish executive or employee dies, an appropriate corporate gesture is to send a basket of fruit to the family of the deceased or to make a donation to a charitable organization (preferably one that relates to the interests of the deceased).

Company employees who were close to the deceased should pay a condolence call to the home where the family is "sitting shivah" (observing the seven-day period of mourning during which families honor their departed loved ones). On such visits, it is traditional to bring gifts of food, as mourners are not permitted to do any work during this period. One should bring kosher food (or fruit) if the family is known to observe the dietary laws or if one does not know the religious practices of the family.

A note of condolence is always appropriate, particularly from a close business associate who is unable to pay a condolence call.

A Donation Made to a Nonprofit Institution "In Memory Of"

Colleagues of the late executive may band together and decide on a charity to which they can make a donation in memory of their friend. In the case of the late Fredrik Jon McLean, an ardent Kenyon College graduate and trustee, his colleagues, knowing of his love for his alma mater, might send a check to Kenyon College in his name. This would set off a flurry of acknowledgements, according to the rules of etiquette. For example:

- The donor group would send the check to the president of Kenyon.
- The president of Kenyon would write them a grateful letter of acknowledgment.
- The president of Kenyon would write to the McLean family, informing them of the gift.
- A McLean family member would write to one of the donors, thanking him or her and the whole group on behalf of the family.

This may seem like a lot of letter-writing, but it is a nice, efficient way of handling the matter and communicating the gesture properly.

Setting Up a Memorial

Occasionally a special memorial is established in the name of a beloved executive by family, personal friends, and business colleagues. Senior management would make a corporate contribution to a memorial for their executive, and the employees could make contributions if they wished to. (They should not be solicited, however.) When employees initiate a memorial project for one of their colleagues, it is customary for management to contribute as well. A list of names of those who contributed to the memorial should be sent to the family.

A memorial should be in keeping with the philosophy and interests of the person for whom it is named. The funds collected might be used to pay for the education of children of the deceased who are not yet old enough for college, for scientific research in the field of the illness that killed the executive, to buy new books for the local library, or to purchase badly needed equipment for the hospital where he died.

No one in the office, executive or employee, should feel compelled to contribute to any kind of memorial fund. It should be done quietly and anonymously.

Keeping in Touch with the Surviving Spouse

The colleagues of the late executive should take turns calling the widow once a month to see if there's anything she needs, and to help advise her. Obviously, the same would apply to the husband of a woman executive who has died.

It is very important to mark the first anniversary of the executive's death. The family should be called; the widow or widower might be invited to dinner in a good restaurant for a quiet evening of reminiscing. A big bouquet of flowers sent to the family with a card signed by senior managers would be a nice gesture, too. All that needs to be written on the cards is "We'll always miss him."

Published Tributes When Someone Dies

- When an executive (or a beloved employee of any rank) dies, it is nice to have a special article written about that person, in tribute, published in the house organ. (Be sure to send the family a copy of it.)
- At the Board of Directors' meeting, a tribute to the late executive should be read aloud and entered into the minutes of the meeting. The text should be hand-lettered in calligraphy, on paper, framed and sent to the surviving family.
- An excerpt of this tribute should be sent to the deceased's college class representative, so that the glowing words will be included in the next class notes of his alumni magazine.
- A tribute should be written into the next annual report of the company detailing his or her accomplishments for the company, giving a few personal anecdotes, and perhaps including a wonderful candid photo of the person.

When an Executive Dies at a Post Abroad

The body of an employee who dies "en poste" in another country is usually brought back to this country for burial. If the family agrees, the company should first arrange a simple memorial service in the city where death occurred.

The American consulate should assist in arrangements to transport the body to the United States. The corporation should pay for the memorial service abroad, the disposition of the employee's foreign home and the return of his personal effects to the United States, and the cost of transporting the body and family home.

It is thoughtful for senior management to invite the surviving family members to lunch in the executive dining room upon their return to this country, as a small gesture that the company shares in their sorrow.

When an executive dies abroad, corporate headquarters should send an updated obituary and photograph to the newspapers in the city where the executive died, as well as to the local newspapers where the corporation has its headquarters.

Condolence Letters

(See also "Letters for Difficult Circumstances," Chapter 7)

It is very gracious for colleagues of an executive who dies to write to his or her spouse or family, and by colleagues, I mean anyone from the receptionist to the CEO. A good condolence letter conveys not only feelings of sadness and praise of the deceased, but also the offer of a helping hand to those left behind. A well-written condolence letter is treasured, is usually passed around, and is often passed down through future generations.

Sending flowers to the funeral or attending the funeral is no substitute for a condolence letter. The letter or short note should be sent regardless of any other gestures you make.

A condolence letter should be written by hand in black ink on good personal notepaper (but using office stationery is better than not writing the letter at all). If your handwriting is totally illegible (like mine), type your letter.

From an Executive to the Mother
of an Unmarried Colleague

Let the bereaved know:

Dear Mrs. Jenkins:

We heard of Ritch's death only yesterday and were shocked to learn that someone so young, physically fit, full of energy, and blessed with the love of life could be struck down so tragically by a heart attack.

That you know what a terrible loss it is . . .

I know what this loss means to you and your children. When one of my brothers died at Ritch's age, the family felt as though our own family structure had disintegrated—forever. Fortunately, life does go on for the survivors, while the family grows closer. You'll realize that Ritch's spirit will help sustain all of you in your sorrow.

. . . but things will get better.

Mention your relationship with the deceased and praise him.

Ritch was a favorite of every person in this company with whom he came in contact. My staff and I welcomed his periodic visits to my division. He had a warm, mischievous smile, a wry sense of humor, and a genuine interest in other people that was a great asset to his career. I personally will miss him both as a friend and as a business colleague.

Say how much he will be missed.

Offer your assistance to the family.

Please let me know if there is anything I can do for you; it would give me great pleasure to be of service, and if you come to our city, I hope you will let me

know, so I can take you to lunch in our company
dining room, where Ritch and I often lunched.

You and your family are in our thoughts and our
prayers.

Sincerely yours,

From an Employee to an Executive's Family

Dear Mrs. McLean:

My deepest sympathy goes to you and to each member of your family in this
time of terrible sorrow. I admired your husband more than I could ever express. As
head of the Mail Room, I saw him quite often. He had a habit of sticking his head in
the door on his way to the Board Room, asking with a smile, "And how's everything
going today in the nerve center of this organization?"

There has never been a chief executive officer who showed more concern for
his employees, not just the senior officers. He made us all feel part of the team. He
knew many of our names (including mine), and we looked up to him as a leader and
as a gentleman.

Everyone in the Mail Room joins me in sending you our prayers and heartfelt
condolences. Mr. McLean will *always* be missed in this company.

Sincerely,

To a National of a Foreign Country Whose Leader Has Died

When a head of state or any beloved leader dies in a country where your company
does business, the death should be noted and acted upon.

Send a Fax to your offices and plants in that country, expressing the sympathy of
your senior management as well as all of your company's local employees. If you are
writing a business letter to a colleague in that country during the following weeks, be
sure to enclose a short hand-written note saying "how saddened we all are for your
country during these difficult days. . . ." When a foreign leader or a crowned monarch
dies, the people in that country usually feel the loss for a long period of time.

It is courteous for a business executive to call on the foreign country's embassy
or consulate in his city. The diplomatic representatives often place a ceremonial book
in the reception area of the office. Diplomats, friends, and business associates of that
country pass by to sign the book as a mark of respect and mourning. The book is
eventually sent to the officials of the foreign country so they may know who paid tribute
to their leader.

On a Personal Note: A Condolence Letter
from a Former Senior Executive to the Family
of Another Senior Executive

When my father, H. Malcolm Baldrige, died at a ripe old age, my brothers, Mac and Bob, and I received many wonderful condolence letters. Not many of them came from my father's peers, because very few were still alive, but one of the most cherished ones we received came from Alton Hyatt, a Yale classmate of the class of 1918. (If you learn how to write a good letter of condolence, you have no idea of how many pairs of eyes will eventually read it.)

> Dear Children of Malcolm Baldrige,
>
> As secretary of the Class of 1918, I write to you expressing sincere sympathy upon the death of your dad. There are only about 30 of us left who would be able to join in expressing the sentiments of this letter, but I am certain that the entire original class of 400-plus would have wanted to be included if they were still with us.
>
> It is a well-known fact amongst us all that Mac was a truly outstanding member of our class. He was not only a great athlete in both football and wrestling, but he also had a great personality, backed up perfectly by an impressive stature and a stentorian voice. His public services throughout his life were of the highest quality, and I never heard a word spoken against him.
>
> Many were the good times we all had together, and it was always a pleasure to see him at our annual Class of 1918 lunches at Mory's in New Haven.
>
> With great admiration for our outstanding classmate,
>
> /s/ Alton R. Hyatt

Acknowledging Expressions of Sympathy

The Family Acknowledges Friends' and Colleagues' Gestures

When a prominent person dies, there is an inevitable flow of mail (sometimes hundreds of letters and Mailgrams) and telephone calls, flowers, and donations made in the memory of the deceased. It becomes difficult to send a personal note to every person who extends his or her sympathy. An engraved or printed card may be sent to everyone, acknowledging the individual's gesture of sympathy in a general manner, such as the following message, engraved or printed on a black-bordered white card:

> The Family of the late Fredrik Jon McLean gratefully acknowledges your expression of sympathy. We shall always remember your kindness.

It is much more gracious, of course, if a member of the family personalizes the card by writing a sentence or two by hand, with a signature beneath, on the card. A sentence or two will suffice, mentioning the specific act of sympathy of the recipient:

Thank you for coming to the funeral. Fred always spoke of you with affection.

Thank you for coming to the funeral home. We feel we know you, because Fred has often mentioned you.

Your flowers were particularly beautiful, and your card was very kind.

We are very touched by your generous donation to Kenyon College. You know how much Fred loved his college. Thank you from us all.

If the executive who dies was not a well-known person, the acknowledgment list would not be long, and therefore it would not be necessary to order sympathy acknowledgment cards. A family member should write a short note to acknowledge each person's expression of sympathy (within three months maximum):

. . . You were so nice to bring us that wonderful basket of fruit. The whole family enjoyed it.

We are all doing pretty well, considering our terrible loss. Having friends like you helps sustain us. Thank you, Richard.

The Family Acknowledges the Company's Gestures

When a company takes an active role in helping the family of the deceased, someone from that family should write to the head of the company, thanking everyone on the family's behalf. In Fredrik McLean's case, his widow should write to the executive who is temporarily in charge of the company:

. . . You cannot imagine how grateful our entire family is to the company for the many kind and wonderful things done for us. From the first minute you brought me the news of Fred's death, through the sad, confusing days that followed while we planned and executed the funeral, I don't know how we would have coped without you. Every thoughtful gesture meant so much to us, including the fact that you taped the children's eulogy of their father at the services, and we now have a precious family record to be passed down to future generations.

I hope you noticed that the wonderful basket of lilies from the employees was placed right next to the casket, where it was seen and admired by everyone. And I must thank you again for the loan of your superb secretary the first two days to handle the telephones for us. That allowed Fred's secretary to join us as a member of the family, sharing our grief. You made everything so much easier for us. Our gratitude can never be properly expressed.

I'm sure you know how much Fred loved this company, and he would have been very proud that Texocon in a moment of crisis took such wonderful care of his family.

This kind of letter from the wife of the late CEO should be published, with her permission, in the company newsletter for the sake of the employees.

Nothing brought up the solemnity, pomp and protocol of the final rite of passage more poignantly to me than when my brother Mac, the Secretary of Commerce for

Ronald Reagan for two terms, was killed while he was roping in a rodeo, when his horse fell on him. It occurred toward the end of President Reagan's term in 1988. His funeral at the National Cathedral in Washington was attended by all the leaders of our government and many diplomats. President Reagan gave a beautiful eulogy. There was another memorial service for Mac the next day in his home town of Woodbury, Connecticut, at which Vice-President George Bush, Mac's close friend, gave the eulogy, and Senator Alan Simpson from Wyoming, a cowboy friend, also spoke. The beauty of ceremony, tradition and ritual that unfolded at both these events with flags, organ music, choirs, bands, honor guards, and taps, did honor to Mac's name, and I could see the pride in the eyes of his widow, Midge, and his two daughters, Megan and Molly. Actually, I felt in my heart that those two days did honor to all Americans.

Mac's name lives on in the "Malcolm Baldrige International Quality Awards" Program for Business, administered by the Department of Commerce since 1987. It's a great memorial to him. If he were alive today he'd probably be on his horse "riding the fences" on a ranch somewhere, but he'd be mighty proud of that award named for him.

Index

F

R

S

T

W

Y